SPECIAL EDUCATION FOR THE '80s

Victory is sweet to a winner in the Special Olympics.

SPECIAL EDUCATION FOR THE '80s

BILL R. GEARHEART, Ed.D.

Special Education and Rehabilitation,
University of Northern Colorado, Greeley, Colorado

with 44 illustrations

The C. V. Mosby Company

ST. LOUIS • TORONTO • LONDON   1980

Copyright © 1980 by The C. V. Mosby Company

All rights reserved. No part of this book may be reproduced in any manner without written permission of the publisher.

Printed in the United States of America

The C. V. Mosby Company
11830 Westline Industrial Drive, St. Louis, Missouri 63141

Library of Congress Cataloging in Publication Data

Gearheart, B   R
  Special education for the '80s.

  Includes references and index.
  1. Handicapped children—Education.
I. Title.
LC4015.G383   371.9   79-20647
ISBN 0-8016-1759-6

C/VH/VH 9 8 7 6 5 4 3 2 1   05/D/604

PREFACE

The initiation of any textbook must be accompanied by some misgivings, and preparing a text about the wide variety of needs presented by the broad range of exceptional persons in our nation is a particularly challenging task. Recent changes in what are considered to be acceptable educational practices for handicapped students, plus parallel changes in treatment and management philosophy as applied to the adult handicapped, only add to the challenge.

It is possible to write "multipurpose" texts, but they tend to result in either omission of essential information or inclusion of information that is either useless or confusing to certain segments of the various intended audiences. Therefore, this book, in style of presentation and scope of information, has one particular group—beginning special educators—in mind. Further, it presumes that all potential teachers and clinicians who plan to work with exceptional children, youth, or adults must possess at least a minimum amount of basic information about all exceptionalities. The importance and universality of this principle have been demonstrated again and again. Even the most specialized teachers or clinicians will sooner or later encounter those individuals who do not fit any "pure" diagnostic type or category. They must then know enough to provide appropriate immediate assistance, gain consultative help as needed, and crossrefer to other professionals as required.

The presentation of information in this book is based on the belief that in the beginning stages of any training program an eclectic point of view (as opposed to a primarily "behavioristic," "clinical teaching," "task analysis oriented," or any other more specific point of view) will make possible a more objective, widely applicable, nonbiased base for further learning. As students proceed into their chosen fields of specialization, the emphasis of any given college training program can be implemented with minimal philosophical interference from this type of information base.

This text is about special education programs for exceptional children, youth, and adults, recognizing the value of joint efforts (by regular and special educators) but emphasizing the role of special educators. It relates in part to my conviction that although the least restrictive educational environment is essential, the importance of the role of the special educator must not be minimized or discounted. Special education is required for children and youth who have very special needs. It must include a variety of services

PREFACE

and be provided in different settings in different amounts, with objectives related to individual needs and specific age and developmental levels. It requires services provided through a combination of educational programs involving both regular classroom teachers and special educators, developed with the active assistance of parents or guardians and students.

The book is organized in a manner that seems, in practice, to be most conducive to learning for those who have little or no background in education of exceptional children. The first three chapters include a general review of the history of development of special education as it exists today. Education of the handicapped has changed extensively in the last 15 to 20 years, and an understanding of the past has continuing value in interpretation of the present.

The majority of this text (Chapters 5 through 12) is dedicated to the provision of objective information about the various types of handicapping conditions that have led to the need for special educational services and about the unique needs of the gifted, talented, and creative students who have been overlooked for much too long. Unlike some other efforts to discuss the needs of exceptional children and youth, there will be no attempt in this book to call the mentally retarded by terminology that implies that they are not mentally retarded. Full recognition is given to the factors that led to overinclusion of students in classes that were said to be organized for mentally retarded but were badly managed and misused. This unfortunate situation (reviewed and discussed in the first section of the text) will haunt special educators for some time to come, but it does not change the fact that there are mentally retarded persons who are in critical need of effective special programs and services. In a similar manner, the hearing impaired have unique needs that must be met and can be best met by first recognizing the fact that those needs relate to their hearing impairment. Thus they will be called deaf or hearing impaired. This same principle applies to all generally recognized handicapping conditions. In each instance, unique characteristics will be considered, and the various ways in which educational needs may be met will be reviewed. In all cases, the guiding principle will be provision of *appropriate* services in the least restrictive educational environment. The major emphasis is on programs for exceptional minors who will more likely be served by the public schools; however, some mention of programs for adults will be found even in these education-oriented chapters. The final two chapters of this text relate almost exclusively to adults.

Chapter 4 provides a look at some of the ways in which special education in Canada compares with special education in the United States. This chapter will have greater value in some geographical areas than others and may be omitted without affecting the flow of information in the following chapters. The four chapters that make up the final section were included because of the unusual importance of the topics under consideration. These topics are similar in that they cut across the various areas of exceptionality and they are well recognized as critically needed but "underdeveloped." The concerns of this section include early childhood programs for the handicapped, educational programming for handicapped or disabled adolescents, programs and services required by the handicapped or disabled adult, and services provided through rehabilitation and other community programs. These areas of concern represent educational "frontiers" and are fertile ground for those who wish to be pioneers. It seems even more certain that these are destined to be areas of great professional potential since services at these levels have been either strongly encouraged (through incentive funds) or actually mandated by Public Law 94-142 or the Vocational Rehabilitation Act of 1973.

This text was prepared in the hope that it might provide the reader with an understanding of the historical basis for programs for exceptional persons, an accurate picture of the present status of such programs and services, and a glimpse of what the future may bring. This information and these understandings may then provide the base on which special educators of tomorrow may build and develop.

Bill R. Gearheart

ACKNOWLEDGMENTS

In 30 years as an educator, I have attempted to learn from children, parents, and other educators and have tried to share what I have learned. However, in embarking on the development of this text, it seemed particularly important to verify basic information and make certain that the book was organized for maximum usefulness in the college classroom.

Three individuals made unusual contributions in the conceptualization and preparation of this text. *Mel Weishahn* assisted in conceptualization, read critical sections of this text, and provided a variety of valuable suggestions. In addition to his experience in teaching special-educators-in-training, Professor Weishahn has the advantage of experience as a teacher of the mentally retarded and of the visually impaired. His expertise was greatly appreciated. *Elaine Uhrig* provided suggestions relating to both organization and content, based on teaching several thousands (she asked that I not tell how many) of undergraduate students in the very type of introduction-to-exceptional-children course for which this text was prepared. In addition to extensive college teaching experience, Professor Uhrig is an experienced teacher of the hearing impaired. Her ideas were most important in the completion of this text. *Carol Kozisek Gearheart* wrote the chapter on teaching the emotionally disturbed, read and provided helpful comments on the entire manuscript, and provided essential support and encouragement. As a former teacher of emotionally disturbed children and now a college professor, she gave essential assistance. To these three fine professionals (and beautiful people) I extend a special word of appreciation.

Another colleague provided assistance that will be of value to professors who may select this text for use in a college course. My sincere thanks to *Tom Sileo* for his work in developing the instructor's manual and for general comments about text content.

A number of other special educators provided assistance by reading specific sections of the manuscript or providing input regarding organization, scope, or content. Suggestions and ideas were solicited and received from respected professsionals in various areas of the United States. We received some widely divergent suggestions and ideas, but also some remarkably similar input from a majority of these individuals. The final section of this text, in which preschool programs, programs for adolescents, programs for adults, rehabilitation services, other community services, and counseling needs are emphasized, is primarily a result of their input.

ACKNOWLEDGMENTS

Those who provided the above-mentioned assistance include:

William Carricker, *University of Virginia*
Jack Dinger, *Slippery Rock State College*
Joseph Eisenbach, *Western Michigan University*
Dale Lundeen, *University of Northern Colorado*
Herbert Prehm, *Arizona State University*
George Sheperd, *University of Oregon*
Richard Schofer, *University of Missouri*
Dean Tuttle, *University of Northern Colorado*
Billy Watson, *University of New Mexico*
Howard Stutt, *McGill University*
Mary Solanus Ufford, *Eastern Michigan University*
James Walker, *Illinois State University*

An additional group of individuals deserve recognition for their very special help. In conversations with professors who teach in some of the northern states, it was suggested that an introductory text would be of more value if it could relate to some of the needs and practices of our special education neighbors in Canada. Although there are many similarities between special education programs in the United States and Canada, there are certain differences that may be of interest. Special educators in Canada were quick to respond to a request for more information about their programs for exceptional children. Although the chapter outlining some of the unique characteristics of Canadian special education cannot be called comprehensive—and I must take full responsibility for any misinformation that may be inadvertently included—I want to thank the following educators who provided information for the "Canadian" chapter:

C. K. Andrews
T. Baron
G. D. Bergman
G. E. Beuree
E. J. M. Church
J. A. G. Gittins
A. G. Jones
D. Kendall

D. Little
R. M. Livingston
K. McKie
E. MacLellan
E. J. Owens
A. J. Rathgeber
H. Stutt
D. Treherne

Finally, may I say a simple "thanks" to others, too numerous to be specifically mentioned by name, who have unselfishly provided encouragement, assistance, and information along the way. This includes teachers and directors of special education with whom I have been privileged to work through the years, staff members of state departments of special education, the Bureau of Education for the Handicapped, and former students who are now professors of special education in colleges and universities in some forty states of the nation. All who comprehend the true nature of learning will understand as I say: "Thanks for what you taught, as we attempted to learn together."

Bill R. Gearheart

CONTENTS

SECTION ONE
Special education for the '80s historical, legal, and philosophical foundations

1 Special education in the '80s: historical forces and vectors, 3

Introduction, 4
Early treatment of the gifted and the handicapped, 4
New hope for the handicapped: mid-eighteenth through nineteenth centuries, 6
    Program development in the United States, 7
Establishment of special classes in the public schools (1900 to mid-1960s), 8
    General trends: 1920 to 1960, 10
Legislation and litigation: prelude to comprehensive programming (mid-1960s to Public Law 94-142), 12
    Legislation and programs for the handicapped, 13
Litigation on behalf of the rights of the handicapped, 16
    Types of litigative efforts, 17
    Right to free, appropriate public education, 18
    Inappropriate or incorrect classification or labeling, 19
Parent and professional groups: advocates for the handicapped, 21
    Parent groups, 21
    Professional groups, 24
Legislation and advocacy on behalf of the gifted, talented, and creative, 25
Summary, 26
    Handicapped, 26
    Gifted and talented, 27

2 Legal and financial framework for services to exceptional students, 33

Introduction, 34
Legal basis for public education, 35
    Effect of litigation, 35
    Local school board, 35
Financial structure of public schools, 37
    Variations in financial base, 37

CONTENTS

        Special education reimbursement, 38
    Public Law 94-142: a major statement of public policy, 39
        Purpose, 40
        Children served, 40
        Related services to be provided, 40
        Appropriate education: individualized education program (IEP), 41
        Other important provisions, 42
        Financial potential, 42
    Section 504: Vocational Rehabilitation Act of 1973, 43
    State and federal assistance for special programs for the gifted, talented, and creative, 44
    Summary, 45

3 Providing programs and services: a philosophical base, program guidelines, and basic issues, 51

Introduction, 52
Education of exceptional children: a philosophy and related principles, 52
    A philosophy of education for exceptional children and youth, 52
    Related principles, 53
Prevalence of exceptional children, 54
Program guidelines, 54
    Screening, referral, and assessment, 55
The placement decision and the need for a full continuum of services, 59
    Regular class placement with consultation from special education personnel, 59
    Regular class placement with consultation from special educators, plus provision of special materials, 60
    Regular class placement plus itinerant services, 60
    Regular class placement plus assistance in the resource room, 61
    Cooperative plan, 62
    Special class in regular school, 62
    Special day school, 62
    Hospital and homebound service, 63
    Residential or boarding school, 63
    Placement decision variables, 63
Basic issues in educating exceptional children, 63
    Mainstreaming/integrating the handicapped, 64
    Nondiscriminatory assessment, 67
    Labeling, 69
Education of the gifted: how, where, and when, 72
Summary, 72

SECTION TWO

Special education in Canada

4 Educational programs for exceptional students in Canada, 81

Introduction, 82
Canada: a constitutional monarchy, 82
    Education in Canada, 83
        Special purpose commissions and seminars; other federal efforts, 85

CONTENTS

The Official Languages Act of 1969, 86
Activities of the Canadian Council for Exceptional Children, 86
Canada: size and population, 87
Special education in the Atlantic provinces, 88
The Atlantic Provinces Special Education Authority, 88
New Brunswick, 88
Newfoundland and Labrador, 90
Nova Scotia, 91
Prince Edward Island, 91
Special education in Quebec, 92
Special education in Ontario, 94
Special education in Manitoba, 96
Special education in Saskatchewan, 97
Special education in Alberta, 98
Special education in British Columbia, 100
Unique and noteworthy programs and activities in Canada, 102
Summary, 104

SECTION THREE

Sensory impairments

5 Education of children and youth who are hearing impaired, 109

Introduction, 110
Historical origins of education of the hearing impaired, 111
Early history, 111
Establishment of schools in Europe, 112
Establishment of schools in the United States, 113
Anatomy and physiology of the auditory system, 115
Definitions: types and degrees of hearing impairment, 117
Other classification systems, 118
Causes of hearing impairment, 120
Medical and surgical treatment of hearing impairment, 121
Audiometry and the role of the audiologist, 122
Prevalence of hearing impairment, 122
Identification of children who are hearing impaired, 123
Major methods used to teach the hearing impaired, 124
Manual communication systems, 126
Other educational considerations, 129
Educational settings: the question of maximal integration of the hearing impaired, 132
An educational placement system: application of the variable service continuum concept, 134
Summary, 136

6 Education of children and youth who are visually impaired, 143

Introduction, 144
Historical origins of education of the visually impaired, 144
Early history, 144
Establishment of schools in Europe, 145
Establishment of schools in the United States, 146
Anatomy and physiology of the visual system, 147
Definitions: terminology used to describe visual impairment or handicap, 148

xiii

CONTENTS

Types and causes of visual impairment, 150
Prevalence of visual impairment, 152
Medical and surgical treatment of visual impairment, 153
Identification of children who are visually impaired, 154
Teaching the visually impaired: approaches and techniques, 155
    Reading and writing for the visually impaired, 155
Orientation and mobility training, 157
Other educational considerations, 160
    Early childhood and preschool needs, 160
    Adapted educational materials and/or equipment, 163
    Techniques of daily living (TDL), 163
Educational settings: the question of maximal integration of the visually impaired, 164
An educational placement system: application of the variable service continuum concept, 166
Summary, 167

SECTION FOUR
Learning disabilities and speech/language disorders

7 Education of children and youth with learning disabilities, 175

Introduction, 176
Historical origins of education of the learning disabled, 176
    Foundations of learning disabilities (prior to 1963), 176
    Learning disabilities: a recognized entity (1963 to the present), 178
Definitions and prevalence, 179
Identification of students who are learning disabled, 181
Approaches, theoretical constructs, and educational implications, 183
    Multisensory approaches, 183
        Educational implications, 187
    Hyperactivity: theories and approaches, 187
        Educational implications, 189
    Perceptual-motor approaches, 190
        Educational implications, 195
    Language function—related approaches, 196
        Educational implications, 199
    Behavior modification approaches, 200
        Educational implications, 201
    Medically oriented approaches, 201
        Educational implications, 202
Educational provisions: application of the variable service continuum, 202
Summary, 204

8 Education of children and youth with speech and language disorders, 213

Introduction, 214
Historical origins of speech/language services, 215
    Establishment of programs in Europe, 215
    Establishment of programs in the United States, 216
Development of speech and language, 217
    Speech development: mechanics of speech, 217
    Language development: the human miracle, 218

Speech and language disorders: definitions and classifications, 221
    Speech disorders, 223
    Language disorders, 223
Disorders of articulation and resonance, 225
Disorders of voice (phonation), 227
Fluency or speech-flow disorders, 228
Language disorders, 230
Prevalence of speech/language disorders, 232
Identification of students with speech and language disorders, 233
Causes of speech and language disorders, 233
Medical and surgical treatment of speech and language disorders, 235
Educational provisions for students with speech or language disorders, 236
    Assessment of speech and language disorders, 236
    Therapy or remediation of speech and language disorders, 237
        Models for therapy, 237
Summary, 238

SECTION FIVE

Other handicapping conditions

9 Education and training of the mentally retarded, 247

Introduction, 248
Historical origins of programs and services for the mentally retarded, 248
    Early history: an era of superstition, 248
    Nineteenth century: the rise of institutions, 249
    Twentieth century: development of comprehensive public programs, 251
A definition and selected terminology used in mental retardation, 253
    Levels of mental retardation, 253
Systems of classification, 254
    Legal classification systems, 255
    Educational classification systems, 255
    Medical classification systems, 255
Prevalence of mental retardation, 257
Causes of mental retardation, 258
    Infections and intoxications, 258
    Trauma or physical agents, 260
    Disorders of metabolism and nutrition, 260
    Gross brain disease, 262
    Unknown prenatal influence, 262
    Chromosomal abnormalities, 263
Identification of the mentally retarded, 264
Education and training of the mentally retarded, 266
    Educable mentally retarded, 266
    Trainable mentally retarded, 269
    Severely retarded, 270
An educational placement system: application of the variable service continuum concept, 271
Summary, 273

10 Education of children and youth who are emotionally disturbed, 283

Introduction, 284
History, 284

CONTENTS

Definitions, characteristics, and prevalence, 291
    Characteristics, 292
    Prevalence, 293
Theoretical models and related interventions, 294
    Biophysical theory, 294
        Interventions, 296
    Psychoanalytic theories, 296
        Interventions, 298
    Behavioral model, 298
        Interventions, 300
    Sociologic theories, 300
        Interventions, 303
    Ecologic theory, 304
        Interventions, 305
    Countertheories, 305
An educational placement system: application of the variable service continuum concept, 305
Issues relating to educational concerns for the emotionally disturbed, 308
    Juvenile delinquency, 308
    Child abuse, 309
Summary, 309

11 Education of children and youth who have physical or health impairments or are multihandicapped, 317

Introduction, 318
Historical origins of special programs for children and youth with physical disabilities, 318
Physical disabilities and health impairments: a definition and a conceptual frame of reference, 321
Classifications of physical disabilities and impairments, 322
Major physical disabilities and educational implications, 323
    Amputations, 323
    Arthritis, 324
    Asthma, 325
    Cerebral palsy, 326
    Convulsive disorders (epilepsy), 329
    Diabetes, 330
    Muscular dystrophy, 332
    Poliomyelitis, 332
    Rheumatic fever, 333
    Spina bifida, 333
Multiple disabilities or handicaps, 334
Role of medical specialists, 335
Educational settings: maximal integration of the physically disabled, 336
Summary, 339

SECTION SIX
Those "most often overlooked" exceptional students

12 Education of children and youth with unusual gifts and abilities, 347

Introduction, 348
Historical development of education for the gifted, talented, and creative (the beginning until 1960), 349

Historical development of education for the gifted, talented, and creative (1960 to the present), 351
Definitions: the gifted, talented, and creative, 353
    Creativity, 358
Identification of the gifted, talented, and creative, 360
    Step 1 in identification, 360
    Step 2 in identification, 364
    Step 3 in identification, 365
Characteristics of gifted, talented, and creative students, 366
Number of children and youth who need special services, 369
Teachers of the gifted, 369
Federal leadership in stimulating programs for the gifted, talented, and creative, 371
State leadership in establishing programs for the gifted, 371
Components essential to good programs for the gifted, 372
Educational provisions for the gifted and talented in Connecticut: a study of the efforts of one state, 374
Implementing the local program for gifted, talented, and creative students, 379
Summary, 380

SECTION SEVEN

Program areas of special concern

13 Early education of handicapped children, 387

Introduction, 388
Terminology, 388
Historical development of early educational programs for disabled/handicapped children, 389
Structure and focus of early childhood programs for the disabled/handicapped, 390
Critical need of handicapped children for early intervention, 392
Existing programs for children who are handicapped or at risk, 393
    University of Washington model preschool center for handicapped children, 394
    Marin County Atypical Infant Development (AID) program, 396
    The Portage Project, 398
    University of Illinois program for gifted/talented handicapped preschool children, 401
A national perspective on early childhood programs for handicapped children and children at risk, 403
    Children served, 403
    Program budgets, 404
    University affiliation, 404
    Amount (quantity) of programming, 404
    Parent involvement, 405
    Source of referral, 405
    Program emphasis, 405
Summary, 406

14 Education of handicapped adolescents: unique problems associated with secondary school programming, 411

Introduction, 412
Historical roots of secondary level programs for the handicapped, 412
  The secondary school: conflicting concepts about its basic functions, 416
  Adolescence: implications for secondary school programming, 419

CONTENTS

Various approaches to successful secondary school programming, 421
Vocational training programs for the handicapped, 423
    Major vocational training programs, 424
        Work experience, 425
        Work-study, 425
        On-the-job training (OJT), 425
        Off-campus work station, 425
        Cooperative programs, 425
        Higher-cost skill training, 425
    General guidelines for establishing an adapted vocational program for handicapped or disabled students, 426
    Common errors and weaknesses of vocational training programs for the handicapped, 428
Summary, 428

15 Programs and services for the adult handicapped, 435

Introduction, 436
College programs for handicapped and disabled adults, 437
Residential programs for the handicapped, 440
    Programs for the mentally retarded, 441
    Programs for the mentally ill, 441
Vocational programs for the adult handicapped, 443
    The sheltered workshop, 443
Community and/or personal adaptation programs, 445
    Environmental adaptations, 446
    Adapted transportation facilities, 447
Temporary or intermittent support services, 449
Legal rights of the adult handicapped or disabled, 450
    Rights guaranteed by federal laws, 451
    Rights guaranteed by state laws, 454
    Litigation and legal rights, 455
Summary, 456

16 Rehabilitation and other programs and resources for the handicapped, 463

Introduction, 464
Historical development of publicly supported rehabilitation programs in the United States, 464
Private rehabilitation programs and resources, 466
Scope and philosophy of rehabilitation programs, 467
Other community programs and services, 468
Summary, 474

Glossary, 477

SPECIAL EDUCATION FOR THE '80s

SECTION ONE

Special education for the '80s: historical, legal, and philosophical foundations

Special education in the 1980s is quite comprehensive in scope; its goal is to provide appropriate educational assistance for all handicapped students at no additional cost to parents. To those new to this field this will seem logical and proper—the way it should be in a nation where education is an accepted birthright—but it has not always been this way. In fact, appropriate education for all handicapped students is a phenomenon of the last decade.

The major goal of this text is to provide a description of special programs and services now available to most children, youth, and adults, regardless of handicap or disability. Chapters 5 through 16 will provide this description and will help the reader to understand much of what is now accepted practice in programs of education and assistance to and for the handicapped.

To fully understand these programs, one must possess some knowledge of the historical evolution that led to this present stage of development. It is also necessary to understand something about the laws that direct and control such special programs and the financial base that makes such programs possible.

Chapters 1, 2, and 3 present the minimum amount of information about these topics necessary to provide a base for the remainder of the text. The litigation that accelerated the process of change and the sequence of federal laws that led to present educational guidelines will be considered. A philosophy of education for the handicapped will be outlined to illustrate the thinking underlying most educational programs for the handicapped in the United States today; some of the basic issues still under debate will be reviewed. In total, the content of this section should prepare the reader to more fully understand the remainder of this text.

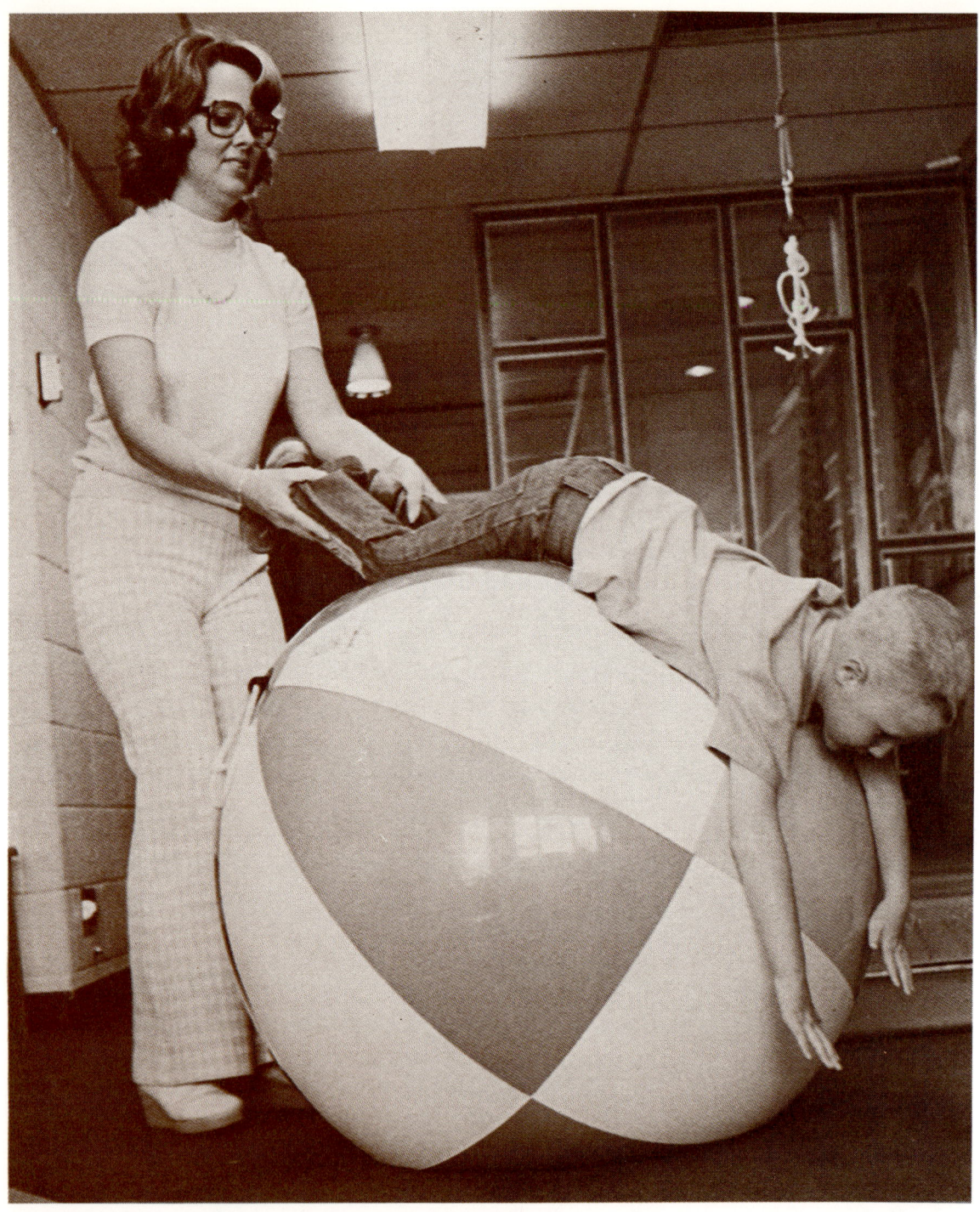

Until recent years, assistance in the development of physical abilities was not considered the responsibility of the public schools in much of the nation. Such assistance was often provided through parent-sponsored programs.

chapter 1

Special education in the '80s: historical forces and vectors

objectives

To trace the historical antecedents of presently existing programs and services for exceptional children and youth and to understand the role of superstition, religion, science, and the concepts of human rights and human dignity in the evolution of education for exceptional individuals.

To emphasize and present examples of the manner in which federal legislation has promoted recent progress in the provision of education for exceptional children and youth.

To indicate how litigation has forced public agencies to reconsider their responsibility to the handicapped and has thus further accelerated existing educational trends.

To describe the role of parent organizations and other advocacy groups in the movement to obtain appropriate, equitable programs and services for the handicapped.

To consider how the promotion of appropriate, specialized educational provisions for the gifted, talented, and creative has been less successful than provision for the handicapped and may require renewed efforts with a somewhat different basic focus.

Introduction

When we consider educational programs and services for exceptional children and youth today, we think of a variety of handicapping conditions and of the gifted, talented, and creative. Some disagreement exists as to acceptable definitions, and different terminology may be in use in various parts of the United States, but for the most part, educators would agree that the handicapped include the mentally retarded, the hearing handicapped, the visually handicapped, the speech handicapped, the emotionally disturbed, the learning disabled, and those with handicaps relating to physical or other health impairments. In recent years, added attention has been paid to children with more than one handicapping condition, children usually called multihandicapped. Alternate terms such as acoustically handicapped or disabled (rather than hearing handicapped), socially maladjusted or behavior disordered (rather than emotionally disturbed), and terms that describe the degree or type of mental retardation are in common use, but regardless of specific terminology, these are recognized as conditions requiring special educational provisions. This is the scope of special education today, but it was very different in the past, as we will see from the following historical review.

Only a limited number of details will be provided in this historical overview, for additional details are included in the more extensive history included in chapters addressed to each exceptionality. The purpose of this general outline of early history is to provide a frame of reference for events that are outlined later in this chapter.

Early treatment of the gifted and the handicapped

Perhaps the *least* widely recognized programs for exceptional students today are those for the gifted, talented, and creative. In contrast, these children were the first to be recognized and provided special educational assistance by various governments or governmental leaders. In fact, several centuries before the time of Christ gifted and talented boys were recognized for their unusual potential and specialized educational programming was provided. The motivation for such assistance was quite different from that to which we subscribe today, but gifted and talented children were sought out and educated to provide leadership for the nations involved. This type of special treatment was not really common, but special provisions for gifted and talented children and youth have existed on a sporadic basis for centuries.

Blindness, deafness, mental retardation, and mental illness have been recognized for centuries, but educational assistance for those with such handicaps is relatively new in the course of recorded history. In times past the deaf, blind, and retarded served as court jesters, walked the streets as beggars, and, in some cases, were put to death as infants. Stigma has been attached to almost all conditions of humanity that are significant deviations from the normal, an effect that has led to expulsion from existing society, loss of rights of citizenship, and, in the case of "witches," burning at the stake. The actions of "normal" members of society were usually justified through the exercise of some sort of pseudolegal procedure, but as is often the case, "legal" and "moral" were not synonymous.

In describing the history of treatment and education of the handicapped, various authors have established "eras," corresponding with major time periods in the recorded history of mankind. There are certain differences in various historical accounts, but most agree that very little of substance regarding educational provisions took place before the last half of the eighteenth century. However, a great deal was happening to those individuals we would now called the handicapped during this earlier time period.

In a comprehensive discussion of the historical origins of education of the handicapped, Hewett (1974) notes that there have been four major historical determiners of treatment of the handicapped; (1) the need for survival, (2) the force of superstition, (3) the findings of science, and (4) the desire to be of service. Using a swinging pendulum analogy, Hewett notes that progress toward the state of development that exists today has been accomplished through a continuing series of swings of the pendulum, with the early swings primarily between survival and superstition. He also notes that during the entire time period from the beginnings of recorded history until the sixteenth and seventeenth centuries, although the pendulum at times swung in the direction of science and service, apparent gains were systematically negated as it moved back toward superstition and survival. In fact, except for the widening of the movement of this hypothetical pendulum at times, during the fourteenth and fifteenth centuries the handicapped received poorer treatment than had been the case many centuries earlier. The only major characteristic that could be ascribed to this long historical period is variation: variation from one geographic area to another and from one decade to the next.

For hundreds of years, gains in the direction of more scientific attitudes and the desire to be of service to the less fortunate were regularly counteracted by the leftover effects of superstition and fear of what could not be fully understood. For example, during the Roman period, as different Roman rulers assumed power, radically different attitudes prevailed. Whereas one emperor would encourage the acceptance of societal responsibility for the handicapped and promote humane treatment, the next might personally participate in such practices as using crippled individuals for personal target practice. And, although the spread of Christianity led to many instances in which service to the less fortunate was taught and practiced, the same force, in the form of church-led attacks on heresy, was a major factor in the reemphasis of demonology, witchcraft, and the belief that forces of evil cause what we would now call mental illness. The effect of this emphasis was felt for centuries and was a strong force in retarding what might otherwise have been much earlier recognition of the needs of the handicapped.

Throughout the entire period from the beginning of recorded history up through the fifteenth and sixteenth centuries, there were those who attempted to establish more rational, scientific, or humanistic points of view regarding the handicapped, but their voices were regularly silenced. In 1584, when Reginald Scot took the position that some of the so-called witches were actually mentally ill (and made his case quite effectively in writing) King James I of England personally condemned this position and ordered Scot's book seized and burned (Coleman, 1972). As recently as the seventeenth century, most scientists and physicians appeared to have accepted the idea that the mind and abnormalities of behavior that might be a result of mental functioning were more the domain of the philosopher and theologian than of those involved with physical ills (Zilboorg and Henry, 1941).

In summary, despite some meaningful attempts to assist the handicapped, the picture from the beginnings of recorded history until the mid-1700s was primarily a bleak one. Because the handicapped looked and acted differently from others, because they were an economic burden in a world in which many nonhandicapped persons could barely keep from starving, because the church persisted in its belief in demons, witches, and evil spirits, and because the nature of handicapping conditions was not understood, whenever a step in the right direction was taken, its effect was nullified by these other factors.

It was noted at the start of this consideration of early history that the gifted were first among the exceptional children to have been recognized and provided special educational opportunities. Throughout this period there were times when, through governmental action, specialized provisions were made. At other times the organized church provided special opportunities for youths thought to be unusually capable, but this too was sporadic rather than general. For the most part, these efforts, whether church or state sponsored, applied primarily to males of the upper middle or upper classes. Fortunately, as the eighteenth century progressed, forces that were to bring about much-needed change were in motion. The events that would lead to the even more momentous changes of the twentieth century are the topic of the next section of this historical review.

New hope for the handicapped: mid-eighteenth through nineteenth centuries

Although there had been widely scattered efforts to educate the deaf and the blind prior to the middle of the eighteenth century, such efforts for the most part were short-lived. Some were recognized but viewed by outside observers as miracles, not educational efforts; others ran counter to existing political philosophy and were terminated by authorities; but all may have had some effect on what was about to happen. What did take place was the formal initiation of schools for the deaf and the blind, schools that were open to students of various social levels and were intended to educate, not protect or shelter. These first programs were initiated in France, Germany, and England in the last half of the eighteenth century and were to be followed in the early 1800s by similar efforts on behalf of the mentally retarded. These were not total national efforts but were promoted by individuals who had developed a belief in the ability of the deaf, blind, or mentally retarded to profit from education or training.

These early programs were sufficiently prominent that the word soon spread throughout Europe and the United States. The viability of education of the handicapped was now an established fact. For all practical purposes we can say that the nineteenth century was the first in which there was some sort of concerted effort to train or educate the handicapped throughout the entire century; it was the dawning of a new age of concern for the handicapped. This concerted interest in education of the handicapped, an interest that crossed national boundaries and won generally wide acceptance in a relatively short period of time, was the beginning of a movement that was to have tremendous impact on the face of public education.

Along with the fact that educational programs became established and well recognized during the nineteenth century, another fact deserves special notice. From the very beginnings, although there was considerable cooperation among professionals interested in educating the handicapped, there were disagreements, sometimes quite strong and heated, as to *how* to educate. Nowhere was this more evident than among early educators of the deaf. As soon as there were two major programs established to educate the deaf, there were two conflicting approaches: one primarily manual, the other strictly oral. This philosophical conflict, which has had so many practical implications, continues to this day.

For the first half of the nineteenth century, Western Europe remained the center of the stage on which the developing drama of education of the handicapped was acted out. Programs for the deaf and blind, already in existence at the start of the century, were improved and expanded. And, although the story of the "Wild Boy of Aveyron" (Itard, 1962) will be told in greater detail in Chapter 9, it is a story that must be mentioned in any general history of the handicapped. It is the story of a boy (given the name Victor) discovered running "wild" in the forest of Aveyron in southern France in 1799. It is also the story of a physician, Jean-Marc-Gaspard Itard, who spent long years attempting to cure Victor. Unfortunately, Itard expected too much and became quite discouraged in the end, but the written record of his efforts was the catalyst that lead to increased interest in providing training for the retarded. Thus by the middle of the nineteenth century, the viability of educational programs for the deaf, the blind, and the mentally retarded was an accepted fact. In addition, efforts were underway to provide for the mentally ill but were less well developed than the others.

In the remainder of this chapter we will consider primarily the educational programs as they developed in the United States. There was a great deal of activity beginning in the United States, and although much of this activity was triggered by events and personalities in Europe, things were truly beginning to happen in the New World.

PROGRAM DEVELOPMENT IN THE UNITED STATES

Many important events took place in the United States at mid-century that were indications of the kind of concern for the handicapped that would soon develop in this nation. Edouard Seguin, Itard's protegé in France and the founder of the first successful school established exclusively for education of the mentally retarded in Paris, emigrated to the United States at mid-century. At about this same time a number of schools (residential institutions) for the mentally retarded (then called feeble-minded or idiots) were opened in various states in the eastern United States. By 1880 there had even been a few institutions for the retarded established west of the Mississippi, and by the turn of the century, institutions for the mentally retarded were an accepted sign of growing maturity for any developing state (Gearheart and Litton, 1979).

During this same period, a number of "asylums" or "institutions" for the deaf were established throughout the United States. The name "asylum" was brought over to the United States from France when the first such program was established as the American Asylum for the Deaf, at West Hartford, Connecticut, in 1817. Acceptance of the need for this residential type setting for the deaf helped to pave the way for the rapid expansion of residential institutions for the mentally retarded just noted.

In a parallel development, residential schools for the blind were under development in the United States. In 1831 an internationally recognized school, presently known as the Perkins School for the Blind, was started in Watertown, Massachusetts, by Samuel Gridley Howe, a Boston physician. By 1850, there were a number of such schools in the United States, and Howe was involved in starting residential schools for the feebleminded. (Howe was Seguin's major contact in the United States and greatly influenced his move to the United States.)

One other movement must be reviewed to complete the picture of the manner in which education of the handicapped first developed in the United States. Dorothea Dix, a retired school teacher, acted anything but retired as she pursued her belief that the mentally ill were among the most mistreated persons in our society. In addresses to the U.S. Congress in 1848, Ms. Dix roundly chastized legislative groups for their indifference. Between 1841 and 1881, she was instrumental in the establishment of thirty-two modern mental hospitals (Zilboorg and Henry, 1941). Though others provided support, hers was the voice that could not be silenced, a voice that was all the more notable in a time when women were not well received in such roles.

The nineteenth century has been called the era of institutions for reasons that should be readily evident in light of the preceding discussion. Residential settings, whether called hospitals (for the mentally ill) or asylums (for the blind), were still residential settings. They tended to serve those with more severe handicaps, and treatment, especially in the case of institutions for the mentally retarded and mentally ill, left much to be desired. On the other hand, they were a great improvement on the kind of treatment that such persons had received for centuries, and they were an important step in the development of educational programs of today. For the most part, programs in the United States, which had started behind those in Europe, were on their way to catching up or even forging ahead as the nineteenth century came to a close.

• • •

Before proceeding to the next section of this historical account, we should note another type of variable that may lead to confusion. In addition to variations having to do with long-term swings of the historical "pendulum," there are variations of record, which are a result of the manner in which information is reported. These apparent contradictions are not highly significant in interpreting the development of programs for exceptional children and youth but may give rise to questions in the minds of readers who are unfamiliar with the origin of such contradictions. This may certainly be the case if a number of different historical accounts are read. One such source of conflicting information has to do with the manner in which certain developments are reported by different historians. This type of apparent discrepancy and its origin can be illustrated by considering, for example, the date given for the time when the first state residential school for a given handicapping condition was established. In such cases, a resolution by a governing legislative body establishing an official study of the need for such a school may pass in a given year. After the study is completed, legislation authorizing such a school may be passed and the date of such legislation may be 2 years after the original date. A superintendent may not be appointed for the school (which still must be built) until 18 months later, and the first resident may not enter the school for another 10 months. When we read conflicting dates for the "establishment" of a given school or program, a situation like this may be the reason. Similarly, when we consider any time period in the United States, we must remember that there are fifty states. While one state may be entering a new period or era, others are in the middle of the preceding era. This sort of variable development must be kept in mind as we proceed with this historical account. It is particularly applicable when rapid changes are taking place.

Establishment of special classes in the public schools (1900 to mid-1960s)

Although a limited number of public school special classes were established before the turn of the century, for the most part this was not the accepted practice. A separate residential facility, serving both children and adults and under the direction of a physician, was the general rule as the twentieth century was ushered in. There were a number of program variations but separate facilities were still the norm. This separation of children from their age peers was of concern to Dr. Alexander Graham Bell. In a speech given at the closing session of the National Education Association (NEA) national convention in 1898, Bell recommended that programs for handicapped children should become:

> an annex to the public school system, receiving special instruction from special teachers, who shall be able to give instruction to little children who are either deaf, blind, or mentally deficient, without sending them away from their homes or from the ordinary companions with whom they are associated.

As a result of his recommendation, and with support from those few school systems that had tried out this then-revolutionary idea, the Department of Special Education was initiated as part of the NEA in 1902. Special classes for handicapped children, supported by and housed in the public schools, became an accepted part of the educational scene during the years that followed, and although they were known by different names in various cities and states, most were established as self-contained classes.

Reliable information as to class size, variability of degree of handicap, and eligibility criteria is not available, but there are indications that classes for the mentally retarded tended to range from about half the number enrolled in a normal class to almost as many as enrolled in a normal class. Classes for the deaf or blind were apparently considerably smaller. At these early dates there were no specific limitations imposed because of state reimbursement standards, and practices varied widely, particularly regarding the mentally retarded. Another complicating factor was the absence, prior to 1916, of any reliable assessment device to determine the actual presence of mental retardation. The original Binet-Simon scales had been developed in France in 1905 and were generally recognized as the first really meaningful individual test of intelligence. In 1916 they were revised extensively by Lewis Terman at Stanford University, thus giving birth to the *Stanford-Binet Intelligence Scale* (Anastasi, 1976). The Stanford-Binet provided a means of determining the degree of mental retardation that was superior to any previous method. This had several effects on education of the mentally retarded in the United States.* First, it provided an effective way to separate those children who actually had significantly lower than average range IQs from those who had higher level ability but were not achieving consistent with this ability. This usually led to further, more comprehensive evaluation of children with average or above intelligence, which in turn often led to discovery of other handicapping conditions. (Mild to moderate hearing losses were among the more common such difficulties discovered through such additional evaluation. Without the information provided by the Stanford-Binet, many of these children might have remained in classes for the mentally retarded for many years with no assistance directed toward their hearing loss, and with inadequate, inappropriate educational programming.) This effect of the Stanford-Binet was a favorable one, with generally positive results regarding the improvement of educational programming for handicapped children and youth.

A second effect must also be recognized, an effect that was not positive as far as provision of better programs for the handicapped is con-

---

*Most readers are aware of the various controversies surrounding the use of intelligence tests. This controversy will not be considered in this chapter, but is further discussed in Chapter 3. In addition, a number of references to this problem, including anecdotes that we hope will shed further light on this problem, will be found in various chapters of this text as appropriate to specific exceptionalities.

cerned. Because the individual test of intelligence provided a more precise way to determine *levels* of ability, there was a tendency to deny programs to those children who were below certain established levels of intelligence. Although there was no immediate, nationwide establishment of a certain level below which the schools would not ordinarily provide services, over a period of several years an IQ of approximately 50 was established as the lower limit. The term "educable mentally retarded" (or handicapped) evolved for those above 50, and "trainable" for those below 50 IQ. In most instances, schools began to deny service to the "trainable," although a few schools continued to serve them. For those who were not served through public education, the alternatives were private schooling, institutional settings, or no formal program. This denial of free public education in some public schools continued until the late 1970s and in a few instances may still exist today. However, special classes for the educable mentally retarded grew and flourished to an extent that eventually led to other problems, as will be discussed later in this chapter.

GENERAL TRENDS: 1920 to 1960

From 1920 to 1960, certain other general trends developed throughout the nation. *When* each of the specific sequential steps actually occurred in various parts of the nation may have varied as much as 10 to 20 years, but the direction of movement was similar, and much of what happened was directly attributable to the phenomenon of special reimbursement. Very briefly, reimbursement for special education programs is a method whereby the state government, supplying funds from the state level, attempts to stimulate the establishment and maintenance of special programs and services for handicapped children. In later years, several states initiated reimbursement for certain programs and services for the gifted. These special funds are provided through several different types of formulas, but the general idea is to pay part of the per-pupil cost, which was presumed to be unusually high. The manner in which reimbursement was provided led to similar programs throughout any given state, and because there has been considerable similarity in reimbursement from state to state, some national similarities have been generated. However, as noted previously, the rate at which various parts of the nation moved through this evolution has varied.

Trends that developed during this period include those outlined in the following section.

1. Self-contained classes for the educable mentally retarded in the local public schools increased in popularity, as noted above.

2. State residential schools for those mentally retarded who were not served in the local public school classes flourished. The population served in such schools (often called the "State Home and Training School" or the "State Home and Hospital" or some similar name) varied greatly from state to state. Because of the lack of public school programs for the educable mentally retarded (EMR) in some localities, because some EMR children became wards of the state for any of a variety of reasons, or because EMR children might have other handicapping conditions and were difficult to manage, such children were regularly placed in state residential schools. During one period, many EMR children were so placed because they had epileptic seizures and medical services were readily available in such residential facilities.

Residential schools were also provided for those children whom educators often call trainable mentally retarded (TMR). Many children with Down's syndrome were placed in state residential schools soon after birth, with the approval of the medical profession and the courts. TMR individuals often provided a significant part of the work force for functions such as laundry work, routine kitchen work, garden work, cleaning, and others. The so-called back wards of these residential facilities also included the very severely mentally retarded and multiply handicapped. Many such individuals were placed in the state residential facility and remained for life. Preparation for life outside the institution as a regular part of the training program was not common until the 1950s and 1960s. The picture was not all bleak or negative, but because of overcrowding, underfunding, and the multiple tasks given to most such residential facilities, the picture was not a pleasant one.

3. State residential schools for the visually impaired increased in popularity during this same time period. These were different from residential facilities for the mentally retarded in that students typically did not attend over the summer and went home over longer holidays, and some who lived closer to the schools went home on weekends. Also, unlike residential facilities for the mentally retarded, these were schools, not holding facilities, and although the upper age range was often extended beyond age 21, it was not a facility for adults. Commencing in the 1950s more public schools added classes or other support programs for the visually handicapped, and since that time public school programs have increased steadily.

4. State residential schools for the hearing impaired increased in popularity. The information outlined above with regard to the visually impaired applies almost equally to the hearing impaired.

5. Special classes in the public schools for children who had physical disabilities such as crippling conditions, heart defects, asthmatic conditions, and the like were started in various parts of the nation in the late 1920s or the 1930s. These programs operated in various ways and such classes were known as classes for the physically handicapped, health impaired, crippled and delicate, or other similar names. These were programs for students who could not participate in regular physical activities, and in smaller school districts these were usually special classes housed on the first floor of an elementary school. In larger communities during the 1950s and 1960s, separate schools with special adaptations (e.g., elevators, therapy pools, ramps, and modified doors, toilet areas, and desks) became popular, and a number of wealthy individuals throughout the nation gave money or left provision in their wills for such schools to be built. As the 1960s neared, it became obvious that many such programs had overreached their intended purpose. In too many cases children who could have stayed in their home schools with neighborhood peers attended special schools. These schools were an easy "out" for a school district and made it unnecessary to adapt other facilities for these students. They also provided a "too easy" environment for some of these students, which did not prepare them for the real world.

6. Another type of service, provided as an adjunct service by itinerant specialists, was started as early as the second decade of the century, but did not receive its real impetus until the 1940s and 1950s. This was a remedially oriented service for students with speech impairments, provided by personnel who were, in the early days of such programming, called speech correctionists or speech therapists. (The title of professionals providing such service began to change in the 1950s and 1960s to include such titles as speech pathologist, speech clinician, or speech and language clinician.) This service was regularly provided in more advanced school systems by the 1950s and was common in a majority of school systems by 1960. The scope of service varied from one geographic area to another,

and rural areas often had less service or no service at all. Between 1950 and the mid-1960s, the function of the speech clinician changed appreciably, with a general broadening of function and additional emphasis on more severe difficulties and those related to language disorders. By 1960, there were more students being served by this component of the total special education program than by any other in most of the nation, and in those instances where this service was not "first," it was usually second.

7. One other handicapping condition was slowly beginning to achieve recognition as an area requiring service by 1950. Larger cities had initiated classes for "delinquent" students many years earlier, but these could not really be equated with services for children who were emotionally disturbed. However, it was finally recognized that there were children and youth who were not necessarily delinquent, but needed special assistance with problems that were obvious in the classroom and were primarily related to very poor emotional adjustment. It is certainly true that most such problems were noticed as a result of acting-out behavior, but as more capability to recognize true emotional disturbance was developed, it became clear that there were a number of children who should receive special services for emotional difficulties that were the underlying cause of their antisocial or generally maladaptive behavior. By 1960, it was becoming clear that this was a handicapping condition, which had been overlooked by virtue of the fact that, in many cases, such children were simply not allowed to attend school. It was equally clear that, using the same rationale as that applied in the case of the deaf, blind, or mentally retarded, they should receive special educational services.

As the period from 1900 to the mid-1960s came to a close, the necessity of special educational provisions for the handicapped (as then defined) was an established fact. There were variations in range and quality of service, but this is generally recognized as being true of all of education, not just education of the handicapped. As for special educational provisions for the gifted, only a few states gave recognition of the gifted and talented prior to the passage of the National Defense Education Act (NDEA) in 1958. This federal legislation, enacted in response to the fact that the USSR was able to loft a space satellite ahead of the United States, provided additional help to public schools in the areas of the sciences, mathematics, foreign languages, and guidance. It might be considered a first step, but predicated as it was on *national* interests, not the needs and rights of individual children, it did not provide a solid base for further efforts for the gifted.

In summary, the first 60 to 65 years of the twentieth century led to significant advances in educational programming for most handicapped children and to the establishment of a new subdiscipline of education, commonly called special education. Considering the events of the many centuries that had preceded this one, it was indeed a good time for the handicapped, and it appeared that if the present rate of improvement were to continue, the picture might become even brighter. But the "present rate" of improvement was destined to change, and events of unparalleled importance and impact were about to occur, as may be seen as this historical account continues.

Legislation and litigation: prelude to comprehensive programming (mid-1960s to Public Law 94-142)

As American society evolved through the turbulent '60s, a number of forces were at work that were to bring about permanent changes in special education. Many of these forces were not deliberately directed toward change in procedures for education of handicapped children, and their leaders did not know about philosophical debates regarding stigma effect, the environment in which children were educated, or negative aspects of institutions for the retarded. However, their efforts were perhaps more effective and permanent because they were *not* directed at one narrow concern, but rather at broad societal changes. This combination of forces and the societal concerns that spawned them related to a war in Vietnam, to concern for the consumer, to protection against the effect of monopolistic practices, to the rights of the elderly and the unborn, and to the needs of the poor and minority groups. These and other similar concerns might be generalized and characterized as increased concern for the "little people," those who traditionally had no one to speak for them, and those who were not always considered worthy of much attention and respect in a society that had for so long recognized beauty, intelligence, position, and the power of the dollar. Coupled with these various concerns was growing recognition of the potential power of *organized* efforts of those who had little power individually. In the midst of this already energized set of forces, there was a President, John F. Kennedy, who had experienced mental retardation in his immediate family, a number of congressional leaders who had similar experiences and concerns, and powerful business leaders of like persuasion. Activist parent groups clamored for their rights and the rights of their children; Congress wanted to support some positive programs; education of the handicapped was sufficiently developed so that it appeared the handicapped *could* be helped if given the proper opportunities: the time for change was at hand. And change came, stimulated by all of these factors simultaneously, with results that certainly equaled more than the sum of the individual efforts. In fact, all of these factors were so interrelated that it is impractical, if not impossible, to attempt to determine which came first, which had the greater effect, and so forth. Because of this difficulty and for ease of presentation and consideration, these factors will be arbitrarily divided into categories. Within these categories, events will be considered in chronologic order, with only occasional comments as to interrelationships. Major categories considered include: (1) legislation, (2) litigation, and (3) parent and professional associations.

LEGISLATION AND PROGRAMS FOR THE HANDICAPPED

Prior to the 1950s there were certain legislative provisions for handicapped persons, but the emphasis tended to be on older youth or adults. Then, in 1958 came the first of the significant enactments that would culminate in Public Law 94-142. We will start our consideration of significant federal legislation with this 1958 law, even though it predates the time period under consideration. The listing of laws that follows is by no means complete, but it includes most of the more significant legislative enactments of this period.

1958
PL 85-926 Public Law 85-926 is generally considered to be the most significant of the early enactments on behalf of the handicapped. This Act provided funds, in the form of direct grants, to the states and to institutions of higher learning. The purpose of these funds was to train college instructors who would then train teachers of the mentally retarded. Public Law 85-926 was important for several reasons. First, it established the principle of federal support of students at institutions of higher learning in pursuit of established national educational priorities. (This principle was even more definitely established in that the National Defense Education Act [NDEA], also representing a national

educational priority, was signed within 1 week of the signing of PL 85-926.) Second, PL 85-926 became even more important because of amendments that were soon to be added (noted later in this description). Third, PL 85-926 confirmed the principle of categorical assistance to persons with various handicapping conditions, a principle that became increasingly important as years went by.

1963
PL 88-164

When it was passed in 1963, supporters of this legislation believed it to be the culmination of all their earlier efforts and just about the best kind of legislation that might ever be expected of Congress. Supported by President Kennedy, it was a fairly complex bill and was entitled the Mental Retardation Facilities and Community Mental Health Centers Construction Act. Like a great deal of other federal legislation, this Act was concerned with more than its title might indicate. One of the parts of PL 88-164 having the most effect on provision of direct services to handicapped children in succeeding years was an amendment to PL 85-926 to expand the earlier provision to include training professional personnel to serve other major handicapping conditions. Earlier provisions, with amendments, had provided for both the mentally retarded and the deaf, and data provided from these programs indicated that the intended "chain letter effect" (one teacher trainer may train fifty teachers, each of whom may affect the lives of 100 children in a 5-year period) was working. Another section of this law provided for research and demonstration projects in the education of handicapped children. Another effect of the passage of PL 88-164, though not actually included in the law, was the establishment of The Division of Handicapped Children and Youth. As he signed this law into effect, President Kennedy established the Division to administer all existing programs for handicapped children and youth and to administer this new Act. In addition, Dr. Samuel Kirk, viewed by many as the top person in the nation in the field of special education, was appointed as director of the Divison, confirming its intended stature.

1965
PL 89-10

Public Law 89-10, the Elementary and Secondary Education Act (ESEA), was the first truly broad-scale aid to education act to be enacted by the U.S. Congress. The primary focus of ESEA was better educational opportunities for educationally disadvantaged children, and although not actually directed toward handicapped children (in the way that "handicapped children" are usually defined) it did provide massive amounts of money, compared to any previous enactments, some of which was used to initiate new programs for the handicapped. Unlike much of the earlier legislation, which was directed toward provision of better qualified teachers, PL 89-10 allowed the local districts to spend this money directly for teacher wages, if these were in fact *new* programs. In some districts, the entire amount received under Title I of PL 89-10 (a section of the law based on the number of low income families in the district) was spent to expand programs for the handicapped.

Another section of this Act, Title V, was directed toward improvement of state level educational leadership. In some instances, significant amounts of these Title V monies were used to improve special education programs; however, in too many instances this extended only far enough to take care of the increased state administrative loads generated by the development of new local programs.

One side effect of the passage of this precedent-breaking law was detrimental to the interests of handicapped children. To handle the enormous increase in federal management responsibilities brought on by PL 89-10, the U.S. Office of Education found it necessary to undertake a major reorganization. One result of this reorganization was the disbanding of the Division of Handicapped Children and Youth after only 18 months of existence. In ordering this reorganization and the resultant dismantling of the Division, there was no indication that the Division had not carried out its job effectively. It was simply one of the things that happen in Washington in reponse to heavy demands and immediate priorities. Although unfortunate for the moment, this temporarily negative effect led to other events that would prove to be highly advantageous in the long run.

1965 and 1966 A number of acts were passed during 1965 and 1966, continuing the "special purpose focus" on specific concerns, and very often on specific handicapping conditions. This included enactments on behalf of the deaf, the blind, and handicapped children in state-operated residential facilities. These were very good years for the handicapped as Congress was in the mood to attempt to correct earlier neglect of this long-forgotten population.

1966 PL 89-750 Late in the legislative session, the Eighty-ninth Congress was convinced that something must be done about the spin-off effect created as a result of earlier congressional action in the passage of PL 89-10. This effect was the dismantling of the Division of Handicapped Children and Youth. Congressional committee hearings brought out the strong feelings of various leaders in both the professional community and parent groups regarding the negative effects of this action. Evidence was presented that convinced committee members that the dispersal of programs for the handicapped among the various bureaus and divisions of the U.S. Office of Education had led to reduced services and other undesirable results. With the support of most special education leaders throughout the nation, the congressional committee recommended a Bureau for the Handicapped (one administrative level above the Division that had been disbanded). PL 89-750 was passed, adding Title VI to the Elementary and Secondary Education Act. Title VI was specifically a special education title and mandated the establishment of the Bureau of Education for the Handicapped, along with various other provisions. These included provision for preschool programs for the handicapped and the establishment of a National Advisory Committee on Handicapped Children charged with the responsibility to advise the Commissioner of Education regarding the nation's pressing needs and priorities.

1967 and 1968 Additional acts passed relating to such concerns as physical education and recreation for the handicapped, regional deaf-blind centers, regional resource centers, architectural barriers, and so forth. During this same time period the practice of earmarking parts of other enactments (for example, the Vocational Education Act) for exclusive use for the handicapped was initiated.

1969 PL 91-230 The Elementary and Secondary Act Amendments of 1969 included a consolidation of all existing legislation for the handicapped into one section, Title VI, which was then called The Education of the Handicapped Act. In addition, a new handicapping condition was recognized in PL 91-230. This was learning disabilities, added through the inclusion of Part G, a separate part of Title VI. This addition had been strongly urged in the initial report of the National Advisory Committee on Handicapped Children (established through PL 89-750) and included a variety of provisions such as research efforts, model programs, teacher training assistance, and others. Another new area was added as a part of PL 91-230, but was not a part of Title VI. This was a section authorizing certain actions on behalf of gifted children and a report to the Congress regarding their actual needs. This was particularly important in that it was based on the principle that gifted and talented children had the right to appropriate educational provisions, simply because this is the right of all children. This is quite different from the idea that the gifted and talented should be assisted in relation to defense needs (as in the case of the earlier National Defense Education Act), or from the point of view of national interests.

1973
PL 93-112 The Rehabilitation Act of 1973 (PL 93-112)—more specifically, Section 504 of this Act—had far-reaching implications for the handicapped. However, there were many difficulties in spelling out the regulations for this Act, difficulties reflected by the fact that the regulations were not signed by the Secretary of Health, Education and Welfare until late April, 1977. By the time it was implemented, Public Law 94-142 had been passed, a law that included many of PL 93-112's most important features as they related to handicapped children in the public schools. Certain features of 93-112 were not covered in later legislation and will be noted here. Most important among these features are guarantees of nondiscrimination in such areas as employment practices, program accessibility, and postsecondary education. This law relates to any program that receives federal assistance and thus in many instances applies to private facilities.

1974
PL 93-380 The Education Amendments of 1974 (PL 93-380) may be described as an umbrella act, for in fact this law relates to almost all aspects of education in the United States. Like PL 93-112, this act contained much that was to be expanded and clarified in PL 94-142, which was already in the planning and writing stage when this law was passed. It directed the states to plan for all handicapped children, to protect the rights of handicapped children and their parents in relation to placement, and to provide as much of the education of each handicapped child as possible in the "mainstream" of education, rather than in segregated settings. It extended most of the earlier Handicapped Act through fiscal year 1977, in anticipation of the Act (PL 94-142) that was soon to be recognized as the legislative mandate toward which parents and other advocates of the handicapped had worked for many years. Public Law 93-380 was the prelude to the climax of this series of legislative enactments, the passage of Public Law 94-142.

Although this legislative review has covered a period of 16 years, a time which must have seemed long to parents waiting for services for their children, it must be noted that this is a relatively short period of time as far as legislative history is concerned. The forces that reflected interest and concern for the handicapped had been sufficiently strong to bring about a radical change in the manner in which Congress viewed its responsibility for handicapped children and youth, and some limited concern for the gifted had also been shown. This was the state of affairs as the Ninety-Fourth Congress met and considered, among many other things, a truly comprehensive law that might properly be called an educational bill of rights for the handicapped. This law will be reviewed in considerable detail in Chapter 2 as part of a description of the framework within which services are provided for exceptional children in the 1980s. This historical account will continue as we consider the various litigative efforts undertaken from 1960 to 1975 that had a great effect on the type of legislation enacted.

Litigation on behalf of the rights of the handicapped*

Litigation has played an important role in the establishment of the rights of the handicapped and in the type of legislation passed at both the state and the national levels. When the courts decide that certain groups or classes of individuals have specific rights or should receive certain services, appropriate legislation usually follows. This has been true with other minority groups and is no less true with the handicapped. An understanding of litigation on behalf of the handicapped may

---

*Much of this discussion of litigation is adapted from a more comprehensive discussion of litigation in Gearheart, B., and Litton, F. *The trainable retarded.* St. Louis: The C. V. Mosby Co., 1979.

provide several insights: (1) it may help indicate how the evolution of certain practices took place, (2) it may provide some indication of what is likely to happen in the future as additional issues regarding the handicapped become the subject of litigation, and (3) it may provide guidance for others who are forced to establish their rights in this manner.

Special educators have obvious reasons to focus on *education* and those court decisions relating directly to education. However, to understand the total picture, it is important to be aware of *all* litigation that relates to the rights of the handicapped, whether or not it dictates such matters as which students will be taught in the public schools, what setting must be utilized, or what types of assessment tools can be used. We will consider those court actions that relate most directly to education in more detail but first will take a brief look at the variety of litigative actions that have been undertaken on behalf of handicapped children or adults.

TYPES OF LITIGATIVE EFFORTS

The following listing parallels that used in *Mental Retardation and the Law,* a publication of the U.S. Department of Health, Education and Welfare. Categories of litigation having obvious application to the handicapped include the following.

Architectural barriers. This includes such concerns as construction of public buildings without regard for accessibility by the physically handicapped, public transportation (subways, buses, trains, etc.) that does not provide for the handicapped, and other barriers to services or facilities.

Classification. This includes a concern for the methods through which students are classified as mentally retarded (primarily those classified as educable mentally retarded). See pp. 19-21 for a discussion of the *Larry P. v. Riles* case.

Commitment. This includes major concerns regarding individual constitutional rights (primarily equal protection of the laws and the requirement of due process), as related to commitment procedures. In many jurisdictions juveniles can be committed upon the application of parents or guardians without benefit of counsel or even a hearing, and without regard for the wishes of the juvenile. Also included are concerns regarding the rights of persons adjudged mentally incompetent to stand trial, as they may be committed indefinitely based on such a finding.

Custody. This concern relates to the rights of children to be raised in a home where parents can provide proper stimulation, care, and treatment. Also at issue is the right of mentally retarded parents to raise their own children.

Education. The concern in these cases is the right of *all* children to a free, publicly supported education. See pp. 18-19 for a discussion of the *Pennsylvania Association for Retarded Children v. The Commonwealth of Pennsylvania* and *Mills v. the Board of Education of the District of Columbia.*

Employment. Several concerns are involved in this general classification. At one level, there is the matter of payment (as opposed to nonpayment) for services performed. Prior to initiation of this type litigation, some workers in institutions performed long hours of work with no real wages. At another level, the question is whether individuals should be paid as "handicapped" employees, thus legalizing subminimum wages, or whether the minimum wage and overtime provisions of the Fair Labor Standards Act should be enforced.

Guardianship. This relates to state guardianship statutes that permit the state to assume control of the assets of individuals deemed to be incompetent. Due process and equal protection of the law are major concerns.

Protection from harm. This issue concerns the rights of both children and adults to have reasonable care and protection from harm while the responsibility of the state.

Sterilization. This relates to sterilization statutes in the various states. Issues considered are whether sterilization is truly in the "best interest" of the individual or is accomplished for institutional convenience, proper representation of the individual to be sterilized, and coercion. Also, the question of the "fundamental right to bear a child" has been a significant consideration in some of these cases.

Treatment. This area of concern, often called the "right to treatment," has grown rapidly in importance. One major principle involved is that those in institutional settings have a constitutional right to receive such individual treatment as will lead to their maximal development as individuals. Such cases have also often included the concern for protection from harm.

Voting. This concerns denial of the right to vote.

Zoning. This highly emotional issue concerns zoning regulations that have been interpreted to mean that group homes for the mentally retarded or mentally ill cannot be operated in residential areas restricted to single-family dwellings.

These are the areas into which advocates of the handicapped have moved through court action. In general, the rights of the handicapped have been expanded through such action. The tool of litigation has proved to be quite effective in establishing the responsibility of society regarding the handicapped and has led to greatly expanded school services to handicapped children. Specific court cases, which are described in the following sections, should provide more details regarding litigation that has been particularly important to special educators.

RIGHT TO FREE, APPROPRIATE PUBLIC EDUCATION

Several cases have involved the right of the handicapped to a free, public education, but two of these cases are often considered of unusual importance. The first, *The Pennsylvania Association for Retarded Children v. The Commonwealth of Pennsylvania,* questioned educational policies of the state of Pennsylvania, which led directly to practices that denied an appropriate education at public expense to retarded children of school age. This case was filed on January 7, 1971, by the Pennsylvania Association for Retarded Children on behalf of fourteen specifically named children and all other children similarly situated. This was a typical *class action* suit, filed in such a manner as to affect those fourteen children named, all others of a similar "class" now residing in the state, and all children similarly situated who will be living in Pennsylvania in the future.

Pennsylvania, like a number of other states, had compulsory school attendance laws, provided certain types of special classes for handicapped children within the public schools, and provided residential schools for some handicapped children. But within the Pennsylvania School Code, there were two specific ways in which the trainable mentally retarded child could be excluded from public education. First, if a qualified psychologist or personnel from a mental health clinic certified that a given child could no longer profit from public school attendance, the child could be excluded. Second, because the law provided that the local board of directors could refuse to accept or retain children who had not reached the mental age of 5 years, most trainable retarded were never admitted to the public schools. Even if a child were not excluded under either of these two provisions, there was a third provision that permitted the local board to provide training outside the public schools: "If an approved plan demonstrates that it is unfeasible to form a special class."

The Pennsylvania Association for Retarded Children (PARC) set out to establish three main points in their case: (1) mentally retarded children can learn if an appropriate educational program is provided, (2) "education" must be viewed more broadly than the traditional academic program, and (3) early educational experience is essential to maximize educational potential.

After considerable testimony by the state and by a variety of "expert witnesses," the case was won by the PARC. In a finalization of earlier decrees, the court ordered, on May 5, 1972, that each of the named plaintiffs be immediately reevaluated and that each be provided free access to public education and training appropriate to his or her learning capabilities. It further ordered that all retarded persons between the ages of 6 and 21 years be provided such access and programming as soon as possible, but in any event, no later than September 1, 1972.

The order and agreement also contained a number of added benefits for the retarded of Pennsylvania: (1) The state department was made responsible for supervision of educational programs in state institutions; (2) children served through homebound programs must now be automatically reevaluated every 3 months; and (3) any district providing preschool education for other children must now provide preschool for the retarded.

The Pennsylvania Association for Retarded Children v. Pennsylvania suit, like many that were to follow, was settled on the basis of a *consent agreement*. This is an out-of-court agreement, usually formally approved by the court. In this suit, the state was ordered to provide free public education, appropriate to the learning capabilites of retarded children, and the consent agreement provided the working framework. To make certain that the consent agreement was carried out, the court established a time schedule for implementation and appointed two "masters" to oversee the total process.

A second case, *Mills v. the Board of Education of the District of Columbia,* is of unusual significance because it applied to *all* handicapped children. To a certain extent, it established a principle that was to tend to lead to the inclusion of all handicapped children in furture class action suits. This case, like the *PARC v. Pennsylvania* suit, led to a court order that required the public schools to provide for handicapped children, even if they did not fit the educational mold. As in the Pennsylvania case, the court appointed masters to oversee the operation.

Unlike the Pennsylvania case, which resulted in a consent agreement between the parties, the *Mills v. District of Columbia* case was decided through a judgment of the court and was based on a constitutional holding. Because of the constitutional base for this judgment, *Mills v. the Board of Education of the District of Columbia* provided a much stronger precedential base for future decisions than *PARC v. Pennsylvania*.

INAPPROPRIATE OR INCORRECT CLASSIFICATION OR LABELING

A case known as *Larry P. v. Riles* was filed November 18, 1971, on behalf of certain specific plaintiffs and all black children in the state of California who were wrongly placed and retained in classes for the educable mentally retarded. All children specifically named in the suit were in attendance in elementary schools in the San Francisco Unified School District. Defendants were Wilson Riles, superintendent of public education of California, members of the state board of education of California, and the superintendent and members of the board of education of the San Francisco Unified School District. In the complaint, plaintiffs alleged that they (and the class they represented) had been wrongly placed in classes for the mentally retarded as a result of inappropriate testing procedures, which ignored their unique home experiences and failed to recognize their unfamiliarity with white, middle class culture. The complaint also alleged that such a placement procedure violated the Civil Rights Act and the right to equal protection as guaranteed by the California Constitution and the Fourteenth Amendment of the U.S. Constitution, which prohibits discrimination based on race or color.

The *Larry P. v. Riles* case was similar to an earlier suit, also brought in California. That suit, *Diana v. State Board of Education*, alleged the use of biased tests to place Mexican-American and Chinese children in classes for the educable mentally retarded. In the *Diana* case, the charges related to the bilingual status of the plaintiffs, along with ethnic and cultural differences. The *Larry P. v. Riles* case was in many respects an extension of the principles involved in the *Diana* case to include black children who spoke English but who were not a part of the white, middle class culture on which the tests of intelligence were normed. The *Diana* case was resolved through a court approved stipulation in which the parties agreed to develop a test that would not be biased against Mexican-Americans, to provide statistical data on the numbers and percentages of various ethnic and racial groups in classes for educable mentally retarded, and to retest and evaluate all Mexican-American and Chinese children presently placed in such classes. (This case, like many others, has included the need for plaintiffs to later initiate contempt proceedings because certain aspects of the agreement were not properly carried out.)

In the *Larry P. v. Riles* case, a preliminary injunction was granted on behalf of all black school children in classes for the educable mentally retarded in San Francisco, on June 20, 1972. The court ruled that because the use of IQ tests as the basis for placing students in classes for the educable mentally retarded had resulted in a disproportionate share of black students in such classes, the burden was on school officials to prove that the test was a valid measure of intellectual ability and did not discriminate against blacks on the basis of race.

On August 16, 1974, the Ninth Circuit Court affirmed the preliminary injunction, and on December 13, 1974, the District Court:
1. Granted a motion to modify the class to include all California black children who had been or might in the future be classified as mentally retarded based on IQ tests.
2. Restrained public educators in the state of California from (a) using tests that do not properly account for cultural background and (b) placing black children in classes for the mentally retarded on the basis of such tests.
3. Ordered state officials to furnish all school districts in the state with copies of the court order within 20 days.
4. Ruled that if, in 120 days, the percentage of black children in classes for the educable mentally retarded exceeded the percentage of black children in total enrollment of any given district, and if an IQ test had been used in any manner in placement in such classes, the plaintiffs may require school officials of that district to show how the IQ test, used properly, accounts for the cultural background and experiences of black children.
5. Ruled that within 150 days the defendants must provide the plaintiffs information indicating the percentage of black children in total enrollment and the number of EMR classes on the 120th day after the

court order. At the same time, a list of all IQ tests used in each district must be provided.

6. Ruled that the use of any test that failed to comply with the injunction would be viewed as grounds for contempt.

Many important principles regarding the rights of the handicapped have been established by these and other related cases. These principles include, among others, the right to due process, the necessity to use assessment instruments that are appropriate to the individual and to the purposes of the assessment, the need for frequent reassessment, and a broadened definition of education. In many cases, litigation has preceded legislation and has, in effect, determined both its scope and content. In other instances it has followed legislation or regulations. Litigation has had some effect on individuals from all areas of handicap, but has had greater effect on certain specific groups. (As yet it has no direct effect on establishing the rights or the need for services for the gifted, talented, or creative.) Those most greatly affected by litigation have been the mentally retarded (affecting all of the mentally retarded, although in different ways at the opposite ends of the total range of retardation) and all of the more severely handicapped persons of the United States.

Most of these issues are now addressed in Public Law 94-142, as will be seen in the following chapter, but they did not magically come to the attention of legislators. These principles were hard-won in courts of law, and as society refuses to acknowledge the rights of the handicapped in the future, litigation will continue to be a potent weapon. A number of other interesting examples of litigation might be reviewed, but these few should provide an idea of how this tool may be effectively used on behalf of the handicapped.

Parent and professional groups: advocates for the handicapped

Legislation and litigation on behalf of the handicapped do not take place simply because lawmakers and attorneys decide that something should be happening in this arena. Catalysts and initiators are essential, and certain individuals and groups have served this function well. The reader should understand that this review is provided to show *what* happened and *how* it happened, but will not include specific mention of each and every group that played a role in this real-life drama. The manner in which history was influenced will be illustrated, both for purposes of general understanding of how we got to this present point of development of programs and services for exceptional persons and to indicate how coming generations may wish to proceed as additional goals must be accomplished in the future.

PARENT GROUPS

Parent groups have, according to Cain (1976), "been a part of our nation's history since colonization." The first of the parent groups organized on behalf of handicapped children was the National Society for Crippled Children, which had its beginnings in 1921. This group and others related more to health and welfare concerns were active in the 1920s and 1930s and remain active today. For the most part, organizational impetus for these groups came from professionals in the field of medicine, and emphasis was primarily on physical rather than educational needs. Then, in the late 1940s and throughout the 1950s, parent groups that were to play a major role in shaping special education came into existence. Two organizations that perhaps had the major impact on early legislation for the handicapped were the National Association for Retarded Children (NARC), which was later changed to the National Association for Retarded Citizens, and the United Cerebral Palsy Association (UCP). They were pioneers in actively calling the attention of the general public to their children's needs and then providing various services, including educational programs, when public agencies did not provide them. Although these two groups enlisted aid of those who were not parents (or grandparents) of handicapped children, their strength was through their *personal* need and drive to provide programs for their children. Most of their early efforts concerned direct provision of special classes that they established. Later efforts were directed toward pressuring public agencies to provide appropriate services for handicapped children, thus assuring that other children, in years to come, would have such services at public expense.

Another group must be noted for its unusual influence since the late 1960s. The Association for Children with Learning Disabilities (ACLD) was organized in the early 1960s and became very politically active by the late 1960s. As a more recently recognized exceptionality, the learning disabled had not been served through the establishment of special classes and programs in the same manner as children with other handicapping conditions, and ACLD initiated its major impact by pushing for legislation, a task at which it proved to be most effective. The earlier efforts of other parent groups provided the pattern, and ACLD followed this pattern with much success.

The evolution of efforts of parent groups may be summarized as follows:

After organizing to attempt to find ways to assure better programs and services for their children, whose needs had been ignored by public education and health agencies, these parent groups established special classes and schools for their children. They also became active in attempting to upgrade the programs and services of state institutions that had been established for various handicapping conditions. Much of their early efforts involved the direct provision of services through their organizational structure.

Before long they began to pressure local educational agencies to provide programs for children with more severe handicaps (often the local schools would, for example, provide for the mildly mentally retarded, but rejected responsibility for the moderately mentally retarded). In many instances they were able to work out some sort of cooperatively financed programs, which gave them "one foot in the door" of the public schools. Concurrently, they began to attempt to convince state officials that those programs and services provided by the parent groups were actually the concern of public education.

As the national organizational structure of these groups became more effective and as members of local groups became convinced that, in the long run, more might be accomplished through national planning and emphasis, a nationwide plan of attack was established. Certain key states became the center of focus for intensive efforts to establish the rights of the handicapped in comprehensive legislation.

At about the same time, national efforts to promote federal research monies, training grants to train teachers of the handicapped, demonstration programs, and other high-visibility projects were launched. To the surprise of some, these efforts were well received by Congress.

As these national efforts were pursued, parent groups discovered valuable allies in a number of professional organizations such as the Council for Exceptional Children (CEC) and others. Though each organization had to compromise its own goals to some extent at times, it was soon discovered that much more was gained by combined efforts.

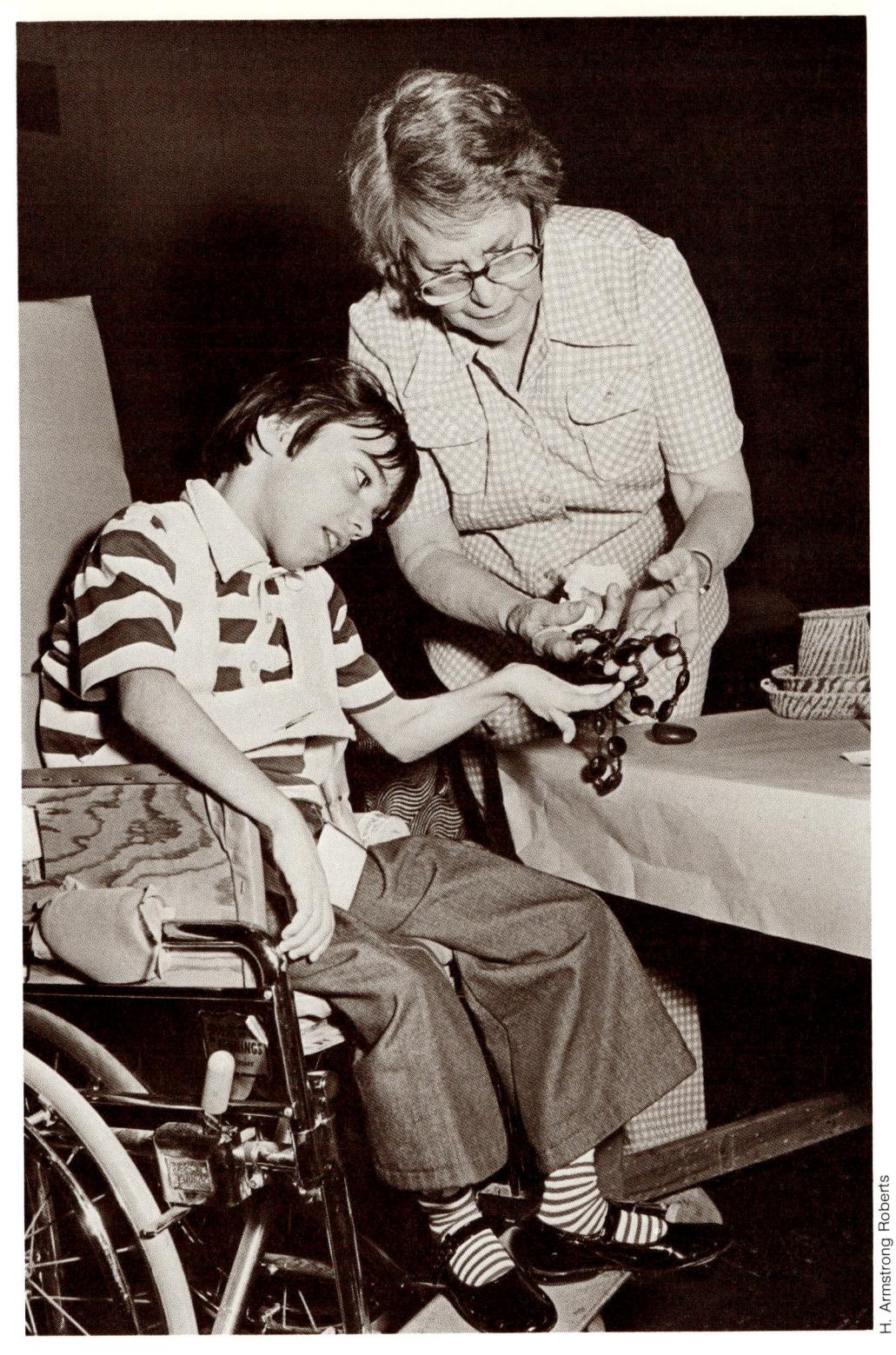

Individual assistance is essential to maximum development.

Other groups interested in the rights of minorities led the way in litigative efforts, and parent organizations for the handicapped soon followed. In some cases, educators even welcomed certain litigation, but they could not bring legal action against themselves. Parents could, and did, initiate a variety of lawsuits and, as a result, the judicial process established the rights of handicapped children and directed the public schools to provide appropriate educational programs.

Along with litigation, which forced the schools to do what they should have been doing all along, parent groups worked hard for legislation that could provide the legal framework for such education and reduce the need for further litigation. Professional organizations worked hand-in-hand with parent groups in the promotion of this much-needed legislation.

As efforts on behalf of handicapped *children* began to bear fruit, parent group efforts were expanded to include handicapped persons of all ages. Handicapped *persons* or *citizens* rather than handicapped *children* became the center of focus. At the same time, after many years of competing with each other for local funds, parent groups began to realize the many benefits of combined efforts on behalf of all handicapped persons. Closely coordinated efforts became the rule rather than the exception in most areas of the nation.

Parent groups have played an extremely important role in the development of the present level of programs and services for handicapped children and youth and have made similar contributions to the establishment of the rights of handicapped citizens of all ages. Many of their original purposes have been fulfilled, but even in those states where it appears that nearly all major goals have been reached, they are needed to monitor the activities of public agencies and to play an important role in assisting the parents of newly born handicapped children. Because all states have not reached the same level of services, national organizations are badly needed to assist state groups to improve with respect to various unique state level needs.

PROFESSIONAL GROUPS

A number of professional groups have participated in a variety of roles in the struggle to secure the rights of the handicapped. Although sometimes at odds, professional and parent groups have for the most part worked together for the past 20 to 30 years. As with any professional organization, a degree of protectionism must be recognized, but the efforts of professionals who work with the handicapped have been tied to those they serve to an unusual degree because of mutual efforts in the area of legislation. Legislation that was designed to benefit the handicapped usually provided benefits to professionals who worked with the handicapped, thus this close relationship was nurtured.

There is one national professional organization that welcomes all educators who work with the handicapped. This organization, the Council for Exceptional Children (CEC), also includes a division for those who work with the gifted, but does not include most of those in the medical arena whose efforts are directed primarily toward the handicapped. The Council for Exceptional Children has played many advocacy roles, but perhaps its most effective efforts have been in relation to legislation. CEC has unusual power potential; its headquarters are in the greater Washington, D.C., area, it has many contacts with the Bureau of Education for the Handicapped, and it has membership in all fifty states. In addition to membership of professionals who presently work with exceptional children, student membership (college students in training to work with exceptional children) is strong and provides a base for continuing influence in this field. CEC is actively involved in legislative efforts, assisting in litigation, publication of professional materials, professional development, research and demonstration projects, and other related activities. CEC was particularly active in support of PL 94-142, which will be reviewed in detail in Chapter 2.

A variety of other professional organizations, most of which are concerned with one or a few closely related professional disciplines, have also played a significant role in the historical development of services for exceptional children. The oldest of these organizations, the American Association on Mental Deficiency (AAMD), was organized in 1876. The AAMD has at times joined parent groups in litigative efforts, and members of this group have appeared as "expert witnesses" in court cases. AAMD has also been active in the promotion of research efforts in the area of mental retardation. Other groups, such as the American Speech and Hearing Association (ASHA), have tended to make their major contributions through the promotion of higher professional standards for professionals in their area of specialty. A number of other groups play some role with regard to their area of specialty, but among professional groups, CEC plays the greatest role in general advocacy efforts.

Legislation and advocacy on behalf of the gifted, talented, and creative

Throughout this chapter there has been an attempt to view the history of exceptional children in general, rather than to consider history and the factors influencing it by exceptionalities. In the area of legislation and advocacy on behalf of the gifted, there is justifiable reason to provide separate consideration. In the first place, legislation enacted on behalf of any one handicapping condition has tended to have spin-off benefits for all handicapped children. This spin-off has not, in most cases, benefited the gifted. Second, parent organizations that act as advocates for the various handicapping conditions have in many cases banded together to provide the strength that comes from joint efforts. Typically, these coalitions do not include parent organizations that are concerned with the welfare of the gifted. Third, the effects of court rulings in the case of litigation on behalf of one particular handicapping condition are often felt with respect to other handicapping conditions, and, as may be seen from the *Mills* case (p. 19), the handicapped may be considered as a general class. This has not been the case with regard to the gifted. Certain state legislation exists that is of value to the gifted, but only in a limited number of states. Federal legislation has been enacted, but that too is quite different from legislation relating to the handicapped. Organizations of parents and professionals who are interested in promoting the special needs of the gifted exist, but they have not, as yet, taken the kinds of actions taken by those involved with the handicapped. Further information on this legislation and these organizations is provided in Chapter 12 and will not be reviewed here. As one educator of the gifted put it: "Parents of the gifted are not in the same ballgame as parents of the handicapped, but we are watching them [parents of handicapped] closely, and may try to use some of their tactics soon. They are accomplishing things which we feel should be accomplished for the gifted, and their approach may be the only way we can accomplish our goals."* It can be noted that present federal efforts, stemming from the Gifted and Talented Act and subsequent legislation that has

---

*Statement to the author by a professor who teaches teachers of the gifted. He indicated that many of his colleagues feel the same, but there is reluctance to pursue the route of open advocacy because it is so difficult to be an effective advocate for children with above-average ability.

expanded its scope and mission (see pp. 352-353), may lead to increased recognition of the needs of the gifted, talented, and creative, but in its present form, such recognition has neither the force of a national mandate nor significant encouragement in the form of special funding. It would appear that the need for special programming for the gifted, talented, and creative may depend primarily on philosophical and theoretical considerations, a situation that has not been particularly promising in the past. On the other hand, if enough educators can be convinced that such programming is truly needed and that to do less is unfair to this segment of our population, perhaps past trends can be changed, and the gifted, talented, and creative will receive the special consideration they deserve.

Summary

Handicapped. The history of treatment of the handicapped is primarily an unpleasant story of misunderstanding and mistreatment based on fear and superstition. In the pre-Christian era it was common for young children who were "defective" to be abandoned or otherwise put to death. Those who lived often became beggars or court fools. If physically strong and not too unpleasant in appearance, they sometimes survived as little more than slaves, but many of the adult handicapped were eventually put away in prisons or dungeons, for society was offended by their presence. At times, there were notable attempts to understand and provide for certain of the handicapped, but progress, when it did come, seemed destined to fade away, replaced by vestiges of early superstition. This variable treatment of the handicapped continued for centuries, until the mid-eighteenth century, when a permanent change for the better was initiated. During the latter half of the eighteenth century and the early nineteenth century, special schools were established to serve the deaf, the blind, the mentally retarded, and, to a very limited extent, the mentally ill.

Only short years earlier, deviations or illnesses of the mind (as opposed to illnesses of the body) had been related to demons and spirits and were left to the clergy. Now, physicians and others with unusual social concern began to show interest and urge societal responsibility for these handicapped persons. The handicapped were viewed as the concern of science, rather than as purely spiritual concerns, a change that brought new hope for positive change. Throughout the 1880s, institutions for the handicapped were established in Europe and in the United States. The institutional setting seemed to be the logical place for the handicapped, and although some handicapped persons were returned to the mainstream of society, many remained institutionalized for life.

As the twentieth century dawned, a new point of view was adopted regarding the proper physical setting for education of the handicapped. It was proposed that, rather than sending handicapped children to separate schools or institutions, they should be provided special classes within the public schools. This special class concept, although initially embraced with caution, became the accepted service mode by the middle of the twentieth century. Until the mid-1960s, this was the century of special classes.

During the 1960s and with increased force in the 1970s, the concept of mainstreaming, or return to the least restrictive educational environment, became popular. This mainstreaming movement in the public schools was paralleled by a similar movement affecting the institutional setting. More often called "normalization," when applied to the more severely handicapped, this movement meant deinstitutionalization and return to the home community whenever possible. As these two general trends were taking place (some would say that they are simply two facets of the same trend), there was also a movement toward more service for more of the handicapped population, all provided at public expense. This was promoted primarily by parent (advocacy) organizations but was supported by professional associations. This increase in service was further stimulated by litigation in which the denial of equal rights to the handicapped was spotlighted, and by legislation that made it mandatory for public agencies to serve the handicapped. This significant increase in the scope of services provided, coupled with a different frame of reference for the provision of these services, was the status as the year 1975 was ushered in. For purposes of this historical review, this date will be considered the end of an era. Events of the years that followed will be considered in the following chapter.

Gifted and talented. Early in human history there was limited recognition of the potential contribution of gifted children and youth, particularly with relation to some specific national purpose and goal. However, any general recognition of the gifted, a recognition related to *their* needs and *their* right to an appropriate education, did not develop on any appreciable scale until mid-twentieth century. There were some exceptions, and administrative provisions, such as acceleration through the twelveth-grade school system, were common, commencing during the second or third decade of the twentieth century, but it was not until the 1950s that any significant number of special programs developed.

By 1970 a number of states had some legislative provision for special programs for the gifted, and Congress had enacted a law directing the U.S. Office of Education to investigate the needs of gifted students of the nation. However, in comparison to the handicapped, program provision was woefully inadequate in most of the nation. By 1975, some improvement was noted, and there was growing interest and much lip service to the needs of the gifted, but very little financial support, the ingredient most authorities agreed was essential. Whether comprehensive programs for the gifted were to actually materialize remained a matter of debate, with insufficient data to form a strong argument for either a negative or a positive conclusion.

Special education for the '80s

focus

The statements presented below provide a point of focus with respect to the more important, basic concepts presented in this chapter. These statements have been repeated as they appear in the chapter narrative and are given in order, following the heading or subheading under which they are found in the chapter. This should facilitate turning back to these statements, as desired, to reconsider the context within which they were given. This focus on critical statements will promote more meaningful consideration of the salient content of this chapter, both immediately following original reading of the chapter and for purposes of review.

introduction

Some disagreement exists as to acceptable definitions, and different terminology may be in use in various parts of the nation, but for the most part, educators would agree that the handicapped include the mentally retarded, the hearing handicapped, the visually handicapped, the speech handicapped, and emotionally disturbed, the learning disabled, and those with handicaps relating to physical or other health impairments.

early treatment of the gifted and the handicapped

Special provisions for gifted and talented youth have existed on a sporadic basis for centuries.

There have been four major historical determiners of treatment of the handicapped: (1) the need for survival, (2) the force of superstition, (3) the findings of science, and (4) the desire to be of service.

For hundreds of years, gains in the direction of more scientific attitudes and the desire to be of service to the less fortunate were regularly counteracted by the leftover effects of superstition and fear of that which could not be fully understood.

Despite some meaningful attempts to assist the handicapped, the picture from the beginnings of recorded history until the mid-1700s was primarily a bleak one.

new hope for the handicapped: mid-eighteenth through the nineteenth centuries

For all practical purposes we can say that the nineteenth century was the first in which there was some sort of concerted effort to train or educate the handicapped throughout the entire century.

By the middle of the nineteenth century, the viability of educational programs for the deaf, the blind, and the mentally retarded was an accepted fact. In addition, efforts were underway to provide for the mentally ill but were less well developed than the others.

program development in the United States

The nineteenth century has been called the era of institutions. They tended to serve those with more severe handicaps, and treatment, especially in the case of institutions for the mentally retarded and mentally ill, left much to be desired. On the other hand, they were a great improvement on the kind of treatment that such persons had received for centuries. For the most part, programs in the United States, which had started behind those in Europe, were on their way to catching up or even forging ahead as the nineteenth century came to a close.

establishment of special classes in the public schools (1900 to mid-1960s

Special classes for handicapped children, supported by and housed in the public schools, became an accepted part of the educational scene during the years that followed Dr. Bell's recommendations in 1902, and although they were known by different names in various cities and states, most were established as self-contained classes.

general trends: 1920 to 1960

The first 60 to 65 years of the twentieth century led to significant advances in educational programming for most handicapped children and to the establishment of a new subdiscipline of education, commonly called special education.

litigation on behalf of the rights of the handicapped

Litigation has played an important role in the establishment of the rights of the handicapped and in the type of legislation passed at both the state and the national levels. When the courts decide that certain groups or classes of individuals have specific rights or should receive certain services, appropriate legislation usually follows.

inappropriate or incorrect classification or labeling

Those most greatly affected by litigation have been the mentally retarded (affecting all of the mentally retarded, although in different ways at the opposite ends of the total range of retardation) and all of the more severely handicapped persons of our nation.

parent groups

Parent groups have played an extremely important role in the development of the present level of programs and services for handicapped children and youth and have made similar contributions to the establishment of the rights of handicapped citizens of all ages.

legislation and advocacy on behalf of the gifted, talented, and creative

Legislation enacted on behalf of any one handicapped condition has tended to have spin-off benefits for all handicapping conditions. This spin-off has not, in most cases, benefited the gifted.

It would appear that the need for special programming for the gifted, talented, and creative may depend primarily on philosophical and theoretical considerations, a situation that has not been particularly promising in the past. On the other hand, if enough educators can be convinced that such programming is truly needed and that to do less is unfair to this segment of the population, perhaps past trends can be changed, and the gifted, talented, and creative will receive the special consideration they deserve.

References and suggested readings

Anastasi, A. *Psychological testing.* 4th ed. New York: Macmillan Publishing Co., Inc., 1976.

Cain, L. Parent groups: their role in a better life for the handicapped. *Exceptional Children,* 1976, *42*(8), 432-437.

Coleman, J. C. *Abnormal psychology and modern life.* 4th ed. Glenview, Ill.: Scott, Foresman, & Co. 1972.

Gearheart, B. *Organization and administration of educational programs for exceptional children.* Springfield, Ill.: Charles C Thomas, Publisher, 1974.

Gearheart, B., and Litton, F. *The trainable retarded: a foundations approach.* St. Louis: The C. V. Mosby Co., 1979.

Hewett, F. *Education of exceptional learners.* Boston: Allyn and Bacon, 1974.

Itard, J. *The wild boy of Aveyron.* New York: Appleton-Century-Crofts, 1962.

Mental retardation and the law: a report on status of current court cases. Washington, D.C.:. President's Committee on Mental Retardation, U.S. Department of Health, Education and Welfare, September, 1975.

Public Laws: 85-926, 88-164, 89-110, 89-750, 91-230, 93-112, 93-180, 94-142. Washington, D.C.: U.S. Government Printing Office.

Zilboorg, G., and Henry, G. *A history of medical psychology.* New York: W. W. Norton & Co., 1941.

This illustration has appeared in many professional journals and popular magazines. This type of "advertising advocacy" is financed by the federal government through *Closer Look*. (Courtesy U.S. Office of Education, Bureau of Education for the Handicapped.)

chapter 2

Legal and financial framework for services to exceptional students

objectives

To understand the legal basis for public education in the United States and how interpretation of this responsibility has changed over the years.

To describe the financial structure of U.S. public schools, consider some significant (and difficult to defend) variations, and show how special education reimbursement has been a major factor in the development of programs for exceptional students.

To introduce and explore the provisions of Public Law 94-142, The Education for All Handicapped Children Act of 1975, and their implications for the future of special education.

To explore the provisions of the Rehabilitation Act of 1973 and its support role in assuring education, training, and equal opportunities for all handicapped persons.

To develop a more complete understanding of the efforts of federal and state education agencies to encourage appropriate, stimulating educational programs for gifted, talented, and creative students.

Special education for the '80s

Introduction

The composite effect of the various factors outlined in Chapter 1 led to a point in history that was unparalleled in the annals of concern for and services to handicapped children and youth. This historical moment is often specifically pinpointed as November 29, 1975, when President Gerald Ford signed the Education for All Handicapped Children Act (Public Law 94-142). This day may be the proper time to be remembered, or perhaps it should be when the *Regulations for PL 94-142* were published in the *Federal Register* (August 23, 1977), the opening of school in 1978, when the major part of the law took effect, or 1980 when the entire law was scheduled to be implemented. However we wish to view specific times and dates, the period from late 1975 to 1980 was the time when a comprehensive legal framework within which public agencies must provide services to the handicapped was established.

Before proceeding to an extensive review of Public Law 94-142 and what it means to all handicapped children and youth, certain other facts must be noted. First, it must be recognized that a number of states had passed laws very similar to PL 94-142 prior to 1975. There were differences among these various laws, but they were much more similar to than different from PL 94-142. We should also note that other states, following the lead of PL 94-142, enacted similar legislation soon after 1975. The importance of PL 94-142 is that it became a *national* statement of the rights of the handicapped to a free, appropriate education. In some respects it can be likened to the civil rights enactments of the recent past. Like the civil rights laws it may take some time before the total intent of the law is realized, but a national statement of the rights of the handicapped has been made and, hopefully, the American public will accept this statement, internalize it, and attempt to implement both the letter and the spirit of the law.

A second point to recognize is that PL 94-142 is really an extension and expansion of PL 91-230 and PL 93-380 (discussed in Chapter 1). Without the groundwork provided in these laws, PL 94-142 could not have been passed. It is also closely related to the Rehabilitation Act of 1973 which, in its Section 504 regulations, actually expands the meaning of 94-142.

Third, it must be noted that the various local educational agencies that provide educational programs to handicapped children and youth operate under constitutional guidelines, legislative enactments, and administrative regulations that are state-level guidelines and directives. This matter will be further pursued in the following section.

Fourth, we must remember the extent to which financial support for education—more specifically, special education—determines program implementation. We will see how this is the major leverage of both 94-142 and the state legislative enactments that govern the provision of programs and services to handicapped children and youth.

Education of exceptional children and youth is the major concern of this text, and for the most part emphasis will be on the nature of the various exceptionalities and the ways in which special educational services can be of maximum assistance to exceptional students. However, practical experience has convinced those who have worked for many years on behalf of the handicapped and the gifted that legal concerns and financial considerations are at the heart of adequate program provision. When we consider the fact that certain states had programs for the gifted in 1968 that were still not available in many others in 1980, the matter becomes very clear. The states that had programs also had special legislation plus special financial incentives; the other states did not. A similar situation exists with regard to the handicapped but the passage of PL 94-142 and similar state legislation plus reimbursement provisions is helping to close such program gaps. Improvement is taking place but special educators must remember why it has come and remain alert to any efforts that will reduce the strength of legal mandates and financial incentives. This is the rationale for a chapter such as this in a text dedicated to an understanding of educational programs.

Legal basis for public education

Public education in the United States, both historically and legally, has been the responsibility of the various states. The Tenth Amendment to the U.S. Constitution indicates that "the powers not delegated to the United States by the constitution nor prohibited by it to the states are reserved to the states respectively, or to the people." From this starting point, the various states developed their own school laws, which were theoretically designed to provide a free public education to citizens of the state. In practice, however, many states provided education only to children who were relatively easy to serve. In fact, until the past few years, there had been a number of states whose constitutions directed the legislature to educate only those children who had "sufficient mental and physical ability." Others omitted terminology that would specifically include *all* children, thus leaving the interpretation of which children to serve to the understanding of the lawmakers who were in office when school legislation was actually passed.

EFFECT OF LITIGATION

Between 1970 and 1975, after being prodded into action by a variety of litigation (see pp. 17-21), many states initiated action to change the constitutional language providing the basis for school legislation. At the same time, most began to change educational practices even before legislation or constitutions were changed. In some instances, state officials apparently hoped to avoid the need for constitutional or legislative change by providing more comprehensive educational opportunities for the handicapped (through liberal interpretation of existing statutes) but for the most part, advocates for the handicapped pressed for new laws. Most had learned that this was essential to the continued provision of adequate educational programs, and thus they would settle for no less.

As noted earlier, the U.S. Constitution leaves the matter of planning and providing educational programs to each state. This is what led to different interpretations of what was meant by "free, public education" in the various states. However, certain federal court rulings had an effect on education even before the cases noted in Chapter 1, and one such ruling provided a major part of the foundation on which many of these cases rested. This ruling, a 1954 holding by the U.S. Supreme Court, stated: "In these days it is doubtful that any child may reasonably be expected to succeed in life if he is denied the opportunity of an education. Such an opportunity, where the state has undertaken to provide it, is a right which must be made available to all on equal terms." This case, usually referred to as *Brown v. Board of Education*, provides an excellent example of how the judicial branch of government has entered the matter of education within the states.

LOCAL SCHOOL BOARD

Another factor of major importance in determining the manner in which education will be provided to the children of the various states is the considerable power of the local school board. Although the states establish the legal framework within which education is provided, many major decisions regarding educational matters are left to local school boards or committees whose members are elected by popular vote of the citizens of the school district. The strong influence of these local decision-makers can be easily understood by anyone who has viewed the obvious differences in quality of educational programs provided in various local educational agencies within the same state. Even greater differences may be found if we expand this comparison to the nation as a whole. In actual practice, local boards or committees adopt and monitor the policies within which the local educational program must be administered. Their decisions play a major role in the determination of whether the local program is designed to meet the minimum acceptable standards of the state, or whether it will be an expanded and enriched program. Numerous examples could be given to indicate the influence of this local decision-making, but with a little imagination, any reader can envision the possibilities inherent in this function.

In summary, the legal base for public education throughout the United States is relatively similar from state to state. First, the primary responsibility for education in the United States belongs to the states. It is determined within the state on the basis of (1) the state constitution, (2) legislation designed to carry out the intent of that constitution, and (3) regulations established by state educational officials to assist in the administration of state legislation. Second, most of the responsibility for actually providing an education to the children of the state is delegated to local education agencies whose policies are established by local school boards or committees. The members of these local boards are elected by popular vote of the citizens of the school district and are likely to reflect the beliefs and interests of those who elect them. If this includes a belief in the right of each child to an appropriate educational program and an interest in providing such programs even if they require special efforts and additional costs, then all is well for exceptional children. If those beliefs are that a generally acceptable program for "normal" children should be provided and that children should "adjust" to the program, exceptional children will not be properly served. More specifically, if holding down the school budget is the primary interest, any program that involves excess cost is subject to elimination as costs continue to rise.

Finally, the legal base for provision of educational services to students in the public schools may at times be dramatically, and in some cases traumatically, affected by federal legislation or rulings of the courts. An obvious case in point, which affected a very large proportion of the schools of the nation, was the legislation and the various court decisions dictating racial integration of the schools. Although the schools were primarily controlled by state legislative enactments and were administered locally, the federal government, through federal legislation and decisions of the federal courts, had a significant, lasting effect on education at the local level. In some cases, then, federal prerogatives can overrule state and local control.

As this chapter proceeds it will become obvious that the major emphasis is on the handicapped child. Some of the legal framework for services for the gifted, talented, and creative students of the United States will be reviewed in a separate section but, unfortunately, the provisions of PL 94-142, mandatory education through state legislative enactments, and broad-spectrum special financial incentives, are not extended to the gifted, talented, and creative in the same manner as they are to the handicapped. This is a battle that remains to be waged, and the likelihood of equal recognition remains in doubt.

Financial structure of public schools

Inadequate funding is undoubtedly blamed for more of the problems of education than can be supported in fact, but it is obvious that above-average funding permits consideration of more alternatives than are available under minimal funding. Nowhere has this been more obviously and consistently demonstrated than with regard to educational programs for exceptional children. This fact must be kept foremost in mind by special educators, and each new educational proposal, at either the state or the national level, must be carefully reviewed for its potential effect on continued support for education of exceptional students.

In addition to the amount of funds available for education, the source of these funds is of great importance. In the case of special education for the handicapped, additional special reimbursement from the state level has been a key factor in the development of new programs and services. Over the years, in nearly every state in the nation, local school board members and the citizens who elect these individuals have tended to accept new programs for the handicapped with cost factors that at times have increased the local school budget by significant amounts, *if the additional monies required to implement these programs came from the state or federal level.* Education dollars come from the citizens of the nation, regardless of details of collection, but educators must realize that *who* collects those dollars and *how* they are collected are very important considerations when it comes to initiating new programs. This is particularly important in budgeting for programs for exceptional children; thus we will review, very briefly, the source of the dollars that provide the budgetary base for the public schools of the United States.

VARIATIONS IN FINANCIAL BASE

The financial base of public schools varies from state to state, leading to unique problems in the fifty states and, in some instances, very unequal opportunities to properly fund educational programs throughout the nation. In a very general way it may be said that essentially all of the funds that support the various local educational agencies come from some combination of local, state, or federal government sources. In combination, local and state sources make up the major part of the budget, with federal funds representing a small, but growing budgetary factor. In commenting on this increase in federal funding for programs for the disabled, Braddock (1978, p. 1) notes:

> In the 1960's, significant new trends in funding developed. The Federal Government began implementing literally hundreds of specific programs. During this period of the "Great Society," 1964–1969, the number of individually authorized project grant programs more than tripled—from 120 to 380—and these numerically constituted over 80 percent of all federal grant programs. A tremendous upswing in funding for human services and also for specific disability programs occurred.

This significant increase of federal aid as a percentage of total public school expenditures is well illustrated in Table 2-1. If the rate of increase indicated in the past 10 to 15 years is maintained, the federal government could be contributing as much as one-half of total public school expenditures in the not too distant future; however, it is unlikely that this will happen if federal involvement in the schools remains that of promotion of special needs.

In some states, locally collected funds make up a greater share of the budget than state funds, but there is an increasing tendency for the states to provide the major part of the lo-

TABLE 2-1

Federal aid as a percentage of total school expenditures: 1902-1978*

Fiscal year	Federal aid (billions)	S & L total expenditures (billions)	Total expenditures (billions)	Federal aid total expenditures (percent)
1902	$ .006	1.2	1.206	.5
1932	.249	9.5	9.749	2.6
1942	.837	13.0	13.837	6.0
1950	3.0	22.3	25.3	11.9
1965	13.0	75.3	88.3	14.7
1973	39.3	181.2	220.5	17.8
1977	70.4	282.8	353.2	19.9
1978	80.0	308.9	388.9	20.6

*Data adapted from *Programs for the Handicapped,* December, 1978.

cal educational budget. (One exception to this generalization is in the case of funds used to build school buildings. These more often come from local funds and usually require a positive vote of the local citizens permitting the board of education to borrow funds with which to build buildings.)

Money that eventually finds its way into the local school budget comes from a variety of sources, including local or state property taxes, local or state sales taxes, local or state income taxes (both personal and corporate), taxes on items such as tobacco, alcoholic beverages, mineral leases, automobile licenses, severence taxes (a tax on minerals that is levied when the minerals are "severed" from the earth), and literally dozens of others. Generally speaking, the fund source that causes the most local controversy is the property tax and, in many cases, attempts to provide additional budgetary needs through the collection of increased property taxes are turned down, either by the citizens of the community or by the local board of education.

SPECIAL EDUCATION REIMBURSEMENT

The tendency to oppose the collection of additional dollars at the local level, regardless of the purpose for which such dollars are intended, has promoted the practice of special state support for certain special needs. This special categorical support has extended to a variety of areas including vocational education, bilingual education, transportation, and, more consistently than any other area, special education. The states have used this approach to encourage the establishment and maintenance of programs for exceptional children for many years, and more recently the federal government has also entered this arena. Variously called categorical support, excess cost funding, incentive funding, special incentive grants, or special education reimbursement, this special funding is critically important as a means whereby the higher-than-average costs of special education may be offset through assistance from the state and federal levels of government. Past experience indicates that: (1) such reimbursement is necessary if comprehensive special education programs are to be maintained, (2) it must be provided at a level that provides most, if not all, of the extra costs of special education programs, and (3) it must be provided categorically for special education, not as a part of some "lump sum" for education in general.

In addition to providing the funds necessary to maintain adequate special educational programs for exceptional children, this reimbursement provides a source of leverage through which the state and federal government can monitor local programs and attempt to establish quality control of local educational opportunities. As with any other type of government regulation, there are potentially negative aspects to be considered, but like regulations established in such diverse areas as civil rights, pure food and drugs, and quality of the environment, such regulations appear to be necessary to protect the rights of the exceptional persons of our nation.

The need for local education agencies, particularly in poorer communities, to be assisted in the provision of special educational services, was noted by Wilken and Callahan (1976) in a study they completed for the Legislators' Education Action Project of the National Conference of State Legislatures. With regard to the wealth of local educational agencies, they concluded:

> Communities with strong support for special education, whether from school officials or parents, usually need only one other attribute to trigger high quality services for handicapped children—wealth. Wealth can exercise more control over the quality of local special education services in some states than all other influences combined. The richer the local school system, the more it is likely to do for handicapped children. This fact, of course, has been recognized in many special education funding formulas. States usually pledge themselves to pay most of the extra costs of special education in the belief that a high support level will enable poorer communities the same opportunity to serve handicapped children as wealthy ones. (1976, pp. 15-16)

In commenting further on the various methods of special education reimbursement, Wilken and Callahan note that in Georgia, a special funding arrangement is used that contains a "carrot" and a "stick." Providing special education services brings state aid; not providing them brings both a loss of state aid and no reduction in the state-mandated school tax (1976, p. 16).

The Georgia system is not unique in the way in which it encourages local districts to provide special education services. It is much more complex than the above description might lead one to believe, and, in fact, so are the systems in use in the other forty-nine states. They must be complex to provide for the differences inherent in the various local school districts within the states, but all have a similar purpose and all are essential to special education. In the following section we will review various aspects of PL 94-142, which has been mentioned so frequently in this text. Although a few states may not attempt to qualify for the funds provided through this law, most are doing so. As noted earlier, there are variations among the states with regard to existing legislation and regulation, but the vast majority are similar to PL 94-142, and as changes are made, it is likely that others will enact legislation very similar to the federal law. Through the review of PL 94-142, we will be able to consider the major components of the laws of the fifty states, even if certain details are not the same.

Public Law 94-142: a major statement of public policy

Public Law 94-142, The Education for All Handicapped Children Act of 1975, was the result of many forces. It was an amendment of earlier legislation, and, as noted by Weintraub (cited by Abeson and Zettel, 1977, p. 114), "P.L. 94 142 represents the standards that have over the past eight years been laid down by the courts, legislatures, and other policy bodies of our country." It may be considered as a formalization of what, by that time, had become accepted practice, if the handicapped were to be provided their rights and equal protection of the law. The following description and discussion of salient parts of PL 94-142 will provide some insight into the potential strength of this legislation and the manner in which the federal government has attempted to bring together the various policy components that seem essential to assure the educational rights of handicapped children.

PURPOSE

Public Law 94-142 has one broad, major purpose. It is designed to assure that:

> all handicapped children have available to them . . . a free appropriate public education which emphasizes special education and related services designed to meet their unique needs, to assure that the rights of handicapped children and their parents or guardians are protected, to assist states and localities to provide for the education of all handicapped children, and to assess and assure the effectiveness of efforts to educate handicapped children.

CHILDREN SERVED*

"Handicapped children" to be served through PL 94-142 include those who are evaluated as being: (1) deaf, (2) deaf-blind, (3) hard-of-hearing, (4) mentally retarded, (5) multihandicapped, (6) orthopedically impaired, (7) other health impaired, (8) seriously emotionally disturbed, (9) specific learning disabled, (10) speech impaired, or (11) visually handicapped. Definitions of these handicapping conditions and regulations for evaluation and determination of the existence of these conditions are detailed in the *Rules and Regulations* published in the *Federal Register*. When applying for federal funds under this Act, the various states must affirm that they have followed the pertinent regulations in determining which children in their state are in fact handicapped.

The intent of PL 94-142 is to provide needed programs and services to all handicapped children and youth between the ages of 3 and 21 who require special services; however, the mandate does not apply to children age 3 to 5 years or 18 to 21 years if such requirement is inconsistent with state law or practice or any applicable court decree.

RELATED SERVICES TO BE PROVIDED

The question of just which services should be considered as appropriate and/or necessary to the handicapped child and included in any reimbursement plan has been answered differently in various state regulations. For federal purposes, related services were outline in some detail in the actual Act and were further delineated in the *Rules and Regulations*. The following terms are specifically included in the regulations: (1) audiology, (2) counseling services, (3) early identification, (4) medical services, (5) occupational therapy, (6) parent counseling and training, (7) physical therapy, (8) psychological services, (9) recreation, (10) school health services, (11) social work services in schools, (12) speech pathology, and (14) transportation. In comments included in the *Rules and Regulations*, it is noted that this list of related services is not to be considered exhaustive but might include other developmental, corrective, or supportive services such as artistic and cultural programs, dance therapy, and the like, if they are required to assist the handicapped child. It is also noted that "each related service defined under this part may include appropriate administrative and supervisory activities that are necessary

---

*In this, and the following discussion of Public Law 94-142, definitions, descriptions, regulations, etc., come directly from the actual law as passed in 1975 or from *Rules and Regulations* for implementation of the law that have been placed in effect in subsequent years. These rules and regulations, which are published in the *Federal Register*, have the effect of law.

Public Law 94-142 encourages the establishment of preschool programs.

for program planning, management, and evaluation." It is abundantly clear that the intent is to provide services necessary to implement a plan for appropriate special education for the handicapped child.

APPROPRIATE EDUCATION: INDIVIDUALIZED EDUCATION PROGRAM (IEP)

IEPs have been the topic of dozens of journal articles, and thousands of workshops and planning sessions in the public schools of the nation. The development of IEP's has been, and continues to be, the target of commercial publishers who hope to benefit from the need of local school districts to find a simple way to expedite the required individual planning and save valuable staff time. It is presumed that most readers of this text will proceed into training programs in some specific area of exceptionality and thus will become involved in methods courses that include training and practice in the development of individualized educational programs. Thus we will consider only the general requirements of the IEP as a basis for greater understanding of the effect of PL 94-142.

The IEP was specifically defined in PL 94-142 (p. 4) as follows:

> The term "individualized education program" means a written statement for each handicapped child developed in any meeting by a representative of the local educational agency or an intermediate educational unit who shall be qualified to provide, or supervise the provision of, specially designed instruction to meet the unique

needs of handicapped children, the teacher, the parents, or guardian of such child, and, whenever appropriate, such child, which statement shall include (A) a statement of the present levels of educational performance of such child, (B) a statement of annual goals, including short-term instructional objectives, (C) a statement of specific educational services to be provided to such child, and the extent to which such child will be able to participate in regular educational programs, (D) the projected date for initiation and anticipated duration of such services, and (E) appropriate objective criteria and evaluation procedures and schedules for determining, on at least an annual basis, whether instructional objectives are being achieved.

The IEP is not actually a detailed instructional plan, but rather a tool for management of the special education program. If properly developed and followed, it should assure that the plan is designed for that particular child and that it is appropriate to his or her special needs. It also provides a vehicle for monitoring the delivery of this special program.

Other key requirements relating to the IEP include a provision to ensure parent participation, provisions to ensure that parents understand the proceedings of IEP meetings (interpreters for parents who are deaf or those whose native language is not English), and record-keeping guidelines.

OTHER IMPORTANT PROVISIONS

PL 94-142 includes many other important provisions and every school district receiving its federal entitlement under this law must submit an application that contains assurances that the rights and protection promised by this Act will be assured by the district. These include the following major assurances:
1. Provision of a free, appropriate public education for all handicapped children in the district, with guarantee of the availability of such education no later than the dates specified by the Act.
2. The development and maintenance of an individualized educational program (with appropriate renewal and revisions as required by federal regulations) for each handicapped child.
3. The provision of special education in such manner that handicapped children are served in the "least restrictive" environment consistent with the most appropriate educational program.
4. Policies and procedures that guarantee due process.
5. Policies and procedures that protect the confidentiality of records.
6. Establishment and maintenance of regular parent consultation and involvement.
7. Testing and evaluation procedures that are nondiscriminatory.

FINANCIAL POTENTIAL

Much of the basic strength of PL 94-142 lies in the federal funding formula that was established as an integral part of the law. However, two important factors regarding this funding must be recognized to fully appreciate both its strength and its weakness. First, it is stronger than many previous federal programs designed to encourage assistance for handicapped children in that it does not have an expiration date. It is permanent, to the degree that any law may be permanent, and although it could be repealed or significantly amended in a manner that would weaken its impact, this is highly unlikely for the present. Therefore, unlike many previous laws, educational planners do not have to be involved in planning what to do when the law expires.

A second factor, and one that is of concern to many educators, is that the dollars generated by PL 94-142 are potential dollars only. The law includes a payment formula which, in effect, established a ceiling, but each succeeding Congress must appropriate the necessary funds. This is not unlike the process followed in most states, but Congress has a record of more variability (which can only be interpreted at state and local levels as less reliability) in funding such programs. The funding formula, which will be described in the following paragraphs, must be understood and interpreted with this fact in mind.

PL 94-142 provides a payment formula that most agree is quite good and will be a powerful incentive for compliance if fully funded. This formula is based on an escalating percentage of the national average educational expenditure per public school child times the number of handicapped children served in each state. The fiscal year authorizations are: 1978, 5%; 1979, 10%; 1980, 20%; 1981, 30%; 1982, 40%. The authorization (ceiling) would remain at 40% from that point on, and the formula carries an inflation factor that provides for inflationary-deflationary adjustments.

Estimates of the actual dollar cost involved, if the Congress appropriates funds to the extent of the appropriation ceiling for each year, vary, but it appears that the 20% ceiling for 1980 would require funding in excess of $1 billion. Because of the limitation in the law regarding number of children who may be counted as handicapped (no more than 12% of the school age children between the ages of 5 and 17, inclusive), there is a predictable upper limit to the costs of PL 94-142, but even so it carries with it a total cost much greater than the Congress has seen fit to provide in the past. On the other hand, this law passed almost unanimously, and if advocacy groups and professional associations play their proper roles, perhaps the full potential of the law may be realized.

One of the questions most often asked in the 2 or 3 years following the passage of PL 94-142 was, "Do we have to follow this law?" This question will have particular importance if future Congressional appropriations turn out to be too low. The answer is "yes," if the school district wants PL 94-142 funds, but, as we will see in the discussion of Section 504 of the Vocational Rehabilitation Act of 1973, a school district or a state that does not participate in PL 94-142 may lose more than just the PL 94-142 funds. In conclusion, we may note that if PL 94-142 is funded and implemented as designed, it is undoubtedly the greatest single event of the century in the history of education of the handicapped. Because of the continuing nature of the law and the adequate appropriation ceilings, the actions of Congress can be monitored by all who maintain a continuing interest in the handicapped, and with constant pressure perhaps its great potential can be realized.

Section 504: Vocational Rehabilitation Act of 1973

Unlike PL 94-142, the Vocational Rehabilitation Act of 1973 (PL 93-112) is seldom referred to by special educators in any way other than by mentioning Section 504. This is because the real impact for handicapped persons is a result of fewer than fifty words contained in this small section (Section 504) of this law:

> No otherwise qualified handicapped individual in the United States shall, solely by reason of his handicap, be excluded from the participation in, be denied the benefits of, or be subjected to discrimination under any program or activity receiving Federal financial assistance.

In commenting on the tremendous impact of Public Law 94-142, Abeson and Zettel (1977, p. 127) note that it may eventually prove that "while P.L. 94-142 is the premier educational policy attainment for the handicapped, the most notable overall policy for this group is Section 504 of the Vocational Rehabilitation Act of 1973 (Public Law 93-112)." As noted in Chapter 1, although this law was passed in 1973, it was not until 1977 that the regulations for Section 504 were published.

This was, at least in part, because its potential effects are so far reaching. Since its regulations were not finally developed and implemented until 1977, they were both similar and complementary to the requirements of PL 94-142. If a state or a local school distict were to decide to not follow the dictates of PL 94-142 and thus lose its direct financial benefits, they would likely be in violation of Section 504 and could lose *all* federal funds. Thus Section 504 adds much clout to the impact of PL 94-142. In addition, the 504 regulations apply to preschool and adult level programs and to private facilities that receive federal funds.

Section 504 regulations also include a specific requirement regarding notification of those who might be affected by its regulations. This regulation requires that all federally supported schools and programs that employ more than fifteen persons must notify students, employees, and applicants that they do not discriminate on the basis of handicap. It also requires that a specific employee be designated to review policies and practices with regard to this requirement. This monitoring employee must consult with a representative of an organization representing the handicapped and ask for suggestions for modifications in employment practices, accessibility, and other related considerations. This deliberate involvement of a member of an advocacy organization may prove to be an unusually effective way to regulate at no cost to the federal government. Actual regulations that relate to schooling of the handicapped (as contained in the 1977 regulations for Section 504) are less extensive than those in PL 94-142, but require, in a less detailed manner, essentially the same procedures as those required by PL 94-142. Although special educators may not hear much about Section 504, they should feel reassured because of its behind-the-scenes power and support.

State and federal assistance for special programs for the gifted, talented, and creative

Special programs for the gifted, talented, and creative student are not supported or provided by either the U.S. Office of Education or state education agencies in the same manner as applies in the case of the handicapped. Unlike the handicapped, the student with above-average abilities has not been historically denied entrance to the public schools, and their superior performance may seem to indicate that present educational programs are meeting their needs. In some cases the more accurate point of view might be that they are succeeding *in spite of* the system, but they do seem to be "doing O.K." In addition, it is difficult to make the case that most of them will not be self-supporting if society does not provide special programs, and it is equally difficult to generate any large amount of concern for the "poor little unfortunate gifted child." These factors, plus the substantiated fact that some of the better school systems provide advanced class sections at the secondary level, weaken the case for special programming for the gifted student. However, the need for special programming has been gaining acceptance in the past 10 to 15 years, and some increased effort both nationally and at the state level can be seen.

PL 94-142, state laws relating to the handicapped, and the litigation outlined in Chapter 1 do not apply to the gifted, talented, and creative, but PL 91-230 (1970) and PL 93-380 (1974) contain sections that hold some promise for the gifted. Although much more limited in scope than efforts on behalf of the handicapped and permissive rather than mandatory, these legislative enactments (and those which may be found in a number of the states) indicate growing interest, which may eventually lead to meaningful programming in much of the nation. A discussion of these laws, national program efforts, and a review of the programming available in one of the leading states in serving the gifted may be found in Chapter 12. There is no question as to the legality of special programming for the gifted, talented, and creative, and in some specific curriculum areas, such as special programs for students who are talented in athletics, special high-cost programs already exist. Questions that must be asked are: (1) Are the various states sufficiently interested in the above-average student to provide special programs? (2) Are state and local education agencies willing to support such programs even if they mean additional costs? (3) Will the general public be able to accept the fact that such programs, if properly planned and implemented, will *widen* the academic or talent gap between the gifted and the average student? Bringing the handicapped student more nearly "up to average" is quite different from assisting students who are above average to become even more superior.

A considerable variety of programs for the gifted, talented, and creative are presently provided in the various states that attempt to provide special programs in this arena, but in no case is the programming as broad in scope or as widespread throughout the state as is true for the handicapped. In some states programs for the gifted are considered a part of special education and are administered at the state and local level by the department of special education. In others, programs for the gifted are in no way connected with state or local departments of special education. In many states there is essentially no organized special program for gifted, talented, and creative students. Although there is increased interest at the federal level, and considerable lip service is paid to the concept of special provisions for the gifted, it is too early to determine whether this interest will develop into anything similar to the programs for the handicapped that have grown so rapidly in recent years.

Summary

Education in the United States is primarily a function of the state, with many decisions delegated to elected members of local school boards. These local governing boards have provided adequate (however quite varied) educational programs for most children and youth, but to varying degrees have denied or provided inadequate programs for the handicapped. Although all states have made at least minimal attempts to encourage better local programs for the handicapped, in most instances it has been those handicapped who are most easily served who have received such services. Prior to the 1960s this encouragement to provide programs usually took the form of permissive laws and minimal special reimbursement to those districts that undertook to provide programs. This set of practices resulted in widely varied programs of education for the handicapped throughout the nation and eventually led to court action on behalf of handicapped students in which it was alleged that they and/or their parents had been denied rights guaranteed under the state or the federal constitution. In a growing majority of cases, advocates for the handicapped won such litigation, and the states slowly started to respond to these actions, either by changing their interpretation of existing laws or by passing new legislation designed to provide adequate programs for all handicapped students.

In the mid-1960s, the federal government began to play an increasingly significant role in assisting the states through specific legislation to upgrade and expand educational programs and services for the handicapped. In many cases federal legislation was shaped by the results of litigation or by the legislative enactments of some of the more progressive

Special education for the '80s

states. In all cases it involved some sort of special funding designed to encourage state and local education agencies to initiate some specific type of program improvement. The effect was to "encourage" rather than "force" local change, and the unspoken hope was that once the merits of such efforts were seen, such programs would be continued and expanded.

Finally, in 1975, a highly comprehensive federal law (PL 94-142) was passed that could be likened to a bill of rights for the handicapped. Most of its content related to principles already established in various places in the nation, either through litigation or state legislative enactments, but its passage brought all of these components together. PL 94-142 included funding authorizations which, if fully funded, were a powerful incentive to compliance. If inadequately funded, school officials could elect to not comply, but if they did not comply with PL 94-142, they would likely be in noncompliance with the Vocational Rehabilitation Act of 1973, thus running the risk of losing *all* federal funds. As a result, most states now have special education laws, regulations, and practices that are quite similar to these required by PL 94-142.

Education of the gifted, talented, and creative is much more variable throughout the nation, and the future of such programs is unclear. There is some indication of growing national interest, but certain factors militate against significant expansion of the type witnessed with regard to the handicapped. These and related topics are treated in more detail in Chapter 12.

focus

introduction

The importance of PL 94-142 is that it became a *national* statement of the rights of the handicapped to a free, appropriate education.

Practical experience has convinced those who have worked for many years on behalf of the handicapped and the gifted that legal concerns and financial consideration are at the very heart of adequate program provision.

legal basis for public education

Public education in the United States, both historically and legally, has been the responsibility of the various states.

local school board

Although the states establish the legal framework within which education is provided, many major decisions regarding educational matters are left to local school boards or committees whose members are elected by popular vote of the citizens of the school district.

Legal and financial framework for services to exceptional students

If the beliefs of the school board are that a generally acceptable program for "normal" children should be provided and that children should "adjust" to the program, exceptional children will not be properly served.

financial structure of the public schools

In addition to the amount of funds available for education, the source of these funds is of great importance.

variations in financial base

The financial base of public schools varies from state to state, leading to unique problems in the fifty states and, in some instances, very unequal opportunities to properly fund educational programs throughout the nation.

special education reimbursement

Past experience with special education reimbursement indicates that: (1) such reimbursement is necessary if comprehensive special education programs are to be maintained, (2) it must be provided at a level that provides most, if not all, of the extra costs of special education programs, and (3) it must be provided categorically for special education, not as a part of some "lump sum" for education in general.

In addition to providing the funds necessary to maintain adequate special educational programs for exceptional children, this special reimbursement provides a source of leverage through which the state and federal government can monitor local programs and attempt to establish quality control of local educational opportunities.

purpose of PL 94-142

Public Law 94-142 has one broad, major purpose. It is designed to assure that:

> all handicapped children have available to them . . . a free appropriate public education which emphasizes special education and related services designed to meet their unique needs, to assure that the rights of handicapped children and their parents or guardians are protected, to assist states and localities to provide for the education of all handicapped children, and to assess and assure the effectiveness of efforts to educate handicapped children.

children served through PL 94-142

The intent of PL 94-142 is to provide needed programs and services to all handicapped children and youth between the ages of 3 and 21 who require special services; however, the mandate does not apply to children age 3 to 5 years or 18 to 21 years if such requirement is inconsistent with state law or practice or any applicable court decree.

appropriate education: individualized education program (IEP)

"The term individualized education program means a written statement for each handicapped child developed in any meeting by a representative of the local educational agency or an intermediate educational unit who shall be qualified to provide, or supervise the provision of, specially designed instruction to meet the unique needs of handicapped children, the teacher, the parents, or guardian of such child, and, whenever appropriate, such child . . ."

The IEP is not actually a detailed instructional plan but rather a tool for management of the special education program.

financial potential

If PL 94-142 is funded and implemented as designed, it is undoubtedly the greatest single event of the century in the history of education of the handicapped. Because of the continuing nature of the law and the adequate appropriation ceilings, the actions of Congress can be monitored by all who maintain a continuing interest in the handicapped, and with constant pressure perhaps its great potential can be realized.

Section 504: Vocational Rehabilitation Act of 1973

Although special educators may not hear much about Section 504, they should feel reassured because of its behind-the-scenes power and support.

state and federal assistance for special programs for the gifted, talented, and creative

Special programs for the gifted, talented, and creative student are not supported or provided by either the U.S. Office of Education or state education agencies in the same manner as applies in the case of the handicapped.

In some states, programs for the gifted are considered a part of special education and are administered at the state and local level by the department of special education. In others, programs for the gifted are in no way connected with state or local departments of special education.

References and suggested readings

Abeson, A., Bolick, N., and Hass, J. *A primer on due process: education decisions for handicapped children*. Reston, Va.: The Council for Exceptional Children, 1975.

Abeson, A., and Zettel, J. The end of the quiet revolution: the education for all handicapped children Act of 1975. *Exceptional Children,* 1977, *44*(2), 114-127.

Ballard, J., and Zettel, J. Public Law 94-142 and Section 504: what they say about rights and protections. *Exceptional Children,* 1977, *44*(3), 117-184.

Ballard, J., and Zettel, J. Fiscal arrangements of Public Law 94-142. *Exceptional Children,* 1978, *44*(5), 333-337.

Braddock, D. Securing federal funds from state and local governments. *Programs for the handicapped.* Washington, D.C.: Office for Handicapped Individuals, December, 1978.

Mental retardation and the law: a report on status of current court cases. Washington, D.C.: President's Committee on Mental Retardation, U.S. Department of Health, Education and Welfare, September, 1975.

Public Laws: 91-230, 93-112, 93-380, 94-142. Washington, D.C.: U.S. Government Printing Office.

Rules and regulations for the implementation of Part B of the Education of the Handicapped Act (PL 94-142). *Federal Register,* Aug. 23, 1977. Washington, D.C.: U.S. Government Printing Office.

Wilken, W. H., and Callahan, J. J. *Disparities in special education services: the need for better fiscal management.* Legislators' Education Action Project; National Conference of State Legislatures. Unpublished report, 1976.

The Individualized Education Program (IEP) must be based on comprehensive assessment. This is particularly important in unique cases; this youngster has mild cerebral palsy but is also intellectually gifted.

chapter 3

Providing programs and services: a philosophical base, program guidelines, and basic issues

objectives

To establish and explore a basic philosophy of education for exceptional children and youth.

To establish comprehensive program guidelines that are consistent with the previously stated philosophy of education and sufficiently practical to be implemented within the existing public school structure.

To describe and discuss what is meant by a "full continuum of services" for exceptional students.

To discuss a number of critical issues basic to educational planning for exceptional students.

Special education for the '80s

Introduction

Legislation and regulations, both state and federal, provide the legal framework for programs for exceptional children and youth and imply a philosophical base, but the local educational agency must develop its own philosophy, program guidelines, and practices. These locally developed guidelines and practices clearly indicate local philosophy whether or not there is a formal philosophical statement. In every state there are regulations, program flow-charts, and the like, which tend to direct local programs, but it is abundantly clear to special educators who have worked with a wide variety of programs in many different parts of the nation, that local interest, knowledge, and support make the vital difference. Therefore, the intent in this chapter is to provide an acceptable general philosophical statement and to review guidelines and practices that are consistent with this general statement. It is important to note that specific guidelines and practices will not be exactly the same throughout the nation, or even throughout a given state. For example, guidelines for pupil transportation practices in some rural areas may be quite different from guidelines in a compact, densely populated school district. Actual practices may be even more different. Therefore, the guidelines and practices indicated here will require modification in many instances, but they should provide some understanding of factors and variables that must be considered and may be helpful as a point of departure for local planning in a variety of settings.

The final section of this chapter will relate to a number of basic issues or controversies that continue to be of major concern in planning to provide programs and services to children. These have been mentioned in the two preceding chapters and their existence will be inferred by the philosophical statement and the principles that will be derived from this statement. For the most part, these issues are more complex than might appear on the surface, and there are no simple answers or easy solutions. The purpose of consideration here will be to better understand these issues so that we may see how they apply in attempting to more effectively serve the unique needs of exceptional students.

Education of exceptional children: a philosophy and related principles

The following philosophy of education of exceptional children and youth, like all philosophical statements, is quite general. However, certain more specific principles may be derived from this general statement. Some of the more significant principles will be indicated immediately following the statement of philosophy.

A PHILOSOPHY OF EDUCATION FOR EXCEPTIONAL CHILDREN AND YOUTH

Exceptional students, like all other students, must be provided an opportunity to fully develop their abilities. Therefore, public, tax-supported educational agencies must adjust and adapt existing educational programs and offerings and provide additional services and programs as required to make this possible. Educational planning must emphasize the learning strengths and abilities of the handicapped, and "labeling" children according to handicap should be avoided when possible. On the other hand, children who are hearing impaired or visually impaired must have certain specific assistance that relates directly to their sensory loss, and thus it will often be advantageous to such children and to their educational programming to think of them as visually impaired (handicapped or disabled) or hearing impaired. In a similar manner, gifted, talented, and creative children must be recognized so as to make special educational planning and programming possible. It would be a serious error to be so concerned about labeling that we permit or encourage teachers to overlook special abilities or disabilities.

Exceptional children and youth should be served in the regular classroom whenever possible, and additional efforts should be directed toward increasing the effectiveness of such programming. If a child must receive specialized assistance in a small, separate grouping of children with special needs, we should provide such help but keep the normal classroom setting as much as possible. If the child has been removed for all or part of the school day, careful attention should be given to ensure that he or she is returned to the regular classroom at the earliest possible time, consistent with the child's social and educational well-being.

Special educators are needed because (1) the child's needs may be so unusual that the regular classroom teacher cannot adequately meet them; (2) the child and the regular classroom teacher may require the support provided through specialized or adapted materials and equipment; and (3) assistance in assessment or direct consultative efforts may spell the difference between success and failure.

In all assessment, planning, and programming parents must be involved to the greatest possible extent with procedural due process and the right to privacy maintained at all times.

RELATED PRINCIPLES

A number of important principles are closely related to the preceding statement of philosophy:

1. The provision of a maximum amount of information to parents is essential. This should be provided with consideration given to such factors as the parents' level of education, basic language, and experience in child rearing. Education gobbledygook should be removed, and the right of parents to free access to school records must be recognized.
2. Regular classroom teachers are highly important members of the educational team that must plan and implement programs for exceptional children. As such, they must be fully informed and must participate in all decisions affecting them. Their problems—such as having to deal with a large number of children with highly varied needs—must be recognized.
3. Assessment must be flexible, broadly based, and ongoing. It must be organized so as to tap information from all possible sources. Minority or low socioeconomic status may present unusual problems in assessment, and special care must be taken where this may be a factor.
4. Prevention, where it may be pursued, should receive top priority. This often requires cooperative efforts with other agencies.
5. Early intervention is highly desirable; however, the possible effects of misidentification and inappropriate labeling must be considered.
6. Some disabilities may be more appropriately viewed as symptoms rather than as specific physical disorders and may exist at one time in life and not at another.
7. Even in the case of a specific, irreversible disability, the need for special educational services may vary from full-time, special class service at one time in the child's life to little or no specialized service at another time.
8. Services for a broad age range, preschool through high school, are essential.
9. A wide variety of services and the total spectrum of service delivery capabilities is essential.

Prevalence of exceptional children

Before proceeding with a discussion of program guidelines, it would be of value to consider the prevalence of exceptional children with which society must be concerned. Prevalence means "how many" and refers to the number of children who might be called exceptional at any given time. As will be seen in the chapters dealing with the various exceptionalities, the number of children involved in each area of exceptionality depends on the definition in use, and there is no absolute agreement among authorities as to definitions; thus there is no agreement as to prevalence. Nevertheless, there is some general agreement as to a *range* of prevalence. As for the handicapped, the U.S. Congress indicated in 94-142 that no more than 12 percent of the children in any one educational agency can be served with *federal funds* at any one time.

Table 3-1 reflects a range of prevalence derived from a composite of federal estimates and those in use by the various professional and advocacy organizations. It indicates the lowest percentage commonly reported as the minimum of this range and a median figure as the upper limit. It may be noted that using the minimum percentages for the handicapped from Table 3-1 we would find a total of 10.6 percent, well below the 12 percent federal maximum. The maximum percentages for the handicapped would total 15 percent, significantly more than the federal maximum. Estimates of gifted, talented, and creative are even more variable for reasons that will be explored more fully in Chapter 12.

Program guidelines

All special education programs have program guidelines, although the length and complexity of such guidelines may vary. Prior to 1970 and the widespread litigation relative to improper assessment and placement procedures, open records, and other similar legal concerns, some smaller school units operated on the basis of very minimal guidelines, but today even smaller educational agencies tend to have fairly extensive descriptions of procedures and guidelines. In the following section we will consider some of the more basic guidelines likely to be found in most school district policies or procedures. The format of these guidelines and procedures will vary, but

TABLE 3-1
Prevalence of exceptional children in the United States

Handicap	Percent of population	Number of children (ages 5 to 18)*
Visually impaired (includes blind)	0.1	55,000
Hearing impaired (includes deaf)	0.5-0.7	275,000- 385,000
Speech handicapped	3-4	1,650,000- 2,200,000
Crippled and other health impaired	0.5	275,000
Emotionally disturbed	2-3	1,100,000- 1,650,000
Mentally retarded (both educable and trainable)	2-3	1,100,000- 1,650,000
Learning disabilities	2-3	1,100,000- 1,650,000
Multihandicapped	0.5-0.7	275,000- 385,000
Gifted, talented, and creative	2-4	1,100,000- 2,200,000
TOTAL	**12.6-19.0**	**6,930,000-10,450,000**

*Number of children based on 1980 population estimates.

certain concerns will be addressed in all school districts. Available space in this text would not permit full coverage of *all* of the details of such guidelines, even if such inclusion were appropriate.*

SCREENING, REFERRAL, AND ASSESSMENT

For a child to be considered for possible need for special education services, certain events must take place prior to a planned staffing. These steps are:

Screening　　　　　　　**Preliminary**
　or　　(leading to)　　**review**
referral
　　　　　　　　(which may
　　　　　　　　lead to)　**Assessment**

The entire process of referral or screening, preliminary review, assessment, staffing, development of an IEP and placement is shown in Fig. 3-1. The following discussion expands each of these topics.

Screening usually refers to a process whereby all children in given grade levels are assessed or evaluated in some simple, preliminary manner to determine whether additional investigation and assessment procedures should be initiated. Vision and hearing screening are common in most school systems and have been for years. Speech screening to determine which children should be considered "high risk" in terms of future learning difficulties is becoming much more common and is more likely to assist in the discovery of children who may later be determined to be mentally handicapped or learning disabled. More will be said about various screening procedures in the chapters relating to specific exceptionalities; however, we should note here that the screening process, when applied to all children in a given class, does not ordinarily require special parent permission. We should also note that the screening procedure is more applicable to the discovery of mildly handicapped children; the more severely handicapped will usually be relatively obvious and will usually be referred directly by the teacher or perhaps by a parent or the child's physician. Obvious examples would be blind, deaf, or moderately or severely retarded children.

Referral, which may include teacher, parent, outside agency, or physician referral, means exactly what the term would seem to imply. It means referring for further investigation or consideration. In the case of teacher referral, most good school districts have guidelines to assist the regular classroom teacher in evaluating whether such referral should be made. This may consist of lists of descriptive characteristics of, for example, hearing impaired, mentally handicapped, and learning disabled children. Also included in such guidelines will be a description of the referral process and referral forms. Typically, these forms will include a structure that encourages teachers to objectify their observations to assist those who will further consider the referral. Almost always, teacher referrals are processed through the building principal, and at times they will also require information from appropriate special educators who are assigned to that particular building.

The child who is referred or who gives indication in the screening process of need for further investigation is *not* to be "automatically" considered an exceptional child as a result of the referral or screening process. He or she

---

*As an example, one set of guidelines from a Midwestern city of approximately 200,000 population (pupil population of 45,000) which I believe to be comprehensive but not overly wordy, contains 142 pages. It is entitled "A Handbook and Guide to Special Education Programs and Services" and was compiled to help educators within that school system understand the local special education program. Such guidelines for larger school districts that have more complicated administrative structures are even more comprehensive.

Special education for the '80s

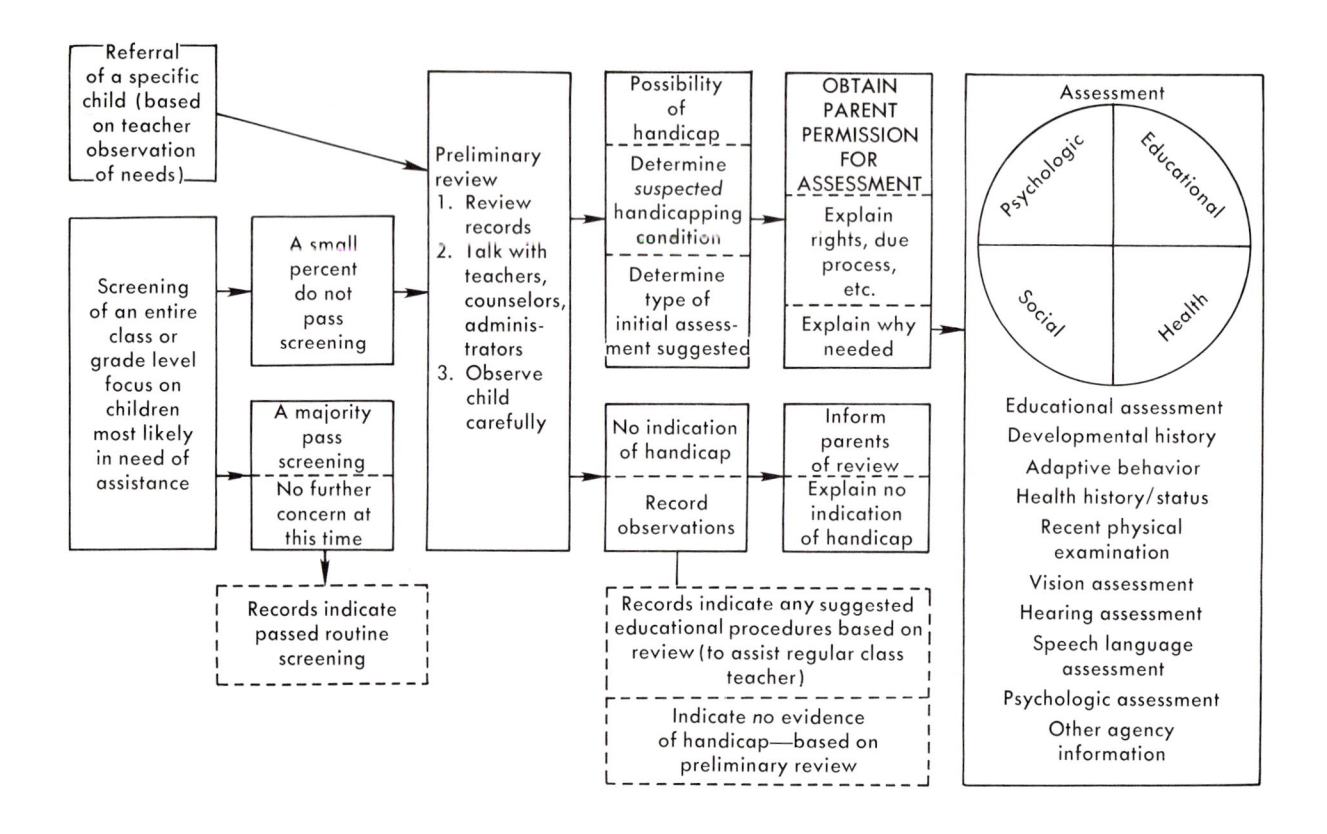

is simply a child who should be given further consideration as one who *may* either now or in the future need additional educational assistance. If screening procedures or referrals were 100 percent accurate in "finding" exceptional children, there would be no need for involved assessment procedures. Screening and referral are simple methods whereby we focus additional attention on specific children, so that we will not overlook children who need special assistance. As indicated in Fig. 3-1 screening and referral may lead to further review, which may be called preliminary review.

Preliminary review is a procedure that may or may not be used between referral or screening and further formal assessment. It appears to be growing in acceptance as a means of further considering either teacher referrals or the results of screening that indicate assessment procedures may be necessary. It is not a substitute for assessment but may prevent further unnecessary efforts. It may also prevent unduly alarming the parents in cases where the screening or referral process has been based on incomplete or inaccurate information. After searching out and reviewing additional records, conferring with other school personnel, or observing the child in the learning setting, the evaluator may decide that no

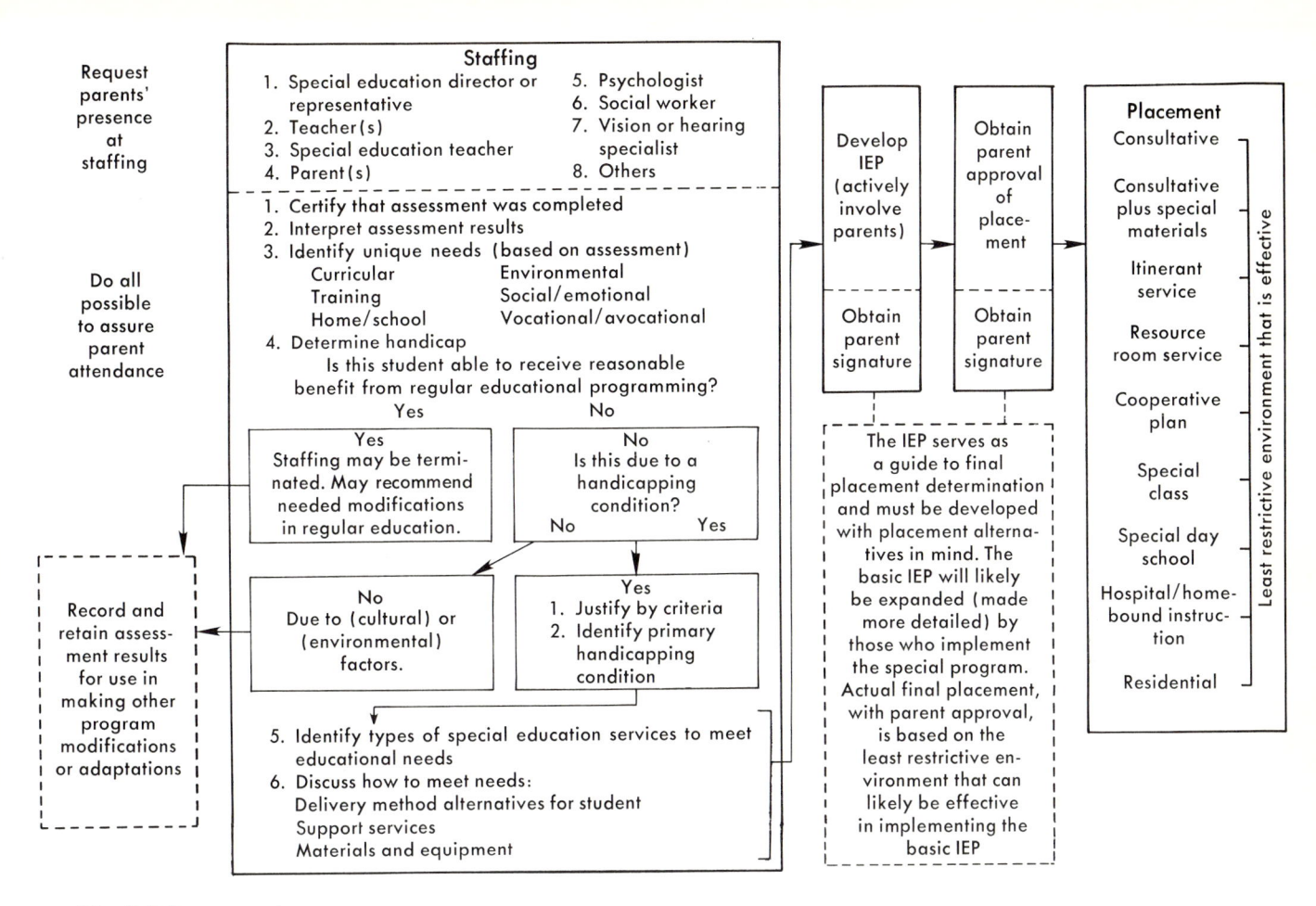

Fig. 3-1. Assessment.

Staffing
1. Special education director or representative
2. Teacher(s)
3. Special education teacher
4. Parent(s)
5. Psychologist
6. Social worker
7. Vision or hearing specialist
8. Others

1. Certify that assessment was completed
2. Interpret assessment results
3. Identify unique needs (based on assessment)
   - Curricular
   - Training
   - Home/school
   - Environmental
   - Social/emotional
   - Vocational/avocational
4. Determine handicap
   Is this student able to receive reasonable benefit from regular educational programming?

Yes — Staffing may be terminated. May recommend needed modifications in regular education.

No — Is this due to a handicapping condition?
- **No** — Due to (cultural) or (environmental) factors.
- **Yes** —
  1. Justify by criteria
  2. Identify primary handicapping condition

5. Identify types of special education services to meet educational needs
6. Discuss how to meet needs:
   - Delivery method alternatives for student
   - Support services
   - Materials and equipment

Request parents' presence at staffing

Do all possible to assure parent attendance

Record and retain assessment results for use in making other program modifications or adaptations

Develop IEP (actively involve parents) → Obtain parent signature

Obtain parent approval of placement → Obtain parent signature

The IEP serves as a guide to final placement determination and must be developed with placement alternatives in mind. The basic IEP will likely be expanded (made more detailed) by those who implement the special program. Actual final placement, with parent approval, is based on the least restrictive environment that can likely be effective in implementing the basic IEP

Placement (Least restrictive environment that is effective)
- Consultative
- Consultative plus special materials
- Itinerant service
- Resource room service
- Cooperative plan
- Special class
- Special day school
- Hospital/homebound instruction
- Residential

---

further assessment is required. This review process must be approached carefully, for we must *not* negate the purpose and value of screening and referral. On the other hand, additional information may lead to the obvious conclusion that no more investigative efforts are needed. In such cases, the procedure should be terminated through the filing of a short report indicating that although some difficulties were suspected, there is, in fact, no evidence of handicap. The reasons for this conclusion, stated succinctly, plus any appropriate recommendations should be made a matter of record. If the procedure has gone this far, parents should be informed that there was a question as to whether or not the student needed specialized educational assistance, but that preliminary review indicated no handicap existed. Parents must know when concerns have been expressed and should know how it was determined that there was no real likelihood that a handicapping condition (as defined by the local educational agency) existed.

Assessment is the next logical step when preliminary review indicates that a definable handicap may exist. *Parent permission, in writing, must be obtained before formal assessment is initiated.* Parents must know *what* is to be done and *why* it is planned, and they should know that they will be a part of the process at every step of the way. They must know their rights, and they must be told in their native language. When properly approached, most parents want the assessment completed. This is especially true when they know that they will be a part of program planning and that they have the right to say no to programs that do not make sense to them. The whole matter of appeals, rights to a hearing, and the like is beyond the scope of this discussion, but the reader should know that such procedures are now required throughout the United States.

Assessment, as indicated in Fig. 3-1, has many facets and components. Among the more common are assessment of visual and auditory abilities, educational (achievement) level, adaptive behavior level, speech and language development, level of intellectual functioning, and general developmental level. In gathering related information that may be of value in providing the most complete picture of the child, a physical examination, a health history, and related data from other agencies (if available) are also highly important. In addition, psychologic testing in addition to an estimate of level of intellectual functioning as appropriate to the suspected handicap may also be required.

All such information will not necessarily be needed in all cases, but the preceding types of data are the most common. Additional information on assessment procedures will be provided in the chapters on the various exceptionalities, and a later section of this chapter will be devoted to the issue of nondiscriminatory assessment. For special-educators-in-training, the subject of assessment will be the topic of additional courses and related experiences.

As indicated in Fig. 3-1, *B*, *staffing* immediately follows assessment. If it is determined that the problems experienced by the student are caused by an identifiable handicapping condition, an IEP must be developed, program placement alternatives must be considered, and programming must be initiated. As with previous steps in this process, the parents must be a part of these considerations and must give permission.

Staffing guidelines are established by PL 94-142 and by state laws and regulations. In general, staffing procedures are similar for most handicapping conditions, except that (for example) they are more complex for learning disabilities and less complex if the only difficulty is speech impairment. In general, a number of professional disciplines should be represented at the staffing. These might include the special education director or representative, teacher(s), psychologist, social worker, vision or hearing specialist (as appropriate), speech pathologist, and others as dictated by the individual case (for example, a specialist in the area of physical handicapping conditions when this is the obvious need). In addition, the parents and anyone else representing them must be included. The objective is to assemble and interpret assessment results so as to identify the unique needs of the student and determine the nature of the handicap.

Certain questions should be asked at the staffing, including:

1. Is the student able to receive reasonable benefit from regular educational programming (with appropriate modifications) but without direct, special education intervention? (If the answer is *yes*, and it appears that no formal, ongoing special educational intervention is required, the staffing may be terminated with appropriate recommendations going back to the original source of referral. If the answer is *no*, then question 2 is asked.)

2. Is there need for specialized programming other than regular class efforts due to a handicapping condition? (If the answer is *no*,

then some statement as to the likely cause is needed. If this likely cause relates to cultural or environmental factors, the student should be referred for further consideration in programs established for that purpose. If the answer is *yes*, then question 3 is asked.)

3. What is the primary handicapping condition, and are there additional related impairments?

It must be noted that the answers to the above questions may at times be easily determined, but at other times are quite difficult to determine. The purpose of the staffing is to consider all data and by using the expertise of the specialists in the meeting plus knowledge about the child that perhaps is best provided by the parents, to come to meaningful—albeit tentative—conclusions.

If the child is handicapped and requires special services, specific planning relating to goals, types of services needed, placement required, materials and equipment required, and other related factors must be completed. An IEP must be developed, parent permission for placement must be obtained, and a program must be initiated. This entire process is illustrated in Fig. 3-1.

The placement decision and the need for a full continuum of services

Most school districts use a decision-making process somewhat similar to that illustrated in the preceding two sections and in Fig. 3-1. However, it is critical that there be a full continuum of services available for the handicapped child, or much of the value of careful consideration and planning will be lost. Not too many years ago, if, for example, a 10-year-old child were diagnosed to be mentally retarded and in the educable range, the only placement alternatives related to which classroom in which building. There might have been a question as to whether he would fit better in a "level two" or a "level three" class (a variety of names were used to designate different achievement/age level classes, but level designations were common), or perhaps there were decisions about the time he would have to ride a school bus to get to the special class, but the only service delivery alternative was the self-contained class. Today, a great many program alternatives are available in most school districts, and the principle of the least restrictive environment is a part of the philosophy of most programs. Therefore, it is important to understand what is meant by a *full continuum* of services and how essential this full continuum is to the ability of any local district to make the right placement decision.

The concept of a full continuum of educational services is based on the belief that, considering the wide range of types of handicapping conditions, the varying degrees of severity, and the fact that students will need different amounts and types of assistance at various age levels, many different combinations of assistance may be required. These may range from nothing more than consultative assistance for children with mildly handicapping conditions to separate programming for students with severe disabilities. Fig. 3-2 is one way to illustrate these varying needs. The discussion that follows will provide more details as to what is involved at each of these levels of service. This discussion is an adapted version of a similar discussion presented in *The Handicapped Student in the Regular Classroom* (Gearheart and Weishahn, 1980).

REGULAR CLASS PLACEMENT WITH CONSULTATION FROM SPECIAL EDUCATION PERSONNEL

In this program the student is enrolled in the regular class on a full-time basis. Supportive assistance from special education personnel may involve observation of a student in the regular classroom and consultation with

Special education for the '80s

1	2	3	4
Regular class and consultative assistance from special education	Regular class and consultation plus special materials from special education	Regular class and itinerant teacher service from special education	Regular class and resource room, resource teacher service from special education

Regular class teacher—primary responsibility

*The regular class teacher may (1) assist the homebound-hospital teacher through the use of telephone or electronic equipment or (2) not be involved in the teaching process in any way.

---

the teacher to relate specific suggestions or procedures that may be helpful. The services of the special educator may be needed for a limited time only; however, some problems require repeated observation and consultation.

The special educator must be a master diagnostician to be able to analyze the situation and develop meaningful educational recommendations. This type of service requires open communicaton between the regular teacher and the special educator; the regular teacher must feel comfortable in asking for assistance and in trying the recommendations offered. The special educator, by nature of his or her experience and preparation, should be competent in analyzing problems and offering tentative solutions to the identified problem.

REGULAR CLASS PLACEMENT WITH CONSULTATION FROM SPECIAL EDUCATORS, PLUS PROVISION OF SPECIAL MATERIALS

Services at this level may be essentially the same as the previous level except that specific materials may be recommended and tried. For example, the regular classroom teacher and special educator may agree on an approach that involves special resource materials, which may be provided on a trial basis.

REGULAR CLASS PLACEMENT PLUS ITINERANT SERVICES

In this plan the student remains in the regular class in the neighborhood school, but the child and teachers receive direct assistance from special education personnel. The itinerant teacher plan with which most educators are familiar is that followed by public school speech pathologists. The itinerant plan has also been used by teachers of the visually or hearing impaired when there is a limited number of students in a school district.

Though there are variations in the manner in which this plan is implemented, the itinerant or traveling teacher generally works with students on a regularly scheduled basis (three to five times a week) or whenever necessary, depending on the child's needs. The itinerant teacher provides instruction either in the regular classroom or in a designated area outside

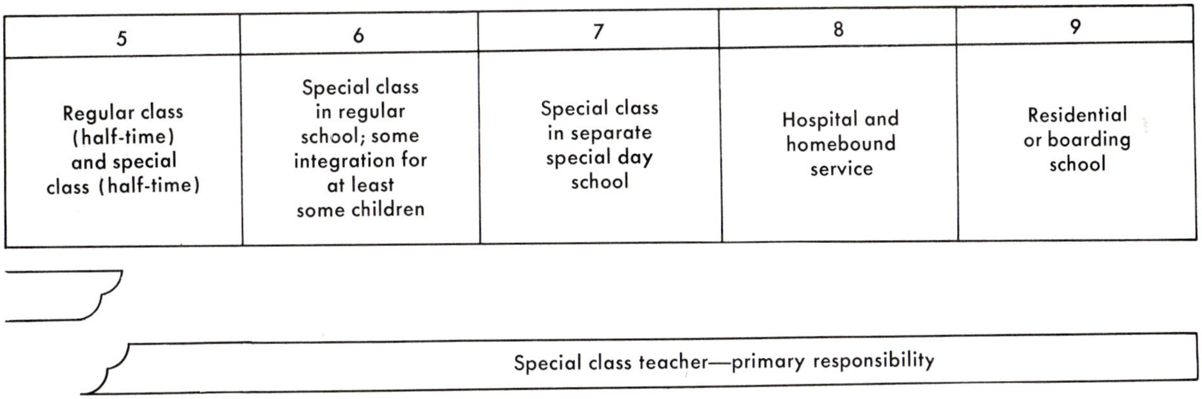

5	6	7	8	9
Regular class (half-time) and special class (half-time)	Special class in regular school; some integration for at least some children	Special class in separate special day school	Hospital and homebound service	Residential or boarding school

Special class teacher—primary responsibility

Fig. 3-2. **A full continuum of educational placement alternatives.**

the classroom. Itinerant teachers may use a van or station wagon to transport necessary equipment and materials; some also use the van for instructional purposes. The itinerant teacher may assume a helping or assisting teacher role by working with a small group of students who need the same remedial work as the handicapped child.

Certain conditions lead to adoption of the itinerant teacher plan, and in some of these situations it appears to be the best method of service delivery. In sparsely populated areas of the United States, where schools tend to have small pupil enrollment, it is difficult to justify a full-time resource room program at one school; and because of long distances between schools it is equally difficult to justify busing children to a specific school to enlarge the population of children requiring special services. The itinerant teacher plan does not seem to be as practical as the resource room plan (see below) for children with learning disabilities, behavior problems, or limited intellectual ability because it typically does not provide intensive services on a daily basis.

REGULAR CLASS PLACEMENT PLUS ASSISTANCE IN THE RESOURCE ROOM

In this plan the student is enrolled in a regular classroom but receives supplemental or remedial instruction in a resource room. This plan differs from the itinerant teacher plan in that the student is provided more specific assistance on a regularly scheduled basis (probably daily) from the resource teacher, and there is a specific room in which this assistance is given.

There are many variations in the ways resource rooms operate. In some instances the resource teacher may serve the student on a temporary basis while completing assessment techniques and planning instructional strategies that will be carried out in the child's regular classroom. In this situation the child may go to the resource room for a brief period each day until assessment procedures have been completed and a program plan has been implemented. In most school systems, however, a placement or program planning committee will have reviewed the information about any child referred for possible assistance in the resource room, and programming will be initiated only if this committee determines that the program is feasible for the child and consistent with local school district policy. In all cases the parents should be involved in such placement planning committee deliberations and must have given express permission for resource room intervention.

The resource room teacher should have the time, materials, and specific training to find effective ways to teach children with special needs. This function becomes a dual one: (1) to initiate alternative strategies and help the child find success in the resource room, and (2) to provide suggestions to the regular classroom teacher that may increase the likelihood that the child will find success in that setting.

Often the resource room teacher will provide valuable "unofficial" assistance to various teachers, sometimes in terms of general instructional ideas, but often in relation to a specific child. This is one of the more highly effective functions of the resource room teacher, but in some states it must be done unofficially because of state reimbursement guidelines and restrictions on the number of children who may be served.

In recent years some resource teachers have been providing their services in regular classrooms rather than in a separate room. By assisting the child in the regular classroom, it is assumed that there will be greater transfer and maintenance than if programming is provided only in a special setting. Although this practice is presently being employed on a limited basis, it should be given serious consideration if the nature of the problem is not so significant that it calls for very intensive work in the resource room.

COOPERATIVE PLAN

Under this plan the student is enrolled in a special class but attends a regular classroom for part of the school day. One basic difference between this plan and the resource room plan is that the child's homeroom is the special class. In the resource room plan, the child's homeroom is in the regular classroom. The amount of time spent in the regular class depends on the child's ability to profit from regular class instruction. This plan has been popular in past years; however, there is a definite movement toward resource rooms. Under this plan, both the regular teacher and the special education teacher have instructional reponsibilities for these students. It is necessary to establish close lines of communication to ensure maximum carry-over from one situation to the other.

SPECIAL CLASS IN REGULAR SCHOOL

Under this plan, the student receives academic instruction from a special education teacher but may attend school-wide activities, such as assemblies, concerts, clubs, and athletic events, and would usually share luncheon facilities. In a few instances some children may attend classes such as industrial arts, physical education, and home economics.

In the past, students classified as educable mentally retarded have often been served on this basis. There has been a definite move away from such programming except for the more seriously involved or multiply handicapped. This type of service delivery has been criticized since it has served to segregate these students, but it may be the only appropriate educational plan for some students.

SPECIAL DAY SCHOOL

The special day school plan is generally designed for students who are very seriously involved or multiply handicapped and need comprehensive special education services for their entire school day. They return to their homes at the end of the day to be with their families. Often this type of facility will offer all of the needed services for these students, such as physical and occupational therapy, counseling, special vocational workshops, and the needed adapted equipment. Like the special class plan, this type of service delivery has been criticized, but there remains a need for such services for some students. A variation of this plan, which addresses some of the criticism just mentioned, is a specially designed wing in a regular elementary or secondary school.

HOSPITAL AND HOMEBOUND SERVICE

Students with chronic conditions requiring long-term treatment in a hospital or in their homes receive special instruction from home-bound-itinerant special education personnel. The nature of the educational program depends on the student's ability, level of achievement, prognosis, and likelihood of returning to school. Some students who are hospitalized or homebound because of a short-term illness may also be served on this basis. In this instance, the instruction is closely related to the programming in the regular classroom and is planned with teachers of the classes to which the child will return. In situations in which the child requires long-term care, a two-way communication system between the child's home and regular classroom may be set up. This system may employ a telephone or a videotelephone to reduce the isolation of being at home or in a hospital. This two-way telephone or videotelephone system provides an opportunity for full-time educational programming and maximal interaction with other students.

RESIDENTIAL OR BOARDING SCHOOL

Residential and boarding schools are the oldest type of educational delivery system. These schools were generally established for students who were visually impaired, hearing impaired, emotionally disturbed, or mentally retarded because local school districts did not offer the needed services. In these programs the students may attend only during the 9-month school year or on a year-round basis, depending on the extent of the handicap. Because of the trend toward mainstreaming and integration of mildly to moderately handicapped students, these programs presently serve only the more seriously involved and multiply handicapped. In addition to educational programming, they can also provide the needed 24-hour, comprehensive services required by many of these students.

PLACEMENT DECISION VARIABLES

A number of variables would be considered when determining the best possible educational placement for a particular student. The following, although not inclusive, would be considered by the staffing committee when making placement decisions for a particular student:

1. Chronologic age
2. Type and degree of impairment or disability
3. Age at onset (birth or acquired)
4. Level of achievement
5. Measured intellectual ability
6. Level of adaptive behavior
7. Social maturity
8. Presence of multiple handicapping conditions (thus the need for related, noneducational services)
9. Ambulation or mobility (particularly important when considering crippled and other health impaired and visually impaired)
10. Success of past and present placement
11. Speech and language
12. Wishes of student and student's parents

Basic issues in educating exceptional children

There are many basic issues that must be considered when planning educational programs for exceptional children, but certain of these are of major magnitude and have been the topic of long and heated debate. In many cases, the heat has been much more noteworthy than any light generated, but these issues must be understood and considered by all special educators. We will consider some of these concerns, emphasizing those that have ramifications for all or nearly all areas of exceptionality. The unusual significance of these issues will become more apparent as we discuss the various exceptionalities in the following chapters.

MAINSTREAMING/INTEGRATING THE HANDICAPPED

There is little question as to the desirability of maximum integration of the handicapped within the mainstream of education. The questions relating to mainstreaming are those concerning when, where, with whom, and to what extent. If *all* children could stay in the regular classroom *all* of the time, this would be undoubtedly best, but special education was established as a subdiscipline of education because it was not practical, in terms of effective accomplishment of educational goals, for all children to remain in the regular program all of the time.

In one of the more critical references to the potential damage of overapplication of the principle of mainstreaming, Moores (1978, p. 12) reviews the reasons (as he perceives them) for the reaction of some educators of the retarded to the concept of mainstreaming. He notes that (1) testing and placement procedures had been biased racially and ethnically and (2) there was no justification for segregating children "purely on the basis of an I.Q. score . . . especially those children using a different language or dialect from that of the tester." He notes that in some cases, major advances have been claimed when, in fact, "One must wonder how such educators can perceive their efforts as anything more than a belated attempt to right past wrongs." Moores' point in his discussion of the phenomenon of mainstreaming is that educators of other handicapped children (in this case educators of the hearing impaired) should feel free to proceed with program planning and placement without feeling that they *must* respond to influence or pressure from other areas of special education.

In a study that included an assessment of issues of major concern to special educators, Monson and Paul (1977) discovered that the single most important issue, as indicated by faculty, doctoral, and master's students in the eighteen public and private universities in North Carolina that had special education training programs, was mainstreaming. Though there is no direct evidence that this would necessarily have been true nationwide, there is considerable likelihood that it would have, given the attention the subject has received. In the introduction to the summary of their findings, they refer to mainstreaming as a slogan. This reference to mainstreaming as a slogan may be objectionable to some mainstreaming advocates, but in fact it has often been treated more like a slogan than a complex principle requiring consideration and understanding before it can be intelligently applied.

A number of school districts across the nation have responded to the confusion generated by the concept of mainstreaming by providing a practical definition for local use. One such definition, from the special education handbook of a large Eastern school district, follows:

> Mainstreaming refers to a continuum of services which handicapped youngsters may receive in regular school settings and which
> - Are based on the educational needs of children
> - Provide coordinated services from classroom teachers, resource room teachers, itinerant

This "mainstreamed" student is receiving help in understanding geometric shapes.

teachers, and other ancillary personnel, as an aspect of shared responsibility
- Provide individual educational management plans for each handicapped child through cooperative team planning, including the development of structured learning environments for those with intensive needs
- Provide the most appropriate education for each child in the least restrictive setting (in other words, as much time as possible participating in the regular program)
- Provide the multiple opportunities for a child whose educational needs may change
- Enable a special education resource room teacher to service a child a minimum of one unit of time (for example, half an hour); or as much as a majority of the day while the need is intensive. For example, at the beginning of a year, one child may be spending 90% of the day in a resource room, three may spend 40%, while others may be spending less than 10% of their time in the resource room.

Mainstreaming does *not* mean:
- Return of all handicapped children to regular classes
- Permitting children with special needs to remain in regular classrooms without the support services that they need
- Elimination of centers, wings, units, classes, and non-public schools for youngsters with handicaps so severe that they cannot benefit from a regular school setting and/or program

The principles and practices implied by the preceding definition of mainstreaming appear to be gaining national acceptance. The factors that provided the motivation for the original efforts to promote the concept of mainstreaming were related to (1) inadequate or biased assessment, (2) a tendency to place students in special classes as a substitute for developing other programs, and (3) increased recognition of the value of interaction with nonhandicapped peers, even if a student were definitely handicapped. These factors led to the acceptance on the part of some of the idea that being with nonhandicapped peers was more important than any other single factor, including effective learning of basic skills. The pendulum swung much too far, as is so often the case in education, and some students suffered as much from mainstreaming as their predecessors had suffered from the lack of mainstreaming. The original intent of mainstreaming will be realized if (1) the type of referral, assessment, staffing, and placement procedures suggested on pp. 55-59 are implemented; (2) due process procedures are followed; (3) the variable needs of students are recognized; and (4) the *least restrictive, educational environment* (which is also the most facilitative in terms of learning goals) *is provided*. As all of this is accomplished, the needs and concerns of the regular classroom teacher must be recognized.

Some so-called mainstreaming programs have been mainly window dressing, and little has really changed in how school districts have planned to maximize integration of handicapped and nonhandicapped students. Others have appeared to be successful initially, but after special funds ran out, even those who originally believed the programs to be successful concluded they had failed (O'Donnell and Bradfield, 1976). Many have been of marginal value because those in charge had more energy and enthusiasm than knowledge and information. Special educators must be especially careful to approach this topic with care and to understand the emotional reactions that may result in regular classroom teachers who may feel special educators are shirking their responsibilities. If we will remember that the goal is to provide the advantages of both special educational assistance and maximal interaction with nonhandicapped peers, perhaps we can plan meaningful *individualized* programs for handicapped students. If mainstreaming is primarily a slogan or a battlecry, it will be difficult to predict who will ultimately be injured most in the battle that will surely take place.

NONDISCRIMINATORY ASSESSMENT

Nondiscriminatory assessment is explicitly required by PL 94-142 regulations as follows:

Evaluation procedures

State and local educational agencies shall insure, at a minimum, that:
(a) Tests and other evaluation materials:
   (1) Are provided and administered in the child's native language or other mode of communication, unless it is clearly not feasible to do so;
   (2) Have been validated for the specific purpose for which they are used; and
   (3) Are administered by trained personnel in conformance with the instructions provided by their producer;
(b) Tests and other evaluation materials include those tailored to assess specific areas of educational need and not merely those which are designed to provide a single general intelligence quotient;
(c) Tests are selected and administered so as best to insure that when a test is administered to a child with impaired sensory, manual, or speaking skills, the test results accurately reflect the child's aptitude or achievement level or whatever other factors the test purports to measure, rather than reflecting the child's impaired sensory, manual, or speaking skills (except where those skills are the factors which the test purports to measure);
(d) No single procedure is used as the sole criterion for determining an appropriate program for a child, and
(e) The evaluation is made by a multidisciplinary team or group of persons, including at least one teacher or other specialist with knowledge in the area of suspected disability.
(f) The child is assessed in all areas related to the suspected disability, including where appropriate, health, vision, hearing, social and emotional status, general intelligence, academic performance, communicative status and motor abilities (Federal Register, August 23, 1977, pp. 42496-42497).

These regulations indicate what must be done and how to do it in as specific a manner as possible, but many questions are left unanswered. For example, since tests are obviously expected to "discriminate" between those who have "much" of some factor or ability as compared to those who have "little" of that factor or ability, they do, and will, discriminate. Obviously, the intent is that they measure in a meaningful manner and not unfairly prejudice the decisions of those who must use test results in program planning. Alley and Foster indicate that four popular procedures have been advocated to attempt to negate unfair discrimination in test results (1978, p. 3). These include: (1) translating existing (traditional) tests into the minority language, (2) norming existing (traditional) tests on specific minority groups, (3) using an examiner of the same minority group as the children being tested, and (4) identifying the competencies required for majority culture survival, evaluating which of these competencies are underattained by minority children, and directly teaching these competencies.

In their consideration of these four approaches, Alley and Foster (1978, p. 6) conclude that "all four procedures to obtain nondiscriminatory testing have serious flaws inherent in their rationale and/or use." They have no "pat" answers but suggest a number of recommendations for further investigation. They suggest (and I heartily agree) that a complete moratorium on testing until truly nondiscriminatory tests can be developed can only rationally lead to more subjective appraisals, which are most likely to increase the possibility of discrimination against minority students if they are not achieving or performing socially as majority group teachers expect.

Full-scale efforts to produce truly nondiscriminatory assessment approaches (tests and other assessment methods) must continue, but in the meantime we must pursue whatever alternative approaches appear to be most potentially fruitful. In an article entitled "Nondiscriminatory assessment: is it achievable?" Ysseldyke (1978) asks the very unpopular question indicated in the title of his article. He points out that bias occurs in relation to such factors as parent's occupation (regardless of racial or ethnic considerations), physical attractiveness of children, and other similar variables. He draws the following conclusion and makes five specific recommendations:

> Clearly, bias does occur in assessment, but I believe that bias is more a function of the ways in which assessment devices are used than of the devices themselves. Let me review the factors we must consider if we are to make progress toward nondiscriminatory assessment practices.
>
> 1. *The decisions to be made.* Assessment data are collected to help educators make decisions. Tests are used in the data-collection process. We must begin to differentiate our assessment devices and procedures in light of the kinds of decisions we make. Norm-referenced measures of intelligence, for example, are useful in making classification and placement decisions. They provide very little information, however, for planning instructional programs for children. Instructional planning requires assessment of a pupil's specific skill development, a goal more nearly approximated by using criterion-referenced tests.
> 2. *Acculturation.* When norm-referenced devices are used, a pupil's performance is compared to that of a reference group. To the extent that the background experiences and opportunities of the child assessed differ, either positively or negatively, from those of the group on whom the test was standardized, norm-referenced interpretation of performance will be biased.
> 3. *Technical adequacy.* Data for use in making decisions about pupils should be collected with the most technically adequate devices and procedures available. Tests used to make important decisions about students should have *reliabilities* that exceed .90. Unfortunately, too many of the tests currently used in educational settings have reliabilities far below .90, yet they are used daily to provide data for decision-making. Furthermore, as noted by the Office of Civil Rights in its recent publication of regulations for Section 504 of the Rehabilitation Act of 1973, tests must have demonstrated validity for the purposes for which they are used. Few test authors provide data in their manuals regarding the validity of their tests for specific purposes.
> 4. *Bias in assessment.* I have noted that evidence is mounting to support the contention that naturally-occurring pupil characteristics affect the assessment decisions made for and about children. I firmly believe that naturally-occurring pupil characteristics such as race, sex, physical attractiveness, socioeconomic status, and parental power have a tremendous effect on who is referred, the settings to which pupils are assigned, and the particular kinds of instructional programs they receive. Educators must, individually and collectively, examine the extent to which the decisions they make are, in fact, biased decisions.
> 5. *Bias following assessment.* We must not only strive for a reduction of bias in the process of assessing children, but also for a reduction of bias following assessment. Educators must learn that labels connote little if anything about the ways in which pupils actually behave and must, somehow, learn to treat child behavior objectively.*

Ysseldyke notes that most of his recommendations are "just plain common sense" and concludes that "we will make little progress by looking for *the* fair tools to be used in decision-making; we must begin to address fair-

---

*From *centerfoLD*, Jan./Feb., 1978; The Network of Innovative Schools, Inc., National Learning Disabilities Assistance Project.

ness in the process of decision-making itself" (1978, p. 3). This statement provides a fitting conclusion to our consideration of this complex, critically important issue.

LABELING

A third issue that is inextricably interwoven with assessment and mainstreaming is the emotionally laden question of labeling. It has been one of the central questions of many of the court actions outlined in the preceding two chapters, and it is far from being resolved.

Labels, categories, and classification systems are the logical outgrowth of our system of communication. They are often used to save time, to serve as shortcuts in communicating more involved and complex concepts. When we say that someone is "president of his or her own company," we convey certain ideas regarding success, prominence, or respect. If we lengthen the "label" and indicate "president of a major, international corporation," the message conveyed is even more definite. If we are speaking of a baseball team, terms such as "pitcher," "second baseman," and "outfielder" are self-explanatory to those familiar with the game and provide considerable information about the position played and numerous related factors.

Labels such as "conservative" and "liberal" have varied meanings in relation to the frame of reference of both the person who uses the term and the person who hears it. During a period of time not too many years ago, the label "communist" was a much more derogatory label in the United States than it is today. In other parts of the world it is a very positive label. Labels are not inherently negative, but they may be made negative through usage. This, then, is the dilemma. How do we speak of handicapping conditions (what terms can we use) so as to *not* communicate negative concepts? Given the need to communicate (evaluate unique educational need, complete planning, implement remedial or adapted programs), how do we do it so as to avoid, or at least minimize, stigma or negative connotations?

Considering the history of treatment of handicapped persons and the tendency to respect and reward those who are "intelligent," "successful," and "attractive" (these terms are among the many labels we use each day), it is not surprising that some negative feelings and reactions are at times related to the handicapped. Most experienced teachers know that children tend to "label" other children, whether or not educators establish labeling systems.

A number of labels have been used to refer to children who have less than average intelligence. In a study, sponsored by the federal government, of the various effects of labeling and the establishment of categories of handicap, Hobbs (1974) concluded that there were both positive and negative aspects to labeling. The negative included:

1. Possibility of permanent stigmatization
2. Rejection by peers
3. Possible assignment to inferior educational programs
4. Unwarranted, unnecessary institutionalization
5. Misdiagnosis (especially of minority persons) through the use of inappropriate tests

The advantages, or potentially positive aspects, of labeling included:

1. Obtaining needed legislation
2. Facilitating communication (about needs, etc.)
3. Designating appropriate services
4. Organizing volunteer advocacy agencies

Various legal rulings indicate that we must carefully avoid the potentially negative, stigmatizing effect of labels, but most of such litigation has dealt with *mis*labeling. To my knowledge there have been, for example, no court cases where the term "visually impaired" has been declared to be a stigmatizing label when used in educational program planning. In contrast, in a number of court cases, parents have demanded and received services for their children whom *they* have declared to be (labeled) mentally retarded. These were children in the moderate to severe range of mental retardation. The major conflict relates to the mildly handicapped, especially those children labeled mildly (or educable) mentally retarded.

Various states have attempted to do away with labels through substitute mechanisms (Birch, 1974). Included are attempts to emphasize the educational needs of the child rather than applying a label emphasizing the handicap or disability; and attempts to broaden categories, as in California's use of the term "learning handicapped" for all mildly handicapped children.

Since the attack by Dunn (1968) on the type of programming he characterized as often ineffective and too often overinclusive of minority children, the literature of special education has been filled with articles about the problems of labeling, the stigma effect, misplacement of minority children, and the self-fulfilling prophecy effect. It is possible to provide a well-documented "Who's Who" of antilabel, anti–special class writers, particularly from 1968 to 1975, and although their concerns and criticisms were justified, at times some may have gone overboard in their fervor. In fact, most of their concern was about the mildly handicapped and the overrepresentation of minority children in special classes, although some readers did not understand the limitations of their protests, perhaps because of their eloquence.

An interesting example of what may happen even if we abandon the traditional labels is cited by Payne and Mercer (1975). In a school program in which unlabeled handicapped children were involved in DISTAR reading instruction while enrolled in a regular classroom, the handicapped children were taunted by nonhandicapped children by being called "DISTAR, DISTAR," apparently to reflect their lower academic or ability status. Both sides in the controversy understood that in this instance "DISTAR" was a bad word. Aside from the *mis*labeling, which must be avoided with great care, perhaps it is, as Gottlieb (1974) observed, the behavior of handicapped children, not their label, that leads to rejection.

Following the lead of President Kennedy, the U.S. Congress has provided significant financial support for special services for the mentally retarded. It would appear that the term "mental retardation" is known by society and that efforts to combat mental retardation have been of great importance to the retarded of today and those who may be with us in the future. Such efforts have been highly beneficial in the fight to prevent mental retardation, and it is doubtful if such efforts could have been mounted without a term (label) to provide a point of focus. McMillan (1977) believes that one of the strongest arguments for retaining categorical labels is that they assist in relating diagnosis to treatment. This may be disputed by some, but it seems to have been supported by historical records.

In summary, labeling must be approached with full understanding of potentially negative effects. Diagnosticians must be well aware of the limitations of assessment tools and techniques and must appreciate the unusual problems inherent in the assessment of minority students, especially those for whom standard English is not the first language. Unless there is the potential of advantageous special programming, there is no need for labels; certainly they have little value in and of themselves. Labels such as "mentally retarded" and "emotionally disturbed" have unusually

Happiness is contagious.

great potential with regard to permanent stigma, and their use may require even more careful attention than most others.

Students who are suspected of being *mildly* handicapped form another subgroup requiring special attention. As with most other situations in life, borderline cases may not be what they first appear to be, thus the need for even more care than in the case of the more obvious, severely handicapped. Children with sensory impairments (the blind and the deaf) have seldom been the subject of concern regarding labeling. In their case, it is most important to provide the best available programming and work to educate the nonhandicapped regarding the many strengths and abilities of these persons. In so doing, it is right and proper to speak of the hearing impaired and visually impaired. The obviously physically handicapped are in a similar situation. It is highly important that we use some properly descriptive terminology in our efforts to be certain that they may enter buildings with maximum ease, gain employment, and the like.

The use of labels to provide a focal point for special interest groups who work in behalf of the handicapped appears to remain highly important. Special funding for the handicapped is essential, and to provide such funding, some type of commonly recognized terminology (labeling) is necessary. Past attempts at general "block funding" (which requires no use of labels) have usually led to the misuse of funds intended for the handicapped.

Objectively, labeling cannot be characterized as either "good" or "bad." Some of its effects have been good; others have been bad. This has resulted from ignorance and misunderstanding, and perhaps in some cases deliberate ill will, but it does not mean that we should not, in any case, use labels. Rather, it means that we must approach the topic of labeling with a full understanding of the factors that make it effective and useful or ineffective and detrimental. It is up to those who are empowered to use or not use labels to do so only when it is in the best interests of those involved. This is essentially the message of the litigation related to labeling; and this is what must be done.

Education of the gifted: how, where, and when

Many of the questions raised with respect to education of the handicapped may also be raised with respect to the gifted, talented, and creative. They are not commonly articulated with such urgency, and in some parts of the nation may be seldom mentioned, perhaps because there is no strong legal pressure to attend to this issue. Nevertheless, there are serious questions as to how to identify the gifted, including questions that concern the use of biased testing instruments; and there is little consensus as to whether gifted students should receive educational services in a segregated or semisegregated setting.

Although any stated philosophy of education of exceptional children, such as the one proposed at the beginning of this chapter, is thought to apply primarily to handicapped students, most of any such philosophy will apply equally well to the gifted, talented, and creative. In a similar manner, screening and referral procedures for the gifted in many respects are identical to those in use for the handicapped; and although assessment procedures are usually less rigorous than required for the handicapped, there are many similarities in this arena also. All of these questions, issues, and concerns will be explored in more detail in Chapter 12.

Summary

Most school districts today have a philosophy of special education, either a formal statement or a set of established practices that, in effect, serve as the philosophical statement. A general philosophical statement was presented at the start of this chapter, which is similar to statements in actual use throughout the United States. In addition to a formal statement of philosophy, most school districts also have a number of program guidelines that are the basis for action in the local district. In many cases, the content of these guidelines is determined largely by state regulations and, of course, all states are influenced to some extent by PL 94-142 and Section 504 of the Rehabilitation Act of 1973.

Among the more important guidelines in any district are those establishing the procedures whereby students are referred for review and assessment, assessed, staffed, and considered for possible inclusion in some type of special educational program. This procedure must be very carefully constructed so that parents are fully informed and part of the decision-making process, and the process must ensure that all pertinent information is collected and properly considered before decisions are made. The final decision must be made in such a manner that: (1) students who are not actually handicapped are not considered as such, (2) students who are handicapped and in need of special services receive appropriate services, (3) services received are provided in the least restrictive environment, consistent with an effective, appropriate program, and (4) all concerned (parents, teachers, other concerned professionals) are fully informed and thus have all necessary information to carry out any required action. In cases where it is determined that the student is *not* handicapped, it is important that all pertinent data be forwarded to those who will continue to teach the student.

In those instances where the student is determined to be handicapped, it is essential that all possible service delivery modes be considered. The full continuum of services (which, when required by a given student, should be available—in all school districts) includes: (1) continued regular class placement with consultative assistance from special education personnel, (2) regular class placement and consultative assistance plus provision of special materials, (3) regular class placement plus itinerant services, (4) regular class placement plus assistance in the resource room, (5) the cooperative plan (approximately half-time in a special class, half-time in the regular class), (6) special class placement in a regular school setting, (7) a separate special school, (8) hospital or homebound service, or (9) residential or boarding school placement. Many children will require one type program at one point in their educational program, and different services at another time. Placement decision variables include: (1) chronologic age, (2) type of disability or impairment, (3) degree of disability or impairment, (4) age of onset of disability, (5) level of academic achievement, (6) level of intelligence, (7) level of adaptive behavior (8) social maturity, (9) other handicaps, (10) degree of ambulation or mobility, (11) success of past and present placement, (12) level of speech and language, and (13) desires of the students and parents.

Three major issues were discussed in this chapter; though highly interrelated they were considered separately. These were mainstreaming/integration, the effects of labeling, and nondiscriminatory assessment. These remain issues because there are no clear-cut answers or solutions that can be said to apply in all instances.

Special education for the '80s

focus

introduction

In every state there are regulations, program flow-charts, and the like, which tend to direct local programs, but it is abundantly clear to special educators who have worked with a wide variety of programs in many different parts of the nation, that local interest, knowledge, and support make the vital difference. It is important to note that specific guidelines and practices will not be exactly the same throughout the nation, or even throughout a given state.

a philosophy of education of exceptional children and youth

Educational planning must emphasize the learning strengths and abilities of the handicapped, and "labeling" children according to handicap should be avoided when possible. On the other hand, children who are hearing impaired or visually impaired (for example) must have certain specific assistance that relates directly to their sensory loss, and thus it will often be advantageous to such children and to their educational programming to think of them as visually impaired (handicapped or disabled) or hearing impaired.

Exceptional children and youth should be served in the regular classroom whenever possible, and additional efforts should be directed toward increasing the effectiveness of such programming.

In all assessment, planning, and programming parents must be involved to the greatest possible extent with procedural due process and the right to privacy maintained at all times.

related principles

Regular classroom teachers are highly important members of the educational team that must plan and implement programs for exceptional children. As such, they must be fully informed and must participate in all decisions affecting them.
- Assessment must be flexible, broadly based, and ongoing.
- Prevention, where it may be pursued, should receive top priority.
- Early intervention is highly desirable; however, the possible effects of misidentification and inappropriate labeling must be considered.
- Some disabilities may be more appropriately viewed as symptoms rather than as specific physical disorders and may exist at one time in life and not at another.
- Need for special educational services may vary from full-time, special class service at one time in the child's life to little or no service at another time.
- A wide variety of services and the total spectrum of service delivery capabilities is essential.

prevalence of exceptional children

Prevalence means "how many" and refers to the number of children who might be called exceptional at any given time.

screening, referral, and assessment

Screening usually refers to a process whereby all children in given grade levels are assessed or evaluated in some simple, preliminary manner, to determine whether additional, more in-depth investigation and assessment should be initiated.

The child who is referred or who gives indication in the screening process of need for further investigation or consideration is *not* to be "automatically" considered an exceptional child as a result of the referral or screening process.

staffing

The purpose of the staffing is to consider all data and, by using the expertise of the specialists in the meeting, plus knowledge about the child that perhaps is best provided by the parents, to come to meaningful—albeit tentative—conclusions.

regular class placement plus itinerant services

The itinerant teacher plan does not seem to be as practical as the resource room plan for children with learning disabilities, behavior problems, or limited intellectual ability because it typically does not provide intensive services on a daily basis.

mainstreaming/integrating the handicapped

Mainstreaming refers to a continuum of services which handicapped youngsters may receive in regular school settings.

Mainstreaming does not mean return of all handicapped children to regular classes.

The factors that provided the motivation for the original efforts to promote the concept of mainstreaming were related to (1) inadequate or biased assessment, (2) a tendency to place students in special classes as a substitute for developing other programs, and (3) increased recognition of the value of interaction with nonhandicapped peers, even if a student were definitely handicapped.

nondiscriminatory assessment

A complete moratorium on testing until truly nondiscriminatory tests can be developed can only rationally lead to more subjective appraisals, which are most likely to increase the possibility of discrimination against minority students if they are not achieving or performing socially as majority group teachers expect.

Full-scale efforts to produce truly nondiscriminatory assessment approaches (tests and other assessment methods) must continue but in the meantime we must pursue whatever alternative approaches appear to be most potentially fruitful.

We will make little progress by looking for *the* fair tools to be used in decision-making; we must begin to address fairness in the process of decision-making itself.

labeling

Labels, categories, and classification systems are the logical outgrowth of our system of communication.

Labels are not inherently negative, but they may be made negative through usage.

Various legal rulings indicate that we must carefully avoid the potentially negative, stigmatizing effect of labels, but most of such litigation has dealt with *mis*-labeling.

Labeling must be approached with full understanding of potentially negative effects. Diagnosticians must be well aware of the limitations of assessment tools and techniques and must appreciate the unusual problems inherent in the assessment of minority students, especially those for whom standard English is not the first language.

References and suggested readings

Abeson, A. Legal forces and pressures. In *Mainstreaming and minority children*. R. L. Jones (Ed.). Reston, Va.: Council for Exceptional Children, 1976.

Alley, G., and Foster, C.: Nondiscriminatory testing of minority and exceptional children. *Focus on Exceptional Children*, Jan. 1978, 9(8), 1-13.

Beery, K. *Models for mainstreaming*. Sioux Falls: Adapt Press, 1972.

Birch, J. W. *Mainstreaming: educable mentally retarded children in regular classes*. University of Minnesota: Leadership Training Institute/Special Education, 1974.

Blatt, B. Public policy and the education of children with special needs. *Exceptional Children*, 1972, 38, 537-546.

Bryan, T. H. Learning disabilities: a new stereotype. *Journal of Learning Disabilities*, 1974, 7, 304-309.

Calhoun, G., and Elliot, R. N. Self-concept and academic achievement of educable retarded and emotionally disturbed pupils. *Exceptional Children*, 1977, 43, 379-380.

Cantrell, R., and Cantrell, M. Preventive mainstreaming: impact of a supportive services program on pupils. *Exceptional Children*, 1976, 42 (5), 381-385.

Dunn, L. M. Special education for the mildly retarded—is much of it justified? *Exceptional Children,* 1968, *35,* 5-22.

Federal Register, Aug. 23, 1977, pp. 42496-49497.

Foster, G. G., Ysseldyke, J. E., and Reese, J. I wouldn't have seen it if I hadn't believed it. *Exceptional Children,* 1975, *41,* 469-473.

Franks, J. Ethnic and social status characteristics of children in EMR and LD classes. *Exceptional Children,* 1971, *37,* 537.

Gallagher, J. J. The special education contract for mildly handicapped children. *Exceptional Children,* 1972, *38,* 527-536.

Gampel, D. H., Gottlieb, J., and Harrison, R. H. Comparison of classroom behavior of special-class EMR, integrated EMR, low IQ, and nonretarded children. *American Journal of Mental Deficiency,* 1974, *79,* 16-21.

Gearheart, B., and Weishahn, M. *The handicapped child in the regular classroom.* 2nd ed. St. Louis: The C. V. Mosby, 1980.

Glicking, E. E., and Theobald, J. T. Mainstreaming: affect or effect. *Journal of Special Education,* 1975, *9,* 317-328.

Gottlieb, J. Attitudes toward retarded children: effects of labeling and academic performance. *American Journal of Mental Deficiency,* 1974, *79,* 268-273.

Gottlieb, J., Agard, J. A., Kaufman, M. J., and Semmel, M. I. Retarded children mainstreamed: practices as they affect minority groups children. In *Mainstreaming and minority children.* R. L. Jones (Ed.). Reston, Va.: Council for Exceptional Children, 1976.

Hobbs, N. *The futures of children.* San Francisco: Jossey-Bass Publishers, 1974.

Jensen, A. R. Test bias and construct validity. *Phi Delta Kappan,* 1976, *58,* 340-346.

Jones, R. L. Labels and stigma in special education. *Exceptional Children,* 1972, *38,* 553-564.

Jones, R. L. *Mainstreaming and the minority child.* Reston, Va.: Council for Exceptional Children, 1976.

Kolstoe, O. P. Programs for the mildly retarded: a reply to critics. *Exceptional Children,* 1972, *39,* 51-56.

Lilly, S. M. Special education: a teapot in a tempest. *Exceptional Children,* 1970, *37,* 43-48.

MacMillan, D. L. *Mental retardation in school and society.* Boston: Little, Brown and Co., 1977.

MacMillan, D. L., Jones, R. L., and Aloia, G. F. The mentally retarded label. *American Journal of Mental Deficiency,* 1974, *79,* 241-261.

Mercer, J. R. *Labeling the mentally retarded.* Berkeley: University of California Press, 1973.

Moores, D. F. *Educating the deaf: psychology, principles, and practices.* Boston: Houghton-Mifflin Co., 1978.

O'Donnell, P. A., and Bradfield, R. H. (eds.). *Mainstreaming: controversy and consensus.* San Rafael: Academic Therapy Publications, 1976.

Payne, J. S., and Mercer, C. D. Definition and prevalence. In *Mental retardation: introduction and personal perspectives.* J. M. Kauffman, and J. S. Payne (Eds.). Columbus, Ohio: Charles E. Merrill Publishing Co., 1975.

Salvia, J., Sheare, J., and Algozzine, R. Facial attractiveness and personal-social adjustment. *Journal of Abnormal Child Psychology,* 1975, *3,* 171-178.

Salvia, J., and Ysseldyke, J. *Assessment in special and remedial education.* Boston: Houghton-Mifflin Co., 1978.

Ysseldyke, J. Nondiscriminatory assessment: is it achievable?" *centerfoLD,* Jan./Feb., 1978, *3*.

SECTION TWO

Special education in Canada

This section, comprised of just one chapter, is designed to provide basic information regarding existing programs for exceptional students in the schools of Canada. Although educational programs for exceptional students in Canada and the United States are similar in many ways, there are also certain differences of considerable interest. Knowledge of these differences may be helpful for those who have an interest in teaching in Canada, and there is always potential value in better understanding the educational practices of other geographic areas. This is true when considering various cities within a state, states within the United States, or the United States compared to other nations of the world. Perhaps the consideration of similarities and differences between the United States and Canada may lead the reader to futher investigation of programs and practices in other parts of the world, thus greatly expanding his or her knowledge base.

Teachers often use auditory input to support visual learning.

chapter 4

Educational programs for exceptional students in Canada

objectives

To describe educational programming for exceptional students in Canada.

To contrast and compare both general education and special education in Canada in the United States.

To illustrate the effects of varied legislative enactments governing education of the handicapped.

To present examples of legislation and actual educational programs in the ten Canadian provinces.

To present examples of unique and noteworthy programs and activities designed to served the handicapped in Canada.

Introduction

There are more similarities than differences in the education of exceptional students in Canada and the United States, particularly if we think, for example of how the teacher in a given school assists a visually impaired 10-year-old. Most of the presentation of how handicapped or gifted individuals are served—as presented in Chapters 5 through 16—is applicable in either the United States or Canada. Significant differences may exist in how a student with a given handicap or disability is served in a large city compared to a rural area, but this is a function of geography, not political boundaries. There are, however, differences in structure, procedures, and the matter of which agency provides a particular service, which lead to differences between the United States and Canada. These differences and the factors leading to them plus a brief overview of programs in the various provinces will comprise the major content of this chapter.

Canada: a constitutional monarchy

Canada is a federation of ten provinces (Newfoundland, Nova Scotia, New Brunswick, Prince Edward Island, Quebec, Ontario, Manitoba, Saskatchewan, Alberta, and British Columbia) and two territories (the Yukon Territory and the Northwest Territories). It is a member of the Commonwealth of Nations and is a constitutional monarchy. Canada is governed under a basic constitution, The British North America Act, adopted in 1867 (the time of Confederation). This constitution provides somewhat different and greater powers to the provinces than is reserved for the states in the United States. The provincial governments, by virtue of the constitution, have authority in the areas of property, civil rights, education, and local government. The Canadian federal government has authority in all matters not specifically reserved to the provinces, and retains power to veto provincial laws. Unlike the United States, where education is a state function but has been partially relinquished to the federal government (as may be witnessed by the amount of federal aid accepted by state and local governments, see p. 38), education in Canada remains a provincial function. There is, therefore, considerable variability in educational matters throughout the nation, and there is no agency similar to the Bureau of Education for the Handicapped of the U.S. Department of Education, or national legislation similar to Public Law 94-142. In Canada, provincial acts and regulations determine the scope and direction of educational services for the exceptional student.

The Canadian federal government is officially under the authority of the sovereign (King or Queen), who is also the sovereign of Britain, Australia, and New Zealand. Although the Canadian government has a legislative branch, a judicial branch, and an executive branch, the nature of a constitutional monarchy is such that the House of Commons is the final authority. The judicial branch does not have similar powers to those presently exercised by the judiciary in the United States and thus may have less influence in matters such as education of exceptional students.

The Canadian government is headed by the Prime Minister, who is the leader either of the party that has the most members in the House of Commons or of a coalition of parties that together have a majority of members. The Prime Minister is also an elected member of the House of Commons. An important distinction between Canada and the United States concerning the executive branch is that the Canadian cabinet is made up of people who are also members of the House of Commons. It is, therefore, chosen by the Prime Minister from elected members of his party. (In the United States it is possible for a senator to be made a cabinet member but this is unusual. In Canada one can be appointed to the cabinet pending election but one must resign if one fails to be elected.)

A number of matters that might easily be considered as educational in the United States (for example, efforts on behalf of adult handicapped, identification of preschool children with sensory impairments) are provided within the provinces at least in part with the assistance of federal agencies that are part of the Department of National Health and Welfare and the Department of Manpower and Immigration. Special education services in the form of *direct* educational programs for school-age children and youth are administered by provincial and local authorities with little or no federal direction or impact.

Some similarity of programs in education among the provinces may be brought about through the existence of the Council of Ministers of Education in Canada (established in 1967), a group that has been studying special education needs in Canada for a number of years. As yet, however, the effects have been minimal and the provinces sometimes have widely varied practices and services, because of the absence of direct federal involvement in education.

Before initiating our consideration of special education programs in the various provinces, we will consider a number of topics that together may provide a "feeling" for Canada and for special education in Canada. We will attempt to focus on ways in which Canada and the United States are quite different or similar. To some extent, the information provided in the following sections will be fragmentary; that is, it will represent samples of information relating to a variety of education-related activities or endeavors. It is hoped that the reader may integrate this information to the maximum extent possible, thus providing a basis for better understanding of the province-by-province review of special education.

EDUCATION IN CANADA

To understand special education in Canada, it is first necessary to have some understanding of education in general in Canada. By the Constitution (under the British North America Act) "the provinces are generally responsible for education, except for federally-sponsored schools for Indian and Inuit (Eskimo) students, children of servicemen in Europe, and inmates of federal penitentiaries." (*Canada Handbook*, 1978, p. 96) The federal government helps support tertiary (postsecondary) education, and in recent years has expanded and diversified its involvement in this arena.

In the past 10 to 20 years, certain trends in the elementary and secondary programs were evident across most of the provinces. These trends include: reorganization of school districts, resulting in a greatly reduced number of individual boards and districts, introduction of many educational innovations, nongraded systems and flexible promotion practices, elimination of departmental examinations, increased provision of kindergarten, emphasis on continuous evaluation, and increased offerings of technical and commercial subjects in secondary grades.

At the postsecondary level there has been increased development of community colleges, vocational and technical schools, schools of nursing, and other expanded vocationally related offerings. Teacher training was at one time carried out by two different systems; elementary teachers were trained primarily in teachers colleges or normal schools while secondary teachers were required to have university degrees. In the western provinces, teacher education has been part of the university domain for 20 or more years; however, in many provinces in the eastern part of the nation, this phasing out of teachers colleges and normal schools did not begin an any general basis until the early 1970s.

Each province in Canada operates the public schools under a "school act," which provides the basic framework for the local school boards. Until fairly recently, in some provinces there were large numbers of denominational boards, representing a wide variety of religious denominations. In Newfoundland, for example, there were literally dozens of strictly denominational, public school boards. Then, as the result of a comprehensive study of the educational needs of the children and youth of Newfoundland, the number of denominational systems was reduced to twenty one "integrated" (mergers of major groups) Protestant boards, twelve Roman Catholic districts and boards, one Pentecostal, and one Seventh Day Adventist board. This situation in Newfoundland was unusual compared to the rest of Canada, but separate denominational systems, supported by public funds, continue to exist in a number of Canadian provinces. (In contrast to the very specific way in which public schools in the United States have been directed *not* to include any activity that might be interpreted as religious in nature, the education act in some provinces in Canada directs the schools to include such exercises. There are provisions under which the student may be excused from such exercises and instruction, and a teacher may claim exemption from teaching religious education, but the situation is quite different from that in the United States.)

Public school programs in Canada are moving toward the provision of kindergarten in most provinces, but this is not yet nationwide. (This same situation exists in the United States.) But Canada does have a variation at the upper end of the system that is not found in the United States. For some provinces the final grade before graduation from high school is the eleventh, for some the twelfth, and for some the thirteenth. In each setting, the school curriculum is planned so that the full sequence of elementary and secondary program offerings is provided by completing this final grade. In certain provinces, through the vehicle of flexible scheduling and promotion by subject, even greater differences are possible. For example, the traditional 12-year program may be replaced by four major divisions, each made of 3 years work for a normal student making normal progress. With flexible promotion, students may move through these four divisions at their own pace.

In summary, the educational system in Canada is more widely varied than that in the United States, and it includes elements of every major innovation or development that may be found in the United States. Its continuance of church-related, denominational educational programs in some provinces and the nationwide program to encourage or permit most students to learn to speak and read in both of its official languages are among the major differences between the two nations. The transfer of teacher education functions from normal schools to universities is, on the surface, several years behind a similar move in the United States, but the very small teachers colleges in the United States are not too different from some of the normal schools and teachers colleges in Canada. The federal government in Canada plays very little role in elementary and secondary schools but may play an even greater role in post-secondary education than does the federal government in the United States. From my vantage point, with many years of contact with education in the United States at the local, state, and federal levels, Canadian educational programs are just enough like United States educational programs to be comparable and just enough different to be highly interesting.

SPECIAL PURPOSE COMMISSIONS AND SEMINARS; OTHER FEDERAL EFFORTS

Although there is no federal education agency in Canada, the Department of National Health and Welfare becomes involved in areas of concern that cross the boundaries of health and education, welfare and education, or health, welfare, and education. A good example of such interrelated concern and effort was the establishment in 1966 of a national Commission on Emotional and Learning Disorders in Children, with welfare grants from the Department to support both a manpower study and an incidence study relating to the efforts of this commission (King, 1968). The Commission was jointly sponsored by six national voluntary organizations: the Canadian Association for Retarded Children, Canadian Council on Children and Youth, Canadian Education Association, Canadian Mental Health Association, Canadian Rehabilitation Council for the Disabled, and Canadian Welfare Council, plus a related organization from Great Britain. These efforts led to the publication of *One Million Children* (Townsend and others, 1973), a most influential report.

The work of this group was not too different from similar national efforts initiated in the United States at about the same time. In fact, some of the first studies of learning disorders in the United States were initiated in the Office of Health (rather than Education), but eventually became the domain of the Bureau of Education for the Handicapped of the U.S. Office of Education. Such studies, resulting in basic national information and recommendations to the provinces, are possible through grants from the Department of National Health and Welfare to consortia of national voluntary organizations. Given the Canadian constitutional mandate regarding the responsibility of the provinces for education, this is perhaps the most effective way to accomplish important educational goals.

Another example of the manner in which national concerns with regard to handicapped persons may be addressed in Canada can be seen in various informational seminars conducted by agencies such as the Social Services Division of the Department of National Health and Welfare. One such seminar on the employability of the handicapped conducted in Toronto, Ontario, in November 1976, included top-level representatives of such agencies and organizations as the Canadian Chamber of Commerce, the Canadian Association for the Mentally Retarded, major insurance companies, the Department of National Health and Welfare, the Department of Manpower and Immigration, provincial ministers of labor, directors of rehabilitation services, and various representatives of business and industry. A publication detailing the proceedings of this meeting was published and widely distributed by the Department of National Health and Welfare, thus extending this information far beyond the direct participants in the seminar (Proceedings, 1976). This procedure has apparently been quite successful in encouraging the provinces to take advantage of federal assistance programs, where such programs exist, and also to encourage the establishment of provincial legislation relating to such concerns as removal of environmental barriers and employment of the handicapped.

The Canadian federal government has been involved with certain programs for the handicapped since at least 1914, when prosthetic and orthotic services were provided for veterans of World War I through the Department of Veterans Affairs. A more general vocational rehabilitation program has been in effect since 1952, and in a somewhat similar manner to that used in the United States, the federal government offers cost-sharing programs to the provinces, including a wide range of social services designed to encourage and prepare disabled persons to move into (or back into) the labor market.

Medical and hospital care are primarily within the jurisdiction of the provincial governments, but the federal government makes significant contributions to such health services, which are now a universal right in Canada (Canada Handbook, 1978). Although there is variation in the implementation of health services in the various provinces, in many, appliances such as hearing aids and various orthopedic devices are a part of this service. In addition, a variety of preschool services for children with sensory impairments may also be covered. Although these may be called "health" services, they are obviously an important part of educational programming.

In total, Canadian governmental agencies are engaged in many activities that generally parallel similar efforts in the United States. Although federal governmental organization does not permit the type of direct involvement with education of the handicapped seen in the United States, it does permit direct involvement in rehabilitative functions, and national agencies play a role in providing information and direction for certain educational programs, especially if they may be viewed as health related.

THE OFFICIAL LANGUAGES ACT OF 1969

A highly interesting development has had far-reaching implications for education and for many other aspects of life for Canadian citizens. The Official Languages Act of 1969 stipulates that "The English and French languages are the official languages in Canada." As a result of that act there is a Commissioner of Official Languages for Canada whose responsibility is:

> to take all actions and measures within his authority with a view to ensuring recognition of the status of each of the official languages and compliance with the spirit and intent of this Act in the administration of the affairs of the institutions of the Parliament and government of Canada and, for that purpose, to conduct and carry out investigations either on his own initiative or pursuant to any complaint made to him and to report and make recommendations with respect thereto as provided in this Act. (Section 25, Official Languages Act)

Language programs to increase the opportunity of French-speaking Canadians to be educated in their own language and to encourage English-speaking Canadians to become better acquainted with the French language are supported through federal aid to the schools. This bilingual system has had more effect in Quebec, Nova Scotia, New Brunswick, Ontario, and Manitoba than in the rest of Canada, and the flow of immigrants to Canada from all over the world has added another linguistic dimension, especially in certain metropolitan areas. Schools have been greatly affected, along with all other segments of Canadian society.

ACTIVITIES OF THE CANADIAN COUNCIL FOR EXCEPTIONAL CHILDREN

The Council for Exceptional Children (CEC) (see pp. 24-25) originated in the United States and remains primarily oriented toward the concerns of education of exceptional children and youth in the United States. However, Canadians are playing an increasingly significant role in all aspects of the Council.

The Canadian Council for Exceptional Children, apart from its contributions to the international CEC organization, plays an unusually important role in Canada, in part because of the absence of any national governmental body to provide leadership in the education of exceptional children. Canadian CEC leadership may be seen in the development of unique and innovative programs for children, successful efforts to influence provincial legislation, and the development of a number of highly valuable position papers and publications. The Canadian Council for Exceptional Children publishes a quarterly journal, *Special Education in Canada**and in recent years, Canadian CEC members have held biannual national congresses in addition to yearly conferences at the provincial level. It should be noted that, although there are active CEC members in Quebec, that province also has a large organization of French-speaking special educators, the Conseil du Quebec de L'Enfance Exceptionnelle (CQEE), which is not affiliated with either the Canadian CEC or the CEC organization in the United States.

A number of efforts of the Canadian CEC have been particularly noteworthy in shaping teacher education and general educational policy (see Hardy, 1971; Little, 1976; Roberts, 1970; Treherne, 1974); one of the more interesting was that of the Ontario Federation of Chapters of CEC which culminated in the document *We Are Not Alike* (Townsend and others, 1973). The Ontario government had arbitrarily abolished the Special Education Branch of the Ministry of Education, and it was only through the concerted efforts of the Ontario Federation of Chapters of the CEC that this very damaging action was reversed. This effort exemplifies the combination leadership/watchdog role that the Canadian CEC will undoubtedly continue to play.

Canada: size and population

For those familiar with the size of the various states in the United States, a comparison of the Canadian Provinces with different states in the United States may provide a meaningful perspective.

---

*It is interesting to note that *Special Education in Canada* evolved from *The Bulletin*, a publication relating to handicapped children started in 1924.

Province	Area (sq. miles)	Comparison
Quebec	594,860	Larger than Alaska
Ontario	412,582	Between Alaska and Texas
British Columbia	366,255	Considerably larger than Texas
Alberta	255,285	Texas
Saskatchewan	251,700	Texas
Manitoba	251,000	Texas
Newfoundland	156,185	California
New Brunswick	28,354	Slightly larger than West Virginia
Nova Scotia	21,425	West Virginia
Prince Edward Island	2,184	Slightly larger than Delaware

The approximate populations of these ten provinces (in order of size) are: Ontario, 7,800,000; Quebec, 6,100,000; British Columbia, 2,250,000; Alberta, 1,650,000; Manitoba, 1,000,000; Saskatchewan, 950,000; Nova Scotia, 800,000; New Brunswick, 650,000; Newfoundland, 540,000; and Prince Edward Island, 115,000.

The Northwest Territories has an area of 1,304,900 square miles, only slightly smaller than the area of all of the provinces but Ontario and Quebec combined. The Yukon Territory has an area of 207,000 square miles. The problems that result because only 60,000 people live in an area totaling over 1.5 million square miles necessitate unique service delivery approaches. We will not attempt to speak to these needs and these approaches, but rather will focus on educational planning and programming in the ten provinces, recognizing that although they contain such major population centers as Montreal, Toronto, Ottawa, Winnipeg, Calgary, Edmonton, and Vancouver, they also have some very sparsely populated areas.

With this brief review of the size and population of Canada, and a reminder that Canada is the second largest nation in land area in the world (second only to the USSR), we will conclude this section and proceed to our review of special education in the ten provinces. We will start in the east, with the Atlantic Provinces, and move to the west, concluding with British Columbia.

Special education in the Atlantic provinces

The four provinces east of Quebec (New Brunswick, Newfoundland, Nova Scotia, and Prince Edward Island) are the smallest of the ten provinces in both land area and population. As a group they are known as the Atlantic provinces. An important study was initiated in 1972 by the ministers of education of these four provinces and a report that came out of this study became the basis for a number of program changes and improvements in services for children with low-incidence handicaps (see Kendall, 1973). This report is commonly referred to as the Kendall Report (Professor D. C. Kendall of the University of British Columbia was chairperson of the study committee) and is referenced in a number of later papers and reports prepared by provincial education officials. This is not to suggest that special education prior to 1973 was seriously neglected in the Atlantic provinces, but rather that as a result of a local interest and support from the ministers of education, a comprehensive, objective study of the needs of this area led to expanded programming and services and increased cooperation among the four Atlantic provinces through the creation of a new administrative structure, the Atlantic Provinces Special Education Authority (APSEA).

In our review of these provinces, we will first consider the Atlantic Provinces Special Education Authority, then consider the provinces in alphabetical order. We will attempt to provide sufficient information to permit the reader to begin to sense the flavor of special education in the Atlantic provinces.

The Atlantic Provinces Special Education Authority. In January, 1975, the Atlantic provinces entered into an agreement establishing the Atlantic Provinces Special Education Authority. This agreement provided for cooperative efforts on behalf of low-incidence handicaps—visual, hearing, or multiple handicapping conditions in which visual or hearing handicaps are a component. In initiating this agreement, earlier agreements that involved only two or three of these provinces and that were limited to only one handicap (for example, the School for the Deaf Act of 1960 between New Brunswick and Nova Scotia) were terminated. With relatively small populations, this type of cooperation may greatly benefit the handicapped population and at the same time permit more fiscally efficient programming. These provinces continue to plan and program for other handicapping conditions in a manner consistent with their individual legislative directives and philosophy, as will be noted from the descriptions to follow.

NEW BRUNSWICK

New Brunswick, immediately adjacent to and only slightly smaller than Maine, has about two-thirds the population of Maine. With coastline making up about half of its boundary, it has valuable fisheries, farms, mineral deposits, and a widely varied population.

Early special education programs in New Brunswick were provided through private schools for the deaf and blind prior to 1890, but special education services first became an official government function in 1892, with the passage of legislation providing residential care and training of blind persons. Similar legislation relating to the hearing impaired was passed in 1903, in the Deaf and Deaf Mute

Persons Act. These programs were provided through contracted services outside of New Brunswick (McGuigan, 1974). In 1957, the Auxiliary Classes Act was passed, providing services for the retarded and the cerebral palsied. This act, and the various regulations accompanying it, made it possible for private societies to sponsor programs for certain handicapping conditions and to be repaid, at least in part, for the provision of such services. In effect, the Auxiliary Classes Act tended to encourage private, incorporated associations, with permission and supervision from the Minister of Education, to serve as a special school board for cerebral palsied or mentally retarded children. The Auxiliary Classes Act indicates that:

> Subject to the regulations, a society
> (a) may establish auxiliary classes and conduct in the classes or privately such courses of instruction and training as are best adapted to secure the mental and physical development of children who are from any physical or mental cause unable to take proper advantage of the public school courses provided for under the Schools Act. (Chapter A-19; 4)

The Auxiliary Classes Act specifies personnel who may be employed, where classes may be held, transportation, residential provisions, fees that may be charged, and other essential details. Required authorizations to the Minister of Finance (of the province) to make payments to approved societies, for provincial health officers to visit and monitor such classes, and for such things as assistance to indigent parents or guardians for the purchase of special appliances for cerebral palsied students are also included. The Auxiliary Classes Act is regularly updated through legislative action or appropriate changes in regulations and serves a highly useful purpose in the province regarding these two handicapping conditions.

In 1974, the government of New Brunswick, through the office of the Minister of Education, issued a comprehensive white paper, entitled *Opportunities for the Handicapped*. Referring to the Kendall report and two others, this paper, in its introduction, indicated that:

> The objectives of this White Paper are to ensure: that every handicapped child has an opportunity to be educated; that district school boards become responsible for the initial identification of handicapped children, and finally, that educational programs are of high quality. These objectives can be realized through a system of program strengthening and development and service-sharing.

Opportunities for the Handicapped summarized available services, outlined needs, and recommended alternative courses of action so that New Brunswick might meet the objective of providing every handicapped student a high quality educational program. In this 1974 paper, which has served to provide guidelines for additional programming since that time, the following handicapping conditions were recognized: (1) trainable mentally retarded, (2) seriously physically handicapped, (3) homebound and hospitalized, (4) educable mentally retarded, (5) emotionally disturbed, (6) visually handicapped, (7) hearing handicapped, and (8) learning disabled. In addition, the critical need for staff development and a separate, but equally important need for additional administrative leadership were detailed. Learning disabilities, the newest area and thus least well implemented in 1974, has since been given special attention through the initiation of a Comprehensive Plan for the Delivery of Educational Services to Learning Disabled Pupils. New Brunswick education officials realize that there is still much to be accomplished, and in all of their program improvement efforts they are attempting to systematically include local education officials, parents, medical professionals, and other interested citizens. Their efforts are characterized by careful, deliberate change, based on a broad range of citizen-educator input and interest.

NEWFOUNDLAND AND LABRADOR*

Newfoundland consists of an island (Newfoundland), which is the easternmost part of Canada, and a mainland area (Labrador) with very limited population. Until 1927, Labrador was disputed territory, being claimed also by Quebec. Newfoundland did not become a part of Canada until 1949, the last province to join The Canadian Federation.

Newfoundland has long provided services to the deaf and blind and, in more recent years, the mentally retarded. However, a separate Division of Special Services was first established in 1969 when the Department of Education was reorganized, providing a new level of leadership to programs for the Handicapped. The Special Services Division is responsible for the initiation and coordination of educational programs for handicapped children and for the provision of other pupil personnel-related services. Operational principles for the Division include the following goals (Educational Services, Province of Newfoundland, 1978, p. 2):

(1) the disabled child be given opportunities and facilities to enable him to develop physically, mentally, morally, spiritually, and socially in a healthy and normal manner and under conditions of freedom and dignity.

(2) the child who is physically, mentally, or socially handicapped be given special treatment, education, and care required of his particular condition.
(3) the disabled child be given an education to promote his general culture and to enable him, on the basis of equal opportunity, to develop his ability for individual judgment and his sense of moral and social responsibility.

Newfoundland provides at least some services for hearing impaired, visually impaired, hospital-bound students, homebound students, the trainable mentally retarded, and the learning disabled. In addition, certain students with unusual or very special problems (for example, multi-impaired) are served on an individual basis, often through assistance to parents to send the student to schools or programs outside the province.

The provincial Department of Education operates a Learning Disabilities Centre in St. John's, which assists local districts in assessment and determination of appropriate learning programs. The department also operates ten special school programs for the trainable mentally retarded and special classes in hospitals at four different sites, and transports students with more severe visual impairments to Halifax, Nova Scotia, to The Atlantic Provinces Resource Center for the Visually Impaired. On the other hand, many local school boards are now assuming responsibility for classes for the trainable mentally retarded, and itinerant service is provided within the province for the more mildly visually impaired through the APSEA board.

The area of mental retardation seems to be unusually well served, with recent emphasis on work-study programs at the senior high level, designed to serve either the educable mentally retarded or the learning disabled. Local school boards are apparently quite attracted to the vocational/occupational potential in such programs, and although special

---

*The dual title "Newfoundland and Labrador" is used interchangeably with "Newfoundland." For example, near the top of the cover of a program description booklet for the province (1978), we find "Province of Newfoundland and Labrador" along with the provincial seal. The title of the booklet on this same cover is *Educational Services; Division of Special Services, Department of Education, Province of Newfoundland*. Throughout this section only Newfoundland will be used for the sake of brevity, but I do want to officially recognize the existence of this dual title.

education is still permissive in Newfoundland, support for most areas of handicap seems to be strong. Legislation which would make programs for the handicapped mandatory is under consideration and would provide additional leverage for the provincial government to use in meeting the goals of the 1978 statement of operational principles.

NOVA SCOTIA

Nova Scotia is second smallest in land size of all the Canadian provinces, but it is the largest in population of the four Atlantic provinces. Nova Scotia has two parts, a peninsula, connected to New Brunswick by a common boundary approximately 30 miles long, plus a small island (Cape Breton Island) to the east. In contrast to Newfoundland, Nova Scotia was one of the four original members of the Canadian confederation. Nova Scotia is one of two provinces with mandatory special education legislation and, according to Beuree (1978), has had some form of special educational services in the schools for nearly 80 years. For many years special education was simply a matter of accepted practice, and with the small geographical area involved, there seemed to be little need for more than a bare minimum of formal statements or guidelines. With constantly changing and evolving practices, however, a more formal set of policy guidelines is now being completed. The Education Act of Nova Scotia provides for special teachers, materials, regular school facilities, appropriate adaptations for the handicapped (i.e., ramps, modified toilet facilities, and the like) and special transportation services for those students who require such special consideration.

> The Nova Scotia Department of Education believes in the rights of parents, relative to the placement of children into any Special Education program, for a complete explanation and justification of special programs. Parents also have the right to refuse any consideration that is different than that provided for the child in the regular program. (Beuree, 1978)

Nova Scotia, as a member of the Atlantic Provinces Special Education Authority, provides for some of the hearing impaired, visually impaired, and multihandicapped through this agreement. With mandatory legislation for children in need of special education, with a long history of programs for handicapped students in the public schools, and with increasing efforts to inform parents of their right to a special education for their children, Nova Scotia obviously supports the concept of broad-range provision of meaningful programs for handicapped students. It would appear, however, that additional funding for programs for the handicapped and improvement in teacher certification requirements are essential if Nova Scotia is to meet its established goals.

PRINCE EDWARD ISLAND

Prince Edward Island is the smallest in both size and population of the ten Canadian provinces. For a short period (1763 to 1769) it was annexed to Nova Scotia and strongly considered joining the Canadian Federation with the original four provinces, but delayed 7 years and joined in 1873. With limited raw materials and sources of power, the citizens of Prince Edward Island are primarily engaged in fishing and agriculture.

Education legislation in Prince Edward Island does not refer to specific groups of children (i.e., various handicapping conditions) except as specified in the Atlantic Provinces Special Education Authority. Provincial legislation indicates that the Department of Education of the province is responsible for the "education of all children, ages 6 to 21 years, who have not completed high school." According to Elinor MacLellan (1978), Special

Education Consultant for Prince Edward Island:

> Within this context [the general authority] we try to provide for the different handicaps. Those who are served in special classes include the deaf, mentally retarded, and a group of severely physically handicapped. These classes are located in regular schools and [certain] children are included in regular music and physical education classes, as well as in a few instances where they go into regular classes for some academics. We do not have self-contained classes for emotionally disturbed or . . . learning disabilities, but we do provide individual tutoring for many of these.

Considering the size of Prince Edward Island and the fact that specific legislation for handicapped students does not exist outside of the involvement in the Atlantic Provinces Special Education Authority, it would appear that the province is making a most acceptable effort to provide for handicapped students.

Special education in Quebec

Quebec is the largest in land size, second largest in population of the Canadian provinces, and has approximately three times the school population of the total of the four Atlantic provinces combined. Perhaps as much as any other factor, it is known internationally for its French language, French-Canadian culture, and periodically renewed interest in the possibility of becoming a separate nation. In the words of Professor Roger Magnuson (1969) of McGill University:

> Politically, Quebec is one of Canada's 10 provinces, but in terms of language, religion, and heritage, it departs strikingly from the rest of the country. Home of most of Canada's French-speaking citizens, Quebec cherishes a culture that is both unique and cohesive. French is the mother tongue of more than 80 percent of Quebec's population, and of that majority almost all are Roman Catholic. Whereas English Canada has its roots in Great Britain, French Canada traces its heritage to . . . prerevolutionary France.
>
> Mistakenly, Quebec is often thought of as a cultural extension of contemporary France in North America. With the exception of language and some social values, France and Quebec hold widely differing conceptions of education, religion, government, and economics. Since the time of the Third Republic, church and state have existed separately in France; whereas in Quebec, lay and religious authorities traditionally have worked closely together. Public education in France is secular and the schools are centrally controlled. In French Canada public education is denominational and central, and local authorities share in the control and operation of the schools.

Although the visibility of the role of religion is emphasized by the existence of separate school systems, the actual effect on educational *content* of these church-related boards may be no greater than the indirect effect on educational content exercised by churches in the United States. The extent of this effect varies from district to district in both nations.

With respect to educational services for handicapped children and youth, Quebec, like the Atlantic provinces, has provided some services for the deaf and blind for decades. In addition, since about 1940, a number of schools have accepted other handicapped students. However, for the most part, these services were provided on the initiative of parent groups, charitable associations, or religious communities (Morin, 1978). Beginning in the middle 1960s the schools began to accept more and more handicapped children, and today comprehensive programming is an accepted practice in most of the province. This responsibility is generally accepted as a result of interpretations of the language of the preamble of the law creating the present Ministry of Education.

Handicapped children in Quebec have been referred to in a number of ways over the past

20 years, but the most recent terms are "children in difficulty" and "children with adjustment and learning problems." Most of the present efforts were influenced by a lengthy (693 pages) governmental study published in 1976, entitled *The Education of Children with Learning and Adjustment Problems in Quebec.* This report and the various position papers that have followed have played a major role in an increase in services from 6,400 handicapped pupils served in 1961 (0.5 percent of the total student population) to 103,000 handicapped students served in 1978 (8.2 percent of the total student population). This total of 103,000 includes an unusually high percentage of students in the category of learning disabilities, as indicated in Table 4-1.

In 1978, the Office of the Minister of Education issued a document entitled *Quebec Schools; Children with Adjustment and Learning Difficulties. Statement of Policy and Plan of Action* (Morin, 1978).* This document serves as the basis for most of the remainder of the information in this consideration of special education in Quebec. In addition to a statement of policy, it is a review of the status of special education in the province. It was published in part in anticipation of an annual meeting of the Conseil du Québec de l'Enfance Exceptionnélle.

In reviewing recent history, it may be noted that in 1969 an interministerial committee was formed, which included the ministries that might be most directly concerned with children in difficulty (Education, Social Affairs, Health, Justice, and Labor). This committee defined and described the responsibilities of the various governmental agencies as they relate to such children. The Ministry of

---

*This report was later published, slightly revised, as Chapter Five of *L'école 'uébécoise: énoncé de politique et plan d'action* (Quebec, 1979) (an English version of this chapter is available as a separate, paper-bound document).

TABLE 4-1

Handicapped students receiving special assistance in Quebec, 1977-1978*

Handicap	Student population served
Learning disabilities	64,295
Mental retardation	20,450
Sensory handicaps (hearing, vision)	1,251
Physical handicaps	985
Social and emotional	9,888
Multiple handicaps	6,249
TOTAL	103,118

*From report by the Minister of Education. Province of Quebec.

Social Affairs (the agency other than education with major involvement with handicapped students), developed a network of reception and hospital centers, which in 1975 received more than 12,000 children. Since 1975, school boards have gradually expanded their services so that today they are accepting a number of students with more severe handicaps who might have earlier been the responsibility of the Ministry of Social Affairs or specialized private institutions.

With the increasing acceptance of the responsibility of the schools to provide direct services to the more severely handicapped population, it became clear that many school districts could not effectively or efficiently provide services within their local schools. Therefore, many school districts entered into ententes (agreements) whereby other school districts or private institutions would provide appropriate schooling. In some situations, the student might be attending a school that was very similar to the one he or she would have attended several years earlier, but now the local schools boards arrange for the program and accept responsibility to see that it results in an appropriate education. In some cases, the schools were also providing assistance to the parents for board and costs of transportation. The important point is that educational provisions for the handicapped student have become an *educational* responsibility, not a social or welfare responsibility.

In the introduction to the actual policy statement regarding children with adjustment and learning difficulties (1978) the following basic statement of intent may be found:

> The goal of the policy is to look at the prevention of learning and adjustment difficulties, to assure that pupils in difficulty have access to appropriate and quality educational services in the most normal setting possible for them, and to prepare these students for harmonious entry into society. (p. 12)

This statement, according to the Ministry of Education, is based on earlier educational laws and on The Charter of Personal Rights and Liberties, a law adopted June 27, 1978 by the government of Quebec.

The plan and policy statement for Quebec, as articulated by the Minister of Education, includes the following facets, which are essentially parallel to Public Law 94-142 requirements and guidelines in the United States:

1. Free access to a public system of education for all handicapped children
2. Early intervention, from the age of 4 years
3. Close collaboration with the Ministry of Social Affairs
4. Regionalization of services (especially to assist remote regions of Quebec) led by the Ministry of Education
5. Promotion of more individualization of instruction, which may serve in part as a preventive measure
6. Early detection measures in conjunction with the Ministry of Social Affairs
7. Planned rehabilitative efforts and promotion of team effort on behalf of handicapped children
8. Extended schooling (ages 16 to 21) for those who need it

The preceding are major areas of concern as indicated by the Ministry of Education; they have been presented to indicate the scope of planning and are not intended to represent every facet and detail of Quebec's plan for exceptional children. Available data from this province indicate that implementation is underway, with both financial and program planning support from the provincial level. How well the local school districts carry out the intent of the provincial government remains to be seen, but an expanded, improved program is certainly well underway.

Special education in Ontario

Ontario, the largest of the provinces in population and the second largest in size, is the site of the Canadian capital, Ottawa. (Ottawa is actually on the boundary between Quebec and Ontario, on the Ontario side of the Ottawa River.) Ontario, Alberta, and British Columbia are the only three provinces that have been experiencing steady population growth in the past 20 years. Ontario provides a broad range of special education services, including programs for the gifted, but at present such services are provided on a voluntary basis by local school boards.*

---

*Ontario, along with several other provinces, is considering making services to the handicapped mandatory. In late 1978, the director of the Special Education Branch, Province of Ontario, indicated that "intensive studies are underway regarding changing the *may* to *shall*" in the existing Education Act of 1974. He further noted that "P.L. 94-142 in the U.S., the Warnock Report, and recent legislation in the province of Saskatchewan are strongly influencing the direction of our studies." (Bergman, 1978) This is cited to illustrate how legislation in other provinces, in the U.S., and significant studies in other lands (i.e., the Warnock Report in the British Isles) continue to influence deliberations in the various provinces.

In many respects, Ontario is similar to the other larger provinces in its provision and delivery of special education services. Ontario Ministry of Education official's use the term "exceptional students" in their written descriptions of the services provided the handicapped and the gifted in the province. Exceptional students in Ontario are defined as "those who have behavioural, communication, intellectual, or physical exceptionalities to such a degree that changes in the regular curriculum must be made and/or special services provided for them in school." (Education for Exceptional Students in Ontario, 1978, p. 1). The Special Education Branch of the Ministry of Education has established the following goals and objectives Education for Exceptional Students in Ontario, 1978, p. 5):

Goal

The overall goal of the Special Education Branch is to ensure that appropriate and equal educational opportunities of recognized quality are made available to all exceptional students in Ontario.

Objectives

1. Policy: To develop and recommend provincial policies that encourage and assist school boards, regional offices, and other agencies to identify and place in programs all exceptional children and to evaluate their educational progress.
2. Standards: To develop standards in provisions for exceptional children in Ontario and to review programs, making recommendations when necessary.
3. Research: To monitor and, when necessary, initiate planning and research in the education of exceptional children.
4. Operations: To operate schools and classes in certain provincial institutions.
5. Teacher Education: To conduct education programs for teachers of the blind and teachers of the deaf.

Consistent with these stated objectives, the Special Education Branch operates three residential schools for the deaf and one residential school for the blind. Since 1971, these schools have also served as resource centers and therefore provide clinical assessment, special materials, and consultive assistance to local school boards. The major goal of this service is to keep visually or hearing impaired students living at home and attending their home school district whenever possible. A home-visiting program to assist parents to play the most effective role possible in the educational and social development of their children is also provided through the Special Education Branch. All of these services—the residential program, the consultive/special materials program to local schools, and the home-visiting program—are provided wholly through provincial funds with no direct cost to the parents or local school boards.

In addition to service provided through the schools for the deaf and the blind, the Special Education Branch provides school programs as required by various minors who are in one of several regional developmental centers operated by the Ministry of Health or the Ministry of Community and Social Services. Admission to such institutional centers is controlled by these other two ministries, but the Ministry of Education operates the school program through the Special Education Branch.

Local school boards operate programs for students classified as emotionally disturbed or socially maladjusted, hearing impaired, visually impaired, educable mentally retarded, trainable mentally retarded, and orthopedically or otherwise physically handicapped. They provide programs for students with speech and language disorders, those classified as aphasic or autistic, the multiply handicapped, and the gifted. Ontario provides for each of the preceding exceptionalities in its regulations established pursuant to the Education Act and, in addition, indicates assessment and placement procedures, maximum class sizes, and teacher approval procedures. At present, officials of the Special Education Branch are developing early identification procedures and additional guidelines for education of the learning disabled. Cooperative programs (between local boards) are encouraged and seem to be receiving increased acceptance in areas of the province where they are particularly needed. Services for exceptional students receive a fair share of attention in Ontario, and special educators are involved in ongoing planning in their efforts to reach their stated goal of "appropriate and equal educational opportunities of recognized quality . . . [for] . . . all exceptional students in Ontario."

Special education in Manitoba

Manitoba is the easternmost of the prairie provinces and is approximately the same size as its two neighboring provinces to the west, Saskatchewan and Alberta. Manitoba contains one major metropolitan area (Winnipeg); otherwise, it is relatively sparsely populated. This type of population distribution leads to a need for very careful planning for handicapped students, especially the low incidence handicaps. Manitoba does not have a "department of special education" or "special education branch," but it coordinates services for handicapped students through the Child Development and Support Services unit of the Department of Education.

For many years the Manitoba Department of Education has been responsible for blind and deaf children of the province and has assisted local units to provide for certain other groups of handicapped students through individually negotiated agreements. In 1967, education of the mentally retarded was given special recognition through specific, mandatory legislation. Other handicapping conditions were served to varying degrees, depending at least in part on local interest and the desire to negotiate agreements with the Manitoba Department of Education. Parent groups have played a prominent role for many years, but certain handicapping conditions were obviously overlooked or, at best, underserved.

In 1975, the Manitoba legislature passed a highly important amendment to the Public Schools Act, popularly known as Bill 58. This bill requires the provision of appropriate educational alternatives for all handicapped students in the province—students known in Manitoba as "special needs" students. The Manitoba definition of children with special needs is such that this is essentially just another term for handicapped children; however, the emphasis is on the needs of the students rather than their handicap.

Bill 58 was passed in 1975, but has not yet been proclaimed. Because of the complex implications of Bill 58, the Manitoba government elected to provide an implementation and "tooling-up" period during which the local districts could become involved in preparing for full implementation. This preparation includes such activities as: (1) evaluating existing programs for the handicapped, (2) establishing identification programs, (3) initiating professional development programs for teachers, (4) evaluating financial needs, and (5) evaluating the most effective cooperative roles of other departments of the government.

The Child Development and Support Services office was given responsibility for Bill 58 during the implementation years, and at present the province is promoting implementation through a series of special grants. School boards are invited to apply for such grants via specific program proposals. Each year a particular target area is suggested (for the 1978-1979 school year it was low incidence handicapping conditions such as hearing and visually impairment, orthopedic handicaps, and severe multiple handicaps) thus leading to province-wide experience with program variations, service delivery alternatives, and opportunity to compare and analyze results within specified areas of handicap. The Child Development and Support Services staff views each year of special program emphasis as another step in the direction of full implementation of Bill 58, but no definite predictions are available as to when Bill 58 might be actually proclaimed.*

An amendment to the Public Schools Act, when Bill 58 is proclaimed, will state: "Every school board shall provide or make provision for the education of all resident persons who have the right to attend school and who require special programs for their education." Present attempts to gear up for the full implementation of this bill have included the initiation of local advisory committees throughout the province, assessment of present resources and development of procedures for such activities as screening, placement procedures (including placement appeals), and program evaluation procedures. Professional development activities with regular classroom teachers and efforts to fully involve the public have also been a part of the plan established by the provincial coordinator of Child Development and Support Services and his staff.

Special education in Saskatchewan

Saskatchewan, like Manitoba, is a prairie province and also includes major developments in potash, oil, gas, and uranium. When purely legislative comparisons are made, Saskatchewan must be considered ahead of most of the other provinces. Saskatchewan has had mandatory legislation for the handicapped since 1971 supported by parallel funding. Saskatchewan's mandatory special education legislation was reaffirmed in 1978 when the legislature passed a new education act that consolidated a variety of legislation previously contained in nineteen separate acts. In this 1978 consolidation, Saskatchewan legislators made it clear that they were satisfied with the intent, and apparently with the results, of earlier legislation. Saskatchewan's mandatory legislation is all the more important in that it has had a considerable influence on other Canadian provinces.

Although the Education Act of 1978 (Section 184 [2]) states that "a board of education shall provide educational services on behalf of handicapped pupils," the board is allowed a number of alternatives in providing such service. Education in the home school is encouraged by both the law and by department regulations, but when other alternatives are utilized, it is the responsibility of the board (often with help from the provincial level) to provide for maintenance, tuition, transportation, and support of such handicapped students. The Education Act (1978) also prescribes that: "All diagnostic and investigative procedures which precede a recommendation or decision with respect to placement of a pupil in a specialized institution or program shall be conducted with the knowledge of, and in consultation with, the parents or guardian of the pupil." (Section 184 [5])

Handicapped pupils under the Act include all of the traditionally recognized handicapping conditions and are separated, for fiscal support purposes, into "high-cost" handicapped pupils and "low-cost" handicapped pupils. Saskatchewan's provisions also include funding for multiply and severely

---

*In communications with education officials in Manitoba, two impressions were received again and again: (1) progress in the "implementation" stage was underway—handicapped students were receiving better, more comprehensive services—and (2) with recent changes in government in the province, no one would venture a prediction as to when Bill 58 might be actually proclaimed. It must be noted, however, that it has already led to a number of worthwhile advances on behalf of handicapped students.

handicapped children from age 3. In total, the regulations for the Education Act include essentially the same guarantees of a free appropriate education for the handicapped, due process procedures, provision for appeal, and the like, that are found in the United States in Public Law 94-142.

Special education services in Saskatchewan are administered under the Regional Services Division, one of three major divisions of the Ministry of Education. The Chief, Special Education Section, is responsible for services throughout the province, but considerable responsibility is delegated to regional special education consultants who serve under the direction of regional superintendents in eight regional offices located throughout the province. The major service of the provincial representatives is that of supervisory and consultative help to local education personnel and parents, but in jurisdictions where specialized staff is limited, provincial consultants will, on request, provide direct service to students.

In addition to such consultative, and at times direct service, the provincial department is involved in interagency cooperative ventures and in the promotion of further specialized training and professional development for special education teachers. A summer school bursary (grant) program regularly provides for teachers from the province to receive advanced training each year.

As with other provinces, education for the visually and hearing handicapped has long been recognized in Saskatchewan. The Saskatchewan School for the Deaf is the direct responsibility of the Associate Deputy Minister of Education (rather than the Regional Services Division), for reasons which appear to the outsider to be primarily a matter of historic procedure. This program appears to receive good support and to have a program quality consistent with that of other special education programs in the province. Other visually impaired and hearing impaired students are, for the most part, served through resource room and itinerant programs, thus remaining in the local community. A small number of very severely visually impaired, hearing impaired, and multihandicapped students are served in residential programs outside the province.

Saskatchewan has long been involved in health services for its citizens. Hospitalization and Medicare plans introduced in Saskatchewan in 1948 and 1962, respectively, have since spread throughout Canada. In the early 1970s the Saskatchewan Hearing Aid Plan was introduced as part of the available health services, and a more recent plan, the Saskatchewan Aids to Independent Living (SAIL) has made various appliances and devices available through the health department.

A number of preschools have been funded throughout Saskatchewan, certain pilot projects are underway, and additional cooperative programs with parent groups and other departments of the government are being comtemplated. Curriculum committee activity, a slow, but perceptible move to provide even more of the existing special education services within the regular classroom, and attempts to provide more direct in-service to both special and regular educators seem to indicate that momentum for improvement continues in Saskatchewan.

Special education in Alberta

Like its neighbors Saskatchewan and Manitoba to the east, most of Alberta is a prairie province, but the western boundary of the southern half of the province is the continental divide. Therefore, the southwest section of Alberta contains the foothills and the eastern slope of the Canadian Rockies. With rich farmland, agriculture is a major industry, but because Alberta contains approximately half of Canada's coal reserves and a majority of its operational oil and gas fields, the energy industry is first in importance. The fact that Alberta accounts for about 85 percent of the total Canadian oil and gas production provides a very solid economic base, and has led to considerable population growth.

Alberta is unique in another way in terms of geographical location of its cities. In all of the other provinces, which stretch from the United States to the Yukon or the Northwest Territories, the capital is located in the south, sometimes almost on the United States border. Edmonton, the capital and largest city of Alberta, is approximately in the center of the province, thus it is by far the northernmost major city in Canada.

The Department of Education Act and the School Act of Alberta provide the basic authority for special education services. The Director of Special Education Services is responsible for the Alberta School for the Deaf, for counseling and guidance services, and for special education. Consultants in education for the handicapped are attached to regional offices and are directly responsible to a regional coordinator of education. Although special education services are not specifically mandated, the Department of Education assumes that the School Act, Section 133, both authorizes and directs the local school boards to provide such services. Section 133 states that "every child who has attained the age of six years is a pupil . . . and unless excused for any of the reasons mentioned in Section 134, shall attend a school over which a board has control." In practice, it is likely that the rather generous grant system, funded at the provincial level, is a major factor in the provision of full educational services without mandatory legislation. These grants specifically provide for teachers in the following specialty positions: (1) educable mentally retarded, (2) learning disabled, (3) socially maladjusted, (4) resource room, (5) language deficit, (6) trainable mentally retarded, (7) institutional, (8) homebound, (9) severely learning disabled, (10) hard of hearing, (11) low vision, (12) speech disorders, (13) specified special school, (14) braille, and (15) deafness. Grants to local boards for the employment of these teachers ranged, in 1978, from over $10,000 to nearly $20,000, depending on the area of specialty.

Alberta apparently recognizes and responds to the requirements of supply and demand when needed. Evidence of this recognition may be seen when we consider, for example, that local boards in 1978 received a grant of $15,875 for a teacher of the deaf, but if that teacher was a "total communication" teacher of the deaf, the grant was $19,875. In addition to grants for teachers to be employed by the local school board, the province will pay rather substantial grants for students who are: (1) under the jurisdiction of the board, (2) who would be pupils in the local district if the district had an appropriate program, and (3) who are attending private programs approved by the Deputy Minister of Education. These grants apply to the trainable mentally retarded, the severely learning disabled, or the socially maladjusted. Further specific payments are made for the board to employ the part-time services of a mobility training instructor or to enroll handicapped children in early childhood programs.

Alberta Department of Education regulations provide for private school programs and to some extent seem to encourage them. They must be nonprofit, must meet a number of specific criteria, and of course must provide services sufficiently satisfactory so that local school boards will elect to send students to them. Alberta's interest in private programs apparently relates to a history of satisfactory programs for the trainable mentally retarded and the language impaired administered by parent associations. In more recent years, some local boards have begun to assume such responsibilities, but since the provincial government will pay a significant part of the cost of building a private school for the handicapped (under certain conditions), thus relieving the local board of such planning, it might be assumed that such programs may be in existence for some time.

Alberta has a unique program that provides services to young handicapped children. The Early Childhood Services (ECS) branch of the government, established in 1973 to coordinate services of other departments, appears to be making highly significant progress in early intervention efforts. The ECS has a stated priority with regard to young children with special needs and seems to have very good results in working with the various agencies in jointly planned programs directed toward young handicapped children and their families.

Although many special education teachers in Alberta have specialized training in special education, the province does not require such training or provide specialized certification procedures. It is assumed that the local school jurisdictions will consider such matters when employing and assigning teacher personnel.

There appear to be some efforts among parents of handicapped students in Alberta to push for more services provided more directly by the public schools. The system whereby private schools are, in effect, encouraged has relieved school boards of concern about some handicapped students, but this separate school practice is not consistent with what parents are hearing about in advocacy group meetings, and is very different from practices in effect in neighboring Saskatchewan. At least one court case relating to lack of appropriate service is presently underway in Alberta, but the outcome remains in question. It is possible that a ruling in favor of the parents might lead to some philosophical changes in this province, which is so rich in financial resources and thus well able to provide whatever services are determined to be most appropriate.

Special education in British Columbia

British Columbia, the westernmost of the Canadian Provinces and third largest in land size, is unique among the provinces in that it is almost wholly mountainous. With little land for farming, the forests of British Columbia make up almost half of all Canada's timber. Lumbering and lumber-related industries, mining, and fishing are major industries. British Columbia is one of three Canadian provinces showing consistent population growth, apparently sharing some of the same attractions as its neighbor to the south, the state of Washington. This has led to the need for an expanding school system, including expanding services for handicapped students.

Special education programs in British Columbia are in many ways similar to programs in other provinces. The Special Programs Branch, a part of the School Division of the Ministry of Education, has primary responsibility for the provision of special assistance to local school districts to provide for handicapped students. One major vehicle for such encouragement is that of "special approvals" —permission for school districts to provide mutually approved special education programs, which become a part of the local district's sharable operating costs. British Columbia uses this approach rather than direct grants, and finds it workable and effective.

Under British Columbia law, education is the responsibility of locally elected boards of school trustees, as directed by Section 158 of the Public Schools Acts. Provincial interpretation of this responsibility is that "the Act requires each school board to provide the basic education program in a classroom, or in a hospital, or in a home, or in an institution using teachers on either regular or special assignment." (*Education Today,* 1978, p. 6)

The Ministry of Education has made a number of formal statements in support of integration or mainstreaming of the mildly handicapped, but has also warned of the problems inherent in inappropriate mainstreaming. In one such statement we find the following summary: "What this paper recommends as practice in the schools of British Columbia is a rational and flexible eclecticism in providing for the handicapped, accepting no single theory or process as a panacea for all needs." (Webber, 1979, p. 4) Although related primarily to the topic of mainstreaming, this statement may characterize much of the approach of special educators in British Columbia to all aspects of special education.

In terms of handicapping conditions served, British Columbia regulations list approved programs in the areas of moderately retarded (TMR), severely mentally retarded, hospital-bound, home-bound, physically handicapped, visually impaired, hearing impaired, speech impaired, and autistic. These are referred to as "specific programs." In addition, "learning assistance" programs are provided for mildly handicapped students who might be called learning disabled or mildly mentally handicapped in some other provinces and the United States. As noted earlier in this description, a system of "special approvals" is used to provide financial encouragement for programs for the handicapped in British Columbia. Such approvals are of two types: (1) noncategorical, population-based approvals, to provide "learning assistance" programs, and (b) categorical approvals to support specific programs. Learning assistance programs are approved on the basis of population units of 350 nonhandicapped pupils. Specific programs are approved based on school district requests and established need.

The provincial school for the deaf enrolls both day and residential students, and fairly extensive work-study programs are supported at the secondary level. Some services for handicapped students, especially those containing a residential component, are largely funded by the Ministry of Human Resources.

A number of special education programs other than the residential programs receive joint support from various ministries, and therefore require coordinated planning at the provincial, regional, and local levels. Such planning has taken place for some time, but in 1978 an Interministry Children's Committee (IMCC) was formed, linking the ministries of the attorney general, education, health, and human resources. These four ministries will attempt to provide additional assistance and guidance in determining how handicapped students needs may best be met, and will likely be of most assistance with respect to the severely handicapped and in planning services in sparsely populated areas. A procedure is being established whereby, in problem situations, an attempt will first be made at the local level, then if necessary at the regional level. If the regional IMCC cannot arrange for the needed resources, the provincial IMCC will be consulted.

British Columbia does not have mandatory education of the handicapped as specific, separate legislation, but it appears that most handicapped students are receiving an education, and the Inter-Ministry Children's Committee system may prove to serve an advocacy role for students who are not being appropriately educated. Although British Columbia has had services for some handicapped students for many years, certain of its programs are relatively new and the effectiveness of the IMCC has yet to be fully established.

Unique and noteworthy programs and activities in Canada

There are many unique and noteworthy programs and activities related to exceptional individuals in Canada, certainly too many to attempt to review in any detail. On the other hand, it is consistent with the purpose of this chapter to mention a sample of such efforts to provide the reader with some concept of their nature and scope. It should be kept in mind that those mentioned are representative of a much larger number of such efforts. Those described in this section are of two major types: (1) those that have some widely recognized international impact or (2) local programs that have potential for application elsewhere.

The National Institute on Mental Retardation, affiliated with York University in Toronto, certainly qualifies as an internationally recognized program. Sponsored by the Canadian Association for the Mentally Retarded, the National Institute on Mental Retardation has become a focal point for many efforts on behalf of the mentally retarded in Canada. It has also made significant contributions throughout the English-speaking nations of the world. Perhaps its best known efforts have been those related to the concept of normalization and *The Principle of Normalization in Human Services* (1972), published by the Institute and authored by Wolf Wolfensberger. Wolfensberger worked at the Institute as a visiting scholar, and his and the Institute's efforts in this area contributed greatly to such statements as the *United Nations Declaration of the Rights of Mentally Retarded Persons* and the implementation of the normalization principle in Canada and the United States. Normalization also was a major factor in the consideration that has been given to the concept of mainstreaming, which caught on more rapidly in the United States than in Canda. (See pp. 64-67 for further discussion of these issues.)

The *Blissymbolics Communication Foundation,** with international headquarters in Toronto, Ontario, is playing a very important role in promoting the use of a unique system of communication for nonvocal, motor impaired individuals. This system was developed by Charles K. Bliss as an international language. It was adopted in 1971, at the Ontario Crippled Children's Center, after considerable study of various symbol systems, for use with nonvocal, cerebral palsied children aged 4 to 6 years (McNaughton, 1977). Its use there brought sufficient success to create considerable demand and interest, and as a result the Centre supported the establishment of the Blissymbolics Communication Foundation. Bliss Symbols were originally used at the Centre with pupils of near normal or above intelligence, but have shown promise for use with mentally handicapped pupils with motor impairments as well. Blissymbolic workshops are now held in various parts of Canada and the United States, and the potential of this communication system has led to considerable attention on the part of educators of the physically impaired throughout the world. Objectives of the Blissymbolics Communication Foundation include: (1) international dissemination and encouragement of the use of Blissymbolics, (2) provision of training and consultive services, and (3) development, production, and distribution of symbol communication materials.*

The international impact of the Blissymbolics Communication Foundation and the National Institute on Mental Retardation characterize some of the more noteworthy efforts of Canadian special educators. There are undoubtedly other programs deserving similar mention, but these two represent Cana-

---

*Further information is available from Blissymbolics Communication Foundation, 862 Eglinton Avenue East, Toronto, Ontario M4G 2L1.

dian efforts on behalf of the handicapped that have had influence far beyond the borders of Canada.

Certain other programs will be described briefly in the following paragraphs to indicate the nature of local or provincial level efforts that exemplify some of the more progressive practices taking place in Canada today. As was the case with the more internationally recognized Canadian efforts, there are many more programs or activities that could be mentioned here.

One example of excellent cooperative effort is that provided by the activities of the Institutional (Educational) Services Divisions of the Edmonton and Calgary public school boards. In this cooperative model, interdisciplinary teams representing separate administrative divisions (health, psychology/psychiatry, social welfare, justice, and education) have devised a plan through which they jointly serve the needs of individuals in regional or provincial sheltered settings, treatment centers, or detention homes, with appropriate authority and responsibility delegated to planners of the various program components. This service is provided without detrimental professional rivalries. Perhaps this should not be surprising but, in fact, divisional and professional rivalries relating to which agency provides what services, what department receives the funding, and who receives credit for the project are major problems in almost all interdepartmental projects in most governmental efforts. The existence of effective cooperative programs proves it can be done, and programs like these provide models for those who need guidance in planning or reshaping their own programs.

Another promising model, also in Edmonton but relating to housing for the adult handicapped, deserves special mention and review. In the early 1970s the Handicapped Housing Society of Alberta convened a meeting in Edmonton to try to find some answers to the question of appropriate, functional housing for physically disabled persons. After carefully detailing their critical needs and considerable lobbying of public officials, a thirteen-story high-rise building, providing housing for both the handicapped and the nonhandicapped, was approved. (Note that the handicapped wanted integrated housing, not totally for the handicapped.) The result is Bader Tower (the first part of a three-phase plan), which has such features as a wheelchair wash just inside one entrance to reduce tracking of mud through the building, and lowered buzzer system, mailboxes, light and thermostat controls, door peep-holes, and intercommunication system, and other such conveniences. The more traditional bathroom adaptations and the like are, of course, included.

The Handicapped Housing Society of Alberta, in addition to providing badly needed housing, has called attention to the special needs of the physically handicapped—which has led to modifications in other buildings in Alberta—and has established a model for others to follow. They have provided important leadership in an area of critical need, which exists in all nations, and have certainly demonstrated the feasibility of such buildings in Canada.

In many places throughout all provinces, both local and provincial officials are apparently going considerably beyond the mandate of law to provide services for handicapped students. In most such instances, it is a matter of local and provincial governmental agencies spending additional effort to work together to be of service to students with special needs. This is not the case in some areas and, according to Canadian sources of information, much improvement is needed in certain areas of the nation. Nevertheless, it appears that there may be more deliberate, planning cooperation between agencies serving handicapped students in Canada than has sometimes been the case in the United States.

Summary

Special education in Canada is both different from and similar to special education in the United States. In terms of actual teaching procedures used with a specific handicapped student, exactly the same procedures will often be used in these two neighboring nations. There are considerable variations in terminology and levels of service among the provinces, but probably no more than among states in the United States.

There are certain variations in Canada that are not found in the United States, but these are applicable across all of education, not just with regard to special education. These include: (1) the dual Catholic-Protestant school systems (in several, but not all provinces), (2) the national, two-language system (which has more effect on Quebec, New Brunswick, Nova Scotia, Ontario, and Manitoba), (3) variation in the grade level considered to be the top level of secondary education (eleventh, twelfth, or thirteenth), (4) the role of the departments of health and/or social services in education, (5) the provision (including apparent encouragement in some provinces) of direct funding to private agencies to conduct certain special programs, and (6) the absence of a national educational agency in Canada.

The concept of normalization is well known to educators of the mentally retarded in Canada, and the attempt to educate all handicapped students in the least restrictive environment is also a part of the stated philosophy of most Canadian special educators. However, this mainstreaming philosophy has not been promoted with the fervor at times evidenced in the United States.

Parent involvement is encouraged in Canada, and parent organizations have played a major role in the development of special education there. There is not the federally mandated requirement for parent involvement as in Public Law 94-142 in the United States, a difference that is difficult to analyze in terms of actual results in programming for handicapped students.

Education of the gifted and talented in Canada may be at about the same state of the art as in the United States. In some provinces it is a part of a division or department of special education, in some it is not. In an increasing number of provinces (e.g., Ontario, Saskatchewan, British Columbia) there is provincial support for programs for the gifted. In most of Canada, however, the existence of programs for the gifted reflects the interest of a particular school district rather than clearly articulated provincial policy. Because of the manner in which the gifted and talented are provided services, it is sometimes very difficult to obtain an accurate picture of this matter.

The complete absence of special certification requirements in several provinces is without parallel in the United States, but it must be recognized that many states use the vehicle of "temporary" or "emergency" certification to do essentially the same thing.

Because Canada has a very different health services system than the United States (comprehensive, universal medical care as compared to private medical practice), there are differences in diagnostic services and preschool services, especially for children with hearing and visual impairments, cerebral palsy, and developmental disabilities.

If, for whatever combination of reasons, a representative sample of teachers of the handicapped from the United States were suddenly to be transported to Canada to teach the same type of handicapped student there, the chances are that much of what they did would be as acceptable and effective as it was in the United States). Two major differences that might be readily apparent would most likely relate to: (1) in some settings, the need to speak French and (2) matters concerning the "framework" within which services are provided (terminology, roles of school board, department of health or social services, type of service delivery, etc.).

Epilogue

In addition to those who provided a wide variety of information regarding education of exceptional students in Canada, four Canadian special educators were of unusually valuable assistance in reviewing this chapter after it was completed. They provided ideas and suggestions that have made it more accurate and meaningful. Those individuals are: David Kendall, The University of British Columbia; Donald Little, Acadia University; Howard Stutt, McGill University; and David Treherne, Governor-at-Large for Canada, CEC.

Many of their suggestions (and corrections of my misconceptions about Canadian education) were such that they could be easily integrated into the already developed chapter. Certain ideas, however, were such that it seemed best to include them here. These ideas were not necessarily reflected by all four reviewers, but were, in each case, prominently mentioned by more than one reviewer and sufficiently well-documented to warrant inclusion.

One reviewer noted that, although this chapter may reflect stated public (governmental) policy, there are many instances where handicapped students do not receive the services indicated by policy statements. (This phenomenon is hardly unique to Canada.) Another noted that the lack of mandatory legislation in most provinces and the fact that specialized teacher education programs for teachers of the handicapped have been slow to develop have contributed to a lag in the development of adequate services. In a further comment regarding this situation, it was indicated that "some (but not all) Canadians would like to see stronger regulatory or watchdog powers in the hands of the government with respect to the operation of services" for the handicapped.

One final suggestion provided by the reviewers is of particular merit. They suggested that readers who were seriously interested in knowing more about special education in Canada should do a great deal of additional investigation and reading. Because of the nature of this chapter and its purpose in this text, it was not possible to do more than provide a very general view of special education in Canada. (The same thing is true of all other parts of this text. The assumption is that readers who are truly interested will delve much more deeply before attempting to reach any final conclusions about any topic under consideration.) Publications of the Canadian Council for Exceptional Children will provide the best available starting point in any such attempt to gain an accurate national perspective. For those who do wish to obtain in-depth understandings regarding education of exceptional students in Canada, such additional reading is essential.

References and suggested readings

Andrews, C. (Department of Education, Newfoundland). Correspondence of January 23, 1979.

Bergman, G. (Ministry of Education, Ontario). Correspondence of December 8, 1978.

Beuree, G. (Department of Education, Nova Scotia). Correspondence of December 21, 1978.

Bill 58 (Unproclaimed amendment to Section 465[22]). *Public Schools Act,* Manitoba.

Canada Handbook. Year Book Section, Information Division, Statistics Canada, Ottawa, 1978.

Children with physical handicaps and health impairments: curriculum ideas for teachers. Ontario Ministry of Education, 1978.

Downey, A, *A program guide for senior special education.* Newfoundland Department of Education.

Education of exceptional students in Ontario. Ontario Ministry of Education, 1976.

Educational Services; Division of Special Services. Newfoundland Department of Education, 1978.

Education today. British Columbia Ministry of Education, Vol. 5, No. 3, December, 1978.

Elementary and secondary schools for trainable mentally retarded children. Ontario Regulation 704/78 (under the Education Act), 1974.

Gayfer, M. *An overview of Canadian education.* 2nd ed. Toronto, Ontario: The Canadian Education Association, 1978.

Gifted/talented children: curriculum ideas for teachers. Ontario Ministry of Education, 1978.

Gittins, J. A. G. (Ministry of Education, British Columbia). Correspondence of March 6, 1979.

Hardy, M., and others. *Standards for educators of exceptional children in Canada.* Toronto, Ontario: Crainford, 1971.

"Housing: High-rise apartments in Edmonton Canada." *Arise,* May 1979, *2*(7), 5-7.

Kendall, D. (Chairman). *Atlantic Provinces Report of the Special Education Committee to the Ministers of Education.* Amherst, Nova Scotia: Interprovincial School, 1973.

King, M. Commission on Emotional and Learning Disorders in Children. *Canada's Mental Health,* 1968, *XVI* (1,2), 9-14.

Little, D. *A chance for every child.* A brief on behalf of the CEC Teacher Education Division of the Canadian Committee of the CEC, submitted to the Council of Ministers of Education in Canada, April, 1976.

Livingston, R. (Department of Education, Saskatchewan). Correspondence of January 15, 1979.

MacLellan, E. (Department of Education, Prince Edward Island). Correspondence of December 20, 1978.

McGeer, P. L. *Report on education: 1976-1977.* Province of British Columbia Ministry of Education, 1977.

McGuigan, J. *Opportunities for the handicapped.* Province of New Brunswick, 1974.

McKie, K. (Department of Education, Alberta). Correspondence of December 29, 1978.

McNaughton, D. The use of Blissymbolics as a communication medium for the non-speaking person. *Communication: everybody's business.* The National Easter Seal Society for Crippled Children and Adults, June, 1977, pp. 9-17.

Magnuson, R. *Education in the Province of Quebec.* Washington, D.C.; Office of Education, U.S. Government Printing Office, 1969.

Morin, J. *Quebec schools, children with adjustment and learning difficulties* (Statement of policy and plan of action). Quebec Ministry of Education, 1978.

New Brunswick Regulation 70-91. A regulation under the Auxiliary Classes Act (Consolidated to January 28, 1976), Fredrickton, N.B.

Ontario Crippled Children's Centre. *Symbol communication research project.* 1972-73 Project Report. Toronto, Ontario: OCCC, 1973.

Owens, E. (Department of Education, New Brunswick). Correspondence of December 6, 1978.

Proceedings of the seminar on the employability of the handicapped (Toronto, November 26, 1976). Ottawa: Social Services Division, Department of Health and Welfare, 1977.

Public Schools Act (consolidation of legislation in effect, 1976). Manitoba.

Public Schools Act (consolidation of legislation in effect, 1978). Manitoba.

Quebec, Gouvernement du Quebec. *L'école Québécoise: énoncé de politique et plan d'action.* (Especially Chapter V, L'enfance en difficulté adaptation et d'apprentissage.) Quebec Ministry of Education, 1979.

Roberts, C., and others. *One million children.* CELDIC Report. Toronto: Crainford, 1970.

School grants regulations. Alberta Department of Education, 1978.

Special education programs: guidelines. British Columbia Ministry of Education, 1977.

The Education Act, 1974, Ontario.

The Education Act, 1978, Saskatchewan.

The education of children with learning and adjustment problems in Quebec. Report of the Committee on Exceptional Children, Quebec Ministry of Education, 1976.

The Official Languages Act of 1969, Ottawa.

The School Act, Alberta, 1970.

The Schools Act, Newfoundland, 1970.

Townsend, J., and others. *We are not alike. Policies for the education of exceptional children in Ontario.* Report of the Policy Statements Committee commissioned by the Ontario Federation of Chapters, The Council for Exceptional Children, October, 1973.

Treherne, D., and others. *A matter of principle: principles governing legislation for services for children with special needs.* Niagara Falls, Ontario: The Canadian Committee, Council for Exceptional Children, 1974.

Vision: curriculum ideas for teachers. Ontario Ministry of Education, 1978.

Webber, B. G. Towards clarification of the ministry position of integration (Mainstreaming) of handicapped children. Position paper of the Special Programs Branch, British Columbia Ministry of Education.

Wolfensberger, W. *The principle of normalization in human services.* Toronto; National Institute on Mental Retardation, 1972.

SECTION THREE

Sensory impairments

When considering the various handicapping conditions, there are several reasons why it may be logical to first consider those which are the result of visual or hearing impairments. As with all other handicapping conditions, there are different degrees of impairment, and factors other than the basic impairment may cause a greater degree of handicap than the basic impairment. Also, as in the case of other handicapping conditions, there are controversies as to the best or most effective way to provide educational programming, especially with the hearing impaired. But there are some specific ways in which sensory impairments are quite different from other areas of handicap. First, these are conditions that most educational authorities and the general public agree actually exist. They relate to physical conditions that can be measured and that have some additional acceptance and credibility because of an obvious relationship to the medical profession. Unlike mental retardation, emotional disturbance, and learning disabilities, they have not been the subject of court action in which it is claimed that educators have labeled children handicapped when in fact the educational difficulty resulted from inappropriate planning for children from minority groups. Also, there is not the strong concern with biased tests; if anything, the concern is that minority group children with visual or hearing impairments may not be identified and provided special programs and services.

Education of individuals with sensory impairments is unique in another significant way. These two areas of handicap are the two oldest of the handicapping conditions in terms of how long recognized special educational provisions have existed. As part of this long recognition, it may be noted that the United States government has made certain special provisions for the deaf and the blind for many years; more about this is in the historical review in these two chapters.

There are many other ways in which educational programming for children with sensory impairments is different from that provided for other handicapping conditions. It has long been recognized that preschool programs for deaf and blind chil-

Sensory impairments

dren are essential, and only recently have there been any serious attempts on a nationwide basis to provide preschool programs for other handicapped children. Electronic devices are in common use with some children with sensory impairments, and in certain cases, surgery may reduce or correct the impairment. These and other characteristics of children with sensory impairments (and the educational programs provided them) reinforce the conclusion that there should be a separate section of this text for consideration of these two handicapping conditions.

Children in this class for the severely hearing impaired are involved in a "peanut butter and jelly party." This is one of many such activities used to promote language development.

chapter 5

Education of children and youth who are hearing impaired

objectives

To trace the early history of education of the hearing impaired and to understand its influence on the types of programs in existence today.

To develop a basic understanding of the anatomy of the auditory system and the major causes of hearing impairment.

To outline the various types of hearing impairment, review classification systems, and consider how hearing loss is determined.

To describe the characteristics of individuals who are hearing impaired and to explore identification procedures.

To review and compare the major methods used to teach the hearing impaired.

To discuss a number of educational considerations (other than degree of hearing impairment) that are most important in educational planning for the hearing impaired.

To outline and discuss questions related to providing for maximum integration of the hearing impaired.

Introduction

As noted in the introduction to this section on sensory impairments, education of the hearing impaired and visually impaired predates other areas of special education. Perhaps the most highly recognized authority on the field of special education as a whole, Samuel Kirk, has stated that "education of the deaf is the most special of all areas of special education" (see Moores, 1978, p. xiii). Education of the deaf was the first organized programming for the handicapped in the United States. In addition, it is the only area of handicap that is sufficiently "special" to have warranted a separate college (Gallaudet) for those with such a handicap.

Our concern in this chapter will be to learn more about how this area of special education originated and how it evolved to its present state of development. In so doing, we will consider definitions, classification systems, specific causes of hearing impairment, and educational programming as it exists today. In reviewing educational approaches we will find that an unusual amount of controversy has existed through the years and that major issues are far from settled. Topics such as specific anatomic information about the ear, medical and surgical procedures, and similar concerns will be addressed briefly. The purpose of this overview is to permit those who may want to further pursue this area of specialty to have a basis for such consideration, and to provide others with sufficient information to recognize the basic educational needs of the hearing impaired.

Historical origins of education of the hearing impaired
EARLY HISTORY

Older accounts of the development of educational programs for the hearing impaired often started with a reference to Aristotle and his written comment that, "Men that are deaf are also speechless; that is they can make vocal sounds but they cannot speak." This, coupled with his statement, "Let it be law that nothing imperfect should be brought up," led to the belief that Aristotle actively encouraged the destruction of deaf babies (Moores, 1978). More recent analysis of the historical effect of Aristotle's comments by highly respected educators of the deaf have indicated that perhaps he should not be so soundly condemned as has been the case in the past (Davis and Silverman, 1978; Moores, 1978). Regardless of how we may consider this specific reference to Aristotle, which has been familiar for decades to educators of the deaf, it is a fact that social acceptance of the deaf has been extremely low for hundreds of years, primarily because of their difficulty with language usage and with traditional academic learning.

Interpretations of the effect of statements by early philosophers, of wording in Biblical passages, and other historical references clearly establish that the deaf were held in low esteem, that there was little understanding of the condition of deafness, and that the common assumption was that the deaf had very limited intelligence (Peet, 1851). This assumption, though not nearly the problem today that it was 2,000 (or even 50) years ago, must still be dealt with by the deaf. In a society where language usage and verbal ability are often correlated with intelligence, lack of language ability remains a serious problem.

The history of treatment of the deaf during the early Christian era and through most of the Middle Ages was consistently bad. In some instances it was primarily a matter of deprivation of rights (such as those of inheritance or the right to marry freely) but even more serious was the kind of everyday treatment that goes with the assignment of legally supported second class status. There were a few instances where "cures" were reported, but these were literally viewed as miracles, for it was generally assumed that it was not possible to teach a person who lacked the basic sensory channel through which language acquisition must take place.

Historians of education of the deaf appear to be unanimous about the matter of who was the first actual teacher of the deaf. Peet (1851), writing in the *American Annals of the Deaf*, and other Western writers agree that Pablo Ponce de Leon (1520-1584), a Benedictine monk who established a school for the deaf children of Spanish nobility, was the first successful educator of the deaf. In this instance the instruction was regarded as instruction, not a series of miracles, and the foundation for education of the deaf was thus laid. Unfortunately, the record of *how* this teaching was accomplished was lost, and subsequent analyses seem to reflect the bias of those conducting the analysis rather than solid fact. (Those who favor the use of signs believe Ponce de Leon used signs; those who oppose signs believe he did not.)

In a legal document dated August 24, 1578, it was reported that Ponce de Leon worked with pupils who were deaf and dumb from birth, who were "sons of great lords and of notable people who I have taught to speak, read, write, to pray, to assist at Mass, to know the doctrines of Christianity, and to know how to confess themselves by speech." (Peet, 1851, p. 141) The denial of rights to inheritance was apparently the motivation for Ponce de Leon's first efforts, in that the son of a prominent Spanish nobleman, Don Francisco Velasco, had been denied such rights (based on being deaf and dumb), and Ponce de Leon's efforts led to his regaining his inheritance. According to the limited records available, it appears certain that a number of students, all sons of Spanish noblemen, learned to speak, read, write, and in some instances to speak and read in more than one language. Further, these students later were able to use these skills to attain recognized competence in a variety of fields of endeavor. What is not known is whether all, or even most, were *congenitally* deaf. There is also the question of how they were taught, a question that will likely never be settled to the satisfaction of advocates of the various differing points of view.

A second individual of great historical importance is Juan Martin Pablo Bonet (1579-1620). Bonet is particularly well known because his efforts were recorded in a book, thus providing the basis for further progress. He too worked in Spain, and much of his work was directed toward teaching another Velasco child, the grandson of a brother of the three Velasco brothers who were taught by Ponce de Leon. In an interesting sidelight to this story, it has been noted that in his book, Bonet does not mention the earlier work of Ponce de Leon or the work of Ramirez de Carrion, who may have done most of the actual teaching of the Velasco boy about whom Bonet wrote (Peet, 1851). Bonet advocated a training method that is remarkably like that which became the standard in many twentieth century schools for the deaf (Deland, 1931). Regardless of the extent to which his ideas may be a reflection of those of Ponce de Leon and Carrion, Bonet's writings are generally recognized as remarkably advanced and insightful, highly valuable, and thus a great contribution in the field of education of the deaf. As noted by Moores (1978), some of Bonet's writing and thinking "anticipates aspects of the work of Seguin, Montessori, Pestalozzi, and Piaget, among others." (p. 37)

ESTABLISHMENT OF SCHOOLS IN EUROPE

Great Britain, France, and Germany all contributed valuable efforts to the fledgling area of education of the deaf. In Great Britain, interest in education of the deaf was based, at least in part, on knowledge of the work in Spain. Several individuals, including William Holder (1616-1698) and John Wallis (1618-1703), apparently succeeded in teaching deaf students, and each claimed to have invented the art of teaching the deaf (Moores, 1978). In addition, neither mentioned the earlier work of Bonet, though each was apparently well aware of his work. A third man, George Dalgarno (1628-1687), produced a highly regarded account of methods for teaching the deaf, but did not mention the other two. Thomas Braidwood (1715-1806) established a school for the deaf in Edinburgh in 1767 and is generally acknowledged as the most important early educator of the deaf in Great Britain.

Other individuals in France and Germany were also involved in developing educational programs for the deaf. According to Davis and Silverman (1978) "two individuals . . . tower above all others in their contributions to advancing the cause of the deaf in the latter part of the eighteenth century—the Abbe Charles Michel de l'Epee in France and Samuel Heinicke in Germany." (p. 425) To de l'Epee (1712-1789) goes the credit for establishing the first *public* school for the deaf. At this school, established in 1775 in Paris, de l'Epee first utilized an approach emphasizing oral language, but soon, because of the press of numbers (l'Epee found it most difficult to turn potential students away) a system of manual communication (signs) was established. This soon became a distinguishing characteristic of de l'Epee's approach.

In Germany, Samuel Heinicke (1729-1790) became interested in the deaf while in the military service and later (in 1778) established the first school for the deaf in Germany. Heinicke believed strongly in an orally based method and was opposed to de l'Epee's manualism. His approach came to be known as an oral approach and his method, the German method. These two men, Heinicke in Germany and de l'Epee in France, started a controversy (oralism versus manualism) that has been fought by various educators of the deaf down to the present time (see pp. 124-129).

ESTABLISHMENT OF SCHOOLS IN THE UNITED STATES

The first permanent school for the deaf in the United States was established at Hartford, Connecticut, and was called the American Asylum for the Education and Instruction of the Deaf and Dumb. This school (now the American School for the Deaf) was established as a result of the determination of a deaf girl's father (Dr. Mason Fitch Cogswell) and the interest of Thomas Hopkins Gallaudet (1787-1851). Gallaudet, a divinity student in Connecticut, became interested in attempting to teach Dr. Cogswell's daughter, had some limited success in teaching her to communicate, and after being convinced he should leave his ministerial calling, went to England to study under the Braidwood's and learn their methods. (The Braidwood family operated their school in England for many, many years, and wealthy Americans often sent their deaf children to Braidwood's school.) Gallaudet also planned to spend time in Paris learning about the French method of de l'Epee, a proposal to which the Braidwoods objected. Thus, because of his open, eclectic point of view and the fact that the Braidwoods considered their method a family secret, Gallaudet reluctantly gave up his plan to use the best from both approaches and went on to Paris. In Paris he was welcomed enthusiastically and he spent a year there. (It should be noted that Gallaudet even tried to enlist the help of a former Braidwood teacher, but that teacher had taken an oath of secrecy from which the Braidwood's would not release him; thus the first schools in the United States were strongly influenced by the French approach.)

Gallaudet returned to the United States, bringing with him a young deaf man, Laurent Clerc (who had also trained in Paris), and in 1817 the American Asylum for the Education of the Deaf and Dumb was officially initiated. The school opened with seven deaf students and enrollment grew to twenty-one students during the first year. At first the school was quite dependent on donated funds, but in 1819 the U.S. Government gave a gift of land to the school, which was sold to provide the necessary permanent endowment. Before long, a number of other states sent students—and tuition—to the Hartford school, and it was firmly established as the center of education for the deaf in the United States. New York opened a school for the deaf in 1818, and a third school was opened in Philadelphia in 1820.

Although three schools were opened in this initial 3-year period, only three more schools were opened in the next 24 years. Then, during the 20 years from 1840 to 1860, seventeen new schools were established. In the beginning, a few of these schools included day school components, but all eventually became residential schools. In addition, all were manual schools; that is, they did little to teach articulation and speechreading; rather they emphasized the French (manual) approach.

More will be said about the oral versus manual controversy in the section of this chapter dealing with educational methods, but it is timely to note that the disagreement as to which approach is most valuable (or acceptable, appropriate, beneficial, etc.), which originated with the debate over the French (l'Epee) versus the German (Heinicke) methods, was to continue in the United States. We may speculate that the whole course of events in education of the deaf in the United States might have been changed if the Braidwoods had been less secretive when Gallaudet asked for their help, but this must remain in the realm of speculation. In any event, oral schools did develop in the United States, after Horace Mann and Samuel Howe visited the German schools and gave glowing reports on the success of oralism there. (Although not educators of the deaf, Mann and Howe were among the most famous and influential educators of their time. Such schools did not develop overnight, for there was opposition from manualists, especially those who believed such schools might endanger existing programs. Nevertheless, oral schools such as the Clarke School for the Deaf in Massachusetts and in New York the school that became the Lexington School for the Deaf were established and prospered. Many of the students who were enrolled in these schools were adventitiously deaf or were not profoundly deaf, but there was certainly good reason to believe that they made more—or at least a different kind of—progress in these schools than they would have in purely manual schools. A side benefit of this controversy was that schools that had been purely manual began to employ speech teachers.

In 1857, another Gallaudet initiated a career that was to lead to prominence as an educator of the deaf and to a major role in combining programs of articulation and lipreading with manual methods in schools for the deaf throughout the nation. Edward Miner Gallaudet, the son of Thomas Hopkins Gallaudet, was, at age 20, appointed principal of the Columbia Institute for the Deaf and Dumb in Washington, D.C. He was quite successful and in 1864 was made president of a college division of this institution, which became Gallaudet College. Gallaudet College is now internationally recognized, grants undergraduate, master's, and doctor's degrees, carries out a variety of research programs, and is the only such institution in the world.

As just noted, E. M. Gallaudet was destined to participate in the oral versus manual controversy in a significant manner. After visiting many programs in Europe, Gallaudet called a meeting of the principals of all the schools for the deaf in the nation, and at that meeting advocated the use of *both* the oral and manual approaches. As a result of this meeting, a resolution was passed indicating that it was the duty of administrators of schools for the deaf to provide instruction in lipreading (now called speechreading) and articulation to all pupils who might profit from it (Moores, 1978). For these efforts, Gallaudet was strongly criticized by some manual advocates, and it seems clear that his efforts did, in fact, contribute more than any other single factor to the development of combined oral-manual approaches. By the end of the century, oralism had won so many advocates that Gallaudet felt compelled to defend the value of manualism, in a manner somewhat similar to his earlier defense of oralism.

One additional pioneer in the development of educational programs for the deaf must be mentioned to make the picture complete. Alexander Graham Bell, whose father and grandfather had been teachers of speech and whose mother was deaf, was destined to play a major role in the continuing war between oralists and manualists. Bell is best remembered by most Americans for his invention of the telephone, but to educators of the deaf he is better known for his role in the oral vs manual controversy. After working for a time with E. M. Gallaudet, Bell became strongly concerned with the continued isolation of many deaf people and marriage of deaf men and women. He came to believe that the system of residential schools, sign language, and the resulting encouragement of the deaf to marry the deaf (thus tending to propogate deafness) must be stopped. He therefore formally recommended educational integration and the elimination of sign language and deaf teachers in programs for the deaf.

The oral versus manual controversy, which originated in Europe, has continued in the United States until the present, although during the past few decades there has been a degree of reconciliation and recognition of the value of the *simultaneous* method (the oral method plus signs and fingerspelling). Most programs for the deaf, especially those in the public schools, have followed a primarily oral method since the early 1900s, but the change that appears to be taking place is one that might eventually lead to the goal which Thomas Hopkins Gallaudet was seeking when he approached the Braidwoods in England.

Anatomy and physiology of the auditory system

The auditory system is very complex and it is not necessary that we understand it in great detail to understand the needs of hearing impaired students. On the other hand, an understanding of the functioning of the ear will be most helpful in developing a better conceptualization of the unique needs of those individuals who do not hear normally and in understanding the remainder of this chapter.

The ear is usually considered in relation to the functioning of the outer ear, the middle ear, and the inner ear (Fig. 5-1). Generally speaking, impairments of the outer ear are less serious than those of the middle ear, and those of the middle ear are less serious than those of the inner ear. Since sound first enters the auditory system through the outer ear, it will be considered first.

The *outer ear* includes the *pinna* (sometimes called the auricle) and the *external auditory meatus or canal*. The pinna and the external auditory canal (meatus) are the only parts of the ear that most individuals usually see and they serve primarily as a "funnel" for sound waves. This part of the ear may collect too much earwax (cerumen), which may cause hearing problems. This cerumen plays the very useful role of keeping the skin of the canal and typanic membrane moist and also serves as a protection against dust and insects, which would seriously injure the middle ear.

The *middle ear* begins with the *tympanic membrane* (often called the eardrum), which moves when driven by sound waves. The function of the middle ear is to transmit sound (vibrations of the tympanic membrane) to the inner ear. This is accomplished through the interconnected movement of three small bones (ossicles), which most grade school chilren learn to call the hammer, anvil, and stirrup. The actual names of these bones are the *malleus*, *incus*, and the *stapes*, respectively. These bones are attached to the walls of the middle ear cavity by flexible ligaments and are uniquely constructed to carry vibrations of various frequencies to the oval window, which looks into the inner ear. The workings of the middle ear include a series of checks and balances to prevent the ossicles from moving too much and thus causing damage in this complex mechanism. The movement of the malleus, incus, and stapes have been observed in action and are fully understood. As we shall see in a later section, this understanding permits surgical assistance in many cases where the cause of hearing loss is in the middle ear, and although characterized as complex, the middle ear is simple compared to the inner ear.

Sensory impairments

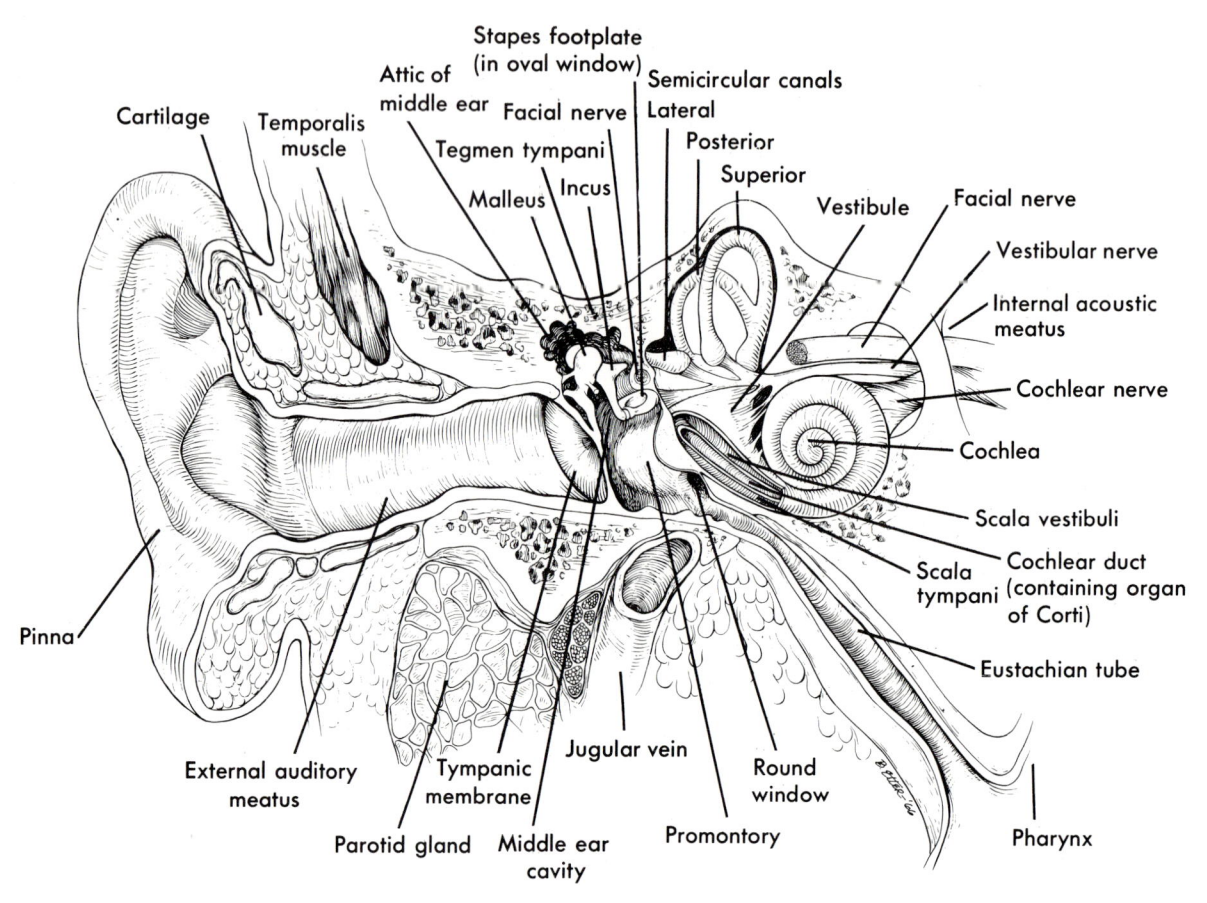

Fig. 5-1. The human ear. (From Saunders, W. H., and Paparella, M. M. *Atlas of Ear Surgery,* ed. 2. St. Louis: The C. V. Mosby Co., 1971.)

The *inner ear* is extremely complicated and involves so many channels and chambers it is called the labyrinth. The inner ear is filled with fluid (the middle ear is filled with air) and contains many sensory cells and specialized structures. The central portion, or *vestibule,* of the inner ear connects with the *semicircular canals* and the *cochlea.* The primary purpose of the *semicircular canals* is to provide a sense of balance, while the *cochlea* is the major organ for hearing in the ear.

The cochlea looks much like a snail (see Fig. 5-1) and is extremely important. A part of the cochlea called the *organ of Corti* is the end organ of hearing. It includes the sensory cells, which finally receive the vibrations that initially enter the outer ear. There are some 24,000 hair cells in the human ear, which can respond to sound. If all is working properly, when the vibrations reach the hair cells of the organ of Corti, an impulse is sent to the brain. Certain details of this part of the total system are still not fully understood. It is known that in some manner when the hair cells are mechanically bent, an electrochemical transmission effect is energized at the opposite end of the hair cell and the message (sound) is recorded in the brain. Specialized functions of some parts of the inner ear have been determined but much remains to be learned. Many of these parts must be studied by electron microscope because of their very small size. From our general point of view, the following sequence of events, which leads to hearing, should be understood:

1. Sound enters the outer ear, moves to the tympanic membrane, and causes vibrations.
2. The malleus, embedded in the tympanic membrane, vibrates, causing the incus to vibrate, thus causing the stapes to vibrate.
3. The stapes strikes the oval window initiating vibration in the fluid in the inner ear.
4. A complex series of vibrations through different types of fluid in the inner ear eventually lead to movement in the organ of Corti.
5. The hair cells of the organ of Corti move, causing an effect that is essentially electrochemical, which results in the auditory message reaching the brain. When all of this system is working normally, sounds of differing frequency and volume lead to accurate recording of these differences in the brain.

In addition to the way in which the organ of Corti "feels" sound that enters the outer ear and travels through the ear in the normal manner, it may also "feel" vibrations transmitted directly through the bones of the skull. This is called *bone conduction* and may be important in telling diagnosticians whether the basic cause of a hearing impairment lies in the process whereby the sound gets to the inner ear or in the inner ear itself.

Two additional functions served by sensory cells located in the ear should be noted. First, the sense of balance, or turning in space, is determined through the semicircular canals. Second, sensitivity to the pull of gravity and to acceleration (as we might feel in a roller coaster) is centered in the *vestibule* of the inner ear. In both cases, these sensations are the result of movement of cells and resultant "messages" to the brain. The fact that these nonauditory functions are so closely related physiologically to auditory functions leads to valuable diagnostic potential in certain types of hearing loss. The remainder of the detail provided in Fig. 5-1 helps to indicate the complexity of the ear and how closely it relates to other parts of the head.

Definitions: types and degrees of hearing impairment

The term "hearing impaired" is a very general one that includes all degrees of hearing loss from very mild to profound. The major problem of the hearing impaired is their hearing loss, but a number of other factors play highly significant roles as they interrelate with the loss in hearing. *Therefore, in considering educational programming, it is imperative that a host of related factors and their probable composite effect be considered.* The following discussion of types and degrees of hearing loss must be considered in light of the fact that, important though they may be, each is only one part of the picture when we consider the social, educational, and vocational problems of the hearing impaired.

This principle is well illustrated by the following anecdote, which relates to only *one* variable other than degree of hearing loss. When we consider the many variables that may be affecting the performance and educational needs of any hearing impaired student, the importance of this principle becomes abundantly clear.

Several years ago, when I was showing a member of the local board of education (who had voted generous funds for a new program for profoundly deaf students in a local school district) through a wing of a building in which the elementary aged students received special assistance, we observed two deaf students in approximately the same academic setting. One was obviously doing much better in reading and language usage than the other. The board member asked about their degree of loss, and I told him it was almost exactly the same. He asked about a number of variables, attempting to guess why one child was doing so much better than the other. When he thought he had covered all but one, he said, "It must be intelligence; Rod must be much brighter than Timmy." He was wrong. The one difference was that although both were born with normal hearing and both had the same type of loss, Timmy had lost his hearing at the age of 4 months, Rod at the age of 5 years. This one factor made a tremendous difference in the academic performance of these two boys.

There are several ways to categorize types of hearing losses, but one of the more common is as follows:

Conductive loss, in which there is reduced or impaired conduction of sound to the sense organ. This type loss relates to problems in the outer or middle ear.

Sensorineural losses, in which the inner ear is the basic source of the problem. The presumption here is that although sound is conducted normally, the inner ear (which may be conceptualized as the "receiving unit") is not working properly.

Mixed losses, in which both conductive and sensorineural losses are involved.

There are two major generally recognized degrees of hearing impairment. The Conference of Executives of American Schools for the Deaf has traditionally been the accepted source for definitions of this sort, and their latest interpretation of these terms (slightly simplified) is: A *deaf* person is one whose hearing disability is so great that he or she cannot understand speech through use of the ear alone, with or without a hearing aid. A *hard-of-hearing* person is one whose hearing disability makes it difficult to hear but who can, with or without the use of a hearing aid, understand speech.

In practice, many authorities simply indicate that "deafness" means total loss of hearing. "Hard-of-hearing" means that although there are difficulties in hearing, there is some remaining functional ability to hear speech. As indicated earlier, "hearing impaired" includes both of these categories.

Other ways to classify hearing impairments are by cause, by age of onset, and by location (physiologically). Students who major in the area of education of the hearing impaired or in audiology will learn much more about all of these classification systems. For our purposes in this overview treatment, we will consider just a few.

Other classification systems

One of the more important factors in determining the type and amount of special educational services a given student may require is the matter of when that student became hearing impaired (age of onset). *Prelingual deafness* refers to deafness that was present at birth or occurred prior to the development of speech and language. *Postlingual deafness* refers to deafness that occurred following the development of speech and language. The age of onset of hearing impairment is a highly critical factor. Other terms commonly used include *congenitally deaf* (deaf at time of birth) and *adventitiously deaf* (acquired after birth).

The most common, simple categorization of degree of hearing impairment is that mentioned in the previous section, i.e., deaf and hard-of-hearing. This categorization is based on sensitivity to sound, which is normally expressed in *decibels*. A decibel (dB) is a unit of intensity or loudness of sound; the more significant the hearing loss, the larger the number value of the decibel (dB) loss.

For purposes of educational planning it is also important to know at which frequencies the loss occurs. Therefore, the *audiogram* (a graphic presentation indicating decibel loss by frequencies) is an important part of the information required to permit meaningful educational planning for any given hearing impaired child.

Table 5-1 indicates several common environmental sounds expressed in intensity (decibels). If a given child's decibel loss is greater than any of the indicated levels, the child would have great difficulty in hearing that sound.

In terms of decibel levels, we find variations among authorities as to precisely where the dividing point between deaf and hard-of-hearing should be placed, but most would include the 27/35 to 69 dB range as hard-of-hearing, and the 91 dB and above range as deaf. There is some debate as to how to consider the 70 to 90 dB range (Davis and Silverman, 1978). However, regardless of precisely where the dividing line may be drawn (and this may be important for some legal purposes), this type of classification is based on the concept of *sensitivity* to sound. For another four-level classification system based primarily on decibel loss, see Table 5-2, p. 134.

A classification often used when speaking of dimensions of hearing impairment that *cannot* be measured in terms of a simple loss of sensitivity is *dysacusis*. This condition and hearing loss expressed in terms of simple losses of sensitivity are not mutually exclusive; they may, and often do, exist simultaneously. As with other terms used in this field, dysacusis may be characterized as "central" or "peripheral" dysacusis to indicate more about the origin of the impairment. Loss of auditory discrimination is one fairly common example of dysacusis; another is pain produced by loud or even moderate sound levels.

At times, hearing losses are characterized in terms of the cause or pathology of the loss. One example is *otitis media*, a conductive loss normally caused by inflammation in the middle ear. This will be further discussed in the section on causes of hearing impairments. However, certain other conditions (classifications) will be mentioned briefly. *Diplacusis*, a condition that involves "hearing double," may be evidenced in several ways. One occurs when the individual no longer hears a pure tone as a single pure tone; it becomes "fuzzy" or "noisy" or may sound like a mixture of tones. A second type of diplacusis occurs when the two ears hear different tones. Also, mixtures of these two varieties may occur. When this occurs in only a limited part of the frequency scale, the effect is not disastrous. In its most severe form, ability to discriminate speech in a normal manner may be lost.

A second condition is *tinnitus*, or "ringing in the ears." This, of course, means ringing in the absence of any exterior sound stimulus. Tinnitus may have a number of natural causes, one of the most common being an

TABLE 5-1

Decibels (dB)	Sounds
140	Threshold of pain
100	Riveting machine at 30 feet
80	Loud music (radio or stereo) at home
60	Normal conversation or average restaurant sounds
40	Minimal level; outdoor sound in a city
20	Very quiet conversation
0	Threshold of hearing

after-effect of hearing a loud noise, particularly an explosion. This ordinarily is temporary, but in some cases may persist. Other causes exist, some of which will be explored in the following section of causation.

One final classification system, which is neither medical nor based purely on sensitivity, might be called an *educational placement system*. This system is of the most importance to educators, but should not be used as a system completely isolated from the others. This system will be described on pp. 134-136 as we consider how the concept of a continuum of special educational services applies to the hearing impaired.

Causes of hearing impairment

There are numerous studies of the causes of hearing impairment with somewhat different results because different definitions have been used and different populations surveyed. Also, there are differences attributed to when (what year) the surveys were taken. Causes have varied because of factors such as the rubella epidemics of 1958-1959 and 1964-1965. Nevertheless, there seems to be fair agreement that *hereditary deafness* is the most common of the known causes, and that *maternal rubella, Rh incompatibility, meningitis,* and *prematurity* are the other generally recognized causes. However, as noted by Moores (1978), "although . . . prematurity is more common among the deaf population than among the normal hearing, the degree to which it is a causative factor is debatable." (p. 91) It has, however, been listed as among the top three factors in a number of regional studies, and it seems to be generally recognized as a cause of deafness. It is true, however, that in many studies of deafness (or hearing impairment) somewhat less than half of the cases can be related to known causes, thus resultant data must be considered in this light.

Other specific causes include the following.

Otitis media is an inflammation of the middle ear, which is most often caused by infection. A significant percentage of young children experience otitis media, and if treated (or if the condition clears despite lack of treatment) damage is not likely. However, a conductive loss will occur while the inflammation persists. There are indications that there is a great deal of untreated otitis media among the various low income populations, and in addition to the discomfort and temporary partial loss of hearing, there may be more permanent after-effects. Another form of otitis media, caused by allergies, has received added attention in recent years. Pollen allergies and allergies to foods such as eggs, milk, chocolate, nuts, etc., may cause this type reaction. The treatments for infection and allergy-caused otitis media are obviously quite different, but the symptoms, in terms of reduced ability to hear, are the same.

Otosclerosis is a bone disease that is fairly common among whites but rare among those of all other races. Recent research indicates that otosclerosis (the condition involves new bony growth in the areas surrounding the inner ear) is more common than earlier believed, but quite often it does not seriously impair hearing. Usually the loss of hearing is moderate, and this condition is most serious when found in combination with other hearing impairments.

Excessive noise levels, which may come from any of a variety of sources, are receiving increasing recognition as a cause of hearing impairment. Unusually loud rock music may be a cause of hearing impairment in some young people, and industrial noises are a definite cause with adults. Because of increasing recognition of this problem, the wearing of "ear plugs" in certain settings has increased rapidly over the past 15 to 20 years.

Aging (presbycusis), though not a concern for children and youth, is a major, highly predictable cause of hearing impairment in older adults.

Tinnitus, mentioned in an earlier section, is often the after-effect of loud noise and thus may be related to excessive noise levels. In other instances, the ringing in the ears may be caused by something altogether different. It probably relates to a spontaneous discharge from auditory nerve fibers, a discharge that *may* be associated with loud noises, or may be occasioned by other physiologic factors. It is also sometimes considered as a part of the hearing loss that comes with age, but this may or may not be the case. Tinnitus is a good example of a condition that is defined primarily with regard to the symptoms (ringing in the ears) but may be *caused* by any of a variety of factors.

This list could also include various childhood diseases (in addition to rubella and meningitis), after-effects of taking various medication, especially some antibiotics, and physical blows to the head. What is most important is that we understand that any one condition may be the result of any of a variety of causes.

Medical and surgical treatment of hearing impairment

Although the major emphasis of this text is on educational efforts on behalf of the handicapped, some knowledge of the medical aspects of various handicapping conditions is of value. The potential role of the physician is as great or greater with respect to the hearing impaired than with any other handicapping condition. The physician's role includes prevention, surgical treatment, and more exotic treatments such as cochlear implantation of electrodes that can deliver electrical stimulation to auditory nerve fibers. (This latter procedure is at a stage of development that many would call experimental, but it reflects some of the bolder efforts of those who are attempting to find ways to reduce the effects of total deafness.)

Otology (the medical specialty that deals with diagnosing and treating pathologic conditions of the auditory system) has made highly significant advances, including many accepted, proved treatment procedures during the past 30 years. A few of these will be mentioned very briefly in the following paragraphs.

Prevention of hearing loss includes many facets such as the use of protective devices to reduce sound levels reaching the hearing mechanisms, use of antibiotics in the case of infections (especially chronic nasal infections and middle ear infections), monitored use of ototoxic drugs, early treatment of otitis media, and use of specific medication to retard the development of otosclerosis. Surgical treatment includes such procedures as the rebuilding of congenital malformations, removal of tonsils and adenoids, removal of diseased tissue (for example, mastoidectomies), reconstruction of various parts of the hearing mechanism through grafts, and the use of prostheses, as in the case of otosclerosis.

Medical procedures such as the use of drugs to control conditions causing hearing impairment, blowing out the ear, and cleaning out impacted ear wax should be added to the long list of established types of medical management or intervention in cases of hearing loss. Recent advances in treatment of allergies (which in some cases lead to blockage of the eustachian tube) have also added to the many ways in which the physician can assist in reducing the number of children with significant hearing impairment. However, it must be noted that, despite these advances and the improvements effected from presently ongoing research, the hearing impaired population will apparently remain sufficiently large in the foreseeable future to require continued effort, both medically and educationally.

Audiometry and the role of the audiologist

Audiometry is the measurement of hearing. According to Davis and Silverman (1978), there are at least four major purposes of audiometry. These are: (1) to assist in medical diagnosis, (2) to determine the fitness of the individual for certain duties, probable need for special education, or other special assistance, (3) to screen individuals, and (4) to determine the existence of changes in hearing that may have occurred as a result of some recognized hazard to hearing. Of these four general purposes, school personnel will usually be more familiar with screening audiometry and the audiometric evaluations of children who need special education services. School-originated audiometric evaluation that results in further medical assessment—and in some instances, corrective surgery—may be among the most beneficial of the audiometric work taking place in the schools.

Although otologists (physicians who deal with medical management of hearing, especially diseases of the ear) may satisfactorily use tuning forks that have been standardized at certain frequencies, audiometry in the school will more often be done with the Pure-Tone Audiometer. In the typical procedure a *sweep test* is conducted, on an individual basis, at established frequencies. These frequencies range from 500 hertz (Hz) to 6,000 Hz. If possible problems are detected in this sweep test, a more extensive evaluation will be made, covering a wider range of frequency, usually from 125 to 8,000 Hz. The range of tests and procedures are much too complex to present here. There are sensitivity and discrimination tests, bone-conduction and impedance tests, tests designed especially for infants and for older adults, continuous-tone versus pulsed-tone threshold audiometry, and a variety of other specialized tests.

In summary, the audiometric procedures carried out by the audiologist are designed to measure various aspects of hearing in order to provide guidance for the efforts of others. When the field of audiology first developed, most audiologists had a purely medical role, but in recent years they have become regular members of the special education team in the public schools. Their role is critically important to any successful program for the hearing impaired.

Prevalence of hearing impairment

As indicated in Table 3-1 on p. 54, there are estimated to be some 275,000 to 385,000 hearing impaired children between the ages of 5 and 18 in the United States. This estimate, which includes all degrees of severity, means that from 0.5 to 0.7 percent of the school age population is hearing impaired. Of this group, perhaps as many as 100,000 have received some type of special educational services, and the estimate that there are more than 200,000 more to serve is based on data from school districts where a very concerted effort to find and serve the mildly and moderately hearing impaired have been instituted. Unfortunately, at present there is no accurate way to establish the number of such children who may be making fair progress through our schools but who would certainly fare much better academically if they were to receive appropriate assistance.

Since we cannot establish the actual number of hearing impaired with certainty, it serves little purpose to speculate more on actual numbers, but certain characteristics and facts regarding the hearing impaired population should be noted. These include the following:

1. Since the beginning of record-keeping in the United States, males have outnumbered females among the known population of hearing impaired.
2. Though our major concern in this text is

hearing impairment among children and youth, it must be noted that a higher percentage of hearing impairment exists among the adult population, primarily because of hearing loss related to the aging process.

3. The incidence of new cases of hearing impairment may vary from year to year because of factors such as major rubella epidemics. This leads to predictable variations in prevalence (total number).
4. Included in prevalence data are an increasing number of multihandicapped children. This may be the result of better medical procedures leading to lower infant death rates among the multihandicapped, to laws that have led to such children being served, or both.
5. A growing percentage of minority children are being served in programs for the deaf. This probably results from legislation and general societal changes leading to more nearly equal educational opportunity for all children.

As better audiometric procedures are available to more areas of the nation, and as we attempt to truly serve *all* handicapped children and youth, we will more nearly approach the estimated prevalence of 0.5 percent of all school-age children being served—at some point in their school career—as hearing impaired.

Identification of children who are hearing impaired

Children who are hearing impaired may have a number of observable behaviors, which we tend to call "characteristics" and which are direct results of their basic difficulty, a hearing loss. As for identification, in the 1980s most children who are severely or profoundly hearing impaired will have been properly identified at a relatively young age (a few months to 1 or 2 years of age),* but the mildly and moderately hearing impaired may not be identified until they reach school. In the public school, they will be recognized as having educational difficulty, but this difficulty may be inaccurately believed to be related to mild mental retardation, emotional disturbance, or learning disability. In some instances, depending on the child's coping mechanisms, he or she will be viewed as simply "stubborn" or "unusually quiet." It is therefore well for the teacher to be aware of the indicators that *may* indicate the presence of a mild or moderate hearing loss. The following behaviors are commonly observed in children with mild or moderate hearing impairment, and should be the basis for referral for further evaluation by a diagnostic/assessment team (Gearheart and Weishahn, 1980).

Lack of attention: If a child does not pay attention, it is possible that he cannot hear what is being said. Another possibility may be that the child hears sounds but that they are so distorted it is difficult for him to understand. Consequently, he tunes them out or does not make the effort to attend to them.

Turning or cocking of head: Another behavior that may indicate the child has a hearing loss is an unusual amount of cocking the head to one side. The child may need to turn one ear toward the speaker to hear more effectively. In addition, the child with a hearing loss may make frequent requests for repetitions.

Difficulty in following directions: The child

---

*In contrast, 20 to 30 years ago, even the severely and profoundly hearing impaired were at times mistakenly identified as mentally retarded and proper identification was not made until they were much older. A few were even institutionalized on this basis, and their handicap was not properly diagnosed until they were adults. This is unlikely today, but still must be considered as a possibility.

who has little difficulty with written directions and considerable difficulty with oral directions may have a hearing loss. Also, if a child often loses his place in oral reading assignments, it could be because he has difficulty hearing what the others are reading.

Acting out, stubborn, shy, or withdrawn: Have you ever tried to listen to a speaker who was talking so softly you had difficulty hearing him? You could see his lips move but were unable to hear what was being said. This may help explain why a child with a hearing loss may seem stubborn, disobedient, shy, or withdrawn. If the child is unable to hear, personality and behavior problems may arise. He or she may be compensating for an inability to hear by acting out in the classroom. Other hearing impaired children compensate by withdrawing, acting stubborn, or appearing to be shy.

Reluctance to participate in oral activities: A less extreme behavior sometimes characteristic of the hearing impaired child is a reluctance to participate in oral activities. Another possible identifying characteristic of the child with a hearing loss is a lack of a sense of humor. The child who does not laugh at a joke may not be hearing the joke.

Dependence on classmates for instructions: Another characteristic involves the tendency to watch classmates to see what they are doing before starting to work. The child may not have fully heard or understood the directions given and will look for a cue from classmates or the teacher.

Best achievement in small groups: If the child seems to work best in small groups or in a relatively quiet working area, this may be an indication of a hearing loss. More success with tasks assigned by the teacher at a relatively close distance or in an uncluttered auditory area (compared with tasks assigned at a distance or in a noisy situation) may also be an indication.

Speech defects: Although children with speech defects *may* have perfect hearing, children with hearing losses tend to develop speech defects. It is fairly common that these would include omissions or distortions, and may often occur in instances where the listener must be able to make fine discriminations between similar sounds such as between /f/ and /th/ or between /f/ and /s/. In other instances the child may talk too loudly or too softly. In case any of the above seem to be occurring, the child should be referred for an audiologic examination.

Disparity between expected and actual achievement: Another possible indication of a hearing loss is a disparity between expected and actual achievement. Obviously, there may be many reasons for a child not achieving in a manner consistent with ability, but the teacher should be aware that one of the reasons may be a hearing loss.

Medical indications: There are certain medical indications of a hearing loss that should not be ignored by the teacher. These include frequent earaches, sore throats, or fluid running from the ears. Such physical characteristics should be brought to the attention of the school nurse and the parents for further medical examination.

Major methods used to teach the hearing impaired

According to Moores (1978) educators of the hearing impaired in the United States today are *oralists;* that is, all are concerned with developing a child's speaking ability and ability to understand the spoken word to the highest degree possible. The controversies exist between the "pure oralists" and those who advocate an "oral-plus" approach. There are also a number of controversies, some quite bitter, between those who advocate variations of the major approaches. We will consider some of the more regularly recognized approaches in the discussion that follows. Readers should be aware that variations of these approaches may be supported by teachers or parents in various areas of the nation (under some specific name), and those supporters may believe their approach is the "only" way and that it must not be subsumed under any other title or label or it will lose its viability. Outside observers may find it difficult to understand the fervor with which some individuals defend their system or approach; however, this has been a part of the history of education of the deaf since its very beginning.

The *pure oral, or the oral-aural, method* is one in which children receive language input only through speechreading and amplification of sound. They are permitted to express themselves only in speech; signs and gestures are prohibited. At times the oral method has meant that in early years, both reading and writing were discouraged because of their possibly inhibiting effect on the development of speech. Not too many years ago, in some such programs, children were punished for using signs and gestures, but evidence indicates that they did so secretly anyway.

Methods such as *acoupedics* or others that might be called *auditory methods* are similar to the oral, but in addition they discourage speech-reading. These methods, more likely to be used by children with moderate hearing losses, are designed to develop listening skills to the maximum. In both the oral and the auditory methods, reading and writing are added to the curriculum after maximal speech development is attained.

The *Rochester method* combines many aspects of the oral method with fingerspelling (Fig. 5-2). Children are taught to use speechreading to the fullest, are encouraged to receive all possible information through whatever residual hearing they may have, and are taught to use fingerspelling while speaking. In contrast to some versions of early oralism, reading and writing are given considerable emphasis.

Total communication, according to Garretson (1976) of Gallaudet College, is "neither a method nor a prescribed system of instruction." (p. 90) Rather, it is a philosophy "that encourages a climate of communication flexibility for the deaf person free of ambiguity, guesswork, and stress." (p. 90) Some type of total communication appears to be the direction in which education of the hearing impaired is presently moving. A committee to define total communication established by the 1976 Conference of Executives of American Schools for the Deaf reported the following definition to the CEASD meeting in May, 1976: "Total communication is a philosophy incorporating appropriate aural, manual, and oral modes of communication in order to ensure effective communication with and among hearing impaired persons." (1976 CEASD Conference Proceedings) Data presented by Garretson (1976) indicates a rapid move to some form of total communication system by a majority of the larger schools for the deaf, and public school programs also appear to be moving in this direction. Total communication programs require acceptance of the following assumptions and principles if they are to be maximally effective (adapted from Garretson, 1976):

1. All visual, manual, oral, and auditory roles in the communicative process can be complementary.
2. Early identification and acceptance of hearing impairment by both parents and school and immediate provision for opportunities for communication and language development are essential. (This means communication by whatever combination of modes appear to be most effective.)
3. Multisensory approaches are of great importance. The hearing impaired require a totality of visual support, but other sensory

modes must also be recognized and exercised as required.
4. Provision must be made for different levels of ability in the various modes of communication. Increased likelihood of incidental learning occurs when teachers and staff members utilize all modes when communicating among themselves in the presence of a deaf child.
5. A staff development program must be implemented in which skills in amplification, manual, and speechreading approaches are emphasized.
6. Staff must be aware of the implications for total communication beyond the classroom. This may involve social and cultural as well as the more traditional instructional roles of the teacher. Such areas as personal counseling, peer interaction, and after-school activities must be used if total communication is to be fully effective.

In commenting on what they call "the communication controversy," Davis and Silverman (1978) recognized two major methods or general strategies. The first they call the "auditory global method." They indicate that the terms "auditory-oral," "aural-oral," "acoupedic," "natural," and "unisensory" are all synonyms for the same fundamental method. They describe this method as one in which "the primary, though not always exclusive, channel for speech and language development is auditory and . . . the input is fluent, connected speech." (p. 442) They note that although the more enthusiastic followers of this approach believe it will work with essentially all hearing impaired children, they think that "the Auditory Global Method will not be attainable, for whatever reason, for all children." (p. 443) They further note that even when the major goal is oral competence, "alternate methods or modifications need to be considered—for example, those that stress multisensory stimulation . . . deliberate development of and drill on speech sounds and their combinations . . . and more structured language instruction." (p. 443)

The second method recognized by Davis and Silverman is one they characterize as "best subsumed under the rubric *Total Communication*." (p. 443) Advocates of this method accept the possibility that manual forms of communication may be of value in some cases. These advocates cite the possibility that sole reliance on speechreading and residual hearing (if such exists) may lead to ambiguous or deficient communication, which in turn leads to retarded cognitive development. They also accept the need for an active "deaf community," which can provide a security for deaf adults that may not be present in the hearing community. Davis and Silverman note that there are many variations within this general category and numerous disagreements regarding the effects of sign language on the development of other language functions, and the question of when, how, and what type of manual communication is acceptable.

Other authorities in the education of hearing impaired might use other systems to identify existing methods, but most would be somewhat similar to these two systems. However, that is far from the end of the methods controversy. Further differences exist regarding which of the manual systems should be used in combination with whatever oral methods are used. These differences serve to retard the development of better understanding of the benefits that may be derived from the approaches Davis and Silverman characterize as "total communication." These manual systems will be considered in the following section.

MANUAL COMMUNICATION SYSTEMS

The oldest of the recognized manual communication systems in use in the United

States today is *American Sign Language (ASL)*. In a study completed in relation to the Bilingual Courts Act, it was noted that ASL is the fourth most commonly used language in the United States today; only English, Spanish, and Italian are regularly used by more citizens (O'Rourke, 1975). Most television viewers have become accustomed to seeing some sort of manual system on selected television programs, and a number of cities have started to provide manual translation in such functions as city government as city council meetings, school board meetings, and special election notices on television. Some churches provide manual communication as part of religious services, and the American public generally accepts this as one of those things we do for handicapped persons—but most non—hearing impaired probably do not fully understand the intricacies and difficulties involved in manual communication.

Since the mid-1960s there has been a rush to develop modifications of American Sign Language to better represent English. These attempts have succeeded to some extent, but the manner in which they have developed has led to another confusing situation for those who train teachers for the hearing impaired, and, more importantly for the hearing impaired themselves. It is difficult to find a really objective discussion of this situation, since many who are writing about it have some considerable emotional or financial investment, but those training to teach the deaf are forced to enter the controversy, and often become dogmatic converts to one system or another.*

Among the recognized systems (other than ASL) are the following:

Seeing Essential English (SEE$_1$) was the attempt to provide a formal sign system that would provide a more definite parallel to English but be related to ASL. It was developed by David Anthony. SEE$_1$ follows the English word order, has signs for all English pronouns, and is syntactically very similar to English. SEE$_1$ appears to have the largest vocabulary of the various systems described here, and probably should be called the most complex. Its complexity and the possibility that it might be too difficult for many of the deaf persons for whom it was intended were part of the reason for the development of SEE$_2$.

Signing Exact English (SEE$_2$) was developed by Gustason, Pfetzing, and Zawalkow (former members of the SEE$_1$ group) in an attempt to provide a substitute for SEE$_1$, which they believed was becoming too distant from ASL (Bornstein, 1973, p. 461; Davis and Silverman, 1978, p. 409). Like SEE$_1$ it follows English word order, a need acknowledged by most educators of the hearing impaired. One major difference in SEE$_1$ and SEE$_2$ is that of printed presentation. SEE$_1$ is presented in a system that includes symbols for many different handshapes, two hand positions, and different directions for these two positions. SEE$_2$ symbols are presented in drawings and apparently are more similar to ASL.

Linguistics of Visual English (LOVE or LVE)

---

*I have attempted to gain further insight into this situation from a number of professional colleagues who train teachers of the deaf. Most have definite "preferences" if not biases, but the substance of what they have said is that the writings of strong advocates of any specific system will likely lead to added confusion. I would suggest that those who wish to read further about this controversial but highly interesting topic should read Moores (1978, pp. 15-18, 154-185); Davis and Silverman (1978, pp. 400-415); and Bornstein (1973, pp. 454-463). Each of these references provides a good resource for those who want to examine this question from an objective point of view. Most of the information presented in this section was derived from these three sources.

Sensory impairments

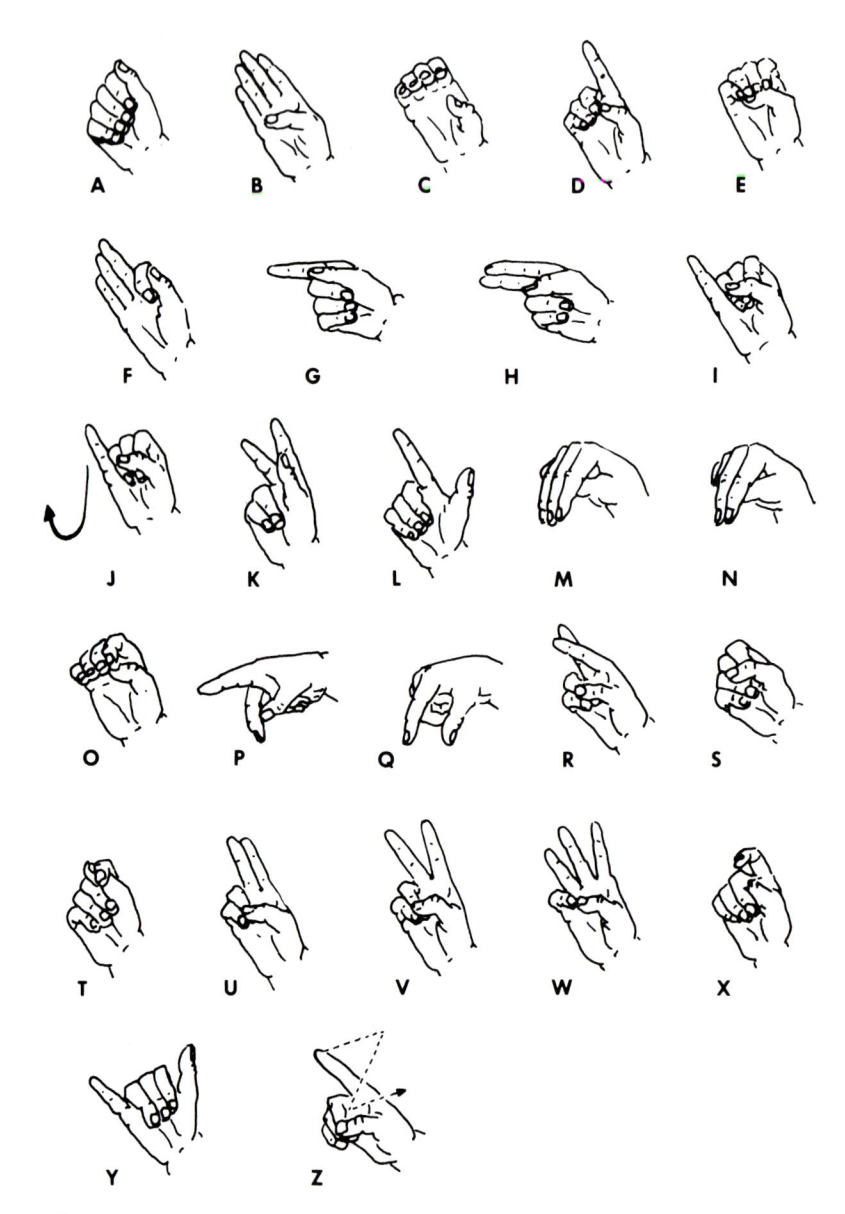

Fig. 5-2. Traditional manual alphabet. (From Litton, F. W. *Education of the Trainable Mentally Retarded.* St. Louis: The C. V. Mosby Co., 1978.)

was developed by Wampler, primarily for use with preschool and kindergarten children. Its intent is very similar to that of SEE$_1$ and SEE$_2$ and, like them, it follows English word order. LOVE is primarily a modification of an ASL symbol system.

Signed English was created for a specific group of preschool children as part of a Gallaudet project. A 2500-word vocabulary was assembled, which was felt to represent normal spoken vocabulary for children, plus words needed by parents for proper parenting and management of young children. It was discovered that approximately 1700 of these words were represented by existing ASL words. Sign words for the remaining 800 were taken from other systems or developed specifically for this project. This system has had the advantage of controlled use in this experimental project and has led to some of the same type of positive reports as may be found for the previous three. Like the others, it follows English word order.

There are other less formal sign systems in use in the United States, and an English system in use in England called Systematic Sign Language. One obvious result of the existence of all of these systems is some confusion and some limiting of communication among the deaf who know only one system and must communicate with someone who uses another system. To the extent that all have some similarities to ASL, there can be *some* communication, but it seems very unfortunate that a group of individuals whose major difficulty is with communication skills must have further difficulty because of this state of affairs. This confusion is one of the arguments oralists use to indicate that theirs is the best answer to the controversy. Those who support some sort of total communication program point to the fact that some deaf children *never* learn through oral methods and thus insist on some use of signs. It would seem that before too long some order should come out of this newer interest in sign systems that parallel English, but those who are familiar with the long history of education of the deaf are not too optimistic regarding any such agreement and cooperation. Perhaps some special educators now entering the field can help to bring more order to this important but often confusing area of specialty.

Other educational considerations

Certain other educational considerations should be explored to permit the special educator who will *not* specialize in teaching the hearing impaired to better understand the nature of this particular specialty. Those who will specialize in teaching the hearing impaired will go far beyond the contents of this chapter in the first course in their chosen specialty. Others, for example those who will teach the mentally retarded, the learning disabled, or the emotionally disturbed, should know enough to understand the needs of multihandicapped children who have some mild degree of hearing impairment along wih other more serious primary handicaps. These topics will include: (1) The critical need for preschool education, (2) hearing aids, (3) auditory training, (4) speechreading, and (5) classroom adaptations.

Preschool education for the hearing impaired remains a very high priority concern for all educators who work with this population. Despite differences in how children should be taught to communicate, there are essentially no disagreements as to the critical need for preschool for the hearing impaired and for the training of parents to play their proper role prior to formal preschool. With audiometric procedures that permit identification of hearing impairment in newborn infants, parents can be trained to assist in the maximization of language development, and thus improve readiness for academic learning. It is critical that we: (1) arrange for early (infant) hearing screening, (2) make certain that physicians who work with young children conduct meaningful hearing screening as part of regular physical examinations and make further referrals as needed, and (3) make certain that the public schools and other appropriate community agencies work together to assure the existence of preschool programs for hearing impaired children and their parents. Appropriate preschool programs can greatly improve the performance of hearing impaired children and reduce the need for costly services when they are older. Such programs are in existence in many parts of the nation and must be initiated in other areas, if hearing impaired children are to attain maximum benefit from later formal education efforts.

Hearing aids are quite important for most hearing impaired students. On the other hand, some hearing impairments are such that a hearing aid cannot help. Determination of the type of aid, how it is worn, and other such details are quite technical and must be left to the experts, but two generalizations can be safely made. First, the hearing aid for any given student must be designed to amplify speech with a minimum of distortion but must not subject the user to distraction or discomfort from overly loud volume. Second, the teacher should play a role in checking to see if the batteries are functioning, whether the ear mold is properly inserted, and other such details (it may be particularly important to assist very young children); but the teacher should *not* get into the business of recommending a specific type or brand of hearing aid. If a student is not using the aid (will not wear it or constantly turns it off), the parent should be told, but selection of hearing aids is a personal matter, just as is selection of the medical doctor.

In addition to a variety of personal hearing aids, group hearing aids are in relatively common use in classes for the hearing impaired. The more modern of these systems are wireless, with (for example) the teacher wearing a small radio transmitter and each student wearing a small receiver and earphones. Students who pursue further training in education of the hearing impaired will become familiar with a variety of such systems; with the development of better electronic devices, such systems will undoubtedly continue to improve.

It must be recognized that the hearing aid *cannot* fully compensate for a hearing loss. Practical limits are imposed both by the type of hearing loss and by the nature of the sounds that we expect to hear. Because human speech is a mixture of sounds of different intensities, to make some sound audible (in certain types of hearing impairment) other sounds may become nearly intolerable. The final, basic reason for using a hearing aid is to make *speech* more intelligible, and certain compromises must be made in many instances. Knowledge regarding the simplicity of this goal, yet the complexity of accomplishing it in some instances, is most important.

Auditory training simply means training the student to use all available auditory sense to the fullest in the development of language and communication. Most normally hearing students acquire language in an almost automatic manner, because of their continued interaction with others in their environment (this occurs, presuming that they have no other handicapping conditions and that their environment is relatively normal). The hearing impaired child, particularly the child with congenital hearing impairment, must receive planned, systematic auditory training to maximize his or her ability to communicate through oral language.

The usual first step in auditory training is selection and evaluation of the appropriate

These hearing impaired students are discussing a videotape they have just viewed.

hearing aid(s) (Davis and Silverman, 1978). With young children, this may be quite difficult because the child may have little vocabulary with which to describe sensory impressions. However, guidelines have been established that usually work satisfactorily for initial selection. After doing all possible to increase amplification, the most common procedure is to do whatever possible to increase the child's awareness of the sounds of the general environment and especially of speech. This may be accomplished both at home (parents need training to perform this task with maximum effectiveness) and in the school setting. Listening games are effective with young children and can be used to motivate them and maintain attention for a relatively long period of time.

The final goal of auditory training is auditory comprehension of connected speech, and in many hearing impaired children this is possible with an adequate hearing aid and auditory training. With others, the degree of loss may be such that auditory training can only lead to the development of cues by which other modes of communication may be utilized. One of these other approaches, speechreading, will be considered next.

Speechreading (earlier called lipreading) means understanding through visual means what a speaker is attempting to communicate. Most speechreading must take place in a setting where the speaker is communicating orally (to others) and the speechreader must decode visual cues that in many ways are only incidental to the oral communication.

Speechreading is in some ways similar to reading the printed page, except the reader can control the speed of reading printed language, and speechreading cannot be "re-read" unless the speaker repeats. Also, in speaking, it is common to be less precise and follow less formal rules than in written communication. Still other problems include: (1) many "sounds" look alike on the lips of the speaker, (2) lighting and distance cause difficulties, (3) the speaker, particularly the classroom teacher who is also using a chalkboard, often turns away for a moment at an inopportune time, and (4) at times there is little or no oral punctuation.

The preceding list could be lengthened, but the point has been made—speechreading as the major tool for understanding the oral language of others is difficult. As a tool to *assist* with limited auditory ability it is most valuable. Speechreading, according to Moores (1978), has not been improved in recent years because it has not had concerted attention. Although speechreading is considered a part of total communication, it has apparently received less attention than many other facets of total communication. According to Moores (1978), "aside from the utilization of film in teaching speechreading, no new methods have been developed since 1930 . . . new techniques in reality involve combinations of old methods." (p. 240) It should be noted that most of the speechreading methods presently in use in the United States were apparently developed for use with hard-of-hearing or deafened persons who had already developed spoken language. It would seem that new methods are needed, focusing on the needs of the congenitally hearing impaired.

Classroom adaptations may be made by the various teachers who may work with the hearing impaired, if they remain aware of the child's special needs. One of the major concerns will relate to how the teacher teaches. Is it mainly lecture and does the teacher sometimes talk with his or her back to the class? How about instructions given while writing at the chalkboard? Does the teacher enunciate clearly, use complete sentences, and repeat involved instructions? Distinct articulation is good; overly loud or exaggerated speech is not desirable.

Seating of the hearing impaired child is most important. He or she should be close to the teacher but should be in a position to see other children whenever possible. The teacher should be aware of proper lighting (adequate light on the face, avoiding strong light behind the teacher) and of the need to repeat more often than usual and to question and encourage questions from the students. Such practices are essential to assist the hearing impaired to learn effectively despite the impairment.

In composite, most of the suggestions and ideas presented in this section are just good common sense. But they are common sense only as we more fully understand the unique educational needs of the hearing impaired. Much of the highly specialized education of hearing impaired students will take place with a qualified specialist, but to the extent that these students are in the regular class, all educators must understand their needs. Also, to the extent that specialists in other areas of handicap will work with students who have some degree of hearing loss in addition to their primary handicap, all special education teachers should have a basic understanding of the educational needs of the hearing impaired.

Educational settings: the question of maximal integration of the hearing impaired

There is little question that the direction of movement of special education programming since the late 1960s has been toward the return of mildly handicapped children to the regular class program, and maximum integration of all others. The question still unanswered to the satisfaction of all concerned (parents, children, and educators) is how to determine with certainty what "maximum" means when considered in individual cases. This question has been particularly troublesome in planning educational programs for the hearing impaired, and there has perhaps been *less* strong support from within the ranks of educators of the deaf than has been the case in other areas of handicap. Moores (1978) makes the point that further integration of deaf children with the nonhandicapped has been proposed by those outside the area, and seems to indicate that perhaps they should get their own areas of specialty in order before getting into this field of specialization. Other educators of the hearing impaired also seem less concerned about making radical program changes regarding "mainstreaming" than their contemporaries in mental retardation. Also, parents do not seem to be agitating for integrated or mainstreamed classes on a nationwide basis, although there have been instances where they have initiated litigation directed toward forcing the local school district to provide educational programs in the home school district rather than sending all deaf children to state funded residential schools (Biklen, 1975). It should be noted that in such cases the question was apparently not the "label" of deaf, but rather the desire to have the children at home—a desire that was rather quickly met, thus the court suit was dropped.

A point made by Moores (1978) and echoed by others is that residential schools for the deaf cannot be equated with institutions for the retarded, which were the subject of court decisions that seemed to indicate that institutional placement was, in nearly all cases, highly undesirable. Educators of the hearing impaired *have* supported integration of hearing impaired children, but apparently believe that the issue cannot be applied to the hearing impaired in exactly the same manner as it has been applied to other handicapped children. The lack of court decisions relative to this question would seem to indicate that: (1) parents of the hearing impaired are not as active and/or interested in their children's welfare or (2) the issue of placement in various types of educational programs (residential, special classes, resource rooms, etc.) is appreciably different from placement of the mentally retarded or (3) both. Because all evidence indicates that parents of the hearing impaired are quite active and interested in their children's welfare, we can only reasonably conclude that the second factor is in effect. Although a significant number of parents of hearing impaired students are asking (or demanding) that the program for their child be provided in the local school district, they seem to be more concerned with the quality of instruction the child receives than with the percentage of the school day the child spends with nonhandicapped children. It must also be noted that many parents remain satisfied with the state residential schools, particularly parents of children with severe and profound hearing losses. As for the nationwide trend toward mainstreaming, which was given further impetus by the wording of PL 94-142, the hearing impaired and the visually impaired were perhaps *less* affected by this trend, because each of these areas had been involved in various degrees of mainstreaming for many years. Perhaps the only major effect was that local districts became more involved in providing programs, as opposed to sending children to state schools. This was considerably different from the activity that occurred with respect to the educable mentally handicapped—activity that included the abandonment of many self-contained classes and, in some cases, abandonment of any effective pro-

Sensory impairments

gramming for those with milder impairments. In many instances, the number of self-contained classes for hearing impaired children (especially for the young, profoundly hearing impaired) have *increased* in the past several years.

An educational placement system: application of the variable service continuum concept

It has been repeatedly emphasized that educational placement of the hearing impaired child must be based on many factors. The most important of these factors include: (1) age of onset of hearing loss, (2) degree of hearing loss, and (3) level of intelligence. Other factors of importance include: (4) nature of early childhood training and experiences, (5) degree of involvement of parents and whether they are hearing impaired, and (6) in some instances, type of hearing loss. Because of the manner in which these factors interrelate, there is no meaningful way in which we may chart or otherwise predict with total accuracy

TABLE 5-2
Guidelines for educational placement of the hearing impaired

Hearing threshold levels	Probable communication/ language impact	Educational placement	Probable need
Level I 26-54 dB	Mild	Regular class and consultative assistance	Most frequent
		Regular class and resource room assistance	Most frequent
		Regular class and special class half/half	Infrequent
		Special class and limited integration	—
		Special day school	—
		Residential school	—
Level II 55-69 dB	Moderate	Regular class and consultative assistance	Infrequent
		Regular class and resource room assistance	Frequent
		Regular class and special class half/half	Most frequent
		Special class and limited integration	Frequent
		Special day school	Infrequent
		Residential school	Infrequent
Level III 70-89 dB	Severe	Regular class and consultative assistance	Infrequent
		Regular class and resource room assistance	Infrequent
		Regular class and special class half/half	Most frequent
		Special class and limited integration	Most frequent
		Special day school	Frequent
		Residential school	Frequent
Level IV 90 dB and above	Profound	Regular class and consultative assistance	Infrequent
		Regular class and resource room assistance	Infrequent
		Regular class and special class half/half	Frequent
		Special class and limited integration	Most frequent
		Special day school	Most frequent
		Residential school	Most frequent

just which educational setting may prove to be the most effective. We must also remember that the appropriateness of any given placement may change as a child grows older or as other factors change. Nevertheless, it is possible to provide very general guidelines to serve as a starting point for planning. The guidelines in Table 5-2 are adapted from a variety of sources, including recommendations of national study groups and various state guidelines. In each case, the least restrictive setting (consistent with maximum educational effectiveness) should be selected. In addition, regular program reviews (preferably twice annually) should be made to determine the need for possible changes in placement.

The most important facet of the principle of the variable service continuum is implied by the term *variable*. In addition to variations dictated by degree of hearing loss, time of onset, and level of intelligence, there are important variations relating to the phase of the total educational program through which the student is proceeding. Especially in the case of students with severe and profound losses, some educational levels require much more specialized programming than others. In general, these are the preschool, very early grade levels, and secondary levels. *The degree of emphasis will vary from student to student, and overgeneralization is inconsistent with the principle of individualization, but the fact that the needs are variable, and thus require the capability (on the part of the local educational agency) to respond differentially in the case of various students, is of prime importance.*

The Office of Demographic Studies of Gallaudet College is responsible for providing reliable status reports regarding various important questions in the field of education of hearing impaired children and youth. In one such report, entitled "Who are the deaf children in 'mainstream' programs?"* Karchmer and Trybus (1977) summarized data they had

TABLE 5-3
Where do hearing impaired children go to school? (N = 49,427)

	Percent
Residential schools for the deaf	38
Full-time special education classes	22
Integrated or "mainstreamed" programs	19
Day schools for the deaf	11
Other programs	10

*This report is a good example of the manner in which even highly recognized groups/authorities may use the terms "deaf" and "hearing impaired" interchangeably. This report is specifically about various levels of hearing impairment, and "hearing impairment" is used throughout the report. However, "deaf" is used in the title.

TABLE 5-4
Distribution of hearing loss by type of program

Hearing loss	Residential schools (%)	Day schools (%)	Full-time class in local public schools (%)	Integrated programs (%)
Mild	1	2	4	22
Moderate	9	18	26	40
Severe	27	28	29	20
Profound	63	52	42	18

gathered from several sources. They analyzed placements with regard to five major categories: (1) residential schools for the deaf, (2) day schools for the deaf (all classes for deaf children but no residential accommodations), (3) full-time classes (full-time in class with only hearing impaired children, but in a regular public school), (4) integrated or "mainstreamed" (part-time special classes, resource rooms, or itinerant services) and (5) others. Some of their more interesting findings are given in Tables 5-3 and 5-4.

This study also reported that integrated programs have the lowest proportion of children with two deaf parents and the highest proportion of children who have "intelligible" or "very intelligible" speech. This is highly consistent with the fact that they also have the lowest proportion of children with severe or profound hearing losses. The concluding statement in this part of the report is: "For the present . . . it is clear that the integrated programs are generally serving a group of hearing impaired children *who are very different on many educationally critical dimensions* from those children who attend other types of special education programs." (p. 3) This statement of what Karchmer and Trybus (1977) call "the current realities of the field" (p. 1) reflects the reasons why we must always provide a full continuum of programs and services and serves as a fitting conclusion to this discussion of integration of the hearing impaired and the application of a variable service continuum concept.

Summary

Education of the hearing impaired appears to qualify for the title of "oldest" among the handicapping conditions as far as organized efforts to serve students is concerned. From earliest times, the deaf have had serious difficulties because they did not develop language, and the phrase "deaf and dumb" became accepted as a statement of fact. Because of the assumption that they would be unable to develop language and thus would be unable to think, some deaf infants were put to death; however, the most common practice was to consider the deaf unfit to hold the normal rights of citizenship. As a result of their second-class status, the deaf were often mistreated, were not eligible for rights of inheritance, and in some cases could not marry. Attempts to assist deaf children to regain these rights, particularly the right of inheritance, was the major motivation for some of the first successful efforts to teach the deaf. The fact that learning to speak and write led to reinstatement of normal rights indicates that it was not the deafness, but the resultant effect on communication skills that led to the early difficulties of the deaf. This result of deafness remains the major difficulty to this day. There is little historical record regarding those individuals with mild or moderate hearing impairments. It is safe to assume that if they had enough hearing to develop language, they were, for the most part, simply overlooked as a recognized group. They could not have made accomplishments in proportion to their intellectual abilities, but until the twentieth century, there was little concern for this principle with regard to any of the more mildly handicapped.

From the earliest of times, there has been controversy as to the best way to teach the deaf. In general it is a question of whether oral or manual communication should be used or how much manual communication can be properly used in combination with oral approach components. The following statements seem to reflect the actual status of this approach controversy at this point in history: (1) a majority of educators of the deaf appear to be "oralists" in principle, but many will accept the use of some manual communication with some children, (2) "total communication," a combination of oral approach components plus a version of manual communication designed to be more similar to spoken English than American Sign Language (ASL) is growing in acceptance for use with the severely and profoundly deaf *(which version* of manual communication remains open for debate), (3) American Sign Language, the type of manual communication that many educators of the deaf are trying to get away from is used by a very large number of deaf adults, and is taught (by parents) to many congenitally deaf children. (ASL is the fourth most commonly used language in the United States; English, Spanish, and Italian are the only ones spoken by more persons.)

The causes of hearing impairment are relatively well known, and medical and surgical treatment of hearing impairment is well established. Audiometric procedures, commencing with techniques to identify hearing losses in infants and continuing through efforts to assist the elderly with the hearing loss that comes as part of the aging process, have advanced a great deal in the last 20 years, as has the science of amplification. In addition to much better personal hearing aids, we now have excellent group training equipment for use in programs for students who need auditory training. These advances are a result of recent strides in electronic technology, and in some cases have led to improvements that educators must still learn to use with maximum effectiveness.

There are many ways to categorize hearing losses, including where (physiologically) the loss occurs, when it occurred, how great the loss is, or, in some cases, behavioral manifestations. A great deal is now known about diseases that lead to hearing loss, and great strides have been taken in reducing the effect of a wide variety of causal factors.

For educational purposes, the hearing impaired, like other handicapped students, should be in the most "normal" environment consistent with achieving major educational goals. On a national basis there has been an increase in public school programs for the hearing impaired, and most of these programs are designed to maximize the amount of the school day spent in a regular class setting. Preschool programs have continued to expand, and there have not been the questions regarding negative effects of labeling that sometimes occur when preschool efforts for the learning disabled and the mildly mentally retarded are considered.

Educational programs for the hearing impaired have made great progress since the first actual schools for the deaf were established some 200 years ago. With ongoing research in a number of critical program areas and with recent advances in electronic technology and medical knowledge, the future of the hearing impaired in the United States looks very bright.

Sensory impairments

focus

introduction

Education of the deaf was the first organized programming for the handicapped in the United States. In addition, it is the only area of handicap that is sufficiently "special" to have warranted a separate college for those with such a handicap.

early history

Social acceptance of the deaf has been extremely low for hundreds of years, primarily because of their difficulty with language usage and with traditional academic learning.

establishment of schools in Europe

Great Britain, France, and Germany all contributed valuable efforts to the fledgling area of education of the deaf.

Heinicke in Germany and de l'Epee in France started a controversy (oralism versus manualism) that has been fought by various educators of the deaf, down to the present time.

establishment of schools in the United States

The first permanent school for the deaf in the United States was established at Hartford, Connecticut, and was called the American Asylum for the Education and Instruction of the Deaf and Dumb.

Gallaudet College is internationally recognized, grants undergraduate, master's and doctor's degrees, carries out a variety of research programs, and is the only such institution in the world.

anatomy and physiology of the auditory system

The pinna and the external auditory canal (meatus) are the only parts of the ear that most individuals usually see and they serve primarily as a "funnel" for sound waves.

The function of the middle ear is to transmit sound (vibrations of the tympanic membrane) to the inner ear.

There are some 24,000 hair cells in the human ear, which can respond to sound. If all is working properly, when the vibrations reach the hair cells of the organ of Corti, an impulse is sent to the brain.

In addition to the way in which the organ of Corti "feels" sound that enters the outer ear and travels through the ear in the normal manner, it may also "feel" vibrations transmitted directly through the bones of the skull. This is called *bone conduction.*

definitions: types and degrees of hearing impairment

A *deaf* person is one whose hearing disability is so great that he or she cannot understand speech through use of the ear alone, with or without a hearing aid. A *hard-of-hearing* person is one whose hearing disability makes it difficult to hear but who can, with or without the use of a hearing aid, understand speech.

causes of hearing impairment

In many studies of deafness (or hearing impairment) somewhat less than half of the cases can be related to known causes, thus resultant data must be considered in this light.

medical and surgical treatment of hearing impairment

The potential role of the physician is as great or greater with respect to the hearing impaired than with any other handicapping condition. The physician's role includes prevention, surgical treatment, and more exotic treatments such as cochlear implantation of electrodes that can deliver electrical stimulation to auditory nerve fibers.

audiometry and the role of the audiologist

The four major purposes of audiometry are: (1) to assist in medical diagnosis, (2) to determine the fitness of the individual for certain duties, probable need for special education, or other special assistance, (3) to screen individuals, and (4) to determine the existence of changes in hearing that may have occurred as a result of some recognized hazard to hearing.

major methods used to teach the hearing impaired

Educators of the hearing impaired in the United States today are oralists; that is, all are concerned with developing a child's speaking ability and ability to understand the spoken word to the highest degree possible. The controversies exist between the "pure oralists" and those who advocate an "oral-plus" approach.

Total communication is "neither a method nor a prescribed system of instruction." Rather, it is a philosophy "that encourages a climate of communication flexibility for the deaf person free of ambiguity, guesswork, and stress."

Sensory impairments

manual communication systems

The oldest of the recognized manual communication systems in use in the United States today is *American Sign Language* (**ASL**). **ASL** is the fourth most commonly used language in the United States today; only English, Spanish, and Italian are regularly used by more United States citizens.

other educational considerations

Despite differences in how children should be taught to communicate, there are essentially no disagreements as to the critical need for preschool for the hearing impaired and for the training of parents to play their proper role prior to formal preschool.

The hearing impaired child, particularly the child with congenital hearing impairment, must receive planned, systematic auditory training to maximize his or her ability to communicate through oral language.

The final goal of auditory training is auditory comprehension of connected speech, and in many hearing impaired children this is possible with an adequate hearing aid and auditory training.

Speechreading (earlier called lipreading) means understanding through visual means what a speaker is attempting to communicate.

educational settings: the question of maximal integration of the hearing impaired

Residential schools for the deaf cannot be equated with institutions for the retarded, which were the subject of court decisions that seemed to indicate that institutional placement was, in nearly all cases, highly undesirable.

As for the nationwide trend toward mainstreaming, which was given further impetus by the wording of PL 94-142, the hearing impaired and the visually impaired were perhaps less affected by this trend, because each of these areas had been involved in various degrees of mainstreaming for many years.

an educational placement system: application of the variable service continuum concept

Placement of the hearing impaired child must be based on many factors. The most important of these include: (1) age of onset of hearing loss, (2) degree of hearing loss, and (3) level of intelligence.

"Integrated programs are generally serving a group of hearing impaired children who are very different on many educationally critical dimensions from those children who attend other types of special education programs."

References and suggested readings

Biklin, D. Deaf children vs. the board of education. *American Annals of the Deaf*, 1975, *120*, 382-386.

Bornstein, H. A description of some current sign systems designed to represent English. *American Annals of the Deaf*, June 1973, *118*, 454-463.

Conference of Executives of American Schools for the Deaf, Conference Proceedings, 1976.

Davis, H., and Silverman, S. R. *Hearing and deafness.* New York: Holt, Rinehart, and Winston, 1978.

Deland. *The story of lipreading.* Washington, D.C.: The Volta Bureau, 1931.

Frisna, R. (Ed.) *A bicentennial monograph on hearing impairment: trends in the USA.* Washington, D.C.: The Alexander Graham Bell Association for the Deaf, 1976.

Garretson, M. Total communication. *The Volta Review*, May 1976, *78*(4), pp. 88-95.

Gearheart, B., and Weishahn, M. *The handicapped student in the regular classroom.* St. Louis: The C. V. Mosby Co., 1980.

Karchmer, M., and Trybus, R. *Who are the deaf children in "mainstream" programs?* Research Bulletin, Series R, No. 4. Washington, D.C.: Gallaudet College, Office of Demographic Studies, 1977.

Moores, D. *Educating the deaf: psychology, principles, and practices.* Boston: Houghton-Mifflin Co., 1978.

O'Rourke, T., and others. National Association of the Deaf Communicative Skills Program. Programs for the handicapped, 75 (No. 2). Washington, D.C.: Office for Handicapped Individuals, Department of Health, Education and Welfare, April 15, 1975.

Peet, H. Memoir on origin and early history of the art of instructing the deaf and dumb. *American Annals of the Deaf*, 1853, *3*, 129-161.

Vernon, M. Deaf and hard of hearing. In *Psychological diagnosis of exceptional children.* M. Wisland (Ed.) Springfield, Ill.: Charles C Thomas, Publisher, 1974.

Wilbur, R. Linguistics of manual languages and manual systems. In *Communication assessment and intervention strategies*, L. Lloyd (Ed.). Baltimore: University Park Press, 1976.

A variety of magnification devices may be used by the visually impaired.

chapter 6

Education of children and youth who are visually impaired

objectives

To describe the historical basis for education of the visually impaired as it exists today, emphasizing critical events or turning points.

To present basic information regarding the anatomy and physiology of the visual system, sufficient to permit an understanding of the varying needs of visually impaired students in the schools.

To outline major types of visual impairment, their causes, and medical and/or surgical treatment.

To understand the most common procedures for identification of visually impaired students and why some identification systems are totally ineffective for certain types of disabilities.

To outline and discuss major issues in education of the visually impaired, emphasizing both the teaching of academic/cognitive skills and orientation and mobility training needs.

To explore the variables that must be considered to determine the most appropriate, least restrictive educational environment for the visually impaired student.

Introduction

The visually impaired, unlike the hearing impaired, have not been historically confused wtih the mentally retarded, especially if the visual impairments were severe. Blindness is relatively obvious, and young children who are born blind are usually recognized as being blind at least within a few weeks. On the other hand, the mildly visually impaired, like the mildly hearing impaired, often go unrecognized for many years, their handicap being sufficiently mild that they perform, academically and socially, almost as well as nonhandicapped children. The responsibility of educators of the visually impaired is to discover and assist children with any degree of impairment to use any remaining visual abilities to the maximum or, in the case of total blindness, to learn to use the other senses to compensate for the missing sense of vision.

Our concern in this chapter will be to consider the nature of visual impairment, how educational programs for the visually impaired were started, and how they evolved to the programs existing today. We will review the early history, the development of schools in Europe and the United States, and see that there were considerable parallels between the evolution of programs for the visually impaired and the hearing impaired. The anatomy and physiology of the visual system, a discussion of definitions and terminology, and some consideration of the types and causes of visual impairment will precede the discussion of educational procedures. Other topics such as prevalence data, medical and surgical treatment, and identification procedures will also be considered.

A variety of educational considerations, including reading and writing for the visually impaired, the importance of orientation and mobility training, and the necessity for preschool programming will be highlighted. The chapter will conclude with a discussion of the question of maximum integration of the visually impaired and various educational placement considerations. The need for the provision of a full continuum of educational programs and services and the application of the variable service continuum concept will become obvious.

Historical origins of education of the visually impaired
EARLY HISTORY

As was the case with the hearing impaired, early treatment of the visually impaired (specifically the blind) was varied, but for the most part included primarily negative aspects. The most "negative" was that blind children were sometimes put to death, in a legally approved manner, just as had been the case with the deaf. This appears to have been true in Athens, Rome, and Sparta at various times during the "flowering" of Western civilization. On the other hand, some blind individuals were venerated as sages, another approach that provided a way to remove the blind individual from normal society.

A second evolutionary stage, noted by Lowenfeld (1973) in his account of the history of education of the visually handicapped, was establishment of a type of *ward status*. In the pre-Christian Jewish communities and in the newly developing Christian church, it was a part of religious teaching to consider three groups—orphans, the aged, and the blind—as special wards of the church or synagogue. As a result of this type of thinking, some asylums for the blind were established, but it was more common for the blind to become beggars and to expect alms from the church.

As a result of the protection afforded by the ward status, a number of blind persons became noted as musicians, and by the eighteenth century, other blind individuals had distinguished themselves in various fields of endeavor. Lowenfeld (1973) notes persons such as Nicholas Saunderson (1682-1739), who became a noted professor of mathematics at Cambridge; John Metcalf (1717-1810), an engineer and bridge builder; Thomas Blacklock (1721-1771), a Scotch minister and poet; and Francois Huber (1750-1831), a Swiss naturalist. Another well-known blind person, Maria Theresia von Paradis (1759-1824), a Viennese vocalist and pianist, became a favorite of French society and in an indirect manner played a role in the establishment of the first school for the blind.

ESTABLISHMENT OF SCHOOLS IN EUROPE

Valentin Haüy (1745-1822) was educated in Paris where he was in tune with the intellectual climate and social concerns that were to lead to the French Revolution. Haüy was interested in the work of Abbé de l'Épee in education of the deaf (see p. 112) and after a personal encounter with a Parisian mob in its cruel treatment of ten blind men, he vowed to play a role in providing education for the blind. Haüy became acquainted with Maria Theresia von Paridis and was impressed by her efforts to provide tactile reading for the blind. After observing a blind pupil reading through recognition of the embossed negative of printed letters (on the back of a page), he developed a system of negative type that produced embossed letters. These embossed letters proved to be of great value and established the fact that the blind could read effectively "through their fingers."

Haüy established the first actual school for the blind (The National Institution for Young Blind People) in Paris in 1784. He attempted to pattern educational practices in his school as nearly as possible after the practices in schools for sighted persons and taught the full range of subjects usually provided in most schools. He emphasized handicraft-related education (basketry, chaircaning, sewing, spinning, weaving) and thus established a pattern that was to be followed for years to come. Though overemphasis on these skills later became a problem, at that time these were reasonable vocational skills with good potential for providing independent support. Haüy wrote about his methods and, unlike some of the earliest educators of the deaf, was apparently eager to share his knowledge and promote the establishment of other educational programs for the blind.

Before the turn of the century, there were other schools for the blind established in Liverpool (1791) and Bristol, England (1793), and in Edinburgh, Scotland (1793). By 1810, educational programs had been established in Vienna, Berlin, Milan, Amsterdam, Prague, Stockholm, Zurich, and Dublin (Napier, 1972). These schools, established by interested individuals and church groups, were primarily elementary schools, although they did often include crafts-oriented vocational training. Unlike the early programs for the deaf, there were no highly significant methodologic controversies; most of these programs were similar in most respects to Haüy's program. Blind students in these schools were taught to read through some type of embossed letter type, although other symbolic representations were also tried, for the most part unsuccessfully. With few exceptions, the blind were taught to read, but little attempt was made to find a substitute for writing. This important step was to come later, along with the development of a better means of tactual reading.

To complete the story of the life of Haüy, we must note that he fell into disfavor with Napoleon and left Paris in 1806. He assisted in the opening of a few other schools, tried to assist in establishing a school in Russia, and eventually returned to Paris where he died in relative obscurity. His accomplishments were considerable, and the field of education of the visually impaired is much indebted to his insight and energy.

ESTABLISHMENT OF SCHOOLS IN THE UNITED STATES

The motivation for the first solid concern for education for the blind in the United States apparently was reports of the success of the Haüy school given by Dr. John D. Fisher when he returned from medical studies in France in 1826 (Napier, 1972). In Boston, sentiment among a number of leaders, including some state legislators, ran high. As a result, the New England Asylum for the Blind was incorporated in 1829, and in 1831, Dr. Samuel Gridley Howe, a wealthy Boston physician, was appointed director. Howe went to Europe to study their schools and to find teachers and came back with certain principles that he believed should be used to guide education of the blind in the United States. These principles were (Farrel, 1956):

1. All blind children should be educated in accordance with their personal needs and the likelihood that they can apply such training in their community.
2. The curriculum for schools for the blind should be similar to educational programs for nonhandicapped children, but should include more music and crafts.
3. The major goal of education of the blind should be that they might be able to be contributing members of their home communities.

These educational principles, although simple, can also be considered profound in potential if applied to the fullest. Except for the emphasis on music and crafts and the "home community," these might well be statements of principles provided today.

In an interesting sidelight on the man who gave education of the visually impaired its start in the United States, Lowenfeld (1973) comments about Howe's innovative, adventurous nature. He notes that after attending Harvard Medical School, Howe went to Greece to assist in the struggle for independence there. It was on his return from Greece that he was engaged to "educate sightless persons" by the governing board of the New England Asylum for the Blind. Then, while in Europe, because he was deeply concerned over Polish refugees who had been interned in Prussia, he went to Prussia where he was "imprisoned as a dangerous radical, and was only extricated . . . by the aging Lafayette, who tactfully suggested that he come back to America and look after liberty here." (Lowenfeld, 1973, p. 7) In later years Howe became involved in such issues as the Abolitionist movement, improvement of institutions for the insane, and prison reform. And, although he was involved in the establishment of many institutions for the blind, he was on record as indicating that institutional living conditions were unnatural and that the number of institutions and their size should be kept to a minimum (Howe, 1866).

After the founding of the New England Asylum for the Blind (which was soon renamed the Perkins Institution and Massachusetts Asylum for the Blind), a number of other schools were initiated in other states in the eastern part of the nation. In the beginning, residential schools provided the educational program for nearly all blind students, and by 1870 there were twenty-three schools for the blind in the United States, many of them state supported (Napier, 1972). Residential schools, following the pattern established by Howe in the 1830s, were the major vehicle for education of the blind for more than 100 years. Only recently has this pattern changed substantially, and today only about one third of all visually impaired children are educated in residential programs. The remainder are a part of some type of special educational day program, with most of these programs housed in the public schools.

Anatomy and physiology of the visual system

Like the auditory system, the visual system is quite complex, yet its basic function can be outlined and described in fairly simple terms. Perhaps this is because the eye, unlike the ear, has just one basic purpose: vision. (The ear, in addition to being the organ of hearing, also houses the sensory components permitting both a sense of balance and of acceleration.) Fig. 6-1 provides an enlarged, semidiagrammatic representation of the human eye.

One of the more common descriptions of the functioning of the eye likens it to a camera. As with the camera, in the absolute absence of light, we cannot see, but with sufficient illumination, light rays reflecting off the object being seen go through several parts or layers of the eye to the back of the eye where

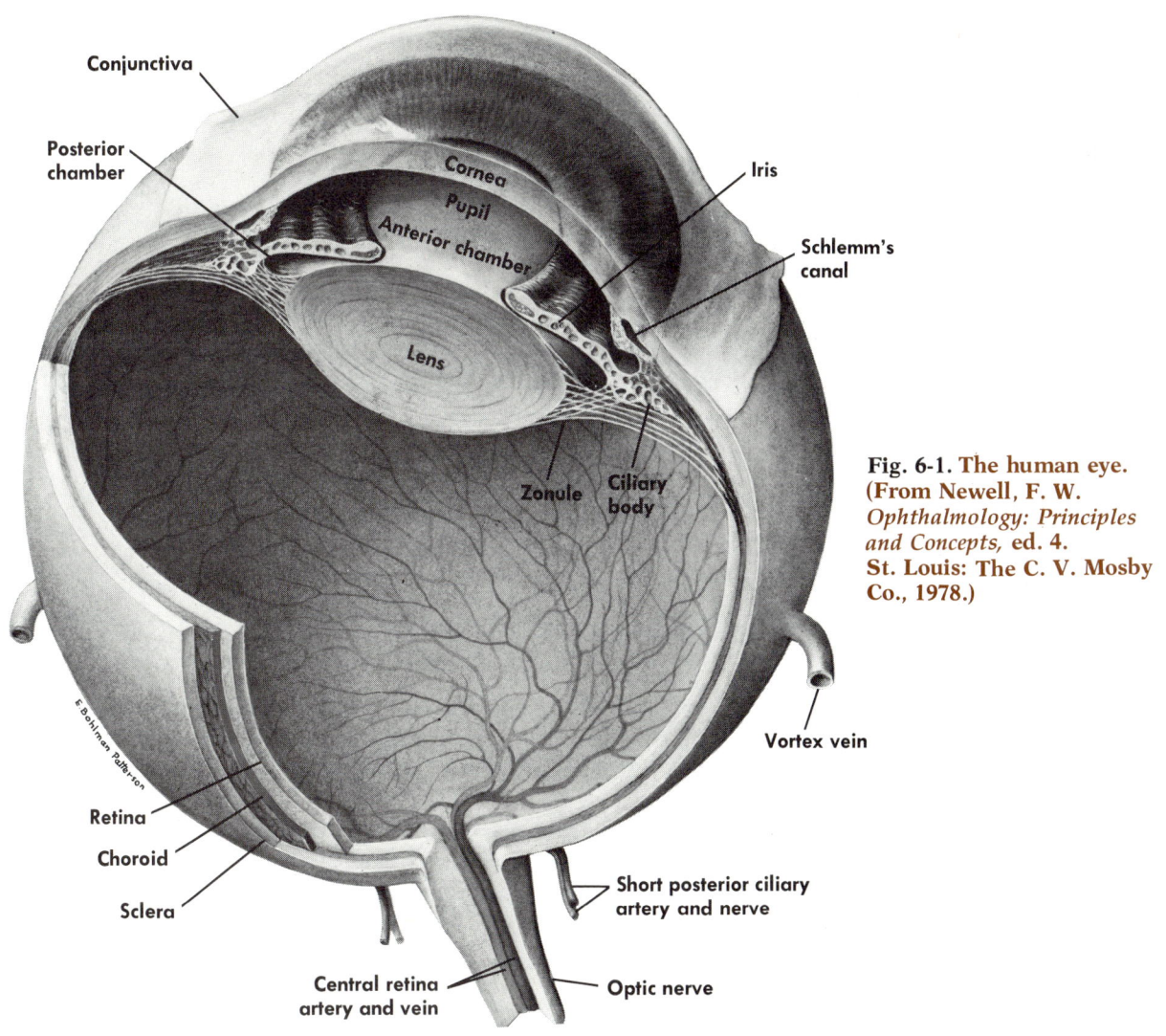

Fig. 6-1. The human eye. (From Newell, F. W. *Ophthalmology: Principles and Concepts,* ed. 4. St. Louis: The C. V. Mosby Co., 1978.)

they are focused on the retina. From here they go via the optic nerve to the brain where they are interpreted. As we look at an object, the process may be outlined as follows:

1. In the presence of sufficient light, and as we look at an object, light rays reflecting off the object pass through the *cornea*, the transparent, outer cover of the eye.
2. These light rays pass through the *pupil*, an apparently black opening in the center of the *iris* of the eye. The *iris* is the part of the eye that gives apparent color to the eyes. It is made up of membraneous tissue and muscles that adjust the size of the pupil to regulate the amount of light entering the eye.
3. The light rays next strike and pass through the *lens*, which changes the direction of the rays so that they will focus on the *retina*.
4. The *retina* is the inner layer of the back part of the eyeball and consists of light-sensitive cells. It is sensitized or activated by the image that falls on it, and this image is carried to the brain by the *optic nerve*. The image is then interpreted by the brain. For practical purposes the retina may be considered a sort of expansion of the optic nerve endings in the eye, and as various images fall on the retina, different parts of the optic nerve are stimulated to differing degrees, thus accounting for the almost infinite variety of messages that can be transmitted to the brain.

It is of utmost importance to note that "normal" interpretation of the image falling on the retina depends on normal, consistent operation of the total visual system, including the brain, and that in many instances visual messages received through this system are processed in conjunction with information received simultaneously through other sensory channels. This is a complex system that is ordinarily used in some combined way with other sensory systems of the body, and although we have considered it here as a single system, for educational purposes it must be considered as it interrelates to other systems supplying information to the brain.

All functions of the visual system require the use of some of the many muscles that are a part of the system. Some of these, such as those used in focusing, tracking, and fixating, must be developed, and if a visually impaired student has very little light reaching the retina, he may have difficulty in such development. The child with normal visual ability and environmental stimulation begins to develop the skills of fixation and tracking in the early stages of infancy in a manner that is primarily reflexive and, once started, they are exercised for many hours each day. In contrast, the child with impaired visual ability may have to be specifically taught certain of these skills. Various of the muscles, such as, for example, the oculomotor muscles which bring the eyeballs into convergence, may be intact and have the potential for normal functioning, but without practice they are essentially useless. It is obvious that in the case of total blindness such matters are of no concern, but for the low vision or visually limited student, an understanding of the physiology of this part of the visual system and knowing how to maximize visual efficiency are of critical importance. A complete understanding of the functioning of the eye and how this leads to differing educational procedures for students with differing degrees of visual impairment will be a basic part of the educational program for those who elect to become specialists in education of the visually impaired.

Definitions: terminology used to describe visual impairment or handicap

Barraga (1976) states that "as far back as the early 1800's, there has been a lack of precision in the use of terms relating to those who have visual impairments or who are totally without sight." (p.12) Barraga also notes that this inconsistency or divergency has existed among professional disciplines (medicine, psychology, and education) and within each discipline. In a representative list of labels used over the past 150 years we find such terms as medically blind, braille blind, economically blind, legally blind, vocationally blind, subnormal vision, partially seeing, visually defective, visually disabled, visually impaired, and many others.

Barraga indicates that in very recent years there has been an attempt, within and across disciplines, to refine terminology and definitions and to minimize confusion. Many of the following terms and accompanying discussion are adapted from Barraga's presentation of this topic (1976, pp. 13-16).

Visual impairment is a term used to describe any clinically diagnosable deviation in the structure or functioning of any part or parts of the eye. For educational purposes we are primarily concerned with an impairment that cannot be totally corrected and/or that leads to the need for modified or adapted educational procedures.

Visually handicapped is a term used to indicate children who have impairments in the structure or functioning of the visual sense organ, regardless of the extent or nature of this impairment. The use of the term "handicapped" specifies that the impairment interferes with learning and that special education procedures are required to optimize learning. This is a very general term and does not indicate the type or degree of impairment or the type of services required for optimal learning.

Blind is one of three commonly used terms that indicate degree of visual impairment but do not indicate cause or time of onset. The term *blind* indicates total loss of vision or only minimal light perception. Braille and related media are used in the school situation, but if the child has some light perception, it may be of considerable use in orientation and mobility.

Low vision, a second term indicating degree of impairment, is used for those who have limitations in distance vision but may be able to see objects or materials at a distance of a few inches or perhaps a very few feet. Low vision children will be able to use their vision for a number of school activities, including, in some cases, reading. Others will require braille and tactual materials. *Low vision children should not be considered blind and must be encouraged to use whatever vision they may have.*

Visually limited, a third level of degree of impairment, refers to the condition in which a student has some visual limitations under some circumstances. These students may require special lighting, optical aids, or other special materials. They should be considered *seeing* children who require some special aid.

The three preceding terms are commonly used to indicate the three major groupings of students who receive some level of special education services because of a visual handicap. Other terminology may be used, but as indicated previously, there is a concerted attempt to reduce this proliferation to facilitate meaningful communication about the visually handicapped.

Certain other terms are necessary to develop minimal understanding of this area of concern. The following are of central importance (Barraga, 1976) or are terms that appear quite often in the literature. This should be considered a minimal list.

Visual acuity refers to the ability to discriminate the details of an object (including abstract symbols) at specified distances. One of the most common expressions of visual acuity is that arbitrary notation of 20/20, indicating "normal" vision. It must be noted that it is quite possible to see at 20 feet what others see at 20 feet and still have serious difficulties at the distance at which a book is normally held for reading. This is critically important in the educational setting, and for educational purposes, we must know visual acuity at *various* specified distances. It may also be noted here that a student may have 20/20 vision but have such a markedly restricted field or periphery (the circular area right, left, above, and below that the individual can effectively see while looking straight ahead) that he or she may be called legally blind.

Legally blind indicates a degree of visual impairment that has been established for identification purposes in relation to the capability or legality of various agencies to serve individuals as "blind" persons. This may result from a requirement in the charter of incorporation or from the legislative enactment through which agency funds are supplied. Legal blindness in the United States usually means central visual acuity of 20/200 or less in the better eye after correction; or a field defect in which the widest diameter of the visual field subtends 20 degrees (or in some states, 30 degrees). Even among the legally blind some individuals may have sufficient overall ability to be considered low vision persons, rather than blind persons. This is usually considered to be a matter of *visual efficiency*, which will be defined later in this section.

Visual perception means the ability to interpret what is seen. This ability relates to the process whereby visual input is related to other information, and will be given more consideration in Chapter 7 in the discussion of learning disabilities. It is possible to have serious visual perceptual difficulties despite having normal visual acuity. From a slightly different point of view, it might be said that visual perception relates to the associative abilities of the brain rather than to the eye.

Visual efficiency is viewed by Barraga (1976) as the most *inclusive* of all terms relating to vision and the most important for educational purposes. It depends on all of the physiologic, psychologic, and environmental variables in effect in the life of any child whose visual abilities are under consideration. A child with less visual acuity than some other child may be more visually efficient because he or she makes better use of the available visual ability. This may be the result of motivation, early training, parental attitudes, intelligence, or other purely visual factors such as width of visual field. Educators consider visual efficiency when planning for any given student, and improvement of visual efficiency should be a major goal of educational programs for the visually impaired.

Individuals may be classified according to visual acuity or visual efficiency or by (1) age categories; (2) anatomic part affected (i.e., cornea, retina, lens); or (3) cause (birth defects, disease, trauma). However classified, it is essential to remember that *classification does not automatically determine program setting or content*. Classification may be for statistical purposes, to establish eligibility for certain types of services, or in some cases it may provide part of the information needed for program planning.

Types and causes of visual impairment

Refractive errors are the most common causes of visual impairment. Of these, the most common is *myopia*, or nearsightedness (Barraga, in Lowenfeld, 1973). Usually caused by improper structural alignment of the eye, this may result in an increased curvature of the cornea, or an eyeball that is "too long." In myopia there is too much refractive power for the size of the eye and the rays of light focus in front of, rather than on, the retina. Because the eye can often accommodate for near vision, this condition may have little effect in normal play or in activities in the home. Therefore, it may be overlooked, and the child may literally not know that other people see things clearly when they are 100 or 1000 feet away. This is particularly limiting regarding incidental information, and may, over a period of time (for example, if this condition continues during most or all of the pre-school years) reduce a child's ability to learn effectively any new information. Fortunately, most refractive errors are correctable with lenses and are of little educational consequence if discovered before they have caused a serious reduction in the development of a normal information base.

A second refractive error, *hyperopia* (farsightedness) is the result of a flattened corneal surface, or an eyeball that is "too short." In this case the point of focus of light rays is beyond (behind) the retina. This condition has more effect on clarity of focus when working on detailed visual material, as in looking at a book or working a puzzle, and unless it is quite severe, it may have little effect until school entrance. Once again, the ability of the visual system to compensate may permit the child to miss very little, but there may be resultant headaches if too much close work is attempted. There will be essentially no effect on distant vision, and thus on the incidental learning that is so important. After the child enters school, the problem may quickly become more significant, depending on the degree of hyperopia. Because simple visual screening takes place at 20 feet, hyperopia is often not detected in screening programs.

A third refractive error, *astigmatism*, is a result of unevenness in the surface of the cornea. Rays of light are refracted differentially and thus do not converge at one point. The result is blurring and confusion, and as the eye (and the brain, working as part of the visual system) attempts to compensate, headaches may occur. It is quite common for fairly serious astigmatism to cause no obvious problems until the child enters school and thus must focus on and gain meaning from written symbols (letters and words). Astigmatism may be found as a separate entity or in combination with either myopia or hyperopia.

These three conditions all lead to abnormal light refraction and are thus grouped together as refractive errors. Refractive errors, though common and potentially serious if left uncorrected, can usually be corrected with eyeglasses or contact lenses.

Lens abnormalities are among the more serious causes of visual impairment. One such impairment, cataracts, is often thought of in connection with older persons but may develop during childhood or be present at birth. In cases where both eyes are clouded, the effects can be very severe because of a general reduction in both the quality and the quantity of sensory information received through the visual system; color discrimination may be virtually impossible. Because they have almost no experience with normal visual learning, children with congenital cataracts may appear to be almost totally blind. With planned experiences and much concentrated effort, it may be discovered that a good deal of visual acuity and potential visual efficiency remains.

Another type of lens defect, less common but also quite debilitating, occurs as a result of sharp blows to the face or head (Barraga, 1973). This defect is *dislocation of the lens*, and if it cannot be restored to its proper position, the result can be serious visual loss or even total blindness.

Choroid or retinal defects (see Fig. 6-1) may be genetic, occur during fetal development, or result from other unknown causes leading to a break in the tissue of the choroid or retina (Barraga, 1973). The seriousness of this type defect relates primarily to the area of retina affected. Most choroid or retinal defects result

Sensory impairments

in weak and/or disorganized sensations being transmitted to the brain and greatly reduced ability of the brain to interpret these sensations accurately. One such condition, *retinitis pigmentosa*, is progressive and is first apparent as night blindness. In most cases it eventually leads to total blindness.

Muscle control problems may lead to diminished binocular ability, which may take a variety of courses. Since the brain will not process and interpret two different visual images, one must be "selected." In some cases, a child may unconsciously shift from one eye to the other; in others the child will use only one eye; and in extreme cases this will lead to loss of ability to use the other (the cells actually lose their sensitivity to light). *Strabismus* (crossed eyes) and *nystagmus* (involuntary, rapid movement of eyes—rolling, rotating, and so forth) are two specific examples of muscle control problems with which many persons are familiar, but other, less well-known difficulties are also common.

Other types of conditions may also cause visual impairment, including actual damage to the optic nerve. This damage may occur from a number of causes, but its effect is obvious; a damaged pathway to the brain cannot carry the visual message accurately.

In closing this section we should note that visual impairment may have a variety of causes: (1) congenital, including impairment resulting from diseases, (i.e., syphilis or rubella in the mother), general developmental defects, and other purely hereditary conditions, (2) physical trauma (blows to the head or direct damage to the eyes), (3) infectious or other diseases, (4) poison (e.g., lead poisoning), and (5) other unique causal factors that may be time- or area-specific.* In addition, the aging process is a major cause of visual impairment but has little application to education of the visually impaired as it is approached in this text.

Prevalence of visual impairment

The figure most often used to indicate the prevalence of visually impaired children in the school age population is 0.1 percent. If we include all visually limited students who often require some special educational assistance, the prevalence figures should be increased. This 0.1 percent estimate is derived from data on legally blind pupils as registered with the American Printing House for the Blind and estimates of low vision and visually limited students based on data from certain states where services are quite broadly based. It does not include those students whose visual impairment can be corrected with eyeglasses or contact lenses. If we were to consider the total population, including adults whose vision is significantly impaired due to aging, this percentage would definitely be increased.

Before leaving the topic of prevalence of visual impairment, it might be well to recognize that the incidence of visual impairment in any given year (new cases within the year) may fluctuate considerably, but that it would take several successive years of greatly increased incidence to have an appreciable effect on the prevalance within the school-age population. In recent history the two factors that have had a great effect on year-to-year variations are the retrolental fibroplasia "out-

---

*An example is *retrolental fibroplasia (RLF)*, a condition in which scar tissue forms behind the lens. This condition, which first appeared in the 1940s, caused a remarkable increase in the number of visually impaired children born during the 1940s and early 1950s. RLF was then dramatically reduced when it was discovered that oxygen given to premature babies had been administered in excessive amounts, thus causing this condition.

Education of children and youth who are visually impaired

break" citied earlier and rubella outbreaks that occur from time to time. Hopefully, these may be kept under control in the future.

Medical and surgical treatment of visual impairment

Prevention and *correction* are key words when considering the many contributions of the medical field to the concerns of the visually impaired. Perhaps half of the readers of this text will be using some type of corrective lens to read. This fact alone reflects a tremendous advance over some years ago; and with recent advances in the use of contact lenses, certain preventive functions can be accomplished at the same time correction is provided. However, for the most part, these two functions are separate and will be discussed separately.

Prevention of blindness is a cause that most enlightened persons in the world would support, and much of the preventive effort in the United States today is led by the National Society for the Prevention of Blindness. Perhaps because so many nonhandicapped persons can readily believe that it could happen to them, and because blindness is conceptualized as such a devastating condition, there has been relatively good cooperation with the activities of the National Society for the Prevention of Blindness through the years. In addition, the fact that so many Americans have some type of continuing contact with an *optometrist* (licensed, nonmedical specialist who treats refractive errors and eye muscle problems through prescriptive lenses and/or exercises) or an *ophthalmologist* (a physician who may specialize in defects and diseases of the eye, in addition to those functions carried out by the optometrist) makes the preventive effort easier to accomplish.

A leading example of the preventive thrust accomplished both through special clinics and through the urgings of optometrists or ophthalmologists is the national attempt to better control *glaucoma*. Glaucoma, which can be detected relatively easily, is a disease of the eye in which there is excessive pressure from within the eyeball. Its cause is presently unknown, but if detected early, its effects (partial or complete loss of vision) can be prevented. Because it could potentially affect so many persons, particularly those past age 30, this one effort can substantially reduce the prevalence of blindness, especially among adults.

Other examples include (1) the use of silver nitrate or other medication in the eyes of newborns to prevent a disease called *ophthalmia neonatorum* (once a leading cause of blindness), (2) prevention of rubella and syphilis, (3) genetic counseling, and (4) increased knowledge about the treatment of infections of the eye.

Correction of visual impairments by means other than surgery certainly must rank high as an important advance of the twentieth century, but it is one that we now take almost for granted. This includes correction of refractive errors and of muscle imbalance and correction in which the contact lens is used to hold the cornea in its proper configuration. We will not further belabor this point, but hope that all who now use corrective lenses may learn to appreciate them for their tremendous effectiveness rather than deprecate them for their inconvenience.

Surgical procedures to assist in improving visual efficiency or regaining vision are also an important part of the contribution of medical specialists. Perhaps the most dramatic of the surgical procedures is that of corneal transplants, which may result in a blind person regaining sight. Less spectacular are the surgical procedures applied with some types of cataracts and those used in the case of strabismus. In these last two instances, timing is all-important (with cataracts in relation to an

Sensory impairments

optimal time for removal—not too early and not too late; and with stabismus, the sooner the better, to reduce the chance of deterioration of the unused eye). In all three of these procedures medical science has made rapid strides in the past 10 years, and additional knowledge is gained yearly.

Identification of children who are visually impaired

The screening device that has been in use for many years, both in the public schools and in the offices of many general practitioners and pediatricians, is the *Snellen chart*. The Snellen chart has rows of letters corresponding to distances, i.e., 15, 20, 30, 40, 50, 70, 100, and 200 feet. If a child at 20 feet can properly identify the letters on the 20 feet row, he is said to have 20/20 vision (interpreted as "normal"). This is a measure of *central visual acuity for distance vision*. If the child can just barely see the letters on the 50 feet row, he is said to have 20/50 vision. The Snellen chart is of value in screening for distance vision but is

TABLE 6-1
Symptoms that may indicate visual difficulties*

Observable signs	Behavioral indications
1. Red eyelids	1. Rubs eyes excessively
2. Crusts on lids among the lashes	2. Shuts or covers one eye; tilts head or thrusts head forward
3. Recurring styes or swollen lids	3. Sensitivity to light
4. Watery eyes or discharges	4. Difficulty with reading or other work requiring close use of eyes
5. Reddened or watery eyes	5. Squinting, blinking, frowning, facial distortions while reading or doing other close work
6. Crossed eyes or eyes that do not appear to be straight	6. Holds reading material too close or too far or frequently changes the distance from near to far or far to near
7. Pupils of uneven size	7. Complains of pain or aches in the eyes, headaches, dizziness, or nausea following close eye work
8. Eyes that move excessively	8. Difficulty in seeing distant objects (preference for reading or other academic tasks rather than playground or gross motor activities)
9. Drooping eyelids	9. Tendency to reverse letters, syllables, or words
	10. Tendency to confuse letters of similar shape (o and a, c and e, n and m, h and n, f and t)
	11. Tendency to lose place in sentence or page
	12. Poor spacing in writing and difficulty in "staying on the line"

*From Gearheart, B. R. and Weishahn, M. W. *The Handicapped Student in the Regular Classroom.* St. Louis: The C. V. Mosby Co., 1980. This list is quite similar to, although somewhat more inclusive than, a list provided by the National Society for the Prevention of Blindess in various publications.

of little or no value for the child who has adequate distance vision but has visual difficulty at distances used for reading (12 to 16 inches). Other specialized instruments including a modified Snellen test for use at a distance of 14 inches, have been developed for use in screening for near vision, but at present these are not widely used for screening purposes for all school children. In the absence of such near vision assessment, the best tool for identification (in addition to the Snellen chart for distant objects) is an alert classroom teacher who will refer children with symptoms indicating possible visual problems to the school nurse and the parent. A list of symptoms that may indicate the possibility of visual problems appears in Table 6-1.

Since the Snellen chart does not identify strabismus, many recommend the titmus fly test as part of the vision screening procedures.

The National Society for the Prevention of Blindness specifically recommends that in addition to the Snellen test, visual screening should include testing for muscle balance, depth perception, and hyperopia. Certain more progressive school districts conduct such screening prior to entrance to kindergarten and at regular intervals thereafter.

Teaching the visually impaired: approaches and techniques

There appears to be much less controversy regarding how to teach the visually impaired than exists with respect to the hearing impaired. There was a time when a controversy existed regarding which of the tactual reading systems was the best, but most of this has been resolved, at least in the United States. Different methods must be used with the blind, as contrasted with those who have some residual vision, but this is generally accepted. There are certain variations in preferred techniques in orientation and mobility, some relating to age, some to personal ability, and some to personal preference, but the overall feeling is one of general harmony. With this positive note, we shall initiate our review of some of the major approaches, methods, and techniques used in teaching the visually impaired.

READING AND WRITING FOR THE VISUALLY IMPAIRED

There are at least two major areas in which the visually impaired must receive very special education and training. These are: (1) reading and writing and (2) orientation and mobility. We will consider the special problems of reading and writing first and will initially focus on these problems as they relate to students who are blind.

As outlined in the historical review at the start of this chapter, formal education of the blind began with successful attempts to teach the blind through tactual senses. Some reading was accomplished, even though the tactual presentations were inconsistent and highly varied. They included embossed letters, wood carvings, string glued or otherwise fastened to paper, writing on waxed tablets, letters pinpricked into felt, and any other method that could permit the blind to "see" through their hands. In the United States, Howe developed embossed type (Boston line type), which was then used in the first American attempt to provide printed materials for the blind (Lowenfeld, 1973). There was no way for the blind to write, but at least the problem of reading had been solved—or so it seemed in the 1850s in the United States. But events were taking place elsewhere, again near Paris, which were soon to change the scene. Those events involved a young man named Louis Braille (1809—1852).

At the age of 3 Louis Braille injured one of his eyes and soon after lost the sight in both eyes. His father apparently made embossed letters for him with upholsterers nails ham-

Sensory impairments

mered into a board and he thus learned to read. At the age of 10, he entered the same school that had been started by Haüy and remained at the school first as a student, then as a teacher. While there he developed the first version of his dot system, which is now known internationally and which bears his name.

At the school, Braille met Charles Barbier, a cavalry officer who had developed a system whereby messages could be read under battle conditions in the dark of night. This code utilized twelve raised dots, a system that Braille soon reduced to the six-dot system in use today. Braille developed an alphabet that blind persons could read and, better yet, write. He devised a series of contractions, a system for mathematics, and one for musical notations. He had some difficulties with sighted teachers and administrators at the school who did not believe that a viable system could come from a blind person. Also, they apparently wanted a system that resembled the alphabetic system with which they were already familiar (Napier, 1972). Braille and some others who believed in the eventual merit of his system taught it secretly, and in fact it was not officially adopted until 1854, 2 years after his death. Thus began what is now the single, most often used method of reading and writing by the blind. Since its adoption in France, it has been recognized and adapted to most other languages.

Braille was not readily accepted in the United States, and because of the influence and power of Samuel Gridley Howe, who believed in embossed type, some others who tried to adopt it were ridiculed. Controversy continued in the United States and between British and American educators of the blind, but what came to be called the "battle of the dots" was finally settled in 1932 (Lowenfeld, 1973). Standard English braille, a compromise between American and English versions, was formally accepted by educators of both nations at that time (Fig. 6-2).

Braille may now be "typed" on mechanical braillewriters or printed by computers. In addition, a slate and stylus system is used by the blind for notetaking and, all in all, the blind can both read and write. When taken in the longer historical perspective, this has developed with considerable speed.

Reading and writing for limited or low vision students is another matter and varies with the degree of visual limitation. Depending on visual efficiency and type of visual im-

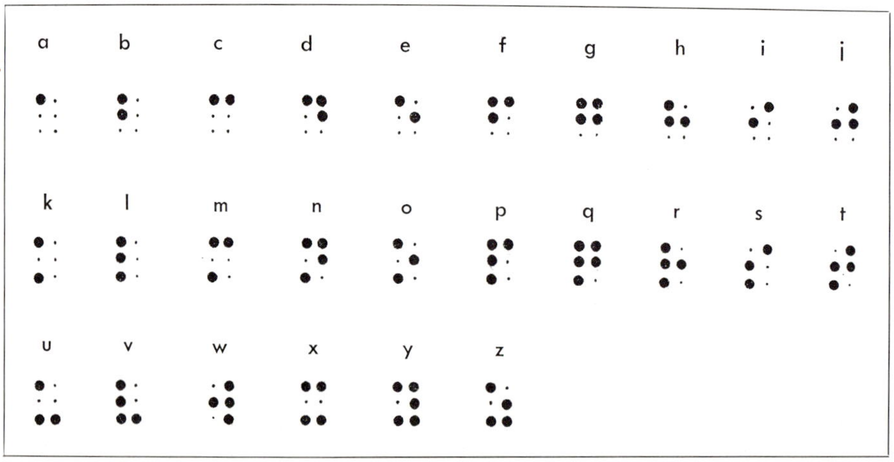

Fig. 6-2. Braille alphabet. (From Gearheart, B. R. and Weishahn, M. *The Handicapped Student in the Regular Classroom,* ed. 2. St. Louis: The C. V. Mosby Co., 1980.)

pairment, some partially seeing students may read normal print with the help of magnification; some can read large print, and some can read normal print by holding the text up to within an inch or two of the eye. An interesting device, the *Optacon*, converts print into tactual images through the use of "pins," which are activated through a highly sensitive camera lens. This allows the reader to read normal print through the index finger. However, because of its considerable cost, the fact that such reading is relatively slow, and the apparent level of intellectual ability required to use it successfully, it has received only limited use since its invention in 1965.

Certain substitutes for reading are also used to good advantage by the visually impaired. One of the most effective is any of various types of sound recording. A number of ways to "compress" and thus speed up recorded speech have made such an approach even more practical.

The visually impaired, including the blind, learn to use an ordinary typewriter to communicate in writing with sighted persons.

Orientation and mobility training

A second broad area of concern for the visually impaired is developing the ability to move safely, efficiently, and gracefully from place to place. This had been accomplished, many years ago, by seriously restricting the environment, thus assuring a safe and known environment. Today, the concern is to train the visually impaired so that they may do all, or almost all, of the things that seeing persons can do. There are some limitations—such as driving an automobile—but these are very few.

Orientation means the establishment of position in space and relative position to other objects in the environment. This is accomplished through the proper use of the remaining senses and is much more complex than most seeing persons initially perceive. It is an ongoing process and requires reestablished knowledge of position after each new step is taken. For example, at one moment, the sharp corner of a table may be directly to a person's right, and after taking a step forward, it will be behind and thus no longer of concern. In contrast, anything that is moving (another person, an automobile, an unfriendly dog) must be reassessed after every step taken.

A seeing person learns, through years of practice, to continually reestablish this position in space automatically. The visually impaired must do this with little or no visual sensory input and must be *trained* to accomplish this task.

Mobility is the actual locomotion (self-generated movement) of an individual from one fixed position to another position in the environment. Included in this process are such skills as proper heel and toe gait, control of the body's center of gravity, ability to detect inclines and declines, obstacle detection, and others. We must remember that seeing persons learn a great deal more through the visual channel than most of us realize and that a visually impaired person must learn these same things with no or limited vision. In combination, orientation and mobility should provide the visually impaired person the ability to move about *independently*. In fact, in many cases the person is semi-independent or "almost-independent," but the goal is to assist the individual to be as independent as possible.

Independent travel is accomplished by using the auditory, tactual, kinesthetic, olfactory, and any remaining visual senses to maximal advantage. The blind cannot hear better than others, but to be able to travel independently and efficiently, they may (and usually do) learn to use their auditory powers more effectively than others who can use their vision as the basic travel guidance system. This

157

Sensory impairments

Use of the long cane requires very specific training, which can result in efficient, independent travel.

principle applies in a similar manner to the other intact senses. The work of the orientation and mobility instructor is to assist the visually impaired student to learn to use these other senses in concert to travel independently. The five modes of travel commonly used by visually impaired persons are: (1) independent travel without the use of devices or any other outside assistance, (2) the sighted guide, (3) the long cane, (4) dog guides, and (5) electronic devices.*

Independent travel, without any assistance or device, is probably the most commonly used, considering that most school-age children do not use a cane, dog, or electronic device. There are, however, certain basic skills that are prerequisite to other modes and are designed to achieve efficient and safe travel. These basic skills are taught at a very early age and are essential if the child is to achieve independent travel in the school and community. A few of the basic techniques that would be taught by the resource/itinerant teacher or orientation and mobility specialist are as follows:

1. Upper hand and forearm (raised position)—protection for head and upper body from half-open doors, walls, and so on.
2. Lower hand and forearm (lowered position)—protection for the lower body and location of desks, tables, and so on.
3. Trailing—following lightly over a straight surface with back of fingertips to locate specific objects or to get a parallel line of direction.
4. Direction taking—using an object or sound to establish a course of direction toward or away from an object.

---

*The following description of the five modes of travel is adapted from materials prepared by Dr. Mel Weishahn (1979). Dr. Weishahn's experience as a former teacher of the visually impaired and his unusual ability to share his knowledge in simple terms are greatly appreciated.

Patterns of familiarization, geographic directions, hearing acuteness for travel, sound localization, and the use of residual vision would also be provided by the resource/itinerant teacher or orientation and mobility specialist.

The *sighted guide technique* (p. 165) is one of the first taught to most visually impaired students. It is an efficient way to orient an individual to an unfamiliar area and is also a viable mobility technique. This technique involves the visually impaired individual grasping a sighted person's arm just above the elbow. He or she will place the thumb on the outside and the fingers on the inside of the guide's arm and will walk about one-half step behind the guide. In effect, the visually impaired person is "reading" the sighted individual's arm or elbow, and any movement of the guide's body and arm will be communicated to the student. By following approximately one-half step behind, the student will know when the guide is stepping up or down, turning left or right, and so on.

All students in a class with a visually impaired child should know the procedures to be used in serving as a sighted guide. The resource/itinerant teacher or orientation and mobility specialist may conduct a type of in-service session for students. The students may want to wear blindfolds to gain a better understanding of traveling without sight. Some caution should be exercised here so that the students do not develop a sympathetic attitude but rather an objective understanding of travel techniques used by the visually impaired.

A common method of travel is with the use of the *long cane* (p. 158). The age at which a child is provided formal training in the use of a cane depends on the student's maturity, need for more independent travel, and ability to profit from rather extensive one-to-one training. The decision to initiate formal training in the use of a cane is made after careful consideration. Generally, instruction in the use of the cane is not started until age 14 or 15, but some children have succeeded in learning cane techniques as early as 11 or 12. The reasons for waiting until the student is 14 or 15 generally relate to his or her ability to profit from instruction and, more importantly, the need for a more independent mode of travel. There are many types of canes, but the most common are made of aluminum or fiberglass and are approximately 1/2 inch in diameter. Some have a crook for balance and easy placement; others have a golf-club–type grip. The tip of the cane is usually made of steel or nylon.

Another mode of independent travel is the *dog guide*, which is not usually recommended until the student is at least 17 or 18. Prior to this age the student may not have either the maturity to handle a dog properly or the need for more independent travel. Often young visually impaired children indicate an interest in obtaining a dog guide as a pet or companion but not necessarily for independence in traveling. The dog guide should not be considered a pet but rather a partner in achieving independent travel. Contrary to popular opinion, less than 2 percent of the visually impaired population uses dog guides. Although there may appear to be many advantages to using a dog, the disadvantages outweigh the advantages for all but a very few individuals. Specific information concerning dog guide agencies, cost, and nature of training can be provided by either the resource/itinerant teacher or the orientation and mobility specialist.

A final mode of independent travel is through the use of an *electronic mobility device*. There are a number of electronic devices available; they are used either as a primary mobility device or a supplement to other devices such as the long cane. Although it is encouraging to see research being conducted in this most important area, it does not seem that any one device will meet the needs of all individuals. Some of the devices enhance hearing efficiency, some detect obstacles, others enable the individual to walk in a straight line, whereas others are directed at revealing the specific location of obstacles in the environment. Most of these devices are still in the field-testing stage, and it is difficult to predict when they will be available for general use.

The decision as to which type of mobility aid or device will be best in a given case is a purely individual matter. It must be made by the student, parents, and the orientation and mobility specialists with whom they work. For most blind persons, a combination of modes of travel, depending on immediate location and circumstances, seems to be best.

Other educational considerations

When planning for the education of the visually impaired the goals are the same as for all other children: preparation for citizenship, occupational effectiveness, and social competence. In practice, social competence is best assured if a combination of other factors are provided, with reading/writing and orientation/mobility skills high on the list. However, to achieve social competence, emphasis must be given to the all-important early childhood period.

EARLY CHILDHOOD AND PRESCHOOL NEEDS

Special attention must be paid to early childhood needs of visually impaired children if they are to experience maximal potential for development in later years. According to Barraga, (1976), "the visually handicapped child . . . because of his impairment, may have less opportunity to experience the emergence of a strong identity of self and understanding of feelings." (p. 20) In further discussion of this potential problem, Barraga notes that, because parents often do not know what to do with a visually impaired child and are afraid of doing the wrong thing, they may simply leave the child alone except to provide physical care. This is exactly the *wrong* thing to do, for the visually impaired baby needs human attachment as much as any other baby. Since he or she cannot experience affection through *seeing* it expressed, as other children may be able to do, parents must work even harder to provide touching, body manipulation, and sound stimulation (talk with the baby, talk with others in the infant's presence, and, if anything, "overdo" sound input).

Careful attention must be given to concept development. Although concept development in nonhandicapped children is not fully understood and in visually impaired children is an even greater puzzle, it is clear that concepts may be developed only after the child has successfully processed and coded a variety of information. Research suggests that differences in concept development between blind and sighted children relates primarily to the time required to attain satisfactory cognitive organization (Tisdall, 1968; Tillman and Osborne, 1969; Witkin and others, 1971). Once attained, it is apparently of equal quality to that of sighted children. This time lag, which may have serious consequences when we educate blind children with their sighted age-peers, may be significantly reduced by carefully planned, enriched preschool experiences. Thus we find additional impetus for planned experiences during the early years. With proper early experiences we can apparently greatly increase the chances for normal cognitive organization on the part of the young blind child, promoting a closer approximation to that expected for sighted peers.

Without going into detail regarding the voluminous research relating to the great influence of the early years (especially the first 18 to 24 months) on the development of any child, let us simply agree that this time period is of utmost importance. With this in mind, and with what is known about the effects of deprivation during these years on any child, it is easy to see why parents need assistance in thinking through a basis for interaction with their visually impaired child. Without the opportunity and encouragement to explore the physical environment and develop tactile and kinesthetic abilities, these abilities may develop very slowly. Yet they are the very abilities that may be required to substitute for the visual in reading and writing. Without concerted effort to provide maximal language development through direct language interaction, the child may not have the language base that is so necessary for all of the basic skill areas in school, a base that is even more important because of the visual impairment. The following case history (which is true except for the name of the child and a few details that have been changed to assure anonymity) provides a striking example of these principles. Fortunately, it had a happy ending.

> Ellen was almost 3 years old when Susan B., an itinerant teacher of the blind, first saw her. Ellen was in the state residential home school for the blind, and some questions about her future had been raised because she was apparently multihandicapped—blind and mentally retarded. She had been in the home since just before her first birthday, being placed by her parents on the advice of the family physician, after examination led to the conclusion that in addition to congenital blindness, she was undoubtedly mentally retarded, probably in the 25—35 IQ range. At the age of 2 years 11 months she could not (or did not) (1) feed herself, (2) understand more than a dozen spoken words, (3) walk alone with any confidence, or (4) respond (by showing pleasure) to attention by others. She was, of course, not toilet trained. Ellen still drank milk from a bottle a good part of the time

but would grab certain foods that she could smell and eat them with apparently great enjoyment.

At earlier ages, some of the personnel at the home had attempted various activities with Ellen, but she did not seem to respond, and because she was identified as mentally retarded, they soon had given up. In all fairness to those who worked at the home, it must be said that they were seriously overloaded with duties and tended to work with those who seemed to show the most promise.

Susan B., one of several itinerant specialists who worked for the state department of public instruction, was asked to observe Ellen, help determine her potential for education, and assist with a possible replacement in the state home for the mentally retarded. Officials at the institution for the mentally retarded did not particularly want her and felt that blindness must be her major handicap. Officials at the home/school for the blind could see no potential for education or preparation for employment.

After her initial contact with Ellen, Susan B. felt she had some indication that there was more potential than was earlier believed. She came back for a series of visits and eventually gave the opinion that Ellen might have near-normal potential. (At this point we will shorten what was in actuality a long procedure during which Susan B. legally adopted Ellen. She then worked with her for a period of 3 years; I first saw Ellen at age 6.)

At age 6, Ellen was formally reevaluated regarding intellectual ability. Her IQ was in the 110 to 120 range. She was self-assured, had very good language skills, was doing well in first grade, and gave promise of becoming a good braille reader. Her memory was described by her regular class teacher as "fantastic."

The obvious questions are: (1) What happened in that 3-year interim? (2) Could a similar thing happen in other cases? (3) What does this infer for other blind children? First, it must be recognized that Ellen lived—full-time—with an expert teacher of the blind, her adoptive mother. Had it not been for that, it is doubtful that the severe early disadvantage could have been overcome so effectively. Given our recognition of that unusual circumstance, let us examine the answers to the questions.

During the 3-year period, Ellen was literally bombarded with experiences, exercising fully all available sensory channels. She heard stories, both those told to her by her mother and those provided on tape. After some socialization was obtained, she began to participate in such activities as Sunday school, preschool for the blind, story reading at the library, and many others that provided an abundance of language input from a variety of sources. Ellen was given many motor experiences. Using various reward systems she was taught to explore her environment. She was not "protected" once she overcame her fear. She was placed in swings, tossed into the air and caught, given small objects to manipulate, taught to climb the jungle gym, and other such experiences. She could *not* have benefited so fully from these experiences if she had not had above average mental ability, but all visually impaired children would benefit to some degree from such experiences. And yes, she learned that she was loved—not smothering/protecting love, but caring love; the kind of love that at times turned to reasonable discipline, but always was clearly honest-to-goodness caring. Because she was so developmentally retarded, her progress seemed miraculous, but it does illustrate what can be done.

The question of whether or not a similar thing could happen in other cases must be answered yes, but with certain disclaimers. Few children will likely "recover" from the severe lack of stimulation in very early childhood as well as Ellen. She was an exception because of the very great opportunity presented by her unusual mother. But this true case history does show it can happen and illustrates the effect of lack of caring and stimulation. It tells us that we must assist parents very early to work effectively with their young visually impaired children. It tells us that we must be very careful about assessment of intelligence of blind children, and it gives us hope even if we have, at times, done the wrong thing.

ADAPTED EDUCATIONAL MATERIALS AND/OR EQUIPMENT

There are many types of adapted materials for the visually impaired; some are exclusively for the child who must read braille, others are useful with visually impaired children who are print readers. The following list is presented to provide an idea of the variety of aids which exist. Because the purpose of this text is an overview of special needs of special children, no expanded explanation of these materials will be given; a teacher training to teach the visually impaired will learn a great deal more about these and other materials.

GENERAL AND MISCELLANEOUS AIDS/MATERIALS

Braillewriter
Braille clocks and wristwatches
Adapted sports equipment (audible balls, etc.)
Audible locators (to be used as a base, object locator, or warning device)
Real objects (sometimes called realia): This might include a real pair of pliers, a real iron, a real golf club, etc.
Model: This includes a model of any larger object that can be used as a reference point in further learning. For example, a model of a building, a school bus, or anything else about which the child must learn, especially in relation to learning about dangerous situations. These must be to scale and, if possible, have appropriate working parts
Braille or large type answer sheets
A variety of children's table games

MATHEMATICS AIDS

Special slates to be used in computation
Abacuses
Raised clockfaces
Geometric area and volume aids
Wire forms for matched planes and volumes
Braille rulers

GEOGRAPHY AIDS

Braille atlases
Molded plastic dissected and undissected relief maps
Relief globes
Landform model (a set of three-dimensional tactual maps illustrating forty geographic concepts)

SPECIAL WRITING AIDS

Raised-line writing paper
Longhand writing kit
Script letter sheets and boards
Raised-line check books
Signature guide

The list, although not endless, is extensive. This preceding list is only a sample. In addition, the teacher may often be able to assist with day-to-day innovation, and itinerant specialists will have their own resources, including the resources of the American Printing House for the Blind, the American Foundation for the Blind, and The Library of Congress, Division for the Blind and Physically Handicapped.

TECHNIQUES OF DAILY LIVING (TDL)

Although some of the adaptations already mentioned in this chapter relate directly to the development of techniques of daily living, it is essential that they be viewed as a whole. Tuttle (1974) has discussed these techniques in some detail. Major headings in his discussion include: personal care and grooming, dressing, eating, care of clothing, housecleaning, the kitchen, sewing, use of tools for home repair, and a miscellaneous section that includes such areas as use of the telephone, identification of money, and others. In the introduction to his chapter, Tuttle provides the following rationale for planned teaching of techniques of daily living (Tuttle, 1974, p. 38):

> Techniques of daily living (TDL) for the visually impaired are more than optional "frills" for the school curriculum; they are an essential complement to the academics. Some teachers and administrators question that this is a function of the school. Others question their own

abilities to handle this area of the curriculum. Neither of these positions is justifiable.

Philosophically, the function of the schools in this country is to provide educational opportunities to all irrespective of race, creed, or disability, and to enable all to take their rightful places in society. "To take a rightful place" requires more than just being able to read, write, and calculate. It means being able to: manage affairs (personal hygiene, dressing, grooming, etc.), live independently in a community housecleaning, cooking, sewing, repairs, etc.), and handle a job suited to the potentials (training and placement). It means being able to integrate into the life of the community (civic, social, recreational, etc.), and to travel independently to meet obligations (orientation and mobility). To the nondisabled, these skills seem superficial and elementary. To the visually impaired who are limited in the ability to learn by observation and visual imitation, such skills are stumbling blocks unless specifically taught and mastered.

Schools, generally, have provided the academic skills required by visually impaired children. The Department of Vocational Rehabilitation has provided job training and placement and re-training for the newly blinded adult. In recent years schools have begun to meet their orientation and mobility obligations by hiring a trained mobility instructor.

However, too many public, private, and residential school graduates simply do not know how to manage their own personal affairs, nor do they know how to live independently and happily integrated into the life of a community. Traditionally, parents of normal children have assumed responsibility for such development and growth; but, parents of visually impaired children look to the professionals for help, direction, and guidance. Historically, residential schools have developed formal and informal ways of teaching self-care skills for personal management. However, more than half of the visually impaired school age group is enrolled in community school programs today. Therefore, more and more teachers must assume a greater responsibility for teaching techniques of daily living.

Apparently the teaching of techniques of daily living is a highly important and often overlooked component in education of the visually impaired. This specific area of concern provides just one more example of the way in which we may focus on one facet of the total life needs of a handicapped population (in this case, academic skill needs of the visually impaired) and run the risk of overlooking other skills required to permit the individual handicapped person to fully utilize those skills that have been mastered.

Educational settings: the question of maximal integration of the visually impaired

As with the hearing impaired, visually impaired children are commonly accepted as a part of the local educational program; this has been the case for a number of years, except in some sparsely populated areas of the nation and in the case of some blind children who have other handicapping conditions. State schools for the visually handicapped have been steadily decreasing in student population, and their enrollment has included an increasing percentage of multihandicapped students. Therefore, the major question is how visually impaired students can be most effectively served in the local schools.

At the preschool level we may find both integrated and segregated programs, with integrated programs more common outside residential schools.

From kindergarten through grade 12, visually impaired children are ordinarily integrated for a major part of the day, with specific help from specialized teachers provided in the resource room. One exception is the blind child who has other significant handicaps. This child may attend special classes for a half day or full day, depending on a variety of factors.

Education of children and youth who are visually impaired

Try using a sighted guide. It may further "open your eyes" to the world of the blind.

Sensory impairments

Programs for the visually impaired might be considered as among the leaders with regard to integration with the nonhandicapped. Such integration was regularly practiced long before the more recent, highly publicized concern with the need to integrate the handicapped with the nonhandicapped (mainstreaming). With this in mind, we shall consider an educational placement system, with the understanding that many factors must be carefully considered and that regular reevaluation of needs is essential.

An educational placement system: application of the variable service continuum concept

Planning for the visually impaired requires careful consideration of a variety of factors. These factors include: (1) age of student, (2) age of onset of visual impairment, (3) level of achievement, (4) level of intelligence, (5) presence of other handicapping conditions, (6) nature of visual impairment, and (7) emotional stability. Other factors, such as wishes and feelings of the student and parents and avail-

TABLE 6-2
Guidelines for educational placement of the visually impaired: application of the variable service continuum concept (most probable educational/placement needs)

Degree of visual impairment	Preschool	Elementary	Secondary
Mild	Regular nursery school Consultative assistance for parents	Regular class Limited consultative assistance for regular class teacher	Regular class Limited consultative assistance for regular class teachers
Moderate	Regular nursery school More intensive consultative assistance for parents Some direct observation and monitoring by specialist	Regular class Consultative assistance for regular class teacher Training with optical aids as indicated Development of visual efficiency Typing, handwriting	Regular class Consultative assistance for regular class teachers Vocational/career counseling as indicated
Severe (including blind)	Regular and/or special nursery school Intensive consultative assistance for parents Direct contact by specialist Early orientation and mobility training Early basis for braille (where indicated) Early experience with optical aids (as appropriate)	Regular class and/or part-time special class Consultative assistance for regular class teacher Special orientation and mobility training Braille as appropriate Directed experience with optical aids (as appropriate) Listening	Regular class and/or part-time special class Consultative assistance to regular class teachers Orientation and mobility training Braille and/or optical aids as appropriate Vocational career counseling Special class or special school vocational program as indicated

ability of services, will also be of importance. Each child must be considered individually, but there are some general placement considerations that should be taken into account. For example, there seems to be a relationship between the age of the child, the nature and extent of the visual impairment, the level of achievement, and the amount of direct special education service and instruction needed.

During the child's early education, he or she may spend as much as 1 to 1½ hours each day with the resource teacher. When the child has developed braille-reading skills and a familiarity with all of the necessary tangible apparatus, he or she may attend regular classroom for increasing amounts of time. If the child is able to read printed materials, with or without an aid, it would not be necessary to spend as much time with the resource/itinerant teacher. The student at the secondary level probably would not require a great deal of direct service from the resource/itinerant teacher.

The guidelines in Table 6-2 are a composite of general practices, but as is the case with many such guidelines, local variables may lead to specific variations. For example, with parents *and the student* playing an increasing role in placement decisions, the final placement may not be what the professional educators would have chosen without such input.

The most important concept implied in the phrase "variable service continuum" is that related to variability. This means that different types and amounts of service will be provided, *depending on the present needs of the child. The provision of services must remain flexible, with regular reassessment of present needs.* Therefore, the guidelines given in Table 6-2 are *general,* and may provide a starting point for future consideration.

The presence of additional handicapping conditions will usually lead to a need for more intensive special educational services and in many instances may dictate a special class or a special school setting. In all cases, level of intelligence, level of academic achievement, and psychologic adjustment to visual impairment will have a significant effect on the final determination of the most appropriate educational placement.

Summary

The more severely visually impaired have long been recognized as handicapped, because of the obvious physical nature of their impairment. On the other hand, until very recently, children with mild visual impairments often were not recognized, and their lower than average level of achievement was thought to be related to other causes. In either case, the visually impaired child is very much *like* all other children, with similar basic needs and motivations. In the various areas of growth and development (which form much of the basis of existing educational practices for nonhandicapped children) the blind child moves through the same sequence of development as all other children, but the rate of change may be slower or appear to be erratic, because of the effects of the visual impairment. These effects may be either direct (resulting directly from the visual impairment) or indirect (environmental restrictions imposed as a result of the impairment) and are the point of focus of special educational provisions for the visually impaired.

Historically, provisions for the visually impaired have ranged from separation or segregation at best to infanticide at worst. We have now moved to planned attempts to provide a near-normal educational program in the local public school systems of both the United States and Canada. If such programs are truly needed, they cannot be called "normal" since a number of special provisions are required—provisions that may vary greatly when comparing the mildly visually impaired and the blind. For the mildly visually impaired, an effective program may be little more complex than full knowledge by the child's parents and teachers of the limitations imposed by the impairment and availability of such optical aids as may be required. In the case of the more severely impaired, a more involved program is essential.

The concept of legal blindness is important in relation to such considerations as whether certain agencies can serve a particular individual, but the matter of degree of functional vision or *visual efficiency* is perhaps the most important consideration for educational purposes. This depends on all of the physiologic, psychologic, and environmental variables in effect in the life of the individual under consideration. Visual efficiency must be the concern of educators, and improving or maximizing visual efficiency is the goal of education of the visually impaired. With the more severely visually impaired it is imperative that this goal be pursued from the earliest possible time; in the case of congenital visual impairment, this should be undertaken when the child is only a few days old and must be continued throughout the preschool and school years.

To a considerable extent, the blind must apply the sense of touch for purposes of cognition, and although this is a powerful tool, it cannot be used with all objects or in all situations. As noted by Lowenfeld (1973), "Though touch has some unique advantages, vision functions as a unifying and structuring sense and in this it cannot be replaced by any or all of the remaining senses." (p. 56) Nevertheless, with proper early childhood planning and assistance and with adequate programming through the school years, the blind may very closely approach the learning efficiency they might have attained through vision.

Special educational provisions for the blind include a whole variety of methods whereby concrete experiences may substitute for the type of experiences sighted children may have almost without planning or effort. They particularly need experiences that will lead to the unification of information, an understanding of the wholeness or totality of both objects and situations. They may learn to read by using braille, but without planned opportunities to understand more fully those things about which they read, this skill will have greatly reduced meaning. They must have enriched language opportunities and must learn to interpret, through language, what others gain through visual scanning. This may be well illustrated in the situation where the blind must operate without the facial expressions that have so much meaning in social situations.

Another area of special concern, which has received full attention only in the past few decades, is the matter of orientation and mobility skills. These are the skills that allow the blind to move safely, efficiently, and gracefully from place to place, so that they can use those other skills and abilities that are the focus of normal educational/cognitive learning. Orientation is the establishment of position in space and relative position to other objects in the environment. Mobility is actual locomotion from place to place. In combination, these skills allow the blind person to move about independently, and they can be taught, though such teaching must be specifically planned and carefully implemented. Early encouragement for the blind child to crawl about and learn about the surroundings, to learn to explore bimanually, and to develop a base for further cognitive learning is also the best base for these skills. This is also commonly denied the young blind child by parents who are overprotective and have not been given information and training regarding this specific need.

Although the visually impaired child is operating under an obvious disadvantage in a world of sighted persons, the combination of proper early childhood opportunities, a full range of special educational opportunities in the schools, and acceptance by the general public as a worthy, competent member of society can lead to a full, satisfying life. This opportunity is greater today than at any previous time in history, and the challenge to those who might choose to become educators of the visually impaired is equally great. This is a fascinating professional field and one worthy of further exploration by those who find it truly interesting.

focus

introduction

The responsibility of educators of the visually impaired is to discover and assist children with any degree of impairment to use any remaining visual abilities to the maximum or, in the case of total blindness, to learn to use the other senses to compensate for the missing sense of vision.

establishment of schools in Europe

Haüy established the first actual school for the blind (The National Institution for Young Blind People) in Paris in 1784. He attempted to pattern educational practices in his school as nearly as possible after the practices in schools for sighted persons and taught the full range of subjects usually provided in most schools.

establishment of schools in the United States

Residential schools, following the pattern established by Howe in the 1830s, were the major vehicle for education of the blind for more than 100 years. Today only about one third of all visually impaired children are educated in residential programs.

anatomy and physiology of the visual system

It is of utmost importance to note that "normal" interpretation of the image falling on the retina depends on normal, consistent operation of the total visual system, including the brain, and that in many instances visual messages received through this system are processed in conjunction with information received simultaneously through other sensory channels.

Sensory impairments

definitions: terminology used to describe visual impairment or handicap

Visual impairment is a term used to describe any clinically diagnosable deviation in the structure or functioning of any part or parts of the eye.

Visually handicapped is a term used to indicate children who have impairments in the structure or functioning of the visual sense organ, regardless of the extent or the nature of this impairment.

The term *blind* indicates total loss of vision or only minimal light perception.

Low vision is the term used for those who have limitations in distance vision but may be able to see objects or materials at a distance of a few inches or perhaps a very few feet. Low vision children should not be considered blind and must be encouraged to use whatever vision they have.

Visually limited refers to the condition in which a student has some visual limitations under some circumstances. They should be considered seeing children who require some special aid.

Visual acuity refers to the ability to discriminate the details of an object (including abstract symbols) at specified distances.

Legally blind indicates a degree of visual impairment that has been established for identification purposes in relation to the capability or legality of various agencies to serve individuals as "blind" persons.

Visual perception means the ability to interpret what is seen. Educators consider *visual efficiency* when planning for any given student, and improvement of visual efficiency should be a major goal of educational programs for the visually impaired.

However classified, it is essential to remember that classification does not automatically determine program setting or content.

types and causes of visual impairment

Visual impairment may have a variety of causes: (1) congenital, (2) physical trauma, (3) infectious or other diseases, (4) poisoning, and (5) other unique causal factors that may be time- or area-specific

prevalence of visual impairment

The figure most often used to indicate the prevalence of visually impaired children in the population is 0.1 percent.

identification of children who are visually impaired

The Snellen chart is of value in screening for distance vision but is of little or no value for the child who has adequate distance vision but has visual difficulty at distances used for reading (12 to 16 inches). Other specialized instruments including a modified Snellen test for use at a distance of 14 inches have been developed for use in screening for near vision. The National Society for the Prevention of Blindness recommends that in addition to the Snellen test, visual screening should include testing for muscle balance, depth perception, and hyperopia.

teaching the visually impaired: approaches and techniques

There appears to be much less controversy regarding how to teach the visually impaired than exists with respect to the hearing impaired.

reading and writing for the visually impaired

There are at least two major areas in which the visually impaired must receive very special education and training: (1) reading and writing and (2) orientation and mobility.

orientation and mobility training

Orientation means the establishment of position in space, and relative position to other objects in the environment. It is a continually ongoing process and requires reestablished knowledge of position after each new step is taken.

Mobility is the actual locomotion (self-generated movement) of an individual from one fixed position to another position in the environment. Included in this process are such skills as proper heel and toe gait, control of the body's center of gravity, ability to detect inclines and declines, obstacle detection, and others. In combination, orientation and mobility should provide the visually impaired person the ability to move about independently.

The five modes of travel commonly used by visually impaired persons are: (1) independent travel without the use of devices or any other outside assistance, (2) the sighted guide, (3) the long cane, (4) dog guides, and (5) electronic devices.

techniques of daily living (TDL)

"Techniques of daily living (TDL) for the visually impaired are more than optional 'frills' for the school curriculum; they are an essential complement to the academics."

an educational placement system: application of the variable service continuum concept

Planning for the visually impaired requires careful consideration of a variety of factors: (1) age of student, (2) age of onset of visual impairment, (3) level of achievement, (4) level of intelligence, (5) presence of other handicapping conditions, (6) nature of visual impairment, and (7) emotional stability.

References and suggested readings

Abel, G. *Concerning the education of blind children*. New York: American Foundation for the Blind, 1959.

Barraga, N. *Visual handicaps and learning: a developmental approach*. Belmont, Calif.: Wadsworth Publishing Co., 1976.

Barraga, N. Utilization of sensory-perceptual abilities. In B. Lowenfeld (Ed.). *The visually handicapped child in school*. New York: John Day, 1973, pp. 117-154.

Cratty, B. *Movement and spatial awareness in blind children and youth*. Springfield, Ill.: Charles C Thomas, Publisher, 1971.

Davidow, M. *A guide for social competency*. Louisville, Ky.: American Printing House for the Blind, 1974.

Farrell, G. *The story of blindness*. Cambridge, Mass.: Harvard University Press, 1956.

Gearheart, B., and Weishahn, M. *The handicapped student in the regular classroom*. St. Louis: The C. V. Mosby Co., 1980.

Howe, S. Address delivered in 1866 at Batavia, New York. (Republished: *Blindness 1965*, Washington, D.C.: American Association of Workers for the Blind, pp. 165-188.)

Knight, J. Mannerisms in the congenitally blind child. *New Outlook for the Blind*, 1972, 66, 297-302.

Lowenfeld, B. (Ed.). *The visually handicapped child in school*. New York: John Day, 1973.

Lowenfeld, B., Abel, G., and Hatlen, P. *Blind children learn to read*. Springfield, Ill.: Charles C Thomas, Publisher, 1969.

Napier, G. The visually disabled. In Gearheart, B. (Ed.). *Education of the exceptional child; history, present practices, and trends*. Scranton, Pa.: Intext, 1972, pp. 75-123.

Tisdall, W. J. The visually impaired child. In *Exceptional Children research review*. Johnson, G. O., and Blank, H. (Eds.). Washington D.C.: Council for Exceptional Children, 1968, pp. 110-134

Tillman, M., and Osborne, R. The performance of blind and sighted children on the Wechsler Intelligence Scale for Children: interaction effects. *Education of the Visually Handicapped*, 1969, 1, 1-4.

Tuttle, D. In *Handbook for teachers of the visually handicapped*, ed. 3. Napier, G., Kappan, O., and Tuttle, D. (Eds.). New York: American Printing House for the Blind, 1974.

Weishahn, M. Modes of travel. Unpublished paper, 1976.

Witken, H., Oltman, P., Chase, J., and Friedman, F. Cognitive patterning in the blind. In *Cognitive studies—deficits in cognition*. J. Hellmuth (Ed.). New York: Brunner-Mazel, 1971, pp. 16-46.

SECTION FOUR

Learning disabilities and speech/language disorders

In this section we will consider one very newly recognized area of disability and one that has been known for hundreds of years. Learning disabilities became a recognized entity in the early 1960s, whereas speech disorders, especially stuttering, have been recognized since long before the time of Christ. What do these two conditions have in common? Learning disabilities, an umbrella term that includes a number of more specific disabilities, includes some subareas, such as asphasia, that have been the target of efforts by some speech/language pathologists for years. In addition, both include language disabilities as part of their domain, although each includes more than language disabilities.

A third commonality (which is not necessarily a reason for grouping these two areas together, but is a common feature) is the level of social acceptability of these two conditions. Handicapping conditions such as mental retardation and emotional disturbance are often viewed in a quite negative manner by much of the general public and have been recognized as negative in connotation by courts of law. Learning disabilities and speech/language disorders do not usually carry this high degree of stigma. In fact, some parents have gone to considerable lengths to have their handicapped children "reclassified" as learning disabled, in preference to an earlier classification as mentally retarded.

One final common feature of learning disabilities and speech/language disorders is that both are considered potentially remediable. Although such remediation is not always accomplished, the fact that remediation is considered possible makes these two areas somewhat unique.

In this section we will consider these two types of disabilities, the "old" and the "new," and attempt to better understand causes, characteristics, educational approaches, and the future professional possibilities of those who may consider entering either of these fields of interest.

Visual perception is an important facet of learning.

chapter 7

Education of children and youth with learning disabilities

objectives

To describe and discuss the manner in which learning disabilities evolved from a number of conditions or syndromes previously recognized as separate entities.

To consider the problem of definitions of learning disabilities and the resultant difficulties in establishing acceptable prevalence data.

To review the characteristics of learning disabled students and present practices in identification of the learning disabled.

To consider and discuss the major approaches to teaching the learning disabled, the underlying theoretical constructs, and the educational implications of each approach.

To outline the manner in which the principle of the least restrictive environment applies to programming for the learning disabled student.

Introduction

Learning disabilities is the newest of the recognized subareas of special education, although its historical roots go back nearly 200 years. The generally recognized "birthday" of this special area of interest came in 1963; this was actually a time of integration of a number of earlier, more narrow efforts, and a time when the name "learning disabilities" was formally suggested. Since that time, the term "learning disabilities" has been popularized and at times overused to the point that some skeptics suggest that it may be just a figment of the imagination.

In this chapter we will review the historical antecedents of the area of learning disabilities, look at its recent growth, and attempt to describe the field as it presently exists. To accomplish this we will examine definitions, procedures for identification, and some of the major theoretical constructs on which remedial efforts are based. Following the description of each theoretical base, we will consider the educational implications growing out of this base. We will conclude this chapter with a look at the manner in which the various types of service delivery systems may apply to learning disabled students at both the elementary and secondary level. In total, this information should permit the reader to determine whether he or she wishes to delve further into this interesting, but sometimes confusing, area of special education.

Historical origins of education of the learning disabled

Many authors who have described the development of the field of learning disabilities have indicated that it came into being in the early 1960s or perhaps specifically in 1963. However, nearly all note that it has its origins in a number of efforts and events that can be traced back at least as far as 1800. Rather than review this development in terms of a series of stages or time periods, we will consider only two major periods. We will review some of the earlier efforts as they led up to the 1963 "date of birth" of this field of specialization, then consider the developments since 1963. It should be obvious that if this newborn infant required a period of gestation of more than 150 years, it should have been born full of energy, ready to grow and develop. Our historic account bears out this premise and also indicates that the field of learning disabilities remains an infant, with a great deal more "growing up" to accomplish.

FOUNDATIONS OF LEARNING DISABILITIES (PRIOR TO 1963)

Franz Joseph Gall, a Viennese physician, is credited by Wiederholt (1974) with being among the earliest pioneers in the investigation of disorders of spoken language, an area that became part of the foundation of what we now call learning disabilities. Gall, in 1802, published an account of his theories in which he attempted to relate specific brain activities with identifiable parts of the brain. Gall had worked with brain-injured adults who had injuries resulting from a variety of causes. These patients had acquired language difficulties immediately following known injuries, and Gall believed he could relate specific areas of damage to what we would now call aphasia. He described patients who, after their brain was damaged, were unable to express feelings and ideas in spoken language. Unfortunately, Gall became connected with phrenology (a system that allegedly could predict personal characteristics through knowledge of the shape and character of protuberances of the skull) and was soon discredited. Thus any lasting value that might have come from his earlier work was lost, except as it was carried on by some of his followers who rejected his interest in phrenology (Head, 1926). Dember (1964) provides a record of specific contributions relating to visual perception in 1801, another strand that was to become a part of learning disabilities at a later date. Thus we see at least two specific instances of contributions at the very start of the nineteenth century, which were to grow through a series of additional investigations into much more scientific research by the end of the century.

By 1900, a number of other physicians had carried forward the work started by Gall; a great deal more had been learned about the differing functions of the two sides of the brain and relationships with language disorders. In the area of visual perception, some specific efforts that were to result in the popularization of the term "word blindness" were taking place. In 1895, James Hinshelwood, an ophthalmologist, published a report on word blindness that documented the existence of severe reading disabilities in children with normal intelligence. In 1896, two British investigators, James Kerr, a physician, and W. P. Morgan, an ophthalmologist, reported similar cases of severe reading problems despite normal intelligence (Gearheart, 1977).

It is of some interest that the earlier work in the area of aphasia was primarily with adults, whereas the work of those interested in word blindess (a term that was to later become dyslexia) was with children. The aphasia studies had to do with abilities that had been developed and then were lost. The word blindness studies related to children and youth who had apparently normal intelligence but had been unable to unlock the mysteries of learning to read.

Hinshelwood, in 1917, published the first comprehensive description of a specific disorder of written language (word blindness) which also included methods of teaching students who suffered from such a condition. His method included three major steps: (1) teaching the student to "store," in the visual-memory part of the brain, the individual letters of the alphabet, (2) teaching the student to spell words out loud, thus developing, through auditory memory, the ability to retrieve the entire word, and (3) transferring this auditory retrieval to the visual memory center of the brain. His methods were based on his understanding of brain functioning, and he was pragmatic enough to note that "no amount of argument can decide the question as to the best method of instruction in these cases. The test of experience alone can definitely settle this point." (Hinshelwood, 1917, p. 107)

The theories of brain functioning advanced by James Hinshelwood are now recognized to have been inaccurate, but his contributions provided important stimulation for further investigation and certain of his educational recommendations are used, with little modification, today. The fact that he attempted to understand the phenomenon called word blindness, and viewed it as a problem amenable to intervention through educational procedures, was a most important step in the right direction. Some were content to consider the student who could not read as mentally retarded and let the matter go at that. Hinshelwood, and others who would soon follow, recognized that some youngsters had otherwise normal intelligence but could not read for unknown reasons. Their efforts were directed toward understanding these reasons and providing special educational assistance.

Following this early work, which was not always associated with "learning disabilities," we encounter the efforts of individuals who are commonly recognized as learning disabilities pioneers. These include individuals who were primarily interested in students who were unusually hyperactive, individuals whose major interests were the disorders of reading and written language, those interested in disorders of spoken language, and a fourth group, called perceptual motor theorists. In a major section of this chapter devoted to various theoretical constructs and the educational implications that grow out of these constructs, we will discuss the efforts of Grace Fernald, Samuel Orton, Anna Gillingham, Alfred Strauss, Laura Lehtinen, William Cruickshank, Newell Kephart, Gerald Getman, Marianne Frostig, Helmer Myklebust, and Samuel Kirk. These individuals and others developed the field of learning disabilities. Until the 1960s it was not called learning disabilities, but they worked with students who had remarkable similarities, and would later come to be called learning disabled. A review of their contributions will provide an important part of the discussion of theoretical constructs, which begins on p. 183.

LEARNING DISABILITIES: A RECOGNIZED ENTITY (1963 TO THE PRESENT)

Learning disabilities programming was taking place prior to 1963, but it existed under a variety of labels, and viable programs were not available in much of the United States. Students who would now be called learning disabled were served in classes for: (1) hyperactive students, (2) brain-injured students, (3) Strauss syndrome students, (4) dyslexic students, (5) students with perceptual disorders, (6) students with perceptual-motor disorders, (7) minimal brain dysfunction (MBD) students, (8) dysgraphic students, (9) asphasic students, (10) neurologically impaired students, and others. In some states, students whose disability led to unacceptable behavior were not permitted in the schools. Parents of these children who were not being served banded together to attempt to learn more about their children's needs and to try to convince the public schools to provide appropriate special educational programs. The time was ripe for action.

On April 6, 1963, one such parent group, the Fund for Perceptually Handicapped Children, Inc., was holding its first annual meeting, hoping to establish direction for future efforts. Dr. Samuel Kirk, one of the most highly respected and widely recognized special educators of that time, was attempting to provide these parents with additional insight regarding the futility of the various labels that were then used for their children. In his speech, Kirk (1963) said:

> I have felt for some time that labels we give children are satisfying to us, but of little help to the child himself. We seem to be satisfied if we can give a technical name to a condition. This gives us the satisfaction of closure. We think we know the answer if we can give the child a name or a label—brain injured, schizophrenic, autistic, mentally retarded, aphasic, etc. As indicated before, the term "brain injured" has little meaning to me from a management or training point of view. It does not tell me whether the child is smart or dull, hyperactive or under-active. It does not give me any clues to management or training. The terms cerebral palsy, brain injured, mentally retarded, aphasic etc., are actually classification terms. In a sense they are not diagnostic, if by diagnostic we mean an assessment of the child in such a way that leads to some form of treatment, management, or remediation. In addition, it is not a basic cause, since the designation of a child as brain injured does not really tell us why the child is brain injured or how he got that way. (pp. 2-3)

Kirk continued by noting that he had recently been using the term "learning disabilities" to describe children "who have disorders in development in language, speech, reading, and associated communication skills needed for social interaction" (pp. 2-3). He noted that he did *not* include within this group children who have sensory handicaps such as blindness or deafness or those with generalized mental retardation.

Ironically, in a speech suggesting that both parents and educators often become overdependent on labels that provide little meaningful educational guidance, Kirk suggested a new label—learning disabilities—which quickly became the fastest growing term ever seen in special education. Parents attending this convention voted, while still convened, to organize the Association for Children with Learning Disabilities (ACLD) and thus the term learning disabilities began a rapid ascendance to national prominence. Since 1963 the ACLD has developed into a powerful advocacy organization, which successfully lobbied for special national legislation for the learning disabled that later became part of Public Law 94-142.

During the first half of the 1960s there were no full-length texts about the broad area of learning disabilities. Ten years later (1970 to 1975) new books about learning disabilities outnumbered new books about any other recognized area of handicap. In a parallel comparison we may note that in 1965 there were two states that provided special programs specifically for the learning disabled, through special state legislation and/or regulations referring to learning disabilities by name. Ten years later, all fifty states had such provision. Learning disabilities programs literally exploded upon the nation during this 10-year period.

As we enter the first half of the 1980s, the explosive nature of earlier programming efforts has subsided. Some expansion at the secondary level still must be accomplished, but for the most part learning disabilities programs have spanned the nation. It is now time for a more careful reappraisal of what we are doing and how well we are doing it. It is a time for investment in quality rather than quantity.

Definitions and prevalence

Definitions of learning disabilities as they appear in state regulations have been varied ever since learning disabilities were first recognized. In some states, it was a matter of modifying some existing definition to include what was now recognized as learning disabilities. In most cases, it was the theoretical or philosophic biases of those in decision-making positions within the state, rather than any type of research evidence, that influenced the first definitions. The first truly national definition was provided by a committee established coincident with the establishment of the Bureau of Education for the Handicapped (BEH) in the Office of Education. This group, the National Advisory Committee on Handicapped Children, was headed by none other than Dr. Samuel Kirk. In its first annual report, the committee made ten major recommendations, including a recommendation that high priority be given to funding that would encourage the development of learning disabilities programs throughout the nation. And, recognizing the need for a definition, the committee report noted that:

> Confusion now exists with relationship to the category of special learning disabilities. Unfortunately it has resulted in the development of overlapping and competing programs under such headings as "minimal brain dysfunction," "dyslexia," "perceptual handicaps," etc.*

The committee then suggested the following definition:

> Children with special learning disabilities exhibit a disorder in one or more of the basic psychological processes involved in understanding or in using spoken or written languages. These may be manifested in disorders of listening, thinking, talking, reading, writing, spelling, or arithmetic. They include conditions which have been referred to as perceptual handicaps, brain injury, minimal brain dysfunction, dyslexia, developmental [a]phasia, etc. They do not include learning problems which are due primarily to

---

*First Annual Report of the National Advisory Committee on Handicapped Children, Washington, D.C., Office of Education, Department of Health, Education and Welfare, 1968.

visual, hearing, or motor handicaps, to mental retardation, emotional disturbance, or to environmental disadvantage.*

This definition is obviously quite different in form from definitions of many of the other handicapping conditions, but there were good reasons for the way it was first established. Major among these reasons were:

1. At the time this definition was proposed, there were established programs for the mentally retarded, hearing handicapped, visually handicapped, and so forth. The definition was necessary to provide an administrative funding vehicle whereby special state level reimbursement could be provided to assure the existence of special programs for children who did not have these other handicaps and therefore could not be served through existing programs. Local school districts should provide for the needs of all children, whether or not special state funds are forthcoming, but we know that this has seldom been the case and that special incentive monies are the best answer at present.

2. There was agreement regarding the existence of a number of conditions that led to unique learning difficulties but which, taken singly, provided insufficient numbers of children for economical special programming. These conditions had (or were assumed to have) a variety of causes, but in fact all led to the existence of significant discrepancies between apparent ability to learn and actual learning. The concept of learning disabilities provided a convenient "umbrella" under which most of these conditions could fit without having to specify causation.

3. Although some members of the specialty professions that banded together to form the initial learning disabilities cadre disagreed with the use of this general term, there was even more disagreement as to precisely what caused these problems and what to do about remediation. Even if it had been decided, for example, to use a series of terms more consistent with the model suggested by the terms "blind," "deaf," or "mentally retarded," there could have been no agreement as to causation and thus to acceptable terminology. "Learning disabilities" provided a middle ground on which these specialists could meet.

The federal government was interested in the establishment of some sort of framework within which they could provide funds for demonstration projects and research efforts, and thus welcomed this definition. Their interest was in part a reflection of the genuine interest of professionals employed by the Bureau of Education for the Handicapped and in part a result of the need to do something about the considerable "heat" generated by the membership of the Association for Children with Learning Disabilities, which had gathered great strength in its first 5 years of existence. At any rate, a definition now existed, though it was due to be the target of continuing controversy and criticism.

The "definition controversy," as it was referred to in various journal articles, has continued to this day and has included such unusual actions as the U.S. Congress imposing limitations on the percentage of students who could be served with federal funds under this categorical label when it passed Public Law 94-142. These limitations have now been eliminated, but professionals are on notice that they must not attempt to overuse the learning disabilities category to the detriment or exclusion of other categories of handicap.

Certain terms are in regular use in the various definitions of learning disabilities. In a study of the various components used in defining or describing learning disabilities, Bai-

---

First Annual Report of the National Advisory Committee on Handicapped Children, Washington, D.C., Office of Education, Department of Health, Education and Welfare, 1968.

ley (1977) surveyed the definitions used in the laws of the various states and the definitions or descriptions used by nearly thirty recognized authors in this area of specialty. Her study indicates that language disorders and perceptual disorders are the two leading components in such definitions, closely followed by the concept of a significant discrepancy between academic achievement and the potential to achieve, and the exclusion of those who are mentally retarded, blind, deaf, and so forth. Her study also suggests that the states are growing toward more similar definitions and that the focus might be the national definition proposed by the Bureau of Education for the Handicapped.

After considerable vacillation while attempting to achieve some sort of meaningful consensus from learning disabilities practitioners through a series of public hearings, the final definition enunciated at the federal level, as part of the regulations of Public Law 94-142, is as follows:

> *Specific learning disability* means a disorder in one or more of the basic psychological processes involved in understanding or in using language, spoken or written, which may manifest itself in an imperfect ability to listen, think, speak, read, write, spell, or to do mathematical calculations. The term includes such conditions as perceptual handicaps, brain injury, minimal brain dysfunction, dyslexia, and developmental aphasia. The term does not include children who have learning problems which are primarily the result of visual, hearing, or motor handicaps, of mental retardation, of emotional disturbance, or of environmental, cultural, or economic disadvantage.

This definition is from an amendment of earlier Rules and Regulations for PL 94-142, and was published in the *Federal Register*.*
The reader will note how very similar this definition is to the first proposed definition, quoted earlier in this discussion. Perhaps we can maintain this definition until we learn enough about learning disabilities to make a meaningful change.

The matter of prevalence of learning disabilities is also the subject of some debate. Also, because learning disabilities are accepted as being remediable, there is likely to be a higher percentage at the lower grade levels with a lower percentage at higher grades after some remediation has taken place. The overall percentage of children with learning disabilities is generally accepted to be between 1 and 3 percent, with more authorities apparently supporting a 2 to 3 percent figure. Some estimates as high as 10 to 15 percent may be found in the literature, but they are generally discounted. A great deal more could be said about prevalence, with numerous sources cited, but for purposes of consideration in this text, we will accept the 2 to 3 percent estimate.

Identification of students who are learning disabled

The definition presented in the preceding section makes it difficult to identify young children who are learning disabled until they have actually attempted academic tasks. It is possible to identify a significant lag or discrepancy in oral expression or listening comprehension for a preschool child, but it is more common to think of younger children as being "at risk" of becoming learning disabled. There are certain recognized characteristics of children with learning disabilities, which include hyperactivity, hypoactivity, incoordination, general motor difficulties, perseveration, inattention, overattention, visual perceptual difficulties, or auditory perceptual difficulties which might be noted in young children, but any one of these characteristics is not sufficient to identify a young child as

---

*Vol. 42, No. 250, December 29, 1977; p. 65083.

learning disabled. These characteristics are more common to learning disabled students than to the population as a whole, *but with any one student they are nothing more than indicative of the possibility of identification as learning disabled.* Identification depends on the existence of significant learning/academic problems as specified in the "Criteria for Determining the Existence of a learning Disability," outlined in the same *Rules and Regulations (Federal Register)* from which the definition in the last section was derived. The criteria follow:

Criteria for determining the existence of a specific learning disability

(a) A team may determine that a child has a specific learning disability if:
  (1) The child does not achieve commensurate with his or her age and ability levels in one or more of the areas listed in paragraph (a)(2) of this section, when provided with learning experiences appropriate for the child's age and ability levels; and
  (2) The team finds that a child has a severe discrepancy between achievement and intellectual ability in one or more of the following areas:
      (i) Oral expression;
      (ii) Listening comprehension;
      (iii) Written expression;
      (iv) Basic reading skill;
      (v) Reading comprehension;
      (vi) Mathematics calculation; or
      (vii) Mathematics reasoning.
(b) The team may not identify a child as having a specific learning disability if the severe discrepancy between ability and achievement is primarily the result of:
  (1) A visual, hearing, or motor handicap;
  (2) Mental retardation;
  (3) Emotional disturbance; or
  (4) Environmental, cultural or economic disadvantage.

As with other handicapping conditions already reviewed in this text, students are brought to the attention of those who may consider the possibility of an identifiable handicap, in the manner outlined on pp. 55-57. Usually there is a specific teacher referral, or the student's possible needs are identified through some screening program. In either instance, if preliminary review indicates the possibility of learning disabilities, parental approval for further assessment will be sought. If such approval is obtained, a series of tests, examinations, and data gathering will be initiated. To determine the possibility of a learning disability, the first step may be tests of visual and auditory acuity to rule out sensory deficits as a cause of the educational problems. At the same time, requests for a physical examination and the gathering of developmental history will be initiated. A speech/language assessment will also be obtained.

Some measure of the child's level of intellectual functioning must be completed; this will usually be the Stanford-Binet or one of the Wechsler tests of intelligence. If there is any indication of below average intelligence or variable results on these tests indicating possible sources of test bias, an additional nonverbal test of intelligence will be administered. If, at this point, there is any possibility that the student might be considered mildly mentally retarded, or even within several IQ points of the upper limits of mild mental retardation, a measure of adaptive behavior should be used to further establish the validity of the IQ test results.

The appropriate assessment personnel should be alerted to the possibility of emotional components in the spectrum of causation. Where available data indicate this is not the case, such assessment may not be necessary.

Educational assessment must be completed to obtain accurate, norm-referenced data as to the students' functional level in the various academic areas. Appropriate diagnostic tests should be used, as indicated by the assessment or data supplied by the referring teacher(s). Assessment of auditory and visual processing abilities will be required in some cases; in others, such assessment may be administered after the student is accepted for special programming. (When a very severe discrepancy between achievement and intellectual ability exists, extensive tests of specific processing abilities may not be required for identification and program placement but will be administered after placement in the special program setting.)

Identification is accomplished when the assessment team has completed the staffing procedure and has concluded that the student is in fact eligible for assistance as a student with learning disabilities. Since the parents must be a part of this staffing (see p. 58), they too must accept the diagnosis. Identification is thus a matter of evaluation of a wide variety of educational, psychologic, and health related information by a team of individuals who can integrate these data and make a meaningful educational judgment, following the identification guidelines that grow out of the definition of learning disabilities.

Approaches, theoretical constructs, and educational implications

In the discussion of various approaches, underlying theoretical constructs, and the educational implications of these approaches and constructs, three objectives will be achieved. These are:

1. The history of learning disabilities will be extended to consider a number of authorities who have had recent major impact on this developing field. In fact, this discussion might be considered to be a type of "Who's Who" in the field of learning disabilities.
2. The nature of the condition we presently call learning disabilities will be further amplified through this review of major authorities and the approaches they espoused.
3. The brief discussions of the educational implications deriving from each of these approaches will give us a better understanding of what can or must be done by educators who enter this field of specialty.

We will initiate this review with the "oldest" approach (in terms of actual historical appearance) and will not attempt to pinpoint the time when the seeds that eventually germinated into each of these approaches were sown. Some theorists are most difficult to place within just one theoretical structure, although we will attempt to do so for this review. The degree of overlap between some of these approaches is considerable, and in some cases some authors consider one approach as a component of other more comprehensive approaches. We will not enter this debate, for it is based on theoretical considerations, and perhaps on personal biases of some of the debaters. We will begin our consideration of these various approaches with an approach or method that was just getting well underway in the early 1920s.

MULTISENSORY APPROACHES

"Multisensory" may mean different things to different people. In general, it means the use of more than one sensory channel or modality, but whether it means the use of two, three, or all sensory modalities can be a point of disagreement. There is also the question as to whether multisensory means or infers *simultaneous* use of several sensory modalities. It is obvious that most individuals, when reading aloud, are using more than one sensory modality. It is equally obvious that many commercial learning materials could be called "multisensory." What, then, is so special about multisensory approaches? Let us first provide a definition for multisensory, then proceed with an answer to this question.

For purposes of this chapter, multisensory will be defined to mean the "deliberate use of three or more of the sensory channels in the teaching/learning process. More often it will refer to the use of four modalities: visual, auditory, kinesthetic, and tactile." (Gearheart, 1977, p. 91) A majority of students with normal learning abilities learn through all of the sensory modalities, with some depending more on the auditory, others more on the visual. Blind students learn through a combination of auditory, tactile, kinesthetic, and, to some degree, olfactory. Deaf students learn through the visual, tactile, kinesthetic, and, to some degree, olfactory. Thus individuals with these two handicaps provide positive evidence that neither of the two modalities most often emphasized in school, vision and hearing, is absolutely essential for success in academic pursuits. Most would agree, however, that a combination of visual and auditory learning is the most effective for most students.

In our later discussion of perceptual-motor approaches, we will consider how early kinesthetic and tactile experiences and related motor development lead to later visual and auditory abilities. Most of us realize that young children are very oriented to tactile and kinesthetic experiences; they must touch and feel new objects as part of learning about them. But somehow we expect all young children who enter kindergarten or first grade to very quickly switch to a learning environment that emphasizes visual and auditory experiences as the major tools for developing basic academic skills, almost to the exclusion of the tactile and kinesthetic. Happily, this works relatively well for a large majority of such students, but for some it does not work. These students, whom we may define as remedial reading cases, students with learning disabilities, or perhaps dyslexics, are those with whom most of the multisensory approach authorities would advocate the multisensory approach.

One of the earliest of the *educators* who developed an established, recognized special approach for students we would now call learning disabled was *Grace Fernald*. Her approach may represent the most comprehensive, total, balanced multisensory system yet devised. It requires the simultaneous use of *v*isual, *au*ditory, *k*inesthetic, and *t*actile sensory channels and has often been called a VAKT approach. Her method has also been called a "tracing" approach, because of the planned use of tracing.

Fernald used her approach in a clinic school at the University of California at Los Angeles, established in 1921 (Fernald, 1943). She maintained her program at UCLA through the years, further expanded the clinic, and perfected her methods. The following description of Fernald's approach is derived from the first full-scale, nationally published account of her methodology, a text published in 1943 (Fernald, 1943). This book is regarded by many as a classic and was still in publication in the late 1970s.

Before initiating the actual VAKT procedure, Fernald believes that it is essential to do something to attempt to reverse the very low self-concept that many students who have had consistent learning problems will have. Her belief has been reaffirmed by many other recognized remedial and learning disabilities practitioners, and many, like Fernald, call this procedure "positive reconditioning."

The major steps in the Fernald method are indicated here. Although Fernald developed procedures for use in various academic subjects, her major emphasis was in reading; therefore, we will illustrate her methods with respect to reading.

1. The first major step is to explain that there is a new way of learning words that really works. The student is told that others have had similar problems and have learned through this new method. The *newness* of the method is emphasized.
2. The student is asked to select any word he wants to learn, regardless of length.
3. The word is written for the student, usually with a crayon in plain, blackboard-size cursive writing. In most cases, regardless of age, cursive writing is used rather than printing, because it permits the student to see and "feel" the word as a single unit rather than a group of separate letters.
4. The student traces the word with his fingers in contact with the paper, saying the word as he traces it. This is repeated as many times as necessary until he can write the word without looking at the copy.
5. The student writes the word, demonstrating that it is now "his" word. Writing with large letters seems to be more effective than using small letters. Several words are taught in this manner, and as much time as necessary is taken to completely master these words.
6. When the student has internalized the fact that he can write and recognize words, he is encouraged to start writing stories. These stories are whatever he wishes them to be at first, and the instructor "gives" him any words (in addition to those he has mastered) he needs to complete the story.
7. After the story is written, it is typed, and the student is to read it in typed form while it is still fresh in his mind. It is important that this is done immediately to relate cursive with printed words.
8. After the story is completed and the new word has been used in a meaningful way, the student writes the new word on a card, which is filed alphabetically in the students individual word file. This word file is a meaningful way to teach the alphabet without undue emphasis on rote memory.

This procedure has been called the tracing method because tracing is an added feature in contrast to the usual methods of teaching reading or word recognition. However, it should be noted that the child is simultaneously *feeling, seeing, saying, and hearing* the word. Thus this is truly a multisensory approach.

There are several other points to be observed and followed for greatest success. We will simply list these points, with minimal amplification, to illustrate Fernald's method for maximizing multisensory input.*

1. Words should be selected *by the student* to maximize motivation.
2. Finger contact is essential while tracing.
3. After tracing a word the number of times required to permit writing with success, the student should write the word several times *without* looking at the copy.
4. In case of errors, the word should be written over from the beginning; erasures should not be permitted since the total word must be "felt" accurately.
5. Stories must be used at the earliest possible time to reinforce the idea that words carry a message; words should be used in normal context.
6. The student should say the word aloud as it is traced or written. This provides auditory support and additional kinesthetic support through the "feel" of the word (in the lips, tongue, jaws, and throat) as it is said.

Fernald provided for a transition stage in which tracing was seldom or never required, and then to a stage at which printed rather than cursive words were used. The final goal is to return to normal reading methods; however, case studies provided in Fernald's 1943

---

*For a more detailed description of the Fernald approach, see the chapter of Multisensory Systems, in *Learning Disabilities: Educational Strategies* (Gearheart, 1977, pp. 91-111).

text indicate that some students who learned through this approach continued to use tracing intermittently throughout their school career as they had difficulty in remembering specific new words. We might also note that many college students, perhaps the majority, "copy" words, phrases, or ideas they want to remember when studying for tests. They too have apparently found that the kinesthetic and tactile modalities (used in copying) provide excellent support for a sagging or recalcitrant memory.

Another recognized pioneer in this field whose efforts led to a multisensory method was *Samuel Orton*. Dr. Orton, a professor of psychiatry at the University of Iowa, became involved in a number of mobile clinics designed to serve the needs of rural areas of Iowa. In his work in these clinics, he encountered an unusual 16-year-old boy he called M.P. This boy had never learned to read, despite adequate intelligence, and became the subject of intensive study by Dr. Orton and staff at the university. In addition to M.P., Orton found others with similar disabilities. In laboratory testing it was determined that many of them had difficulty with reversals (for example, reading *saw* as *was*), confusion of *b* and *d*, and other such confusion of visual symbols. Orton became involved in this problem, and after further study established hypotheses relating to both reading methodology and what was actually taking place neurologically.

Orton had been involved in a study that correlated clinical symptoms with anatomic findings in adults who had suffered language impairment before death (a postmortem, human brain study), and had the interest and the background to pursue the question of possible neurologic causation in reading disability. Orton presented his field findings and theories to the American Neurological Association meeting in 1925. As a result of enthusiastic acceptance and interest in his report, he received a Rockefeller Foundation Grant to carry on his work. He organized an excellent clinical team and completed a number of studies of interest. Orton coined the word "strephosymbolia" (twisted symbols) to describe the memory-for-word-pattern and letter orientation problems of those with whom he worked.

Orton's impact on the type of disability that was soon to be called dyslexia, and later to be merged with learning disabilities, was multiplied by a later contact with *Anna Gillingham*, a remedial reading specialist. At the Neurological Institute, Columbia-Presbyterian Medical Center in New York, they worked together and evolved a multisensory method that was soon to be called the Orton-Gilligham method. Orton's theoretical postulations (now believed to be unacceptable) were based on the belief that the dominant hemisphere is opposite the preferred hand. He believed, in the case of mirror writing and reversals, that at times when the "image" of a word or letter was stored on the dominant hemisphere, a mirrored image was stored on the opposite hemisphere. Then, with mixed dominance, the individual might select inconsistently, leading to reversals, mirror writing, etc.

The Orton Society, a group of individuals who carry on many of the Orton-Gillingham methods, remains active today. Their major concern is reading difficulties that they would describe as dyslexia, and a number of school districts throughout the United States use certain of the Orton-Gillingham approach components with various handicapped students, especially the learning disabled and the educable mentally retarded; some regular class teachers use them also.

The Orton-Gillingham approach is a multisensory approach, but it is significantly different from the Fernald method. In the Orton-

Gillingham approach the initial effort is phonetic, learning to recognize and properly reproduce certain specific sounds. Words are then put together one letter at a time, starting with certain very simple words. Whereas Fernald encourages student selection of words, the Orton-Gillingham approach specifies the initial words. However, many important elements are the same. Both use positive reconditioning prior to launching actual remediation, both use visual, auditory, kinesthetic, and tactile channels; both emphasize tracing; and both prefer cursive writing as a starting point for remediation.

Educational implications. The educational implications of multisensory approaches relate both to specific approaches and the various components of such approaches in use by many teachers every day. Some teachers use such components and ideas because they are so basically logical; they may know little or nothing of the existence of the VAKT or Orton-Gillingham approach. Other teachers study one or both of these approaches and experiment with elements that are consistent with their present teaching style.

In addition to multisensory approaches, a number of spin-off techniques have developed as a result of the fact that multisensory approaches call the teacher's attention to the value of the kinesthetic and tactile modalities. For example, various tracing techniques may be of value for young students who have difficulty with letter or word recognition. This includes tracing of sandpaper words or letters, tracing of raised words or letters, tracing in a small sandbox, or any technique in which the surface of the letter feels different from the background. In other variations, words may be traced on the student's hand or back, or the student's arm may be moved in a pattern that represents the form of a given letter. Other techniques such as "feeling" objects or plastic letters in a sack or inside a box where they cannot be seen also make use of the kinesthetic and tactile senses.

The various multisensory approaches have been of great value with some learning disabled students and of no apparent value with others. It is difficult to say whether, in all cases, it was a matter of the appropriateness of the method, or some other factor(s) that made the difference, but there has been sufficient success to suggest the careful consideration of such approaches for some learning disabled students.

HYPERACTIVITY: THEORIES AND APPROACHES

Hyperactivity is one of the more often mentioned characteristics of learning disabled students, and one of the early approaches to teaching hyperactive students with learning problems was initiated by *Alfred Strauss*. Strauss left Nazi Germany in 1933 and, after a 3-year stay in Spain, came to the United States as a research psychiatrist (Hallahan and Cruickshank, 1973). Strauss had considerable earlier experience with brain-injured persons in Germany and soon began to apply his knowledge in the United States with children who acted like brain-injured children but who had no definite evidence of brain injury. Strauss worked with a number of other individuals who were later to become well known in the field of learning disabilities and, in a joint effort with *Laura Lehtinen*, authored a classic text entitled *Psychopathology and Education of the Brain Injured Child* in 1947. This text was widely used for at least 20 years and received some usage beyond that time. Strauss's work was based in part on his experience and research, in part on the theoretical formulations of Heinz Werner, and in part on the educational expertise of Laura Lehtinen. Strauss and others initiated Cove Schools for brain-injured students who were not admitted to public schools, and formulated and perfected methods for manipulating and controlling the environment so that brain-injured students would not become overstimulated.

The procedure for manipulating the environment, which we shall refer to as the *environmental control* approach, became so closely related to Strauss that students who had the symptoms described by Strauss were often called "Strauss syndrome students," and in a few instances classes for such students were called "Strauss syndrome classes," even in state regulations.

Other individuals have also been associated with the concept of controlling the environment to reduce hyperactivity in learning disabled students who exhibit such characteristics. Among the best-known is *William Cruickshank,* who worked for a time with Strauss. His recommendations for environmental control are quite similar to those of Strauss and Lehtinen.

Environmental control is based on the assumption that for some reason or combination of reasons the receipt of what would be normal auditory, visual, tactile, or kinesthetic stimulation to most other individuals causes serious problems for the hyperactive student. This effect is regularly observed in students who are known to be brain damaged, and a similar effect may be seen in students who exhibit some of the symptoms commonly associated with brain damage but cannot be so diagnosed with certainty. The matter of how hyperactivity interferes with learning has been subject to a great deal of speculation, but two interesting theories, outline by Keogh (1971), deserve further consideration.

One of these theories assumes that, although the student is neurally intact, *the nature and extent of the excess motor activity are such that the activity interferes with the basic acquisition of information.* For example, if such students cannot attend to what they are attempting to read, what they are seeing in a film, or what the teacher is presenting long enough to actually acquire the information, they will not learn effectively. This learning loss soon becomes cumulative, and these students eventually may be diagnosed as learning disabled. This theory seems to be supported by investigations indicating that if motor activity is reduced, many students are able to learn more effectively.

A second theory or hypothesis may be called the *decision-making hypothesis.* This hypothesis assumes that the decision-making process (rather than the information acquisition stage) is the basic source of academic difficulty for the hyperactive student. This hypothesis, in very simple terms, indicates that the hyperactive student makes decisions too quickly and thus makes them on the basis of too little information. This too-fast, impulsivity model would help to explain these students' lack of thoughtfulness, apparent inability to consider and think things through, and inability to delay responses. Studies indicating that learning to take longer to respond usually improves performance in such students seem to support this decision-process hypothesis.

Either of the preceding hypotheses may be applied whether or not there is demonstrable brain damage or dysfunction. Either is also consistent with the idea of environmental control.

Two other general theoretical assumptions underlie two other approaches to assisting the hyperactive learning-disabled student. One, *a medical approach,* assumes that there are specific causes, which may be managed through the administration of tranquilizers, stimulants, antihistamines, or anticonvulsants. In another application of the medical approach, elimination of various foods (sources of allergy), allergic desensitization, administration of megavitamins, or even air filtration may be utilized. Each of these paths of treatment could easily become the topic of a separate chapter, and some are the subject of a number of separate books. Almost all of these approaches presume some sort of chemical effect on the nervous system brought on by allergies, malfunction of some part of the glandular system, or some cause requiring medical intervention. Since these types of treatment are beyond the realm of responsibility of educators, we shall only note their existence and voice the hope that researchers in this area will have continued success in reducing hyperactivity amenable to this type treatment.

The second of the two general approaches (other than environmental control) is *behavior modification*. In most such approaches, behavior is "shaped" and undesirable behavior is reduced through the planned, programmed use of reinforcements (Simpson and Nelson, 1974). Behavior modification techniques will be discussed in a later section of this chapter as a general approach for use in learning disabilities (not just to control hyperactivity).

Educational implications. Three major approaches for dealing with the hyperactive student were mentioned in this section: (1) environmental control, (2) a medical approach, and (3) behavior modification. It was noted that medical approaches are not implemented by educators; however, teachers may be asked to play a role in record keeping or reporting with respect to the effects of medical treatment. Behavior modification will be discussed in a later section of this chapter. Environmental control techniques are within the realm of responsibility of the educator and may be of value in managing learning disabled and other students. We will further consider environmental control methods or techniques but should first note that in some instances a teacher may have reason to use behavior modification techniques and environmental control methods with a student who is also under some sort of drug or medical regime. These three approaches *can* be used simultaneously in some cases to good advantage, and in most instances there would be little or no loss of value in the effectiveness of one as a result of the use of the other.

The idea behind the controlled environment approach is that through such control we may counteract or reduce (by not stimulating) the undesirable behavioral characteristics. In the original formulation of ideas by Strauss and Lehtinen, this would dictate that such students be as uncrowded physically as possible, and that their classroom should have a minimum of pictures, bulletin boards, and decorations. We should note that many of the recommendations provided by Strauss and Lehtinen are difficult to implement within a regular classroom setting, for the very things that are of value for normal students may have a negative effect on hyperactive students. In the regular classroom it may be a matter of making compromises so as to assist the hyperactive student but not sacrifice the interests of other students.

In a separate, special class setting, the following might be implemented:

1. Relatively bare walls
2. Learning carrels or booths
3. Opaque covering on bottom half of windows
4. Workbooks, etc., provided one page at a time
5. Desk facing blank walls
6. Avoidance of jewelry by the teacher, since it may be distracting.

The preceding list might be extended to a considerable extent, but it is the underlying concept that is important. And it is possible to provide some such adaptations within the regular class setting. For example, screens or "offices" can be arranged for specific students. Seating can be arranged to reduce overstimulation. "Ear muffs" can be used in more extreme instances, and class activities, as they involve hyperactive students, can be modified.

The hyperactive student and other students in the class must know that these arrangements are not "punishment." The explanation used can be very simple and straightforward: "Jimmy has trouble concentrating on his work, and if we set up his desk this way and all help, he can do better and so can the rest of you."

There are all levels and degrees of hyperactivity, and the management method to be used must fit the needs of the individual student. It should be the most "normal" arrangement that will work, and with constant awareness the teacher may be able to reduce some of the problem with very simple, nonobvious management techniques. For example, a student who overracts to noise and movement should not be right next to the door to the hall, the pencil sharpener, or a ground level, outside window. With basic understanding of the nature of the problem and with continual awareness of the need to make small adjustments in the environment, the innovative teacher can make significant contributions to this aspect of learning disabilities. If the student is unusually hyperactive and in a special class setting most of all of the day, much greater environmental adjustments can be made.

PERCEPTUAL-MOTOR APPROACHES

Perceptual-motor approaches were among the most popular as the learning disabilities field began to blossom in the 1960s, and such approaches have many staunch advocates today. Cruickshank, briefly mentioned with respect to work with hyperactivity, was better known as a perceptual-motor theorist in the 1960s and 1970s; a number of other authorities are also widely recognized. Prominent among these individuals are *Gerald Getman, Marianne Frostig,* and *Newell Kephart.* Getman and Frostig became best known with relation to visual perception, while Kephart's efforts, although strongly tied to development of visual perceptual abilities, had somewhat more emphasis on general perceptual-motor development. Rather than attempt to separately outline the specifics of the work of each of these individuals, we will review the general framework of perceptual-motor theorists and its implications for learning disabilities. When some specific concept relates to an unusual degree to one of these three individuals, we will note this relationship.

Most perceptual-motor authorities would agree that higher level mental processes are the result of adequate earlier development of the motor system and perceptual systems. According to Kephart (1971): "It is logical to assume that all behavior is basically motor, that the prerequisites of any kind of behavior are muscular and motor responses." (p. 79) This idea is basic to the work of all perceptual-motor theorists. Kephart then continues: "Behavior develops out of muscular activity, and so-called higher forms of behavior are dependent upon lower forms of behavior, thus making even these higher activities dependent upon the basic structure of the muscular activity upon which they are built." (p. 79)

Gerald Getman, an optometrist, developed a learning/developmental theory that relates more specifically to the period from birth to age 5 years, and that illustrates how intellectual development evolves from earlier motor and perceptual development. This theory is graphically illustrated in Fig. 7-1; the description of what the various "boxes" in the model represent follows.

I. *Innate responses,* which normal children have at birth, include: the tonic neck reflex (TNR on the model), the starting point for infant movement; the startle reflex (SR), the reaction to a sudden flash of light or sudden loud noise; the light reflex (LR), eyelid tight-

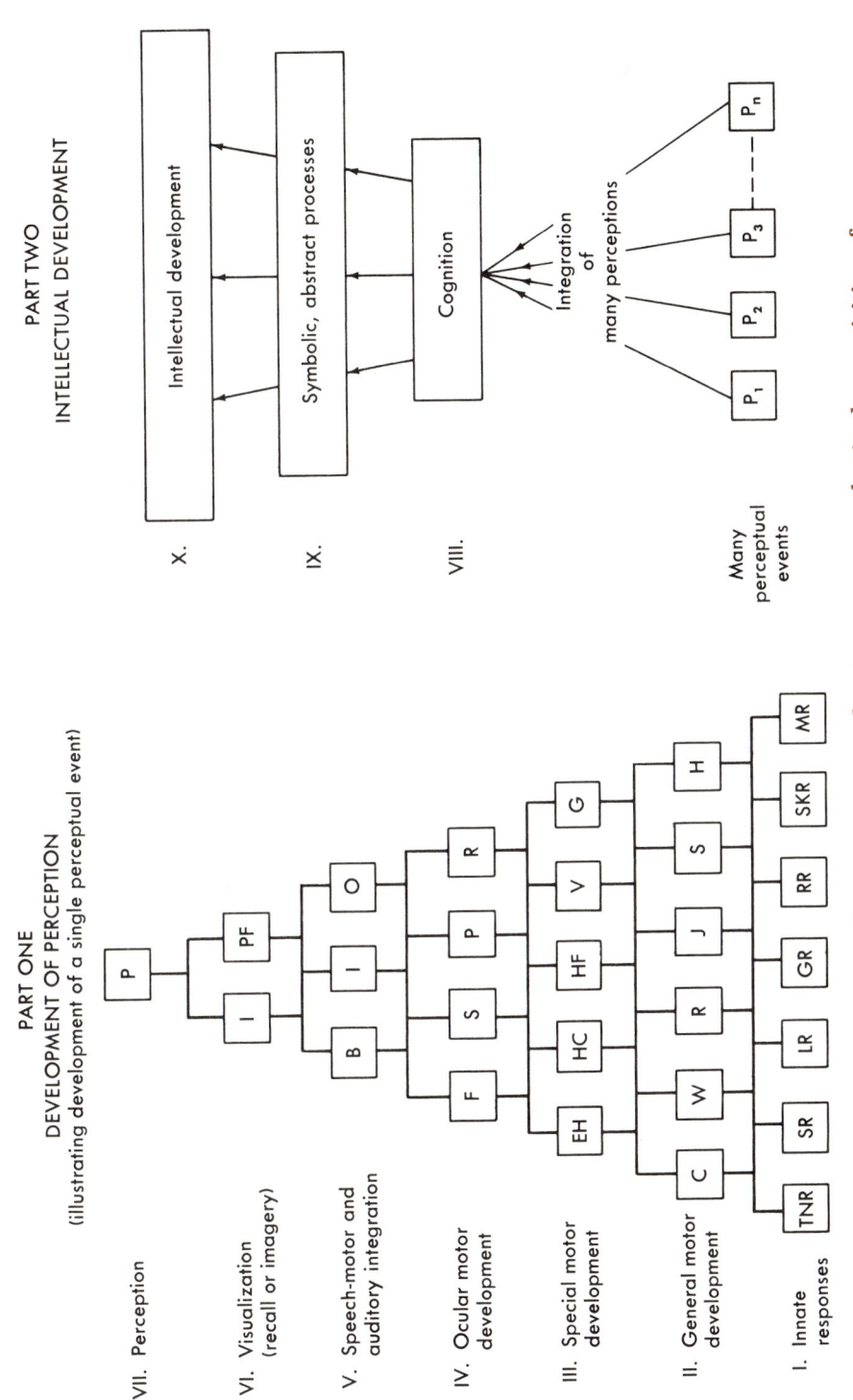

Education of children and youth with learning disabilities

Fig. 7-1. The visuomotor model. (Adapted from Getman, G. The visuomotor complex in the acquisition of learning skills. In J. Hellmuth [ed.] *Learning Disorders*, Vol. 1. Seattle, Wash.: Special Child Publications, 1965, p. 60.)

191

ening (in response to light) and later reduction in pupil size; the grasp reflex (GR), grasping of objects; the reciprocal reflex (RR), the facility of thrust and counterthrust of movements of the body; the statokinetic reflex (SKR), relaxed attentiveness; and the myotatic reflex (MR), a stretch reflex system with a built-in feedback system. These innate response systems become the base for all further learning. To the extent that these are not intact and fully and normally operational at birth, the child will be at a disadvantage in developing intellectually.

II. *General motor development* includes those abilities associated with locomotion or mobility. Development of these abilities is considered important by all perceptual-motor theorists. These include: creeping (C), walking (W), running (R), jumping (J), skipping (S), and hopping (H). Through this series of skills, the child uses and builds on the information obtained at the lower, innate response system. These skills provide the base for higher, more complex skills, which are necessary for continued, effective learning. General coordination, which should develop at this level, is required to permit adequate development of more specific and specialized coordination at higher levels. Children who have not developed these more general motor skills must have planned opportunities to do so or suffer the consequences later.

III. *Special motor development* includes a variety of special motor systems. These abilities, like those in level II, are given high priority by all perceptual-motor theorists. These include: eye-hand relationships (EH), two hands working in combination (HC), hand-foot relationships (HF), voice systems (V), and skill in gestures (G). Getman believes we may often ask children to perform at this level before they have developed requisite skills at levels I and II. This might lead to learning difficulties.

IV. *Ocular motor development* includes the ability to move and control the movement of the eyes. This involves two separate systems—one for each eye—which must be matched and balanced constantly. Getman is undoubtedly the best informed of all major perceptual-motor theorists in relation to this complex system, and he believes many children have reduced effectiveness in learning because of problems that appear at this level. Of particular concern is the fact that many educators attempt to teach children at levels above this one without being certain that skills at this level are well developed. Although children have 20/20 vision, they may have problems in bilateral relationships, problems that may have serious negative effects in reading. Too often we check only mid-point vision and ignore near-point vision, which is of the greatest importance in reading.

Ocular skills indicated in Fig. 7-1 are: fixation (F), the ability to fixate on or visually locate an object; saccadics (S), the visual movement from one target (object) to another; pursuit (P), the ability to successfully follow a moving target with both eyes; and rotation (R), the ability to rotate or move the eyes freely in any direction.

V. *The speech-motor and auditory integration system includes:* babbling (B), imitative speech (I), and original speech (O). Getman believes that skill in the speech-motor and auditory integration system is interrelated with vision.

VI. *Visualization (recall or imagery)* means the ability to recall what has been seen, heard, or sensed tactually. It means the ability to revisualize what is not now present. Getman recognizes two types of visualization, immediate (I) and past-future (PF). An example of immediate visualization would be feeling a key in a pocket or purse and "seeing" it simultaneously. Revisualizing a near-accident in an automobile 2 days ago would be past-visual-

Some learning disabilities authorities emphasize the importance of early motor development.

ization. Thinking through how to get through that same dangerous corner tomorrow would be future-visualization.

VII. *Perception,* often simply called vision by Getman, is the ability to differentiate between similar but different sensory stimuli. Unless an individual can visualize (level VI) accurately, there will at times be problems in perception. According to Getman's model, unless each of the levels below the level of perception has been fully developed, perceptual difficulties can occur.

VIII-X. VIII (cognition), IX (symbolic processes), and X (intellectual development) are developed as a result of interrelating and integrating a wide variety of perceptions. These are those abilities about which most educators are most concerned, and it is these abilities that have permitted the human race to develop so rapidly through generalizing, conceptualizing, elaborating, and recording thoughts and ideas in writing, which may be understood by peers and by future generations.

Getman's visuomotor model is constructed to indicate a pyramid of skills, each dependent on the skill(s) at the next lower level. All skills or abilities indicated on the model and discussed in preceding paragraphs are widely recognized as actually existing, and the sequence of development indicated in the model is generally recognized by many authorities. It would be possible to divide these skills in a number of ways, using more (or fewer) than the seven levels indicated as necessary to reach the goal of perception. Getman's model was used here because it provides a simple and graphic way to illustrate one version of the basic theory generally recognized by perceptual-motor theorists.

Other perceptual-motor theorists, such as *Newell Kephart,* have played a major role in establishing the value of perceptual-motor approaches in working with the learning disabled. We will consider some of Kephart's basic ideas before proceeding to a consideration of the unique contributions of other theorists. Many of Kephart's theoretical formulations were very similar to those of Getman (the two worked together for a number of years), but certain of Kephart's concepts deserve special attention.

Kephart believed that the way a child learns to process and interpret incoming sensory signals is developed in terms of actual neurologic processes and changes. This is the basis of his idea of perceptual-motor match, a concept that is very important in the total learning process as viewed by Kephart. Kephart uses the development of eye-hand coordination as an illustration of perceptual-motor match. This may be explained briefly as follows.

When a child first moves a hand, it is moved randomly and with limited direction or meaning. Soon, however, the moving hand contacts something. The head turns, and the eye attempts to correlate the visual information with the tactual. The eye learns to see what the hand feels. This is the first step in eye-hand coordination and is *hand-eye,* the hand leading the eye.

As the child becomes more and more experienced and the perceptual and motor information input more closely correlated, the child is able and likely to automatically substitute one for the other without hesitation. The child may occasionally use the hand simply for assurance or in new situations, but motor and perceptual data are so closely matched, they merge as one for most practical purposes. This is what Kephart called *perceptual-motor match.*

The development of perceptual-motor match is viewed by Kephart as highly essential, and those individuals who do not develop accurate and effective perceptual-motor match at the normal age are likely to be retarded in learning. Without it, learning obviously takes more time, and the time loss in learning becomes cumulative. Thus it is especially important that the developing child learn to process incoming sensory signals quickly and effectively and to be able, for example, to determine through the eyes how something will feel, whether it will fit a given space, and other similar information.

Another important concept that was carefully and clearly enunciated by Kephart has to do with the directionality and irreversibility of development. Kephart believes the development of the child is accomplished in a series of stages, each involving the development of a more complex system, or method, of processing data. According to this theory development can go in only one direction—toward greater complexity. Development cannot be reversed or remain stationary. To undo such development would mean to erase neurologic alterations that are permanent in nature. This therefore cannot happen. New stages, resulting in new data-processing methods, are viewed as compulsive—the child must use them in preference to simpler ones.

For students with learning disabilities it is assumed that there is either a general slowdown (as compared to age peers) in the progress of development or that there has been an actual breakdown at some point. The obvious answer is to restore the course of development through remedial or therapeutic methods. A major reason why teaching the child whose development has been interrupted is so difficult is that the child has been forced into stages that he or she cannot handle. However, the child makes some kind of adaptation, and even though we may attempt to go back to redo the earlier stage, techniques usually applicable and appropriate at the earlier stage—and at an earlier age—are not likely to apply.

Although they may feature different aspects of the overall theory, major theoreticians in the perceptual-motor field agree on essential, basic theoretical foundations. Another early authority, *Marianne Frostig*, was particularly interested in visual aspects of perceptual-motor theory. Because she had already developed a recognized test, the *Developmental Test of Visual Perception* (DTVP) before the 1963 "birth" of learning disabilities, this test and a related remedial program were widely used in the early days of evolution of the field. In fact, so much attention was given the DTVP (more often called the "Frostig") that many teachers did not know of Frostig's other valuable contributions and general orientation as a perceptual-motor authority.

One other perceptual-motor theorist will be mentioned because of his unique contributions. *Bryant Cratty*, a perceptual-motor authority from the physical education field, has provided a number of very worthwhile contributions as a result of his research regarding the success syndrome as it relates to learning and the value of games and physical activities in remediation of learning disabilities. Some of Cratty's ideas are: (1) optimal levels of alertness, activation, or arousal are necessary for efficient performance, and such levels may be attained through motor tasks; (2) game participation can motivate and reinforce students in acquiring concepts in academic areas (i.e., reading, language, and mathematics); (3) attention span may be improved through learning self-control via games and motor activities; and (4) success and/or satisfaction in physical efforts can contribute to a "success syndrome," which in turn can assist in academic areas (Cratty, 1967, 1968, 1969).

Educational implications. The educational implications of perceptual-motor theories can be summarized as follows:

1. A student with learning problems may be underdeveloped in any of the basic motor or perceptual areas. A variety of efforts should be initiated to help further develop these abilities.
2. How effectively the student uses his or her visual abilities should be determined. This does not mean just the normal 20/20 Snellen chart, mid-point vision, but also includes near vision, ability to use the two eyes simultaneously, ability to follow a line of reading from left to right efficiently, and all other visual skills. Some of this information may have to be obtained from other professionals.
3. A student may be overusing one type of learning ability to compensate for an underdeveloped ability. In some cases this is a necessity, but in others it is just a matter of underdeveloped ability, and it should become the focus of attention to aid in future learning.
4. Games and physical efforts of various types should be considered to (a) help build or develop concepts, (b) help build a general success syndrome, (c) assist in specific memory tasks, and (d) assist in building self-control.
5. Level of attention or arousal as it relates to readiness to learn should be carefully considered. It must be recognized that for dif-

ferent types of learning, different levels of arousal may be required.
6. A number of specific skills must be assessed when learning problems are present. These include such skills as ability to readily distinguish figure from ground, knowledge of laterality and directionality, eye-hand coordination, and accurate perceptual-motor match in all perceptual areas.

In general, perceptual-motor approaches are more often applicable at the preschool and primary grade levels, but if older students have such needs, they may be critically important. We may also conclude that separate motor or perceptual-motor skills—taught without correlation with academic tasks—may be of little or no tangible value to academic pursuits. To be most effective (especially with children over age 5), such skills should be taught as part of academic tasks whenever possible.

LANGUAGE FUNCTION—RELATED APPROACHES

In the federal definition of learning disabilities (p. 181) the first type of disorder mentioned is a "disorder in one or more of the basic psychological processes involved in understanding or in using spoken or written language." It is therefore somewhat surprising that this theoretical approach had so few supporters among learning disabilities pioneers; however, this may be the result of the fact that "their progenitors, Werner and Strauss, paid relatively little attention to language problems in children." (Hallahan and Cruickshank, 1973, p. 101) Perhaps it was also because other characteristics of those students who were the concern of the early learning disabilities authorities were so obvious and were often the reason why these students were not permitted to remain in school.

Whatever the reason, it was not until the work of Helmer Myklebust and Samuel Kirk that real attention was drawn to the general deficits in overall language functioning of learning disabled students. (A case can be made for the earlier involvement of Orton and Fernald, mentioned in connection with multisensory approaches. Orton was interested in the language problems of brain damaged adults and later in the problems of "strephosymbolic" students, but this concern with general language disorders soon became more specifically focused on reading difficulties through efforts promoted by Anna Gillingham. The work of both Orton and Fernald is language related in that it was concerned with reading, but it did not emphasize more global language disorders as did the later work of Myklebust and Kirk.)

Helmer Myklebust began his work with learning disabled students in the Institute for Language Disorders at Northwestern University in the early 1950s, before the recognition of an organized field of learning disabilities. His earliest efforts were with deaf and aphasic children, youth, and adults, and when aphasia was formally included in the area of learning disabilities, he "automatically" became part of this field. Myklebust, along with Doris Johnson, produced one of the first texts which was, in title and content, exclusively about learning disabilities (Johnson and Myklebust, 1967). In this text, *Learning Disabilities: Educational Principles and Practices*, he outlined a comprehensive theoretical rationale and related teaching practices for what he called "psychoneurological learning disabilities."

Psychoneurological learning disabilities, according to Myklebust, are those learning problems that are related to central nervous system dysfunctions rather than psychodynamic factors or peripheral nervous system dysfunctions. (Psychodynamic factors would include such conditions as autism, schizophrenia, psychogenic deafness; peripheral nervous system dysfunctions refer primarily to handicaps in vision and hearing.) Myklebust's theoretical formulations regarding learning disabilities are based on his concept of how learning takes place, given normal learning abilities. The following description will indicate, in highly condensed form, the essential steps in such normal learning and certain related learning problems, as viewed by Myklebust.

Sensation, or sensory reception, is the lowest level of all learning. Inability to hear or see effectively results in basic deprivation in certain areas of learning. (By definition, the learning disabled individual *has* adequate sensory abilities.)

Perception, the second level, is defined by Myklebust as the ability to accurately recognize sensory input, or information.

Imagery is the next higher level and has often been either confused with perception or overlooked altogether. The imagery concept is necessary to explain the differences between perception and memory. Perception concerns the ability to differentiate between various similar but different ongoing sensations. Imagery pertains to information already received. When a child uses imagery, he is recalling aspects of past experience or is relating to memory of past perceptions. If he describes what he saw at the circus, he is exercising visual imagery of the earlier experience. If he describes and imitates the loud explosion he heard, he is utilizing auditory imagery or memory.

Symbolization is the fourth level of learning. According to Myklebust, it is a level that only humans can attain; all lower forms of life (some of which can engage in perception or imagery) are unable to engage in symbolization. Although both verbal and nonverbal symbolization definitely exist, Myklebust is most concerned with verbal symbolization, the ability to acquire language.

Myklebust is concerned with three major aspects of verbal symbolization. The first, *inner language*, permits a word to have meaning. Without inner language and the understanding of what a word means, the word does not transmit meaning and therefore is not, in truth, language.

Myklebust views inner language as the language in which an individual thinks. He suggests that bilingual individuals may think in their native tongue. If faced by a particularly pressing problem, even though fluent in the second language and in the habit of using it daily, many such individuals use their native tongue to think through the problem. Since inner language is the first language to be acquired and must be learned before an individual can receive or express oral language, it may be very fixed and rigid. If it is not well developed, this will retard all subsequent language development.

The second aspect of symbolization is *receptive language*, which includes at least two major parts—visual and auditory. Normally, auditory receptive language is developed first, but in the normal reading process, both are required. If input (reception) precedes output (expression), any defect in receptive language will inhibit the development of expressive language, that is, written or vocal expression. At this level of the language development hierarchy, small deficiencies at a lower level, multiplied by any resultant higer level deficiencies, become a major problem. For example, a deficiency in perception will result in additional deficiencies at the imagery level, and serious difficulties are likely at this symbolization level. If a child misperceives what he or she hears, the child proceeds at the imagery and symbolic levels on the basis of this misperception, and behavior seems inappropriate. This child may appear to be mentally retarded, emotionally disturbed, or hard of hearing. Misunderstandings or misdiagnosis of such students can be disastrous.

When memory (imagery) functions are impaired, symbolic functions cannot be developed in a normal manner. One common evidence of memory sequence problems is the child's inability to follow instructions that involve three or four acts to be accomplished in a particular sequence. Since sequential behavior becomes increasingly important, particularly as the child grows older and is involved in more complex activities, this disability must be recognized and dealt with.

Expressive language is the third major facet of symbolization. Expressive language, like receptive language, may be either auditory or visual, with auditory developing first in nearly all children. Expressive aphasia, one of the most common types of expressive language problems, was the first language disorder to be separately identified and widely recognized. Expressive auditory language may be indicated through either auditory or written language impairment, with the auditory being much more common.

Conceptualization is the fifth and highest level at which we must consider the possibility of learning disabilities. Although we may often see disabilities affecting perception, imagery, or symbolization, the conceptual process is the most complex and perhaps the most interesting. Conceptualization includes the ability to abstract and the ability to categorize. Although abstraction can take place without conceptualizing, we cannot conceptualize without engaging in abstraction. Conceptual reasoning is somewhat difficult to explain and may be best shown through illustration. Development of the concept of the category of objects we call *dishes* will be considered as an example.

To the very young child, *plate* refers to the plate on which he eats. It may be highly distinctive, have pictures of Wonder Woman or Walt Disney characters, but it is "plate" to him. Later he leans that other objects on which he or others eat are called plates. In the meantime he has learned about cups and glasses or perhaps mugs and may be able to distinguish among them.

Finally, although the word has been in his environment for some time, he becomes aware of the word *dishes*. Soon he learns that all the plates, cups, bowls, etc., on the table are dishes. Through a variety of experiences and through the language that has been used in these experiences, the child learns of the class of objects called dishes. He learns that all plates are not shaped alike, although they have similar uses (except perhaps for the decorative plates on the plate rail overhead). He also learns that all plates are dishes. A plate is observable, but the category dishes is not, except as a group of experiences with a variety of items that others have called dishes. The child has developed the *concept* of dishes.

Children who have greater than average difficulty in relating objects and ideas to classifications and concepts will tend to have related difficulties in academic areas. The degree of difficulty will depend on the type and severity of conceptual difficulty, but unfortunately many teachers do not readily recognize that conceptual problems may be the basis of reading problems, for example.

As a result of this theory of learning (or of language), Myklebust has developed a series of guidelines for remediation. Certain of these guildelines will be included in the discussion of educational implications at the close of this section. First, however, we will briefly consider some of the contributions of Samuel Kirk, the man who first used the term "learning disabilities" in 1963.

Samuel Kirk is closely associated with learning disabilities for at least four reasons. One is his role in suggesting the term "learning disabilities" and, in effect, providing the first definition. A seond is the leadership role he played in assisting the Association for Children with Learning Disabilities (ACLD) to gain initial momentum. A third is his role as chairman of the first National Advisory Committee on Handicapped Children, which in its report to the Bureau of Education for the Handicapped of the U.S. Office of Education recommended top priority to the development of programs to serve the students with learning disabilities. The fourth was his development of an assessment instrument, the *Illinois Test of Psycholinguistic Abilities* (ITPA).

The Illinois Test of Psycholinguistic Abilities was first introduced by Kirk in 1961 as an experimental edition, limited to 250 handmade kits and distributed to a selected group of professionals who were specially interested in psychometric and educational assessment of children with learning problems (Kirk, W., 1974). Because of the critical need for this type instrument and the rapid word-of-mouth spread of positive comments, additional test kits were made and distributed, leading to an unusually large amount of information available for the revised edition, which was published in 1968.

The experimental version of the test, developed jointly by Kirk and James J. McCarthy, was the result of 15 years of clinical experience and much field testing by Kirk and his graduate students at the University of Illinois (Hallahan and Cruickshank, 1973). Kirk's interest was in finding a better way to systematically assess the sometimes widely varied abilities of children, many of whom had been previously diagnosed as being at the upper limits of mental retardation, as then defined.

The ITPA consists of twelve subtests that assess abilities in two main channels of communication (auditory-vocal and visual-motor), three types of psycholinguistic processes (receptive, organizational, and expressive), and two levels of functioning (representational and automatic). The ITPA may serve many purposes, but one major function is to determine discrepancies in scores for the various psycholinguistic functions tested. The total pattern of discrepancies is the most important indicator of potential difficulties, and unlike tests of intelligence, which focus on interchild (between-child) differences, the ITPA is concerned with intrachild (within-child) differences.

The ITPA was at first overused, for it had the potential to do more in the area of learning disabilities than any other assessment tool available. In more recent years, the ITPA has been used more sparingly and sensibly, and those using it have tended to be better equipped to use it correctly. The ITPA provides a broad look at various levels of the language functions, and if used properly, including analysis of actual behaviors that underlie test performance, it can be a highly valuable test. Kirk has provided a number of useful aids (manuals) to assist both the examiner and the teacher who uses the results provided by the examiner, and has thus played an additional role in the development of effective educational techniques based on a language discrepancy approach to learning disabilities.

Educational implications. Myklebust provides a number of general educational recommendations which grew out of his specific theoretical beliefs. These include (Gearheart, 1977, pp. 84-85):

1. *Teach to the level of involvement.* Teaching must be directed toward the lowest level of involvement—perception, imagery, symbolization, or conceptualization.
2. *Teach to the type of involvement.* Does the disability involve intrasensory or intersensory learning? Does it involve verbal or nonverbal factors? Does it primarily relate to integrative functions? Whatever the case, teach appropriately for that type of involvement.
3. *Remember that input precedes output.* Con-

sider the fact that either input or output disabilities or both could be involved in the problem. Remember that output difficulties may actually reflect input problems.

4. *Consider tolerance levels.* Overloading is always a possibility. Certain types of stimulation may be distracting, either by themselves or by interfering with other modalities. The possibility that both psychologic and neurologic tolerance levels may be grossly abnormal in a learning disabled child must be carefully considered.

5. *Consider the multisensory approach.* The multisensory approach, which involves teaching through several or perhaps all sensory channels, is always a possible alternative but must be approached with tolerance level and overloading potential in mind.

6. *Teaching to deficits alone is a limited concept.* Teaching only to and through the deficient areas is a restricted, unitary approach and is unacceptable in the light of available evidence.

7. *Teaching only to and through intact learning channels is limited.* This approach is insufficient when used alone.

8. *Do not assume the need for perceptual training.* Perceptual training alone may be most inadequate. To stress perceptual training, except as diagnostic information so dictates, can be a waste of time or in some cases detrimental.

9. *Control important variables.* This principle calls for teacher control of variables such as attention (control elements that lead to distractions), proximity (to the teacher or to other children), rate (as in rate of presentation of materials), and size (of writing, objects, etc.).

10. *Emphasize both verbal and nonverbal learning.* Deliberately attend to both the verbal and nonverbal components of the learning problem with planned efforts to interrelate the two.

Educational implications and guidelines that could be derived from Kirk's approach and from the ITPA would be quite similar to these specifically taken from Myklebust's recommendations. Each would recommend a careful, total analysis of the strengths and weaknesses of the individual student, including language related factors, but also including information regarding intelligence, health history, educational history, present levels of functioning, and emotional status. A careful consideration of all of these factors, plus levels and types of language (or psycholinguistic) abilities and disabilities, would provide the basis for individual planning for each student.

BEHAVIOR MODIFICATION APPROACHES

Most educators and educators-in-training are familiar with the concept of behavior modification. In practice in the classroom, behavior modification procedures may be called operant conditioning, contingency management, behavior shaping or modeling, or any of a variety of other terms. Each of these techniques or procedures has in common the planned, systematic arrangement of the consequences or resultants of a given action or response, which are designed to alter the response in some way.

One of the behavior modification procedures that has become quite popular in special education classroom is contingency contracting, sometimes called behavioral contracting. This procedure can be used effectively with both elementary and secondary students and involves the establishment of a clear, carefully written contract in which the student is rewarded after the completion of specified tasks. Contingency contracting must be fully and clearly understood by both the teacher and the student. *Contingency con-*

tracting and all other behavior modification techniques can be used to encourage and motivate the student to do what he or she is able to do, but it will not work if the student does not have the prerequisite skills.

Some teachers have difficulty with behavior modification techniques because they are unable to organize *their* efforts and reactions to student behavior and responses. Behavior modification requires a considerable degree of organization and self-discipline on the part of those using it, but it may pay major dividends. It is of most value in working with the learning disabled when applied in conjunction with considerable knowledge about the student's abilities, disabilities, and required skills for the various tasks attempted. A review of several of the suggested readings at the close of this chapter will provide a good initial understanding of this procedure for those who are not fully informed as to the various ways in which it works in the actual classroom setting.

Educational implications. To be able to effectively apply behavior modification techniques, the teacher must understand underlying behavioral theory and, in addition, must study and observe, if possible, several of the various applications of behavior modification. To have success with behavioral techniques the teacher must: (1) identify the precise behavior to be learned and establish the desired level of performance, (2) make reasonably certain that the student has the underlying prerequisite skills to attempt this behavior, and (3) establish a situation and setting in which it is possible for the identified behavior to occur. The teacher must obtain baseline data (normal behavior under normal conditions) for several days and, while so doing observe and attempt to discover patterns of error.

Following each study and collection of baseline data, the teacher must select and schedule a teaching technique that appears, on the basis of present evidence, to be likely to increase the probability of occurrence of the desired behavior. This behavior may be spelling certain basic words, sounding out a certain class of endings, persisting in efforts in the mathematics workbook for a given period of time, etc.

Rewards or resultants for success must be established so that the *student* feels they are truly worth working for. This means knowing what is important to the student (for example, free reading time, time outside or in the gymnasium) and arranging for the possibility of rewarding such contingent events.

A good, practical, concise set of recommendations relating to the use of behavior modification is provided by Lovitt (1975) in the *Journal of Learning Disabilities*. Any teacher who does not have a good command of behavior modification techniques should carefully read and reread this set of recommendations.

MEDICALLY ORIENTED APPROACHES

Medically oriented approaches to remediation of learning disabilities encompass a wide variety of efforts, some of which are under considerable debate within the medical community. We will enumerate certain of the major efforts without attempting to comment as to the relative value of these approaches.

Megavitamin treatment is supported by a number of medical researchers, including Pauling (1968), Cott (1971, 1972), and Hoffer (1971). This approach, often called orthomolecular medicine, involves the administration of very large quantities of vitamins and minerals, plus other nutritional control which, in a number of documented cases, appears to be effective in reducing hyperactivity and various other symptoms of learning disabilities.

Treatment of hypoglycemia appears to be of great value for some individuals. In hypoglycemia the glucose content in the blood is abnormally low; narcolepsy (unusual drowsiness) is often a factor also. The major treatment is dietary control and the elimination of almost all foods that contain simple sugar. The value of this treatment has been documented by such researchers as Powers (1975) and Roberts (1969).

Dietary restriction of various foods, including soft drinks, ice cream, hot dogs, and others, especially those containing food dyes, has been of value in reducing hyperkinesis. It is believed that some children may be allergic to such foods and as a result are hyperactive and have reduced ability to learn in the normal manner. Various physicians, including Wunderlich (1973), Crook (1974), and Hawley and Buckley (1974) have been among the leaders in this area of treatment.

Psychochemicals (drugs that directly influence behavior through effecting temporary chemical changes in brain functioning) are often used to treat extremely hyperactive children. Drug therapy has been used by many physicians for a variety of purposes; we will not attempt to point out any specific authorities or researchers in this area but will note that this type treatment has received a great deal of negative attention in the popular press.

A number of other medical efforts may also prove to be of value in the very near future. Efforts to better understand the effects of alcohol on the fetus, research into the effects of extremely poor general nutrition, and other efforts presently unreported may be of major interest by 1990. Research in other areas of handicap, such as mental retardation, may also bear fruit with respect to learning disabilities. The future regarding this approach to remediation of learning disabilities appears to be unusually promising.

Educational implications. Although all of the preceding approaches must be implemented by physicians, there are certain potential roles for educators. As more is known of these various approaches, educators may become more alert to symptoms and, through referral to physicians, may be able to help bring about the needed diagnosis and treatment. After students are involved in treatment, the teacher may play an important part in the necessary observation and record keeping that will assist the physician in adjusting medication, changing treatment, etc.

The treatments outlined in the preceding section are not, even in the minds of their strongest advocates, a "cure" for all types of learning disabilities. Each has potential value for certain students, and in composite they are of great value, but they appear to be the answer to only part of the diverse set of conditions we have come to call learning disabilities. For at least the immediate future, it appears that a combination of approaches is required, and there are still a significant number of learning disabled students for whom none of the known approaches are effective.

Educational provisions: application of the variable service continuum

Although learning disabled students may be served in various ways, the vast majority are served through the resource room. Therefore, we will concentrate on the role of the resource room teacher.

The viability of resource room service for other handicapping conditions was well established before the initiation of programs for the learning disabled, and it was apparent from the beginning that this type service delivery was tailor-made for most learning disabled students. The very nature of learning disabilities, the emphasis on remediation, and the fact that these children are in the normal range or above in intellectual ability led to an obvious need for retaining these children in the regular class for a maximal amount of time.

The need for close cooperation between the regular class teacher and the specialized teacher is great for all handicapping conditions, and with learning disabilities, the resource room, located in the school building in which the student is normally enrolled, is a highly practical arrangement. The relatively high incidence of learning disabilities, as compared, for example, to conditions such as visual impairment, has made it practical to establish a learning disabilities resource room in each school in some districts. In some smaller schools the learning disabilities resource teacher may be in the building only half of each day and then serve in another building the other half day, but his or her presence in the building on a daily basis provides the type of service necessary for maximal assistance to learning disabled students.

A self-contained class program may be required for some learning disabled students who have other handicapping conditions or for that very small percentage of the learning disabled whose hyperactivity is extreme. In this case, there may be one or several such classes within larger school districts; students are transported to the schools where such classes are located and they remain there throughout the school day. Even in this setting every attempt is made to integrate individual students for small segments of the school day with the hope that they may eventually be returned to a less restrictive setting, perhaps to their home school.

At the other end of the continuum, some students with very mild learning disabilities may be successfully assisted without going to the resource room for regular service. They may go for a short period of assessment-related teaching, but their permanent source of assistance will be their regular teacher, who is assisted by the learning disabilities resource or consulting teacher. Such assistance may include materials, suggestions, and, in a few cases, demonstration teaching. In many instances such mild problems will not come to the official attention of the entire staffing team but, rather, the regular class teacher will ask the resource teacher for suggestions and ideas, and the student will not be officially designated as learning disabled. Although not always officially condoned in the various regulations relating to special reimbursement for special educators who work with the learning disabled, this type of preventive effort (which may or may not ever appear on the records) may be one of the best effects of learning disabilities programming.

At the secondary level, somewhat different educational provisions may be made. In some instances, a program similar to that just described will be effective. However, for many secondary level learning disabled students, it is no longer effective to emphasize the remedial aspects of educational programming. Rather, it is a matter of adapting, adjusting, and accommodating the secondary program to permit maximal learning, given the student's existing difficulties with some of the basic skills. This may include modified assignments, permission to tape, rather than write out class papers, permitting the assistance of a peer helper for reading, or other such accommodations. Because the student contacts a number of different teachers during the day, it is more difficult to be certain that all of these teachers are fully informed. The resource teacher must attempt to "run interference" for the student, try to arrange assignments with teachers who understand and are willing to provide accommodative measures and, in some cases, teach special class sections established exclusively for learning disabled students. At this point in history, secondary level service delivery is much less well organized and, in many school districts, nonexistent. This deficiency is recognized, however, and a number of efforts to upgrade and improve secondary programming are underway. (For a comprehensive treatment of secondary programming for the learning disabled, see Marsh, Gearheart, and Gearheart, 1978.)

We might summarize educational provisions for the learning disabled as follows:

1. The majority of educational programming for the learning disabled takes place through the services of the resource room teacher. The student ordinarily attends the resource room daily, and the resource teacher provides suggestions and at times materials for the regular classroom teacher's use in specified academic areas. The most common point of focus of such efforts is reading and/or mathematics, but the academic problems, and thus the remedial efforts, may be evident in other areas as well.
2. A small number of learning disabled students may have such severe problems that they require a self-contained class setting. This is more likely to relate to students who are unusually hyperactive or multihandicapped.
3. Some mildly learning disabled students may be served by the regular class teacher, with no scheduled contact with the learning disabilities specialist. However, the teacher should receive both advice and materials from the learning disabilities consultant or specialist.
4. At the secondary level, the focus of educational efforts may change from remediation to curriculum adaptation. A wide variety of procedures may be initiated to permit the student to gain information and continue conceptual development in spite of basic skill deficits. Some variation of a work-study or work experience program may be used with some secondary students, especially those who are not college bound. Secondary level programming is still in the developmental stage, and many schools with relatively good elementary programs have not developed comparable effective secondary programs.

Summary

Learning disabilities have become the topic of widespread interest since their recognition in the 1960s, and school districts have responded with a variety of remedial efforts. In parallel efforts, some members of the medical profession have attempted to attack the cause(s) of learning disabilities, although many other physicians apparently have misgivings about certain of these medically oriented approaches. There is a national definition of learning disabilities, provided through the Bureau of Education for the Handicapped of the U.S. Office of Education, but the fact that new definitions are proposed almost every month in various professional journals illustrates the continuing controversy.

In this chapter we have reviewed certain of the major approaches to teaching the learning disabled and have recognized some of the major proponents of these approaches. Approaches discussed included multisensory, hyperactivity-related, perceptual-motor, language function—related, behaviorally oriented, and medically oriented. Most of these overlap other existing approaches, and each appears to have some merit in at least some instances. The reason for such a wide variety of recognized approaches is clear when we consider the learning disability definition. Characterized by some as an umbrella definition, it includes many different conditions; thus various remedial efforts are essential. Without an adequate understanding of this fact, the reader will find it difficult to understand and benefit from the broad range of literature presently available.

In the discussion of educational provisions for learning disabled students, it was noted that the majority of learning disabled students are presently served through the resource room, although a few students with more severe disabilities may require full-time, self-contained class programs. It was also noted that secondary school programs often require an emphasis on adaptation of the educational program, rather than a continuation of the remedial efforts that characterize most elementary school programs. Some variation of work-study type programming appears to be in considerable use at the secondary level throughout the nation.

It is difficult to predict what may happen next in this field, which has literally exploded with sometimes widely divergent efforts in the past decade and a half. It seems likely that with time to more carefully investigate the effectiveness of various approaches, we may soon become better informed as to what works best with which students. Parents who in the past felt it necessary to work to simply *have* a program for their children may now be able to concentrate on obtaining the *right kind* of program. Overplacement in learning disabilities programs will, hopefully, diminish. The future should be bright, but only one prediction seems absolutely safe: learning disabilities programs are here to stay.

focus

introduction

Learning disabilities is the newest of the recognized subareas of special education, although its historical roots go back nearly 200 years.

foundations of learning disabilities (prior to 1963)

Hinshelwood, in 1917, published the first comprehensive description of a specific disorder of written language (word blindness) which also included methods of teaching students who suffered from such a condition.

learning disabilities: a recognized entity (1963 to the present)

Learning disabilities programming was taking place prior to 1963, but it existed under a variety of labels, and viable programs were not available in much of the United States. Students who would now be called learning disabled were served in classes for: (1) hyperactive students, (2) brain-injured students, (3) Strauss syndrome students, (4) dyslexic students, (5) students with perceptual disorders, (6) students with perceptual-motor disorders, (7) minimal brain dysfunction (MBD) students, (8) dysgraphic students, (9) aphasic students, (10) neurologically impaired students, and others.

definitions and prevalence

Specific learning disability means a disorder in one or more of the basic psychological processes involved in understanding or in using language, spoken or written, which may manifest itself in an imperfect ability to listen, think, speak, read, write, spell, or to do mathematical calculations. The term includes such conditions as perceptual handicaps, brain injury, minimal brain dysfunction, dyslexia, and developmental aphasia. The term does not include children who have learning problems which are primarily the result of visual, hearing, or motor handicaps, of mental retardation, of emotional disturbance, or of environmental, cultural, or economic disadvantage.

Because learning disabilities are accepted as being remediable, there is likely to be a higher percentage at the lower grade levels, with a lower percentage at higher grades after some remediation has taken place. The overall percentage of children with learning disabilities is generally accepted to be between 1 and 3 percent, with more authorities apparently supporting a 2 to 3 percent figure.

identification of students who are learning disabled

There are certain recognized characteristics of children with learning disabilities, which include hyperactivity, hypoactivity, incoordination, general motor difficulties, perseveration, inattention, overattention, visual perceptual difficulties, or auditory perceptual difficulties that might be noted in young children, but any one of these characteristics is not sufficient to identify a young child as learning disabled. These characteristics are more common to learning disabled students than to the population as a whole, but with any one student they are nothing more than indicative of the possibility of identification as learning disabled.

multisensory approaches

For purposes of this chapter, multisensory will be defined to mean the "deliberate use of three or more of the sensory channels in the teaching/learning process. More often it will refer to the use of four modalities: visual, auditory, kinesthetic, and tactile."

Before initiating the actual VAKT procedure, Fernald believes that it is essential to do something to attempt to reverse the very low self-concept that many students who have had consistent learning problems will have. Her belief has been reaffirmed by many other recognized remedial and learning disabilities practitioners, and many, like Fernald, call this procedure "positive reconditioning."

educational implications

The various multisensory approaches have been of great value with some learning disabled students and of no apparent value with others It is difficult to say whether, in all cases, it was a matter of the appropriateness of the method or some other factor(s) that made the difference, but there has been sufficient success to suggest the careful consideration of such approaches for some learning disabled students.

hyperactivity: theories and approaches

Environmental control is based on the assumption that for some reason or combination of reasons the receipt of what would be normal auditory, visual, tactile, or kinesthetic stimulation to most other individuals causes serious problems for the hyperactive student.

One of these theories (about hyperactivity) assumes that, although the student is neurally intact, the nature and extent of the excess motor activity are such that the activity interferes with the basic acquisition of information.

A second theory or hypothesis may be called the decision-making hypothesis. This hypothesis assumes that the decision-making process (rather than the information acquisition stage) is the basic source of academic difficulty for the hyperactive student.

educational implications

The idea behind the controlled environment approach is that through such control we may counteract or reduce (by not stimulating) the undesirable behavioral characteristics.

There are all levels and degrees of hyperactivity, and the management method to be used must fit the needs of the individual student. It should be the most "normal" arrangement that will work, and with constant awareness the teacher may be able to reduce some of the problem with very simple, nonobvious management techniques.

perceptual-motor approaches

Most perceptual-motor authorities would agree that higher-level mental processes are the resultant of adequate earlier development of the motor system and the perceptual systems.

Kephart believes the development of the child is accomplished in a series of stages, each involving the development of a more complex system, or method, of processing data. According to this theory development can go in only one direction—toward greater complexity.

Although they may feature different aspects of the overall theory, major theoreticians in the perceptual-motor field agree on essential, basic theoretical foundations.

educational implications

The perceptual-motor approaches are more often applicable at the preschool and primary grade levels, but if older students have such needs, they may be critically important. Separate motor or perceptual-motor skills—taught without correlation with academic tasks—may be of little or no tangible value to academic pursuits.

language function—related approaches

Children who have greater than average difficulty in relating objects and ideas to classifications and concepts will tend to have related difficulties in academic areas.

The degree of difficulty will depend on the type and severity of conceptual difficulty, but unfortunately many teachers do not readily recognize that conceptual problems may be the basis of reading problems, for example.

behavior modification approaches

Contingency contracting and all other behavior modification techniques can be used to encourage and motivate the student to do what he or she is able to do, but it will not work if the student does not have the prerequisite skills.

educational implications

Rewards or resultants for success must be established so that the child feels they are truly worth working for. This means knowing what is important to the student and arranging for the possibility of rewarding such contingent events.

educational provisions: application of the variable service continuum

The very nature of learning disabilities, the emphasis on remediation, and the fact that these children are in the normal range (or above) in intellectual ability led to an obvious need for retaining these children in the regular class for a maximal amount of time.

For many secondary level learning disabled students, it is no longer effective to emphasize the remedial aspects of educational programming. Rather, it is a matter of adapting, adjusting, and accommodating the secondary program to permit maximal learning, given the student's existing difficulties with some of the basic skills.

References and suggested readings

Ayres, J. Improving academic scores through sensory integration. *Journal of Learning Disabilities,* 1972, *5,* 338-343.

Ayres, J. *Sensory integration and learning disorders.* Los Angeles: Western Psychological Services, 1972.

Bailey, E. Learning disabilities definitions in the literature and state regulations. Unpublished study, University of Northern Colorado, 1977.

Bryan, T., and Bryan, J. *Understanding learning disabilities.* New York: Alfred Publishing Co., 1975.

Conners, C. What parents need to know about stimulant drugs and special education. *Journal of Learning Disabilities,* 1973, *6*(6), 349-351.

Cott, A. Orthomolecular approach to the treatment of learning disabilities. *Schizophrenia,* 1971, *3*(2), 95-105.

Cratty, B. *Active learning: games to enhance academic abilities.* Englewood Cliffs, N.J.: Prentice-Hall, Inc., 1971.

Cratty, B. *Developmental sequences of perceptual-motor tasks.* Freeport, N.Y.: Educational Activities, Inc., 1967.

Cratty, B. *Movement behavior and motor learning.* Philadelphia: Lea & Febiger, 1967.

Cratty, B. *Perceptual-motor behavior and educational processes.* Springfield, Ill.: Charles C Thomas, Publisher, 1969.

Cratty, B. *Psychology and physical activity.* Englewood Cliffs, N.J.: Prentice-Hall, Inc., 1968.

Crook, W. The allergic tension-fatigue syndrome. A *Pediatric Annals* reprint. New York: Insight Publishing Co., 1974.

Cruickshank, W. Myths and realities in learning disabilities. *Journal of Learning Disabilities,* 1977, *10,* 51-58.

Cruickshank, W. *The brain-injured child in home, school, and community.* Syracuse, N.Y.: Syracuse University Press, 1967.

Cruickshank, W. (Ed.). *The teacher of brain-injured children.* Syracuse, N.Y.: Syracuse University Press, 1966.

Dember, W. *Visual perception: the nineteenth century.* New York: John Wiley & Sons, Inc., 1964.

Fauke, J., and others. Improvement of handwriting and letter recognition skills: a behavior modification procedure. *Journal of Learning Disabilities,* 1973, *6,* 296-300.

Federal Register, Vol. 42, no. 250, Dec. 29, 1977, p. 65083.

Fernald, G. *Remedial techniques in basic school subjects.* New York: McGraw-Hill Book Co., 1943.

Feingold, B. *Why your child is hyperactive.* New York: Random House, 1975.

Forness, S., and MacMillan, D. The origins of behavior modification with exceptional children. *Exceptional Children,* 1970, *37,* 93-99.

Frostig, M. *Frostig developmental test of visual perception.* Palo Alto, Calif.: Consulting Psychologists Press, 1963.

Frostig, M. *Movement education: theory and practice.* Chicago: Follett Publishing Co., 1970.

Frostig, M. *Selection and adaptation of reading methods.* San Rafael, Calif.: Academic Therapy Publications, 1973.

Gearheart, B. *Learning disabilities: educational strategies.* St. Louis: The C. V. Mosby Co., 1977.

Getman, G. *Instructor's guide: pathway school program.* Boston: Teaching Resources Corp., 1968.

Getman, G. The visuomotor complex in the acquisition of learning skills. *Learning disorders.* Vol. 1. J. Hellmuth, (Ed.). Seattle: Special Child Publications, 1965.

Goins, J. *Visual-perceptual abilities and early school progress.* Chicago: The University of Chicago Press, 1958.

Graber, D. Megavitamins, molecules, and minds. *Human Behavior,* 1973, *2*(5), 8-15.

Hallahan, D., and Cruickshank, W. *Psycho-educational foundations of learning disabilities.* Englewood Cliffs, N.J.: Prentice-Hall, Inc., 1973.

Hammill, D. D., and Bartel, N. R. (Eds.). *Teaching children with learning and behavior disorders.* Boston: Allyn & Bacon, 1978.

Hawley, C., and Buckley, R. Food dyes and hyperkinetic children. *Academic Therapy,* 1974, *10*(1), 27-31.

Head, H. *Aphasia and kindred disorders of speech.* London: Cambridge University Press, 1926.

Hinshelwood, J. *Congenital word blindness.* London: H. K. Lewis & Co., 1917.

Hoffer, A. Vitamin B-3 dependent children. *Schizophrenia,* 1971, *3*(2), 107-113.

Hoffman, M. A learning disability is a symptom, not a disease. *Academic Therapy,* 1975, *10*(3), 261-275.

Isgur, J. Establishing letter-sound associations by

an object-imaging-projection method. *Journal of Learning Disabilities*, 1975, *8*, 349-353.

Johnson, D., and Myklebust, H. *Learning disabilities: educational principles and practices.* New York: Grune & Stratton, Inc., 1967.

Keogh, B. Hyperactivity and learning disorders: review and speculation. *Exceptional Children*, 1971, *38*, 101-109.

Kephart, N. *The brain-injured child.* Chicago: National Society for Crippled Children and Adults, 1963.

Kephart, N. *The slow learner in the classroom* (rev. ed.). Columbus, Ohio: Charles E. Merrill Publishing Co., 1971.

Kirk, S. *Behavioral diagnosis and remediation of learning disabilities.* Proceedings of the First Annual Meeting of the Conference on the Exploration into the Problems of the Perceptually Handicapped Child. First Annual Meeting, Vol. 1, April 16, 1963.

Kirk, S., and Kirk, W. *Psycholinguistic learning disabilities: diagnosis and remediation.* Urbana, Ill.: University of Illinois Press, 1971.

Kirk, S., McCarthy, J., and Kirk, W. *Illinois test of psycholinguistic abilities: revised edition, examiner's manual.* Urbana, Ill.: University of Illinois Press, 1968.

Kirk, W. *Aids and precautions in administering the Illinois Test of Psycholinguistic Abilities.* Urbana, Ill.: University of Illinois Press, 1974.

Lerner, J. *Children with learning disabilities.* New York: Houghton-Mifflin Co., 1976.

Lovitt, T. Specific research recommendations and suggestions for practitioners. *Journal of Learning Disabilities*, 1975, *8*, 504-517.

Lovitt, T., and others. Using arranged and programmed events to alter subtraction performance of children with learning disabilities. In *Behavior modification: applications to education.* F. Keller, and E. Ribes-Inesta (Eds.). New York: Academic Press, Inc., 1974.

Marsh, G., Gearheart, C., and Gearheart, B. *The learning disabled adolescent: program alternatives in the secondary school.* St. Louis: The C. V. Mosby Co., 1978.

Myklebust, H. (Ed.). *Progress in learning disabilities.* Vol. 3. New York: Grune & Stratton, Inc., 1975.

Myklebust, H., and Boshes, B. *Minimal brain damage in children.* Evanston, Ill.: Northwestern University Press, 1969.

Orton, S. *Collected papers, Orton Society monograph II.* Pomfret, Conn.: The Society, 1966.

Pauling, L. Orthomolecular psychiatry. *Science*, 1968, *160*(4), 265-271.

Powers, H., Jr. Caffeine, behavior, and the LD child. *Academic Therapy*, 1975, *II*(1), 5-19.

Powers, H., Jr. Dietary measures to improve behavior and achievement. *Academic Therapy*, 1974, *9*(3), 203-214.

Roberts, H. A clinical and metabolic reevaluation of reading disability. *Selected Papers on Learning Disabilities.* Fifth Annual Convention, Association for Children with Learning Disabilities. San Rafael, Cal.: Academy Therapy Publications, 1969.

Scranton, T., and Downs, M. Elementary and secondary learning disabilities programs in the U.S.: a survey. *Journal of Learning Disabilities*, 1975, *8*(6), 394-399.

Simpson, D., and Nelson, A. Attention training through breathing control to modify hyperactivity. *Journal of Learning Disabilities*, 1974, *7*, 274-283.

Special Education for Handicapped Children. *First Annual Report of the National Advisory Committee on Handicapped Children.* Washington, D.C.: Office of Education, Department of Health, Education, and Welfare, 1968.

Strauss, A., and Kephart, N. *Psychopathology and education of the brain-injured child. Vol. 2. Progress in theory and clinic.* New York: Grune & Stratton, Inc., 1947.

Strauss, A., and Lehtinen, L. *Psychopathology and education of the brain-injured child.* New York: Grune & Stratton, Inc., 1947.

Wiederholt, J. Historical perspectives on the education of the learning disabled. In *The second review of special education.* L. Mann and D. Sabatino (Eds.). Philadelphia: Journal of Special Education Press, 1974.

Wiig, E., and Semel, E. *Language disabilities in children and adolescents.* Columbus, Ohio: Charles E. Merrill Publishing Co., 1976.

Wiig, E., and Semel, E. Productive language abilities in learning disabled adolescents. *Journal of Learning Disabilities*, 1975, *8*, 578-586.

Wunderlich, R. *Allergy, brains, and children coping: allergy and child behavior: the neuro-allergic syndrome.* St. Petersburg, Fla.: Johnny Reads, Inc., 1973.

Wunderlich, R. Treatment of the hyperactive child. *Academic Therapy*, 1973, *8*(4), 375-390.

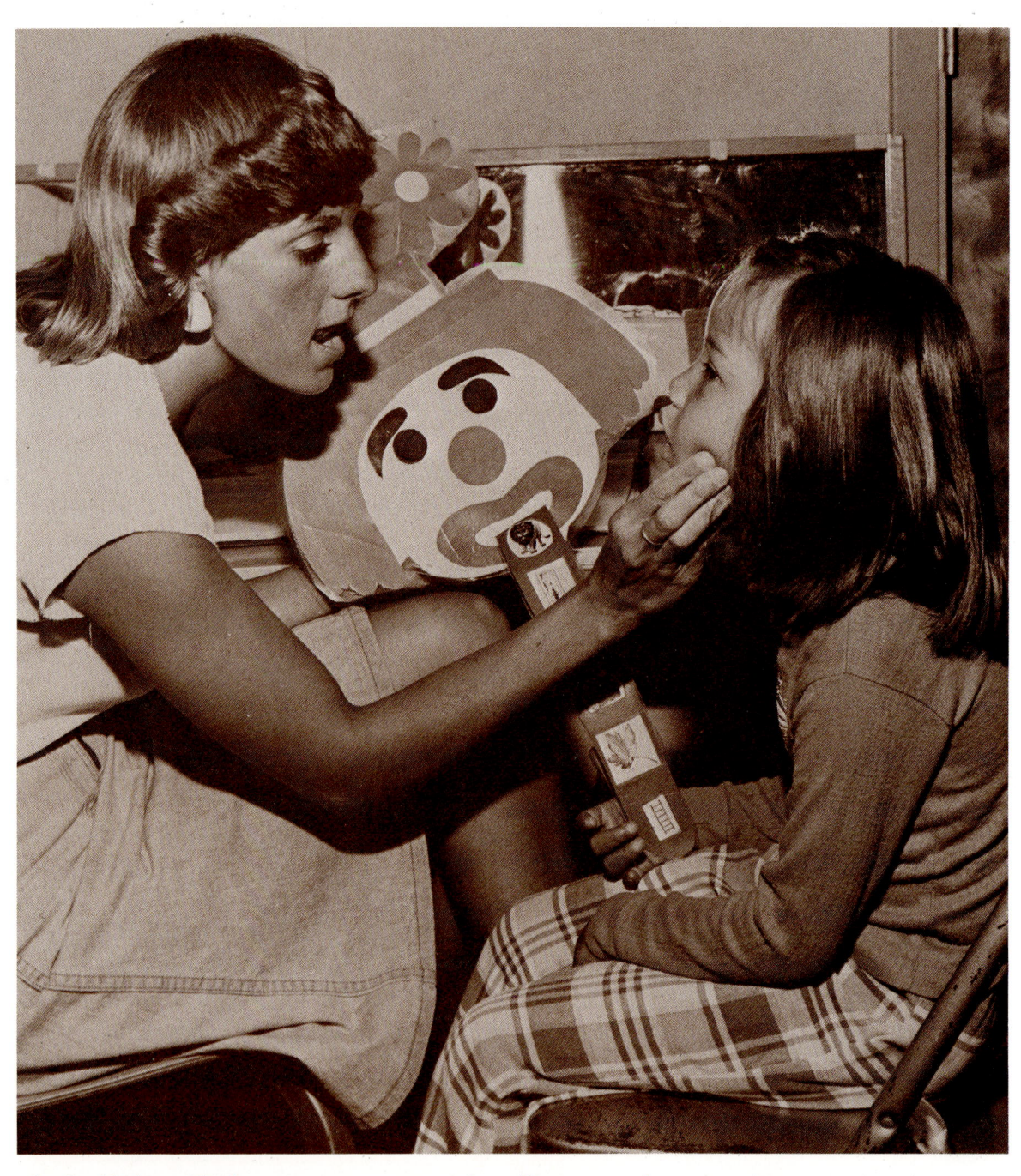

Individual help and high motivation are essential to effective speech services. (From Litton, F. W. *Education of the Trainable Mentally Retarded.* St. Louis: The C. V. Mosby Co., 1978.)

chapter 8

Education of children and youth with speech and language disorders

objectives

To understand the mechanics of speech.

To develop an understanding and appreciation of the complexity of language development.

To describe and discuss disorders of articulation, voice, speech flow, and language.

To discuss the causes of speech and language disorders and understand the differences between organic (biologic) and functional disorders.

To review the basic types of medical and surgical treatment for speech and language disorders.

To discuss and describe four different models for speech therapy and to consider various procedures for assessment and remediation in the educational setting.

Introduction

Speech and language disorders are common handicapping conditions, yet when undergraduate students in teacher preparation programs are asked to name the most prevalent types of handicap found among school-age children, this area may be omitted entirely. This may be the result of a number of factors but certainly would include the fact that some disorders are relatively mild, and in many cases these children do not appear (either to other children or to teachers) to be as "different" as children who are hearing impaired, visually impaired, or mentally retarded. Nevertheless, if appropriate assistance is not provided, such difficulties may have continuing, long-lasting effect on both eduational progress and social acceptance. Severe stuttering is of course noticeable, as are other more severe speech or language disabilities, and remedial intervention on behalf of children with speech and language disorders is highly important.

In the prologue to his speech pathology text, Perkins (1977) provides the following introduction to students entering this professional field. In addition to its general introductory message, it will provide some interesting insight into the various titles by which speech pathologists have been known through the years.

> Early in this century rivulets of interest in communicative disorders began to flow from several wellsprings. Psychology was a fountainhead, as in many ways were education and medicine. Over subsequent years, other disciplines and professions joined in contributing to what is now the mainstream of speech pathology, an interdisciplinary profession rapidly developing an identity of its own.
>
> Like all youth, speech pathology has suffered from, and periodically is still agonized by, growing pains. What is probably a major source of strength for this young field, its multiple roots, has at the same time been a major source of its chief conflict: identity. Who is a speech pathologist? From the answers to this question, two types of bias are often visible.
>
> From one, we can generally sort academicians from clinicians. Those who prefer academic identity may label their area of concern *communication sciences*. This recently developed hybrid has had sufficient vitality to survive and sufficient breadth to include areas that would otherwise be called *experimental phonetics*, *speech science*, and *voice science*. Those interested in these areas are closest to being the "pure" scientists of speech pathology. In fact, some are so pure that they do not want to be speech pathologists at all. Their interests tend to focus on normal processes of communication.
>
> On the other side of this bias are the academicians' applied brethren, the clinicians who dispense service to the speech handicapped. They, too, have preferred identities that often reveal bias toward the related profession with which they are most closely aligned. In public schools are *speech correctionists*, *speech improvement teachers*, and more recently (with some relief to the profession), well-qualified *speech specialists*. *Speech therapists* are a vanishing breed. This label is onerous to the profession only because it implies that as therapists they work under medical prescription. These clinicians seek medical consultation regarding somatic conditions and, in turn, provide consultation for physicians regarding the adequacy of a patient's speech performance. Theirs is therefore a consultative, not a prescriptive, relationship. Finally, reflecting preference for medical affiliation is the *speech clinician* and his more exalted colleague, the *speech pathologist*. It is this name with its obvious, and somewhat erroneous, medical connotation that has been taken as generic for the profession.
>
> This proliferated jumble of titles has been the subject of much discussion—at times approaching contest proportions. Speech pathology's counterpart in hearing, *audiology*, being blessed with an adequate moniker for its scientific and clinical aspects, generously offered its name as an umbrella under which to include speech and its disorders. The offer was declined. Speech pathology seems to be as much with us as ever as a surname for the family of scientists and

clinicians interested in normal and disordered processes of speech. Still, out of this great introspective effort are emerging a few general terms that encompass audiology as well as speech pathology: *speech and hearing,* historically accepted as connoting interest in normal as well as disordered processes of communication; *communicative disorders,* a newcomer that is spreading rapidly; and *communicology,* a name with the proper spirit but little enthusiastic support to nourish it.

So much for what this fledgling among health professions chooses to call itself. The question still remains: what is it? It is an *applied interdisciplinary behavioral science.* This term denotes that, on one side, the profession is an interdisciplinary field of study of disordered oral communication, and, equally important on the other, it is an interprofessional area of clinical practice in which knowledge of problems of speech is applied in their remediation. (pp. 2-3)

In this chapter we will consider speech and language handicaps from the point of view of education and consider speech and language pathologists more as educators than as members of a health profession. Also, in addition to our focus on children and youth, we will take a very brief look at speech and language disorders in adults.

Historical origins of speech/language services

Some aspects of the historical development of the speech pathology profession in the United States were outlined in the preceding section and, if references to historical origins in introductory texts in the various areas of exceptionality are any meaningful indication, there is less effort expended in reviewing history in this subarea of special education than in most of the others. Further, as noted by Perkins' reference to speech pathology as a "fledgling among health professions," there is some question as to whether speech pathology should be considered a health profession providing an assistive role in education or a specialty area in education. Nevertheless, the speech/language pathologist is a very important member of the team that serves handicapped children and youth in the public schools and both children and adults in a variety of community or hospital settings.

Lundeen (1972) notes that speech disorders have been recognized for thousands of years and that references to such problems as stuttering and cleft palate have been found among hieroglyphic records in Egypt. He also notes that Moses apparently had speech difficulties and reportedly used this as an excuse when asked to speak to the Pharoah regarding the release of the children of Israel. In fact, there are numerous accounts throughout history of noted individuals who had speech defects, and various causative factors were postulated (possessed by devils, stiff or weak tongues, punishment for sins, and so forth). Speech disorders have apparently been recognized since the dawn of history, but only during the last two centuries have there been any well-organized efforts to provide systematic remediation.

ESTABLISHMENT OF PROGRAMS IN EUROPE

As was the case with most other exceptionalities, the forerunners of programs for persons with speech disorders in the United States were those developed in Europe, and "a marked expansion of knowledge about speech disorders occurred . . . after the beginning of the nineteenth century." (Paden, 1970, p. 1) In an account of the founding of the American Speech and Hearing Association, Paden, (1970) notes that a number of publications relating to speech disorders and their remediation had appeared by 1850, most of these written by physicians in France, England, Ireland, Austria, and Germany. These included such early authorities as James Hunt and J. S. Bristowe in England, Ainé Chervin and A. Guillaume in France, and Hermann Klencke, Adolph Kuzzmaul, and Albert Gutzmann in Germany.

The development of clinical treatment of speech disorders in Europe in the late 1800s and early 1900s seemed to center in Germany and Austria where the more highly recognized European professors organized their students and followers "into what amounted to schools of practitioners, of which the master served as something of a messiah." (Paden, p. 2) As in some other developing areas of handicap, little exchange of information was accomplished among groups, apparently because of intense group loyalty and a tendency to discount, if not discredit, theories and practices expounded by other groups. In most instances, these European programs were developed as a part of, or in direct relation to, medical service programs; speech disorders were considered to be a medical problem, not an educational problem. There is some question as to the amount of truly scientific investigation involved in the development of the first formally developed theories regarding speech disorders, but apparently such theories were known and recognized by those with similar interests in the United States, and early practitioners in this country tended to follow the European masters. However, some departure from tradition was indicated when speech correction was taught in a nonmedical setting in the United States in 1874 by Alexander Melville Bell (Lundeen, 1972).

ESTABLISHMENT OF PROGRAMS IN THE UNITED STATES

As indicated above, a precedent for consideration or inclusion of speech disorders in a nonmedical setting was established in the United States in 1874, when Alexander Melville Bell was invited by Boston University to instruct speech correction classes. These classes, which continued for 5 years, were apparently the first university classes in this subject area taught in the United States. In 1910, the Chicago and Detroit public schools established formal speech correction services through the hiring of "speech correction teachers" (Paden, 1970; Lundeen, 1972). In the next few years, other school districts, including Seattle, San Francisco, and New York, established similar services. By 1919, there was enough interest in this type of service that an article written by Walter Swift, entitled "How to Begin Speech Correction in the Public Schools," was published in a speech education journal *(Quarterly Journal of Speech Education)*. For all intents and purposes, the interest in speech correction services in the schools, which was to grow to one of the largest of special service areas in special education, was established by the early 1920s.

In addition to public school speech correction programs, many private speech disorder programs had been established by 1920. One, the *Boston Stammerers' Institute*, advertised in early editions of the *Quarterly Journal of Speech Education* and claimed to have been founded in 1867. According to Paden (1970) this institute had an excellent reputation, but there were many other alleged "experts" who were quacks. These others would "for an appropriately large sum of money . . . guarantee a complete cure within a specified time." (Paden, p.3) Many of these "experts" made the clients vow that they would not reveal the secret of their miraculous treatment, undoubtedly a part of the selling mystique. Their continued existence in active practice, despite questionable approaches and practices, testified to the considerable need for responsible, organized speech services in the nation.

Although well underway by the 1920s, the speech correction movement did not receive its major impetus until the establishment of the American Speech and Hearing Association (ASHA), the professional group most often associated with the work of speech pathology. ASHA was established as a result of discussions that took place in 1925, in which a small group of individuals who were members of the National Association of Teachers of Speech decided that a separate subsection for speech correctionists was needed. This association, first named the American Academy of Speech Correction, has grown into the strong, sometimes militant, professional organization so influential in the field today. Its early self-confidence might be inferred by the fact that in 1935, after its paid membership had reached the tremendous total of 87 (the name of the association was then the American Speech Correction Association), the publication of a journal was undertaken (Paden, 1970).

The original concern with "speech correction" has now broadened into wide involvement with language disorders and in more recent years with learning disabilities. Although a relatively new professional group with somewhat diverse interests, the history of concern with speech disorders, and particularly the very rapid development of this professional group since the 1950s, gives indication of a strong, vital profession, providing much needed services to handicapped individuals.

Development of speech and language

In earlier chapters we considered the anatomy and physiology of the auditory and the visual systems before approaching additional details about special educational efforts on behalf of children and youth who were hearing or visually impaired. A similar effort is appropriate in this chapter, but certain observations must be made before initiating such consideration. Here we should investigate two related but separate aspects of the physiologic/anatomic foundations for this area of interest. These two are: (1) *speech*, the mechanical (vocal) operations that produce audible, identifiable sounds (words) and (2) *language*, the ability to communicate thoughts and feelings through sounds (primarily words), gestures, or written symbols.

In the schools, these two areas, speech and language, will not necessarily be considered separately; the speech/language specialist will work with students whose speech is defective (different from normal to the extent that it gives rise to any of a variety of other problems) and who may or may not have language problems. However, the following consideration of speech and language will be presented in separate sections, for reasons that should become evident.

SPEECH DEVELOPMENT: MECHANICS OF SPEECH

Speech is at times identified as the ability to communicate through the use of spoken words, but here we will consider *what the speaker does to produce the sounds we call speech*. This production requires that the speaker modulate the stream of breath so that some type of sound results. Perkins (1977) states that there are three processes required to produce overt speaking behavior. These are phonation (controlling the breath stream), articulation/resonance (moving the organs of the vocal tract to produce distinctively different speech sounds), and speech flow (movement from sound to sound, syllable to syllable, word to word). In combination these three are responsible for the production of speech. In highly oversimplified terms the following events must take place for speech to occur:

1. Air that has been taken into the lungs must be expelled under pressure in order to establish the air flow.
2. In the case of *voiced sounds* (e.g., /a/, /i/) the air being expelled through the trachea causes the vocal bands in the larynx to

vibrate. The rate of this vibration determines what is ordinarily called *pitch* (see Fig. 8-1).
3. In the case of *voiceless* sounds (e.g., /t/, /s/), the larynx is open and the air turbulence is generated at points of constriction or closure in the vocal tract by sudden release of closures in the tract.
4. Beyond (above) the larynx, the breath stream is modified by the tongue, lips, teeth, jaw, and soft palate (the articulators and resonators), which cause the oral chambers to assume any of a wide variety of sizes or shapes (see Fig. 8-2).
5. The preceding steps in the production of speech account for sounds of various pitch, volume, and quality. However, it is the *timing* of the various sounds as they flow from basic speech sounds to syllables to words to phrases and to sentences that produces speech that can be readily understood. This is called *speechflow* and includes sequence, duration, rhythm, rate, and fluency. Speech flow may be limited or constrained by a combination of factors, including functioning of other parts of the system (the articulators, the vocal bands), understanding of grammar, lack of adequate vocabulary, impaired hearing, and others. Speech flow disorders are therefore more complex and more difficult to diagnose with certainty than phonatory or articulatory/resonatory difficulties.

Human speech requires constant monitoring by the speaker, and in normally flowing speech, the speaker is already adjusting all of the physiologic apparatus of speech to produce a different sound, even as any given sound is being heard by the listener. A complicated set of interconnected muscle actions must be constantly directed by the brain for normal speech production. In addition to this muscular movement, the individual must also be directing the entire flow of *thought* (this is

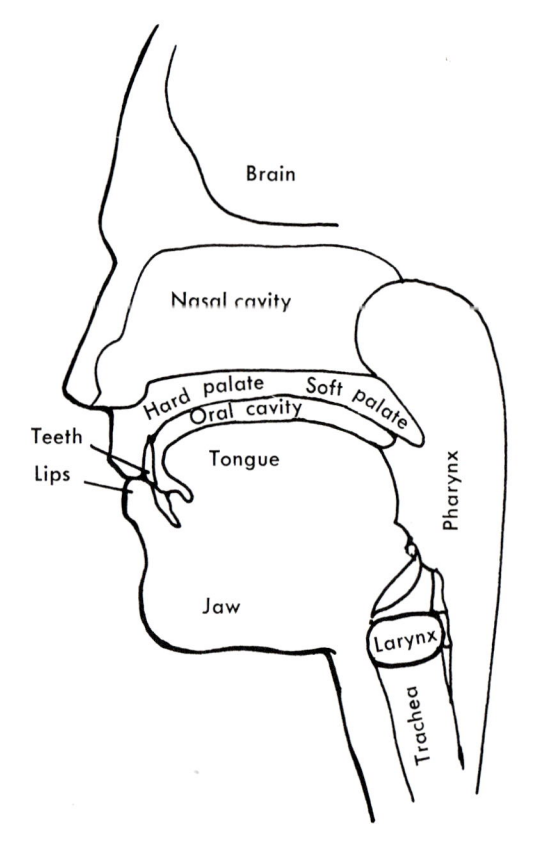

Fig. 8-1. The speech mechanism. (From Weiss, C., and Lillywhite, H. *Communicative Disorders: A Handbook for Prevention and Early Intervention.* St. Louis: The C. V. Mosby Co., 1976.)

quite a different matter from the flow of speech) through a meaningful set of thought processes, which must be in terms of some language system (English, German, Spanish, etc.). This leads to the next consideration, the matter of language.

LANGUAGE DEVELOPMENT: THE HUMAN MIRACLE

Although many of the lower animals produce sounds of different pitch and volume, none is involved in language in the manner common to the human species. Language is

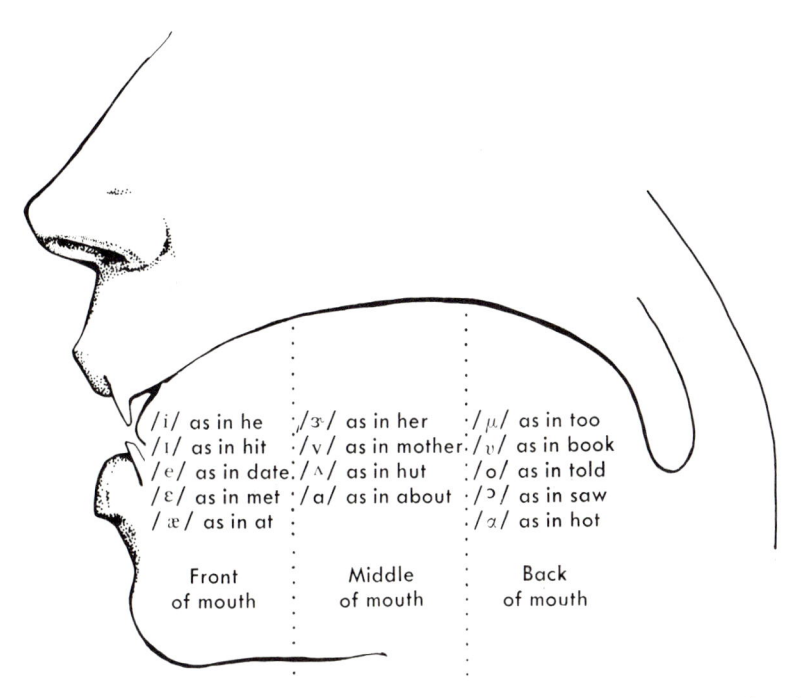

Fig. 8-2. Vowel chart showing approximately where in the mouth the tongue is placed for each of the fourteen vowels. The symbols representing the vowels are from the International Phonetic Alphabet. (From Weiss, C., and Lillywhite, H. *Communicative Disorders: A Handbook for Prevention and Early Intervention.* St. Louis: The C. V. Mosby Co., 1976.)

the one factor that most clearly sets humans above all of the lower animals, and because so many humans develop language with little or no difficulty, we tend to overlook its complexity. This fact is expressed in a variety of ways by authorities from many disciplines. According to Smith and coworkers (1976), "language is the most useful and marvelous invention yet achieved by man, and it is amazing that virtually every child achieves near mastery of at least one language by the time he is five or six." (p. 9) Dale (1976), in speaking of language development, states: "Children—most children—learn how to talk without any difficulty at all. In a sense, we are never going to discover any astonishing *new* facts; *this* is the fact that we are trying to explain." (p. 1) These two quotations are representative of the manner in which scholars and scientists regard language and may serve to emphasize its recognized importance and complexity. But how is language developed? What happens physiologically as a young child learns to communicate? And, most importantly for our consideration here, what is wrong (delayed, dysfunctional, defective) when the child does

219

not develop language within normally expected limits?

In their review of central processing dysfunctions in children, Chalfant and Sheffelin (1969) note that "it is generally agreed that in acquiring auditory language, the child acquires an auditory-vocal communication system . . . used by his speech community. The terminal behavior of the child is agreed to be the comprehension and production of complex and highly structured utterances which conform to the code, the content and form of which are relatively well-known." (p. 76) But they further note that "what is not generally agreed upon is the manner in which children acquire the code." (p. 76)

This does not mean that nothing is known of how the human species acquires language, but rather that the process is so highly complex that there is conflicting information as to how it is acquired. A relatively simple analysis of how auditory receptive language and auditory expressive language ordinarily develop is presented in Tables 8-1 and 8-2. These are in the form of a task analysis of these two skills and are oversimplifications; nevertheless, they effectively demonstrate the process under consideration.

It is beyond the scope of this introductory text to pursue the matter of language development at any great length, but it would appear to be essential to have at least some basic understanding of its complexity, so as to better understand the area of speech/language disorders. As for the physiologic mechanisms that play an active role in language development, it is primarily a matter of a variety of brain functions. In order to develop language the child must have adequate auditory acuity and an opportunity to experience language and interact in the language arena, but language development also requires many complex symbolic manipulations, which take place in the brain. Although it is generally rec-

TABLE 8-1

Acquiring auditory receptive language: a task analysis*

I. **Attention:** Attend to vocally produced auditory sound units, i.e., noises, speech sounds, words, phrases, sentences.
II. **Discrimination:** Discriminate between auditory-vocal sound units.
III. **Establishing correspondences:** Establish reciprocal associations between the auditory-vocal sound units and objects or events:
   A. Store and identify auditory-vocal sound units as meaningful auditory-language signals. Substitute auditory-language signals for actual objects and/or events.
   B. Establish word order sequences and sentence patterns.
IV. **Automatic auditory-vocal decoding:**
   A. Improve interpretation by analyzing increasingly more complex auditory-language signals.
   B. Increase the speed and accuracy of the reception of auditory-language signals through variation, practice, and repetition to the point of automatic interpretation.
   C. Shift attention from the auditory-language signals to the total meaning that is carried by the signal sequence.
V. **Terminal behavior:** Respond appropriately to verbal commands, instructions, explanations, questions, and statements.

*From Chalfant, J., and Scheffelin, M. *Central processing dysfunctions in children*, NINDS Monograph No. 9. Washington, D.C: U.S. Department of Health, Education and Welfare, 1969, p. 77.

ognized that language functions are largely controlled by the left hemisphere of the brain in adults, this is not necessarily true for very young children. Lenneberg and Long (1974) have outlined what is known about this question of equipotentiality of the hemispheres of the brain in a table, which is reproduced here as Table 8-3. Although this tabular presenta-

TABLE 8-2

Acquiring expressive auditory language: a task analysis*

I. Intention:
  A. Possess the need to communicate.
  B. Decide to send message vocally.
II. Formulate message by retrieving and sequencing the appropriate vocal-language signals.
III. Organize the vocal-motor sequence:
  A. Retrieve the vocal-motor sequence for producing the selected vocal-language signals.
  B. Execute the vocal-motor sequence for producing the vocal-language signal.
IV. Automatic vocal encoding:
  A. Combine simple vocal-language signals to form more complex vocal-language signal sequences.
  B. Increase the rate, accuracy, length, total number, and types of vocal-language signal sequences to the point of automatic production.
  C. Shift attention from the mechanics of producing vocal-language signal sequences to the contents of the message to be sent
V. Terminal behavior: To produce appropriate verbal instruction, commands, explanations, descriptions, and questions.

*From Chalfant, J., and Scheffelin, M. *Central processing dysfunctions in children*, NINDS Monograph No. 9. Washington, D.C.: U.S. Department of Health, Education and Welfare, 1969, p. 77.

tion leaves many questions unanswered, it does clarify certain issues about language specialization of the two hemispheres of the brain. This change in the manner in which the human brain can acquire the language function parallels the general development of the central nervous system, and it is possible that after a certain amount of development, the functional plasticity of the brain (in this case the ability of the right hemisphere to direct language functions) is drastically reduced to the point of near uselessness *for this purpose*.

Three areas of the cortex of the brain are recognized with relation to specific speech functions, and certain relationships between these areas and the thalamus have been established. Other similar relationships exist, most of them established and verified through work with subjects with brain lesions or specific brain damage resulting from accidents or war-related injuries. Nevertheless, this is an area with more unknowns than knowns. All of the handicapping conditions we have thus far considered are closely related to brain function, but most of the others (i.e., visual, hearing, and speech impairments) also relate to physiologic/anatomic functions that we can observe and measure to a considerable degree. Language functions take place in the brain, cannot be observed directly, and are thus less understood. Because they are so highly essential to normal learning, they must remain the target of concerted effort on the part of highly trained specialists from various disciplines.

Speech and language disorders: definitions and classifications

In the introduction to this chapter it was indicated that the professional field under consideration has evolved through numerous name changes. Some have related to a changing definition of function, some were designed to more clearly indicate independence from earlier roots in the medical profession, and some are expressions of a desire to be of further professional service or to carve out greater areas of responsibility for a variety of reasons. At any rate, the field of specialization is often called *speech pathology*, although it certainly relates to both *speech* and *language* disorders; and those who serve in the public

TABLE 8-3
Language specialization of the two hemispheres of the brain*

Age	Lateralization of function	Equipotentiality of hemispheres	Explanation
0-20 mo	None: symptoms and prognosis identical for either hemisphere.	Perfect equipotentiality.	Neuroanatomical and physiological prerequisites become established.
21-36 mo	Hand preference emerges.	Right hemisphere can easily adopt sole responsibility for language.	Language appears to involve entire brain; little cortical specialization with regard to language, though left hemisphere beginning to become dominant toward the end of this period.
3-10 yr	Cerebral dominance established between 3-5 years, but evidence that right hemisphere may often still be involved in speech and language functions. About ¼ of early childhood aphasia due to right hemisphere lesions.	In cases where language is already predominantly localized in left hemisphere and aphasia ensues with left lesion, it is possible to reestablish language, presumably by reactivating language functions in right hemisphere.	A process of physiological organization takes place in which functional lateralization of language to left is prominent. "Physiological redundancy" is gradually reduced and polarization of activities between right and left hemisphere is established. As long as maturational processes have not stopped, reorganization is still possible.
11-14 yr	Apparently firmly established, but definitive statistics not available.	Marked signs of reduction in equipotentiality.	Language markedly lateralized and internal organization established irreversibly for life. Language-free parts of brain cannot take over; however, where lateralization is incomplete or has been blocked pathologically during childhood, the right hemisphere may remain language-competent throughout life.
Midteens to senium	In about 97 percent of the entire population language is definitely lateralized to the left.	None for language.	

*From Lenneberg, E., and Long, B. Language development. In *Psychology and the handicapped child.* J. Swets and L. Elliot (Eds.). Washington, D.C.: Office of Education, 1974, p. 138.

schools are commonly called *speech pathologists, speech/language pathologists, speech and language specialists,* or *communication disorders specialists. Speech therapy,* one of the older terms, is in limited use but for all practical purposes is an out-of-date term. Although several states still refer to *speech clinicians* in state guidelines, this term is apparently not acceptable to most modern practicioners in this field. However, all must be recognized as terms that may still be used in some geographic areas (or in older writings in the field), and for some purposes they may be used interchangeably.

Regardless of the various titles by which the personnel who work with speech and language disorders may be called, it is necessary to eventually define or describe what they do. To avoid the potential biases of authors who may prefer some particular definition in relation to their personal perspective, we shall turn to the professional association that best represents this profession for our descriptive definition. According to the American Speech and Hearing Association:

> A *Speech Pathologist* is a professional trained in the study of human communication, its normal development, and its disorders. By evaluating the speech and language skills of children and adults, the speech pathologist determines if communication problems exist and decides the best way to treat these problems.

With the role of the speech pathologist thus briefly defined, we may then proceed with a consideration of classifications and common terminology used to refer to the types of disabilities or disorders these professionals will treat. To a considerable extent, the following classification system is taken from that used by Perkins (1977), in a text that has been used widely as part of the basic source material for review for the National Examinations on Speech Pathology and Audiology. However, in his text, Perkins classifies disorders of language under the broad heading of disorders of speech. For purposes of emphasis in this chapter, disorders of language have been indicated as separate from disorders of speech. A case can be made for either point of view.

SPEECH DISORDERS

Although there is some variation in classification, the major speech disorders recognized by most authorities in this field are:
1. Articulatory disorders (both articulation and resonance disorders)
   a. Omissions
   b. Substitutions
   c. Distortions
   d. Additions
2. Disorders of voice (disorders of phonation)
   a. Pitch disorders
   b. Intensity (loudness) disorders
   c. Flexibility disorders
   d. Quality disorders
3. Fluency of speech-flow disorders
   a. Stuttering
   b. Cluttering

LANGUAGE DISORDERS

There may be somewhat less agreement as to these classifications than with the speech disorder classification, but the following appear to represent general consensus, with certain possible exceptions as noted:
1. Delayed language
2. Aphasia
3. Nonstandard English (not always included)
4. Learning disabilities (not always included)

The indication "not always included" following nonstandard English and learning disabilities does not imply that these are not real or at times serious considerations. It does indicate that they may be considered under some other general classification in the total classification of disorders or impairments.

Learning disabilities and speech/language disorders

LANGUAGE DISORDERS
DELAYED LANGUAGE: marked slowness in the onset and development of language skills necessary for expressing ideas and for understanding the thoughts and ideas one hears or reads.
LEARNING DISABILITIES: something interfering with a child's ability to understand the message that his eyes and ears receive.
APHASIA: loss of speech and language abilities following brain damage sometimes resulting from a stroke or head injury.

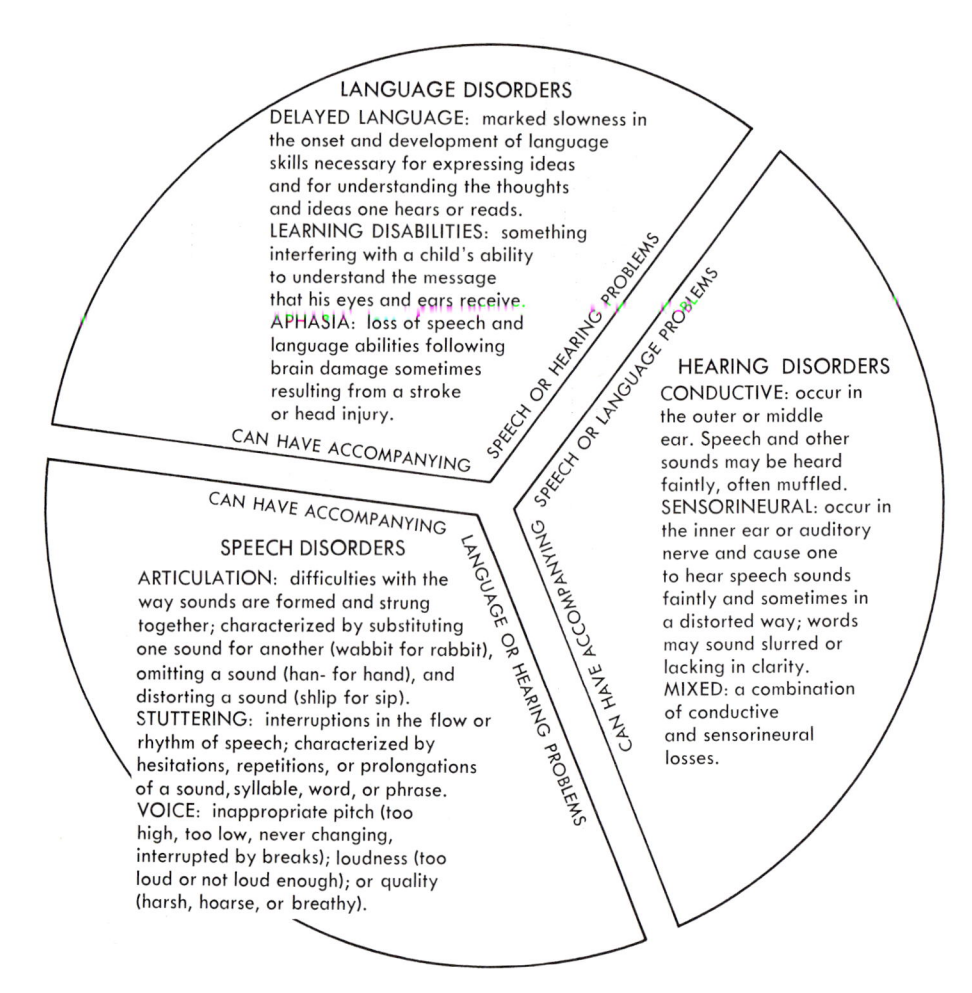

CAN HAVE ACCOMPANYING SPEECH OR HEARING PROBLEMS

HEARING DISORDERS
CONDUCTIVE: occur in the outer or middle ear. Speech and other sounds may be heard faintly, often muffled.
SENSORINEURAL: occur in the inner ear or auditory nerve and cause one to hear speech sounds faintly and sometimes in a distorted way; words may sound slurred or lacking in clarity.
MIXED: a combination of conductive and sensorineural losses.

CAN HAVE ACCOMPANYING LANGUAGE OR HEARING PROBLEMS

SPEECH DISORDERS
ARTICULATION: difficulties with the way sounds are formed and strung together; characterized by substituting one sound for another (wabbit for rabbit), omitting a sound (han- for hand), and distorting a sound (shlip for sip).
STUTTERING: interruptions in the flow or rhythm of speech; characterized by hesitations, repetitions, or prolongations of a sound, syllable, word, or phrase.
VOICE: inappropriate pitch (too high, too low, never changing, interrupted by breaks); loudness (too loud or not loud enough); or quality (harsh, hoarse, or breathy).

CAN HAVE ACCOMPANYING SPEECH OR LANGUAGE PROBLEMS

Fig. 8-3. The interrelationship of speech, hearing, and language disorders. (From Public Information Pamphlet No. 66, American Speech and Hearing Association. Reproduced with permission of The Association.)

Perhaps nonstandard English should not be considered an impairment, and it is not an impairment under some circumstances, but in the real world it may become a definite handicap.

As was noted earlier, language disorders are sometimes simply considered as one type of speech disorder, but as may be seen from Fig. 8-3 the American Speech and Hearing Association apparently recognizes the potential value in viewing speech and language disorders as separate, major categories. Fig. 8-3 emphasizes the relationship of speech disorders, language disorders, and hearing disorders. The relationship of speech and language disorders to hearing disorders will not be pursued in this chapter (see Chapter 4). However, the interrelationships between these areas are most effectively illustrated in Fig. 8-3.

Rather than providing specific definitions

of each of the above terms (pitch disorders, stuttering, etc.) at this point, we will proceed to define and discuss each area of speech and language disorder separately. Definitions will then come as an integral part of these discussions.

Disorders of articulation and resonance

Articulation and resonance disorders are more often grouped together as "articulation disorders" in most popular writing about the subject. According to Perkins (1977), the degree of articulatory *defectiveness* "is determined by the judgment of either speaker or listener." (p. 253) The extent to which such defects or differences in speech are a *problem* is the private concern of the speaker. This determination of the extent of the problem is certainly a matter for any individual adult to determine privately, but in the case of children in school, it is a matter of judgment that must be exercised by the professional speech pathologist and involves a decision that should be determined jointly with the parent, particularly when the defect is minor. Articulation disorders include various types of impreciseness in speech and may be evaluated according to a number of different criteria. The first and foremost is that of *intelligibility*. If speech is primarily for the purpose of communicating thoughts and ideas, then it must be understood—that is, others must recognize what the speaker is attempting to say.

A second criterion concerns *vocational goals*. If an individual plans to be a teacher or a television or radio announcer, or to pursue any vocation or profession that depends heavily on articulatory preciseness, then it is much more important that articulation differences be corrected than if, for example, the student's goal is to acquire the technical skills to become a mechanic, a computer programmer, or an electrician. Another example is to contrast the job requirements of a taxi driver and the dispatcher. This matter of vocational goals may have less immediate applicability when dealing with young children, but it can be an important part of planning a remedial program for older students and adults.

A third consideration is that of the *acceptability of various accents or regional speech patterns*. In the case of ghetto children in schools where there is an attempt to encourage more use of standard English, the child may have to attempt to meet two different standards—one to be accepted in the neighborhood, another to be accepted at school. This criterion is often referred to as a *cultural speech standard*.

The fourth criterion is *personal satisfaction*. This is a matter for the speaker to determine, or for parents and speech specialists to attempt to predict on behalf of some very young children.

Articulation disorders have been estimated to comprise about 75 percent of the total of all speech disorders and are particularly problematic in young children. Because many 5- and 6-year-old children outgrow their articulation disorders by the time they are 10 or 11 years of age, there is some debate as to how much time the speech specialist should spend in working with articulation disorders in young children. An added factor that makes for confusion is that for the most part, articulation disorders "exist only in the listener's ear." (Perkins, 1977, p. 254) However, for classification purposes, there is general agreement that articulation disorders are of three major types: omissions, substitutions, and distortions. Some authorities add a fourth type, additions. These will be considered briefly in the order listed.

Omission errors are quite common in the speech of young children and are usually outgrown with no specialized assistance. Children may say "I uv u," omitting the /l/ and the /y/. In many cases a sound is regularly omitted, but such consistency is not always the case. If the sound omitted is part of a word in a sentence that is otherwise quite coherent, the meaning is usually clear. If the child is attempting to communicate with a single word, or if there are other articulation errors in the communication, it may be difficult to understand what the child is attempting to say. The matter of age-appropriateness is also a part of the general consideration that must be given to any omission error. When 3-year-old Sammy says "I ove u" it may be considered "cute." When 19-year-old Sam says "I ove u" in an amourous moment, it may cause a somewhat different reaction.

Substitutions are the substitution of one speech sound for another. Mike, another 3-year-old, might say "I wuv you." Here the /w/ is substituted for the /l/. Another common substitution of /w/ for /r/ is in the word red (it often becomes "wed"). There are many other similar substitutions, which will be well known to any reader who has recently conversed with young children.

Distortions are sounds that are somewhat like the intended sound but are not quite right. They are usually the result of the tongue, lips, teeth, or jaw not being in precisely the right position, with the tongue often the culprit. In general, distortion errors are more easily corrected than errors of substitution or omission, but there are exceptions to this generalization too.

It was noted that omission errors may be inconsistent. The same is true of errors of substitution and distortion. Reasons for this inconsistency may vary, but one example might be the case of the correctly articulated /l/ or /s/, which may have been learned more recently than some misarticulated sound. Earlier misarticulations are continued because of the strength of habit, but they may be corrected through proper effort. With bilingual children, articulation errors may have a very different origin than for nonbilingual children. In such a case, a specific sound that is part of one language may be used to substitute for a new sound in the second language.

Errors of *addition* are not always listed among articulation errors, and they are not as likely to lead to misunderstandings in communication as are errors of omission, substitution, or distortion. At times these are characteristic of geographic regions, as in the case of addition of /r/ in the words idea (idear) or saw (sawr). In some instances, in some parts of the nation, to *not* make this type of error would be to call attention to oneself. Therefore, this is a particularly good example of a situation in which differing criteria may be applied to the determination of when a difference in articulation is or is not a defect.

Articulation errors are common among young children, and in each case the *type, frequency, and consistency* of errors must be considered in relation to the child's *age, language experience, and background.* Some children will still exhibit articulation errors upon entrance to school, but if they persist or give indication of leading to related errors in academic endeavors, remediation should be initiated. The question of when to provide planned assistance for articulation errors in young children remains a cost-efficiency, effort-efficiency puzzle for the speech pathologist. However, there is some indication that state law or state regulations may, in the near future, limit public school speech pathologists in their involvement with children with minor articulation errors.

In a discussion of speech problems directed primarily at the regular classroom teacher, Mowrer (1978) notes that the state of Wisconsin now stipulates by law "that only those children whose deviant speech can be shown to interfere with the child's learning process may be enrolled in speech therapy classes." (p. 34) In this same article, Mowrer indicates that for years, many speech pathologists have appeared to be working under the philosophy that "the more the better." He quotes one national study indicating that 81 percent of the children seen by speech pathologists were being seen for articulation errors and that 75 percent of the speech pathologists worked primarily with students in kindergarten, first, and second grades. This trend is changing, but in too many instances the "numbers game" continues; articulation disorders lend themselves well to the numbers game, for many children can be seen by the speech pathologist, and the high number of cases of "successful remediation" looks good to administrators and state legislative committees who watchdog school budgets.

Disorders of voice (phonation)

Perhaps the most common way to classify disorders of phonation (voice disorders) is according to pitch, intensity (or loudness), and quality. Only the first two, pitch and intensity, are independent dimensions of vocal production. Quality is multidimensional, a composite of many elements, including pitch and intensity. Quality is judged in relation to various elements in interaction, and in most cases the single elements cannot be identified for separate consideration.

In addition to these three types of voice disorders, we will also note a fourth, which may be considered a part of quality, but also may be considered a separate dimension. This is what Lundeen (1972) calls flexibility.

Voice disorders are noted by those who contact the speaker primarily in terms of esthetics. A given voice may be considered, in very general terms, as being: (1) of noticeably pleasant quality, (2) of noticeably unpleasant quality, or (3) not particularly noticeable regarding quality. Perkins (1977) states that "although *esthetic standards* of the culture and *acoustical standards* of comprehension must be considered in evaluating optimal phonation, the dominant criterion for the speech pathologist is *vocal hygiene*." (p. 274) In the case of these three variables, when good vocal hygiene is promoted, in almost every instance acoustical and esthetic considerations are enhanced. Deviant vocal behavior (in the area of phonation) in most cases means abuse. Abuse can at times lead to such difficulties as benign growths on the vocal cords and in a few cases to malignant growths. Thus the careful consideration of voice disorders (for example, hoarseness) is unusually important.

Pitch disorders may be quite noticeable and in some instances can have negative social consequences. The adult usually has a lower voice than the child, and although there are no significant differences in pitch between male and female voices in children, the male adult's voice is usually lower than that of the female adult. During ordinary speech, there are many transitions from lower to higher and back to lower pitch, but abrupt "breaks" in pitch, as often experienced to the dismay of adolescent males, are a source of distress and discomfort. Pitch disorders seldom cause difficulties in the listener understanding what the speaker is attempting to say, but the effectiveness of communication may be reduced for affective reasons.

Pitch difficulties may be caused by a variety of factors, including both physical and psychogenic, but usually are a result of a combination of factors. They often become a factor in quality disorders and in many cases may be significantly reduced through the assistance of a competent speech pathologist, medical intervention, or both.

Intensity disorders (often called "loudness" disorders, but intensity may be a more appropriate term, since the voice may be either "too loud" or "too soft") are not likely to have the same type of negative social consequences as those of pitch, especially for males, but a person whose voice is too weak or too soft may be unable to communicate effectively. This will be a particularly difficult problem if the speaker must regularly communicate in a noisy environment. The other extreme, the voice that is too loud may be understood but may be irritating and unpleasant. Either difficulty may lead to employment problems, depending on the job requirements. Intensity disorders are more often part of a more complex quality disorder, in which case the effect of the intensity disorder is increased. Reasons for intensity disorders include physiologic problems with some part of the voice mechanism, a hearing problem, or psychologic problems.

Flexibility disorders include such behavioral manifestations as monotone speech (usually a combination disorder of both pitch and intensity) or other unusual, stereotyped speech patterns or inflections. Usually, this will not result in inability of the listener to accurately understand the speaker but does result in speech that is generally undesirable socially. Such disorders may be caused by emotional difficulties (e.g., extreme shyness) hearing loss, or in some cases, physiologic difficulties with some part of the speech mechanism. In some cases this may simply be a case of learned behavior with no other identifiable cause.

Quality disorders are difficult to define, since they are a combination of other disorders. Quality disorders include those requiring medical treatment (for example, vocal nodules, which in a few cases are malignant); however, some authorities would hesitate to call the vocal nodule the "cause" and instead would emphasize that vocal abuse "caused" the nodule. At any rate, immediate attention must be given to various types of persistent quality disorders because of this possibility. Some of the most common descriptions of quality disorders are: nasality, hoarseness, breathiness, harshness, thinness, and the falsetto voice. Other terms used to describe combinations or degrees of the preceding may also be found in the literature relating to quality disorders.

In addition to the possibility of vocal nodules, quality disorders may be caused by such factors as scars (as opposed to growths) on vocal cords, enlarged adenoids, congenital deformities of the palate, emotional problems, speech imitation (such as regional speech habits) and any of a number of physical defects of some part of the speaking mechanism. The speech pathologist can sometimes pinpoint the apparent causes of disorders in voice quality, but more often than with the other phonation disorders mentioned here, the services of a medical specialist or psychologist may also be required.

Fluency or speech-flow disorders

Disorders of speech-flow include stuttering and cluttering. Stuttering is the disorder that first comes to mind when fluency disorders are mentioned, and it is the topic of much research and writing in the area of speech pathology. According to Perkins (1977), "Not long ago more had been written about it [stuttering] than most other communicative disorders combined." (p. 295) Cluttering is an established term in Europe, where it is based on the medical (disease) model, and is discussed primarily in medical terms. Therefore, it is difficult to equate with stuttering, which is understood in speech pathology circles in the United States from a behavioral point of view and is discussed in behavioral terms. Both stuttering and cluttering will be further discussed in the following sections.

Stuttering has long been a source of fascination for those who have studied speech disorders for many reasons; perhaps one of the most significant is the manner in which it has successfully avoided any solid conclusions as to causation or remedial technique. Generally speaking, stuttering involves such forms of disfluency as repetitions, prolongations, hesitations, and interjections. It is obvious that all of these characteristics may be found as part of "normal" speech. How then is a stutterer different from a person with normal speech who occasionally exhibits these characteristics of stuttering? There is some difference of opinion on the question, but it is obviously a matter of how much and how often the stutterer exhibits these types of disfluencies. It is also a matter of judgment on the part of the listener. Unless readers of this text have been hidden away in some small village with a population of only twenty or thirty persons—none of whom stuttered—for all their lives, they certainly have heard stutterers, but can they *(you)* define stuttering? Since the experts cannot agree on a definition, we should not feel too upset if we cannot provide one. Without further attempts to accomplish this difficult task, and with the assumption that all readers have heard what they have identified as stuttering, let us proceed to consider some things that *are* known about stuttering.

1. Those who stutter rarely do so while singing (some apparently never do).
2. Those who stutter rarely stutter while speaking in unison, speaking in syncronization to a rhythmic beat, while alone, or while swearing (these are somewhat less absolute than no. 1 above, but nevertheless usually true).
3. Even for those who stutter regularly, there is no situation that absolutely *ensures* stuttering; that is, it cannot always be induced.
4. Stutterers tend to stutter on the same words when reading and rereading the same passage. They may *not* stutter on these same words in other sentences.
5. As a group, stutterers tend to be able to predict their stuttering.
6. One factor that appears to lead to an increase in stuttering is time pressure.
7. Stutterers cannot be shown to be biologically different from nonstutterers.
8. Stuttering has been eliminated or significantly reduced by totally different procedures in cases that seemed to be very similar. (There is no readily demonstrable, significant correlation between type of stuttering and any particular remedial technique.)
9. Stutterers can hear how their speech flows, and they understand what normal fluency means; they just cannot attain it.
10. In many cases (more than 75 percent by some estimates) stuttering simply ceases without any provable reason.

The above statements are generally accepted by most authorities on the subject of stuttering; much has been learned, but stuttering remains an enigma. Theories regarding the cause(s) of stuttering range from those that are primarily psychologic in nature (role conflict, repressed need, and others that assume the stutterer to be at least maladjusted, if not outright neurotic) to those that are physiologically (organically) based. In summarizing theories of stuttering, Perkins (1977) expresses the opinion that although no single theory has satisfied all who have researched stuttering, "each seems to hold a segment of the answer to the riddle." (p. 320)

Cluttering, although not as commonly referred to in the United States as in Europe, has received sufficient recent attention to warrant further mention here. Although some American authors seem to doubt whether the distinction between stuttering and cluttering is always meaningful, a review of definitions of cluttering indicate that there is emphasis on rate and rhythm, sound transpositions, and the like. According to Perkins (1977) clutterers have problems with fluency, "but additionally clutterers tumble erratically through speech, blurring intelligibility as they go." (p. 325) Cluttering includes garbled speech, lack of awareness of the disorder in some instances, and, in most cases, related symptoms suggesting a more general central language disorder.

Language disorders

Language disorders, for purposes of consideration here, will include delayed language, aphasia, nonstandard English, and learning disabilities. We will consider all four types of language disorder but will place more emphasis on delayed language and aphasia, for they are true language disorders and will not be discussed elsewhere in this text. Nonstandard English will be considered briefly, but because there is considerable debate as to whether it is actually a disorder, it will be given only limited attention. Learning disabilities was the topic of the previous chapter and will be mentioned here primarily to indicate how speech pathologists may consider it from their point of reference.

Delayed language is the failure to develop language at the expected or normal time, and it may relate to the ability to *understand* or to *speak* the language of those in the immediate environment. The underlying assumption is that for some reason(s), the person with delayed language *has not developed an understanding of how language works* in the normal time and/or manner. Children with delayed language may exhibit such delay for any of a variety of reasons: mental retardation, hearing impairment, emotional disorders, and others. Young children who have lived in an apparently normal environment, who apparently have all of the normal learning equipment and yet do not develop language normally may be called *congenitally aphasic.* Such childhood aphasia, which is characterized by a delay in language development from the very beginning of life, must be differentiated from *acquired aphasia* (usually simply called aphasia), a condition in which an individual loses language ability that had already been acquired. Aphasia will be discussed in the following section of this chapter.

Delayed speech or language is one term that means exactly what it implies, and the major debates in this area center around the questions of how much "delay" is necessary for a child to be considered as having delayed speech. Of particular concern are those believed to relate to brain injury, for in many cases, actual brain insult is difficult to prove. The child with delayed language may exhibit a variety of grammatical or syntactical errors, and the only statement that can be made about all children with delayed language is that their ability to use spoken language is retarded well beyond what is expected or normal for children of their age.

Some of the debate surrounding the question of causation in the past has been in regard to which children with delayed language can truly benefit from speech/language development efforts. For example, for years speech pathologists in many parts of the U.S. did not believe it was of value (or at least was so minimally productive that it was questionable, from a cost-benefit point of view) to spend much time with mentally retarded children with delayed speech. The rationale was that, although their speech and language development was delayed, it was a result of their lower level of mental ability and thus it was not productive to work with such children. In other words, their language was delayed, but probably was "normal," in view of their mental ability. This view has been slowly changing over the past several years, and work such as that conducted with Down's syndrome children in various infant stimulation programs around the nation (see Chapter 13) lends credence to the belief that mentally retarded children with delayed language should also receive specific language development assistance. Approaches used in such programs are considerably different from those in more traditional use, but they are effective and thus should be implemented. It is safe to predict that with the increased emphasis on language development efforts with children with other handicapping conditions, plus emphasis on language development of the environmentally deprived child, the study of delayed language, whatever the cause, will increase in the immediate future.

Aphasia, in its classic definition, is impairment of already acquired ability to use language. Aphasia is acquired as a result of injury to the dominant cerebral hemisphere, usually the left. It is quite possible to have brain injury without having aphasic symptoms, but it is one common result of brain injury. Such injury may be the result of a stroke, an accident, a growth within the brain, or some other cause, but by definition aphasia is loss of previously acquired language functions resulting from some type of brain injury or insult. It is relatively common in adults, particularly following a stroke, and in many cases there is some spontaneous recovery. Aphasia may affect any one or all of the various language ability components, and though not as common in children, it can occur in the same manner as with adults. Although there has been a great deal of research attempting to localize the areas of the brain related to specific types of aphasia, such research is not conclusive and many debates remain among the experts.

Aphasia, like most other handicapping conditions, can exist in conjunction with other handicaps. Aphasia is also included under the umbrella definition of learning disabilities (see p. 181), thus leading to some confusion on the part of those who would like to see more discrete descriptions of the various handicapping conditions.

The existence of *nonstandard English* is a recognized fact, but how to regard it or what to do about it is another matter. Some maintain that children who use nonstandard English will be placed in a position of permanent disadvantage if they do not learn to use the dominant language of the general culture. To be consistent with this position such children must be assisted to learn standard English, the language in which most English books and newspapers are written, and in which radio, television, and other mass communication information and entertainment are presented. Others cannot accept this point of view but would support the need for polycultural schools to educate children for a polycultural society. Despite the many pros and cons, certain facts should be noted. One important fact is that in large urban areas where there are many children who speak, for example, a dialect usually called black English, there is a great likelihood of misdiagnosis of basic learning problems because of a lack of understanding of the problems these children face in a standard English–oriented school. Since black English and standard English are essentially dialects, not different languages, some children learn to translate from one code to the other as required by the social situation and have only limited difficulty. There is an obvious loss in progress in the normal standard English setting, but for some children this loss is minimal. For other children, for reasons not fully understood, these transitions from black to standard English may be very difficult. This tends to result in children who are outcasts in the world of formal education. They may resort to nonparticipation, thus leading to erroneous conclusions, particularly since this nonparticipation and lack of understanding are consistent from day to day—*in the school setting*. Their plight is even further worsened by the fact that many of their neighborhood friends are able to function successfully in both black English and standard English settings, something they cannot understand.

The preceding description of problems that may result from this unusual type of language difficulty should be viewed as only the tip of the iceberg. The host of related problems and difficult program decisions, which are likely to be made differently under various sets of circumstances in different geographic areas, are sufficient in magnitude to fill several volumes. The only suggestion we will make here is that the educator who works where such problems exist must be aware of it and must not let the confusion that sometimes surrounds this problem distort diagnostic conclusions. Language disorders (differences?) relating to the existence of nonstandard English are real. They must be recognized for what they are, and solutions must be planned within the framework of existing provisions for service or those additional provisions that can be developed in each individual setting.

Learning disabilities may also be considered language disorders. In some cases the learning disability may be more social in nature, or it may be manifested primarily in mathematics or spatial disorders, but for the most part, learning disabilities may be considered language disorders. Some of the confusion concerning who should work with the learning disabled child has related to the kind of teaching/remedial task required of the teacher who works with such a child. Because the teacher is usually expected to work directly with reading problems, and because, typically, the speech pathologist is not specifically trained to teach reading, the task of working with the large majority of learning disabled children has gone to the learning disability specialist, with supportive assistance from the speech pathologist. One exception is in the area of aphasia, which is included in the learning disabilities definition, but is also very definitely a part of the basic domain of the speech pathologist.

Prevalence of speech/language disorders

Several factors govern the manner in which we arrive at a meaningful estimate of the prevalence of speech/language disorders. One is the question of whether learning disabilities should be considered a part of a general speech/language disorders category.

Another question of importance is what percentage of the 5-, 6-, and 7-year-old population with minor articulation problems should be counted in the speech/language prevalence data. This concern is simply a matter of opinion. We will attempt to take a middle-of-the-road point of view on this issue. Therefore, rather than accept the 5 percent figure in use in many places (federal estimates, many textbooks in speech pathology, and state estimates in many parts of the United States) prior to about 1975, we will consider that 3 to 4 percent of the school-age population have significant speech and/or language disorders requiring special assistance.

Recent federal estimates have tended toward the more conservative 3 percent figure, perhaps because of a limitation that was a part of Public Law 94-142. This limit indicates that only 12 percent of any school district could be served as handicapped with PL 94-142 funds at any one time. This total figure has had the effect of holding down the estimates for the high-incidence handicapping conditions (speech, learning disabilities, mental retardation, and emotional disturbance), since overestimation of one or two of these areas might effectively negate services to children with other handicapping conditions.

According to the American Speech and Hearing Association:

- Nearly ten million Americans, or one out of every 20 persons, suffer from a speech or language disorder.
- Each year, 60,000 Americans suffer from aphasia, the loss of the ability to use speech and language, due to a stroke or head injury.
- There are 30,000 Americans who have undergone surgery for laryngeal cancer, and 8,000 new cases of laryngeal cancer are discovered annually.
- There are more than one million persons in the United States who stutter, one-half of whom are children. Throughout the world, there are an estimated 15 million persons who stutter.
- Articulation disorders constitute the most numerous of all speech disorders. About 3 out of 5 of all speech and language disorders are related to articulatory problems.

This quotation seems to indicate the 5 percent prevalence figure, but it also includes adults; therefore, the estimate for school-age children is not clear. It should be noted that the information pamphlet from which this prevalence quotation was taken also indicates: "too often, normal differences in speech and language are mistakenly identified as disorders. On the other hand, professional help is often not sought for real disorders of communication." Herein lies the real problem with establishing hard and fast rules for maximum prevalence estimates as a basis for provision of service. Speech pathologists today recognize that in the past too many children with minor articulation problems were said to have speech disorders, and they are attempting to avoid this error. However, care must be taken or some children who truly need professional help to improve academic performance and help prevent future problems will be overlooked.

Identification of students with speech and language disorders

As with other handicapping conditions, students may be identified as a result of direct referral from parents, teachers, other professionals, or community agencies. A second source of identification is general speech screening. In either case, *speech disorders*, since they are a matter of how speech sounds to the listener, will ordinarily be determined through the "trained ear" of the speech pathologist. The speech pathologist may use any of a variety of tests, both formal and informal, to attempt to determine type and degree of disorder, but with speech disorders, determination of the existence of the handicap is much more a function of professional judgment than with any other handicapping condition. In the case of specific *language disorders*, much more specific testing may be required. This is particularly true if we consider learning disabilities as part of this general domain.

In addition to assessing the student's speech and language, the speech pathologist may conduct a visual inspection of the throat and various parts of speech mechanism.

The presence of a speech or language disorder may often be quite easily determined; that is, it may be most obvious. However, the cause of such disorder may be quite difficult to determine in some cases. Since the matter of cause may be more important in this area of special education than in many others (note that this certainly is not *always* true), an investigation of cause should at least be considered along with the process of identification. A consideration of major types or categories of causation will be the topic of the following section.

Causes of speech and language disorders

The consideration of causes of speech and language disorders that follows will be brief and general, since various of the causes of speech and language disorders have already been indicated in the section of types of disorders (definitions and classifications), and more consideration of causation will be required in the section on medical and surgical treatment.

Biologic or organic causes constitute one major area of concern when considering speech and language disorders. Damage to or malfunctioning of the neurologic system may be the cause of speech or language disorders that are manifested in a variety of ways. Examples include disorders associated with cerebral palsy, certain types of mental retardation, and aphasia. In some cases, such as mental retardation and cerebral palsy related to brain damage, the situation is permanent. In others, such as aphasia following stroke and the brain trauma that may follow serious head injuries, the disorder may be temporary, or at least the situation will improve with time and treatment.

Some neurologic damage may affect the language center in the brain, causing difficulty in dealing with symbols; other types of damage may lead to poor control of the muscles necessary for normal phonation and articulation. In some cases it may be difficult to pinpoint the exact cause-effect relationship except to conclude that the nature of the difficulty indicates some type of neurologic malfunction.

In the case of a severe stroke or a severe blow to the head that is followed by loss of language ability, the question of causation is fairly obvious. In other cases, especially in young children where there is no evidence of when such severe brain trauma might have occurred, it must remain a matter of conjecture. The following are recognized as possible causes of such damage: (1) fetal anoxia (deprivation of oxygen during fetal life), (2) anoxia during the early developmental years (for example, as a result of a very high fever, perhaps associated with a childhood disease), (3) drugs taken by the mother during pregnancy, (4) maternal-fetal blood incompatibility, (5) damage incurred at birth during a difficult delivery, or (6) physical blow to the head of the child at a time unknown.

Hearing loss may also be the basis of speech or language difficulty. This is not always listed among organic causes of speech/language disorders, but since the hearing loss is organic, it may be properly listed here. The effects of hearing loss on speech and language are discussed in more detail in Chapter 4.

Other physical causes include deformities of the physical apparatus through which humans produce speech. These might be congenitally determined or in some cases could result from one of the causes of neurologic damage listed before. Physical (or organic) causes account for a minor proportion of the speech/language problems with which the speech pathologist typically works in the schools, and knowledge of the cause of the problem or defect does not always contribute to planning and programming for the child. Language difficulties related to deformities of the organs of speech may at times be corrected through surgery or the use of a prosthesis. In some cases orthodontic work leads to significant improvement in speech. The possibility of organic causes of speech or language difficulties must be carefully pursued, since knowledge of such causation may be of concrete value in educational planning and in some cases may lead to correction of the basic problem.

Functional disorders make up the majority of the problems that will be the object of the speech pathologists' efforts in the public schools. "Functional" in this case means that functioning is defective but there is no known, identifiable *biologic* cause. Most articulation problems fall into this category, and the causes may include: (1) the child was given poor models for speech, or (2) parents encouraged (for any of a variety of reasons) inappropriate speech or voice patterns. The cause of some problems is simply unknown. Functional disorders obviously make up a catch-all subcategorization, but if organic causes are not known or identifiable, it is most productive to assume the disorder is functional and proceed from that starting point. Guessing about past events with little or no basis in fact is of questionable merit.

Speech and language disorders, like most other handicapping conditions, may result from a variety of causes, and the "obvious" cause may not be the primary cause. Multiple casuality is probably the rule rather than the exception. Caution is essential in drawing conclusions as to causation, particularly if such conclusions are to be major determinants in dictating remediation.

Medical and surgical treatment of speech and language disorders

It was indicated earlier that some authorities classify speech pathology as a health profession, and in Europe most speech practitioners are definitely medical professionals. We might also note that among the specialties reviewed in this text, only the speech pathologists are not ordinarily considered as "teachers." Therefore, it might be assumed that there is a close and continuing relationship between the efforts of speech pathologists in the schools and physicians.

In practice, this is not necessarily the case. Although speech pathologists who work with adults often work with patients who have undergone medical/surgical procedures or who have had a stroke, the speech pathologist in the schools is not that closely related to the medical profession. However, there are a number of ways in which the medical profession and speech/language pathology are related.

If the speech pathologist, through work with a given child, feels there may be undiagnosed hearing problems, the child should be referred to the audiologist or perhaps directly to the physician. Medical treatment may also be indicated for problems affecting the *larynx*. These include: (1) lesions responsible for impaired vocal cord movement (usually either growths or inflammation), (2) paralysis of laryngeal muscles (either one or both vocal cords), and (3) manifestations of various diseases (such as thyroid or pituitary problems). Medical handling of these disorders will vary, but in some cases there may be need for laryngeal surgery. There are various types of laryngectomy (removal of all or some part of the larynx), with specific names for each surgical procedure, but the speech pathologist will usually be essential to the clients' return to more normal speech. The role of the speech pathologist is actually twofold: (1) referral to the physician to assure early detection, and (2) assistance following any medical/surgical procedures to help the individual attain more normal speech production.

Orofacial and upper respiratory abnormalities can also cause speech disorders. Some disabilities, such as those associated with cleft lip and palate, are quite obvious. Others, such as certain dental abnormalities, although obvious once we focus on them, may be overlooked as a cause for speech disabilities. Still other potential sources of problems include abnormalities of the tongue, problems with tonsils and adenoids, and nasal abnormalities. The condition most commonly thought of among this group is that of clefts. This area is of sufficient interest to various professionals that a separate organization, the American Cleft Palate Association, has as its purpose the study of this disability. Although cleft palate surgery is obviously the responsibility of the medical profession, "with no other structural abnormality is the speech pathologists consultative advice valued more than with cleft palate." (Perkins, 1977, p. 198) The advice of speech pathologists is highly important to the surgeons, orthodontists, and others who work on the cleft palate team, because of their knowledge about how various types of corrective surgery will affect speech production. Sometimes a very small modification in surgical procedure makes significant differences in the potential for near-normal speech production.

This discussion would not be complete without mentioning prosthetic devices or "speech appliances," which are used in some cases in place of surgery. One such appliance, the obturator (a prosthesis used to close a cleft in the palate), may prove to be effective, but the speech pathologist is essential in assisting the client to use the device. Speech pathologists play some role in helping clients to use almost any such prosthesis.

We may summarize this consideration of relationships with medical problems and the medical profession by stating that although the speech pathologist in the public schools may not be involved with many cases such as those reviewed here, when such involvement is required, it is highly essential. In extreme cases, proper referral at the right time may save a life; in cases of less urgency, the speech pathologist may be an important team member in assuring that speech improvement made possible by earlier surgical or prosthetic measures is fully realized.

Educational provisions for students with speech or language disorders

Fortunately, the question of providing for maximal integration of the majority of students with speech and language disorders is not the controversial issue that it is in many other areas of handicap. Perhaps this is because most such students are served through some type of itinerant program that permits them to stay in their regular class for most of the day. This itinerant service pattern has been the standard procedure for many years in speech pathology; the speech pathologist was the original itinerant or traveling special educator in many parts of the nation. As for that small group of students with more severe language disorders, most are served primarily as mentally retarded, learning disabled, or multiply handicapped. Therefore, we will address the manner in which the speech pathologist may serve children and youth within the framework of itinerant service. The work of the speech pathologist will be viewed as, first, determining the type(s) and degree(s) of speech defect and, second, planning and implementing appropriate remedial or therapeutic strategies.

ASSESSMENT OF SPEECH AND LANGUAGE DISORDERS

Examining speech and language behavior is the first important task of the speech pathologist. It may be evident that "something" is wrong, but the speech pathologist must conduct a scientific examination to determine the nature of that "something." Perkins indicates that "speech is examined for three purposes: description, diagnosis, and assessment." Description is the necessary first task and forms the basis for diagnosis and assessment. If medical diagnosis seems to be indicated, a referral is made to the physician. In the meantime, the speech pathologist should assess the various abilities and disabilities of the student, for such assessment will form the basis for educational procedures and may, in many cases, be of concrete assistance to the physician in those cases where medical treatment is indicated. It might be again noted that of those children normally seen by the speech pathologist in the public schools, only a minority will require medical referral.

Assessment is not always required for *identification* but is essential to provide the basis for educational programming. It may include

various components, depending on the type of information gathered in the original descriptive phases of the investigation, but may include assessment of:
1. Vocabulary, grammar, and functional language usage
2. Articulation, phonation, and fluency
3. Speech mechanisms (to determine any possible bases for speech problems)
4. Other relevant abilities such as sensory, perceptual, motor, intellectual, emotional, etc. (skills of other professionals may be required)

The information derived from the assessment combined with other descriptive information previously gathered will provide the basis for the therapy or remediation, which is the speech pathologist's major task.

THERAPY OR REMEDIATION OF SPEECH AND LANGUAGE DISORDERS

Changing speech or language behavior, whether it be a matter of modifying unacceptable speech, encouraging the development of delayed language, or assisting in the process of rehabilitation in adult aphasia, is often a very complex process. In some instances the whole process may proceed exactly according to theoretical planning (the perfect textbook cases), but more often than not—except in very simple articulation cases with young children—there are complications and complexities that defy prediction and lead to the need for regular reassessment and replanning. This is not necessarily because of lack of expertise on the part of the speech pathologist (though adequate training and a great deal of supervised experience are essential) but rather because of the complexity of the speech/language functions.

In carrying out their professional responsibilities, speech pathologists tend to work from the point of view of either action or behavior therapies, that is those directed primarily toward directly modifying specific speech behaviors, or psychoanalytic or psychodynamically based therapies. There are, of course, all varieties of middle ground, and most action-based therapy also includes a component in which the client is assisted to develop insight and thus hopefully reduce anxiety. In addition, there are certain models for therapy that Perkins (1977) believes all speech pathologists work from, whether or not they realize it. These models may be given somewhat different titles, depending on the authority who describes them, but the following description, adapted from Perkins, provides a simple view of these models and the theory underlying them. (Perkins notes that the differences between these four models are theoretical and may not exist in fact. However, in this overview, consideration of these differences appears to be a most effective way to view these four bases for therapy, which apparently speech pathologists follow or ascribe to.) Speech pathologists may follow all of these models as seems appropriate to a given case.

Models for therapy (adapted from Perkins, 1977, pp. 366-367)

THE "BAD HABIT" MODEL

1. Assumes that, whatever the cause(s), the wrong speech patterns were learned and persist only because the correct pattern has not been learned.
2. Most typically assumed in the case of articulation disorders, but can be assumed with any speech behavior that likely can be altered with relative ease.
3. If speech remediation is accomplished with not too great effort, this may be considered operational evidence that this was, in fact, the appropriate model.

THE "VICIOUS CYCLE" MODEL

1. Assumes that whatever the cause(s) the wrong speech patterns were learned and

persist because the speaker's struggles to avoid this defective speech have intensified, and to some extent further exaggerated, the existing problem.
2. Often assumed in the case of stuttering and when the aphasic client has a catastrophic reaction to failures. May apply to some articulation difficulties not associated with other known problems or conditions.
3. If remediation is accomplished after the client is able to reduce the tendency to struggle against the problem, this may be considered operational evidence that this was, in fact, the appropriate model.

THE "BAD HABITS WITH BENEFITS" MODEL

1. Assumes that, whatever the cause(s), the defective speech patterns were established and persist, at least in part, because there are various reinforcing or rewarding elements associated with them.
2. Examples might include the older, aphasic person who enjoys the special attention given by other family members, or lisping or persistent "baby-talk" by children, which adults might reward as "cute."
3. If speech improves following specific therapy and opposition to speech modification is reduced, this may be considered to have been the appropriate model. (This may include reducing benefits of present speech patterns or providing greater rewards for corrected speech.)

THE "SYMPTOMATIC DISORDER" MODEL

In most respects this is similar to the "bad habit with benefits" model. Theoretically, psychodynamic conflict is the basic cause of the speech disorders, which are then viewed as symptomatic. In both models, the basic problem is the matter of needs, which are expressed symptomatically. In this model (as compared to the bad habits with benefits model) resolution of the psychodynamic conflict with no actual attention to the symptom (the defective speech) is recommended. As with the other models, if it works, it must have been the right theoretical rationale.

Speech pathologists must know the appropriate therapy for specific types of speech remediation, must understand how to assist the client in reducing anxiety (so that remediation may be effectively approached), and must understand speech and language development, so as to be able to work effectively with children who are experiencing delayed language. They must know enough about the physiology of speech to be able to conduct basic examinations of the speech apparatus and must be able to provide directive counseling to assist those who cannot correct their speech defects to live gracefully with those defects. Specific therapeutic methods that might be effective in modifying various types of speech disorders are beyond the scope of this text and will not be presented. Readers who wish to know more about the work of the speech/language pathologist may want to select readings from the references and suggested readings at the end of this chapter. Free general information is available from the American Speech and Hearing Association, 9030 Old Georgetown Road, Washington, D.C. 20014.

Summary

The professional role of speech and language pathologists is precisely what their title infers; the remediation of defective speech or language, including the development of delayed language and rehabilitative efforts for adult aphasics. In a few cases, (for example, a person who has lost hearing suddenly) the task might be to maintain adequate speech. Although this field of specialization has passed through a number of name changes since its inception early in the twentieth century, the name "communication disorders," a name presently growing in acceptance, may be the most accurate description of its real focus. Disorders of communication, with all their variations and complexities, is what speech and language pathology is all about.

"Speech is defective when it is ungrammatical, unintelligible, culturally or personally unsatisfactory, or abusive of the speech mechanism." (Perkins, 1977, p. 3) From some version of this basic definition has grown a profession that serves 3 to 4 percent of the population of the United States who suffer some form of communication disorder. If we include even half of those students whom we call learning disabled, the percentage is increased to 5 to 6 percent, and perhaps even more when we consider adult aphasia, adults who have had laryngeal surgery, and others. The purpose of this chapter has been to develop a general picture of the varied roles of speech/language pathologists, with some attention to services normally provided to adults, but with emphasis on school-related duties.

Speech pathology in the schools has been historically directed toward children with articulation disorders, including disorders characterized by omissions, substitutions, distortions, and additions. Articulation disorders outnumber all other speech/language disorders combined and continue to receive attention, but the emphasis has slowly shifted to fluency and language disorders. Fluency, or speech-flow, disorders, especially stuttering, have received a great deal of research attention in the past; however, the record of remediation of speech-flow disorders has not been particularly good, and stuttering remains the number one enigma of speech pathologists. Remediation (cessation) of stuttering has occurred after the utilization of so many different approaches that any sound conclusion as to the "best" approach is not possible. In contrast, with increased attention to various types of language disorders, speech/language pathologists appear to be making concrete progress. With the rapid growth of interest in learning disabilities, the speech/language pathologist's expertise in the language area is sorely needed; however, the precise manner in which his or her efforts should be coordinated with those of the learning disabilities specialist remains to be determined.

Causes of speech and language disorders can be generally classified as organic (e.g., neurologic damage, defects in the structure of some part of the speech mechanism) or functional (e.g., no known biologic cause, but could be poor speech model or reinforcement of inappropriate speech patterns). Medical and surgical treatment, including the use of prostheses, is indicated in some types of disorders. In these cases the speech pathologist plays an important role in assisting the client to learn to speak appropriately following surgery or after the initiation of use of a prosthetic device.

Most speech and language service to students in the schools is provided through use of the itinerant service model, thus there has been minimal concern about the degree of educational segregation of such children. Speech and language therapy in the schools is usually based on the use of one of four models. These models, with names which are unusually descriptive, are: (1) the "bad habit" model, (2) the "vicious cycle" model, (3) the "bad habit with benefits" model, and (4) the "symptomatic disorder" model. With a well-developed professional field, with a history of relatively strong support from public school administrators, with little debate as to whether communication disorders actually exist, and with the mandate of recent federal legislation, the speech/language (or communication disorders) professional is in an excellent position to make continued, significant contributions in the field of special education.

Learning disabilities and speech/language disorders

focus

establishment of programs in Europe

The forerunners of programs for persons with speech disorders in the United States were those developed in Europe, and "a marked expansion of knowledge about speech disorders occurred . . . after the beginning of the nineteenth century."

establishment of programs in the United States

Interest in speech correction services in the schools, which was to grow to one of the largest of special service areas in special education, was established by the early 1920s.

The original concern with "speech correction" has now broadened into wide involvement with language disorders and in more recent years with learning disabilities.

speech development: mechanics of speech

It is the timing of the various sounds as they flow from basic speech sounds to syllables to words to phrases and to sentences that produces speech which can be readily understood. This is called speech flow and includes sequence, duration, rhythm, rate, and fluency.

A complicated set of interconnected muscle actions must be constantly directed by the brain for normal speech production. In addition to this muscular movement, the individual must also be directing the entire flow of thought (this is quite a different matter from the flow of speech) through a meaningful set of thought processes, which must be in terms of some language system.

language development: the human miracle

Language is the one factor that most clearly sets humans above all of the lower animals, and because so many humans develop language with little or no difficulty, we tend to overlook its complexity.

Although it is generally recognized that language functions are largely controlled by the left hemisphere of the brain in adults, this is not necessarily true for very young children.

All of the handicapping conditions we have thus far considered are closely related to brain function but most of the others (i.e., visual, hearing, and speech impairments) also relate to physiologic/anatomic functions that we can observe and measure to a considerable degree. Language functions take place in the brain, cannot be observed directly, and are thus less understood. Because they are so highly essential to normal learning, they must remain the target of concerted effort on the part of highly trained specialists from various disciplines.

speech and language disorders: definitions and classifications

"A Speech Pathologist is a professional trained in the study of human communication, its normal development, and its disorders."

speech disorders

The major speech disorders recognized by most authorities in this field are articulatory disorders (both articulation and resonance disorders)—omissions, substitutions, distortions; voice disorders (disorders of phonation)—pitch, intensity (loudness), flexibility, quality; fluency or speech-flow disorders—stuttering, cluttering.

disorders of articulation and resonance

The degree of articulatory defectiveness "is determined by the judgment of either speaker or listener."

Articulation disorders have been estimated to comprise about 75 percent of the total of all speech disorders and are particularly problematic in young children.

Omission errors are quite common in the speech of young children and are usually outgrown with no specialized assistance.

Substitutions are the substitution of one speech sound for another.

Distortions are sounds that are somewhat like the intended sound, but are not quite right. They are usually the result of the tongue, lips, teeth, or jaw not being in precisely the right position, with the tongue often the culprit.

Articulation errors are common among young children, and in each case the type, frequency, and consistency of errors must be considered in relation to the child's age and language experience and background.

disorders of voice (phonation)

Pitch disorders seldom cause difficulties in the listener understanding what the speaker is attempting to say, but the effectiveness of communication may be reduced for affective reasons.

Intensity disorders are not likely to have the same type of negative social consequences as those of pitch, especially for males, but a person whose voice is too weak or too soft may be unable to communicate effectively.

Flexibility disorders include such behavioral manifestations as monotone speech (usually a combination disorder of both pitch and intensity) or other unusual, stereotyped speech patterns or inflections.

Some of the most common descriptions of quality disorders are: nasality, hoarseness, breathiness, harshness, thinness, and the falsetto voice.

fluency or speech-flow disorders

Generally speaking, stuttering involves such forms of disfluency as repetitions, prolongations, hesitations, and interjections.

Theories regarding the cause(s) of stuttering range from those that are primarily psychologic in nature (role-conflict, repressed need, and others that assume the stutterer to be at least maladjusted, if not outright neurotic) to those that are physiologically (organically) based.

language disorders

Delayed language is the failure to develop language at the expected or normal time and may relate to the ability to understand or to speak the language of those in the immediate environment. The underlying assumption is that for some reason(s), the person with delayed language has not developed an understanding of how language works in the normal time and/or manner.

It is safe to predict that with the increased emphasis on language development efforts with children with other handicapping conditions, plus emphasis on language development of the environmentally deprived child, the study of delayed language, whatever the cause, will increase in the immediate future.

Aphasia, in its classic definition, is impairment of already acquired ability to use language. Aphasia is acquired as a result of injury to the dominant cerebral hemisphere, usually the left.

Aphasia may affect any one or all of the various language ability components, and though not as common in children, it can occur in the same manner as with adults.

identification of students with speech and language disorders

Speech disorders, since they are a matter of how speech sounds to the listener, will ordinarily be determined through the "trained ear" of the speech pathologist. The speech pathologist may use any of a variety of tests, both formal and informal, to attempt to determine type and degree of disorder, but with speech disorders, determination of the existence of the handicap is much more a function of professional judgement than with any other handicapping condition.

causes of speech and language disorders

Functional disorders make up the majority of the problems that will be the object of the speech pathologists' efforts in the public schools. "Functional" in this case means that functioning is defective, but there is no known, identifiable biologic cause.

Speech and language disorders, like most handicapping conditions, may result from a variety of causes and the "obvious" cause may not be the primary cause. Multiple causality is probably the rule rather than the exception.

educational provisions for students with speech or language disorders

The question of providing for maximal integration of the majority of students with speech and language disorders is not the controversial issue that it is in many other areas of handicap. Perhaps this is because most such students are served through some type of itinerant program that permits them to stay in their regular class for most of the day.

assessment of speech and language disorders

Examining speech and language behavior is the first important task of the speech pathologist.

Assessment is not always required for identification but is essential to provide the basis for educational programming.

therapy or remediation of speech and language disorders

Speech pathologists must know the appropriate therapy for specific types of speech remediation, must understand how to assist the client in reducing anxiety, and must understand speech and language development so as to be able to work effectively with children who are experiencing delayed language. They must know enough about the physiology of speech to be able to conduct basic examinations of the speech apparatus, and they must be able to provide directive counseling to assist those who cannot correct their speech defects to live gracefully with those defects.

References and suggested readings

American Speech and Hearing Association. Selected pamphlets. Washington, D.C. Undated.

Chalfant, J., and Scheffelin, M. *Central processing dysfunctions in children,* NINDS Monograph No. 9. Washington, D.C.: U.S. Department of Health, Education and Welfare, 1969.

Dale P. *Language development: structure and function* 2nd ed. New York: Holt, Rinehart, and Winston, 1976.

Eisenson, J. *Aphasia in children.* New York: Harper and Row, Publishers, 1972.

Hayden, A., and Dmitriev, V. The multidisciplinary preschool program for Down's syndrome children at the University of Washington Model Preschool Center. In *Exceptional infant.* Vol. 3: *Assessment and intervention.* B. Friedlander, G. Sterritt, and G. Kirk (Eds.). New York: Bruner/Mazel, 1975.

Irwin, J., and Marge, M. (Eds.). *Principles of childhood language disabilities.* New York: Appleton-Century-Crofts, 1972.

Lenneberg, E., and Long, B. Language development. In *Psychology and the handicapped child.* J. Swets, and L. Elliot (Eds.). Washington, D.C.: Office of Education, 1974, pp. 127-148.

Lundeen, D. Speech disorders. In *Education of the exceptional child,* Gearheart, B. (Ed.). Scranton, Pa.: Intext Publishers, 1972.

Menyuk, P. *The development of speech.* New York: Bobbs-Merrill, 1972.

Mowrer, D. Speech problems: what you should and shouldn't do. *Learning,* Jan. 1978, *6*,(5), 34-37.

Paden, E. *A history of the American Speech and Hearing Association, 1925-1958.* Washington, D.C.: The American Speech and Hearing Association, 1970.

Perkins, W. *Human perspectives in speech and language disorders.* St. Louis: The C. V. Mosby Co., 1978.

Perkins, W. *Speech pathology: an applied behavioral science.* 2nd ed. St. Louis: The C. V. Mosby Co., 1977.

Schiefelbusch, R., and Lloyd, L. (Eds.). *Language perspectives—acquisition, retardation, and intervention.* Baltimore: University Park Press, 1974.

Smith, E., Goodman, K., and Meredith, R. *Language and thinking in school.* 2nd ed. New York: Holt, Rinehart, and Winston, 1976.

Travis, L. (Ed.). *Handbook of speech pathology and audiology.* Englewood Cliffs, N.J.: Prentice-Hall, Inc., 1971.

Van Riper, C. *Speech correction: principles and methods.* 6th ed. Englewood Cliffs, N.J.: Prentice-Hall, Inc. 1978.

Van Riper, C. *The treatment of stuttering.* Englewood Cliffs, N.J.: Prentice-Hall, Inc., 1973.

Weiss, C., and Lillywhite, H. *Communicative disorders: a handbook for prevention and early intervention.* St. Louis: The C. V. Mosby Co., 1976.

Wiig, E., and Semel, E. *Language disabilities in children and adolescents.* Columbus, Ohio: Charles E. Merrill Publishers, 1976.

SECTION FIVE

Other handicapping conditions

As the title indicates, this section will include the "other" generally recognized handicapping conditions. These three, mental retardation, emotional disturbance (or mental illness), and physical handicaps have been recognized for some time, although mental retardation and mental illness were often confused until about the middle of the nineteenth century. Mental retardation and emotional disturbance were also blamed on devils, evil spirits, and the like for many centuries, and persons with such handicaps were severely ostracized and even burned as witches in relatively recent times.

In contrast to mental retardation and emotional disturbance, which are sometimes difficult to diagnose, physical handicaps are relatively obvious and tend to be much more readily accepted by the general public. There are exceptions—cases where facial characteristics are extremely grotesque or the body is greatly deformed—but for the most part we tend to be able to relate better to individuals with physical handicaps than to those whose handicap involves emotional or intellectual components. However, as we will see in Chapter 11, attempts to empathize with the physically handicapped child often lead to overprotection and result in retardation of the development of personal independence.

Our goal in this section will be similar to that of preceding sections. We will learn more about the history of education of individuals with these handicaps, investigate characteristics, identification procedures, and medical dimensions of the handicap, and finally focus on educational provisions for students with varying degrees of handicap. Consideration of the multihandicapped as part of Chapter 11 will conclude our categorical overview of handicapping conditions.

With specific instruction and "hands-on" experience, the mildly mentally retarded may learn to perform a number of useful tasks.

chapter 9

Education and training of the mentally retarded

objectives

To develop a historical understanding of the treatment of the mentally retarded and the effects on programs and services provided today.

To describe the systems of classification used in the field of mental retardation, emphasizing the educational and the medical systems.

To indicate the major causes of mental retardation as recognized by the American Association on Mental Deficiency (AAMD)

To demonstrate the interrelatedness of the definition of mental retardation, identification of the mentally retarded, and educational programming implications.

To develop a basic understanding of educational programs and services for the educable, trainable, and severely mentally retarded.

Introduction

A general awareness of the condition we now call mental retardation has existed since the dawn of history, but it has been only during the past two centuries that real momentum to assist the retarded has taken place. More specific knowledge of the needs of the mentally retarded has become a matter of general public awareness since the mid-1960s as a result of programs enacted or encouraged by the federal government and a high level of activism on the part of advocates, effectively led by the National Association for Retarded Citizens (NARC). In this chapter we will review the historical development of the field of mental retardation, examine terminology, and outline a number of different classification systems. Major causes of mental retardation will be discussed, and educational programs will be overviewed. We will see that two major trends in serving this population of handicapped persons are: (1) programming that encourages more normal life activities, be it classroom environment or community participation, and (2) more meaningful attention to the mentally retarded at the lower ranges of intelligence. We will initiate our consideration of mental retardation with a summary of the historical origins of present day programs and services for the mentally retarded.

Historical origins of programs and services for the mentally retarded

The history of mental retardation has been documented by many authors using a variety of frameworks or constructs depending on the purposes at hand. Because our interest in this chapter is mental retardation in its very broadest sense, we will review historical events as they may be keyed to major changes in philosophy, attitudes, treatment, and training or education. Because such changes were very limited up until the seventeenth and eighteenth centuries, we will consider all events prior to the 1800s as one time period or era. The nineteenth and twentieth centuries will then be considered separately.

As we move on to the consideration of mental retardation within the framework of these three major time periods, we should emphasize that no fine line of demarcation exists between such time divisions. Many historical occurrences were carried over or were precipitated by related happenings in a prior era. Therefore, these time frames must be recognized as being basically arbitrary.

EARLY HISTORY: AN ERA OF SUPERSTITION

Both the Greeks (in 1552 BC) and the Romans (in 449 BC) recorded official references to the condition of mental retardation (Barr, 1913; Lindman and McIntyre, 1961). In these writings, such persons were typically called "fools" or "monsters." The legal system of the Athenian and Spartan city states dealt severely with mental defectives because societal interest was in developing nations free of defectives. The mentally retarded were thought of as essentially nonhuman and were treated accordingly. The laws of Lycurgus called for the deliberate abandonment of idiots and fools, and as a result such persons were thrown off mountains, drowned in rivers, or simply left to the elements to die. They were considered incapable of human feeling and therefore undeserving of human compassion. Extermination was the generally accepted practice.

In Rome, it was customary for the rich to keep fools and jesters for the amusement of the household and its guests. Kanner (1964) reports that many who kept the mentally retarded for such purposes acquired greatness and fame as a result of their presence. Unfortunately, most mentally retarded and deformed persons did not fare even this well.

Chains, cages, or sentences of death were the fate of many, while others were left alone to wander and care for themselves and eventually to perish.

During this same period, some of the more wealthy provided much better treatment, but for the most part this too was based on superstition. Whitney (1954) describes a unique circumstance in Belgium at the village of Gheel. Many of the retarded migrated to Gheel in hopes of being cured, based on reports of earlier miracles there. When no miracle occurred and the town became overpopulated with these people, many of the richer residents took these wanderers into their homes. They were given special treatment based on the belief that they might have some connection with God or the unknown, and their labor was also useful to the household.

Taking defectives under care during this period of history is amply illustrated by Tycho Brahe, the great astronomer. He is said to have kept a mentally retarded male as a close companion in hopes that the mutterings of the defective would give him a "divine revelation." (Davies, 1959)

Christianity provided the first real hope for many of these less fortunate members of society. The teachings of Christ, with their compassion for the unfortunate and handicapped, resulted in isolated instances when society recognized its responsibility. Doll (1962) reports that Christian institutes provided care and compassion for imbeciles and idiots (as the mentally retarded were called). As early as the fourth century AD, St. Nicholas Thaumaturges (the wonder-worker and Bishop of Myra) is said to have urged giving care and protection to the feebleminded (Kanner, 1964).

From the thirteenth century, churches of Europe (mainly Roman Catholic) began to provide asylums for the mentally handicapped (Kott, 1971). The most famous was the Bicetre of Paris established by St. Vincent de Paul and his Sisters of Charity. These monasteries or asylums were not designed for treatment or education but were intended to provide sanctuary and separation from society.

The Protestant Reformation brought with it still another view concerning the mentally ill and retarded. Both were thought to be "possessed with the devil" and "filled with Satan." The strange behavior some retarded individuals displayed (for example, convulsions) was interpreted with religious overtones. As a result, many were tortured, tormented, and punished in an attempt to exorcise the demons within.

With only a few exceptions, the mentally retarded were treated with ridicule, persecution, even extermination. In those cases where they were treated more humanely, it often related to inaccurate ideas about some special "connection" with God. The idea that they might be worthwhile persons, capable of some learning and with inherent rights as citizens, did not seem to occur to a society that could only view such differences through the tunnel-vision of superstition.

NINETEENTH CENTURY: THE RISE OF INSTITUTIONS

The future of programs and services for the mentally retarded was destined to be profoundly changed as a result of an accidental discovery that took place in the fall of 1798. Three men, hunting near Aveyron, France, came upon a most unusual sight. They found a naked boy of 11 or 12 apparently looking for acorns or other edibles on the forest floor. When seen by the hunters, he tried to escape by climbing a tree. After capture, the boy was taken to the hospital of Saint-Afrique for a short stay. It was then decided to turn the "savage" over to Abbe Sicard Bonnaterre, a professor of natural history at the Central School of the Department of Aveyron. Bonnaterre bestowed the scientific name of Juvenis Averionesis or Victor upon the boy. After being pronounced an incurable idiot, Victor (now called the Wild Boy of Aveyron) was taken to Paris for observation and study. Dr. Jean Marc Gaspard Itard, chief medical officer at the National Institute for the Deaf and Dumb, observed Victor and refused to accept the idea that Victor's condition was incurable and irreversible. He believed the boy was an idiot because of social and educational neglect and could be reinstated to normalcy by intensive training. Being a follower of John Locke and Abbe de Condillac who stated "sense provides all," the 25-year-old Itard embarked upon a carefully planned series of sensation training. Itard's goals with Victor were:

1. To interest him in social life
2. To awaken his nervous system
3. To extend the range of his thought
4. To lead him to the use of speech
5. To make him exercise simple mental operations to satisfy his physical needs

This five-point program was divided into development in the functions of the senses, training of intellectual skills, and control of emotions.

Itard described his efforts and progress of the first 9 months in a publication in 1801. It was noted that although concrete evidence of progress had taken place, it was very minimal. After changing tactics and 4 more years, Itard concluded that his experiment with the "wild boy" was a miserable failure since his goals were not accomplished. Victor was then placed in the home of Madame Guerin, an assistant of Itard's, where he lived the remaining 20 years of his life. He died in 1828 at the approximate age of 40.

Itard's efforts had a number of worthwhile results, which he did not recognize because of his disappointment over not effecting a "cure." These results included: (1) the development of many excellent teaching techniques, which led to considerable progress with Victor and were to provide the basis for later successful efforts with the retarded, (2) increased recognition and enthusiasm for education and training of the mentally retarded, brought about through wide (for that day and age) dissemination of written reports about his efforts, and (3) encouragement of one of his students, Edouard Seguin, who was destined to soon stimulate international progress in treatment of the mentally retarded. As is so often case, history was to reverse the negative perspective with which Itard viewed his work with the Wild Boy of Aveyron.

Itard's pupil, Edouard Seguin, developed a teaching approach, which he called the "physiologic method." Seguin was also influenced by the work of a number of other French educators including Abbe de Condillac, Jean Rousseau, and Abbe Sicard. They tended to deviate from accepted practices in education; their beliefs supported the ideas of observation, active involvement in what was being studied, and an experiential approach to learning. Seguin's successes led to the formation of an experimental class for idiots in an asylum, the Salpetriere, in Paris. In 1842, he was made director of the school for idiots in another famous French asylum, the Bicetre, and by 1844 his work was so highly recognized that a commission of scholars from the Paris Academy of Science declared that he had solved the problem of "idiot education." Observers from all over the world came to observe his programs, and his book, *The Moral Treatment, Hygiene, and Education of Idiots and Other Backward Children*, published in 1846, won international acclaim.

When Louis Napoleon came into power with the revolution of 1848, Seguin believed that the personal liberty of thought and action of all Frenchmen would be ended. So in 1850, Seguin emigrated to the United States, practicing medicine in Ohio and then serving briefly as director of the Pennsylvania Training School for Idiots. He lived in New York from 1861 till his death in 1880 and played a major role in establishing new residential facilities for the mentally retarded in New York, Massachusetts, Pennsylvania, Ohio, and Connecticut. Seguin served as the first president of the newly established Association of Medical Officers of American Institutions for Idiotic and Feebleminded Persons, which was to later to become the prestigious American Association on Mental Deficiency (AAMD).

Seguin's efforts in France were just one part of the beginnings of the institutional movement in Europe.* By 1846, institutions for the mentally retarded had been founded in Switzerland (1839), France (1834), Germany (1845), and England (1846). The first institutions were founded in the United States in 1848 and were followed within the next 8 years with institutions in Latvia, Scotland, Netherlands, and Denmark. By the end of the nineteenth century, institutions had been initiated in many other countries of Europe, and a total of twenty-four institutions existed in the United States.

Early institutions were founded in the hope that the condition of mental retardation might be remediated and patients returned to the community. Most of these institutions used some variation of Seguin's physiologic methods. By the close of the century, it had become clear to most who worked in this field that mental retardation could not be "cured" in the sense that diseases could be cured. But even though Seguin's basic goals could not be met, many of the instructional techniques he espoused are still in use today, and the institutional movement provided the base for the next important step, the development of public school classes for the retarded.

TWENTIETH CENTURY: DEVELOPMENT OF COMPREHENSIVE PUBLIC PROGRAMS

There were at least four programs for the mentally retarded initiated in the public schools prior to 1900 (Providence, R.I., 1896; Springfield, Mass., 1897; Chicago, 1898; and Boston, 1899), but the first three decades of the twentieth century was the time when such classes became firmly established in the nation. Prior to the standardization of the Binet test of intelligence in 1916, there was some question as to how accurately the identification of mental retardation was accomplished, but with the enforcement of compulsory education laws, school officials were faced with the question of what to do with children who were very slow mentally. A special program provided in a special class seemed to be a logical answer. Previously, if such children were no serious problem in the community, they often attended school intermittently for a few years and then dropped out. Those at the upper end of the range of mental retardation sometimes learned certain low level work skills and made some minimal adaptation to the community. Those at the lower end were placed in an institution, where they spent the rest of their lives. The coming of special classes permitted many more of the mildly mentally retarded to become self-sufficient as adults, and such programs were hailed as a great step forward in efforts to effectively serve the mentally retarded.

Unfortunately, the special class program was not provided on a total basis in all states. Larger cities established programs first, but it took special state legislation providing financial incentives for such programs to obtain action. Such legislation eventually became generally accepted, and by the 1950s special class

---

*Much of the discussion of institutional development is adapted from Gearheart, B. and Litton, F. *The trainable mentally retarded: a foundations approach*, St. Louis: The C. V. Mosby Co., 1979.

programs for the educable mentally retarded were nationwide.

The move to public school classes in the first half of the century provided for many of the mildly retarded minors of the nation but did not, in most cases, address the needs of the moderately or severely mentally retarded. In addition, the lot of most mentally retarded adults (of all levels of severity) was not significantly improved during this time period. But new interest and concern for the mentally retarded of all ages began to surface in the United States in the 1950s and 1960s. This interest is believed by Kott (1971) and Sarason and Doris (1969) to have had its origins immediately following World War II. They believe this awakening related to four factors: (1) disgust and horror with the Nazi practice of exterminating retarded persons, (2) growing interest in mental retardation on the part of biologists and sociologists, (3) growing awareness on the part of the general public that little was being done for the mentally retarded, and (4) the beginnings of a well-organized parent movement.

After internalizing the full impact of the slaughter of mentally retarded persons in Germany, a number of American citizens who wanted to do something to compensate for these obvious wrongs set about to better provide for the mentally retarded in the United States. This included efforts to assure better medical, educational, and recreational facilities, and it took the form of both public and private efforts.

Biologists researched the causes for and treatments of those syndromes that had been earlier identified, and gathered new information about those conditions. Social scientists initiated new investigations on the actual (as opposed to the assumed) effects of the mentally retarded on society.

Public awareness was in part a result of reports in the popular press of the efforts just mentioned but also of expressed interest of a growing number of political figures. President John F. Kennedy, in October, 1961, appointed a National Panel on Mental Retardation, which was directed to outline a national plan to combat mental retardation. In October, 1962, the panel presented a detailed report, including ninety recommendations in the areas of research, prevention, clinical and medical needs, educational needs, and law. Also included were recommendations as to how the local, state, and federal government should organize to meet these needs. Kennedy presented, in a major address to Congress, comprehensive program recommendations aimed at prevention, treatment, and rehabilitation of mental retardation.

In 1966, President Lyndon Johnson appointed the President's Committee on Mental Retardation (PCMR), which was to provide continued advice and recommendations on the needs of the mentally retarded. Unlike some national committees, the PCMR has continued to exert a powerful force in guiding the federal government in its efforts to better provide for the retarded, and its influence has spread far beyond the federal level. Another event that has led to continued awareness of the needs of the retarded was the establishment of the Special Olympics. This was initiated by the Joseph P. Kennedy, Jr. Foundation in 1968, and is given wide publicity on local, state, and national levels by sportscasters and professional athletes. All of these efforts contributed to growing awareness on the part of the general public.

In 1950 the National Association for Retarded Citizens was founded. First established as the National Association for Retarded Children, this organization has grown in numbers and power and is an extremely potent force today (see pp. 21-22).

Part of the story of the development of programs for the mentally retarded since the early 1970s has been told in Chapter 1. This was a time of major advances in the education, care, and treatment of the mentally retarded, and for the first time the moderately and severely retarded began to receive their share of societal attention. Through litigation the public schools were forced to provide for the trainable mentally retarded, and retarded adults were moved from institutions back to community settings (see pp. 441-443 for a further discussion of this trend). After a long struggle, mental retardation is no longer viewed with fear, distrust, and abhorrence, based on superstition and lack of understanding; rather the retarded are viewed as citizens who require help, understanding, and an opportunity to live the most normal life possible. Not all of their normal peers are ready to grant the retarded all the rights they deserve, but at present the picture is one of promise and hope.

A definition and selected terminology used in mental retardation

There have been a number of definitions of mental retardation in use in the United States, but the most widely recognized, for all purposes, is that found in the *Manual on Terminology and Classification in Mental Retardation* (Grossman, 1977), the "bible" of the American Association on Mental Deficiency. This definition reads as follows: *"Mental Retardation refers to significantly subaverage general intellectual functioning existing concurrently with deficits in adaptive behavior, and manifested during the developmental period."* (p. 11) "General intellectual functioning" refers to the results of individual intelligence tests, "significantly subaverage" means an IQ of more than 2 standard deviations below the mean for the test, and "developmental period" means between birth and the eighteenth birthday. "Adaptive behavior" is a measure of the degree to which an individual "meets the standards of personal independence and social responsibility expected of his age and cultural group." (Grossman, 1977, p. 122)

Much of the variation in published definitions of mental retardation has disappeared following passage of PL 94-142 and the requirement of a measurement of adaptive behavior as part of the assessment of mental retardation. Thus a number of states in which a few years ago only the IQ measure was required, a measurement of adaptive behavior is now required. It is most important to note that a diagnosis of mental retardation requires both significantly subaverage intelligence and corroborating levels of adaptive behavior.

LEVELS OF MENTAL RETARDATION

In addition to the general diagnosis of mental retardation, it is customary to consider the *level* of mental retardation. The AAMD classification system indicates four levels of mental retardation: *mild, moderate, severe,* and *profound.* They are illustrated in terms of IQ scores in Table 9-1. Adaptive behavior deficits are more difficult to illustrate without very lengthy explanation but relate to the following (Grossman, 1977):

1. *Early childhood:* deficits in sensory motor skill development, communication skills, socialization, and self-help skills

TABLE 9-1

Levels of mental retardation	Intelligence quotient scores	
	Stanford-Binet	Wechsler scales
Mild	67-52	69-55
Moderate	51-36	54-40
Severe	35-20	39-25
Profound	< 19	< 25

TABLE 9-2
Comparison of terminology relating to levels of mental retardation

AAMD levels of mental retardation	Common educational or institutional terminology
Mild mental retardation	Educable mentally retarded (EMR)
Moderate mental retardation	Trainable mentally retarded (TMR)
Severe mental retardation	Severely mentally retarded; dependent mentally retarded
Profound mental retardation	Life support care

2. *Childhood and adolescence:* deficits in application of academic skills in daily life activities, application or reasoning and judgment in environmental mastery, and social skills
3. *Late adolescence and adulthood:* deficits in social and vocational performance

The AAMD *Manual* (Grossman, 1977) provides tables that illustrate typical behavior as measured by various existing scales of adaptive behavior, but diagnostic practitioners (psychologists and assessment specialists) seem to feel that the available tools for assessment of adaptive behavior are not totally satisfactory (Coulter and Morrow, 1978).

Although the AAMD terminology for levels of mental retardation (mild, moderate, severe, and profound) represents the most specific and scientific system available, an alternate system is in common use in public education. This system involves the use of the terms *educable mentally retarded* (or handicapped), *trainable mentally retarded* (or handicapped), and *severely retarded* or *dependent retarded*. These terms (as used by educators) cannot be precisely equated with the AAMD terms describing levels of mental retardation, but Table 9-2 reflects the manner in which these terms are commonly related. Also, see Table 9-3 for a further expansion of the meaning of the terms "educable mentally retarded" and "trainable mentally retarded". An understanding of the terms used in this and the two following sections will be of particular value if the reader elects to pursue additional information through wider reading in the field of mental retardation.

Systems of classification

Defining mental retardation only according to level or degree of retardation is inadequate for many purposes. A more detailed system of classification is of value for a number of reasons. First, it facilitates research efforts because it permits a more meaningful discussion of incidence, prevalence, characteristics, educational strategies, prevention, and treatment. Second, it makes possible increased precision in communication among professional disciplines that conduct research or provide services for the retarded. Third, classification may aid in understanding the behavior of a child or group of children.

Classification systems have been established for many different purposes and employ differing criteria. Though there may be as many as nine or ten systems, the three following—legal, educational, and medical—will serve to illustrate the variety of ways in which mental retardation may be classified.

LEGAL CLASSIFICATION SYSTEMS

Most of the early legal classification systems in the United States were based on England's Mental Deficiency Act of 1913, which used the classifications idiot, imbecile, feeble-minded, and moral imbeciles. Unfortunately, there was no effective objective method established whereby these classifications could be accurately determined. Legal classifications in many states have changed, but restrictions regarding various rights normally accorded other citizens remain in effect in certain states. Also, the question of legal determination of who is retarded has only recently been successfully addressed through litigation. Laws are difficult to change, and change is needed in many parts of the nation; the most powerful agent for change in recent years has definitely been litigation. It is quite possible that rather than becoming involved in a new, complex system of classification, lawmakers may now be moving in the direction of speaking of mental retardation without further classification and leaving the matter of specific interpretation of rights, privileges, etc., to be determined in individual cases. This would certainly be better than the outmoded system that referred to idiots, imbeciles, and morons without any defensible method of differentatiation.

EDUCATIONAL CLASSIFICATION SYSTEMS

Educational classification systems have tended to focus on two or three classifications of mental retardation. The information given in Table 9-3 is adapted from definitions given in the *Dictionary of Special Education and Rehabilitation* (Kelly and Vergason, 1978), and the AAMD *Manual on Terminology and Classification in Mental Retardation* (Grossman, 1977).

Educational classifications were established for two primary purposes: instructional grouping and reimbursement. In practice, it was quickly established that other variables, such as chronologic age, mental age, social age, and previous educational experience, must also be carefully considered when establishing instructional objectives. The requirement in Public Law 94-142 to provide an Individual Educational Plan for each child may help assure that these other variables are actually considered. As for reimbursement, it was inititally a matter of smaller class size and/or greater reimbursement per pupil for the trainable mentally retarded that led to classification procedures to separate these two levels. Newer reimbursement procedures in some states have tended to eliminate "advantages" or "disadvantages" to a local school district in classifying a given student as educable or trainable.

MEDICAL CLASSIFICATION SYSTEMS

The medical classification system of the AAMD is based on the idea that mental retardation is caused by disease or a biologic defect. The following system is offered by the AAMD.

1. Infections and intoxications
    a. Prenatal infection
    b. Postnatal cerebral infection
    c. Intoxication
2. Trauma or physical agents
    a. Prenatal injury
    b. Mechanical injury at birth
    c. Perinatal hypoxia
    d. Postnatal injury
3. Metabolism or nutrition
    a. Neuronal lipid storage diseases
    b. Carbohydrate disorders
    c. Amino acid disorders
    d. Nucleotide disorders
    e. Mineral disorders
    f. Endocrine disorders
    g. Nutritional disorders
    h. Other
4. Gross brain disease (postnatal)
    a. Neurocutaneous dysplasia
    b. Tumors

TABLE 9-3
Educational classification—a system established by common usage

Educational classification	Dictionary of Special Education and Rehabilitation*	Manual on Terminology and Classification in Mental Retardation*
Educable mentally retarded (EMR)	Most can become self-sufficient	Usually can learn basic functional academic skills
	Most can learn academic skills through upper elementary grade levels	Usually can maintain themselves independently or semi-independently in the community
	Most now mainstreamed	
	Equivalent of mildly retarded	
	IQ range: approximately 50 to 70	
Trainable mentally retarded (TMR)	Term used in educational codes for those unable to function well in regular classes or in EMR classes	Can attain only limited achievement in traditional basic academic skills
	Have characteristics indicating capability of profiting from work in (a) self-help skills, (b) social adjustment, and (c) controlled work settings	Capable of profiting from training in: self-care and simple vocational skills
	Intellectual ability from one-third to one-half that of average age-peer	
	IQ range: approximately 25 to 50	
Dependent retarded or severely retarded	May be able to live in group or alternative living system	Requires continuing supervision and/or assistance in: social functioning, academic functioning, and daily living
	Will require extensive supervision throughout life	
	Lower in IQ than TMR	

*Adapted from information/discussion provided in this source.

c. Cerebral white matter, degenerative
   d. Specific fiber tracts or neural groups, degenerative
   e. Cerebrovascular system
   f. Other
5. Unknown prenatal influence
   a. Cerebral malformation
   b. Craniofacial anomaly
   c. Status dysraphicus
   d. Hydrocephalus
   e. Hydranencephaly
   f. Multiple malformations
   g. Single umbilical artery
   h. Other
6. Chromosomal abnormalities
   a. A group—chromosomes 1, 2, 3
   b. B group—chromosomes 4, 5
   c. C group—chromosomes 6-12
   d. D group—chromosomes 13-15
   e. E group—chromosomes 16-18
   f. F group—chromosomes 19-20
   g. G group—chromosomes 21-22
   h. Chromosomal abnormality, X chromosome
   i. Chromosomal abnormaltiy, Y chromosome
   j. Chromosomal abnormality, other abnormality
7. Gestational disorders
   a. Prematurity
   b. Low birth weight
   c. Postmaturity
   d. Other
8. Following psychiatric disorder
9. Environmental influences
   a. Psychosocial disadvantage
   b. Sensory deprivation
   c. Other
10. Other conditions

These major classifications are described in more detail in the AAMD *Manual on Terminology and Classification in Mental Retardation*. Certain of these classifications will be further discussed in the section of this chapter relating to causes and origins (etiology) of mental retardation on pp. 258-264.

Any classification system may be considered aribitrary in that it is based on characteristics chosen by those who established the system. The use of a classification system based on a single criterion is perhaps the least satisfactory because the complexity of the condition of mental retardation almost guarantees that such a system will be meaningless for certain purposes. Even when students are classified as "educable" or "trainable" for purposes of statistical reporting, knowledgeable educators make use of information available from other systems of classification. With the coming of the requirement for an individual educational plan and program for each child, this becomes essential from both a legal and a practical standpoint.

Prevalence of mental retardation

Although some variation exists in the estimates of the prevalence of mental retardation provided by various agencies and authorities, there is much more agreement than, for example, with estimates of the prevalence of learning disabilities or emotional disturbance. Most authorities tend to agree that the percentage is between 2 and 3 percent. As indicated in the prevalence table in Chapter 3 (p. 54) this means a school-age population of between 1.1 and 1.65 million. This also means that there are somewhat more than 6 million mentally retarded in the total population of the United States.

Although there is considerable indication that socioeconomic status is related to the reported incidence of the educable level of mental retardation, it appears to be unrelated to the incidence of lower levels of mental retardation. Some school areas that include an unusually high percentage of very low income families may report higher prevalence data (here we get into the question of pseudoretardation), but for purposes of educational planning it is fairly safe to assume the 3 percent estimate and plan for twenty-five EMR students, four TMR students, and one severely or profoundly retarded student per 1000 school-age children and youth. A more detailed discussion of this matter, including epidemiologic considerations, may be found in Sarason and Doris (1969), Scheerenberger (1971), and Tarjan and co-workers (1973).

Causes of mental retardation

When speaking of the causes of mental retardation, the term etiology is often used. Etiology means either the assignment of causes or the science of causes or origins. Etiology is used by medical doctors in relation to diseases, and since the medical profession is the major group involved in researching the origin of mental retardation, this is common terminology when considering the causes of mental retardation. In an earlier section of this chapter, we considered the medical system of classifying mental retardation; the discussion here will relate to a few examples of each of the major classificiations.

Causes of mental retardation sometimes can be traced to a single factor. This might be genetic, the result of a specific childhood disease, or physiologic damage, such as that resulting from an accident or a blow on the head. In these cases, the matter of etiology is relatively simple (if proper substantiating data can be gathered). In other cases, mental retardation is apparently a result of the complex interaction of many factors—genetic, environmental, or a combination of both. Even with the present state of knowledge about the causes of mental retardation, the cause is unknown in 50 percent of the cases of mental retardation (Moser and Wolf, 1971; Stern, 1973).

Whenever possible, the determination of cause is of value; if conditions leading to mental retardation are known, remedies can be sought and preventive strategies developed. Both may serve to keep the occurrence of mental retardation to an absolute minimum.

INFECTIONS AND INTOXICATIONS

Infections and intoxications are among the major causes of mental retardation. This grouping includes diseases and intoxication that may occur either in the prenatal or postnatal periods of development.

The extent of mental retardation produced by infections and diseases is determined by the extent and location of brain-cell damage. In some cases, the disease inhibits normal development of intellectual functions. In other cases it causes deterioration or loss of these functions after they have been acquired. Destruction of the cortical cells of the brain seems to contribute most to retardation in this category. Causes of mental retardation discussed here will include rubella, hemolytic disease, and poisons.

Rubella, a viral disease, has been recognized since 1815, but it was not until 1914 that the relationship between birth defects and maternal rubella was demonstrated. Investigations of the 1964 United States rubella epidemic indicated this relationship was highly correlated with the first trimester of pregnancy. In addition to causing retardation,

TABLE 9-4
Frequency of specific defects following maternal rubella (367 cases)*

Defect	Frequency
Cataracts, glaucoma, retinopathy (disease of the retina)	267
Deafness	252
Mental retardation	170
Mild	84
Moderate	40
Severe	46
Heart disease	182
No defect	70
Death	61

*Data from President's Committee on Mental Retardation. *The decisive decade.* Washington, D.C.: U.S. Government Printing Office, 1971, p. 10.

rubella may also lead to deafness, heart disease, cataracts and glaucoma, or various neurologic defects. In a small percentage of the cases there may be no damage; however, the child is more often born with multiple defects (see Table 9-4).

With rubella, the expectant mother may experience few symptoms and suspect no damage to the unborn child. If rubella is contracted within the first trimester of pregnancy, the estimate of possible birth defects ranges from 50 to 80 percent, with an additional 10 to 15 percent of the pregnancies being spontaneously aborted. If the infection strikes later in pregnancy, the incidence and severity of damage are lessened but the danger of damage still exists.

An effective rubella vaccine has been available since 1969 and if properly used could eliminate the effects of this disease on newborn infants. Persons recommended for vaccination are girls in prepuberty and puberty; young women who are in regular contact with groups of children (since prevalence is highest in groups); and children older than 1 year. At present it appears that as many as one-fourth of the children of the United States are not protected and the percentage of protection among older girls and young women may be equally low. Rubella is particularly dangerous because pregnant women often do not even know they have the disease. It is essential that we push for better educational and community health programs to combat this known, but often ignored, cause of mental retardation and other handicapping conditions.

Hemolytic disease (destruction of red blood corpuscles) of the newborn has long been recognized but only recently has been fully understood. There are various types of hemolytic disease of the newborn that may result in mental retardation, but Rh incompatibility occurs most frequently.

When the fetus has an Rh-positive blood type and the mother is Rh-negative, a sensitization may occur between the mother and unborn child. The Rh-negative mother forms anti-Rh antigens in response to pregnancy with an Rh-positive infant. Several pregnancies may be required before a dangerous level of antigens is produced, but when this occurs, the red blood cells of the fetus are destroyed. Bilirubin (reddish yellow pigment in the bile) is then secreted and deposited in the nerve cells of the basal ganglia of the brain where damage results. This condition is known as *erythroblastosis fetalis* or, in severe form, *kernicterus*. About 75 percent of infants with kernicterus die in the neonatal period.

Remedies for the Rh problem include: (1) massive amounts of oxygen during and after labor, (2) induction of early labor, (3) injections of Rh hapten to prevent antibody formation, (4) transfusions of blood (partial or complete) to the newborn, and (5) fetal blood transfusions before birth (Clarke and McConnell, 1972). The most successful remedy, when the potential for this condition is known, is Rh gamma globulin injections for the Rh-negative mother after the birth of her first Rh-positive child or following a miscarriage. This prevents initial sensitization and thus prevents the formation of destructive antibodies. Before the availability of such preventive injections, it is estimated that 20,000 infants a year were affected by diseases stemming from Rh-factor incompatibility.

Although fully recognized, Rh incompatibility as a cause of mental retardation has not yet been eliminated.

Poisons are a much more recently recognized cause of mental retardation. Lead poisoning (plumbism) has received the most widespread attention, and much progress has been made since the early 1970s. One of the more significant steps was the passage of PL 91-695, the Lead-Based Paint Poisoning Prevention Act, which provides assistance for

Other handicapping conditions

communities to initiate programs to identify and eliminate the sources of lead poisoning. Although progress is being made and the Food and Drug Administration banned the manufacture of paint with dangerously high levels of lead in 1971, the problem will continue until all housing that has older paint containing dangerous levels of lead is gone.

Lead poisoning from paint is a problem because young children (ages 1 to 3 are the most dangerous years) tend to eat chips of paint or paint-covered plaster. Other potential sources of lead poisoning include improperly glazed earthenware, acidic food stored or cooked in certain lead pewterware, certain canned evaporated milk (because of a defective soldering process in canning), some brands of paint coating on pencils, some coating on toothpaste tubes, some lead-based ink used in magazines (particularly yellow, orange, and red), inhalation of lead fumes produced by burning of lead-based materials (for example, battery casings), accidental swallowing and retention of lead objects, automobile exhausts, and consumption of lead-contaminated "moonshine" whiskey (Lin-Fu, 1973).

Lead poisoning occurs as a result of the activities and products of humans and thus is preventable. Efforts to eliminate lead poisoning must include: (1) continued screening in high-risk areas, (2) treatment and provision for follow-up, (3) continued search for sources of lead poisoning, (4) enforcement of existing laws related to lead poisoning, and (5) continued public education. It is possible that through strict enforcement of existing laws and the passage of time (thus the destruction of older buildings), much of the danger from lead-based paint will pass, but vigilance is required with regard to other sources that may develop as new products are introduced in the marketplace.

In addition to the problem of lead poisoning, other poisons pose the threat of mental retardation. Some, like manganese, arsenic, and mercury, may be part of other mixtures or compounds and must be guarded against as hidden hazards. Others, such as alcohol, drugs, and narcotics, may be deliberately ingested and are probably the greatest poison threat of the 80s if existing trends continue.

TRAUMA OR PHYSICAL AGENTS

Trauma or physical agents as a cause of mental retardation can be discussed much more briefly than infections and intoxications, and many such causes are amenable to prevention. Paradoxically, such retardation may be increasing. This category includes injuries occurring during prenatal, perinatal, or postnatal periods of development and may be on the increase, in part, because better lifesaving procedures are keeping more high-risk infants alive.

Prenatal types of injury include excessive radiation, prenatal anoxia (lack of oxygen caused by a twisted umbilical cord), and prenatal trauma (maternal fall or accident).

Perinatal damage to the fetus may be caused by improper application of forceps, prolonged labor (over 24 hours), precipitous birth (under 20 minutes), pelvic-head disproportion, or perinatal anoxia.

Postnatal damage as a cause can include direct trauma to the head (severe fracture), cerebral hemorrhage (stroke), electric shock, lesions on the brain (tumor), or postnatal anoxia. Postnatal anoxia is often caused by high body temperatures, which result in a shortage of oxygen supplied to the brain and resultant cell damage. Child abuse is another potential cause of mental retardation.

DISORDERS OF METABOLISM AND NUTRITION

Metabolic and nutritional disorders are a third major causal classification according to the AAMD. These include a number of recognized metabolic, nutritional, endocrine, and mineral dysfunctions. Representative disorders include phenylketonuria, galactosemia, and cretinism.

One of the most widely known diseases in the field of mental retardation is *phenylketonuria (PKU)*, a metabolic disease. Phenylalanine is an essential body protein found in most foods, particularly milk. When the infant with PKU is fed a normal total milk diet, the levels of phenylalanine rise very rapidly and can usually be detected at the end of 2 days of feeding, depending on the degree of impairment of the metabolic process.

This disorder may be easily screened in the neonate by the ferric chloride test for phenylpyruvic acid in the urine or by the blood-culture Guthrie test. Early detection and diagnosis (before 1 month) are essential for successful treatment.

PKU is characterized by a lack of pigment, and approximately 90 percent of all children with PKU have blond hair, blue eyes, and fair, sensitive skin. Mental development varies widely, ranging from severe retardation to normal intelligence. PKU rarely occurs in darker-skinned races, and screening tests have indicated an approximate 2:1 ratio, male to female (Hansen and Hoffman, 1970).

Treatment of children with PKU consists of a phenylalanine-restricted diet. A diet used with success by Hunt, Sutherland, and Berry (1971) creates a balance between essential amino acids with a commercial low-phenylalanine protein substitute and supplementary phenylalanine from natural foods. Effective diet treatment programs have existed since 1955, and there has been no significant improvement in this diet since its inception (Berry and others, 1977).

Studies by Berman and Ford (1970) and Wilson (1970) provide convincing demonstration of the value of this special diet. These studies indicate normal IQ levels and prevention of progressive mental deterioration in the majority of cases. These programs of control were initiated before the age of 4 months. Other studies show similar results.

A national screening movement in the mid-1960s resulted in a decreased incidence of retardation caused by PKU, and PKU screening of newborns is now standard procedure for most hospitals.

Bush, Chen, and Patrick (1975) analyzed the cost effectiveness of the PKU screening program in New York State (1965 to 1970) and found that 1 year's operation of the program (annual cost $837,307) identified enough cases (22) to produce the equivalent of 189 years of well life. Massive PKU programs can easily be justified in both humanitarian and economic terms.

PKU is for the most part under control in the United States, but this is not the case in some underdeveloped nations. This certainly is one case where those in more advanced nations must do all possible to share knowledge with others, but the task is quite difficult in areas where babies are delivered without the benefit of an attending physician or available laboratory facilities. However, the PKU story should serve as encouragement for more research, it is a symbol of what can be done with sufficient effort and dedication.

Recognized in the early 1900s, *galactosemia* is now known to be an important and partially preventable metabolic cause of mental retardation. Galactosemia is a disorder in which the patient has the inability to metabolize galactose (sugar).

Galactosemia may be indicated at birth by cataracts, jaundice, cirrhosis of the liver, and low birth weight. When the child first digests milk, vomiting, diarrhea, and colic may develop. Later symptoms include poor weight gains and malnourishment. Diagnosis and treatment very early in life can reduce the possibility of permanent liver damage, severe retardation, and even death. The more common screening test is a urinanalysis.

Dietary restriction of galactose and lactose from an early age, preferably during pregnancy if the mother has already had a child with the disease, is the most effective treatment (Sardharwalla, 1976).

Because of relatively low incidence (1 in 70,000 births), screening programs have not been instituted nationwide. One hope is that multiple metabolic screening programs will be expanded, thus permitting the detection of galactosemia along with other disorders.

Cretinism (hypothyroidism), one of the more readily recognized metabolic endocrine abnormalities, is caused by a thyroid gland disorder. Characteristics of cretinism include short thick hands and neck, hoarse voice, heart problems, large protuding tongue, short extremities, dry scaly skin, delayed bone development, and muscular hypertrophy (enlargement).

Treatment consists of replacement of the thyroid hormone, which reverses many symptoms of hypothyroidism. According to a study by Raiti and Newns (1971), early treatment is essential. Wilkins (1965) reports that 45 percent achieve a normal intellectual level if treatment is instituted before the age of 6 months. The results of treatment depend on both the length of time before treatment is begun and the severity and type of hypothyroidism.

The incidence of cretinism is estimated to be about 1 in 20,000 and is decreasing because of better understanding of the condition and improved treatment procedures.

GROSS BRAIN DISEASE

The classification of gross brain disease recognized by the AAMD, includes a number of hereditary conditions in which tumors appear on the brain and which, for the most part, can be treated only by surgical removal. In some of these diseases tumors may not always appear on the brain and thus there is no mental retardation. In others mental retardation is almost always present. In nearly all diseases included in this classification, tumors or nodules develop on or in various parts of the body and contribute to a greatly reduced life span.

UNKNOWN PRENATAL INFLUENCE

In this classification are the conditions hydrocephalus and microcephalus. *Hydrocephalus*, characterized by enlargement of the cranial vault, may be produced in three different ways (Eckstein, 1966):

1. Excess formation of cerebrospinal fluid
2. Failure of absorption of cerebrospinal fluid
3. Blockage in the circulatory system of the cerebrospinal fluid (by far the most common cause)

Enlargement of the cranial vault leads to other very obvious changes in appearance. The eyes become very widespread, eyelids often cannot be closed, and the nose is flattened. Mental development may be normal or retarded, depending on the extent of the pressure damage to the brain. In cases where the defect is operable and surgery is performed early, mental retardation can be prevented. The extent of expansion of the head depends on the speed of fluid buildup, the severity of the pressure, the age of onset, and (when operable) the success of surgery.

Surgery, directed toward reducing the amount of cerebrospinal fluid produced, rerouting, or draining the excess fluid, is the only accepted treatment for hydrocephalus. When detection and treatment are early, the prognosis for successful management is good.

Microcephalus is diagnosed when the head circumference is significantly (2 standard deviations) below the mean for persons of similar age and sex. The small head may be attributed to a lack of formation of brain tissue or a destructive brain process and, generally speaking, the smaller the head the more severely retarded the individual.

An apparent correlation exists between microcephaly and such factors as radiation, perinatal anoxia, meningitis, head trauma, chromosomal abnormalities, and child abuse (Oliver, 1975).

Apparently, there may be both inherited or acquired microcephaly and, regardless of cause, mental retardation is almost always present. There is no accepted treatment for this condition.

CHROMOSOMAL ABNORMALITIES

There are a number of chromosomal abnormalities recognized as causal in mental retardation, but only the most common, *Down's syndrome,* will be discussed here. Because it has been recognized for so long (Down, 1866), is so easily recognized, and is so common, Down's syndrome has been very extensively researched. Down mistakenly thought that this syndrome was a result of "human degeneration" and related it to the Mongolian race, thus in effect naming such persons mongols or mongoloids. Because the inferred relationship is inaccurate and is obviously insulting to Orientals, there has been a concerted effort to use the term "Down's syndrome," although the term mongolism persists, undoubtedly because of the facial characteristics of Down's syndrome individuals.

Chromosome abnormalities are not unusual, and according to Holmes and co-workers (1972), over 90 percent of those fetuses with chromosomal errors are spontaneously aborted. There are many possible causes of chromosomal aberrations, including radiation, drugs, viruses, and gene mutations. However, the one factor most highly correlated with Down's syndrome births is maternal age. According to Smith and Wilson (1973), the odds that a woman over age 45 will give birth to a Down's syndrome child are over 20 times greater than that of a woman under age 30. In fact, the odds increase very rapidly at ages over 30, as may be seen from Table 9-5.

TABLE 9-5

The relationships of Down's syndrome to maternal age

Maternal age	Frequency of occurrence
< 30	1 in 1500
30-34	1 in 750
35-39	1 in 280
40-44	1 in 130
> 45	1 in 65

*Data from Smith, D. W., and Wilson, A. A. *The child with Down's syndrome.* Philadelphia: W. B. Saunders Co., 1973, p. 17.

The chromosomal disorder common to about 95 percent of all cases of Down's syndrome is one in which there is an extra chromosome in the G group of chromosomes, connected with chromosome 21. Thus Down's syndrome is often called trisomy 21 (rather than a twenty-first *pair* of chromosomes, there are *three,* thus "trisomy"). There are two other chromosomal aberrations that lead to somewhat different forms of Down's syndrome. They are much more rare, but have similar practical results to those of trisomy 21.

Clinical features associated with Down's syndrome are: (1) short, broad head, (2) round, flat face, (3) small, flat nose, (4) slanted eyes, with speckling of the iris common, (5) small, angular, low-set ears, (6) mouth usually held open, (7) tongue fissured and usually protruding, (8) short, broad neck, (9) short (compared to other body features) feet, hands, and fingers, (10) shorter than average at birth and at maturity, (11) low voice that at times is guttural, (12) articulation often faulty, (13) genitals underdeveloped in males, normal to over-

Other handicapping conditions

developed in females, (14) muscle tone poor, especially at birth, and (15) heart problems and unusual tendency to have respiratory infections. *All* individuals diagnosed as having Down's syndrome do not have all of the preceding characteristics (often called stigmata), but they usually have most of them. In addition, almost all individuals with a majority of these characteristics have varying degrees of mental retardation, with most in the moderate range of retardation.

Down's syndrome is a condition present at birth and is usually diagnosed at birth. There are, according to reports of the President's Committee on Mental Retardation (PCMR, 1977), some 15,000 children born each year with Down's syndrome. The major hope of preventing Down's syndrome lies with prenatal screening of high-risk mothers and effective genetic counseling. As this text was going to press, a lawsuit in New York State (where this type of legal action is possible) had successfully passed through a District Court hearing in which it was ruled that the parents of a Down's syndrome child *could* sue their medical doctor for the predictably high costs of raising a Down's syndrome child, because they had received no warning of the chances of such an occurrence (because of the mother's age and other related factors). They maintained that if they had known, they would have insisted on amniocentesis. Then, since the amniocentesis would have presumably warned of the abnormality, the mother maintained that she would have had an abortion. This case will undoubtedly go into additional appeals, but the stage is set for much additional pressure on the medical profession for meaningful genetic counseling.

The causes of mental retardation included under the other major classifications as proposed by the AAMD do not represent any large proportion of the total causes of mental retardation. One possible exception is environmental influences. For the most part environmental factors would either result in very mild mental retardation (considered pseudoretardation by many) or result in conditions that are better classified in another category. It is, of course, possible that there are significant numbers of persons who are actually retarded as a result of purely environmentally related factors. If a child is mentally retarded because he ingested pieces of lead-based paint, it would seem more meaningful to classify the cause as poisoning rather than environmental deprivation, even though the poisoning occurred because the environment was substandard and the child's parents were poorly educated and unaware of the potential danger. However, this point can be argued either way.

Perhaps we may best conclude this consideration of causes of mental retardation by again noting that the cause is known with relative certainty in only about half of all cases; some of these causes are subject to amelioration and some are not, given present knowledge. In many, if not most, cases, the cause is really a matter of cause*s* and may relate to genetic factors, physical damage, or environmental influences. The determination of causes is important because it provides a better basis for both remediation and prevention, unfortunately, knowledge of causation is usually not particularly valuable in educational planning.

Identification of the mentally retarded

Identification of the mentally retarded has, to some degree, been already explained in previous sections of this chapter. The purpose of this section will be to organize these various segments of information into a more integrated presentation.

Early identification of the mentally retarded may take place before birth through amniocentesis. This procedure, which involves analysis of amniotic fluid taken from the uterus of the expectant mother, has proved to be highly reliable for the identification of certain syndromes but somewhat less reliable for others. The results of amniocentesis may be used as a basis for at least two major types of action: (1) remedial measures such as changes in the diet of the mother, blood transfusions, etc., or (2) abortion.

Identification immediately after birth may be based on screening tests (including both chemical tests and an examination of various physical characteristics) which may lead to special diets, surgery, or other steps that will prevent or greatly reduce the degree of mental retardation. One of the best known procedures for rating the indicators of normalcy at birth was developed by Virginia Apgar and usually called the Apgar test. This scoring system should be applied to newborn babies within 5 minutes after birth, and will give a quick indication of conditions requiring emergency measures (Apgar and Beck, 1972). In using the Apgar scale, five vital signs are checked: appearance or coloring, pulse, grimace or reflex irritability, activity, and respiration (Apgar and Beck, 1972) This type of indicator is most valuable in the case of more severe conditions but may provide at least some indication of the need for continued attention to potential (future) needs, even in the case of mild retardation.

As indicated previously, in some cases early identification may lead to special diets or surgical procedures that can reduce or even prevent mental retardation. In others, such as identification of a Down's syndrome infant, the major advantages are the increased chances for an early start in an all-important parent education program and the provision of the earliest possible chance for enrollment in an infant stimulation program such as the program at the University of Washington, described in Chapter 13. This type of early identification is a medical matter and requires full knowledge on the part of attending physicians and proper testing facilities in the hospital or community. Although this level of knowledge and these facilities are not available in all parts of the nation, the past 20 years has been a time of rapid progress.

The parents or a physician may identify the preschool child who is mentally retarded, based on their knowledge about normal child development. When the parent has had forewarning about the possibility of having a handicapped child through earlier genetic counseling, the odds of such identification are greatly increased.

Identification of moderately or severely mentally retarded individuals of school age is no major problem since they are usually identified prior to school entrance. Identification of the mildly mentally retarded is another matter, with more difficulties in early identification. For the most part, students are considered for further evaluation regarding academic difficulties after referral by classroom teachers. With the parent's permission, such evaluation may proceed, and if mental retardation is suspected, the two indications specified in the definition of mental retardation—level of intelligence and level of adaptive behavior—must be assessed.

Level of intelligence (IQ) is most often measured through use of the Stanford-Binet or one of the Wechsler scales. In addition, if there is any question of unusual language difficulties, deprivation of experience, or minority status as a factor tending to reduce the measure of IQ, at least one nonverbal test of intelligence should be used. Measures of adaptive behavior are also essential. These measures, designed to assess the individual's level of functioning in nonintellectual areas, especially those related to social functioning, must be chosen with care. Measures of intelligence and adaptive behavior are required to meet accepted definitions of mental retardation; but all of the other types of information indicated in the Fig. 3-1 (p. 56) must also be obtained. Developmental history, health history and status, and assessment of vision and hearing are also essential.

Identification of the mildly mentally retarded must be approached with unusual caution, because of the variety of factors that can lead to the appearance of mild mental retardation. However, if both IQ and level of adaptive behavior indicate mental retardation and there are no other factors to indicate that this is an erroneous diagnosis, the presence of mental retardation should be accepted and proper educational planning initiated. In some instances educators have become so afraid to identify a child as mentally retarded that some who need special services do not receive them.

Education and training of the mentally retarded

Because preschool programs are discussed in Chapter 13 we will not discuss such programs here except to indicate that they provide experiences and activities that will assist the child to move through the normal developmental steps as quickly as possible, considering the type and degree of mental retardation. Training and involvement of the parents in this entire process appears to be a critically important factor. With their understanding and cooperation, the effort more nearly approaches a 24-hour program, thus maximizing the chances of progress.

Programs for school-age children may be categorized in a number of ways but there are at least three major categories relating to levels of retardation. These are programs for the mildly retarded (educable), the moderately retarded (trainable), and the more severely retarded. Until the 1960s and early 1970s, many school districts provided programs only for the educable mentally retarded, but many more programs for the trainable have since been initiated. Some school districts also provide for the more severely mentally retarded, but acceptance of this level of retardation as part of the responsibility of the public schools is now at about the same point of evolution as acceptance of programs for the trainable was in the 1960s. Although there is considerable variation in scope of program provision *within* states, the major variation is *between* states and reflects state legislation, the level of overall educational development, and the manner in which program responsibilities are assigned to the various governmental agencies within the state. Given this variation, we will explore certain major facets of educational programming for these three levels of mental retardation.

EDUCABLE MENTALLY RETARDED

The educable mentally retarded should receive an education as similar as possible to that received by nonhandicapped students. In the very recent past it was assumed by many educators that the educable mentally retarded would never be able to read beyond the third or fourth grade level, would perform in mathematics at about the same level, and might, with special assistance, develop social and vocational skills at a somewhat higher level. The most serious error in such an assumption was the apparent belief that *all* students diagnosed as educable mentally retarded would be limited to these levels of performance. It was often apparently assumed that whatever worked for the "average" in these classes was also satisfactory for those at the very top of the range and for those at the very bottom. In most schools, regular educators were so happy to get these slower children out of their classes and into a "special" program, there was little interest in attempting to determine whether they might

When appropriately used, a variety of learning material may be quite effective with the mildly retarded. With carefully planned, sequentially presented activities, much more may be accomplished than was generally thought possible 20 years ago. (From Chinn, P. C., Drew, C. J., and Logan, D. R. *Mental Retardation: A Life Cycle Approach,* ed. 2. St. Louis: The C. V. Mosby Co., 1979.)

successfully spend all or part of their school day in the regular class.

As a result of (1) studies questioning the efficacy of existing programs for the educable mentally retarded, (2) lawsuits that attacked the high percentage of minority students in self-contained classes for the educable mentally retarded, and (3) the passage of PL 94-142, it is probably true that most children in this category are mainstreamed (Kelly and Vergason, 1978). Mainstreamed in this case may mean anything from a few hours per day in regular classes to all day in the regular class, with some consultative help from a special education specialist.

The usual academic program for the educable mentally retarded student will have approximately the same components as for any nonhandicapped student. (An exception would be some students at the very lower end of this range of retardation. Their program, planned individually, will often be considerably adapted.) Presuming that these students have significantly subaverage mental ability, they will learn at a slower rate than other students and will require more assistance with highly abstract concepts. They will certainly require more individual help and thus may require a different proportion of time spent on various academic activities than is planned for most other students. Many will continue to become more and more *educationally* retarded, and at some point in the middle elementary grades, through individual planning with parents and all educational personnel who can provide meaningful input, certain parts of the normal program may be reduced in emphasis or even omitted, in favor of additional time spent on basic skill subjects.

Within the basic skill areas (for example, reading) it may become necessary, from the point of view of learning efficiency, to reduce the size of the target word recognition vocabulary, deleting whatever necessary to ensure learning of the words most critical to the development of employment skills. This, too, will vary from student to student. In the area of mathematics skills, there may be some reduction in certain of the more theoretical aspects and increased emphasis on applied mathematics. As each curriculum area is planned, there will be an attempt to integrate learning activities so that, for example, when a student is developing reading skills, he or she is also learning arithmetic skills and social concepts. This is not possible all of the time with all areas of the curriculum, but whenever possible, this integration of learning materials, relating the total program to concrete experiences that may have immediate meaning to the students, will be most effective.

As noted earlier, classes are planned so that the EMR student is in the "mainstream," that is, with non-handicapped students as much as possible. In all instances, the potential benefits of such mainstreaming as opposed to any loss of effective academic learning will be closely monitored, and individual planning will continue throughout the total school program.

At the secondary level, the educational program for the EMR student may become more different from the regular program than was the case in elementary school. However, it should be noted that programs for *nonhandicapped* students also become more varied at the secondary level. For most educable mentally retarded students, a vocationally oriented program, including some variation of a work-study or work-experience program, appears to be the most meaningful and effective. These programs are described in Chapter 14.

Educational programming for the educable mentally retarded can be characterized as being as similar as possible to the "regular" school program, with as much time as possible spent in the regular classroom with non-handicapped peers. In some instances, especially with students who are very near the upper limit of the EMR range, full-time return to the regular class with no continued special programming is possible. This move, though highly desirable when it will work, must be approached with the same care as was taken with original placement in special programming to avoid the possibility of a serious error. This step is also required by PL 94-142 and by most state regulations because this is a radical change of program, which must be accompanied by appropriate data gathering and a formal staffing. Students who are at the very bottom of the EMR range may need to be considered for placement in a lower level program, but this too requires much consideration, data gathering, and a staffing. In practice, many school districts appear to be using some type of "borderline" or "in-between" programming, rather than placing students directly from a program for EMR students into a program for the trainable mentally retarded. However, the advisability of this type of planning may also be debated.

TRAINABLE MENTALLY RETARDED

As recently as the mid-1960s the moderately mentally retarded were considered "too low" in mental ability to be the responsibility of special educators in many parts of the nation. They were still not served by special education in some states in the mid-1970s. However, these children are now receiving increasing attention nationwide. The present level of acceptance of the moderately retarded (more often called the trainable mentally retarded or TMRs in educational circles) has come about through a variety of efforts and changes in attitude. An official stand on attitudes toward institutionalization was stated by the American Medical Association in 1965 in an AMA resource book, *Mental Retardation: A Handbook for the Primary Physician.* Prior to this time, many physicians apparently followed the practice of an almost automatic recommendation that most children in the TMR range (or below) be placed in an institutional setting. The following statement from the introduction to the chapter on placement and alternatives for care indicate this modified attitude: "No type of retardation is in itself an indication for residential care. The mentally retarded individual should remain in his own home or community as long as this environment can provide for his needs." This statement also reflected the feelings of the National Association for Retarded Citizens and supported their efforts to force the public schools to provide adequate programs for all retarded children and youth. Their efforts, plus national support through the President's Committee on Mental Retardation, led to the present state of affairs. That state of affairs, briefly summarized, is that all states have some type of educational programming for the trainable mentally retarded in addition to that provided in the institutional setting, although those programs and services may be provided by an agency other than the public schools or through some sort of cooperative effort. These programs vary in quantity and quality, but most have similar objectives and considerable similarity in the program components used to attempt to reach these objectives. We will outline major curricular areas, emphasizing those common to states with more comprehensive programs. Since TMR programs are on the increase nationally, and there appears to be continued improvement in existing programs, it may be assumed that the curriculum is being broadened and more effective teaching procedures are being developed each year.

For purposes of overview, we will consider seven educational goals:

1. Ability to care for one's personal needs
2. Ability to communicate effectively
3. Appropriate social behavior and emotional stability
4. Effectiveness in perceptual-motor and general physical skills areas
5. *Functional* academic skills (highest level possible)
6. Ability to function in leisure time (recreational skills)
7. Maximal vocational ability/economic usefulness.

Under these goals, major curriculum areas are:

1. Personal needs (self-care skills)
    a. Feeding (all components—drinking, eating with knife, fork, spoon, etc.)
    b. Toileting (bowel and bladder control, clothing management, flushing toilet, etc.)
    c. Clothing (dressing, undressing, buttoning, zipping, selection of appropriate clothing, care of clothing, etc.)
    d. Personal grooming (washing, combing hair, care of nails, teeth, skin, use of razor, deoderants, etc.)

e. Safety (use of household appliances and tools, crossing streets, using stairways, playground safety, etc.)
2. Communication skills
  a. Listening/receptive skills (for information, for directions, for enjoyment, etc.)
  b. Speaking/expressive skills (both gestures and vocal speech; production of words, phrases, sentences, etc.)
3. Social skills
  a. Self-control (general stability, in games, under criticism, waiting turns, in changes of routine, etc.)
  b. Social amenities (in greetings, in eating, etc.)
  c. Group activity participation (team games, in transportation, etc.)
  d. General personality (enthusiasm, honesty, dependability, etc.)
  e. Sex education (recognition of body parts and functions, peer relations, marriage, contraception, etc.)
4. Physical skills; perceptual-motor skills
  a. Basic movement skills (hopping, skipping, sliding, running, etc.)
  b. Perceptual-motor skills (body image, laterality, eye-hand, etc.)
  c. Physical fitness (strength, muscular endurance, agility, speed, balance, and so forth
5. *Functional* academic skills
  a. Reading (all basic skills possible leading to ability to recognize safety words, names, colors, weather, clothing, numbers, food, and "public sign" words)
  b. Writing (all prewriting skills and maximal ability to write such things as name, address, phone number)
  c. Number concepts (time, measurement, money)
6. Recreational/leisure time skills
  a. Ability to participate in bicycling, bowling, hiking, swimming, and other basic recreational pursuits
  b. Knowledge and ability in leisure time pursuits (arts and crafts, music, dancing, various hobbies
7. Vocational ability/economic usefulness
  a. Use of common household items (can opener, dryer, iron, toaster, vacuum cleaner, etc)
  b. Contributions to family (clean floors, wash dishes, fold clothes, set table, wash car, water lawn, etc.)
  c. Use of vocationally related tools (hammer, paint brush, hand saw, screwdriver, etc.)
  d. Work habits and attitudes (adjusting to new assignments, to new co-workers; following verbal instructions, task orientation, acceptance of correction)
  e. Vocationally related academic skills (specific job-related words, knowledge of money, understanding of units of measurement, etc.)
  f. Specific vocational tasks (folding, packaging, sorting, collating, assembling, etc.)
  g. Other independent skills (use of time clock, use of telephone, use of public transportation)

The preceding goals and related areas of curriculum were adapted from Litton (1978, pp. 36-40). The expansion of these topics, using the most appropriate instructional methods and settings, can provide the basis for educational programs for trainable mentally retarded. For some students, some of these goals may be met in a classroom with nonhandicapped students, in these cases, this setting should be used. Many of these goals may be most effectively achieved in a semisegregated or segregated setting. Where this is the case, after development of the IEP and agreement with other staff members and parents, this is the proper setting to be used, and is consistent with the requirements of both federal and state laws and regulations. *Programs for the trainable mentally retarded must be individually planned. The basic abilities and needs of TMR students vary widely; this must be carefully considered in planning.* The fact that a significant percentage of TMR students have one or more other handicaps must also be carefully considered—another reason for careful, individual planning.

SEVERELY RETARDED

The range of mental retardation below the trainable remains less well served, at least by the public schools. According to the AAMD, the more capable of the severely retarded, who do not also have a number of other handicapping conditions, can develop the ability to "perform self help and simple work tasks under supervision." (Grossman, 1977, p. 149) They may, however, be expected to require close continuing supervision throughout life. The "why" of providing training for the severely retarded is obvious—it is a matter of assisting them to develop any potential ability to be productive and to participate in life as fully as possible. The "how" usually includes some of the same methods and approaches used with TMR students. The process will take more time, and tasks may have to be simplified and taken in smaller segments, but training is possible. The "where" is a matter still being decided throughout the nation. There is no question but that the intent of both Public Law 94-142 and many state laws is that they should be trained at public expense. There is evidence that at least some of the severely mentally retarded are being assisted through existing public school programs. (For example, see Gearheart and Litton, 1979, pp. 221-223, for a brief description of the Des Moines, Iowa, program.) However, the question of how to best serve *all* of the severely mentally retarded, including those with various other handicaps, remains to be fully answered. It seems certain that the public schools must play a role, perhaps a major role. It also seems certain that close coordination with other public agencies is necessary, especially in light of the fact that this is a matter of total life planning.

Before closing this consideration of the severely mentally retarded, we should recognize that another, lower level of mental retardation exists. The profoundly mentally retarded are considered to be those whose IQ is more than 5 standard deviations below the norm (i.e., 19 and below on the Stanford-Binet). In the AAMD discussion of this level of mental retardation it is noted that "some . . . may be able to perform simple self help tasks." (Grossman, 1977, p. 149) The line of demarcation between the severe and the profound levels is not really as clear as the definition would lead some to believe. Those familiar with tests such as the Stanford-Binet will recognize that in many cases it will be very difficult to determine whether an individual is profoundly or severely retarded. How an individual functions in a training situation is the real determinant of whether a planned training program will be of benefit. Evidence of this may be inferred from programs in which both the severe and the profound levels of retardation are served. Therefore, many of the statements about where to serve the severely retarded apply to the profoundly retarded.

An educational placement system: application of the variable service continuum concept

In the preceding section we have considered educational programming for the mentally retarded with respect to levels of mental retardation: educable, trainable, and severe. We have noted that the level—as defined by any set of criteria—should not be the only guide to what and how to plan. Such factors as the parents' ability to provide regular effective support, available resources in the immediate area, other handicapping conditions, previous educational experiences, family expectations or attitudes (this may be separate from *ability* to support), and others must be considered. Planning *cannot* be based on a single factor or criterion. It must take into consideration multiple factors and criteria; this is possibly the *only* absolute that may be accepted in the area of planning.

Given the need for consideration of many criteria, we may develop a composite of gen-

Other handicapping conditions

TABLE 9-6
Guidelines for educational placement of the mentally retarded—application of the variable service continuum concept

Level of mental retardation	Preschool	Elementary	Secondary
Educable	Often not identified at this level Enriched environment programs; may be either regular preschool, special program for high-risk children, or combination Parent training important Emphasis on amelioration	Regular class Regular class plus consultative assistance Special class with resource room assistance Special class if multihandicapped or in other unusual situations; more likely to be used after earlier, less segregated efforts prove unsuccessful	Regular class plus resource help Part-time core subjects with special teacher; selected integration in regular class Work-study program in grades 10-12, with limited integration is the most common program for EMRs who still require special assistance at this level
Trainable	Usually identified at this age level Infant stimulation program with other handicapped and with nonhandicapped as possible Parent training *essential* A few TMRs with other handicaps placed in residential setting, but this practice rapidly declining*	Special class with some integrated activities (exception in the case of TMR's whose early childhood program led to near normal developmental levels† A few TMRs with other handicaps or those whose family cannot or will not maintain them in the home placed in residential setting*	Special class in public school Special preparation for sheltered employment In some areas of nation, because of lack of community placement possibilities or inability of parents to maintain, placement in residential setting still utilized*
Severely retarded‡	Almost always identified at this age level Infant stimulation programs, often with other handicapped children Parent training *essential* Placement in residential setting still fairly common*	Special class programs in public school (this provision on increase) Special program in residential setting*	Same as for elementary

*Placement in residential setting *not* a good choice if there are other alternatives. In addition, it must be remembered that "residential" may refer to a small community residential setting.
†In this case placement alternatives similar to those of EMR.
‡Medical needs may have a significant effect on the placement decision, especially at this level.

eral practices to serve as a starting point for planning. As indicated with respect to other handicapping conditions, the concept of providing variable service also implies that different types and levels of service may be necessary for the mentally retarded individual at different times of life, regardless of level of mental retardation. With this caution in mind, the guidelines indicated in Table 9-6 can provide a starting point for planning and illustrate the variety of placement and program possibilities for the mentally retarded.

Summary

Mental retardation is a condition characterized by below-average levels of intelligence and comparably low adaptive behavior. This results in restricted ability to achieve in traditional academic areas and difficulties in abstract thinking. Four levels of mental retardation are recognized by the American Association on Mental Deficiency: mild, moderate, severe, and profound. Educators more often use the terms educable and trainable, rather than mild and moderate, but may at times use the term severe to include both the severe and profound. At this lower end of the continuum there is no established consensus on educational terminology because the schools have not traditionally provided much service for the severely and profoundly retarded.

It is generally accepted that 3 percent of the total population is mentally retarded. At the upper (mild) end of the continuum, such retardation may not be recognized until the

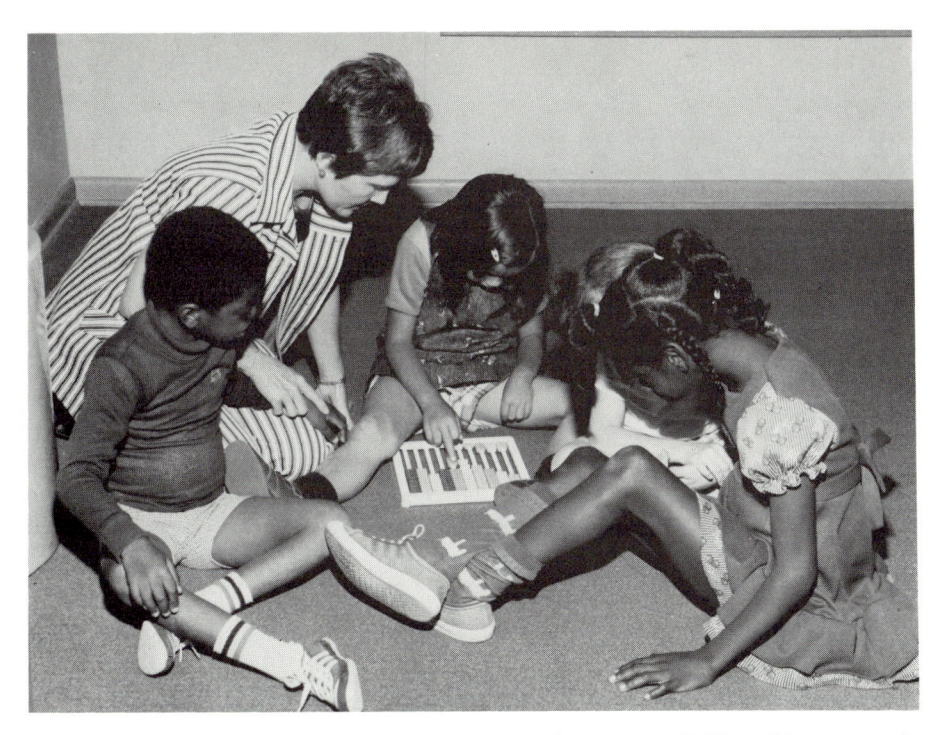

The abacus provides a concrete basis for the development of counting skills and basic number concepts with these trainable mentally retarded children. (From Litton, F. W. *Education of the Trainable Mentally Retarded.* St. Louis: The C. V. Mosby Co., 1978.)

child enters school, but the moderately retarded and those of lower ability levels are usually identified quite early in life. Early identification of young children who are at risk may sometimes result in prevention of mental retardation, depending on the causes.

There are many known causes of mental retardation, but in approximately half of all cases of identified mental retardation the cause *cannot* be determined with certainty. Nevertheless, factors such as rubella (in the mother), Rh-factor incompatibility between mother and infant, and various poisons are known causes. In these causal areas, prevention can be attained. Also, the recognized higher incidence of Down's syndrome among children of older mothers and a variety of genetic information about probabilites of mental retardation under certain conditions have led to greatly increased potential benefits from genetic counseling.

In the public schools, programs for the mentally retarded were initiated at about the beginning of the twentieth century and were primarily for those students we now call educable. For many decades, educable students were served in self-contained special classes, and most school districts essentially ignored all levels of mental retardation below the educable. These children were either kept at home or sent to institutions. Then, starting in the 1940s and 1950s, more and more private classes—often sponsored by a parent group such as the National Association for Retarded Citizens—were initiated.

During the 1960s and early 1970s, many public school systems started classes for the trainable retarded and began to move educable mentally retarded children out of self-contained classes into regular classes, at least on a part-time basis. This trend toward a more normal class environment for the educable mentally retarded was paralleled by "normalization" for many institutionalized adults. In the case of adults, this meant moving back into the community whenever possible. This required the establishment of community support services of many different types, a need that has not yet been fully met in most parts of the nation.

The public schools and all other community state, and federal agencies must work together to prevent mental retardation when possible and to provide an opportunity for maximal development for those who are already mentally retarded. The 1976 report to the President, presented by the President's Committee on Mental Retardation, concluded as follows:

> We ask three final questions:
> - Can mental retardation be significantly diminished as a human problem?
> - Can the mentally retarded person be accepted as a citizen member of the community?
> - Can humane services be so effectively delivered that the retarded person actualizes his full potential for human living?
>
> These questions are the shape of the challenge . . . in the century of decision. (PCMR, 1977, p. 264)

The goal of all who work with or on behalf of the mentally retarded must be to achieve a *yes* to each of these questions. The programs outlined in this chapter and those provided by readers who eventually go into this field of endeavor must be designed to assure these affirmative answers.

focus

introduction

We will see that two major trends in serving the population of handicapped persons (the mentally retarded) are: (1) programming that encourages more normal life activities, be it classroom environment or community participation, and (2) more meaningful attention to the mentally retarded at the lower ranges of intelligence.

early history: an era of superstition

The legal system of the Athenian and Spartan city states dealt severely with mental defectives because societal interest was in developing nations free of defectives. The mentally retarded were thought of as essentially nonhuman and were treated accordingly. They were considered incapable of human feeling and therefore undeserving of human compassion. Extermination was the generally accepted practice.

nineteenth century: the rise of institutions

Early institutions were founded in the hope that the condition of mental retardation might be remediated and patients returned to the community. By the close of the century, it had become clear to most who worked in this field that mental retardation could not be "cured" in the sense that diseases could be cured. The institutional movement provided the base for the next important step, the development of public school classes for the retarded.

twentieth century: development of comprehensive public programs

The move to public school classes in the first half of the century provided for many of the mildly retarded minors of the nation but did not, in most cases address the needs of the moderately or severely mentally retarded. In addition, the lot of most mentally retarded adults (of all levels of severity) was not significantly improved during this time period.

a definition and selected terminology used in mental retardation

"Mental retardation refers to significantly subaverage general intellectual functioning existing concurrently with deficits in adaptive behavior, and manifested during the developmental period." "General intellectual functioning" refers to the results of individual intelligence tests, "significantly subaverage" refers to an IQ of more than 2 standard deviations below the mean for the test, and "developmental period" means between birth and the eighteenth birthday. "Adaptive behavior" is a measure of the degree to which an individual "meets the standards of personal independence and social responsibility expected of his age and cultural group."

systems of classification

Defining mental retardation only according to level or degree of retardation is inadequate for many purposes. A more detailed system of classification is of value for a number of reasons. First, it facilitates research efforts because it permits a more meaningful discussion of incidence, prevalence, characteristics, educational strategies, prevention, and treatment. Second, it makes possible increased precision in communication among professional disciplines that conduct research or provide services for the retarded. Third, classification may aid in understanding the behavior of a child or group of children.

educational classification systems

Educational classifications were established for two primary purposes: instructional grouping and reimbursement. In practice, it was quickly established that other variables, such as chronologic age, mental age, social age, and previous educational experience, must also be carefully considered when establishing instructional objectives.

medical classification systems

Any classification system may be considered arbitrary in that it is based on characteristics chosen by those who established the system. The use of a classification system based on a single criterion is perhaps the least satisfactory because the complexity of the condition of mental retardation almost guarantees that such a system will be meaningless for certain purposes.

prevalence of mental retardation

Although there is considerable indication that socioeconomic status is related to the reported incidence of the educable level of mental retardation, it appears to be unrelated to the incidence of lower levels of mental retardation. Some school areas that include an unusually high percentage of very low income families may report higher prevalence data (here we get into the question of pseudoretardation), but for purposes of educational planning it is fairly safe to assume the 3 percent estimate and plan for twenty-five EMR students, four TMR students, and one severely or profoundly retarded student per 1000 school-age children and youth.

causes of mental retardation

Even with the present state of knowledge about the causes of mental retardation, the cause is unknown in 50 percent of the cases of mental retardation.

infections and intoxications

Infections and intoxications are among the major causes of mental retardation.

Rubella, a viral disease, has been recognized since 1815, but it was not until 1914 that the relationship between birth defects and maternal rubella was demonstrated. If rubella is contracted within the first trimester of pregnancy, the estimate of possible infant birth defects ranges from 50 to 80 percent with an additional 10 to 15 percent of the pregnancies being spontaneously aborted.

There are various types of hemolytic disease of the newborn that may result in mental retardation, but Rh incompatibility occurs most frequently.

Poisons are a much more recently recognized cause of mental retardation. Lead poisoning (plumbism) has received the most widespread attention.

trauma or physical agents

Trauma or physical agents as a cause of mental retardation can be discussed much more briefly than infections and intoxications and many such causes are amenable to prevention. Paradoxically, such retardation may be increasing.

disorders of metabolism and nutrition

One of the most widely known diseases in the field of mental retardation is *phenylketonuria (PKU)*, a metabolic disease. A national screening movement in the mid-1960s resulted in a decreased incidence of retardation caused by PKU, and PKU screening of newborns is now standard procedure for most hospitals. The PKU story should serve as encouragement for more preventive research; it is a symbol of what can be done with sufficient effort and dedication.

Recognized in the early 1900s, *galactosemia* is now known to be an important and partially preventable metabolic cause of mental retardation.

Cretinism (hypothyroidism), one of the more readily recognized metabolic endocrine abnormalities, is caused by a thyroid gland disorder.

gross brain disease

The classification of gross brain disease, recognized by the AAMD, includes a number of hereditary conditions in which tumors appear on the brain and which, for the most part, can be treated only by surgical removal.

chromosomal abnormalities

Chromosome abnormalities are not unusual, and according to Holmes and coworkers (1972), over 90 percent of those fetuses with chromosomal errors are spontaneously aborted. There are many possible causes of chromosomal aberrations, including radiation, drugs, viruses, and gene mutations. However, the one factor most highly correlated with Down's syndrome births is maternal age. The odds that a woman over age 45 will give birth to a Down's syndrome child are over 20 times greater than that of a woman under age 30.

There are, according to reports of the President's Committee on Mental Retardation, some 15,000 children born each year with Down's syndrome. The major hope of preventing Down's syndrome lies with prenatal screening of high-risk mothers and effective genetic counseling.

identification of the mentally retarded

In some cases early identification may lead to special diets or surgical procedures that can reduce or even prevent mental retardation. In others, such as identification of a Down's syndrome infant, the major advantages are the increased chances for an early start in an all-important parent education program and the provision of the earliest possible chance for enrollment in an infant stimulation program.

Identification of moderately or severely mentally retarded individuals of school age is no major problem since they are usually identified prior to school entrance. Identification of the mildly mentally retarded is another matter, with more difficulties in early identification.

Identification of the mildly mentally retarded must be approached with unusual caution because of the variety of factors that can lead to the appearance of mild mental retardation. However, if both IQ and level of adaptive behavior indicate mental retardation and there are no other factors to indicate that this is an erroneous diagnosis, the presence of mental retardation should be accepted and proper educational planning initiated.

education and training of the mentally retarded

Educational programming for the educable mentally retarded can be characterized as being as similar as possible to the "regular" school program, with as much time as possible spent in the regular classroom with nonhandicapped peers.

trainable mentally retarded

All states now have some type of educational programming for the trainable mentally retarded in addition to that provided in the institutional setting, although those programs and services may be provided by an agency other than the public schools or through some sort of cooperative effort.

Programs for the trainable mentally retarded must be individually planned. The basic abilities and needs of TMR students vary widely; this must be carefully considered in planning. The fact that a significant percentage of TMR students have one or more other handicaps must also be carefully considered—another reason for careful, individual planning.

severely retarded

The range of mental retardation below the trainable is one which remains less well served, at least by the public schools.

The question of how to best serve *all* of the severely mentally retarded, including those with various other handicaps, remains to be fully answered. It seems certain that the public schools must play a role, perhaps a major role. It also seems certain that close coordination with other public agencies is necessary, especially in light of the fact that this is a matter of total life planning.

References and suggested readings

American Medical Association. *Mental retardation: a handbook for the primary physician.* Washington, D.C.: AMA, 1965.

Apgar, V., and Beck J. *Is my baby all right? A guide to birth defects.* New York: Trident Press, 1972.

Barr, M. W. *Mental defectives: their history, treatment, and training.* Philadelphia: Blakiston Co., 1913.

Berman, J. L., and Ford, R. Intelligence quotients and intelligence loss in patients with phenylketonuria and some varient states. *Journal of Pediatrics,* 1970, 77, 764-770.

Berry, H. K., and others. New approaches to treatment of phenylketonuria. In *Research to practice in mental retardation: biomedical aspects.* Vol. III. P. Mittler (Ed.). Baltimore: University Park Press, 1977.

Bush, J. W., Chen, M. M., and Patrick, D. L. *Analysis of the New York State PKU screening program using a health status index.* La Jolla, Calif.: University of California Press, 1975.

Challop, R. S. Estimation of childhood lead poisoning in United States—1971. *Mental Retardation,* 1971, 9, 46.

Clark, C. A., and McConnell, R. B. *Prevention of Rh-hemolytic disease.* Springfield, Ill.: Charles C Thomas, Publisher, 1972.

Coulter, W., and Morrow, H. Requiring adaptive behavior measurement. *Exceptional Children,* 1978, 45(2), 133-135.

Davies, S. T. *The mentally retarded in society.* New York: Columbia University Press, 1959.

Doll, E. E. A historical survey of research and management of mental retardation in the United States. In Trapp, P., and Hemelstein, P. (Eds.). *Readings on the exceptional child.* New York: Appleton-Century-Crofts, 1962.

Down, J. L. H. Observations on ethnic classification of idiots. *Clinical Lecture Reports London Hospital,* 1866, 3, 259-262.

Eckstein, H. B. Hydrocephalus. *Nursing Mirror,* Aug. 1966, 122, 10-16.

Gearheart, B., and Litton, F. *The trainable retarded: a foundations approach.* St. Louis: The C. V. Mosby Co., 1979.

Grossman, H. (Ed.). *Manual on terminology and classification in mental retardation.* American Association on Mental Deficiency. Baltimore: Garamond/Pridemark Press, 1977.

Hansen, H., and Hoffman, S. Sex ratio in phenylketonuria. *Lancet,* 1970, 1, 1229.

Holmes, L. B., and others. *Mental retardation: an atlas of diseases with associated physical abnormalities.* New York: The Macmillan Co., 1972.

Hunt, M. M., Sutherland, B. S., and Berry, H. K. Nutritional management in phenylketonuria. *American Journal of Disabled Children,* 1971, 122, 1-6.

Kanner, L. *A history of the care and study of the mentally retarded.* Springfield, Ill.: Charles C Thomas, Publisher, 1964.

Kelly, L., and Vergason, G. *Dictionary of special education and rehabilitation.* Denver: Love Publishing, 1978.

Kott, M. G. The history of mental retardation. In *Mental retardation: readings and resources.* J. H. Rothstein (Ed.). New York: Holt, Rinehart & Winston, Inc., 1971.

Kugel, R., and Wolfensberger, W. (Eds.). *Changing patterns in residential services for the mentally retarded.* Washington, D.C.: President's Committee on Mental Retardation, 1969.

Lindman, F. T., and McIntyre, K. M. *The mentally disabled and the law.* Chicago: The University of Chicago Press, 1961.

Lin-Fu, J. S. Preventing lead poisoning in children. *Children Today,* 1973, 2, 2-6.

Litton, F. *Education of the trainable mentally retarded.* St. Louis: The C. V. Mosby Co., 1978.

Moser, H. W., and Wolf, P. A. *The nosology of mental retardation.* Birth Defects, Original Article Series, vol. 7. Baltimore: The Williams & Wilkins Co., 1971.

Oliver, J. E. Microcephaly following baby battering and shaking. *British Medical Journal,* 1975, 2, 2626-264.

President's Committee on Mental Retardation. *The*

decisive decade. Washington, D.C.: U.S. Government Printing Office, 1971.

President's Committee on Mental Retardation. *Mental retardation, past and present.* Washington, D.C.: U.S. Government Printing Office, January, 1977.

Raiti, S., and Newns, G. H. Cretinism: early diagnosis and its relation to mental prognosis. *Archives of Diseases in Children,* 1971, *46,* 692-694.

Reisman, L. E., and Matheny, A. P. *Genetics and counseling in medical practice.* St. Louis: The C. V. Mosby Co., 1969.

Sarson, S. B., and Doris, J. Psychological problems of mental deficiency. New York: Harper & Row, Publishers, 1969.

Sardharwalla, I. B. Treatment of galactosemia and homocystinuria. In *Early management of handicapping disorders; reviews of research and practice.* T. E. Oppe and F. P. Woodford (Eds.). No. 19. Amsterdam: Associated Scientific Publishers, 1976.

Scheerenberger, R. C. Mental retardation: definition, classification, and prevalence. In *Mental retardation: readings and resources.* J. H. Rothstein (Ed.). New York: Holt, Rinehart & Winston, Inc., 1971.

Smith, D. W., and Wilson, A. A. *The child with Down's syndrome: causes, characteristics and acceptance.* Philadelphia: W. B. Saunders Co., 1973.

Stern, C. *Principles of human genetics.* 3rd ed. San Francisco: Freeman Press, 1973.

Talbot, M. E. *Edouard Sequin: a study of educational approach to the treatment of mentally defective children.* New York: Teachers College, Columbia University Press, 1964.

Tarjan, G., Wright, S. W., Eyman, R. K., and Keeron, C. V. Natural history of mental retardation: some aspects of epidemiology. *American Journal of Mental Deficiency,* 1973, *77,* 369-379.

Wilson, D. (Ed.). Treatment of PKU. *Lancet,* 1970, *1,* 1272-1273.

Whitney, A. E. The ETC of the mentally retarded. *American Journal of Mental Deficiency,* 1954, *59,* 13-25.

The student who is *always* on the fringes of activity may need special help.

chapter 10

Education of children and youth who are emotionally disturbed

by CAROL J. GEARHEART

objectives

To understand the history of the treatment of mental disorders and the early focus on adults.

To explore the manner in which definitions and characteristics of the emotionally disturbed have influenced identification, estimates of prevalence, and treatment.

To describe and discuss several varied theoretical models and the intervention strategies implied by each model.

To consider various educational programs presently in operation in the public schools.

To appreciate the interrelationship between concerns such as juvenile delinquency and child abuse and the more general area of emotional disturbance in children and youth.

Introduction

There have been many attempts to precisely define those behaviors we call "emotional disturbance." By and large, these attempts have been unsuccessful; however, the condition of emotional disturbance is generally agreed to exist. Perhaps one of the major difficulties is that we are also unable to precisely define "normal" behavior; however even if we could, other difficulties would remain. For example, we seem uncertain whether we may simply describe behavior or must also determine an origin or cause for this behavior. A further complication is that the concept of emotional disturbance is such a negative one there is a tendency to avoid considering it at all.

In spite of all these difficulties, the federal government, through the Bureau of Education for the Handicapped, recognizes the existence of emotional disturbance in minors, has supported training programs for teachers of the emotionally disturbed, and provides monetary support for school districts that have special education programs for these students. In addition, all states have some sort of financial support system whereby local districts are encouraged to initiate and continue programs for emotionally disturbed children and youth. Various synonyms are used at the state level but it is agreed that these refer to the same students that federal education officials call emotionally disturbed.

In this chapter we will try to establish some degree of order in this often confusing area of exceptionality. Since there is little agreement in many areas of this field of interest, we will attempt to take an objective view of the various major theoretical approaches and the intervention strategies they seem to suggest.

By Carol J. Gearheart, Ed. D., Associate Professor of Special Education, University of Northern Colorado, Greeley, Colorado.

Prior to such consideration, we will review the general history of this field, with the hope that this may help explain some of the present confusion and diversity. We will briefly consider two topics, juvenile delinquency and child abuse, which have received a great deal of recent attention in the popular press and which may, in some cases, be directly related to emotional disturbance.

Finally, we will consider the matter of appropriate educational placement of the student who is judged to be emotionally disturbed. For the educator, this consideration is of great importance, since it is within this framework that we must provide educational services, regardless of our theoretical leanings.

History

The earliest treatment for mental disorders of which we have knowledge was practiced by Stone Age cave dwellers. This treatment consisted of chipping away a circular portion of the skull until the brain was exposed. This aperture in the skull was to allow the evil spirit to escape. The belief was that once the evil spirit (the cause of the disorder) escaped, the person would no longer demonstrate abnormal behavior. Examination of the skulls of these primitive people indicates that healing took place in some and the individual lived for many years afterward. It is not known whether or not they were "cured" (Selling, 1943).

The writings of the ancient Greeks, Hebrews, and Egyptians contain numerous references to the mentally ill. Generally, the writings infer possession by evil spirits. This is not difficult to understand when it is noted that most incomprehensible events such as earthquakes, lightning, thunder, fire, and physical illness were "explained" by means of good and bad spirits.

During the Golden Age of Greece, some

progress was made in the understanding and treatment of mental disorders. Hippocrates (460–377 BC) has been called the father of modern medicine; he denied the intervention of demons and evil spirits and insisted that mental disorders had natural causes and required treatment just as did other physical illnesses (Lewis, 1941). He further believed that mental disorders were caused by brain pathology.

Hippocrates maintained comprehensive descriptions of his patients, which are surprisingly thorough. It is interesting to note that Hippocrates believed in the importance of dreams in understanding the personality of the patient. In this belief he was anticipating one of the concepts basic to various forms of psychotherapy that were to be further developed in the eighteenth and nineteenth centuries. By encouraging treatment such as regular, tranquil life-styles, vegetable diets, exercise, and abstinence from excess, Hippocrates was in direct opposition to his contemporaries who often practiced exorcism.

Plato (429-347 BC) contended that the mentally ill were not responsible for their acts and if these acts were criminal, the mentally ill should not be punished in the same manner as normal persons. Plato also advocated more humane treatment and emphasized individual differences in intellectual as well as other abilities. He agreed with Hippocrates that dreams were important in understanding an individual's personality.

Later Greek and Roman physicians continued the thought and practice of Hippocrates and Plato. The temples dedicated to Saturn were centers that encouraged humane treatment for the mentally ill. Pleasant surroundings and activities such as parties, walks in the gardens, rowing, and musical concerts were provided. These therapies merged into dieting, massage, gymnastics, education, and hydrotherapy. Occasionally bleeding, restraints, and purging were still employed with the more violent patients (Menninger, 1944).

Asclepiades, Aretaeus, and Galen were among the physicians who made significant contributions to the understanding of mental illness during the period 124 BC to 200 AD. Asclepiades recorded the difference between acute and chronic mental disorders and distinguished between illusions, delusions, and hallucinations. He devised a hammock-like bed whose swaying was considered to be calming to his patients.

It was Aretaeus who provided the first hint that some mental disorders were extensions of the normal psychologic processes. He believed that people who were irritable and violent or unusually joyous and interested in pleasurable activities were prone to the development of mania. Those who were serious and industrious would develop melancholia. Utilizing the information gleaned from his patients, Aretaeus described the various phases of mania and melancholia and considered them as parts of the same illness.

Galen, although not contributing new information to the field of mental illness, performed a major service by compiling, integrating, and systematizing the existing knowledge (Guthrie, 1946). By examining the information made more accessible by this compilation he was able to divide the causes of mental illness into two broad categories: (1) physical, which included alcoholic excess, menstrual changes, and injuries to the head, and (2) mental, which included shock, fear, economic reverses, disappointments in love, and adolescence (Coleman, 1976). Considering the time of his writing, his thoughts are quite advanced. It is important to note here that although significant advances were being made by certain physicians and that humane treatment of the mentally ill was being advocated, the belief in possession by demons or evil spirits continued to be held by many educated people as well as those with much less education.

Many historians consider the collapse of the Roman Empire as the dividing line between ancient and medieval times; however, with the death of Galen in 200 AD the Dark Ages of mental illness began. Advances in the knowledge of causality and humane treatment were forgotten, and those who had continued in the belief in demons and spirits again reigned supreme. The incidence of mental disorders increased during the Middle Ages and there were widespread occurrences of group mental disorders. It was during this historical period that treatment of the mentally ill became the prerogative of the clergy.

During the Middle Ages the clergy attempted to "cure" the mentally ill by a liberal use of prayers, holy water, touching relics, visits to holy places, and the breath and spittle of the priests. Monasteries served as refuges and places of confinement for the mentally ill. Mild forms of exorcism gradually developed into more harsh measures as the populace began to believe more firmly that mental illness was caused by demons and more specifically by the devil inhabiting the body of the ill person. Flogging, starvation, immersion in hot water, and chains were used to either torture the devil enough that he would leave or to punish the person for allowing the devil to inhabit his body.

As is usual during any period when a particular belief or practice dominates, there were quiet dissenters. Paracelsus (1490-1541) was one such dissenter. He rejected witchcraft and demonology, postulated the idea that there could be psychic causes for mental illness, and advocated treatment by "bodily magnetism," later recognized as hypnotism. He also believed that the moon ("lunatic" is derived from the Latin word *luna*, meaning moon) exercised a supernatural influence over the brain.*

Had he been born in another time, Johann Weyer (1515-1588) might have been regarded as the founder of modern psychopathology. He made a careful study of witchcraft and concluded that most if not all those imprisoned, burned, and tortured were actually mentally or physically ill and that great wrongs were being committed against innocent people. Unfortunately, his work was banned by the Church and remained so until the twentieth century.

While the Catholic Church as well as the Protestant churches supported the belief in demons and witchcraft, certain clergymen were in opposition and began to preach that witches are in reality mentally ill people, that mental illness is a disease similar to bodily disease, and that the mentally ill should be treated in a humane and Christian manner.

Continued attacks on the then prevailing ideas concerning possession by demons and witchcraft forced a gradual change in the 1600s and early 1700s, thus paving the way for the later emergence of observation, reason, humanitarian treatment, and the formulation of theoretic models of mental illness.

The emergence of asylums in Europe provided a model for similar types of institutions in the United States. However, in most cases the care afforded the mentally ill left much to be desired. Often these asylums or hospitals were little more than modified penal institutions. The inmates were chained to walls, food was scarce and of poor quality, their heads were shaved, they were given cold baths and

---

*There are current studies that indicate higher rates of crime such as robberies and assaults, more suicides, and increased violent behavior among both the "normal" population and those confined to mental institutions when the moon is full.

were forced to submit to bleeding (Selling, 1943; Deutch, 1946; Coleman, 1976).

Dismayed by the conditions of the asylums in France, Philippe Pinel (1745-1826) received permission to begin various experiments with the inmates. His plan was to remove all chains, provide the inmates with nutritious and sufficient food, and treat them with kindness. His experiment led to drastic changes in the behavior of the patients. He was soon given charge of the Salpetriere Hospital as well as the Bicetre. His successor, Jean Esquirol (1772-1840), continued this humane treatment at Salpetriere and established several new hospitals employing the same methods.

While Pinel was reforming the care provided for the mentally ill in France, William Tuke was establishing similar hospitals in England. Trained women nurses were employed with the belief that the care women could provide would be even more humanitarian. These innovations, quite revolutionary for that time, were not only improving the care of the mentally ill but also slowly changing the attitudes of the public (Kauffman, 1977).

In 1790, Jean Itard, one of Pinel's students, attempted to train the "Wild Boy of Aveyron," a boy about 12 who was captured from the forests. He was unable to speak, responded to food only by smell, and lacked any of the characteristics of "civilized" people (for further details, see pp. 249-250). Pinel, widely recognized as France's leading authority on the mentally ill, pronounced the boy an idiot (a term used to describe the mentally retarded). Itard disagreed with Pinel, believing that the boy suffered from cultural deprivation rather than retardation. The sensory stimulation and techniques for speech formation that Itard used, produced some changes in the boy but not enough for Itard to regard his work as successful. Itard returned to his work with the deaf, feeling he had failed.

However, Edouard Seguin, who had worked with Itard, believed that such educational practices could benefit the retarded and at the invitation of Samuel Gridley Howe emigrated to America (Hoffman, 1974). (A review of the writing of various authorities in the early nineteenth century reveals a blur between mental retardation and the mentally ill. Many descriptions of nineteenth century idiocy are recognizable by today's readers as descriptions of psychosis or autism.)

Prior to Seguin's emigration to the United States, Benjamin Rush (1745-1813), influenced by reports of Pinel's and Tuke's experiments, was revolutionizing the treatment of mental patients in the United States. His encouragement of humane treatment, writings on psychiatry, and organization of the first American course on psychiatry have earned for him the title of father of American psychiatry. He advocated the abolition of cruel punishments and supported more humane methods of behavior control. Because of his efforts and those of others, "moral therapy" became an established means of dealing with the mentally ill in the early part of the twentieth century (Coleman, 1976; Kauffman, 1977).

Dorothea Dix (1802-1887), a former Sunday school teacher for female prisoners, followed the pioneer efforts of Dr. Rush in advocating change in the treatment of the mentally ill. In 1843 she reported to the Massachusetts legislature (one of the more progressive states in regard to treatment of the retarded, deaf, or blind) of conditions she found in her work. She reported persons being kept in barns, chained to stalls, and put in cages. Part of her solution was to provide separate structures for the mentally ill; to remove them from jails and almshouses (these latter were barracks-like buildings in which the poor or cast-offs of society were kept). Her efforts in changing the treatment that was accorded the mentally ill were so widely recognized that the United States Congress presented a resolution that characterized her as an outstanding example of humanitarianism.

Over the next few decades the prevailing trend was to provide special buildings or asylums for the mentally ill. Most were poorly constructed; however, they were an improvement over jails and almshouses. Educative or rehabilitative programs were nearly nonexistent; for the most part these institutions were custodial.

As noted previously, in early efforts to provide services for the mentally ill little differentiation was made between the mentally retarded and the mentally ill. However, the overall tenor was optimistic. The general view was that both the retarded and mentally ill were victims of environment. It was believed that if mentally ill students were provided with sensory stimulation (music to develop auditory powers, manipulation of objects of various shapes and colors to develop visual abilities), individualized instruction, and a teacher who was sincerely interested in them, they could be prepared to later take their place as contributing members of society.

In the case of the more severely disturbed, "reformatories" or "houses of refuge" were established. At their inception these institutions were not meant to be punitive but rather intended to reform and educate the socially maladjusted. In 1846 the first state educational facility for "the socially maladjusted and incorrigible" was opened in Westborough, Massachusetts. Dr. Samuel Howe was directly involved in obtaining funds and establishing the educational philosophy for the school. It was intended that this school and others like it would accept destructive and aggressive children, teach them by providing proper parental role models and much guidance, and later graduate them as decent members of society (Hoffman, 1974). As institutions became more numerous these optimistic hopes did not materialize. Large enrollments and the lack of proper parental models were cited as reasons.

At this same time another force began to affect the treatment of mentally retarded and mentally ill. Darwin had published his *Origin of the Species*, which emphasized heredity and a biologic view of human beings. Spokesmen for social darwinism foretold the destruction of society in the unchecked propogation of lower classes and defective individuals. An explanation accepted by many was that undesirable behavior represented inherited flaws; giving such people instruction and providing institutions for them merely perpetuated the problem; the solution was selective breeding (Kauffman, 1977). Thus the nineteenth century closed with a pessimistic view of the education of the mentally ill. Humane treatment seemed to be almost forgotten; institutions in existence provided impersonal custodial care.

Between 1852 and 1918 all states enacted some type of compulsory education law. Children who up until this time may have not attended school because of their behavior were now compelled to attend. Schools were forced to provide at least minimal education for the mentally ill. Special schools and classrooms were established to meet this responsibility. However, little distinction was made between mentally ill, mentally retarded, or immigrant children whose only problem was an inability to speak English; these classrooms were often merely holding areas.

Among the earliest efforts by the public schools to provide educational services for disruptive children was the establishment of ungraded schools. Such schools were established in New Haven, Connecticut, in 1871, in New York in 1874, and in Cleveland in 1875 (Hoffman, 1974). Several other school districts followed their lead.

During the last decades of the nineteenth century there were relatively few innovations regarding the education of the emotionally disturbed in the public schools; however, a number of other events were taking place that would influence education in the years following World War I.

Clifford Beers, a Yale graduate who had experienced a nervous breakdown and recovered, published *A Mind that Found Itself* in which he described the treatment he had received. His book influenced public opinion and elicited the interest of other prominent mental health personnel. Beers, along with Adolf Meyer, who was known as dean of American psychiatry, and psychologist William James, founded the National Committee for Mental Hygiene in 1909. The mental hygiene movement resulted in efforts in early detection and prevention including the establishment of some programs in schools and the opening of child guidance clinics. Thus the contemporary mental health movement began.

That same year the Juvenile Psychopathic Institute was established to study juvenile delinquency from the psychologic and sociologic points of view. The research conducted by individuals involved with the institute influenced the treatment of juvenile delinquents for many years (Healy, 1915; Kauffman, 1977).

The development of intelligence and psychologic testing evolved into educational practices in use today. Psychologists were employed by school districts to administer and interpret the various psychologic and IQ tests. Information from such assessments was usually used in the determination of the placement of a student in a special class or program and/or in providing the student with vocational advice. Present-day counselors may be primarily vocational advisors or employ counseling therapies or practice some combination of both (Hoffman, 1974; Kauffman, 1977).

The 1920s and 1930s were characterized by attempts to establish classification systems, describe characteristics, and define emotional disturbance. The literature on children's behavior grew in size and quality (Baker and Stullken, 1938). Surveys of teachers' attitudes were completed and attempts were made to estimate the prevalence of children with behavior disorders. Various experimental educational plans, such as special rooms, schools, classes, and consultative help, were initiated (Kauffman, 1977).

Efforts to unify the various services available to emotionally disturbed youngsters were attempted. One such effort was the establishment of the Bureau of Child Guidance in New York City. The bureau was administratively under the board of education with the goal of meeting the emotional and psychologic needs of school-age youngsters. In practice this meant that school psychologists, counselors, social workers, and consulting psychiatrists would pool their knowledge about certain children and, hopefully, devise some unified plan of action that would enable the student to function more successfully in the school system. A slight variation, which included the police, was established in New Jersey in the late 1930s. In this case adolescents were the primary target population. The Children's Bureau, as it was named, was a coordinating agency that served to bring schools, courts (because of various forms of delinquency), police, psychiatrists, and psychologists together to provide unified rehabilitation services to students who had commited crimes, were truant, or were unable to function successfully in schools. These models in a wide variety of modified forms are present today in urban areas. The value of these bureaus is questioned by some who believe the red tape created by increased bureaucratization serves as a detriment to actually assisting those who are in most need of the services.

From the close of World War I to the late 1930s classes for the emotionally disturbed were begun primarily in the urban areas. More often than not these classes were called "disciplinary classes" with teachers selected because they were known to be strong disciplinarians. Employing trained teachers was no easy task; in 1953 while forty colleges and universities offered teacher training programs for the mentally retarded, only ten offered courses for teachers of the emotionally disturbed (Hoffman, 1974).

In 1946, New York City organized special schools for the emotionally disturbed or socially maladjusted, which became known as "600 Schools." Although it was intended that these schools be therapeutic environments, they actually were custodial institutions with minimal rehabilitative effort provided. These schools have undergone various reorganization efforts and name changes, but there are various indications that little of substance has changed over the years. Thus educational programs for the emotionally disturbed remained sparse, variably effective, and largely unorganized until the late 1960s.

Early in the 1960s events took place that were to dramatically affect teacher preparation and, in turn, programs for the emotionally disturbed. The first was passage in 1963 of PL 88-164, the Mental Retardation Facilities and Community Mental Health Centers Construction Act. This provided the federal dollars to establish local mental health centers, which led to the provision of varying amounts of assistance for the mentally ill of all ages.

Also included in PL 88-164 was a provision for training professional personnel in all recognized categories of handicap, including funds for training teachers of emotionally disturbed children. With more trained personnel available, school districts were now able to establish programs for children who were emotionally disturbed. The establishment of classes for the emotionally disturbed continued until the early 1970s, when the newly recognized field of learning disabilities became prominent. It was at this time that students who were emotionally disturbed and were academically below their grade level were more often labeled "learning disabled." This was partially because of the relative ease with which parents could accept this label as opposed to "emotionally disturbed." (Parental guilt feelings on having supposedly caused the emotional problems of their children is at least part of the basis for a general distaste for the label "emotionally disturbed".) It was not until the late 1970s that school districts again attempted to meet the specific needs of the emotionally disturbed; PL 94-142 with its emphasis on an individual educational program for each child played an important role in this change.

The roots of the psychoanalytically oriented theories used as the basis for education of the disturbed child were established primarily during the 1940s and 1950s. The 1960s and 1970s gave rise to behaviorally, sociologically, ecologically, and humanistically oriented intervention strategies. These theories received such nationwide acceptance that some felt compelled to resist them and to begin what are presently referred to as countertheories. These widely divergent theories will be discussed in the theoretical models section of this chapter.

In summary, the treatment of the mentally ill has vacillated from humane to inhumane through the centuries. The mentally ill were regarded as witches and as such were subjected to various forms of torture. The 1800s ushered in a time period during which attempts to provide at least custodial care for the emotionally disturbed were initiated; asylums and institutions were to serve this function. The nineteenth and twentieth centuries brought increased awareness of disturbance in children, and compulsory education laws influenced the establishment of more programs for disturbed youngsters. Various individuals began to study children's behavior and formulate theories that became the basis for the major educational strategies in use today. The past 20 to 30 years have been a time of accelerated interest and expanding scope in programs for disturbed students.

Definitions, characteristics, and prevalence

In the remainder of this chapter we will use the term "emotionally disturbed." This does not imply that "emotionally disturbed" is a more widely accepted term than others but its use will simplify reading. In this section we will attempt to define emotional disturbance, outline the characteristics of emotionally disturbed youngsters, and provide an estimate of the numbers of emotionally disturbed children who need special assistance. In the program publicity prepared for the 1979 meeting of the American Orthopsychiatric Association, the officers of this professional organization noted that although much study and writing had been accomplished, there was no comprehensive, generally accepted definition of emotional disturbance. They further asked the rhetorical question, "Can we reach a workable definition?" Shea (1978) observes that there appear to be as many definitions of emotional disturbance as there are persons who write about them and that the definitions tend to reflect the purposes for which the author is writing. According to Shea, definitions are also influenced by the discipline of the author (educator, psychiatrist, clinical psychologist, etc.) and his or her theoretical perspective (biophysical, psychodynamic, behaviorist, humanist).

Among the reasons cited for the lack of a universally accepted definition of emotional disturbance are *absence of agreement* on the following: (1) agreed upon terminology or even descriptive phrases that mean the same thing to all people; (2) the degree of maladjustment needed to "qualify" one as emotionally disturbed, and (3) the number of inappropriate behaviors required to merit the label "emotionally disturbed."

With even a general perusal of the literature the reader will note terms such as emotionally disturbed, behavior disordered, mentally ill, autistic, socially handicapped, maladjusted, socially maladjusted, mentally disturbed, phobic, psychotic, schizophrenic, emotionally and behaviorally disordered, etc. The list could go on and on. Usually, the authors of articles or books decide on a particular label and define it according to their purpose, thus laying to rest this troublesome issue. However, most definitions are subject to additional interpretation by the reader, and confusion can arise regarding the degree of each characteristic needed to determine emotional disturbance. For example, Lambert and Bower (1976) along with many others suggest that an inability to form interpersonal relationships characterizes the emotionally disturbed. The reader may well ask, "Does this mean no relationships or only one or two?" Woody (1969) defined the emotionally disturbed as one who does not adjust to the socially accepted norms of behavior and thereby disrupts his or her own learning or that of classmates. Again, the reader may question what precisely are "socially accepted norms" and how much does one have to "not adjust"? This is not to disparage the efforts of the various persons who have attempted to define emotionally disturbed, rather, it is to indicate the impreciseness of present definitions. A further compounding factor in arriving at a universal definition is

Other handicapping conditions

that of degree. Wolman (1976) states, "The difference between so-called normal and abnormal behavior is a matter of degree. Every human being is occasionally irrational, some people are more often so than others. Some people are so irrational that they need help in adjusting to life." (p. 9) In a similar vein, Reinert (1976) indicates that an individual's adjustive resources (ability to cope) and the amount of stress present at any given time may affect the emotional stability of that person. Some children live with (what seems to most of us) a great deal of stress and yet never receive the label emotionally disturbed, while others who seem to have little stress are soon categorized by those who must deal with them as emotionally disturbed.

Since many leaders in this field have offered definitions (all with some merit), we will include several that might be considered representative and conclude with the characteristics generally found in state definitions, since these will be especially important to those who may be considering the profession of teacher of the emotionally disturbed. Additional definitions appropriate to the specific theoretical approaches to emotional disturbance will be noted as the various theories are discussed in later sections of this chapter.

Lambert and Bower (1976):

"The emotionally handicapped child is defined as having moderate to marked reduction in behavioral freedom, which in turn, reduces his ability to function effectively in learning or working with others." (p. 95)

Kirk (1972):

"A behavior disorder . . . is defined as a deviation from age-appropriate behavior which significantly interferes with (1) the child's own growth and development and/or (2) the lives of others." (p. 389)

Kauffman (1977):

"Children with behavior disorders are those who chronically and markedly respond to their environment in socially unacceptable and/or personally unsatisfying ways but who can be taught more socially acceptable and personally gratifying behavior . . ." (p. 23)

Reinert (1976):

"Children in conflict . . . describes the children being served in school programs. These children are in conflict (nothing more or less) with their environment. They might be having a relationship problem with their teacher or a peer, they might be in conflict with themselves, or they may be victims of uncontrollable circumstances in their homes." (p. 6)

Morse (1975):

" . . . a disturbed pupil is one who is persistently unable to cope with a reasonable school environment even though expectations are geared to his age and potential. . . . The specific patterns or manifestations of disturbance are many and range in depth . . ." (p. 556)

CHARACTERISTICS

These and other similar definitions could easily lead to some confusion in interpretation by educators who must deal with such students in the public school setting. Therefore, in an attempt to further clarify the situation, most state education agencies have developed a list of characteristics believed to be common to emotionally disturbed children and youth, as defined in that particular state. These characteristics, in composite, should be of some assistance in describing behavior that is common in those students who have been called emotionally disturbed. *It must be very specifically noted that the characteristics listed are commonly found in students who have been identified as emotionally disturbed, but the presence of one, two, or several of these characteristics does not mean that the student exhibiting these characteristics is emotionally disturbed.* The following list is a compilation of characteristics mentioned in various state regulations or guidelines.

Characteristics of emotionally disturbed children*

    Avoids contact with others
    Avoids eye contact
    Behavior that is ritualistic
    Chronically disobedient
    Covert or overt hostility
    Disorganized in routine tasks or spatial orientation
    Displays temper tantrums
    Disturbances of sleep or eating habits
    Emotional isolation
    Exaggerated or bizarre mannerisms
    Few or no friends
    Frequent and/or persistent verbalizations about suicide
    Frequent illnesses
    Frequent unexplained crying
    Frustration level is low
    Hyperactivity
    Inability to complete tasks
    Inappropriate verbalizations and noises
    Inattentive
    Inconsistent in academic performance
    Inconsistent in friendships
    Lethargic
    Out of touch with reality
    Physical withdrawal from touch
    Physically aggressive to others or property
    Rapid and severe changes of mood
    Refuses responsibility for actions
    Requires constant reassurance
    Repetitive behavior
    Seeks attention
    Self-mutilating
    Self-stimulating
    Severe reactions to change in usual schedule
    Sexual deviations
    Truant
    Unexplainable "accidents"
    Unexplained academic decline
    Unmotivated
    Unreasonable and/or unexplainable fears
    Verbally aggressive
    Verbally disruptive

PREVALENCE

The major problem affecting an accurate estimation of the prevalence of emotional disturbance in school-age children is the lack of consensus regarding a definition that includes clear, specific characteristics. The lack of acceptable, standardized tools for diagnosis of emotional disturbance is another closely related problem. Some estimates of prevalence are as low as 0.05 percent (Kauffman, 1977); others are as high as 81.5 percent (Wolman, 1976). More realistic figures range from a conservative 2 percent (U.S. Office of Education, 1975) to 10 percent (Bower, 1969). In their report prepared for the Joint Commission on the Mental Health of Children, Glidewell and Swallow (1968) indicate that 30 percent of the elementary school-age youngsters demonstrate at least mild adjustment problems, 10 percent of the total school population may require professional services, and 2 to 3 percent may require full-time services. More will be said about this later in the chapter.

Regardless of the difficulties encountered in attempting to "count" emotionally disturbed children, teachers are surprisingly accurate in their assessment of the emotional status of the students when compared to the psychologists' and psychiatrists' designations of emotionally disturbed children (Bower, 1969). This does not imply that all tests or other assessment tools should be eliminated or that children are emotionally disturbed *because* their teacher says they are, but rather that teachers *on the whole* can effectively des-

---

*A compilation of characteristics appearing in the regulations of various state guidelines for the placement of children in programs for the emotionally disturbed.

ignate which children may need special services. It seems clear that boys outnumber girls in being considered behavior problems. Boys tend to exhibit aggressive behavior patterns while girls, especially as they become older, show increasing personality problems (Quay, 1972).

Clarizio and McCoy (1976), after reviewing a number of longitudinal studies, concluded that about 30 percent of the children treated for emotional disturbance would continue manifesting some moderate to severe mental problems as adults, while 70 percent would lead normal adult lives. They stated that severe cases of aggression, antisocial, and acting-out behaviors persist into adulthood while shyness and withdrawal tend to decrease.

Although children regarded as emotionally disturbed are generally from 1 to 2 years behind their peers academically, various investigations have shown that their intelligence roughly corresponds to that found in the school population (Shea, 1978). It must be noted, however, that at times it is difficult to ascertain a realistic intelligence quotient (usually accepted as a predictor of school success) because emotionally disturbed youngsters often exhibit behaviors that make test results questionable (i.e., withdrawal, hyperactivity, inattentiveness).

We may conclude our consideration of prevalence by stating that most authorities in the field would agree to an estimate of at least 2 to 3 percent as definitely emotionally disturbed and, following the lead of Glidewell and Swallow (1968), there may be an additional 7 to 8 percent who will require some less intensive professional services. This need for differing types and degrees of service will be further addressed in a later section on various service delivery methods or models. First, we will review the major theoretical models that provide the bases for therapeutic and remedial techniques.

Theoretical models and related interventions

In this section we will consider the various conceptual models that have been used to describe the causes of emotional disturbance and the various interventions that may be utilized under each theoretical rubric. These will be brief overviews to provide the beginner in the field of special education with a "feel" for the diverse approaches to emotional disturbance. The suggested readings at the close of the chapter list sources that will be valuable to the reader desiring more detailed information.

Rhodes (1974) identifies five major theoretical concepts regarding emotional disturbance. These are not mutually exclusive nor are they exhaustive; they do, however, serve as a starting point. Included are biophysical, psychodynamic, behavioral, sociologic, and ecologic. The historical roots, basic tenets, and examples of classroom application will be considered with respect to each of these theoretical models.

BIOPHYSICAL THEORY

As modern experimental science became prominent during the eighteenth century, the knowledge of chemistry, physiology, and neurology increased rapidly. These advances gradually led to a better understanding of the organic pathology underlying many physical ailments. It was hoped that similar discoveries could be made that would link brain pathology to emotional disturbance in a simple cause-effect relationship.

As early as 1757, Albrecht von Haller, in *Elements of Physiology*, emphasized the importance of the brain in functioning of an individual and advocated the postmortem analysis of brains. It was not until 1845 that a systematic presentation of the organic viewpoint was published by William Griesinger in *The Pathology and Therapy of Psychic Disor-*

ders. Griesinger emphasized that psychiatry should examine the physiologic and that mental disorders could be explained by brain pathology. Emil Kraepelin, in 1883, hypothesized that mental illness was a disease that followed patterns similar to those followed by chickenpox or diphtheria. He proceeded to classify these types of mental illness, which became the basis for present-day classifications. This provided widespread speculation that specific causes for mental illness could be discovered and that the illness would follow a predictable course, although the cure for it might not be known (Coleman, 1976). Significant advances in medical science were made, such as the discovery of specific drugs that either prevented or negated the effects of paresis (a mental disorder that generally brought about death), leading many to believe that all variations in behavior could be related to organic disorders within the individual. However, it is likely that there are more authorities in the field of emotional disturbance who discredit this assumption than there are those who accept it (Kauffman, 1977).

Among the biologic factors usually mentioned as influencing the behavior of individuals are: brain damage and/or dysfunction, genetic blueprints, and biochemical imbalances.

Brain damage or dysfunction can occur at any point in life—before birth, during the birth process, or by accident or disease anytime during the life cycle. Brain dysfunction is a term used to describe the brain which apparently has not been damaged but seems not to function properly. Generally, there is little hard evidence that "proves" dysfunction; that is, lesions or other damage cannot be located. Bender (1952), a leader in the field of childhood disorders, has proposed the existence of developmental failure in the nervous system of the emotionally disturbed, which implies the cessation of normal growth patterns so that the child remains immature in certain behavior patterns. The failure is caused by some biologic crisis, such as severe illness or accident which results in poor attention and inadequate perceptual and/or motor skills, which in turn reduces adaptability, creates frustration, and increases anxiety.

Rimland (1969), as a result of his work with severely disturbed children, believes a particular portion of the brain may have been injured in infancy, which prevents the child from relating current and past experiences. Thus the world in which the child lives is ever new and frightening, leading to somewhat bizarre behavior. Rimland further believes that the external environment is unimportant; other authorities disagree, proposing that although some inherent organic predisposition can reside within the individual, the external environment must be such that it contributes to the maladjustment of the individual (Rosenthal, 1963).

Genetic blueprinting is another type of biophysical theory. The reader may recall that the genes carry the "blueprints" for such inherited factors as color of eyes and hair, whether or not an individual will have freckles, and so forth. Certain mental retardation syndromes also have been linked to genetic determination. Direct genetic determination of mental illness has not been proved; however, research indicates an increase in the risk of certain mental illnesses (schizophrenia and psychosis) when individuals have relatives with such conditions. The closer the relationship, the more likely the child will develop the disorder. Environment and interpersonal factors can affect the degree to which the condition manifests itself, but they alone cannot explain the heightened risk (Kauffman, 1977). Some authorities (Rosenthal, 1963; Pollin, 1972) believe that there is an inherited predisposition to behavioral disorders; however, some external catalyst is necessary for the condition to become manifest.

The research in this area seems to proceed slowly in spite of technologic advances because genetic study is a life-long task. In addition, the researcher is unable to control the life-style and relationships of the child, thus failing to control external factors as they influence the development of the individual (Reinert, 1976).

Biochemical imbalances are the third type of biophysical causation we will consider here. Toxic substances, deficiencies or abnormally high amounts of vitamins, minerals, or metals, malnutrition, and other similar imbalances are believed by some to be related to emotional disturbance (Coleman, 1976). Although there are no proved cause-effect relationships, Coleman (1976) indicates that with the reduction of certain minerals and/or the increase of certain vitamins, the behavioral manifestations of emotional disturbance can be alleviated. Malnutrition, if left untreated, can result in social withdrawal and school failure (Cravioto and others, 1967).

The biophysical approach is the oldest theoretical approach to emotional disturbance and there may be, as the science advances, significant breakthroughs that will benefit severely disturbed youngsters. Although there is evidence suggestive of a biologic etiology in emotional disturbance, there is no conclusive evidence of a direct cause and effect. In some cases there is a known biologic cause; however, this cannot be generalized to other youngsters exhibiting similar behavioral disorders. The most accepted view is that biologic and environmental factors interact and that both may be manipulated to exacerbate the disorders.

Interventions. If a biologic cause of emotional disturbance is suspected, the interventions are essentially medical. These might include modified nutrition and diet, megavitamin therapy, or medication. The teacher of the emotionally disturbed must be prepared to cooperate with the various professionals to provide the best education for the youngsters in their charge. If brain damage is suspected, emphasis might be on order and routine in the daily schedule, a reduction of extraneous environmental stimuli, and a sequential, detailed approach to learning tasks.

PSYCHOANALYTIC THEORIES

Under this umbrella term we find many variations of systematic attempts to show how psychologic processes result in mental illnesses of various dimensions. Individuals such as C. G. Jung, Alfred Adler, Carl Rogers, and Frederick Perls, who are known for their development of apparently diverse theoretical approaches to mental illness, are considered psychodynamic theorists (Fine, 1973). However, credit for the initial development of psychodynamic thought must go to Sigmund Freud.

During Freud's lifetime (1856-1939) the view that emotional disturbance was caused by some organic pathology was predominant; however, toward the end of the nineteenth century, researchers such as Jean Charcot and Joseph Breuer began experiments with hypnosis and the "cathartic method" (Coleman, 1976). Breuer urged his patients to discuss their problems under hypnosis, which not only relieved the tensions of the patient but also provided Breuer with considerable insight regarding the nature of the difficulties that brought about the neurotic symptoms. Freud found he could dispense with hypnosis and that his patients could overcome the inner obstacles and discuss their problems freely. He renamed the cathartic method "free association" and prescribed a set of principles that were involved in analyzing and interpreting what the patient had said. This was later called "psychoanalysis." Freud spent the rest of his life developing and refining the psychoanalytic process. His introduction of this procedure in the United States in 1909 led to a great deal of controversy including considerable negative publicity. Psychoanalysis was slowly accepted, and in the 1950s and early 1960s it (or certain variations) was the predominant therapy for emotionally disturbed children (Shea, 1978).

Psychoanalytic theory is too complex to be fully explained here; for students interested in becoming teachers of the emotionally disturbed, this topic will be dealt with in some depth in the introductory or methods classes. However, a brief summary will be presented in order for the reader to gain an appreciation of the contributions this approach has made. It might be added here that most teachers, even those who maintain they are strict behaviorists, utilize at least some of the principles of psychodynamic theory.

According to Freud, the maturing child undergoes a series of psychosexual stages of development before reaching adulthood. These stages (oral, anal, phallic, and latency) represent biologic maturation as well as phases in the sexual and aggressive instincts that play an important part in shaping the personality of an individual. Each stage of development places demands on the individual that must be met and arouses conflicts that must be resolved. If the demands are not met or conflicts are not resolved, the personality of the individual may be affected and/or he may become fixated at that level. An example of becoming fixated at the oral stage would be an adult who is prone to excessive eating or drinking.

Another prominent characteristic of the psychoanalytic model is the concept of anxiety. This may be a warning of impending danger and is a painful experience, so it forces the individual to take some corrective measure to alleviate the pain. If the ego is sufficiently strong, it can cope with the fear or danger by rational measures. In the case of the emotionally disturbed, the ego is rarely strong, and irrational protective measures are taken. These measures are usually referred to as defense mechanisms. They alleviate the pain but do so by distorting reality instead of dealing directly with the problem. An emotionally disturbed person may feel inadequate or have no sense of self-worth. Unable to either deal with the pain or to rationally examine the reasons for the feelings of worthlessness, the person may turn to fantasy and imagine himself performing great feats or (in extreme cases) actually believe that he is some well-known and admired personality. Many of the stereotypic jokes about mentally ill persons imagining themselves to be Napoleon or Jesus have their basis in this theoretical concept as well as reality.

A third important concept in psychoanalytic theory is the role of the unconscious. Freud believed that the conscious is merely the tip of the iceberg, with the unconscious being the submerged portion. The unconscious includes hurtful memories, forbidden desires, and unpleasant experiences that are excluded from the conscious. These memories, feelings, and desires, although the individual is unaware of them, continue to seek expression and will be reflected in fantasies or dreams. This will also lead to irrational and maladaptive behavior until it is brought to the awareness and integrated into the ego structure. The concept of free association, mentioned earlier, has as part of its purpose the bringing of this unconscious material to the awareness of the individual so that it can be resolved satisfactorily.

Psychoanalytic theory places a great deal of emphasis on early relationships within the family unit. Proponents of this theory believe that the influence of mother, father, and siblings is exerted through unconscious processes in which the child's behavioral and (often) academic problems represent symbolic attempts to defend against anxiety or other conflicts.

Interpretations of behavior based on the psychoanalytic model are often criticized as being too subjective. Most support for the psychoanalytic viewpoint is based on anecdotal rather than empirical data (Kauffman, 1977). Although many of Freud's ideas have been revised, his contributions to an increased understanding of emotional disturbance made such an impact on the field that psychoanalytic thought dominated until the middle of the twentieth century.

Interventions. Ordinarily, teachers do not follow a strict psychoanalytic approach in dealing with emotionally disturbed children since this rightly is the domain of psychiatrists and psychologists. However, children who are in classrooms for the emotionally disturbed may be receiving the services of a psychiatrist who utilizes the psychoanalytic approach. As has been stated, there are many widely used variations that may be employed by the psychiatrist so the fact that a particular child is receiving individual therapy does not necessarily indicate a "pure" psychoanalytic treatment. The teacher will want to work as closely as possible with the psychiatrist. Valuable insights regarding the behavioral problems of the child can be gained if a cooperative relationship exists.

Many teachers of the emotionally disturbed employ variations of the psychoanalytic approach in their classrooms. Building a warm, accepting relationship between the child and the teacher so that the child will feel free enough to act out his impulses is one application. Depending upon the child's age a variety of play therapy approaches might also be utilized. Providing music or art activities that allow the child to express angry, withdrawn, or hostile feelings is another variation. Whatever the medium used, the concern is for the unconscious feelings and motivations and the symbolic meaning of the child's behavior. Following this model the teacher views his or her responsibility as enabling the child to overcome these underlying conflicts.

BEHAVIORAL MODEL

While Freud was formulating his views on mental illness, the foundations of the behaviorist model were being laid by a Russian, Ivan Pavlov (1849-1936). During his studies on salivary responses in dogs he noted that when taxed beyond their abilities the dogs would become uncooperative. Using this seemingly unimportant factor, Pavlov began a whole new research attack on the study of abnormal behavior. He speculated that persons of various personality types would, in the event of mental illness, develop predictable abnormal responses. (For example, quiet types would be prone to become obsessive—compulsive and schizophrenic.) Continued research of his hypothesis on the human level did not prove definitive; however, his postulations provided the emphasis needed for a vast amount of research in psychopathology.

An American psychologist, eager to raise psychology to the level of a science, seized upon the pioneer work of Pavlov. J. B. Watson (1878-1958) changed the research focus of mental illness from the study of inner psychic processes to the study of outer, objectively observable behavior, an approach he termed "behaviorism." Watson demonstrated through his research that irrational fears could be learned by conditioning. His now famous experiment included teaching Albert, a small boy, to fear a white rabbit by striking a steel bar with a hammer each time he reached for the rabbit. In time, Albert generalized this fear to all white furry animals. Later experiments with another subject, Peter, indicated that this fear could be reversed. By placing a white rabbit in the far end of the room while

Peter was eating (a pleasurable activity) and gradually moving it closer over a period of time, Peter overcame his fear of white rabbits and eventually his generalized fear of white furry animals (Coleman, 1976). It was therefore concluded that we might eliminate irrational fears by conditioning with little or no attention to the subconscious. This type of conditioning, termed classical conditioning, accounts for much learning especially during infancy and childhood. It can be adaptive, as when fear of actually hurtful things is learned, or maladaptive as when irrational fears are learned.

B. F. Skinner (1904-   ), often considered the foremost authority on behaviorism, formulated a second key concept—*operant conditioning*. He concluded on the basis of his studies that the most understandable determinants of behavior lie outside the individual and that these can be manipulated to control behavior (Skinner, 1953). The individual "operates" on or modifies that environment while seeking some goal. The goal may be avoiding something aversive or seeking a reward.

Behaviorists tend to believe that the unacceptable behaviors of emotionally disturbed youngsters are learned and in some way are rewarding to them, that these behaviors somehow enable them to reach their goal. In order to eliminate the unacceptable (to others) behavior, the environment must be "operated" on so that it no longer serves as a reward or reinforcement to the individual.

The behaviorist theory has several principles of reinforcement as well as schedules for reinforcement and types of reinforcement to establish and maintain a particular behavior. All of these will not be discussed here; however, an example will provide sufficient insight for an introduction to this aspect of behaviorism.

Let us assume that an emotionally disturbed child often fights with other children. The teacher gives him a piece of candy when he is observed to be not fighting. The teacher continues to give the candy (or other reinforcer) at regular intervals, as long as the child does not fight. In time, the type of reinforcer may be changed and provided only after longer periods of acceptable (nonfighting) behavior. It is by manipulation of the different variables in this framework that the child's behavior is changed.

Modeling and shaping are two related concepts often proposed by behaviorists. Modeling is precisely what the term implies: the demonstration of a behavior by one individual to be imitated by another. If this imitation is rewarded, the behavior will likely be repeated. In classrooms for the emotionally disturbed a problem can arise when undesirable behaviors are modeled, imitated, and rewarded. This situation can exist when a child fights with another, the teacher intervenes, and that attention is seen as a reward by another child. He may model the fighting behavior to gain the reward (attention of the teacher).

At times a desired behavior does not appear to be in the child's repertoire of behaviors and therefore cannot be rewarded. The child cannot or will not model a given behavior. In such cases it may be possible to shape the response by reinforcing successive approximations of the desired behavior. The initial responses that are in the right direction, even though they do not achieve the desired outcome, are rewarded. For example, an autistic child might be rewarded for making any sound, then a particular sound, then a recognizable word, and finally a sentence. Utilizing the shaping procedure the final goal of speech might be achieved.

Behaviorist theory as applied to emotional disturbance is concerned primarily with variables in the environment that may be manipulated to eliminate the unacceptable behavior. The basic premise is that the maladaptive behavior was learned and can be "unlearned" if proper reinforcement and motivation are provided.

Although the roots of behaviorism began with Pavlov in the very early 1900s, it was not until the 1960s that this thought took the educational field by storm. It was accepted by many because it was heralded as a panacea for the elimination of all unacceptable behavior. Others apparently accepted it as a reaction against the psychoanalytic approach. Many reports of remarkable changes in behavior in short periods of time were published. All of this was in direct opposition to the imprecise descriptions of behavior, time-consuming therapy, and often minimal observable changes in behavior that were considered characteristic of the psychoanalytic school of thought. Thus it was that one approach to emotional disturbance had unintentionally paved the way for the ready acceptance of another.

Interventions. Perhaps no other approach places more emphasis on the role of the teacher than the behavioral. When one believes that inappropriate behavior is learned and the elimination of that behavior depends upon learning acceptable behavior by means of appropriate reinforcers, the provider of the reinforcers becomes all important. It is the teacher (perhaps in consultation with other professionals) who defines the inappropriate behaviors, decides the type and schedule of reinforcement, and then administers it. Records should be kept in order to determine successes and failures. If the appropriate behavior is not observed, usually it is assumed that the reinforcer(s) is not sufficiently reinforcing. It may be increased (given more frequently) or changed completely to one that *is* reinforcing to the child.

The behavioral approach (along with the ecologic approach, to be discussed in a following section) is used extensively with more mild forms of emotional disturbance. The regular classroom teacher will usually employ various techniques of behavior modification before referring a child believed to be emotionally disturbed. Teachers of the emotionally disturbed who serve a school on an itinerant basis may suggest various behavior modification techniques to the regular classroom teacher. To a greater or lesser degree perhaps all teachers (both special and regular educators) utilize some of the principles of the behaviorist school of thought. A teacher of the emotionally disturbed who espouses this approach accepts responsibility for an extremely important role. Unlike other approaches reviewed, the teacher knows that he or she is in control and the mysticism sometimes associated with other approaches is not present. This is undoubtedly reassuring and reinforcing to most effective teachers and may be the major reason that behaviorism is so widely embraced in classrooms for the emotionally disturbed today.

SOCIOLOGIC THEORIES

Sociologic theories are "borrowed" from the field of sociology, which can be defined as the study of the development, structure, interaction, and behavior of organized groups of people (Shea, 1978). Since these theories are borrowed, they are not as systematized or as developed as either the psychoanalytic or behavioral theory. However, this does not reduce their value in providing a better understanding of emotionally disturbed youngsters.

Among the sociologic perspectives of importance to educators is that of deviance, which focuses on the breaking of social rules. Mental illness is often associated with a lack of conformity in ordinary social interaction (DesJarlais, 1972). Several theoretic propositions are provided by various sociologic re-

Education of children and youth who are emotionally disturbed

"Cooling off" time.

searchers to explain deviance. Among these are cultural transmission, social disorganization, anomie, and labeling. Each of these will be discussed in the following sections.

The cultural transmission theory has as its source social learning theory. It describes deviance as learned rather than inherent in the individual. Proponents (Shaw and McKay, 1942; Sutherland, 1960) have suggested that all groups in a society are comprised of psychologic normals. However, some individuals within that society engage in types of behavior that are very different. This phenomenon is explained by the fact that certain individuals learn from others to act in a certain manner. When these "others" define such activities as theft or the sale of narcotics as acceptable behavior, then the individual learns to act in the same manner. Persons within the larger society label this law-breaking behavior as unacceptable. Within the subgroups, the law-breaking tradition is passed on to succeeding generations in the same manner as all traditions are transmitted. Those who learn from their subgroup to break laws may be emotionally disturbed. It is at this point that the boundary between emotional disturbance and juvenile delinquency becomes somewhat blurred.

The social disorganization theory, originally developed in the field of sociology, was later applied to an examination of mental disorders. The first research was conducted to determine specific characteristics of various portions of large urban areas. Some areas were termed disorganized as a result of high rates of crime, juvenile delinquency, and other forms of deviance. Others were "natural" areas characterized by a lack of the same forms of deviance.

"Disorganization" implies the breakdown of the orderly ways of interacting within the community, which is said to be caused by the inability of the usual social institutions (educational facilities, economic advancement, recreational facilities, etc.) to meet the fundamental needs of the individuals (DesJarlais, 1972). This in turn leads to greater numbers of emotionally disturbed. It is important to note here that disorganized areas produce disorganized persons and also attract persons with disorganized behavior living in "natural" areas (Faris, 1944). It is fully recognized that not all persons living within disorganized areas are or become mentally ill.

The concept of *anomie* was developed by Durkheim (1951) in his attempts to explain the cause of mental illness. He conceptualized society as limiting and regulating individual needs that tend to expand beyond the point at which they can be fulfilled. If society does not limit and regulate, the individual experiences severe frustration, which in turn leads to deviance such as theft, aggression, or suicide. When society fulfills its role of regulating, for example, the wealth or power of an individual within a particular status position in that society, the individual then has reached the "limits" and, theoretically, is satisfied. Durkheim further contends that rapid social change does not allow for society to formulate the necessary norms or limits (societal norms develop and change slowly); therefore, a state of anomie exists. This leads to a marked degree of deviance.

It must be noted that Durkheim's theory of anomie relates more to rates of mental illness rather than to individual cases. Genetic background and the personal history must be explored to determine the cause of mental illness in individual cases (Durkheim, 1964).

The *labeling theory,* although often criticized as incomplete (Matza, 1969; Gove, 1970; Blum, 1970), appears to have a continuing applicability for those interested in emotional disturbance and those currently investigating the effects of labeling on any handicapped person.

According to this theory a society distinguishes between conformists and deviants. Each is labeled and then expected to act in accordance with that label. The label is conferred upon those who have demonstrated or are suspected of rule-breaking within the society. As a result, a role is assigned to the label (for example, addict, discipline problem, pimp) and those so labeled are expected to fulfill the role. Generally, there are covert rewards for fulfilling the role—a "high," attention, money. The rewards tend to provide impetus to the labeled individual to continue to live up to society's expectations. Since not all are labeled deviant who do in fact perform deviant actions and not all so labeled *do* perform deviant actions, the labeling theory does not apply to all individuals or in all situations. The impact of labeling relates to whether or not the system needs to have a deviant role filled, and the frequency and visibility of the rule breaking, the tolerance level for rule breaking, and the relative power of the rule breaker.

Those individuals charged with the responsibility of enforcing social rules, such as teachers, parents, police, and psychiatrists, invoke the labeling process. They select from all rule breakers those who will play the deviant role. This selection usually operates under the guise of rehabilitation, maintaining discipline, or treatment.

The labeling theory, like the cultural transmission theory, stresses the similarities of motives and psychologic make-up of deviants and conformists; however, it goes farther and emphasizes the similarities in behavior. All people conform to some rules and break others; for example, a youngster who steals may also help elderly ladies across the street.

There is considerable debate in regard to whether or not an individual is mentally ill because someone has assigned him the label or his actions were such that they merited the label (Scheff, 1966; Gove, 1975).

Regardless of the lack of clarity of some applications of the sociologic theories, they can be of value in our attempts to better understand and assist the emotionally disturbed student.

Interventions. Because sociologic theory is based more on the behavior patterns of groups than on those of individuals, many interventions, to be fully effective, must be implemented on a large scale. For example, an attempt to alleviate the social disorganization of a community has ramifications that testing a new drug or trying a new form of analysis does not.

The application of sociologic theory to interventions may be much more difficult than is the case with other theories, since there are numerous political implications to be considered. Although anomie may be considered a factor in emotional disturbance, it is beyond the power of any one facet of society to affect the rapid rate of change of society and the resultant problems with norms and limits. Similarly, it is beyond the ability of any one segment of society to change the behavior of those who have been taught a tradition of rule breaking.

This does not mean that the teacher of the emotionally disturbed has no interventions available other than massive social action. An attempt to alleviate individual pathology may be the best way to alleviate group pathology (DesJarlais, 1978). Various interventions from other theories, such as the development of warm, trusting relationships, providing time and structure for discussions of various values, and determining the reinforcement that is maintaining certain deviant behaviors or providing more powerful ones for acceptable behaviors, may be used. The nature of the intervention used will be determined by the predominant problem of the individual and the professional judgment of the teacher. It may even be as simple as teaching a youngster how to set an alarm so that he arrives on school on time and is not designated "tardy" or "truant."

ECOLOGIC THEORY

This conceptual model for examining emotional disturbance is neither as systematized nor organized as the behavioral or psychoanalytic models since it has been the focus of researchers for a relatively short period of time.

Among the first major contributions to the ecologic theory was that of Faris and Dunham (1939), whose research clearly indicated a relationship between community life and mental health. In communities that were highly disorganized the rates of mental illness were significantly higher. Continued research into the relationship between individuals and their environment indicates that suicide rates increase when the community lacks support systems such as economic stability, opportunities for leisure activities, education, etc. Such research also verifies the relationship between social class and psychiatric hospitalization, with the highest rate of hospitalization occuring in the lowest social groupings.

Studies of animals have also contributed to the development of the ecologic theory. When bees, termites, or rats enter a community that is not their own, waves of disturbance are set in motion throughout the colony. The regular inhabitants are agitated and coalesce into a united "army" to evict the intruder. At times they are so agitated and disorganized that they attack members of their own clan in their frenzied efforts to route the intruder (Lorenz, 1967).

Application of this theory to emotionally disturbed youngsters leads to recognition of the fact that each person is an integral part of many separate but interrelated environmental systems. The school, neighborhood, peer group, church, and one or more social agencies, each presenting a unique set of expectations, rewards, and punishments, are just some of the systems within which a child may find himself. It is usually expected that a youngster can successfully negotiate each of these interrelationships; however, in the case of the emotionally disturbed this does not happen. Either expectations are made that the child cannot fulfill or he or she has expectations that are not fulfilled. The resulting frustration provokes responses and counterresponses on the part of the individual and the environmental system. *Each* contributes—and a mutually responsive pattern of maladjustment is established. The problem lies as much within the environment as in the individual.

If an individual experiences this frustration and resulting lack of harmony between self and only one particular environment, he or she is not usually judged emotionally disturbed. However, if this conflict exists between the person and many or all aspects of the environment, that person may be judged to be severely emotionally disturbed.

An important basic tenet of the ecologic theory is that the root of the problem is not perceived to be within the individual alone or in the environment alone but rather in the *interaction* of the two. When one member of a given group acts in a manner unacceptable to the others, some action is undertaken. This in turn calls for a response action (for example, if a child fights in the classroom the teacher must act or choose to ignore; either leads to some sort of response on the part of the fighting child).

At times a person may act in such a manner that the actions are misunderstood by others in the larger society. The reaction of the others may resemble that of the animal societies.

These actions are "different," therefore, that person is an "intruder" and thus begins an agitation process. The person's presence invokes reactions in those around him. They may want to exclude him and his response is again misunderstood by others, which increases their concern. This is an ecologic exchange that is convulsive or disruptive to the normal tempo. According to the ecologic theory, the agitation is not the fault of either the individual or the society but rather in the exchange between the two.

Interventions. At one time residential treatment centers were seen as an ideal resolution of the problem of the emotionally disturbed since they had specially created environments. Soon it became apparent that because the environments were controlled they also tended to be artificial and removed from reality. At present the residential center is believed to be appropriate only for those so severely emotionally disturbed that they cannot remain in their normal environment.

A community liaison person can effectively assist an individual and the environment to accommodate each other. This includes, at times, acting as an advocate, coordinating available services, or modifying the environment.

Teachers of the emotionally disturbed may employ group dynamics methods, such as role playing and discussion to assist the student to understand the human exchanges that take place in various environments. With a better understanding the students are able to choose to modify their own behavior, more fully accept that of another, or create a new, more satisfying system of exchanges. This may be accomplished within a self-contained classroom and then extended to the various environments. The same goal may be achieved when regular class teachers and the special education teacher assist each other and the child to live more comfortably in the environment.

COUNTERTHEORIES

Not all theories, ideas, or methodologies concerned with emotional disturbance can be neatly categorized under the headings of biophysical, psychoanalytic, behavioral, sociologic, or ecologic. There are many people who work effectively with emotionally disturbed youngsters who have conceptualized other theories. Prominent among these are Kohl, Harris, Neill, and Shapiro. (Reinert, 1976). Their conceptualizations are either contradictory to the above theories or are so different that they cannot be included within them. We have chosen not to include a discussion of these individuals and their theories but felt an obligation to mention them. Those who read further into this area of interest will eventually become acquainted with these and other counter-theorists.

An educational placement system: application of the variable service continuum concept

As has been noted in the section on definitions in this chapter, there is no generally recognized set of descriptive statements to characterize emotionally disturbed children. Perhaps no other disability is so difficult to precisely describe and define. If a person is blind, that is relatively easy to determine. If a person is visually impaired, the loss of vision can be defined as 20/400 or 20/100, which indicates to all concerned the degree of handicap. Even "learning disabled", which is believed by some to be difficult to define, has a quantifiable element (in all definitions of learning disabilities there is a statement relating to lack of academic achievement). This is not true of emotional disturbance. Although many emotionally disturbed youngsters are not functioning on an academic level commensurate with their expected ability, some perform very adequately, and others may even perform two or three grades above what might be expected of them.

Because this is true, youngsters suspected of having emotional problems are defined to a large extent by the adults with whom they come in contact. Ordinarily, it is the regular classroom teacher who makes the initial referral. Although often quite accurate in their judgments, classroom teachers may be biased. Researchers have found that the sex or age of the child, sex of the teacher, the fact that they have been told that the child is emotionally disturbed, and other similar factors can influence the judgment of the teacher (Kelly, Bullock, and Dykes, 1977; Rich, 1977; Rubin and Balow, 1978; Ysseldyke and Foster, 1978). It does not seem to be stretching the point to assume that any of the other adults charged with the responsibility of making judgments about a particular child could possibly be equally biased by the same or similar factors.

Therefore, because of the lack of precise definition and the possibility of bias, extreme care must be taken to ensure that only children who are truly handicapped by their emotional difficulties are officially identified as emotionally disturbed. The responsibility of those in attendance at the preliminary review or staffing is great. Every precaution must be taken to determine whether all possible interventions have been used in the regular classroom as well as within the school. Such interventions as changing the child's desk out of the main traffic pattern within the classroom or changing the child's classroom from an unstructured open space to a self-contained classroom are examples of adjustments that can be made to enable a child to interact within the school system in a more appropriate manner.

When interventions such as the preceding are not sufficient and it is determined, in the best judgment of all involved, that the child *is* emotionally disturbed and requires special services, a decision must be made regarding placement. This includes possibilities ranging from remaining in the regular classroom and receiving assistance from the special education teacher to placement in a residential facility.

As in all handicapping conditions the principle of the least restrictive environment is followed. If the child's emotional disturbance is considered mild, he or she may remain in the regular classroom all day. The teacher of the emotionally disturbed may suggest to the regular class teacher various intervention strategies. Usually these follow a behavior modification approach. Strategies such as listing each assignment on a paper so that the child can check them as they are completed, allowing for free time after completion of work during which the child may choose an activity, or providing the child with free time after a fight-free recess are among the many that may be suggested.

For other students who are considered mildly emotionally disturbed, placement may be primarily in the regular class with more direct assistance from the teacher of emotionally disturbed. The student may spend as little as an hour or as much as half a day in the resource room or classroom for the emotionally disturbed. During this time various interventions may be used and will depend upon the theoretical orientation of the teacher and the needs of the student. In some cases the emphasis may be on academic tutoring or counseling. The organization of junior and senior high schools lends itself to this type of placement and, in some cases, is the determining factor in providing services to emotionally disturbed youth.

Moderate to severely disturbed students

may require more full-time special services and thus may be placed in self-contained classrooms. Here, the teacher of the emotionally disturbed provides academic assistance as well as more intense therapy. (This may follow any one of the previously discussed theoretical orientations or be very eclectic, using the aspects of each that best meet the needs of the child.) The teacher in this self-contained classroom is responsible for the academic as well as emotional growth of the students. If and when a child reaches a certain level of appropriate behavior the child may be integrated into selected classes. (Exactly what is "appropriate" is determined by the nature of the child's disturbance; for one it may be maintaining contact with reality because the initial problem was living in a world of fantasy; for another it might be the ability to control extremely aggressive behavior.) As the child successfully negotiates the reintegration process in individual classes, more may be added until full time is spent in the regular class. It must be mentioned that some children may experience emotional disturbance of sufficient magnitude that little or no integration is possible, although they may be learning and succeeding in the smaller, usually more structured environment of the self-contained classroom. Some junior and senior high schools have arranged a "school within the school" for emotionally disturbed students. This may include a separate area such as several rooms or a wing of the school; when facilities permit.

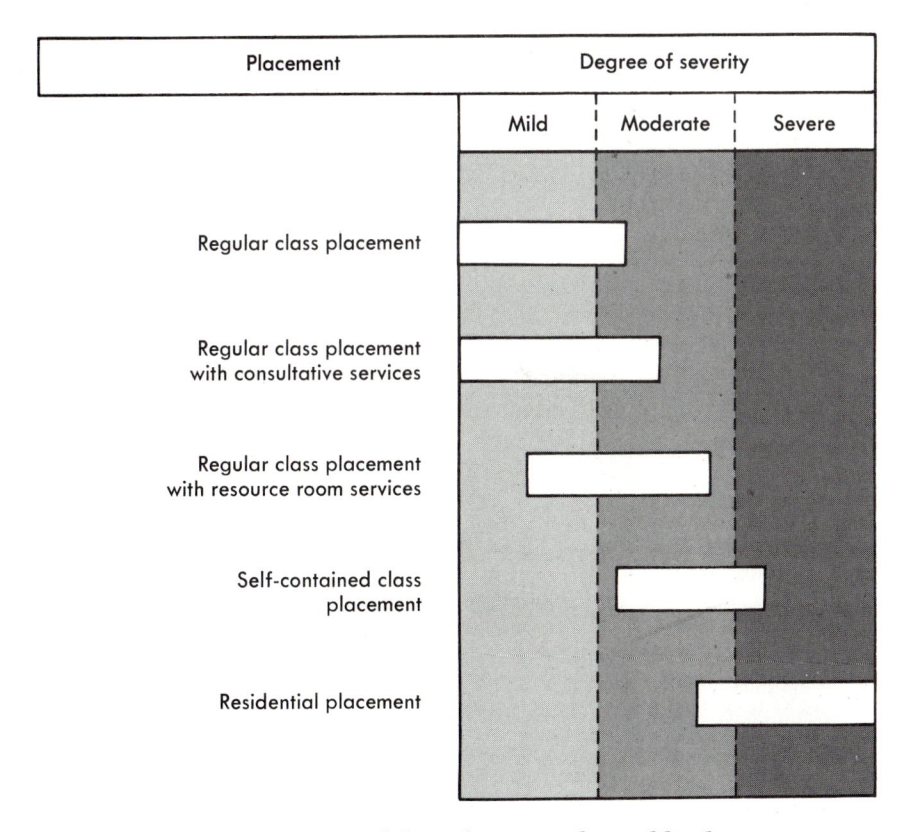

Fig. 10-1. **Degrees of emotional disturbances and possible placement.**

Other handicapping conditions

This may be a separate building on the campus of the main school building. The students are provided with all their classes; however, the numbers remain small, allowing for much more personal contact between teachers and students. At no time are there thirty to thirty-five students in a class, nor are the students required to negotiate the complexities of a school with 1,000 or 2,000 other students.

For certain students even these accommodations are not sufficient, and they require residential placement. Here they receive services on a 24-hour basis. Usually, residential facilities subscribe to a specific theoretical model; however, some are eclectic in their approach. The degree of emotional disturbance of those students in a residential school usually dictates the services of nurses, psychiatrists, or psychologists as well as educators. The residents attend classes as they are able to benefit from a learning situation. This may vary from 30 minutes per day to an entire school day. Ordinarily, the residential school is structured so that as a student progresses, more and more responsibility is allocated until he or she makes most decisions and is functioning adequately in the subject areas. At this point reintegration into the home school is attempted. Support services from the residential school staff or from the teacher of emotionally disturbed in the home school are provided as long as the student requires them.

As mentioned in previous chapters, the school and other community agencies must provide a continuum of services to meet the varied needs of the child. Regular reassessment will determine whether this is being accomplished.

The variability of the characteristics of emotional disturbance and the impact on the life of the child make precise determinations regarding degree of handicap and exact placement difficult. It is often assumed that the degree of emotional disturbance may be characterized as mild, moderate, or severe. There is little agreement, though, in regard to the precise procedure for separating the mild from the moderate or the moderate from the severe. These are frequently overlapping and it is at this point that the impact of the emotional disturbance on the functioning of the individual must be considered in determining the best placement. Fig. 10-1 illustrates the overlap of degrees of severity as well as possible placements.

Issues relating to educational concerns for the emotionally disturbed
JUVENILE DELINQUENCY

Although, strictly speaking, juvenile delinquency cannot be equated with emotional disturbance, a higher proportion of offenders exhibit behavior disorders of varying degrees than do nonoffenders (Smiley, 1977). A juvenile delinquent is one who has broken a law and has been apprehended. The law broken can be as serious as murder or armed robbery or as minor as truancy or running away from home. With this wide discrepancy in what constitutes juvenile delinquency it is difficult to speak of all offenders as a homogeneous group (Smiley, 1977). Often the attitude toward juvenile delinquents depends on the philosophic orientation of the people concerned. Psychiatrists and social workers tend to look for causes in family tensions or poor interrelationships that result in personality problems. Sociologists believe many juvenile delinquents are merely victims of poverty, unequal opportunities, racial bias, or cultural conflicts. Psychologists may view the problem as stemming from overcontrolled hostility, which results in explosive, aggressive behavior. Behaviorally oriented persons tend to overlook the cause but plan modification in terms of rewards or punishment. Some with a religious orientation see delinquency as "disobedience to God" and a result of moral decay (Fox, 1976).

These "reasons" for juvenile delinquency are among those proposed as causes of emotional disturbance; the overlap is obvious. However, there is still another consideration. According to a study by the Educational Testing Service, juvenile delinquents are more than twice as likely to have learning disabilities as nonoffenders (Trends, 1978). Bryan and Bryan (1977) indicate that a variety of negative personality and behavioral characteristics have long been associated with the presence of learning disabilities. It is commonly accepted that learning disabilities may produce emotional problems. Also, since learning disabled children may have difficulty in "reading" social situations, their comments or actions may seem unacceptable. At the present time educators do not have tools sufficiently precise to ensure a clear distinction between emotional disturbance and learning disabilities (Bryan and Bryan, 1977).

It seems important for those anticipating a career in teaching the emotionally disturbed to be aware that they may in fact be working with juvenile delinquents, students who are emotionally disturbed or learning disabled or, perhaps more likely, students with various combinations of these and perhaps other conditions or disabilities. This is especially true when teaching emotionally disturbed adolescents.

CHILD ABUSE

While child abuse cannot be equated with emotional disturbance, a number of the characteristics that describe abused children are the same as those for emotional disturbance. Included are unexplained crying, acting out, withdrawal, lack of friends, and lack of a positive self-concept, (Halperin, 1979; Helfer, 1976).

According to authorities the effects of child abuse may vary. In many cases, after the source of abuse is removed, the child needs little or no assistance in becoming physically or mentally healthy; in other instances the individual may need intensive therapy for a few weeks or for an entire lifetime (Halperin, 1979; Newberger and Bourne, 1978; Gelles, 1978; Helfer, 1976).

Another issue compounding the difficulty in attempting to fully understand the effects of child abuse is the question of the *type* of abuse. It is believed by some that physical abuse or physical neglect (although not acceptable) may have fewer harmful effects on a child than sexual abuse, emotional abuse, or emotional neglect.

Because of the similarities between an abused child and an emotionally disturbed child, and the variations in the effects of abuse on individuals, it is not unusual for a teacher of the emotionally disturbed to suspect that some type of abuse may exist in the home. Therefore, it is imperative that teachers be aware of all pertinent state legislation as well as school policy for reporting suspected child abuse.

Summary

The question of emotional disturbance in children and youth of school age is one that many school districts have attempted to avoid, partly because of difficulties with definition and identification and partly because this particular handicapping condition is "unpopular" with both parents and the general public. This has led to a lack of meaningful service for many students with mild problems, and when the problems become very obvious, particularly if the behavior exhibited can be called "dangerous," placement in segregated facilities has been the common practice. This lack of attention to emotional difficulties until the problem becomes so serious it can no longer be overlooked is somewhat parallel to overlooking early symptoms of various recognized diseases, hoping they will go away.

The question of serving the emotionally disturbed (or "disruptive," "socially maladjusted," or whatever they may be called) may no longer be left up to the local or state school officials. There is no question but that the provisions of 94-142 (and, for that matter, a host of similar state laws) *require* that they be provided an appropriate educational program. The question is, how soon will parents and other advocates for the handicapped press this issue throughout the nation? When they do, the courts will undoubtedly reaffirm the rights of these handicapped students to an appropriate special education program, just as they have done for all other handicapping conditions for which the issue has been raised. It would seem likely that it is only a matter of time.

focus

history

During the Middle Ages the clergy attempted to "cure" the mentally ill by a liberal use of prayers, holy water, touching relics, visits to holy places, and the breath and spittle of the priests. Mild forms of exorcism gradually developed into more harsh measures as the populace began to believe more firmly that mental illness was caused by demons and more specifically by the devil inhabiting the body of ill persons.

Continued attacks on the then prevailing ideas concerning possession by demons and witchcraft forced a gradual change in the 1600s and early 1700s, thus paving the way for the later emergence of observation, reason, humanitarian treatment, and the formulation of theoretic models of mental illness.

Early efforts to provide services for the mentally ill made little differentiation between the mentally retarded and the mentally ill. The general view was that both the retarded and mentally ill were victims of environment.

Among the earliest efforts by the public schools to provide educational services for disruptive children was the establishment of ungraded schools. Such schools were established in New Haven, Connecticut, in 1871; in New York in 1874; and in Cleveland in 1875.

The roots of the psychoanalytically oriented theories used as the basis for education of the disturbed child were established primarily during the 1940s and 1950s. The 1960s and 1970s gave rise to behaviorally, sociologically, ecologically, and humanistically oriented intervention strategies.

prevalence

The major problem affecting an accurate estimation of the prevalence of emotional disturbance in school-age children is the lack of consensus regarding a definition that includes clear, specific characteristics. The lack of acceptable, standardized tools for diagnosis of emotional disturbance is another closely related problem.

Although children regarded as emotionally disturbed are generally from 1 to 2 years behind their peers academically, various investigations have shown that their intelligence roughly corresponds to that found in the school population.

Most authorities in the field would agree to an estimate of at least 2 to 3 percent as definitely emotionally disturbed, and there may be an additional 7 to 8 percent who will require some less intensive professional services.

biophysical theory

The biophysical approach is the oldest theoretical approach to emotional disturbance. Although there is evidence suggestive of a biologic etiology in emotional disturbance, there is no conclusive evidence of a direct cause and effect. The most accepted view is that biologic and environmental factors interact and that both may be manipulated to exacerbate the disorders.

psychoanalytic theories

Psychoanalytic theory places a great deal of emphasis on early relationships with the family unit. Proponents of this theory believe that the influence of mother, father, and siblings is exerted through unconscious processes in which the child's behavioral and (often) academic problems represent symbolic attempts to defend against anxiety or other conflicts.

behavioral model

Behaviorists tend to believe that the unacceptable behaviors of emotionally disturbed youngsters are learned and in some way are rewarding to them, that these behaviors somehow enable them to reach their goal. In order to eliminate the unacceptable (to others) behavior, the environment must be "operated" on so that it no longer serves as a reward or reinforcement to the individual.

Modeling and shaping are two related concepts often proposed by behaviorists. Modeling is the demonstration of a behavior by one individual to be imitated by another.

The behaviorist theory as applied to emotional disturbance is concerned primarily with variables in the environment that may be manipulated to eliminate the unacceptable behavior. The basic premise is that the maladaptive behavior was learned and can be "unlearned" if proper reinforcement and motivation are provided.

sociologic theories (interventions)

Because sociologic theory is based more on the behavior patterns of groups than on those of individuals, many interventions, to be fully effective, must be implemented on a large scale.

The application of sociologic theory to interventions may be much more difficult than is the case with other theories since there are numerous political implications to be considered.

ecologic theory

An important basic tenet of the ecologic theory is that the root of the problem is not perceived to be within the individual alone or in the environment alone but rather in the interaction of the two.

an educational placement system: application of the variable service continuum concept

Youngsters suspected of having emotional problems are defined to a large extent by the adults with whom they come in contact.

Because of the lack of precise definition and the possibility of bias, extreme care must be taken to ensure that only children who are truly handicapped by their emotional difficulties are officially identified as emotionally disturbed. Every precaution must be taken to determine whether all possible interventions have been used in the regular classroom as well as within the school.

juvenile delinquency

Although, strictly speaking, juvenile delinquency cannot be equated with emotional disturbance, a higher proportion of offenders exhibit behavior disorders of varying degrees than do nonoffenders.

It is commonly accepted that learning disabilities may produce emotional problems. Also, since learning disabled children may have difficulty in "reading" social situations, their comments or actions may seem unacceptable. At the present time educators do not have tools sufficiently precise to ensure a clear distinction between emotional disturbance and learning disabilities.

child abuse

While child abuse cannot be equated with emotional disturbance, a number of the characteristics that describe abused children are the same as those for emotional disturbance.

References and suggested readings

Baker, E. M., and Stullken, E. H. American research studies concerning the "behavior" type of exceptional child. *Journal of Exceptional* Children, 1938, *4*, 36-45.

Bandura, A. *Principles of behavior modification.* New York: Holt, Rinehart & Winston, Inc., 1969.

Bender, L. *Child psychiatric techniques.* Springfield, Ill., Charles C Thomas, Publisher, 1952.

Blum, A. Sociology of mental illness. In *Deviance and respectability: the social construction of moral meanings.* J. D. Doublas (Ed.). New York: Basic Books, Inc., 1970.

Bower, E. M. *Early identification of emotionally handicapped children in school* (2nd ed.). Springfield, Ill.: Charles C Thomas, Publisher, 1969.

Bryan, T., and Bryan, J. H. The social-emotional side of learning disabilities. *Behavioral Disorders,* May 1977, *2*(3), 141-145.

Burton, A. *Modern humanistic psychotherapy.* San Francisco: Jossey-Bass, Inc., 1968.

Chess, S., and Thomas, A. (Eds.). *Annual progress in child psychiatry and child development.* New York: Brunner/Mazel, 1977.

Clarizio, H. F., and McCoy, G. F. *Behavior disorders in children* (2nd ed.). New York: Thomas Y. Crowell Co., 1976.

Coleman, J. C. *Abnormal psychology and modern life.* Glenview, Ill: Scott, Foresman & Co., 1976.

Cravioto, J., Gaona, C. E., and Birch, H. G. Early malnutrition and auditory-visual integration in school age children. *Journal of Special Education,* 1967, *2*, 75-91.

Daley, J. W. Freud: the ethics of ambivalence. *The Intercollegiate Review,* Fall 1977, *13*(1), 45-56.

Donahue, G. T., and Nichtern, S. *Teaching the troubled child.* New York: The Free Press, 1968.

DesJarlais, D. C. Mental illness as social deviance. In *A study of child variance.* W. C. Rhodes and M. L. Tracy (Eds.). Ann Arbor: The University of Michigan Press, 1972.

DesJarlais, D. C., and Paul, J. Labeling theory: sociological views and approaches. In *Emotionally disturbed and deviant children.* W. Rhodes and J. Paul (Eds.). Englewood Cliffs, N.J.: Prentice-Hall, Inc., 1978.

Deutch, A. *The mentally ill in America.* New York: Columbia University Press, 1946.

Durkheim, E. *The division of labor in society.* New York: The Free Press, 1964.

Durkheim, E. *Suicide.* New York: The Free Press, 1951.

Faris, R. Reflections of social disorganization in the behavior of schizophrenics. *American Journal of Sociology,* 1944, *50*, 134-141.

Faris, R., and Dunham, H. W. *Mental disorders in urban areas.* Chicago: University of Chicago Press, 1939.

Fine R. Psychoanalysis. In *Current psychotherapies.* R. Corsini (Ed.). Itasca, Ill: F. E. Peacock, Publishers, 1973.

Fox, V. Delinquency and its treatment in current perspective. *Behavioral Disorders,* August 1976, 2(1), 5-15.

Gelles, R. J. Violence towards children in the United States. *American Journal of Orthopsychiatry,* October 1978, 48(4), 580-592.

Glidewell, J., and Swallow C. *The prevalence of maladjustment in elementary schools.* Chicago: University of Chicago Press, 1968.

Gove, W. Labeling and mental illness: a critique. In *The labeling of deviance: evaluating a perspective.* Gove (Ed.). New York: Halstead, 1975.

Gove, W. Societal reaction as an explanation of mental illness: an evaluation. *American Sociological Review,* 1970, 5(35), 873-883.

Group for the Advancement of Psychiatry. *Pharmacotherapy and psychotherapy: paradoxes, problems, and progress.* New York: Brunner/Mazel, 1975.

Guthrie, D. J. *A history of medicine.* Philadelphia: J. B. Lippincott Co., 1946.

Halperin, M. *Helping maltreated children: school and community resources.* St. Louis: The C. V. Mosby Co., 1979.

Hammill, D. D., and Bartel, W. R. *Teaching children with learning and behavior problems.* Boston: Allyn & Bacon, 1978.

Harth, R. (Ed.). *Issues in behavioral disorders.* Springfield, Ill.: Charles C Thomas, Publisher, 1971.

Healy, W. *Mental conflicts and misconduct.* Boston: Little, Brown and Co., 1915.

Helfer, R. E., and Kempe, H. *Child abuse and neglect: the family and the community.* Cambridge: Ballinger Publishing Co., 1976.

Hoffman, E. Treatment of deviance by the educational system. In *A study of child variance. Vol 3.* W. C. Rhodes and S. Head (Eds.). Ann Arbor: University of Michigan Press, 1974.

Iverson, S. D., and Iverson, L. L. *Behavioral pharmacology.* New York: Oxford University Press, 1975.

Kauffman, J. M. *Characteristics of children's behavior.* Columbus: Charles E. Merrill Publishing Co., 1977.

Kelly, T. J., Bullock, L. M., and Dykes, M. K. Behavioral disorders: teachers' perceptions. *Exceptional Children,* Feb. 1977, 43(5), 316-317.

Kempe, C., and Helfer, R. (Eds.). *Helping the battered child and his family.* Philadelphia: J. B. Lippincott Co., 1972.

Key, E. *The century of the child.* New York: G. P. Putnam's Sons, 1909.

Kirk, S. *Educating exceptional children.* Boston: Houghton-Mifflin Co., 1972.

Lambert, N., and Bower, E. In-school screening of children with emotional handicaps. In *Conflict in the classroom: The education of emotionally disturbed children.* N. J. Long, W. C. Morse, and R. G. Newman (Eds.). Belmont, Calif.: Wadsworth Publishing Co., 1976.

Lewis, N. D. C. *A short history of psychiatric achievement.* New York: W. W. Norton Co., 1941.

Long, N., Morse, W., and Newman, R. *Conflict in the classroom: the education of emotionally disturbed children.* Belmont, Calif.: Wadsworth Publishing Co., 1976.

Lorenz, K. *On aggression.* Translated by Marjorie Wilson. New York: Bantam Books, Inc., 1967.

Matza, D. *Becoming deviant.* Englewood Cliffs, N.J.: Prentice-Hall, Inc., 1969.

Menninger, R. W. The history of psychiatry. *Diseases of the Nervous System,* 1944, 5, 52-55.

Morse, W. C. The education of socially maladjusted and emotionally disturbed children. In. *Education of exceptional children and youth.* W. M. Cruickshank and G. O. Johnson (Eds.). Englewood Cliffs, N.J.: Prentice-Hall, Inc., 1975.

Mour, S. I. Teacher behaviors and ecological balance. *Behavioral Disorders,* 1977, 3(1), 55-58.

Newberger, E. H., and Bourne, R. The medicalization and legalization of child abuse. *American Journal of Orthopsychiatry,* October 1978, 48(4).

O'Gorman, G. *The nature of childhood autism.* New York: Appleton-Century-Crofts, 1970.

Polier, J. W. *A view from the bench of the juvenile court.* Chicago: National Council on Crime and Delinquency, 1964.

Pollin, W. The pathogenesis of schizophrenia. *Archives of General Psychiatry,* 1972, 27, 29-37.

President's Commission on Mental Health. Vol. 1. Washington, D.C.: U.S. Government Printing Office, 1978.

Quay, H. C. Patterns of aggression, withdrawal, and immaturity. In *Psychopathological disorders of childhood.* H. C. Quay and J. S. Werry (Eds.). New York: John Wiley and Sons, 1972.

Reinert, H. R. *Children in conflict: educational strategies for the emotionally disturbed and behaviorally disordered.* St. Louis: The C. V. Mosby Co., 1976.

Rhodes, W. C. *A study of child variance. Vol 4. The future.* Ann Arbor: The University of Michigan, 1975.

Rhodes, W. C., and Head, S. *A study of child variance. Vol. 3. Service delivery systems.* Ann Arbor: The University of Michigan, 1974.

Rhodes, W. C., and Tracy, M. L. *A study of child variance. Vol. 1. Conceptual models.* Ann Arbor: The University of Michigan, 1972.

Rich, L. H. Behavior disorders and school: a case of sexism and racial bias. *Behavioral Disorders,* Aug. 1977, *2*(4), 201-204.

Rimland, B. Psychogenesis versus biogenesis: the issues and evidence. In *Changing perspectives in mental illness.* S. C. Ploz and R. B. Edgerton (Eds.). New York: Holt, Rinehart & Winston, 1969.

Rosenthal, D. (Ed.). *The Genain quadruplets: a case study and theoretical analysis of heredity and environment in schizophrenics.* New York: Basic Books, Inc., 1963.

Rothman, D. *The discovery of the asylum.* Boston: Little, Brown & Co., 1971.

Rubin, R. A., and Balow, B. Prevalence of teacher identified behavior problems: a longitudinal study. *Exceptional Children,* Oct. 1978, *45*(2), 102-110.

Scheff, T. *Being mentally ill. Chicago: Aldine Publishing Co., 1966.*

Selling, L. S. *Men against madness.* New York: Garden City Books, 1943.

Shaw, C., and McKay, H. *Juvenile delinquency and urban areas.* Chicago: University of Chicago Press, 1942.

Shea, T. M. *Teaching children and youth with behavior disorders.* St. Louis: The C. V. Mosby Co., 1978.

Skinner, B. F. *Science and human behavior.* New York: The Macmillan Co., 1953.

Smiley, W. C. Classification and delinquency: a review. *Behavioral Disorders,* Aug. 1977, *2*(4), 184-195.

Srole, L., and others. *Mental health in metropolis.* New York: McGraw-Hill Book Co., 1962.

Stephens, T. N. Teaching learning and behavioral disabled students in least restrictive environments. *Behavioral Disorders,* May 1977, *2*(3), 146-150.

Sutherland, E., and Cressey, D. *Principles of Criminology.* Chicago: J. B. Lippincott Co., 1960.

Trapp, E. P., and Himelstein, P. *Readings on the exceptional child.* New York: Appleton-Century-Crofts, 1972.

Trends. *Today's Education,* Nov./Dec. 1978, *67*(4), 7.

Wolman, B. B. (Ed.). *The therapist's handbook.* New York: Van Nostrand Reinhold, 1976.

Wood, M. M. *Developmental therapy.* Baltimore: University Park Press, 1975.

Woody, R. H. *Behavioral problem children in the schools.* New York: Appleton-Century-Crofts, 1969.

Ysseldyke, J. E., and Foster, G. G. Bias in teachers' observations of emotionally disturbed and learning disabled children. *Exceptional Children,* May 1978, *44*(8), 613-615.

Maximal participation in a wide variety of activities is important to all students.

chapter **11**

Education of children and youth who have physical or health impairments or are multihandicapped

objectives

To develop an understanding of the variability in physical impairments and the related variation in the types of physical and educational modifications that may be required by each student.

To become aware of the manner in which some physically impaired students may become emotionally and attitudinally "crippled" by an overly protective or solicitous attitude.

To describe and discuss the major physical disabilities for which the special educator must plan and the educational implications of each of these disabilities.

To consider the unusually complex needs of students with multiple disabilities.

To explore the role of the itinerant or resource teacher, the self-contained class teacher, and the efforts of other team members who may be called upon to serve the physically impaired or the multihandicapped student.

Introduction

In discussing the changing population of individuals with physical disabilities, Best (1978) indicates that "if there is a truism about physical disabilities and their associated features, characteristics, services, and so on, it is that change is continual." (p. 19) An often cited example is the change from 1940, a year in which poliomyelitis accounted for the largest single enrollment of children in schools for the crippled (Kirk, 1972), to the situation in the 70s in which cerebral-palsied children were the major single group of physically disabled students receiving special services. It should be noted that, by nearly unanimous agreement throughout the United States, when we speak of the "physically disabled" or the "physically handicapped," we do *not* include the visually impaired or the hearing impaired, even though these are obviously physical disabilities. We will follow this practice in this chapter. "Physically handicapped" refers to a conglomerate of individuals with many different types of impairment; *their commonality is that their unique educational needs result from physical or health impairments, and in many cases they have multiple disabilities.*

Educational programs established to meet the unique needs of these students have been called classes or programs for: (1) crippled, (2) physically handicapped (or disabled or impaired), (3) orthopedically handicapped, (4) health impaired, or (5) some combination of these terms. In fact, with the advent of substantial federal aid for college and university programs to train teachers for these children in the 1960s, they were so commonly called "crippled and other health impaired" at the federal level that teachers were called "COHI" teachers throughout most of the nation. The various terminology has related to federal or state legislation, the type of children placed in such programs at various points in history, or other similar variables, but, as is the case with characteristics and services provided in such programs, the labels by which they have been known have also been subject to continual change. Nevertheless, unlike some other disabling conditions, there has been little debate over whether congenital heart defects, cerebral palsy, muscular dystrophy, and poliomyelitis are real. Students who are physically disabled exist and their needs are real though highly varied; the programming by which these special needs may be met is the topic of concern of this chapter.

In considering these needs, we will review the history of programming for the physically disabled, the major types of physical disabilities, some pertinent medical information, and the educational procedures that must be implemented in the schools to provide these students with maximal learning opportunities. The historical review that follows should serve to place these other topics and considerations into more meaningful perspective.

Historical origins of special programs for children and youth with physical disabilities

Special classes or programs for crippled children were made available as early as 1900 (Solenberger, 1918); Chicago, New York, Detroit, and Cleveland had classes by 1910. Most children included in these early programs were orthopedically handicapped children who needed special physical surroundings in order to be able to attend public school classes, and these early programs tended to be those in which physical modifications to the school setting permitted attendance and participation in a program that was relatively normal except for these physical adaptations. If children were multihandicapped, they were often excluded, and it was primarily the very large cities that made special schooling available; a child in a smaller community was usually denied public education if he or she could not "fit" the program provided for nondisabled children.

Provision of a wide variety of services for the physically disabled is primarily a phenomenon of the last 20 to 30 years, but additional recognition of the needs of the physically disabled (outside of the major cities) was given a significant boost in 1919 when the Ohio Society for Crippled Children was formed. The National Society was formed in 1921 and has provided many services through the years as the National Easter Seal Society for Crippled Children and Adults (National Easter Seal Society, 1969). Their initial efforts were directed toward establishing special classes through their own organizational structure. Classes were held in any available space, with church buildings and private homes among the more popular options. Cooperative funding for instructional materials and the use of volunteer instructors were common. Early state and local societies for crippled children (much of their basic effort was expended at the state and local level) raised funds in many different ways, and a good deal of their early support came from service groups such as the Rotarians. Easter Seals were not used as a major fund-raising vehicle until 1934 (National Easter Seal Society, 1969). Although most of the very early Easter Seals groups were satisfied with their accomplishments in establishing viable private school programs for their children, it was not long until they began to question why other children should have free public education while their children were denied this opportunity. Thus they began to actively pressure public school officials regarding this question, and they were among the early advocates of the right of handicapped children to free, appropriate educational programs.

Another organization that has played a major role in providing services to physically disabled, health-impaired, and multihandicapped children is the United Cerebral Palsy Associations, Inc., a group mentioned previously in relation to initiating services for the mentally retarded. Organized locally in New York City in 1946, the national organization was formed in 1948 and very rapidly became a major factor and a militant force in promoting programs for handicapped children. Because many cerebral-palsied children have other handicapping conditions, and because many physically disabled children are multihandicapped, the United Cerebral Palsy Association and the National Easter Seals programs tended to serve children who were more alike than different. In many cases it was a matter of which group was organized first in a given community, rather than any definitive description of the children who needed service, that determined which group provided a given program. Like the Easter Seal Society, United Cerebral Palsy, Inc., provided programs in churches, homes, or wherever space could be found. And, after initiating programs on a purely private basis, parents of children served in United Cerebral Palsy sponsored schools soon began to wonder why their children were bypassed by the public schools, and began to apply pressure for a wider opening of the doors of the public schools.

It should not be inferred from the foregoing review that physically disabled children were never admitted to the public schools. To the contrary, if a child's disability were "simple" (that is, if the child were not multihandicapped) or if the crippling condition did not require much specific modification of the program, such children were admitted as part of the "mainstream." In some cases, individual teachers or schools would adapt desks or other materials, and some children progressed adequately through the regular public school program. Their progress was primarily dependent on their individual adaptability, the specific type of handicap, and their good fortune in finding a school or teachers who would adjust to at least some of their individual needs. If they were multihandicapped, especially if one of the handicapping conditions was mental retardation, they were unlikely to be accepted by the public schools. Interpretations of state laws and regulations—as they existed at that time—made it relatively easy for the school to refuse admission. And if these children were admitted, it was generally assumed that any subject at the secondary level requiring considerable adaptation was not open to them. Chemistry and physical education were among those subjects often viewed as "impossible" for certain students, depending on the handicap.

Although the general attitude toward physically and multihandicapped children who could not fit the existing program improved very little in much of the United States until the 1970s* there were some happy exceptions. During the 1940s and 1950s a surge of development of special classes and special schools for the crippled and other health-impaired students occurred in various areas of the nation. Some programs developed even in smaller communities, but for the most part only the larger population of physically handicapped children found in the cities generated sufficient public interest and concern to start good programs.

One of the more popular methods of providing services to crippled and health-impaired children was the separate special school. Many such schools were developed, often resulting from gifts from private foundations or from very wealthy persons who had developed an interest in crippled children. These schools tended to become the showplace of educational services for crippled and health-impaired children and youth, with ramps and elevators, modified toilet areas and drinking fountains, therapy pools, and a full complement of adapted furniture and equipment. In addition, there were physical therapists, occupational therapists, teacher aides, specially trained teachers, and a very low pupil/teacher ratio. Such schools often had their own "handi-bus," to transport children from all over the school district, and they provided an excellent demonstration of how much the school district cared about handicapped children. But like other well-intentioned efforts on behalf of the handicapped, they had their drawbacks.

One of the major errors in many special schools for crippled children was overinclusion of children who should never have left their home district school. In too many cases, children who, because of an accident, were in a cast that temporarily reduced their mobility were sent to the special school instead of making modifications and adaptations in their regular school. *This practice was easy for educators and seemed to indicate interest in the handicapped, but it ignored the need of students to stay with peers whenever possible.* It also overlooked the adjustment a child must make when there are changes in teachers, curriculum approaches, and total atmosphere. In addition, in too many instances this "adjusting to" the student reduced the child's motivation to adjust to the normal physical environment. The intentions of educators involved were undoubtedly good, but the outcomes were often the opposite.

Another major criticism of some of these special schools (or special wings on an existing building) was that some programs were established to serve only the physically handicapped or health impaired who had normal or near normal mental ability. Thus they some-

---

*Section 504 of the Rehabilitation Act, discussed on pp. 43-44, provides ample evidence that the United States Congress recognized this attitude in 1973.

times turned away mentally retarded children who were most in need of special help, and accepted children with temporary problems who did not require the special setting.

The foregoing should not be interpreted to mean that such programs have no merit or that they should be totally rejected today. Special school programs may be highly beneficial and are the most appropriate, least restrictive environment for certain children. And, in the construction of these earlier special schools, a great deal was learned about building modifications, which are now a part of nearly all new school buildings. For the most part, we may assume that these special physical settings are most likely to be needed with the multihandicapped or those children who have very severe handicapping conditions. Physical location in a specially built wing of an existing building seems to be a very good alternative when such special physical surroundings are deemed essential.

Regardless of the controversial aspects of special school programs, they are a major facet of the history of educational programming for the physically disabled, health impaired, and multihandicapped. Many such programs remain, but for the most part they have adjusted their admission practices to correct the problems just reviewed. In the meantime, with the acceptance of the concept of the least restrictive environment and state and federal requirements to provide building adaptations, an increasing number of physically impaired students are educated in the regular class environment. This pattern represents the present state of evolution of this field.

Physical disabilities and health impairments: a definition and a conceptual frame of reference

In this chapter children who are physically disabled are defined as those with non-sensory physical disabilities or health impairments that require the use of modified or adapted physical settings, curriculum presentation, or other specialized materials or equipment to permit maximal social and educational development. Such children may also have other disabilities, such as speech difficulties, hearing or visual impairments, or mental retardation, but to be classified as physically disabled, their primary disability must relate to a physical or health condition.

In a later section we will define and describe a number of specific types of physical disabilities and health impairments. One major question with regard to developing such a section is that of how many such conditions should be described; the potential list is of course finite, but a complete list would include conditions so uncommon as to be of questionable value for discussion here. However, more important than any such list is a frame of reference for considering physical disabilities and health impairments. Why give special consideration to a child with missing limbs, and how much special consideration is too much? How do our actions in providing for special needs affect the self-concept of the disabled child? How much do they affect his peers? When is "making things easier" in the present likely to make life adjustments more difficult in the future? These and many related questions must be asked as we develop a philosophy for educational programming for the physically disabled and health impaired. All would not agree on any single philosophy or frame of reference, but it is important that we have one and that we keep it open to modification as conditions or additional information may dictate.

The statements that follow, applied in conjunction with the more general statement of philosophy for all handicapped children given on pp. 52-53 provide philosophic guidelines for planning and implementing programs for

physically handicapped children and youth.
1. In keeping with the more general philosophy concerning the education of all handicapped children and youth, we must provide appropriate educational opportunity within the least restrictive, least modified framework and setting possible.
2. In planning any physical or educational modifications that may seem necessary, we should consider the actual functional problems, not the medical label. Etiology is important only as it has practical application regarding functional needs; the extent to which the student is normal in learning needs and requirements should be emphasized.
3. Regular reevaluations regarding any program modifications in effect are particularly critical to permit the maximization of normal program components.
4. Although the emphasis must remain that of promoting "normal" learning, we must also be unusually sensitive to the possible need for a number of very unusual physical adaptations so that learning may take place.
5. We must remain sensitive to the possibility of certain subtle needs, especially in the affective area, which are common spinoff effects of various physically handicapping conditions.
6. Finally, and most important of all, we must continually focus on the physically disabled student as a *person*. Personhood, not the disability, is the most critical consideration.

In the following sections we will consider some of the physical conditions that may lead to the need for special program efforts. The word *may* in the preceding sentence is of utmost importance, for in many cases, two children who, for example, have some physical disabilities as a result of cerebral palsy may require very different programming. One may need essentially no special educational modifications; the other may require extensive special assistance. If we understand this principle and are careful to provide all the special assistance needed—when it is needed—and yet hold such provision to the *minimum* required, we will more likely be able to operate by the true spirit of the least restrictive environment.

Classifications of physical disabilities and impairments

The physical disabilities and health impairments discussed in the following section are included because (1) they are likely to lead to a need for special educational provisions and (2) they are among the more common physical disabilities. There are many other types of disability that could be mentioned, which will be of interest to those who decide to teach the physically disabled. Those reviewed here should serve to represent the various types of physical disabilities, and the resultant need for educational and physical environment adaptations that characterize most special programs for students with physical disabilities.

As is the case with deciding which of the recognized physical disabilities to review, there is the question as to how these disabilities should be categorized. Polio is a good example of a disability that has been classified in differing ways by highly respected authors. Kirk (1972) included poliomyelitis under his general grouping of "orthopedically handicapped" rather than "neurologically impaired" even though the poliovirus causes damage to the spinal cord or brain. However, most of the educational adjustments provided for these students are typical of those provided for students who would unquestionably be called orthopedically handicapped (impairments of the normal functioning of the bones, muscles, or joints).

In other texts in which this question has

been confronted, we find as many as ten or eleven classifications or as few as three or four. Some authors elect to not mention classifications at all. In this presentation we will first outline the major classifications under which physical disabilities are sometimes grouped. We will then consider several of the specific physical impairments. The major classifications include:
1. Neurologically related disabilities
2. Musculoskeletal and orthopedic disabilities
3. Cardiovascular and respiratory system disabilities
4. Disabilities of metabolic origin

Among the *neurologically related disabilities*, cerebral palsy undoubtedly deserves the most consideration, because cerebral-palsied students tend to make up the largest single group of handicapped children in our programs for the physically disabled. Also included will be spina bifida, convulsive disorders (primarily epilepsy), and poliomyelitis (polio). Conditions that might be listed under the classification of *musculoskeletal and orthopedic disorders* include amputations, arthritis, and muscular dystrophy. Asthma and rheumatic heart disease could be included under the broad general classification of *cardiovascular and respiratory system disabilities*, and diabetes is a *metabolic disorder*. The discussion of these various conditions follows.

Major physical disabilities and educational implications

Unlike the sequence of information presented in most of the earlier chapters of this text, the various disabilities and certain medical or physiologic information related to that particular disability will be presented in the same subsection. Whenever practical, educational implications will be presented at the same time in an attempt to integrate the description of the disability, some limited medical information, and the resultant need for special education provisions or modifications. This seems most appropriate since, unlike the chapter on hearing impairment, for example, where the basic consideration was one impairment, in this discussion we are considering a number of widely varied disabilities having only two major factors in common. These factors are: (1) the disability is primarily physical in nature and (2) because of the disability, the student requires special educational assistance. As for the "anatomy and physiology" of this area of disability, it is the totality of physiology and anatomy with which we are concerned, except that by definition disabilities relating primarily to hearing or vision are excluded. Therefore, since we do not intend to present an overview of how the entire human body functions, we will focus on limited aspects of the disabilities presented. The physical disabilities will be presented alphabetically, with some notation within each presentation as to the relative severity and incidence of this disability within the total population of physically disabled.

AMPUTATIONS

Many children with amputations require very little special educational planning; therefore, although the amputation is a fact, they would not be considered physically disabled. An amputation may be congenital, acquired as a result of trauma, or elective as a result of a birth defect, disease, or infection. In most instances, the child will be fitted with an artificial arm or leg (prosthesis). Generally, the child with a congenital amputation will be fitted with the prosthesis very early and will have learned to use it effectively by the time he or she begins school. The prosthesis may be made of wood, metal, or plastic, with plastic being used more frequently because it is so lightweight.

The extent of any necessary modifications

will depend on the age of the child, the site of the amputation, and the manner in which the child has adjusted to the disability. In general, the higher the amputation, the more severe the educational disability. A child with a missing leg but with a properly fitted prosthesis and well-developed skill in using it will require very little, if any, planned program modification. A child with a missing arm, especially if it is the arm with which the child had previously learned to write, may have more difficulty. When multiple amputation is involved (for example, the amputation of both arms) a considerable amount of specialized assistance is required.

Proper exercise is very important, particularly in the joints around the amputation. Physical education activities and games may be adapted or individualized for this child to ensure maximal fitness and exercise. It is not uncommon to read or hear about individuals with amputations who not only participate but who excel in competitive athletic events.

Postural habits must be carefully observed to ensure that the child does not develop spinal curvatures such as scoliosis (lateral curvature of the spine resulting in a C-shaped curve). The child may develop habits such as using only one side of the body, causing postural problems that can limit body mechanics and general functioning. If the child has a lower extremity amputation, the teacher must observe to see that unusual gait or ambulation problems do not develop.

Children with amputations may use modified or adapted equipment such as pencil holders, page turners, or other reading and writing aids. Many of these materials are available from commercial sources, and others may be easily adapted or made by the teacher.

Children with amputations usually remain in the regular classroom unless the amputation is only part of a more significant disability. Amputations in children do not usually have the severe effect that they have with some adults, because of a child's adaptability. However, special assistance may be required within the regular classroom and may be provided by the teacher who specializes in teaching the physically disabled, the occupational therapist, or both. Full knowledge about the physical condition, helping the other children in the class to accept the disability and providing adapted equipment as appropriate are the major ingredients in making proper educational provision for the child with an amputation.

ARTHRITIS

Though more often associated with adults, arthritis may occur at any age. The most common form of arthritis in children is called *juvenile rheumatoid arthritis*. Onset may be very sudden or it may be slow and gradual, with effects and complications that are quite variable. In some instances it may only last a few weeks or months and not seriously limit the child. In other cases it may be a chronic condition that continues throughout the child's life, becoming worse as time goes on. Rheumatoid arthritis attacks the joints of the body and may also involve the heart, liver, and spleen. There may be accompanying skin rash, inflammation of the eyes, possible retardation of growth, and swelling and pain in the fingers, wrists, elbows, knees, hips, and feet. As the disease progresses, the joints may stiffen, making movement very difficult and painful.

Treatment for arthritis is designed to permit the child to live as normally as possible. Otherwise, children with arthritis may become "care-cripples," overprotected and not allowed to participate fully in the activities of home or school. Juvenile arthritis is self-limiting, and the child will ordinarily use good sense in determining whether he or she should participate in an activity.

Treatment procedures are generally highly individualized because no two cases are exactly alike. Because of the variance between patients and their individual response to drugs, the drugs prescribed by the physician may be different in each case. Generally, aspirin is the single most effective drug used in the treatment of arthritis because it reduces pain and inflammation of the joints and is among the safest drugs on the market for this purpose. Large amounts may be prescribed on a routine basis, and dosage must be continued even after the swelling and pain have subsided. Special exercises may be prescribed and will involve putting the joints through a full range of motion to prevent joint deformity and loss of strength in the muscles. Heat treatments may also be prescribed to enable joints to move more smoothly and with less pain. Heat treatments take a variety of forms and may be carried out at home or in a clinic. Surgical procedures may be used to prevent and correct deformity caused by this disease, and for some children, splints, braces, or plaster casts are prescribed to subdue inflammation and protect the joints from becoming frozen.

In all but the most severe conditions, the child with juvenile arthritis will be able to function effectively with normal curricular approaches and regular learning materials. However, writing aids and special paper and pencils may be needed. The child will likely have more difficulty in physical education since the hips, knees, and ankles are often involved, and movement may cause pain. Special efforts provided by the physical therapist may be the best answer in some of these more involved cases.

Possible complications such as eye disease (fairly common in association with rheumatoid arthritis) should be regularly monitored. Teachers must also understand the child's need to have more time to finish assignments, because of the pain involved with writing, and more time to move from place to place within the school building. Children with arthritis must not be overprotected, but an understanding of potential difficulties and the various adjustments that may be required is part of special educational planning for these children.

ASTHMA

Asthma is usually related to an allergic state, which leads to an obstruction of the bronchial tubes, the lungs, or both. The basic allergy may be to foods, inhalants, or both, and when such sensitivity flares into an attack, excessive mucus is produced and there is a spasm of the bronchial musculature. Breathing becomes unusually difficult during an attack, and the child may lose color, wheeze, and perspire excessively. The attack may last for a few minutes, for hours, or in some instances for days.

An asthmatic attack can be a most frightening experience because of the labored breathing and other behaviors. In addition to sensitivity to various allergens, an attack may be triggered by excessive physical activity or an emotional reaction. The influence of emotional factors is not well established; some authorities believe that the emotional environment plays an important role in asthma, whereas others see little or no relationship.

Treatment procedures may include administration of epinephrine by injection or inhalation; and since asthma is a chronic condition, long-term treatment procedures must be employed. Teachers must be aware of the factors that precipitate an asthmatic attack and have information concerning the proper course of action should an attack occur. The teacher should also be aware of possible side effects or behavioral changes that may be related to prescribed drugs being used by the child. Teachers are in a unique position to observe the child during a variety of activities throughout the entire school day.

In the past, it was generally believed that asthmatic children should be excluded from physical education and other physically exerting activities. The results of more recent research have clearly indicated that there are many beneficial effects of exercise and activity relative to long-term care and treatment (Seligman, Randel, and Stevens, 1970; Scherr and Charleston, 1958). Many of the limitations formerly placed on these children may have done more harm than good. Generally, the child will regulate himself; if he runs too long, he may start wheezing and will then rest. Physical restrictions may have adverse psychologic effects, which are as great a danger as the physical problem itself.

Not too many years ago, it was common for children with moderate to severe asthma to be assigned to a special school for physically handicapped children. There they had a school nurse constantly available and a greatly reduced program of physical activities. Most parents, educators, and physicians seemed to agree that this was the best possible setting. However, more recently most parents will agree to regular class placement (if they receive that advice from professionals), and with proper support most regular classroom teachers manage children with mild to moderate asthmatic conditions quite effectively.

CEREBRAL PALSY

In some cases, over half of the students in any given program for the physically disabled are classified as cerebral palsied; in others, the percentage is 30 to 40 percent. No other single category of physical disability is represented by a percentage that great.

What is cerebral palsy? The definitions vary to some degree, but considerable agreement is evident. One brief dictionary definition indicates that cerebral palsy is "paralysis due to a lesion of the brain, usually one suffered at birth, and characterized chiefly by spasms." (Webster's New Universal Dictionary; unabridged, 1976) A more detailed definition provided by the United Cerebral Palsy Research and Educational Foundation (1958) includes the following elements:

1. Caused by injury to the brain
2. Motor disturbance, including paralysis, weakness, and incoordination
3. May be most accurately described as a group of conditions
4. Usually originates in childhood
5. May include learning difficulties, psychologic problems, sensory defects, and convulsive and behavioral disorders of organic origin

This list of elements includes most of those to be found in the variety of definitions proposed by various authorities. "Learning difficulties" in this listing of elements may be translated as mental retardation and/or learning disabilities; "sensory defects" means impairments in vision and hearing.

Cerebral palsy is a complex condition, characterized by a number of concurrent symptoms and attributed to brain injury. The child who is cerebral palsied is, in every sense of the term, multihandicapped. The pattern of handicaps will differ among individuals diagnosed as cerebral palsied, but the totality of these common elements leads to the diagnosis. One final note of caution: Brain injury alone does not lead to a diagnosis of cerebral palsy. Brain injury without some degree of motor dysfunction would not be diagnosed as cerebral palsy.

Because cerebral-palsied students make up such a large part of the total group of physically disabled students served in special programs, it seems appropriate to give this condition somewhat greater emphasis. In so doing, we will first review the major recognized types of cerebral palsy, categorized by differing forms of neuromuscular involvement.

Spasticity is the most common type of motor dysfunction, with about half of all cerebral-palsied persons exhibiting spastic symptoms. When a spastic child attempts to initiate voluntary movement, the result is likely to be jerky, with lack of control, particularly of body extremities. In spasticity the balance between the antagonistic muscles and suppressor areas of the brain is absent, thus, although the brain does direct the muscles, movement is attained through a series of "spasms" related to spasmodic contractions. The disability may affect any or all limbs.

Athetosis affects about one fourth of all cerebral-palsied persons and is the second most common type of motor dysfunction. In athetosis the individual tends to writhe and twist, and the head is often drawn back with the neck extended and the mouth open. The athetoid person exhibits more purposeless movements than the spastic person and facial grimaces are more common.

Ataxia, tremor, and *rigidity* are the other three specific types of neuromuscular involvement, and there may also be combined types of motor dysfunction. Ataxia includes unsteadiness in balance and thus in walking. Often the eyes are uncoordinated, and the ataxic child may stumble or fall frequently. Tremor usually includes involuntary vibration of the entire body, while rigidity involves a somewhat rigid posture, and rather than extra movement (as is the case with the other types) there is diminished movement. Ataxia, tremor, and rigidity are somewhat less likely to be diagnosed at birth than are spasticity or athetosis. In some cases, an inexperienced observor might be able to correctly identify the type of motor dysfunction quite easily; in others, it requires the clinical judgment of a medical expert. In all types, the condition may vary from mild to severe.

In addition to characterizing or describing cerebral palsy by type of neuromuscular involvement, it may be characterized by the parts of the body affected. This includes the following classifications:

1. Monoplegia; one limb affected
2. Hemiplegia; one side of the body (an arm and a leg)
3. Triplegia; three limbs involved
4. Quadriplegia; all four limbs somewhat equally affected
5. Paraplegia; only the legs involved
6. Diplegia all four limbs affected, but more involvement with the legs.
7. Double hemiplegia; all four limbs affected, but two sides affected to a different degree

Hemiplegia is the most common, with monoplegia, triplegia, and double hemiplegia quite uncommon (Denhoff, 1976).

In describing or classifying cerebral palsy, the preceding two systems are consistently used; that is, type of neuromuscular involvement (i.e., spastic, athetoid, etc.) and limbs involved (hemiplegic, quadriplegic,etc.). In addition, the description will usually include the degree of involvement (mild, moderate, or severe) and will indicate the existence of associated disabilities.

Because cerebral palsy is nearly always a matter of *several* disabilities, it is a prime example of the need for a multidisciplinary approach. The physician will play varying roles, depending on the characteristics in any given case. The physical therapist, occupational therapist, and speech pathologist will often have specific, continuing roles in the total educational program. An audiologist, a speech and hearing specialist, a learning disabilities specialist, or a teacher of the mentally retarded may be needed to provide direct service or consultation to the teacher who has primary responsibility.

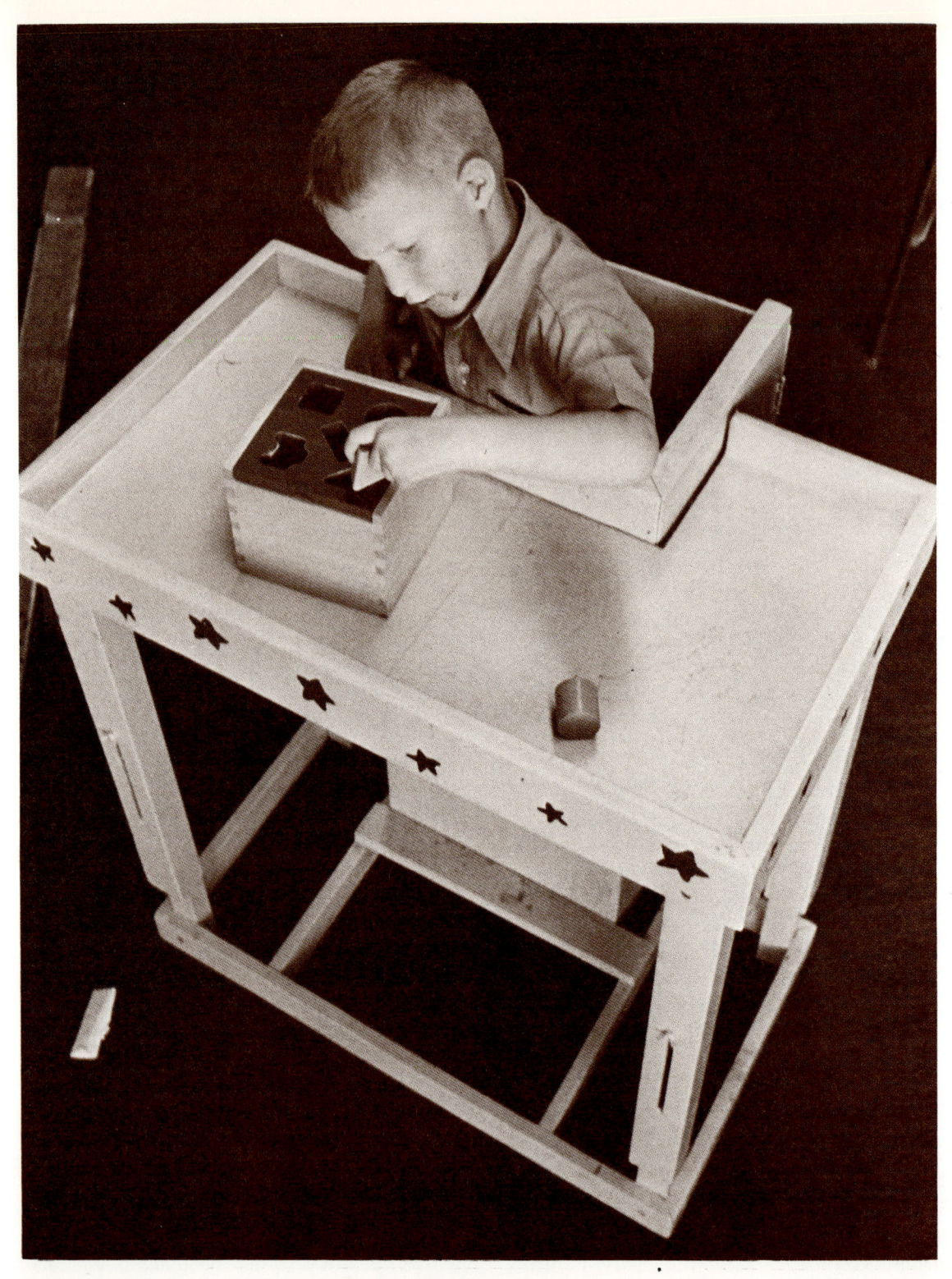

The stand-up table is an essential tool for some physically impaired students.

A variety of specialized equipment, such as adapted typewriters, pencil holders, book holders, page turners, special desks, and braces, may be required. Cerebral-palsied children provide the classic example of why the individualized education plan (IEP) is so essential in special education. They also illustrate the need for teachers with very specialized training and a complete staff of supporting specialists. The "payoff" for such programs is the considerable number of cerebral-palsied adults who are self-sufficient in spite of relatively severe motor dysfunctions.

CONVULSIVE DISORDERS (EPILEPSY)

Many people have some type of convulsion or seizure at some time in their life. In the case of young children, it is not uncommon for convulsions to occur in conjunction with high fever, and a large majority of children who have such fever-related seizures early in life never experience them as adults. All seizures (or convulsions) are apparently caused by the discharge of an unusual amount of electric energy in the brain, leading to a sort of "short-circuiting" of the normal control system. In more severe cases this results in severe muscle contractions, thus the appearance of being "seized" by some outside force. In earlier times, it was thought that the person was being seized by demons or devils, and at times the person so "seized" was subjected to treatment (to chase out the devils) that was much more severe than any normal effect of the convulsion. When such seizures are recurrent, the condition is called *epilepsy*. Fortunately, much of the negative social reaction to epilepsy has been reduced, primarily through public information programs of groups such as the Epilepsy Foundation of America.

Epilepsy can apparently result from a variety of types of brain injury, and since brain injury is the cause of many other types of disabilities, it may occur concurrently with other handicapping conditions. Although most types of epilepsy cannot be cured (in a few cases, brain lesions can be removed, thus "curing" epilepsy) recent advances in the use of various drugs to control seizures have been most successful. In fact, one of the major remaining problems is that of public attitude, which, although greatly improved, remains anchored in ignorance in many cases.

A highly unusual phenomenon sometimes occurs just prior to an epileptic attack in some individuals. This phenomenon, called an *aura*, is difficult to explain but can be specifically "sensed" by some epileptic individuals. The aura is apparently a combination of sensory signals, triggered by the brain just prior to the full-scale short-circuiting, and in some persons this set of internal sensations is an absolute predictor of an epileptic attack.

Epileptic disorders are commonly identified as being of four different types: *grand mal* and *petit mal* are the most common; *psychomotor* and *jacksonian* are much less common, especially in children.

Grand mal seizures are the most severe and may be frightening to those who have never before witnessed them. When a grand mal seizure occurs, the individual loses consciousness, falls, and has general convulsive movements. Breathing may be very labored, the child may produce a gurgling sound or may shout, and saliva may escape from the lips. The seizure may last for several minutes. Afterward the child may be confused or drowsy and will not recall what happened or what was said during the seizure.

Petit mal seizures are generally short in duration, are most common in children, and can occur as often as 100 times a day. Often these children are accused of daydreaming because they lose contact with what is happening in the classroom during the seizure. The child may become pale and may stare into space; the eyelids may twitch, or there may be slight jerky movements. After the seizure the child will continue with activities almost as though nothing had happened, probably unaware of the seizure. Petit mal seizures have a tendency to disappear before or near puberty, but they may be replaced by other types of seizure.

Psychomotor seizures are the most complex because they affect not only the motor system but the mental process as well. The seizure may last from a few minutes to several hours. During the seizure the individual may chew or smack the lips or appear to be confused. In some instances, the indivudal may carry out purposeless activities such as rubbing the arms or legs, may walk, and may pick at or take off clothing. Some individuals experience fear, anger, or rage. After the seizure the person will probably not remember what happened and will want to sleep.

Jacksonian seizures are partial seizures, in that they affect only one part of the body. At times, those who have previously experienced such seizures can control them, that is, they can prevent the spread or expansion of the seizure through intense involvement in other tasks.

The following suggestions, provided by the Epilepsy Foundation of America, are of value to teachers or to anyone who observes a grand mal seizure. In addition to their value in managing a seizure, they may add to a better understanding of epilepsy.

1. Remain calm. Students will assume the same emotional reaction as the teacher. *The seizure itself is painless to the child.*
2. Do not try to restrain the child. Nothing can be done to stop a seizure once it has begun. It must run its course.
3. Clear the area around the student so that he or she is not injured on hard objects. Try not to interfere with the movements in any way.
4. Do not force anything between the teeth. If the mouth is already open, a soft object such as a handkerchief may be placed between the side teeth.
5. It generally is not necessary to call a doctor unless the attack is immediately followed by another major seizure or if the seizure lasts more than 10 minutes.
6. When the seizure is over, let the child rest if he or she needs to.
7. The child's parents and physician should be informed of the seizure.
8. Turn the incident into a learning experience for the entire class. Explain what a seizure is, that it is not contagious, and that it is nothing to be afraid of. Teach the class understanding—not pity—toward the child so that the classmates will continue to accept him or her as "one of the gang."

In the vast majority of instances, special educational modifications are not necessary for the student who has epilepsy. (One exception might be a child who has severe grand mal seizures and who has to be protected from further damage from falls.) However, it is important for teachers to understand the condition and be prepared for it. It actually may be more important for teachers to become alert to the existence of petit mal seizures (which may go on for months or years unnoticed) and the effect they may have on overall learning. Children cannot effectively attend to learning tasks if they have recurrent petit mal seizures. In the case of the multihandicapped child who must make maximal use of all possible learning opportunities, the continuation of petit mal seizures may prove to be a serious additional handicap, which might be avoided through anticonvulsant medication if properly diagnosed.

DIABETES

Diabetes is a metabolic disorder in which the individual's body is unable to utilize and properly store sugar. This condition is a result of the inability of the pancreas to produce a sufficient amount of the hormone *insulin*.

Although diabetes is most frequently seen in adults, it occurs in children and can become a serious problem if the proper treatment procedures are not followed. There are a number of symptoms classroom teachers should be aware of that may indicate diabetes: unusually frequent urination, abnormal thirst, extreme hunger, changes in weight (generally a rapid loss), drowsiness, general weakness, possible visual disturbances, and skin infections such as boils or itching.

If diabetes is diagnosed, treatment procedures will probably involve daily injections of insulin, adherence to a rather strict diet to maintain the correct sugar level, and a balance between the right amounts of exercise and rest. The key to the treatment of diabetes is to maintain a proper balance of medication, diet, rest, and activity. Generally, children with diabetes can have a happy childhood and adolescence and can do almost everything their peers do except they may not fill up on sweets and must maintain a balance among the previously mentioned variables.

The thought of daily injections may sound potentially traumatic, but to the child with diabetes this will become a routine matter. The injections are generally administered at home and become almost as routine as other hygienic practices such as bathing or brushing teeth. Often the child and parents will attend a clinic to learn how to manage daily activities such as injections, diet, exercise, care of the feet (this can be a definite problem because of poor circulation), and necessary changes in life-style to accommodate the condition. As a result of these clinics, the child will know a great deal about the condition and will know how to manage it.

There are potential problems the classroom teacher must be aware of, such as an insulin reaction and diabetic coma. The child may have an insulin reaction resulting from anything that increases the metabolic rate, such as too much exercise, too much insulin, not enough food, or nervous tension. It may occur anytime during the day but most often occurs before meals or after strenuous exercise. General irritability may be the first sign. One child may be despondent and cry readily, whereas another may be exuberant or belligerent. The child may be hungry, perspire excessively, tremble, be unable to concentrate, and complain of being dizzy. These symptoms may vary in duration and will often disappear after providing the child with any of the following: sugar cube, pop, candy, raisins, fruit juice with sugar, or any other carbohydrate. Generally, the symptoms will disappear after 10 to 15 minutes.

The opposite of an insulin reaction is a diabetic coma. Although fairly rare, it does occur and can be serious if not treated immediately. A diabetic coma is the result of failure to take insulin, an illness, or neglect of proper diet. In this instance the child has too much sugar and must have an injection as soon as possible. Generally, it is slow in onset, and the following symptoms may be observed: thirst, frequent urination, flushed face, labored breathing, nausea, and vomiting. Treatment involves rest, injection of insulin, and possible hospitalization.

Except for extreme cases, the child with diabetes will function well in a regular class and will learn to live with the restrictions imposed by the condition. Teachers must learn to help the child avoid certain activities or situations that might lead to an insulin reaction or a coma, but the final goal is to build the child's awareness to the point that *he or she* can handle the condition. Not too many years ago, a large number of diabetic children were in special classes for the physically disabled but today, even if such classes exist, the diabetic child is much more likely to be found in the regular classroom. If the teacher is aware of and informed about the condition and does not panic when a problem occurs, it is likely that all will go well with most diabetic children.

MUSCULAR DYSTROPHY

Muscular dystrophy is a progressive, hereditary disease in which muscle fibers degenerate and are replaced by fatty tissue. The most common, and most serious type, *Duchenne*, occurs in children and is generally considered fatal. The age of onset is usually between the child's first and sixth year and rarely occurs after age 10. Early signs of the condition include a tendency to fall easily, clumsiness in walking, difficulty in climbing stairs, and difficulty in rising from the floor. There is a steady progressive decline in the child's ability to walk. He falls more frequently and eventually will need crutches to move about. As the child continues to lose strength it will be necessary to move from crutches to a wheelchair. Later, nearly all large muscles will be involved and the child will be bedridden. During the later stages, the child may be unable to raise the arms, sit erect, or hold his head up. Fortunately, the small muscles of the hands and fingers maintain some strength even during the most advanced stages.

During the early stages of muscular dystrophy very few modifications and adaptations will be necessary, but as the condition progresses there will be need for some modifications. Eventually, the student may not be able to attend any educational program and will have to receive homebound instruction; however, every effort should be made to maintain the student in regular classrooms as long as possible.

Muscular dystrophy imposes a set of contradictions. On one hand, it is known that it is generally fatal, and on the other, we ask the student, parents, teachers, and others to carry on as though the child were going to live a rich and full life. This apparent contradiction must be dealt with, and guidance and counseling services can do a great deal to accommodate the acceptance of this conflict. There is little question that if the child and parents are to accept this contradiction, ongoing counseling must be offered. Counseling programs should be conducted in cooperation with the child's parents, brothers and sisters, therapists, teachers, and physicians.

It is important that the student attend adapted physical education classes and maintain a balance between diet, activity, and rest since there is a tendency for these children to become overweight. They should be encouraged to participate as fully as possible in recreational and physical activities. Although the effects of the condition cannot be stopped by physical activity, there is some indication that it may assist in delaying some of the debilitative effects. Some caution must be exercised, however, as these children may become very easily fatigued. They should be allowed intermittent periods of rest as needed.

Research into the cause and cure for muscular dystrophy goes on, and in the meantime educators must attempt to stimulate students academically, recreationally, and socially as much as possible within the limits of their abilities. Although the disease is assumed to be fatal, proper exercise and treatment can prolong life, and perhaps that long-sought-after cure may be found, and some who already have this disease can be cured.

POLIOMYELITIS

Poliomyelitis, more commonly known as polio or infantile paralysis, was at one time the leading cause for placement in special classes and programs for the physically disabled (Kirk, 1972). The poliovirus attacks the brain or spinal cord, leaving many persons crippled, muscularly weak, or spastic. In some cases, there are almost no aftereffects; in others, death can result. With the advent of the Salk polio vaccine in 1956 and aggressive immunization programs over the following years, polio no longer "contributes" to special class programs for the physically disabled to any significant extent. A communicable disease that regularly reached epidemic proportions, polio could once again become a serious health hazard if prevention programs are not maintained. Poliomyelitis is mentioned here primarily to illustrate the manner in which medical research can radically change the complexion and composition of special programs for the physically disabled. We can only hope that similar discoveries may soon be made with respect to other serious childhood conditions and diseases.

RHEUMATIC FEVER

Rheumatic fever is a condition in which the joints become inflamed and swollen. It most often occurs following strep throat infections or scarlet fever, and it has few long-lasting effects except as the inflammation also affects the heart. When the heart is affected, it is called rheumatic heart disease, and the damage to the heart may range from mild to very serious. When heart damage is serious, the child must be treated with some additional care (within the limits of instructions from the physician) but most such children can attend regular classes. This is another condition that 15 to 30 years ago was regularly assumed to require the special conditions available only in the separate, special class. This concept has changed for all except children with very severe heart conditions or those for whom the heart condition is just one of several handicapping or disabling conditions.

SPINA BIFIDA

Spina bifida is a serious birth defect in which the bony casing of the spinal cord failed to close during fetal development. It is among the more common birth defects leading to physical disabilities, but its precise cause is unknown. In its more serious forms, a cyst or sac is present in the area of the lower back when the child is born. This protrusion is generally surgically treated during the child's first 24 to 48 hours of life. The extent of the disability resulting from this condition varies enormously. Some will have little or no disability, whereas others have varying degrees of paralysis of the legs and incontinence (lack of bowel and bladder control). In some respects this condition is similar to other crippling conditions that cause degrees of paralysis in the legs, but it is further complicated by the lack of bowel and bladder control. Because of the deficiency of nerve fibers, the child may not be able to tell when the bladder is full. The bladder may overflow, and the child may not be aware of the situation until he or she sees the wetness appearing through the outer clothing.

There are surgical procedures that can assist in accommodating this condition, or artificial devices may be worn to collect the urine. The child may also regulate fluid intake and adhere to a systematic voiding schedule. Generally, the child will be able to take care of toileting needs, but younger children may need some assistance from a classroom aide, volunteer, parent, or resource/itinerant teacher.

It is important for educators to work in close harmony with medical personnel and especially the school nurse to ensure proper health care. The teacher must also maintain a close working relationship with physical and occupational therapists to meet the child's ambulation needs and activities of daily living. Last, but certainly not least, the teacher must implement and maintain an extremely close working relationship with the parents, especially concerning prescribed toilet training programs. A flexible scheduling procedure providing specific times for toileting needs should be implemented.

If not handled properly, the psychosocial limitations imposed by this condition can be very serious. While this may seem to be a trivial matter, it is a very real concern expressed by many spina bifida children. The child may bear the brunt of other children's laughter or joking because of odor or an "accident." It is suggested that the teacher consider explaining, in a most factual manner, the limitations and problems associated with spina bifida to the other children.

The problems imposed by poor ambulation skills must be taken into consideration by therapists and teachers. However, this factor would not be any more significant for the child with spina bifida than for the child with cerebral palsy or any other major crippling condition.

Inasmuch as the child with spina bifida has good use of the upper body, arms, and hands, only minimal educational modifications are necessary. Unless they have multiple handicaps, these children are capable of profiting from regular classroom attendance and instruction with only minor modifications and adaptations.

• • •

Many other specific disabilities could be described, but the preceding are generally representative of the types of disabilities with which educators must regularly work. Wide variations in degree of severity of disability limit the value of generalizations about which of these conditions is the most difficult to plan for educationally, but we can generalize with regard to the difficulty of working with children with multiple disabilities, the topic of the following section.

Multiple disabilities or handicaps

When planning for students with multiple disabilities or handicaps, the principle relating to degree of disability applies to each of the disabilities, but in general we may say that students with multiple disabilities or handicaps present a much more difficult educational problem than those with only a single disability. We should hasten to note that cerebral-palsied students must be considered as having multiple disabilities, even though we may use the single descriptive label to refer to the syndrome. Many other students may have multiple disabilities resulting from a simple cause. A good example is rubella occuring during the first trimester of pregnancy, which commonly produces mental retardation, hearing defects, visual defects, and other disabilities. There is no way to predict in advance just which of these handicapping conditions may occur or how severe each will be, but such multiple disabilities are common.

In a study of post-rubella children in special education programs for the hearing impaired conducted by the Office of Demographic Studies at Gallaudet College, it was clearly demonstrated that these students had more severe hearing losses and more additional handicaps than hearing impaired children whose loss was caused by other factors (Jensema, 1974). In this study, of the 7,739 hearing impaired students whose impairment related to rubella, 38 percent had additional handicaps that were "educationally significant." These included visual disabilities, emotional disorders, cerebral palsy, epilepsy, mental retardation, and others. These additional handicapping conditions existed to a much greater degree in youngsters who had had rubella than in those who were hearing impaired from other causes.

Along with certain obvious differences between hearing-impaired students whose disability related to rubella and those whose impairment related to other causes, this study effectively reflects the variety of handicaps and disabilities related to rubella and suggests the complexity of planning and implementing educational programs for multihandicapped students. Causes such as anoxia (an inadequate supply of oxygen to the body), blows to the head, or other sources of brain trauma may also lead to multiple disabilities.

Children with multiple disabilities or handicaps may be much more likely to require an educational program provided through a special class or special school. As more mildly physically disabled children are placed in regular classes and more severely disabled (including those with multiple disabilities) are admitted to public schools, separate programs for the physically disabled are becoming programs for the multihandicapped for the most part. This is not to say that some children with only a single disability might not require a special class, but rather that the composition of such special classes has changed significantly in the past 20 years.

One result of this change in composition of special classes and special schools for the physically disabled (most of whom are multiply disabled) is that a much smaller pupil-teacher ratio is required to successfully educate these children with more complex learning problems. Other changes include the increased need for teacher aides (to gain this more favorable ratio) and acceptance on the part of special class personnel of a larger percentage of students who are mentally retarded in addition to other disabilities. The federal government has given special recognition to the needs of one particular type of multihandicapping condition through establishment of regional centers for the deaf-blind (this means children with significant degrees of hearing and visual impairment existing concurrently). Although the intent of PL 94-142 was for all school districts to provide for handicapped children within their local school districts when possible, it is apparent that some physically disabled students who have other serious handicapping conditions may not be able to receive the best possible service in some of the smaller, more sparsely populated communities. Regional centers would appear to be the only feasible answer in many areas of the nation, and although some such cooperative programs exist, it may be some years before the entire nation has such programming. This is one of several important goals toward which all special educators must work with diligence.

Role of medical specialists

In the preceding discussions the role of the physician has been specifically indicated in some cases and inferred in others. Because this discussion has related to medically defined conditions, it is obvious that the physician will diagnose the direct remediation of the more purely medical aspects of these conditions. In the case of poliomyelitis, the tremendous effect of medical research in the near-eradication of this disease in the United States is obvious. Research in other areas of disability may pay similar dividends in the near future.

Medical knowledge regarding causative factors such as maternal rubella has led to a significant reduction of disabilities, and antibiotics have reduced the effects of rheumatic fever.

Surgical correction for a number of conditions is possible today, including many cases of congenital heart defects and other congenital conditions such as clubfoot. Other congenital conditions may be corrected by the use of braces or casts or in the case of more severe conditions, through the use of prostheses. In fact, the use of prostheses is of very great value, both for congenital defects and for amputations.

Anticonvulsant drug control of epilepsy and diet plus insulin control of diabetes have made these conditions much less serious and

Other handicapping conditions

infinitely more manageable. Surgical procedures in some cases of spina bifida have worked near-miracles, and recent advances in asthma research holds out new hope for the many affected.

In total, the work of the medical profession has helped prevent some disabilities, and ameliorate the effects of others. Contributions of the medical profession have been a powerful force in permitting the physically disabled child to remain in the regular class, thus promoting the concept of the least restrictive environment. But one other result of the efforts of medical specialists should also be noted. In developing better techniques through which children with birth defects are kept alive, medical advances have contributed to the greater percentage of more severely disabled, multihandicapped children who must receive educational services. This group of more severely handicapped students remains one of the greater challenges to special educators today.

Educational settings: maximal integration of the physically disabled

Attempts to achieve maximal integration of the physically disabled were initiated many years before the concept of mainstreaming came into the national spotlight with respect to the mildly mentally retarded. In the days of overplacement of mildly physically disabled students in separate special schools, the pendulum had swung too far, but for the most part, corrections were made by the close of the 1960s without litigation or negative national press coverage. The use of adaptive equipment, building modifications, etc., is common in more progressive school districts, and even if *all* buildings have not been renovated to provide free access to the physically disabled, students are transported to buildings that permit free access, and thus are in classes with nondisabled students. Students are taught by regular class teachers, with consultative help from a specialist when required.

At the other end of the continuum, more severely involved students with multiple disabilities are usually taught in separate classes, often in separate settings. (Some schools had to be pressured into accepting children with multiple disabilities if moderate or severe mental retardation was among those disabilities, but progress has been made.)

It is possible to say that today programs for the physically disabled have developed to the point that there are two rather distinct types of special educational assistance provided. For the more mildly disabled or for those with a disability that is purely physical and can be in part circumvented through the use of prostheses, adapted furniture, or learning materials, the major service delivery approach is through assistance provided the regular class teacher by a resource or itinerant specialist. For students with multiple disabilities or for those with very complex and severe disabilities, a separate special class is provided. Careful assessment of all pertinent factors, both strengths and weaknesses, is the basis for deciding between these two general approaches. In the following sections we will further amplify typical roles of the specialists who serve in such assignments.

The resource or itinerant specialist is the key to providing effective support services to physically disabled students whose primary assignment is in the regular classroom. Their duties and responsibilities may include (but certainly are not limited to) the following:

1. Coordination of referrals from teachers, administrators, and school health personnel.
2. Coordination of information flow between medical agencies, therapeutic services, parents, and teachers. The resource/itinerant teacher serves as the liaison between the agencies serving the child and regular

teachers and parents. It is often necessary for the resource/itinerant teacher to assist in interpreting medical management recommendations to either the parents or the child's regular classroom teacher. In a similar manner, interpretation of occupational, physical, or speech therapy recommendations may be required. It will often be the responsibility of the resource/itinerant teacher to interpret these various recommendations and to assist in carrying them out. It is also necessary for the resource/itinerant teacher to obtain up-to-date evaluations, recommendations, and changes in treatment procedures.

3. Provision of assistance in program planning and staffing. If the staffing team suggests regular classroom placement, the resource/itinerant teacher will begin specific planning to determine the best possible setting, transportation needs, and availability of therapies.

4. Assistance to the regular classroom teacher in checking braces, crutches, and wheelchairs and observation to see that the equipment is functioning properly.

5. Assistance in planning for the modification of architectural barriers or physical restrictions, such as removing desk bottoms for wheelchairs and providing adjustable chairs and stand-up tables if needed. The resource/itinerant teacher may also arrange for construction of special equipment or assist in modifying barriers, such as installing short ramps or handrails in toilet stalls.

6. Monitoring of physical performance of the child in classroom, playground, or school community to ensure that desired ambulation patterns are being maintained outside of therapeutic settings.

7. Supplementing or reinforcing instruction of the regular classroom teacher or the physical education teacher in areas related to the disability. It may be necessary, for example, to tutor a child in an academic area in which assignments cannot be completed in the normally allotted time. Some resource/itinerant teachers have also had considerable success in working with small groups of children in the regular classroom.

8. Provision of guidance and counseling to regular teachers through in-service meetings. In some instances the resource/itinerant teacher will conduct short in-service sessions or small group discussions with children concerning a particular disability.

9. Coordination of volunteer services or classroom aides used in the regular classroom. This may involve the selection, training, placement, and scheduling of aides for assisting in activities such as physical education, physical therapy, toileting, or adapting materials.

The *teacher of a self-contained class* will be involved in the various activities outlined in the preceding section but for the most part will *actually carry out the duties* rather than assist a regular classroom teacher. The coordinative duties (i.e., between agencies, parents, medical specialists, etc.) will be quite similar, except that because of the degree of impairment of most children placed in self-contained classes, there may be more adaptations needed, more medical involvement, and more need for supportive services from the physical and occupational therapists and the speech pathologist. In addition, the teacher of the self-contained class is usually responsible for teaching the basic skills and perhaps for art, music, physical education, etc. At the secondary school level, some sort of division of teaching responsibilities among the teachers of the physically disabled may be organized to provide specialization in such subject areas as physics, advanced mathematics, bookkeeping, and American history.

Other handicapping conditions

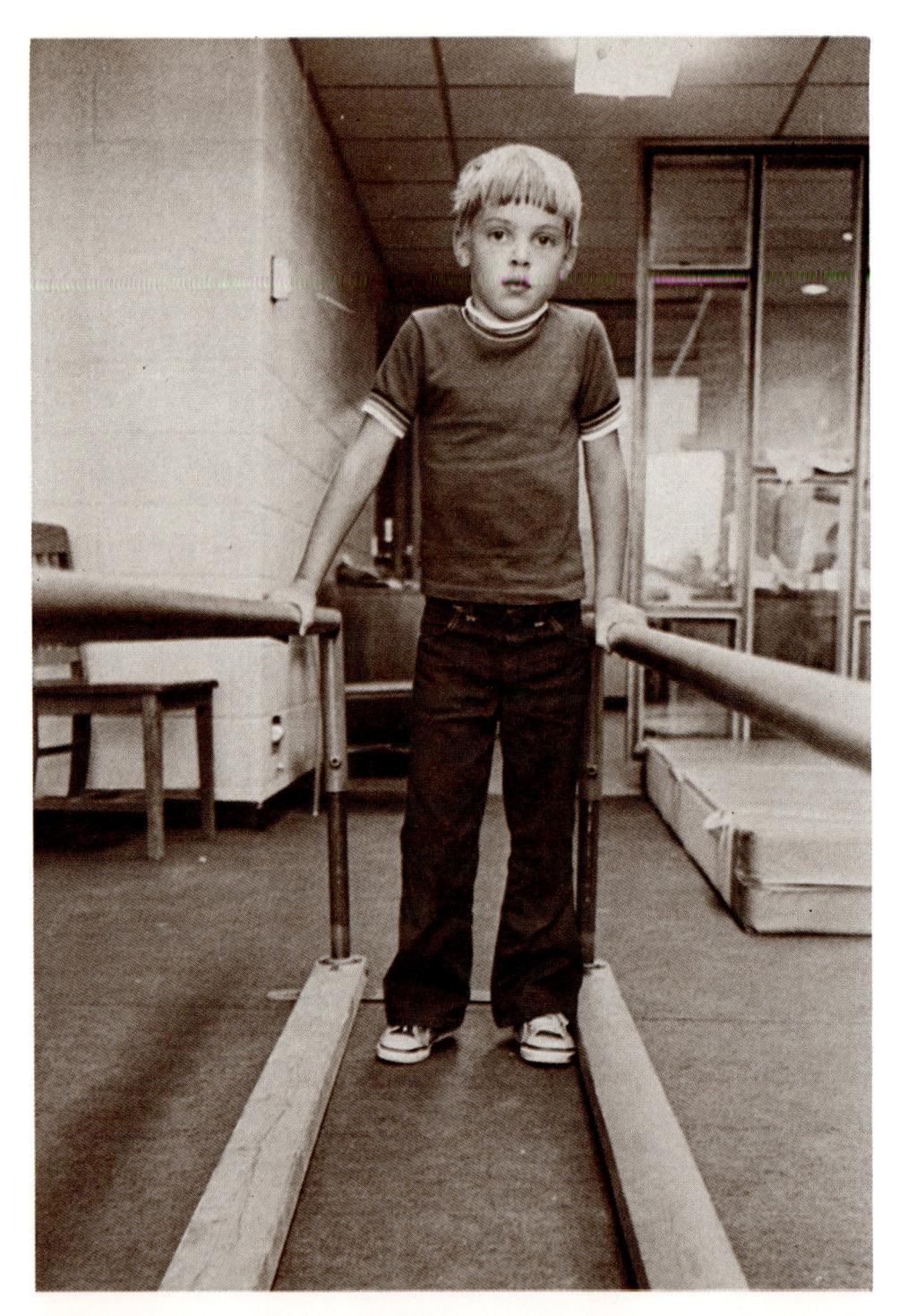

Parallel bars may provide the needed support to assist in increasing ambulation ability.

A variety of organizational arrangements may be used, but the essential underlying rationale of self-contained programs is that the students in such classes are so disabled that integration in the regular class is not feasible. Thus the special teacher must be responsible for the total program and must be sufficiently well trained and organized to carry out all of the many functions and responsibilities. He or she must indeed be a master teacher.

Other team members in the total effort to provide an appropriate educational program for the student with physical disabilities include, in addition to various purely medical specialists, occupational therapist, physical therapist, speech pathologist, other special teachers (i.e., teacher of the hearing impaired, teacher of the mentally retarded, etc.), and the school nurse. This need for the combined efforts of a number of individuals underscores the necessity for a teacher who can *harmoniously* coordinate and orchestrate these efforts. In some areas of handicap, it was at one time believed that the teacher of a self-contained class could primarily "do one's own thing." This is no longer true in other areas of disability, and in teaching students with physical disabilities cooperation is particularly essential. A teacher who can work harmoniously as part of a team effort is an absolute necessity if successful programming is to result.

Summary

Children with physical disabilities represent what is perhaps the most heterogeneous group among the generally recognized categories of disability or handicap. As generally found in established programs in the public schools, this grouping of students has tended to include more and more multihandicapped and severely handicapped or disabled individuals in the past several years. This results from several factors, including: (1) the acceptance in the public schools of more severely impaired students (primarily the result of legislation and litigation, discussed in Chapter 1), (2) inclusion of a higher percentage of the more mildly impaired in the regular school program, and (3) medical advances that have led to the survival of more severely impaired infants.

Certain principles may be applied to program planning for children with physical disabilities: (1) Physical and educational modifications should relate to actual, functional problems, not medical labels. (2) Emphasis should be on the most normal possible learning situation, but we must be sensitive to the possible need for certain very unusual physical adaptations. (3) Other subtle needs, especially in the affective area, are equally possible. (4) After applying the preceding principles and those generally applicable to all handicapped or disabled persons we must make a continuing effort to focus on the *person*, not the disability.

Physical disabilities may be classified or categorized in a number of ways, but one of the more simplified systems is to classify them as (1) neurologically related disabilities, (2) musculoskeletal and orthopedic conditions, (3) cardiovascular and respiratory system disabilities, and (4) disabilities of metabolic origin. Specific disabilities were discussed in this chapter, including amputations, arthritis, asthma, cerebral palsy, convulsive disorders, diabetes, muscular dystrophy, poliomyelitis, rheumatic fever, and spina bifida. It was noted that in most special programs today, students with cerebral palsy comprise the largest single disability grouping. It was further noted that cerebral-palsied students should actually be considered multihandicapped.

As for teachers of the physically disabled, there may be a wide variety of specific assignments, but most are variations of a basic assignment as either an itinerant or resource teacher (serving children whose basic educational assignment is in the regular classroom) or as a teacher of more severely impaired students (providing services primarily through a self-contained classroom setting). Many of these latter teachers are part of a special school setting, or what amounts to a special school within a school. In many such instances the student must also receive assistance from the physical or occupational therapist or the speech pathologist. Teacher aides are also commonly employed in programs for the physically disabled.

Teachers of the physically disabled, especially those who teach the more severely disabled, are more likely to be working with medical specialists than are teachers of children with any other type of disability or handicap. There is also more likelihood that a team of individuals will be regularly working with such students than is the case with other types of disability. This requires that the teacher not only be very well trained but also highly capable of working with others and able to coordinate and integrate the efforts of the entire team. This is a major part of the challenge of working in this complex but highly interesting specialty.

focus

introduction

"Physically handicapped" refers to a conglomerate of individuals with many different types of impairment; their commonality is that their unique educational needs result from physical or health impairments, and in many cases they have multiple disabilities.

Educational programs established to meet the unique needs of these students have been called classes or programs for: (1) crippled, (2) physically handicapped (or disabled or impaired), (3) orthopedically handicapped, (4) health impaired, or (5) some combination of these terms.

historical origins of special programs for children and youth with physical disabilities

One of the major errors in many special schools for crippled children was overinclusion of children who should never have left their home district school.

physical disabilities and health impairments: a definition and a conceptual frame of reference

Children who are physically disabled are defined as those with nonsensory physical disabilities or health impairments that require the use of modified or adapted physical settings, curriculum presentation, or other specialized materials, or equipment, to permit maximal social and educational development.

Two children who, for example, have some physical disabilities as a result of cerebral palsy may require very different programming. One may need essentially no special educational modifications; the other may require extensive special assistance.

classifications of physical disabilities and impairments

The major classifications of physical disabilities include: (1) neurologically related disabilities, (2) musculoskeletal and orthopedic disabilities, (3) cardiovascular and respiratory system disabilities, and (4) disabilities of metabolic origin.

amputations

Amputations in children do not usually have the severe effect that they have with some adults, because of a child's adaptability. Full knowledge about the physical condition, helping the other children in the class to accept the disability, and providing of adapted equipment as appropriate are the major ingredients in making proper educational provision for the child with an amputation.

arthritis

Treatment of arthritis is designed to permit the child to live as normally as possible. Juvenile arthritis is self-limiting, and the child will ordinarily use good sense in determining whether he or she should participate in an activity.

asthma

In the past it was generally believed that asthmatic children should be excluded from physical education and other physically exerting activities. The results of more recent research have clearly indicated that there are many beneficial effects of exercise and activity relative to long-term care and treatment. Many of the limitations formerly placed on these children may have done more harm than good.

cerebral palsy

Cerebral palsy is a complex condition characterized by a number of concurrent symptoms and attributed to brain injury. The child who is cerebral palsied is, in every sense of the term, multihandicapped. Brain injury alone does not lead to a diagnosis of cerebral palsy. Brain injury without some degree of motor dysfunction would not be diagnosed as cerebral palsy.

Spasticity is the most common type of motor dysfunction, with about half of all cerebral-palsied persons exhibiting spastic symptoms.

In describing or classifying cerebral palsy, two systems are consistently used; that is, type of neuromuscular involvement (i.e., spastic, athetoid, etc.), and limbs involved (hemiplegic, quadriplegic, etc.)

Because cerebral palsy is nearly always a matter of several disabilities it is a prime example of the need for multidisciplinary approach.

convulsive disorders

All seizures (or convulsions) are apparently caused by the discharge of an unusual amount of electric energy in the brain, leading to a sort of "short-circuiting" of the normal control system.

Epilepsy can apparently result from any of a variety of types of brain injury and since brain injury is the cause of many other types of disabilities, it may occur concurrently with other handicapping conditions.

Epileptic disorders are commonly identified as being of four different types. Grand mal and petit mal are the most common, psychomotor and jacksonian are much less common, especially in children.

In the vast majority of instances, special educational modifications are not necessary for the student who has epilepsy.

diabetes

Diabetes is a metabolic disorder in which the individual's body is unable to utilize and properly store sugar.

Except for extreme cases, the child with diabetes will function well in a regular class and will learn to live with the restrictions imposed by the condition.

muscular dystrophy

Muscular dystrophy is a progressive, hereditary disease in which muscle fibers degenerate and are replaced by fatty tissue. The most common, and most serious type, Duchenne, occurs in children and is generally considered fatal.

Although the disease is assumed to be fatal, proper exercise and treatment can prolong life and perhaps that long-sought-after cure may be found, and some who already have this disease can be cured.

poliomyelitis

Poliomyelitis, more commonly known as polio or infantile paralysis, was at one time the leading cause of placement in special classes and programs for the physically disabled. The poliovirus attacks the brain or spinal cord, leaving many persons crippled, muscularly weak, or spastic.

multiple disabilities or handicaps

As more mildly physically disabled children are placed in regular classes, and more severely disabled (including those with multiple disabilities) are admitted to the public school, separate programs for the physically disabled are becoming programs for the multihandicapped for the most part.

role of medical specialists

In developing better techniques through which children with birth defects are kept alive, medical advances have contributed to the greater percentage of more severely disabled, multihandicapped children who must receive educational services.

educational settings: maximum integration

Today programs for the physically disabled have developed to the point that there are two rather distinct types of special educational assistance provided. For the more mildly disabled or for those with a disability that is purely physical and can be in part circumvented through the use of prostheses, adapted furniture, or learning materials, the major service delivery approach is through assistance provided the regular class teacher by a resource or itinerant specialist. For students with multiple disabilities or for those with very complex and severe disabilities, a separate special class is provided.

References and suggested readings

Abruzzo, J. L. Rheumatoid arthritis: reflection of etiology and pathogenesis. *Archives of Physical Medicine and Rehabilitation,* Jan. 1971, *52,* 30-39.

Anderson, E., and Spain, B. *The child with spina bifida.* Denver: Love Publishing, 1978.

Best, G. A. *Individuals with physical disabilities: an introduction.* St. Louis: The C. V. Mosby Co., 1978.

Bigge, J. L. *Teaching individuals with physical and multiple disabilities.* Columbus, Ohio: Charles E. Merrill Publishing Co., 1976.

Cobb, S., and Stanislav, K. The epidemiology of rheumatoid arthritis. *American Journal of Public Health,* Oct. 1966, *56,* 1657-1663.

Collier, R. N., Jr. The adolescent with diabetes and the public schools—a misunderstanding. *Personnel and Guidance Journal,* Apr. 1969, *47,* 753-757.

Conine, T., and Brennan, W. T. Orthopedically handicapped children in regular classrooms. *Journal of School Health,* Jan. 1969, *39,* 59-63.

Cratty, B., and Breen, J. *Educational games for physically handicapped children,* Denver: Love Publishing, 1978.

Deahl, T., and Deahl, M. The orthopedically handicapped. *Instructor,* 1971, *80,* 34.

Decker, J. L. Closing in on rheumatoid arthritis: the number one crippler. *Today's Health,* June 1967, *45,* 44-47, 71.

Denhoff, E. Medical aspects. In *Cerebral palsy: a developmental disability* (3rd ed.). W. Cruickshank (Ed.). Syracuse: Syracuse University Press, 1976.

Drash, A. Diabetes mellitus in childhood. *Journal of Pediatrics,* June 1971, *78,* 919-937.

Ducas, D. Winning the battle against asthma. *Today's Health,* Aug. 1967, *45,* 28-32.

Edgington, D. *The physically handicapped child in your classroom.* Springfield, Ill.: Charles C Thomas Publisher, 1976.

Finnell, C. Despite cerebral palsy—I have the chance to try. *Today's Education,* Nov. 1970, *59,* 74-75.

Forsythe, W. I., and Kinley, J. G. Bowel control of children with spina bifida. *Developmental Medicine and Child Neurology,* Feb. 1970, *12,* 27-31.

Harlin. V. K. Experiences with epileptic children in a public school program. *Journal of School Health,* Jan. 1965, *35,* 20-24.

Haslam. R., and Valletutti, P. J. *Medical problems in the classroom: the teacher's role in diagnosis and management.* Baltimore: University Park Press, 1975.

Holley, L. The physical therapist: who, what, and how. *American Journal of Nursing,* July 1970, *70,* 1521-1524.

Jensema, C. Post-rubella children in special education programs for the hearing impaired. *Volta Review,* 1974, *76,* 466-473.

Kirk, S. A. *Educating exceptional children.* Boston:. Houghton Mifflin, 1972, 368.

Martin, J. W. Attitudes toward epileptic students in a city high school system. *Journal of School Health,* 1974, *28,* 144-146

Mitchell, M. M. Occupational therapy and special education. *Children,* Sept.-Oct. 1971, *18,* 183-186.

Moore, M. L. Diabetes in children. *American Journal of Nursing,* Jan. 1967, *67,* 104-107.

Noon, E. F. Don't be afraid of the child with epilepsy. *Instructor,* 1968, *78,* 57.

Puthoff, M. New dimensions in physical activity for children with asthma and other respiratory conditions. *Journal of Health, Physical Education, and Recreation,* Sept. 1972, *43,* 75-77.

Robins, H., and Schaltner, R. Obstacles in the social integration of orthopedically handicapped children. *Journal of Jewish Community Services,* Winter 1968, *45,* 190.

Scherr, M. S., and Charleston, L. F. A physical conditioning program for asthmatic children. *Journal of the American Medical Association,* 1958, *168*(15), 1196-2000.

Seligman, T., Randel, H. O., and Stevens, J. J. Conditioning program for children with asthma. *Physical Therapy Journal,* May 1970, *50,* 641-647.

Şolenberger, E. R. *Public school classes for crippled children.* U.S. Department of the Interior Bulletin No. 10. Washington, D.C.: U.S. Government Printing Office, 1918.

Stratch, E. H. Rehabilitation of young spina bifida children. *Rehabilitation,* April-June 1969, *69,* 17-20.

United Cerebral Palsy Research and Educational Foundation Program for 1958. New York: The Foundation, 1958.

SECTION SIX

Those "most often overlooked" exceptional students

A number of unique features of this section may be noted. First, all other parts of this text relate to handicapped or disabled persons. This section relates to the gifted, talented, and creative—to those who will likely be the major contributors of tomorrow and who, hopefully, may be encouraged to enter positions of political, economic, and social leadership. Their contributions and their leadership are sorely needed, and efforts to encourage their maximal development should pay significant dividends for all, including the handicapped and disabled.

A second feature of this section is that it includes only one chapter. If our concern were details of program implementation, it might be advantageous to subdivide this chapter; but after considering the development of separate chapters for the gifted, talented, and creative, it became obvious that much of the content of the chapters would be the same. In most cases, information that applies to the gifted applies also to the talented and the creative, and the cumbersome phrase, "gifted, talented, and creative," has been shortened to the "gifted" in many cases. However, at various times throughout the chapter, the longer designation will be used to remind the reader that most of the content of this chapter concerns all three.

A third way in which this section is different from the others is that it concerns a population that does not have the assurances or protections of law regarding their right to a special education. There is separate federal legislation regarding the gifted and talented, which will be discussed, but it is very different in scope and in degree of fiscal support from the legislation relating to the handicapped and disabled.

Gifted, talented, and creative students are different in many other ways, differences that will be amplified in this section. In almost half of the fifty states, education of the gifted, talented, and creative is not a part of the state division of special education, which may be either advantageous or disadvantageous. However, it is becoming much more generally recognized that the gifted, talented, and creative students in our schools *are* exceptional, in both their potential and their educational needs. These exceptional educational needs and the manner in which they are being met in certain areas of the nation are the concern of this section.

This young boy actually picked up the ball and mitt as shown. At 30 months of age, this may be an indication of future athletic talent.

chapter **12**

Education of children and youth with unusual gifts and abilities

objectives

To appreciate the history of the recognition of gifted and talented individuals and the varied efforts initiated on their behalf.

To develop an understanding of the more common definitions of giftedness, talent, and creativity.

To describe the characteristics commonly ascribed to the gifted, talented, or creative and how such students may be identified.

To explore the qualifications and characteristics of teachers of these students.

To describe federal efforts to promote programs for the gifted and talented.

To describe and illustrate state leadership in establishing programs for the gifted, talented, and creative.

Introduction

There is little doubt in the mind of many objective observers that of all the normally recognized exceptionalities, the gifted, talented, and creative students of the United States are among the most neglected. There are a few states in which this may not be true, but on a nationwide basis, it is easy to substantiate this neglect. Presuming this to be true, three questions must be asked: Why is this the case? How did it happen? What should be done to correct the situation? The answer to the first two questions lies in the history of development of special programs for exceptional children, the nature of the financial structure of the public schools (including special provisions for exceptional children), and the lack of understanding of the needs of gifted, talented, and creative students. The history of development of special programs for the gifted/talented/creative will be presented in the following section. However, the manner in which programs for *other* exceptional children (the handicapped) have developed may provide much of the answer. This was reviewed in Chapter 1 and involves, among other things, the established need to make the handicapped more independent, as self-supporting as possible, and more "normal." Most gifted, talented, and creative students tend to be quite independent and more able than "normal" students to become self-supporting, even without special programs. In addition, if we do provide the type of program that will lead to maximal development of the gifted, creative, and talented, we often make them *less* rather than more "normal."

A second aspect of the events that led to the development of more effective broad-range programs for the handicapped was the development of militant advocacy groups, including both parents and professional special educators. This element too is missing, for the most part, regarding gifted, talented, and creative students. Coupled with this militant advocacy was another factor which, though not regularly articulated, is highly important. With regard to the handicapped, it was possible to establish a feeling of sympathy. We have, of course, learned that we should assist nonhandicapped students to accept handicapped students with a minimum of such overt feelings, but in the last analysis, it is much more difficult to turn down extra budgetary requirements for blind children than for gifted children. Whether we want to recognize it or not, *a major factor in the present lack of adequate programming for the above-average student in most of the nation is the difficulty in generating much concern for the "poor little gifted child."* Guilt or pity should *not* be the basis for provision for appropriate educational programs for exceptional children, and with the passage of PL 94-142, The Education for All Handicapped Children Act of 1975, a broad range of programs for the handicapped became a matter of mandated public policy. However, prior to that time, as programs for the handicapped evolved through the years, the matter of concern for the less fortunate was a definite factor. Today, we should consider appropriate programming for the gifted, talented, and creative from two different vantage points. *First, they have a right to free, appropriate educational programming, so that they may experience the satisfaction of maximal challenge and full development of their basic potential. Second, they are an important human resource, and as such their development is important to the nation and to the world.* PL 94-142 directs that the handicapped must receive a free, appropriate education in the least restrictive educational environment. The gifted, talented, and creative should receive precisely the same guarantee.

Historical development of education for the gifted, talented, and creative (the beginning until 1960)

Perhaps the earliest special planning for education for the gifted or talented was that proposed by Plato in planning his Republic. He was concerned about the provision of able leadership and thus the successful maintenance of his ideal state. In a similar manner the Romans searched out talented youth for special training in law, politics, and military strategy. This procedure seemed only logical in the development of an expanding empire, and like the recommendations of Plato, it was not related to any concept of the inherent right of individuals to maximal personal development; rather, it was related to the needs of the nation. The Roman Catholic Church was, at various times and to various degrees, interested in development of talented individuals; but interest seemed to center on the good of the church, not the individual.

This tendency to provide some type of more extensive, special educational effort in an attempt to develop leaders continued throughout the years with only minor variations until the seventeenth century when, in response to the political concept of equality and equal opportunity for all, most such educational programs were halted. Because so many of those youths who had been provided a higher level of education were part of what had been the ruling class, and because "equal" was interpreted as meaning "the same," the only acceptable course to pursue at the time was to halt all special educational programs. This was the pattern for nearly two centuries in both Europe and the United States with one notable exception in the New World. Thomas Jefferson, in a formal educational plan developed for the state of Virginia, advocated that able students be sought out and provided special educational programming. This included, among other things, a plan to search among the poor for talented students who might be sent to William and Mary College at public expense. In his treatise it was clear that the purpose of such free public education of talented students was based on concern for the state of Virginia, but it was equally clear that he was advocating special, state-supported education for the gifted. On the other hand we may speculate that the reference to the good of the state was for political purposes, and Mr. Jefferson was actually interested in the development of talented youth for the sake of self-development.*

Although there were earlier examples of private schools providing for the gifted and talented, these were little more than copies of similar private schools in Europe. However, there have been notable milestones in the establishment of educational programs for the gifted in the United States, including the following:

1868   The St. Louis, Missouri, public schools initiated a variable promotion plan, which provided additional opportunity for the gifted student. This was the first application of variable interval promotions (rather than the fixed, rigid, grade-level promotion system); varieties of this plan were adopted in schools around the nation.

1886   The Elizabeth, New Jersey, public schools introduced a type of homogeneous grouping based on academic achievement. The most academically talented group was encouraged to move more rapidly through the established content of the school curriculum.

---

*Historical events noted in this summary were drawn from a variety of sources, including primarily Gearheart, B. *Education of the exceptional child*, Scranton, Pa.: Intext Publishers, 1972; and Rice, J. *The gifted: developing total talent.* Springfield, Ill.: Charles C Thomas, Publisher, 1970.

1898	The Santa Barbara, California, schools began to group more able students together in an attempt to broaden educational experiences. The emphasis in Santa Barbara and in some other larger school districts was to substitute this type of ability grouping for acceleration. This was a variety of what came to be called "tracking."
1900	New York City public schools established what is recognized by some educational historians as the first special classes for the gifted. These classes, in contrast to the tracking type programs, were designed primarily to permit effective acceleration.
1920	The Cleveland, Ohio, public schools established a very extensive program often called the Major Work Program, one of the longest lasting and most comprehensive such programs in educational history. These separate, special classes for gifted students were generally well received by both students and parents and provided the basis for much of the special class programming in other parts of the nation in the years which followed.
1920 to 1940	A variety of combinations of acceleration, enrichment, and special settings were attempted, each apparently with sufficient merit to warrant continuation for several years, and each with inherent disadvantages. It is worthy to note that no one administrative or curricular plan was of sufficient merit to lead to exclusive utilization at any one time. The states of California, New York, and Ohio were among the leaders in developing these programs, but plans were not implemented on a statewide basis, and actually not too many students, in total, were included in these early programs.

In addition to various attempts to establish special administrative provisions and to broaden, enrich, or otherwise modify curriculum to better serve gifted or academically talented students, a number of other events influenced the development of such programs.

In 1921, Lewis Terman initiated his investigations of giftedness, which eventually led to the *Genetic Studies of Genius* publications and what is undoubtedly the most well-known longitudinal study of gifted children and adults accomplished anywhere in the world. Terman's study established one fact beyond any shadow of a doubt: gifted children become adults who contribute in the areas of art, science, journalism, politics, and all arenas of life, far beyond what may be expected of average students. The publication in 1925 of Terman's first volume of *Genetic Studies of Genius* led to a flurry of interest in the gifted. A second publication, *School Training of Gifted Children*, the 1928 report of the Cleveland, Ohio, Major Work Program for the gifted was the first lengthy report of an actual public school program and provided a model that other cities imitated at least in part.

The decade of the 1930s brought with it little that was new in the education of the gifted, either in terms of program implementation or significant writings in the field. Perhaps as a side effect of the depression era, acceleration (often popularly called "skipping" of grades) became more popular during this time, and according to Rice (1970), "Many inaccurate generalizations which prejudice us against acceleration stem from this period." (p. 8)

The year 1941 brought World War II, and in 1942, the Westinghouse Corporation initiated the "Science Talent Search," an attempt to discover high school students who had unusual potential to become creative scientists. This event, with related advertising, emphasized the value of gifted individuals to science-related industries, and helped bring the existence of giftedness to the attention of the general public. In 1947 the American Association for Gifted Children was established, and as an outgrowth of its establishment a highly important text, *The Gifted Child* (Witty) was published in 1951. Contributors to this text included most of the well-known authorities in the area of education of the gifted, and although the total percentage of American educators who were truly interested in the gifted was small, the number was growing.

In 1953, an organization was formed that is known today as The National Association for Gifted Children (NAGC). The NAGC promotes programs for gifted students and their publication the *Gifted Child Quarterly* has become a most useful forum for debate and dissemination of information of interest to professionals and parents who espouse the cause of the gifted.

Dr. James Conant, after returning from a series of observations of educational programs abroad, warned the nation in 1947 that we were inviting future difficulty because we did not do more to promote the academic competence of our talented youth. Ten years later, the USSR launched Sputnik (the first manmade satellite), and the American public became concerned overnight. More important, the U.S. Congress became alarmed. Dr. Conant quickly reminded the nation of his previous warnings, and in February 1958 a conference, chaired by Conant, was held in Washington, D.C. The National Education Association, assisted by a Carnegie Foundation grant, sponsored this meeting dedicated to finding more effective ways to discover and educate the academically talented in our secondary schools. Most Americans seemed to agree that we must not let the Russians beat us at anything. And if it took extra effort— even extra tax dollars—it was probably worth it. The Congress became very busy, and the National Defense Education Act (NDEA) was passed and signed into law by President Eisenhower by the middle of 1958. It was almost as if Congress did not know they were providing federal support to public education (a very unpopular concept at that time), and it is doubtful if they were particularly concerned with the students who would be involved. Their concern was to keep anyone else from bypassing the United States scientifically; winning the "space race" became top priority. The title of the act is certainly significant, and the manner in which our nation has established its priorities must be noted. Like Plato, the ruling powers of Rome, and many others down through the ages, education for the gifted came about through concern for the *state*, not for the individual.

NDEA, although not labeled an "education of the academically gifted" act, was in fact just that. It provided money primarily for improved programs in science, mathematics, foreign languages, and guidance and counseling. It was limited in scope and as expanded through amendments, its effect on the original narrow target area was diluted. NDEA did prove that the federal government could, if properly motivated, assist education of the gifted through direct aid. It was at least a beginning.

Historical development of education for the gifted, talented, and creative (1960 to the present)

Since approximately 1960, some encouraging signs have appeared regarding official recognition of the special educational needs of the gifted, talented, and creative. A majority of the states have shown some recognition of their needs, but all too often this recognition has been limited to the appointment of a state consultant or two and the promise to assist local districts in planning programs.

At the federal level a few publications of value were provided through the sponsorship of such agencies as the Children's Bureau or the Cooperative Research Branch of the Office of Education, but lacking specific congressional directives, not much was done until 1968 and 1969 when proposals were introduced in Congress under the title, The Gifted and Talented Children Educational Assistance Act. Introduction of this act was significant and unique in the history of federal involvement on behalf of the gifted in that it was not promoted in relation to national defense and was not directed toward the culturally different or the economically underprivileged. It was intended to provide federal impetus for improvement of programs for the gifted and talented—for the good of those gifted and talented. Though the act was titled "gifted and talented," and omitted specific mention of the creative student, it defined the gifted and talented as those children who "have outstanding intellectual ability or creative talent." Thus it did, at least indirectly, relate to creative children and youth. The need for the act was dramatized at the time by the fact that, in 1969, only thirteen of the fifty states had even one full-time staff member (at the state department of education level) working with programs for the gifted. As a result of this situation, nine out of ten gifted students then receiving special services or programs were from those thirteen states.

Due to a number of circumstances, the bill was not enacted as separate legislation, but many of its essential components became part of another law, the Elementary and Secondary Act Amendments of 1969 (PL 91-230). PL 91-230 became law on April 13, 1970, and as a result, the Commissioner of Education was directed to do a number of specific things. Section 806(c) of PL 91-230 reads:

> The Commissioner of Education shall:
> (A) determine the extent to which special educational assistance programs are necessary or useful to meet the needs of gifted and talented children,
> (B) show which existing Federal educational assistance programs are being used to meet the needs of gifted and talented children,
> (C) evaluate how existing Federal educational assistance programs can be more effectively used to meet these needs, and
> (D) recommend which new programs, if any, are needed to meet these needs.

The commissioner was further directed to report the findings, together with recommendations, to the Congress within 1 year. In response to this mandate, the Office of Education initiated a status study, in which a variety of approaches were used to determine answers to the questions posed by PL 91-230. According to Senator Jacob Javits (from the foreword to the report to the Congress given by the U.S. Commissioner of Education, Sidney Marland, in 1972), one of the most valuable and productive sources of information for the report was the public hearings held by the ten Regional Commissioners of Education, covering the fifty states. Parents, citizens, gifted children, and graduates of programs for the gifted, along with state and local educators and administrators of programs for the gifted, were invited to testify regarding the importance of specialized programs for the gifted and talented. Another productive aspect of the Office of Education study was a reveiw of existing federal education programs and review of research in the field. A third important source of information was developed through systematic consultation with individuals recognized as leading experts in education of the gifted.

This report, growing out of the mandates of the law, undoubtedly represents the most comprehensive, broad-range documentation ever compiled of needs of the gifted and possible ways to meet these needs. If it is biased, it is biased in the direction of the belief that gifted children and youth *should* receive extra attention and assistance. However, due to the unusually broad base from which information was drawn, and the fact that those gathering and compiling data did not represent any specific philosophic school of thought, it is essentially unbiased as to theoretical/philosophic frame of reference. From the point of view of history, this, and the mandate to provide this report, are of great significance. Contents of the report will be further reviewed later in this chapter.

Following the 1972 report to the Congress, the Office of Education established a minimal but ongoing program at the federal level, which tended at least to keep the idea of federal involvement with the gifted and talented alive. In 1974 PL 93-380 authorized additional assistance for programs and projects to attempt to more adequately meet the special educational needs of gifted and talented children and youth. Like earlier interest in the gifted, this program of assistance included the promise of very limited funds but was greatly expanded in scope and in potential for the future. Finally, regulations governing the program for the gifted and talented were published in the *Federal Register* on May 6, 1976. These provide a comprehensive base for federal assistance to the gifted and talented, which, if supported by adequate federal funds, would have a dramatic impact on the development of such programs. Provisions of these rules and regulations will be outlined in a later section of this chapter.

This historical review may seem to indicate that, although some federal effort was being made, it was very, very minimal. This is, in fact, what is intended, but two observations are required to assist the reader to interpret these implications. First, these federal efforts were indeed minimal compared to efforts being made during the same time period on behalf of handicapped children. From this point of view they seem totally inadequate and patently unfair. However, a second observation must also be made in the interests of objectivity. Congress, for the most part, responds to pressure, and the pressure during this period was on behalf of the handicapped. And, although this interest in the gifted was minimal, it provides a basis for much more comprehensive assistance, *if the public demands it*.

Finally, by the last half of the 1970s, an increased level of broad-scale activity appeared to be underway. Stimulated by what appeared to be a real possibility that the U.S. Office of Education might be permitted, by the provision of adequate funds, to really get into the business of providing substantive assistance to the gifted, university training program directors and state associations for the gifted around the nation increased their individual efforts. The Council for Exceptional Children supported the idea of expanding the Bureau of Education for the Handicapped, by officially removing the term "handicapped" and replacing it with "exceptional" or "exceptional persons" or some other term to indicate inclusion of the gifted and talented. This recommendation, made through congressional subcommittee hearings, is apparently supported by some within the federal establishment and opposed by others. Whatever the outcome of this question, if the provisions for assistance to special projects and services for the gifted and talented are adequately funded, the history of education of the gifted and talented will eventually record a dramatic increase of programs, both in quantity and in quality.

Definitions: the gifted, talented, and creative

The possible sources for definitions of the gifted, talented, and creative are not endless but certainly are numerous. For example, the list of references included in the report to the Congress, entitled *Education of the Gifted and Talented*, includes 198 references. Most of these include either an actual definition of giftedness or an inferred definition. Although some are precisely the same, there are notable differences. Even if we limit our consideration to a definition for the word "gifted," we will find a variety of definitions. When we include "talented" and "creative" the variety is increased. Various studies have been conducted to attempt to resolve this dilemma, but the conclusions that must be drawn when considering such studies in total is that definitions of giftedness vary, and this has become much more noticeable since about 1950. We will review several of these definitions, concluding with the one established as a result of PL 91-230 and affirmed by PL 93-380.

Prior to 1950 nearly all definitions of "gifted" clearly state or strongly infer superior intellectual ability or high IQ. Other factors were sometimes mentioned, but high IQ was the major factor. The usual basis for referral for programs for the gifted was some sort of nomination by teachers. This led to nomination of those "intelligent" students who demonstrated their intelligence in academic pursuits. The word "talent" came to be used to some extent but was used primarily in relation to *academic* talent and almost always related to *demonstrated academic talent*—a practice that led to the inclusion of those whose talent was most obvious through their achievement. In most instances, nomination for inclusion in the "gifted" or "talented" program was the first step, but usually some test of intelligence or academic achievement or both was required if the student were to be considered gifted or talented.

In a succinct, well-presented evaluation of the expanding concept of giftedness, Getzels and Jackson (1958) made a number of important points which deserve consideration here:

1. When any concept becomes the focus of continued attention, the original meaning is likely to be both expanded and differentiated.
2. Giftedness has been primarily related to a score on an IQ test and has been essentially the study of a single IQ variable.
3. One result of the fact that "gifted" has become synonymous with "high IQ" (at least for school-related programs) is that school personnel have been blinded to other forms of excellence.
4. Educators have tended to act as though the results of the IQ test represent an adequate measure of *all* the universe of functions that might be called intellectual functions.
5. Because learning involves the production of *novelty* as well as remembering course content, a measure of creativity should be considered, in addition to measures of IQ, in defining characteristics of giftedness.

Getzels and Jackson would likely be listed among the top four or five authorities in the area of study of creativity, and this point of view, expressed in 1958, suggests the inclusion of the concept of creativity within a broader concept of giftedness. It is more likely that a survey of the beliefs of authorities in the field of creativity today would lead to a recommendation that creativity be considered separate from rather than a part of a broader, general concept of giftedness. This is obviously a semantic controversy, but it is based on the concerns expressed by Getzels and Jackson and the fear that, because of the historical basis for the definition of the gifted, creativity might be neglected.

In one of the earliest U.S. Department of Health, Education and Welfare publications relating to giftedness, published the same year as the Getzels and Jackson's article, we find this discussion of definition (*Your Gifted Child*, 1958):

> What does gifted mean? There are a great many definitions for the term. Some are broad and some precise. One educator described a gifted child as . . . any child whose performance in a potentially valuable line of human endeavor is consistently superior. Another said, . . . every child who in his age group is superior in some ability which may make him an outstanding contributor to the welfare of society. Another

said, ... the top 1 percent of the juvenile population in general intelligence.

Drawing from several definitions [we call] a child gifted when he performs much better than his age group in a way or ways that give promise of future high level achievement or contribution. In other words, they are in the comparatively small group from which are likely to come our most creative and outstanding artists, teachers, scientists, engineers, philosophers, explorers, historians, economists, psychologists, jurists, poets, educators, writers, inventors, ministers, statesmen, and business leaders. (pp. 2-3)

This definition, provided in a pamphlet for parents of gifted children over 20 years ago, is not too out-of-date today in many respects. It recognizes creative efforts and it recognizes professions that obviously require high-level intellectual ability. From its listing of occupational/professional groups, it infers a broad range of talent and creative ability, but it lacks in one important aspect. It seems to require that the child give evidence *through present performance* that he or she will later do something unusual. Unless we are very careful in identification procedures, we are likely to continue with the teacher nomination procedure, which will miss a significant number of children in our search for the potentially gifted and creative. (See pp. 361-362 for the study by Jacobs, which so aptly illustrates this difficulty.)

A number of other writers have provided definitions that deserve mention, both for historical interest and to provide a more complete perspective regarding who the gifted, talented, and creative may actually be. This is important since it appears that the gifted, or talented, or creative student is that student who is described as being such for any particular program or geographic area at any given point in history.

Words change in meaning as concepts change. This discussion of definitions is provided to indicate the broad range of possibilities within which the definition may lie. Some students may be included no matter which definition is used. Others will be included by some definitions, excluded, or never discovered if others are in use. Additional federal guidelines may provide more similarity among the fifty states, particularly if significant amounts of federal monies are provided for programming, but absolute rigidity in definition would be an error. If such rigidity were possible and had been applied 40 years ago, presumably we would now still have the "IQ score" definition, a situation that nearly all would agree is undesirable.

One relatively comprehensive definition of the gifted was proposed in a discussion suggesting classifications of talent as follows (Rice, 1970):

1. *Academic talent:* in general, can be predicted from high scores of general mental ability.
2. *Creative talent:* should not be restricted to students selected by rigid identification procedures. This might include groups ranging from "conforming types such as inventors, theorists, and critics through to extraordinary types such as revolutionaries, avant-garde poets, and creative writers." (p. 12)
3. *Psychosocial talent (leadership):* though admittedly very difficult to measure, the ability to influence others in intellectual, social, religious, political, or military ways is an important talent that should be further researched, identified, and encouraged.
4. *Talent in the performing arts:* in contrast to most others categories, primarily empirical in conception. This would include but not be limited to such areas as music, dance, and dramatics.
5. *Kinesthetic (athletic) talent:* relatively self-explanatory, but historically has received highly varied degrees of acceptance and recognition in American culture.

6. *Manipulative skills:* includes various psychomotor capabilities, such as those of the craftsman, painter, sculptor, and others. This relates particularly to talent that requires above-average ability to coordinate what the eye observes with what the hand produces.
7. *The mechanical-technical-industrial complex of skills:* includes those skills and aptitudes highly prized by the industrial-business complex. This would include many subcategories but certainly includes skills required by the master mechanic, machinist, draftsman, etc.

Rice notes that these are obviously overlapping talents, that some are much more highly recognized than others, but that all should be considered important among the talents that the gifted exhibit or have the potential to exhibit or develop.

An excellent example of the reason why those who are novices in the field of education of the gifted must be careful in drawing conclusions about the definition of giftedness may be seen in a generally well-written, practical guide for educators who work with the gifted. *Gifted and Talented Children: Practical Programing for Teachers and Principals* includes narrative that seems to say that giftedness is a very broad concept, then includes the statement, "generally the label *gifted* refers to children who achieve 132 or higher on the Stanford Binet Intelligence Tests. These comprise the top 2 percent of the general population." (Syphers, 1972 p.5) Additional discussion indicates various factors that might lead to inclusion of those with lower IQ scores, but the statement would lead many to believe that this is *the* definition of gifted.

Dorothy Syphers is former Coordinator of Gifted Programs in California, and this definition may have been consistent with the definition in use *in California* at that time. Her book of suggestions is most worthwhile reading, but it is unfortunate that she did not note the limitations of this definition. She could have added that it *might* apply elsewhere but would be unacceptable in some other states, for example, Connecticut. (The Connecticut definition at that time made specific reference to demonstrated or potential achievement in music, the visual arts, or the performing arts and recognized such areas of talent as part of their programs for the gifted and talented.) This is only one of many examples of the manner in which a small amount of reading in selected texts or journals may lead to misconceptions or at least very limited conceptualizations. One further note of caution: Even the *date* of any particular piece of writing (either textbook or journal article) cannot be used to ensure that the information is the "latest" or the most comprehensive. Note that Getzels and Jackson's (see p. 354) article is 14 years older than the Syphers publication, yet it reflects a point of view that most would agree is more modern. *The fact is that information provided by various authors may be primarily for one specific audience, and if the reader is not cautioned or if only one part of a text or journal article is read, misconceptions may result.* This point also applies to the literature of all other areas of special education.

A different definition has been proposed by an educational psychologist of established reputation. After noting the "distracting array of terminology used in regard to the gifted" and commenting on the manner in which educators "in prescientific fashion . . . have let the gifted identify themselves by demonstrating superior achievement" T. Ernest Newland (1976) proposes a socially based definition. He reasons that society determines the extent to which it needs the gifted. This should be reflected in a "sound first approximation of how many are needed to carry out its high-level operations." (p.11). This then provides a quantitative statement of the magnitude of societal need, which becomes the magnitude of the school's responsibility.

Next (according to Newland), psychologists must identify the conditions and characteristics that differentiate those with top-level responsibilities from those with lower-level responsibilities. This will determine the required behavioral characteristics of those who must be prepared to meet the high-level responsibilities.

Finally, the schools must locate a sufficient number of students who have the essential psychologic characteristics to meet the needs of society. This is how the gifted should be identified. Newland provides a detailed description of how to determine the percentages of leaders needed, how to add additional percentages for "slippage," and reports on some research and computation he has completed that indicates the nation should regard 8 percent of its population as essential to society's high-level, leadership responsibilities. He further notes that this does not necessarily mean this set percentage in any given class, school, or community, for some have greater or lesser percentages of students who should be considered gifted.

Newland is quick to note that this rationale applies only to how the school identifies those who are to be educated as gifted. The matter of how to go about educating them is another matter, which he explores and expands in the remainder of his text.

The final definitions to be considered are those that may have some significant degree of national acceptance because they were developed through the federal Program for the Gifted and Talented, which grew out of Public Laws 91-230 and 93-380. This acceptance, if it in fact develops, will be promoted by two factors. First, these definitions were developed with the input of educators of the gifted from all over the nation, thus they reflect at least some of the thinking of many of those individuals who will play the greatest role in acceptance or rejection. Second, if this act is funded for any significant dollar amount, some degree of acceptance will be assured, at least on paper, because those who want to avail themselves of these funds will find it necessary to play the game by the federal rules.

The 1976 federal definition reads as follows:

"Gifted and talented" means children and, where applicable, youth, who are identified at the preschool, elementary, or secondary level as (1) possessing demonstrated or potential abilities that give evidence of high performance capability in areas such as intellectual, creative, specific academic, or leadership ability or in the performing and visual arts; and (2) needing differentiated education or services (beyond those being provided by the regular school system to the average student) in order to realize these potentialities. (Federal Register, May 6, 1976, p. 18666)

This definition is very similar to an earlier definition included in the report of the Commissioner of Education (Marland) in response to PL 91-230. This earlier definition, established by the first advisory panel to the Commissioner of Education, is widely quoted in the literature of the 1970s and reads as follows:

Gifted and talented are those identified by professionally qualified persons who by virtue of outstanding abilities, are capable of high performance. These are children who require differentiated educational programs and/or services beyond those normally provided by the regular school program in order to realize their contribution to self and society.

Children capable of high performance include those with demonstrated achievement and/or potential ability in any of the following areas, singly or in combination:
1. general intellectual ability
2. specific academic aptitude
3. creative or productive thinking
4. leadership ability
5. visual and performing arts
6. psychomotor ability. (Marland, 1972, p. 2)

It might be noted that the only specific component included in this 1972 definition not repeated in the 1976 definition was "psychomotor ability." It could be argued that high level psychomotor ability would most likely show itself in the performing arts, and thus it is actually included, at least in spirit. It is also important to note that *potential* abilities are recognized and that these definitions are limited to those children and youth who require *differentiated services* (which is defined as services beyond those regularly provided the average student). The gifted, talented, and creative are at times deliberately included in one specific definition or program description while at other times each may be specified as a separate characteristic. However, the most common present practice is to include the gifted and talented together (as in the federal definition) but leave considerable question as to whether the creative are also included, if they do not meet the criteria established for the gifted and talented. Therefore, a limited presentation and discussion of definitions of creativity will be provided in the following section.

CREATIVITY

An interesting interpretation of the problems involved in defining creativity was presented by Yamamoto (1965) in a journal article entitled "Creativity—A Blind Man's Report on the Elephant." Likening the various investigations of creativity to the fable about the blind men who perceived the elephant so differently because of the various anatomic parts they investigated, Yamamoto states: "On some facts, we agree among ourselves; on others we cannot even understand what each is trying to tell the other. But it is precisely this amorphousness which is the elephant—the elephant of creativity." (p. 428) He further notes that most who write about the creative individual agree that creativity is important, perhaps even essential to the continuation of society. But other than this agreement on the importance of creativity, there is very limited agreement. This lack of consensus, this difficulty in communication and understanding, according to Yamamoto, results from the radically different philosophic frames of reference within which investigations of creativitiy have been established. In addition, there have been significant differences in research strategies, and in a few cases, objections to analysis of a trait (creativity) that, in the minds of some, is not subject to empirical investigation. To a considerable extent, this state of affairs as described by Yamamoto in 1965 exists today.

Certain individuals have been recognized as major contributors to the literature describing creativity. Prominent among these are Guilford, Getzels and Jackson, and Torrance. One of Guilford's unique contributions was his presentation of the concept of a three-dimensional "structure of intellect," which predicts the existence of at least 120 distinct intellectual abilities (1959). This theoretical model, including the predication of divergent thinking and convergent thinking as two major types of abilities, has perhaps been more often reproduced in various textbooks and referred to by more authors than any similar conceptual model in the history of the study of intelligence. The description of divergent thinking, which is now commonly associated with creativity, triggered an almost unbelievable amount of both research and theoretical speculation among investigators and authors in many related fields. Guilford's additional contributions through the years have been of great importance to the development of creativity as a recognized, if somewhat controversial, field of endeavor.

Getzels and Jackson (1962) compared a high IQ (average 150), low-creative group of students to a high-creative group with I.Q.s

Creativity has many facets.

averaging 23 points lower. In this study, Getzels and Jackson measured creativity in relation to indications of divergent, as opposed to convergent, thinking. School achievement of the two groups was essentially equal, thus suggesting that in relation to school achievement, high-level creativity might be as important as high IQ. Similar results have been found in some replicative studies but not in all. This leaves some question as to the meaning of Getzels and Jackson's results but provides sufficient support for the concept of separate abilities to stimulate continued research. Like Guilford, Getzels and Jackson have made many other valuable contributions.

One individual seems to stand out more than all others in the literature relating to creativity. E. Paul Torrance has had both feet firmly planted in the area of study of the gifted for some time, and in the past 15 to 20 years has been most regularly associated wtih the creative. In numerous writings, Torrance reaffirms his interest in the gifted and his belief in the value of special educational provisions for those students who are identified primarily in relation to their high IQ., but his major interest appears to be in development of an effective way to identify creative students.

In the test manual for the Torrance Tests of Creative Thinking (1974), Torrance notes that there are definitions of creativity formulated in terms of product (such as invention and discovery), in terms of process, or in terms of the kind of person who may be considered creative. He notes that the production of something new is a part of almost all definitions. Then, for purposes of his research (using his Tests of Creative Thinking) he defined creativity as:

> A process of becoming sensitive to problems, deficiencies, gaps in knowledge, missing elements, disharmonies, and so on; identifying the difficulty, searching for solutions, making guesses, or formulating hypotheses about the deficiencies; testing and retesting these hypotheses and possibly modifying and retesting them; and finally communicating the results. (p. 8)

Identification of the gifted, talented, and creative

Identification of any group of exceptional children is highly dependent on the locally accepted definition or description of that exceptionality. As we have seen in the preceding discussion of definitions, there is considerable variation to be expected with regard to the gifted, talented, and creative. Nevertheless, there is a somewhat standard or typical procedure that is commonly used, and there are also some variations that may be predicted, depending on whether the focus is on gifted (emphasizing academically gifted), talented, or creative. This general or typical procedure will be outlined, with comments as seem appropriate with regard to program focus (gifted versus talented versus creative).

STEP 1 IN IDENTIFICATION

Initial nomination for consideration for possible inclusion in a special program is the usual first step, and in the past, such nominations have come primarily from teachers, principals, and counselors. At the elementary level, the source is more likely to be the classroom teacher, for this is the one individual in the school setting who is able to observe the child in a variety of situations. It is important that consideration for nomination for possible inclusion in a special program be based on the broadest possible range of observations, since gifted, talented, or creative children may give evidence of their unusual characteristics in certain settings, while appearing no different from normal children in others. Gifted and creative children (using "middle-of-the-road" definitions) are perhaps more likely to show their unusual abilities in more than one setting than are talented children if, by definition, talented means unusual ability in only *one* area, for example, art or music. However, even the gifted or creative child (or the potentially gifted or creative child) may not indicate these abilities in many areas of the traditional school curriculum thus ability to observe the child in a wide variety of settings and situations is most important. At the secondary level or in any situation where the child spends only an hour or two with each teacher, one person must be responsible for coordination of information gathering and interpretation, or many children will be overlooked. When properly organized, the counselor, principal, or assistant principal may be able to play this coordinative role. If this is to be accomplished effectively, a careful, deliberately organized structure for gathering information and making meaningful decisions is essential.

As noted before, the gifted and creative may more likely show their unusual abilities in more than one class, area of study, or setting than the talented, with the academically gifted most likely to be readily noticed. Also, certain talents tend to be demonstrated in a variety of areas while others are evident in only one area of the normal public school setting.

Just as is the case with the handicapped, a more effective identification program can be assured if a variety of procedures and a wide range of agencies and individuals are deliberately included in the nomination procedure. Rice (1970) suggests that nominations should be solicited from the following sources, in addition to teachers, counselors, administrators, and other school personnel: (1) community guidance centers, (2) various specialists in the community, (3) parents, (4) student self-referral, (5) work settings in business and industry, and (6) formal screening programs.

Nomination from several sources, as suggested by Rice, takes on additional meaning when we consider the findings of Jacobs (1970). This study has implications for identification procedures and for the accuracy of any listing of characteristics based on studies of students who are identified as gifted. In the following discussion of Jacob's study implications will be reviewed as they relate to characteristics of the gifted, which are discussed in the following section of this chapter.

Jacob's concern was that the identification pattern first established by Lewis Terman in 1921 may have had a limiting effect on nearly all similar studies conducted since that time. Terman's procedures included teacher nomination, high group IQ scores, high gradepoint average, and other similar criteria. Usually, these criteria were used in some combination to identify and thus define the gifted. The rationale for using teacher nomination was, and continues to be, very practical, considering the high cost in time and dollars of most alternate systems, particularly those involving individual testing of large groups of children.

Jacobs reports that his study was directed toward finding *all* gifted children, thus an individual intelligence test was given to all children (654) in the incoming kindergarten class in an entire school district. After 5 months of school, kindergarten teachers were asked to nominate those students in their class who might possibly be gifted. Nineteen of the children who had been discovered (by individual testing) to have full-scale IQ's of 125 or above on the Wechsler Preschool and Primary Scale of Intelligence (WPPSI) were *not* nominated by their teachers. These teachers did, however, nominate others with lower IQ's.

It might be argued that some of these children (if we accept above 125 IQ as a proper definition of gifted) might have shown up as gifted if this study had been continued through first grade, when more formal academic subjects were taught; however, a very important point was demonstrated in this study. Whatever the definition used, the method of screening and referring children for special programs can result in inclusion of only a small part of the special population that should be in such programs. Thus, because present identification procedures define only part of a total gifted population, resultant studies of characteristics relate only to those children whose qualities make it easy for teachers to identify them.

The study reported by Jacobs does not mean that the characteristics of gifted children (however defined) are not accurate for those children studied. It does indicate, however, that this may be only part of the population that should be studied, and that we have no way of knowing whether the rest of the gifted population has the same characteristics. Further, there is the inference that the rest of the gifted population does *not* have the same characteristics, since they were not identified in the first place. Other researchers (Peganto and Birch; Cornish) have suggested that the teacher nomination procedure may miss as many as half of the gifted population; this may in turn significantly affect the accuracy of the lists of characteristics of the gifted.

Still another problem was uncovered in the Jacobs' study. When the nineteen gifted students were discovered in preschool-entrance testing, a random sample of nongifted students were also selected to make certain comparisons possible. The WPPSI was readministered to the nineteen gifted students and the nineteen control students at the close of the kindergarten year. There was no change in the group mean of the control students at the close of the school year, but there was a significant loss in IQ on the part of the nineteen gifted students. The mean full-scale IQ of the gifted group dropped from 130.6 on the pretest to 122.9 on the posttest. The mean verbal IQ dropped from 132.3 to 120.8. The mean performance IQ did not change significantly.

This study was relatively small and should be replicated both under similar conditions and under deliberately different conditions before any definitive conclusions can be reached. However, the implication is clear; the gifted, if they are unrecognized, may lose what may have been potential giftedness. This would seem to be particularly likely to happen for those children who do not exhibit overt behavior of the type teachers usually associate with giftedness.

Jacobs and others have provided indications that teacher nomination alone is of questionable merit. Though it may result in the discovery of many gifted children, it will miss others. Nevertheless, it remains a major first step in identification of the gifted in many parts of the nation. Until it can be replaced with a procedure of greater proven merit, it must be reviewed, carefully analyzed for strengths and weaknesses, and revised to correct all possible weaknesses while retaining its strengths. The following suggestions may be used to increase the ability of teachers to identify (nominate) gifted students with more accuracy.

Teachers must learn to recognize several different sets of characteristics, which may be exhibited under different circumstances. These are characteristics other than high-level academic ability or scholastic productivity. It is not particularly difficult to understand that the children who are obviously among the best in the class in mathematics or reading achievement may be possible nominees for further screening and consideration. On the other hand, these students may not be gifted, creative, or anything other than average students who are highly motivated. They are a pleasure to have in class and we should encourage their continued efforts, but they may not in any way be gifted. However, some very average achievers may be gifted or creative children who are very, very bored with school. This is not necessarily the fault of the present teacher, or any one teacher for that matter, but may be the cumulative effect of many years of unexciting schooling. This child may be one who has learned he can apply almost no effort, do average work, and be left alone. He may have discovered that if he does much more than that, teachers tend to give him many more arithmetic problems, all equally boring.*

However, for the most part, gifted, talented, or creative children do provide clues to the fact that they have these high level abilities, if teachers are alert to them. These clues include the following:

1. *Unusual curiosity* (inconsistent with their academic achievement)
2. *Unusual persistence at any given task* (sometimes this may be persistence at the task of annoying the teacher or other children)
3. *Restlessness, inattentiveness, or even aggressiveness, when given repetitive tasks or superficial activity* (ability to recognize this characteristic requires that the teacher be aware of repetitive tasks and superficial activity, and be able to contrast the child's behavior at those times with behavior when the tasks are more challenging)
4. *Originality* (teachers who structure the classroom so that children have an opportunity to exhibit originality *outside of purely academic tasks or those requiring superior basic academic skills* are more likely to see this)
5. *Imagination* (students sometimes cannot exhibit imagination in written assignments because of their own underdeveloped writing skills or the structure of the classroom; teachers must learn to provide an opportunity for children to display imagination in a variety of ways)

These five clues to possible giftedness or creativity are just a sample of many such clues that may be of value for this purpose. No single characteristic or certain combination of characteristics means that a child is gifted or creative any more than high achievement in mathematics means he or she is gifted. But these are the type of clues often overlooked and must be considered if any nomination program is to be successful. Teachers must be informed of these characteristics, made aware of the clues that suggest them, trained to structure their class so that they may be observed, and encouraged to implement strategies that will permit the observation of indications of giftedness.

One additional nomination procedure may be patterned after that suggested by Gowan (1971). This procedure is particularly valuable in making nominations for secondary

---

*A real case involving a child with the highest IQ that I have ever personally evaluated is one in which the child was referred for evaluation as potentially learning disabled or mildly mentally retarded. This child, a member of a minority group in a school with a large minority enrollment, was so bright that he had completely fooled his teachers. In addition to being intelligent, he was very stubborn, and since he did not want to do the work assigned, he had found it could be avoided most easily by his appearing too "dumb" to be able to do it. English was his second language, and he often appeared not to understand it. Because this could have been possible and provided an explanation— as far as the teachers were concerned—he was highly successful. When presented with the tasks on the Wechsler Intelligence Scale for Children (WISC), he scored so exceedingly high we had difficulty believing the scores. This was in spite of the fact that the test was administered in English. We then had difficulty convincing the teachers and the principal, but eventually got the job accomplished. We conducted a crash course on how they might deal with him both educationally and behaviorally. They tried the program with success, which both pleased and amazed them. This was an unusual case but was a beautiful illustration of the child "bright" enough to appear "dull."

school programs where no one teacher will know any one student very well. Gowan suggests circulating a paper on which the teacher is asked to nominate under such categories as: (1) best student, (2) child who is the best leader, (3) most original or creative child, (4) most highly motivated, (5) most scientifically oriented, (6) most advanced in terms of grade placement, and (7) best liked child. If a specific interest in any area of art, music, the performing arts, or other areas is part of the program goal, then questions relating specifically to these areas should be included.

Multiple listings (a child listed more than once by one teacher or more than once when all teacher listings are compiled) obviously can provide important data. This suggestion by Gowan is only one part of his total recommendation for identification, which will be further pursued in a later part of this section.

STEP 2 IN IDENTIFICATION

The second step in identification of gifted, talented, or creative students involves extensive, intensive evaluation, including a consideration of past academic records, attitudes, motivation, developmental and health history, and various specific tests as appropriate to the type of program under consideration. If additional individual testing is a part of this process, parent permission is required.

In some instances, teacher nomination will have been accomplished on the basis of a brief statement of the purposes of the program, perhaps a short in-service meeting, and a request for teachers to nominate. When this is the case, a great deal of work must be accomplished in step 2. In other cases, the nomination will have been based on multiple nominative factors and only a limited amount of work need be done in step 2. The purposes of the program and the breadth of special programming available will determine the degree of specialization to be found in this step.

If step 3 involves placement, then step 2 should include individual testing with a test of intelligence such as the Stanford-Binet or one of the Wechsler tests (WPPSI, WISC-R, or WAIS), and/or a test of creativity such as the Torrance Tests of Creative Thinking. If there is some specific focus on, for example, ability in the area of sculpturing or creative dance, there should be a procedure whereby experts in these areas provide some sort of rating of potential talent. Because most of the present programs place major emphasis on high IQ and academic talent (or potential talent), we will examine possible procedures in this type program as an example of possible substeps within step 2.

Programs for the gifted, talented, and creative have always been plagued by problems related to shortage of available funds. This shortage extends to the identification procedure and in fact has dictated the use of nomination as part of the screening procedure. Teachers, counselors, and principals can be asked to provide data for selection without actually costing extra dollars from the school budget. True, it takes some of their time, but they can participate as part of their regular duties. On the other hand, individual testing by a psychometrist or psychologist is all "extra time" and requires extra budget provision. Therefore, if a nomination procedure of some sort plus additional "sorting" in step 2 can reduce the number of students who must be individually evaluated by the psychologist, this is the procedure that will be followed.

To reduce the number of students who must be given an individual intelligence test, several different systems can be used. In essence, all follow a similar rationale to accomplish this goal. This rationale is that if multiple criteria are applied or multiple factors considered *prior* to such individual testing, dollars will be saved, which hopefully will be used in the actual provision of special program components. The suggestion made by Gowan (1971), referred to before, regarding use of teacher nominations based on multiple categories is one part of such a multiple factor system. In Gowan's system other factors are systematically used. These include among others, achievement test battery scores, children who are the best representatives of minority groups, children who have held notable leadership positions, and children who have reading difficulties but are thought to be mentally talented. After all of the various factors or criteria are applied and students are named on various lists, those who are mentioned more than a given number of times (Gowan uses three in his system) are automatically included in the program. Those mentioned fewer times are sent for individual testing of intelligence. Those who are mentioned only once may be placed in a "reservoir" for possible further evaluation. This results in additional screening before individual testing, mainly to save time and dollars.

In the system described some students will be placed *without* evaluation on an individual test of intelligence. This procedure is undoubtedly defensible on a theoretical or philosophic basis if enough factors are considered, but in states where special reimbursement is involved and where the state standards require the results of an individual test of intelligence, this would not be possible.

Another device often mentioned in the literature is on its way out. This is the use of group tests of intelligence. For reasons documented in other chapters, especially relating to minority group children and the mentally retarded, a growing number of cities and states are banning the use of group IQ tests entirely. They provided an inexpensive screening tool, but because of their potential bias against the poor and many minority group students, they are rapidly disappearing in the public schools.

In summary, the step that follows nomination for consideration for program placement may vary greatly in relation to: (1) how much effort went into the nomination (was it simple nomination by a teacher, or was it multiple factor nomination including some testing), (2) the type of program for which the student is being considered (an academically talented program, based primarily on IQ and academic achievement; a program that targets specific talents; one that emphasizes creativity), (3) the grade level, (4) state guidelines, especially if the program is tied to reimbursement, and (5) funds available.

STEP 3 IN IDENTIFICATION

The third step in identification of students for programs for the gifted, talented, or creative involves some sort of committee deliberation in which all of the data gathered in step 2 are considered, program alternatives and program space are considered, and one of the following recommendations is made:
1. *The student is recommended for placement.*
2. *The student is placed on a standby status (to wait for program space).*
3. *Further evaluation and/or data gathering is recommended.*
4. *The student is not recommended for placement for specified reasons.*

Whatever the decision, all pertinent school personnel must be notified, and a conference with the child's parents must be scheduled to explain the recommendation. If immediate program placement is recommended, parental consent must be obtained and necessary administrative steps must be implemented.

Identification for programs for the gifted, talented, or creative has come a long way since the first programs where IQ and academic tests scores were the only criteria and there often was only one program alternative. Today, evaluation of a student's unique ability in a single area such as vocal music, poetry, or oil painting has complicated the procedure considerably. Unfortunately, the complexity of such identification may be a major reason why many school systems have elected to retain programs related to IQ and academic excellence in major academic areas, but change is underway and must be encouraged if we are to promote and stimulate a broad range of abilities.

Characteristics of gifted, talented, and creative students

The preceding two sections of this chapter have in effect outlined the characteristics of gifted, talented, and creative students. On the other hand, studies reviewed in those sections indicate that we may have focused on the characteristics of only part of the population that should have been included. Several authors have indicated that giftedness identifies itself (as when a child starts to read at age 2½ years, or plays the violin at age 4), but this limits us to the type of giftedness that is self-motivating or that which exists in children who are fortunate enough to have been born into surroundings that tend to encourage or motivate giftedness. Some of the best listings of characteristics of giftedness, talent, or creativity may be those provided teachers as a basis of nominating children for possible inclusion in special programs, but few lists of characteristics would be acceptable as complete and all-inclusive by all authorities in the field. Therefore, rather than to attempt the impossible, we will review the efforts of several different authors to indicate their views on the characteristics of giftedness, talent, or creativity. These reviews may serve as a sort of status report on some of the characteristics of gifted, talented, and creative students.

One of the most cited recent references on the gifted and talented is a 1972 report made by the U.S. Commissioner of Education to the Congress of the United States. This report, directed by law, involved most of the recognized authorities in the field of education of the gifted, talented, and creative and certain public school program officials (those with programs for the gifted) and included a review of much of the existing literature on the gifted, talented, and creative. In addition, those who prepared the report attempted to find a sort of middle ground rather than some particular philosophic, theoretical, or programmatic bias based on the specific interests of a particular author. This provided a summary that was unique in its objectivity and respected regarding the general accuracy of content. The following quotations are from this report (Marland, vol. I, 1972):

> Probably the area in which the gifted and talented are recognized most frequently is achievement. Large-scale studies over the past 50 years have uniformly agreed that these individuals function at levels far in advance of their age-mates. Beginning at the early primary grades and even at the time of school entry, the gifted and talented present challenging educational problems because of their deviation from the norm.
>
> Typically, half of the gifted have taught themselves to read before school entry. Some of them learn to read as early as 2 years and appreciable numbers are reading at 4. In comparison with their classmates, these children depart increasingly from the average as they progress through the grades, *if their educational program permits*.
>
> In one statewide study of more than 1,000 gifted children at all grade levels, the kindergarten group on the average performed at a level comparable to that of second-grade children in reading and mathematics; the average for fourth and fifth-grade gifted children in all curriculum areas was beyond that of seventh grade pupils. In another study a representative sample of gifted high school seniors took the Graduate Record Examinations in social sciences, humanities, and natural sciences—examinations normally used for admission to graduate study. In all of the tests, the high school seniors made an average group score which surpassed

the average for college seniors; in the social sciences, they surpassed the average of college seniors with majors in that field. These findings on the attainments of gifted students are typical. . . .

In general, gifted children have been found to be better adjusted and more popular than the general population, although there are definite relationships between educational opportunities and adjustment.

Exceptional capacities create problems for most people, even at the earliest ages. Young gifted children encounter difficulties in attempting to manage and direct activities. Since their ideas differ, they lose the participation of others and find themselves marginal and isolated. Of all children in a large gifted population, those at kindergarten level were reported by teachers to have the highest incidence of poor peer relationships. This was ascribed to the lack of experience at this age in adapting to requirements, in coping with frustrations, or in having available a repertoire of suitable substitute activities, as older pupils would.

When conditions are changed and the gifted and talented are given opportunities to satisfy their desires for knowledge and performance, their own sense of adequacy and well-being improves. Those who can function within an appropriate learning milieu also improve in their attitudes toward themselves and others. If education and life experiences for the gifted are what they should be, the likelihood that the gifted and talented will relate to the total society and work within it actually is enhanced.

The gifted explore ideas and issues earlier than their peers. While they enjoy social associations as others do, they tend early to relate to older companions and to games which involve individual skills or some intellectual pursuits. The gifted child is not necessarily a 'grind' or a 'loner,' despite the fact that he develops special interests early. Biographical data from studies of large populations reveal that these individuals characteristically perform in outstanding fashion—not only in widely varied organizations, in community groups, in student government, and in athletics. The total impression is of people who perform superbly in many fields and do so with ease.

While the academic advancement of the gifted has generally been recognized even though it has not been served, the early social and psychological development of the gifted has been less frequently noted.

Gifted pupils, even when very young, depart from self-centered concerns and values far earlier than their chronological peers. Problems of morality, religion, and world peace may be troublesome at a very early age. Interest in problems besetting society is common even in elementary-age gifted children.

The composite impression from studies ranging from childhood to adults is of a population which values independence, which is more task- and contribution-oriented than recognition-oriented, which prizes integrity and independent judgment in decision making, which rejects conformity for its own sake and which possess unusually high social ideals and values.

Of all human groups, the gifted and talented are the least likely to form stereotypes. Their traits, interests, capacities, and alternatives present limitless possibilities for expression; the chief impression one draws from studying this group, at either the child or adult level, is of almost unlimited versatility, multiple talents, and countless ways of effective expression. Because gifted people have many options, they often also encounter problems of choice. When you do well in science but also love music, where does the energy go in a career? Again, there are numerous examples in Terman's longitudinal study of men and women who have been as productive in an avocation as in their chosen careers. (pp. 15-17)

The preceding comments from Commissioner Marland's report are from Chapter II, "Profile of the Gifted and Talented Population." They indeed provide a profile, but it may be a limited profile because it was based primarily on completed research. Some of the extreme difficulty in finding agreement on the characteristics of the gifted, talented, and creative may be due to the contradictory nature of such characteristics. For example, Torrance (1962), who has long been associated with the idea of creative giftedness and more recently with the idea of creativity as a separate entity, has provided a description of nontest ways to identify such children. Included are such descriptive characteristics as: (1) is imaginative, creates fantasies, enjoys storytelling, (2) can occupy time usefully without stimulation from the teacher, and (3) is full of ideas, has conversational fluency. There is little question that many gifted or creative children might have these characteristics, but it is also obvious that many potentially gifted or creative children from bilingual or lower socioeconomic backgrounds will *not* indicate these characteristics in the normal school setting because they have not been preconditioned to think of school as a place to achieve and to please the teacher. Storytelling and conversational fluency may not even surface except with a very unusual teacher. The very bright or gifted child will occupy time in some manner, but it may be just the opposite of what the teacher might call useful. In other writings, Torrance suggests that the creative may be a source of classroom difficulties for some teachers (an observation echoed by many other authors) and also indicates a concern for disadvantaged gifted children. These apparent contradictions in characteristics are real and they exist for obvious reasons. The reader should understand that in addition to the variables involved in defining giftedness, there are the problems of identifying gifted children who are underprivileged, undermotivated, or from different language or cultural backgrounds. Without educational programs that will simulate and predispose these children to show what they can do, many will never exhibit the characteristics found on our many lists.

The following list of characteristics is a composite of lists proposed by many authors. Rather than attempt to categorize them in terms of source and frequency of mention, they are listed in alphabetical order, with no inference as to which is most important or which applies to what ages or to which definition(s) of giftedness or creativity. In a very orderly and systematic (if not creative) manner, an attempt was made to list these characteristics in terms of frequency of mention by various recognized authorities. It was soon obvious that certain lists of characteristics were repeated over and over, often in almost the same order, and often without reference to another source. Thus the value of determining the frequency of mention was essentially lost, except to determine who tended to follow whom within the hierarchy of writers in the field.

Although many of the characteristics will be perceived positively by most teachers, some will be perceived differently by different teachers (those who like conformity will dislike them, others may appreciate them for what they represent), and a small number will cause problems for almost all teachers.

Characteristics of the gifted, talented, and/or creative* (an unranked, alphabetical listing)

Academically superior
Applies systems approaches (often self-devised) to problems
Applies abstract principles to concrete situations
Courteous
Deliberate underachiever under certain conditions
Difficulty in conversing with age-mates
Emotionally stable
Extraordinarily verbal
General curiosity
Gives uncommon responses
High energy level, especially in mental/intellectual tasks
High vocabulary level

---

*In cases where it is not so stated, the assumption is that the characteristic listed is exhibited to a greater extent than normal for age.

Intellectual curiosity
Intellectually superior
Inquisitive
Logical ability above age level
Makes individualistic interpretations of new subject matter
Obnoxious or rebellious when asked to do repetitive tasks
Original (may relate to verbal responses, problem solving, etc.)
Perceives and identifies significant factors in complex situations
Persistent in achieving goals
Physical ability, average or above
Pleasure in intellectual pursuits
Pleasure in pursuing unusually difficult mental tasks
Power of concentration
Recognizes and is uncomfortable with unresolved ambiguity
Rebels against conformity
Scientifically oriented
Sense of humor
Sensitive to problems of others
Skips steps in normal (expected) thinking sequence
Socially aware
Strong sense of responsibility
Superior ability to remember details
Superior ability to see relationships
Unhappy with most group participation projects (with normal peers)
Unaccepting of routine classroom rules
Unusual demonstrated talent (in any area)
Verbally facile
Verbally flexible

Although obvious contradictions exist in the listing of characteristics, most such contradictions can be explained by: (1) the existence of conflicting conceptualizations of giftedness, talent, and creativity, (2) the wide range of possible reactions of different individuals to the same situation (i.e., a given type of classroom atmosphere), or (3) the effect of radically differing environmental backgrounds of the children in our schools.

Number of children and youth who need special services

Assuming the need of special services to assure maximal personal development and self-fulfillment, the question of how many children and youth of our nation require such help is a matter of percentages. With no established cut-off point for the lower level of academic talent based on IQ alone, we cannot establish nationally acceptable estimates even on this type of giftedness. Other, broader definitions lead to even more difficulty in estimation of total numbers. Turning to the oft-quoted Marland report (1972) to the U.S. Congress, we find the following: "Some people put the figure [percentage of gifted] at 3 percent of the total school population while others would range as far as 15 percent to include those children with a special talent who may lack the full spectrum of giftedness. This may be too broad, but even taking the very conservative estimate of 3 percent, the size of the population—1.5 million—demands attention." (pp. 22-23) *Based on estimates of state officials in the states where more comprehensive programs have been implemented, the opinions of various authorities in the area of education of the gifted, talented, and creative, and Marland's report, a range of 3 percent (if we consider primarily those students with high level intellectual ability) to 5 percent (when we include those with special talents or creative abilities who do not fit into the higher IQ range) would seem a supportable, conservative estimate. This means 1.5 to 2.5 million children and youth, a significant part of our future human resources.*

Teachers of the gifted

What are the identifiable characteristics of teachers of the gifted or talented or creative? What should a teacher of the gifted know? What does the superintendent of schools or the school district personnel director look for when a search for such teachers is initiated? Must the teacher of gifted children be gifted?

The above and a variety of closely related questions have been asked and answered by most of the authorities in the area of education of the gifted. A number of sources could be cited, but in general, the answers regarding characteristics of teachers of the gifted fall into two distinct categories. These may be characterized as follows: (1) A teacher of the gifted should be a creative person, be personally gifted, be an original thinker, be an unusually secure person, be highly flexible, have excellent health, possess an excellent sense of humor, understand the basic theories of learning, be an experienced, master teacher, etc., etc. (2) We really don't know what characteristics a teacher of the gifted should possess.

There have been studies in which gifted students were asked about the characteristics of a good teacher and others in which gifted students identified good teachers who were then studied by others. These investigations tend to come up with certain commonsense characteristics such as "maturity," "superior intelligence," "experience," and "caring persons," but these are the characteristics of *all* good teachers. Possibly the best summary of the state of present knowledge about teachers of the gifted was made by Gallagher (1975): "There is probably more nonsense and less evidence dispensed about the needed characteristics of the teacher of the gifted than almost any other single issue." (p. 312) When we consider certain specific areas of talent, for example music, we can perhaps assume that the teacher of the program for those talented in the area of music should be a good musician, but beyond certain specialty areas, the questions essentially remains open to debate.

Two other possible avenues of inquiry regarding teachers of the gifted might logically be considered. One potential source of information is state requirements for certification of teachers of the gifted. Karnes and Collins (1977), in reporting on a 1977 survey of teacher certification in gifted education, indicate that of the forty-seven states replying, only six had specific certification standards. It would seem from an analysis of their replies that this source is of very limited value. One other source is the training institutions that prepare teachers to teach the gifted. A survey of such programs, conducted by the National/State Leadership Training Institute for the Gifted and Talented (1977), indicated that twenty-four states had at least one graduate level training program in gifted education or a program that provided an emphasis in gifted education. Unfortunately, there is no apparent agreement among these institutions as to what a good training program should emphasize. Unlike teacher training in other areas of special education there is no national consensus, and it is difficult to predict when or how such agreement or consensus will develop.

Perhaps all we can say with certainty is that teachers of the gifted should be competent, effective teachers, should be interested in teaching children with unusual ability or talent, and should understand that to be successful, they may be required to remain more alert, think faster, and work harder than they ever thought possible. With additional efforts supported and directed through the Office of Gifted and Talented, perhaps some substantive progress will be made in the near future. However, the fact that programs for the gifted, talented, and creative are viewed as the responsibility of different departments of the educational system in various parts of the nation will likely tend to further retard any consensus regarding the characteristics of teachers of the gifted.

Federal leadership in stimulating programs for the gifted, talented, and creative

For all other exceptionalities, adequate programming has been directly related to stimulation at the federal level. For the various handicapping conditions, the final, essential ingredient was a strong federal law, mandating appropriate education as a basic right of handicapped children and youth.

There has been a start, however minimal, with respect to federal support for programs for the gifted. As this text goes to press there is hope, and there is competent, qualified leadership at the federal level, but the missing component is demonstrated, long-range federal support as evidenced by continued, adequate funding. The Office of Gifted and Talented was created in 1972 but did not receive funding of consequence until 1976. In 1976, 1977, and again in 1978, the Office of Gifted and Talented received $2.5 million with which it funded twenty-five state projects, and eighteen local projects, three teacher training programs, a graduate fellowship program, an internship program, and a national/state leadership training program. The various state and local programs have been of value; the teacher training, fellowship, and internship programs served an important purpose; and the national/state leadership training program has served to stimulate interest on a national basis. But regardless of the quality of present leadership personnel, without more funding and without state funding on a wider basis, appropriate educational services for the gifted, talented, and creative are a long way from realization.

Efforts are underway to achieve a stronger commitment at the federal level to education for the gifted, talented, and creative. The Council for Exceptional Children (CEC) has taken an official position with congressional committees that the Office of the Gifted and Talented should become part of the Bureau of Education for the Handicapped (BEH), which in turn might be renamed the Bureau of Education for Exceptional Persons (BEEP). This would make the federal bureau consistent in scope with the Council for Exceptional Children, and, in the opinion of many, would strengthen the cause of the gifted. There are pros and cons, and there are political considerations too involved to discuss here. This matter may well be settled in the near future, but the matter of federal leadership must be carefully considered, regardless of the office or bureau to which gifted programs are attached. If history provides any meaningful guidance as to the future, continued, expanded federal leadership in this area is critical. Without such leadership, and without related stimulation funding, programs for the gifted, talented, and creative will remain a matter of piecemeal, off-again, on-again services. Therefore, all who are seriously concerned for the future of such programs must remain involved and supportive of strong federal legislation for the gifted and consistent, adequate, year-to-year appropriations to support such legislation. Advocates for the handicapped achieved their goals through a combination of program support and litigative pressure. Although many advocates for the handicapped were at first hesitant to initiate litigation to accomplish their goals, they soon learned that this was an essential, highly effective tool to gain the rights to which handicapped persons were entitled. If the rights of the gifted cannot be attained otherwise, this seems to be the next logical step.

State leadership in establishing programs for the gifted

Although the *needs* of the gifted have been addressed in federal legislation, their *right* to an appropriate education is not protected by law. Most states do not have special legislative recognition of the unique needs of the gifted and, as in federal legislation, the existing state laws and regulations tend to relate to needs, not rights. In many cases, local school officials may actually believe they are providing adequately for the gifted; unlike the handicapped, many gifted children do not stand out as requiring additional assistance, thus it is relatively easy to overlook them. Their very success in school has tended to obscure the fact that they need special educational programs and provisions if they are to fully develop their talents.

Fortunately, in some areas of the nation, good programs have developed despite these inhibiting factors. The events leading to such development differ, but there are certain factors or components common in all states where effective, ongoing programs exist. These are worthy of further consideration as we attempt to better understand the role of state leadership in the establishment of effective programs for the gifted, talented, and creative.

Components essential to good programs for the gifted

Those states with good programs for gifted, talented, and creative students have:
1. Legislation that specifically recognizes the unique needs of a broad range of gifted, talented, and creative students and encourages local education agencies to make special provisions for such students.
2. Adequate special funding on a continuing basis
3. Administrative regulations and program guidelines that provide a practical framework within which effective programs may be provided
4. Leadership from the state education agency to assist local school officials in the establishment and maintenance of effective programs

If any one of these components is missing, the program is less than satisfactory.

Many authorities in education of the gifted would add at least two other factors as essential to the provision of good programming: (1) local belief in and support of the concept of special efforts on behalf of the gifted, and (2) an available source of effective teachers for gifted programs. These two are quite important, but in practice, when states have developed the four basic components indicated above, they have at the same time developed a conviction, on the local level, that such programs and services are worthwhile. Stated another way, a significant number of local officials must become convinced of the value of such programs or it is highly unlikely that good legislation will be passed and stable funding be established. The question of good teachers works out in a similar manner. The legislation/funding matter usually takes several years to accomplish. As this is evolving, local university personnel, who are likely to be a part of this program evolution, become very busy developing programs to: (1) retrain previously certified teachers through summer and extension programs, and (2) train new teachers through the development of new course sequences.

Assuming, for the moment, that the local support and the teacher training functions will in fact develop if the other four basic components are present, let us further examine the four components.

1. Legislation that specifically recognizes the unique needs of a broad range of gifted, talented, and creative students is of primary importance. If state legislation is such that it provides general recognition of all children with exceptional needs, without being specific about the unique needs of the gifted, talented, and creative, it will be quite easy for many school districts to overlook programs for the gifted. In the earlier statement of this component it was also noted that the state should *encourage the local education agency to make special provisions for such students.* At present, even in those states with the best programs, "encouragement" is the essential thrust of the law. If appropriate programs for gifted, talented, and creative students are ever to be nationwide, the word *encourage* will undoubtedly have to be changed to *mandate;* but for the present, it is accurate to say that states that presently have good programs "encourage" special educational provisions for the gifted.

The reference to a "broad range" of gifted, talented, and creative students is most important if the schools are to provide for all such students. In some states, only the top 1 or 2 percent in academic achievement are included in the definition of gifted. When this is the case, those potentially gifted children who are not properly motivated by the regular school program are further disadvantaged by the rigidity of the program for the gifted. This is most likely to happen to certain minority group children but may happen to any child. This must be very carefully avoided through efforts to identify those children with undeveloped potential. Also, if *academic ability*, whether demonstrated or potential, is the only type of giftedness recognized, the program does little to encourage specific types of giftedness or talent in art, music, and other specialized areas, unless that student is also eligible for special assistance because of academic giftedness. Thus the "broad range" concept is essential.

2. *Adequate special funding on a continuing basis* is the best present form of "encouragement." This is not as effective as mandate, but it is a very close second choice approach. It is critically important to note that *legislative authorization* of special funds and *actual appropriation* of special funds are two very different things. Legislative authorization must come first, and thus is essential. But authorization simply means making it possible to appopriate money for that purpose. In too many cases the legislative enactment authorizes adequate funding, but the state legislature does not appropriate even one fourth as much as was authorized.

A second important point regarding special funding is that it should be provided in a manner that reduces the likelihood that the local school agency will attempt to use these funds for other purposes. This is related to the need for good administrative regulations, which will be considered next.

3. *Administrative regulations and program guidelines that provide a practical framework within which effective programs may be provided* is a third, highly important component in any good state program for the gifted. These regulations can be no more effective than the basic legislation that authorizes them and establishes program parameters, but even if good legislation exists, good administrative regulations are a "must." This is especially important as new programs are being initiated, since lack of local experience in providing special educational programs for the gifted can lead to errors that may hold back more effective programs for years.

One example of good administrative regulations is provided by the state of Connecticut (see pp. 375-378).* These regulations

---

*In the continuing discussion of programs for the gifted, talented, and creative, several references will be made to the state of Connecticut. Other states have good programs for the gifted, but the Connecticut model is certainly one of the best and is of particular value to illustrate some of the points about programming which I feel to be most important. My sincere thanks to William Vassar, State Consultant for the Gifted and Talented in Connecticut, for pertinent information and materials.

force the local district to think through the total program prior to initiating it. Because the completion of state forms, reports, and records takes time, and because most local education officials have learned through the years to react negatively to the state bureaucracy, this type of regulation and the paper work required would have little value were it not for the reimbursement that comes with implementation of well-developed programs. (Note that we are once again reminded of the great importance of adequate funding.)

4. *Leadership from the state education agency to assist local school officials in the establishment and maintenance of effective programs* is the final major component that must be present if gifted students across the state are to have the programs and services they deserve. This should include a variety of leadership functions such as: (1) specific guidelines and program materials to assist program development, (2) statelevel personnel who have sufficient expertise and *time* to provide in-person assistance at the local level, (3) planned program development in which outside experts are brought into the state to broaden local perspectives, (4) coordinative efforts with state and regional colleges and universities, and (5) coordinated efforts with specialized facilities (for example, science and performing arts groups, industries) that may be available to assist local educational units in providing unusual opportunities for students. Too many states provide just enough consultative assistance to regulate, leaving no time for actual consultative efforts. When attempting to initiate or improve programs in an area that is not well established, it is critical that state assistance be available and that the quality of such assistance be high. This is just as true in education of the gifted as in any other area; and because gifted programs are permissive programs, it may be even more important. In commenting on the ten top states (as determined in a 1977 survey) with respect to state funds expended for gifted/talented programs, Dorothy Sisk (1978), Director of the Office of the Gifted and Talented, U.S. Office of Education, noted that nine of the top ten states had at least one full-time state consultant for the gifted. Sisk then commented further as to the considerable importance of consultative assistance to successful program development for gifted and talented students.

Educational provisions for the gifted and talented in Connecticut: a study of the efforts of one state

Statewide programming for gifted and talented students in Connecticut was given a significant boost in 1967 when the general assembly enacted into law new guidelines for special education that included a broad conceptualization of gifted and talented, reimbursement that was better than any existing in the nation at that time, and encouragement to establish regional districts, if needed, to serve the gifted and the handicapped. Among the outstanding provisions of this legislation was that programs for the gifted were reimbursed on the same basis as programs for the handicapped. Another was the unusually broad definition of gifted and talented (which in effect also included creative students). One shortcoming of this legislation was that it was permissive rather than mandatory. (Recent efforts in Connecticut have been directed toward inclusion of the gifted and talented under the mandatory provisions of the law relating to exceptional children.)

The Connecticut program, although admittedly still short of ideal, is certainly one of the better programs in the nation. The descriptive information on pp. 375-378 will help illustrate the four components outlined above and will provide a better understanding of the nature of programs for the gifted, talented, and crea-

Text continued on p. 379.

Education of children and youth with unusual gifts and abilities

Policies, procedures and guidelines for gifted and talented programs

I. Overview

The recommendations on the following pages are concerned with programs for those children who have extraordinary learning ability and/or outstanding talent in the creative arts, and who require qualitatively different instructional programs and services. Section 10-76 allows reimbursement for such programs when provided as *part of the public school program* and *prior approved* by the secretary of the State Board of Education.

RESPONSIBILITY OF THE PLANNING AND PLACEMENT TEAM

Many pupils can succeed in the regular school program with some adaptions in the curricular design while others require programs or services beyond the level of those ordinarily provided in the regular school program, but which may be provided through special education as part of the public school program. The determination as to which plan may be effective for these children should be reached by the combined thinking of the special education planning and placement team. In Connecticut the ultimate responsibility for the school placement of any child lies with the superintendent of schools of the school district in which the child attends school. While this responsibility is with the superintendent of schools, this decision should represent the result of inter-professional collaboration on the part of his staff and, if necessary, other consultation of an appropriate nature.

ARTICULATION WITH ADMINISTRATIVE GUIDELINES

These policies and procedures should be used in conjunction with the *General Guidelines for Special Education Programs*, published by the Connecticut State Department of Education. 1976-77.

II. Summary of legal provisions

Section 10-76(a-j) of the Connecticut General Statutes makes it permissive for local and regional school districts to provide reimbursable special instructional and ancillary services for pupils with extraordinary learning ability and/or outstanding talent in the creative arts. A local or regional board of education may do this individually or in cooperation with other school districts.

PRIOR APPROVAL PLAN

To be reimbursable, plans for providing such special education must be approved in advance by the State Department of Education. Reimbursement based on an excess cost concept is explained in Section VII of the 1975-76 *General Guidelines for Special Education Programs*.

III. Definitions of terms

"Extraordinary learning ability" is deemed to be the power to learn possessed by the top five per cent of the students in a school district as chosen by the special education planning and placement team on the basis of (1) performance on relevant standardized measuring instruments or (2) demonstrated or potential academic achievement or intellectual creativity.

"Outstanding talent in the creative arts" is deemed to be that talent possessed by the top five percent of the students in a school district who have been chosen by the special

Policies, procedures and guidelines for gifted and talented programs—cont'd

education planning and placement team on the basis of demonstrated or potential achievement in music, the visual arts or the performing arts.

It should be noted that a local school district could provide for upward to ten percent of its school population, if the broadened concept of giftedness is utilized.

For example, extraordinary learning ability allows for 5% of the population involved (K-4, 5-6-7, etc.). However, if the district elects to work with only one segment of the population i.e. high IQ, high achieving pupils, it is suggested that a single target group such as this be limited to 1-3%. This would allow the district to include other target groups (high creative producers, potential underachievers) to complete the five percent factor.

The five percent factor is not an automatic or magic figure. The school district must assure the Department that these children have been identified through *multiple criteria* and that the five percent factor is not limited to one small segment of giftedness. The same concept is to be applied when utilizing the definitions relative to "outstanding talent in the creative arts."

Screening and identification processes become quite complex when one is developing such criteria in the prior approval process. Each target group of pupils being identified must be processed by multiple criteria which is reasonable and prevents loose or unreasonable criteria from being utilized.

IV. Screening and identification procedures

A. *Responsibility for formulating screening and identification process*

The responsibility for the screening and identification of eligible children and youth rests with the superintendent of schools or a professional staff member of the school district to whom he may delegate this responsibility. This professional person responsible for the screening and identification process will assume the duties of designing a planning and placement team for the gifted and talented as required by Section 10-76.

B. *Screening and identification criteria*

Screening and identification criteria should be based on a study of all available evidence as to the pupil's ability and/or potential by personnel qualified to administer and interpret:
1. appropriate standardized tests
2. judge demonstrated ability, potential, intellectual creativity and leadership
3. recognize outstanding talent in the creative arts

C. *Approval of identification criteria*

Section 10-76 of the General Statutes requires that the screening and identification criteria for those who are gifted and talented must be approved by the State Department of Education.

D. *Items for consideration in screening and identification criteria*
1. *Extraordinary learning ability*
   a. Very superior scores on appropriate standardized tests. Criteria for "very superior" might be the upper two or three percent of an appropriate criterion group or scores which are at least two standard deviations above the local norms. When a school district falls below the national norms, then appropriate measures to measure potential should be applied.

b. Judgments of teachers, pupil personnel specialists, administrators and supervisors who are familiar with the pupil's demonstrated and potential ability.
c. Utilization of a multi-criteria approach is necessary. A number of objective and subjective items should be used to identify and target group. These may include appropriate check lists, rating scales, etc.
d. Intense interest and involvement in a specific intellectual area.
2. Additional items of evidence used in the creative arts category should include:
a. Evidence of advanced skills, imaginative insight, intense interest and involvement.
b. Judgments of outstanding talent based on appraisals of specialized teachers, pupil personnel specialists, experts in the field and/or others who are qualified to evaluate the pupil's demonstrated and potential talent.

The procedures have been designed to avoid arbitrary cut-off points or limitations. The identification process should identify a small percentage of pupils with extraordinary ability and outstanding talent whose needs are such that they cannot be met in the regular school program.

V. Minimum standards for prior approved programs

The designing and developing of programs for pupils in these categories should include the following key components:

A. A *written plan* for the total program *must be submitted* to the State Department of Education for prior approval and should include the following steps:
1. *Need for program*—the extent to which the program is needed by children at specific grade levels and in various target groups and cannot be provided within the general curriculum and regular classroom offerings.
2. *Philosophy of program*—the selection of students, staff, the development of differentiated curriculum and instruction will be dictated by philosophy of the program. Developing a program without articulating purpose with practice is like playing first base without understanding why.
3. *Goals*—program—long range
4. *Objectives*
   a. Pupil
   b. Teacher
   c. Environmental
5. *Target group(s) of pupils to be served*—which group(s) of gifted and talented pupils have the greatest need for a program, grade levels included, and number of pupils to be involved in the program.
6. *Screening and identification procedures*—each target group selected must be screened and identified. The procedures for screening and identification must be sufficiently comprehensive to screen and identify each target group of children and youth included in A-5 above.

   Such procedures *must be accomplished by use of multiple criteria*, such as intelligence tests, achievement and aptitude tests, creativity tests, peer nominations, teacher check lists and rating scales, cultural norms or other predictive measures.
7. *Administrative design(s)*—there are various designs for bringing pupils together or providing space or facilities for the instructional aspects of the program. Such

Policies, procedures and guidelines for gifted and talented programs—cont'd

designs may embrace regional centers, resource centers in the school district or within a school, resource rooms, itinerant teacher approaches, community mentors, seminars, etc.

8. *Differentiated instruction* (program and/or services), the process which is adaptable to varying levels of talent:
   a. *Differentiated curriculum*—one that involves experiences and activities which are *qualitively different* from those provided in the regular classroom, and involve a high level of cognitive and affective concepts and processes beyond those normally provided in the regular classroom.
   b. *Differentiated teaching strategies*—teaching strategies which will accommodate the unique learning styles of the target groups being programmed for. For example, utilizing the higher mental processes of analysis, synthesis and evaluative thinking in working with the target group of high achieving, highly motivated children and youth.
9. *Amount of time spent by pupils in program*—pupils should be involved in these differentiated programs for an appropriate and sufficient amount of time to assure that the "qualitatively different" special education activities will have a significant effect on reaching the objectives set for them.
10. *Articulation and coordination*—the special program should include evidence that it is being developed in relationship to the total school program. Careful planning should be undertaken to articulating and coordinating the special program with the general education program.
11. *Professional staff qualifications*—careful attention should be given to the selection of both the instructional and ancillary staff who will work with the pupils. No special certifications have been established. Teachers should hold a certificate appropriate for the age level of the program and should have professional and personal qualifications judged necessary for work with these children and youth.

    The teacher should be an individual who has a desire to do this special work, and has demonstrated this interest by showing understanding of children as well as by taking graduate courses which are designed to increase this understanding and to develop the competence required to help these children and youth.
12. *Special education consultative services*—there may be a need for special education consultant services provided by personnel other than employees of the school district. Personnel contracted with for these services need not be certified since their services are being utilized in a non-instructional category or under the supervision of certified personnel. For example, the school district may contract with musicians and artists to evaluate outstanding talent in the creative arts; to advise and assist in planning appropriate special education programs for these pupils; to assist in special instruction of pupils under the supervision of certified personnel; and to engage in other activities which assist teachers to work more effectively with eligible pupils.
13. *Evaluation*—both process and product should be taken into consideration. The program and pupil program should be evaluated in terms of the qualitatively different objectives designed for the program and the children and youth involved. This will require the use of both objective and subjective processes that take into account the variety of important program dimensions.

tive. This information is derived from publications provided by the Connecticut State Department of Education.

Implementing the local program for gifted, talented, and creative students

Identifying students, passing state legislation, assuring special funding, and providing special training to teachers are essential prerequisites to implementation of good programs for gifted, talented, and creative students. A number of texts have been written on program implementation and those who may be interested in teaching the gifted should pursue further reading in this area.* For overview purposes, the major approaches to teaching the gifted, the advantages and disadvantages of these approaches along with certain general aspects of local programs will be considered.

Historically, the general administrative modifications used in providing for the gifted have been special classes, acceleration, or enrichment. Special classes may mean self-contained classes at the elementary level, either full- or part-time, or special sections (usually 1- or 2-hour blocks of time) at the secondary level. Any variation of programming in which students identified as gifted, talented, or creative are placed in a separate setting with other children with similar abilities may be considered special classes.

Acceleration means any procedure that leads to more rapid movement through the program of the public schools. This includes early school entrance, more rapid movement through the traditional twelve grades, and early or advanced placement in college. Gallagher (1975) notes that "studies of acceleration and its effects on gifted children are invariably positive, but the concept itself is not well institutionalized or accepted." (p. 305) In fact, it seems safe to say that concerns about acceleration, often expressed by both parents and teachers, are part of the folklore about the gifted, which continues to cause problems as more attempts are made to provide for their unique educational needs.

Enrichment, usually taken to mean the provision of enriched program components or content within the regular class setting, is the third of the traditionally recognized administrative provisions for the gifted. Although there should obviously be a great deal of enrichment within the special class arrangement, the term enrichment, as used in planning programs for the gifted, often means enrichment without placement in a special class setting.

No matter which of the preceding arrangements is used or what organizational pattern is attempted, *the school program must be changed to lead to more meaningful educational results.* Gallagher believes that the schools can modify existing programs in three major areas. "They can change the content or material presented, the method of presentation, or

---

*A good procedure would be to read major sections of a number of basic texts on the gifted and creative. However, if reading is limited to only one text, I would recommend *Teaching the Gifted Child* by James Gallagher. Gallagher's presentation is highly objective and is not influenced by personal interest in any one approach, test instrument, or single component of the gifted-talented-creative continuum. In addition to presentations which may be found in all texts on the gifted (history, administrative adjustments, definitions and characteristics of the gifted, etc.) this text includes chapters on curriculum modifications in mathematics, science, language arts, and social studies, plus detailed consideration of productive thinking, and how to stimulate it. Much of this material is provided in the form of short case studies or examples of dialogue that might take place in an actual classroom. Texts by Torrance, which tend to relate more to the creative child, are also highly recommended.

the learning environment in which the education takes place." (1975, p. 87) *The essence of any good program for the gifted, talented, or creative lies in these modifications, rather than in administrative arrangements.* However, certain administrative arrangements are more conducive to such program modifications than others. Which administrative structure is most likely to provide the best vehicle for a given program modification will depend on many factors and will vary from location to location. These factors include school size, location with respect to other schools, existence of nearby (nonschool) specialized facilities and personnel, existence of nearby colleges or universities, funding structure, community biases, and state regulations, to name a few. As noted before, the administrative changes should be made only for the purposes of facilitating changes in content or material presented, method of presentation, or learning environment.

The *Minimum Standards for Prior Approved Programs* in Connecticut (pp. 377-378) provide a good checklist of components that must be considered in implementing a local program. In addition, William Vassar, State Consultant for Programs for the Gifted and Talented, has provided the following summary of the major features or components of a well designed program.

Major features of a well-designed program

1. Those involved in the total program should have a thorough knowledge of the broadened concept of giftedness.
2. Curriculum, instructional, and pupil personnel should play key roles in designing and developing programs.
3. An assessment of needs should be conducted in the school district to point up the priority needs of the gifted and talented.
4. The philosophy and objectives for both the pupils and program should be clearly established.
5. Identification criteria for the specific target group(s) should be fully developed.
6. The administrative design to serve the pupils should be developed according to local needs.
7. A differentiated curriculum design articulated with differentiated teaching strategies for the gifted and talented should be designed and developed as the core of the program.
8. The differentiated program should be articulated and coordinated with total general education at all levels.
9. Public understanding should be nurtured among the many publics of the community.
10. Instructional and supportive personnel should be carefully selected.
11. A definitive plan for evaluation should be developed to assure that the goals for both pupil and program will be met.
12. Parents should play an integral role in all aspects of the program.
13. Community resources of both the human and physical nature should be fully utilized by those developing and implementing the program.
14. Funding sources from all public and private sectors should be explored.

Programming for the gifted and talented is an integral part of the total educational process. By their special nature, programs will vary from district to district. We should, however, consider each of the factors mentioned when designing, developing and implementing these special education programs for the gifted and talented.

Summary

Special educational programs for the gifted and talented were provided at an earlier point in history than were programs for any of the handicapping conditions, yet they are poorly developed in the United States today compared to programs for the handicapped. The major reason for this apparent contradiction may have been best summarized by Gallagher

(1975) when he stated that "the resistance to special programming for the gifted lies . . . in a basic ambivalence in the society which, on the one hand, wishes to reward talent . . . and, on the other hand, deplores the possible existence or emergence of an intellectual or societal elite." (p. 88) This resistance or lack of acceptance of special programs for the gifted, talented, and creative has led to a situation in which some states provide a broad range of special programs for the gifted, talented, and creative student, some limit programs to just one type of giftedness or talent, and others do essentially nothing

Definitions of giftedness, talent, and creativity have varied during the past three to four decades but have recently evolved in the direction of a broadened definition that includes a wide variety of giftedness, talent, and creativity. On the other hand, general public recognition of this area tends to remain identified with an earlier concept of giftedness, which involves intellectual ability, especially that ability expressed as superior academic achievement. Identification of gifted, talented, and creative students obviously depends directly on the definition in use, and until the broadened definition is fully accepted by most educators, some confusion will exist.

Without complete agreement as to definitions and procedures for identification, it is not possible to agree on characteristics of the gifted; however, a general discussion of characteristics was included in this chapter. Estimates of the number of students who should receive special educational programming range from 1 to 5 percent, depending on breadth of definition. The U.S. Office of Education tends to speak in terms of 1, 2, or 3 percent but in reports to Congress has recognized the possibility that a larger percentage might be defensible.

Federal interest, as indicated by federal legislation and federally sponsored programs, is of very recent vintage. At the close of the 1970s it appeared that the U.S. Congress might decide to play a larger role in promoting programs for the gifted, and the '70s were certainly better than the '60s. The handicapped gained much of their recognition through litigation, an approach yet to be pursued by advocates of the gifted; however, rumblings regarding this possibility are sometimes heard. As for state level interest, the picture is spotty, and even where good legislation has been enacted, it is permissive rather than mandatory.

Certain states have developed good programs for the gifted, which have provided a basis for planning in other states. Guidelines developed in the state of Connecticut may be used to suggest legislative and program options in other states.

In summary, although program provision throughout the nation leaves much to be desired and the needs of the gifted, talented, and creative are not recognized in the same manner as the needs of other exceptional children, the general outlook has improved considerably in the past 10 years, and with continued emphasis will continue to improve. The question of whether the gifted student has a *right* to appropriate special programming (in the same manner as has been established with regard to the handicapped) may be the most important single question to be asked today. The possibility of adequate programs for the gifted, talented, and creative in the next decade may well depend on the answer to this question.

Those "most often overlooked" exceptional students

focus

introduction

If we do provide the type of program that will lead to a maximal development of the gifted, creative, and talented, we often make them less rather than more "normal."

A major factor in the present lack of adequate programming for the above-average student is most of the nation is the difficulty in generating much concern for the "poor little gifted child."

historical development of education for the gifted (the beginning until 1960)

Terman's study established one fact beyond any shadow of a doubt; gifted children become adults who contribute in the areas of art, science, journalism, politics, and all areas of life, far beyond that which may be expected of average students.

definitions: the gifted, talented, and creative

One result of the fact that "gifted" has become synonymous with "high IQ" (at least for school-related programs) is that school personnel have been blinded to other forms of excellence.

Educators have tended to act as though the results of the IQ test represent an adequate measure of all the universe of functions that might be called intellectual functions.

Because learning involves the production of novelty as well as remembering course content, measures of creativity should be considered, in addition to measures of IQ in defining characteristics of giftedness.

The 1976 federal definition reads as follows:

> "Gifted and talented" means children and, where applicable, youth, who are identified at the preschool, elementary, or secondary level as (1) possessing demonstrated or potential abilities that give evidence of high performance capability in areas such as intellectual, creative, specific academic, or leadership ability or in the performing and visual arts; and (2) needing differentiated education or services (beyond those being provided by the regular school system to the average student) in order to realize these potentialities.

creativity

The Torrance definition of creativity is "a process of becoming sensitive to problems, deficiencies, gaps in knowledge, missing elements, disharmonies, and so on; identifying the difficulty, searching for solutions, making guesses, or fomulating hypotheses about the deficiencies; testing and retesting these hypotheses and possibly modifying and retesting them; and finally communicating the results.

step 1 in identification

For the most part, gifted, talented, or creative children do provide clues to the fact that they have high level abilities. These clues include the following: (1) **unusual curiosity**, (2) **unusual persistence at any given task**, (3) **restlessness, inattentiveness, or even aggressiveness when given repetitive tasks or superficial activity**, (4) **originality**, and (5) **imagination**.

number of children and youth who need special services

With no established cutoff point for the lower level of academic talent based on IQ alone, we cannot establish nationally acceptable estimates even on this type of giftedness. Other, broader definitions lead to even more difficulty in estimation of total numbers. Based on estimates of state officials in the states where more comprehensive programs have been implemented, the opinions of various authorities in the area of education of the gifted, talented, and creative, and Marland's report, a range of 3 to 5 percent would seem a supportable, conservative estimate.

implementing the local program

Historically, the general administrative modifications used in providing for the gifted have been special classes, acceleration, or enrichment. Special classes may mean self-contained classes at the elementary level, or special sections (usually 1- or 2-hour blocks of time) at the secondary level.

Acceleration means any procedure that leads to more rapid movement through the program of the public schools.

Enrichment means the provision of enriched program components or content within the regular class setting.

References and suggested readings

Barbe, W. B. (Ed.). *Psychology and education of the gifted: selected readings.* New York; Appleton-Century-Crofts, 1965.

Cornish, R. L. Parents', teachers', and pupils' perception of the gifted child's ability. *Gifted Child Quarterly,* Spring 1968, *XII,* 14-17.

Dennis, W., and Dennis, M. W. (Eds.). *The intellectually gifted: an overview.* New York: Grune & Stratton, Inc., 1976.

Gallagher, J. J. *Teaching the gifted child.* Boston: Allyn and Bacon, 1975.

Gearheart, B. R. *Education of exceptional children.* Scranton, Pa.: Intext, 1972.

Getzels, J. W., and Jackson, P. W. *Creativity and intelligence.* New York: John Wiley and Sons, Inc., 1962.

Getzels, J. W., and Jackson, P. W. The Meaning of "giftedness" an examination of an expanding concept. *Phi Delta Kappa,* Nov. 1958,—*40*(2), 75-77.

Gowan, J. C., and Torrance, E. P. (Eds.). *Educating the ablest: a book of readings on the education of gifted children.* Itasca, Ill.: F. E. Peacock Publishers, 1971.

Guilford, J. P. *The nature of human intelligence.* New York: McGraw-Hill Book Co., 1967.

Guilford, J. P. Three faces of intellect. *American Psychologist,* 1959, *14,* 469-479.

Jacobs, J. C. Are we being mislead by fifty years of research on our gifted children? *Gifted Child Quarterly.* Summer 1970, *XIV,* (2), 120-123.

Karnes, F., and Collins, E. Teacher certification in gifted education: a national survey. *Gifted Child Quarterly,* 1977, *XXI* (2) 204-207.

Labuda, M. (Ed.). *Creative reading for gifted learners.* Newark, Del.: International Reading Association, 1974.

Marland, S. *Education of the gifted and talented: report to the Congress of the United States by the U.S. Commissioner of Education.* Washington, D.C.: U.S. Government Printing Office, 1972.

Newland, T. E. *The gifted in socioeducational perspective.* Englewood Cliffs, N.J.: Prentice-Hall, Inc., 1976.

Pegnato, C. W., and Birch, J. W. Locating gifted children in junior high schools: a comparison of methods. *Exceptional Children,* Mar. 1959, *XXV,* 300-304.

Rice, J. P. *The gifted: developing total talent.* Springfield, Ill.: Charles C Thomas, Publisher, 1970.

Sisk, D. *Groups for gifted and talented,* Newsletter of the National/State Leadership Training Institute for Gifted and Talented, Los Angeles, Jan. 1978.

Syphers, D. F. *Gifted and talented children: practical programming for teachers and principals.* Arlington, Va.: Council for Exceptional Children, 1972.

Torrance, E. P. *Torrance tests of creative thinking technical manual.* Lexington, Mass.: Personnel Press, 1974.

Torrance, E. P. *Guiding creative talent.* Englewood Cliffs, N.J.: Prentice-Hall, Inc., 1962.

Vassar, W. G. (Ed.). *Conn-cept: Connecticut's programming for the gifted and talented.* Hartford: Connecticut State Department of Education, 1976.

Witty, P. A. *The gifted child.* Boston: D. C. Health and Co., 1951.

Yamamoto, K. Creativity—a blind man's report on the elephant. *Journal of Counseling Psychology,* 1965, *12,* 428-437.

Your gifted child. Children's Bureau Publication No. 371, Washington, D.C.: U.S. Government Printing Office, 1958.

SECTION SEVEN

Program areas of special concern

A number of areas of special concern have been mentioned briefly in preceding chapters and deserve special mention in this concluding section. These program areas cut across the various areas of disability and for a variety of reasons have been overlooked or underdeveloped in the past. These areas include: early education of handicapped children, education of handicapped adolescents, education of the adult handicapped, rehabilitation services, community resources and services, and counseling for parents of the handicapped.

There are many more such topics, but these appear to be of sufficient national concern that they should be specifically recognized and discussed here. The following chapters should provide a base for further investigation for those interested in pursuing these topics. Each of these areas of concern has been provided additional impetus by either the Education for All Handicapped Children Act of 1975 (Public Law 94-142) or the Rehabilitation Act of 1973 (Public Law 93-112), and each involves a potential area of professional service that should be considered by college students now entering the field of special education.

Cooking experiences (and the "fringe benefits") are an important aspect of many preschool programs.

chapter 13

Early education of handicapped children

objectives

To learn the terminology used to describe early childhood programs and to understand its implications.

To trace the historical antecedents of early childhood programs as a basis for understanding present efforts, particularly the variable settings and structures for these efforts.

To emphasize the critical need for early childhood efforts for handicapped children and for infants and children at risk.

To demonstrate certain of the major types of existing early childhood efforts through the description of representative programs.

To develop a national perspective on early childhood programs regarding a number of critical variables, such as types of children served, areas of major program emphasis, parent involvement, and program costs.

Introduction

Early education of children who are handicapped or disabled or who are at risk of becoming handicapped or disabled is highly variable both among the states and with respect to the various disabilities and handicapping conditions. This degree of variability may soon be reduced through financial inducements built into Public Law 94-142, but because of federal recognition of the states' responsibility in providing educational programs, the very states that are most in need of improvement in this critical area may be exempt from the mandate to provide such programs. (This will be explained in the historical section, which follows.) There is evidence that some early childhood programs are effective while others are not. There is another concern, expressed by some legislators and echoed by some educators, that programs for "potentially handicapped" children may result in early labeling of children who are not actually handicapped or disabled—and these children may never be able to escape or recover from the related stigma effect. Problems abound, but early childhood programs continue to expand. Our intent will be to take a brief look at historical origins, program needs, and characteristics and then to review certain successful programs.

Terminology

The variety of terminology used when referring to programs for young children must, at best, be called varied. In some cases, especially when we attempt to make program comparisons on the basis of limited information, this variation can be downright confusing. There has been no attempt to correct this situation in this chapter with some sort of semantically precise usage of these terms. Because this chapter includes descriptions of actual programs, it seems best to describe these programs using the terms employed by those who actually implemented them. However, by considering the nature and variability of these terms as commonly used, we can perhaps reduce confusion and permit the reader to read this and other accounts relating to early childhood programs with more understanding.

Early childhood education often means the range of educational programming from birth to age 5, but in some cases this might be considered to extend up through ages 7 or 8. This term may be shortened to *early education*.

Preschool programs probably more often mean those that serve children of ages 3 to 5 or 6, but in some instances preschool programs funded by the federal government start with infants a few days or weeks old. Some authors, such as Safford (1978), dislike using the word "preschool" because it may imply to some that anything prior to kindergarten is not really school. This point of view has considerable merit; however, as long as governmental agencies promote and fund "preschool programs," the term will be regularly used.

Nursery school means prekindergarten, and programs are for children age 5 and younger.

Infant programs or *infant stimulation programs* usually refer to programs for children from birth through age 2 or 3. Very seldom is the term infant used for children over age 3.

High-risk children usually means those children for whom certain factors, such as environmental deficits, delay in normal development, or the presence of a number of siblings who are handicapped, would seem to indicate considerably greater-than-usual likelihood of future handicapping conditions. If they present the characteristics of a known syndrome (for example, Down's syndrome), then they are already *identified* and would not ordinarily be called high risk.

Developmental disabilities or *developmental delay* may include any identifiable delay in normal development. This term is often used as a substitute for "suspected mental retardation" and has become a catch-all term used to describe most young handicapped children (or those at considerable risk) who cannot be readily identified as visually impaired, hearing impaired, physically handicapped, or having some specific syndrome such as Down's.

Intervention, as used in relation to programs for young children, means actual involvement in the life of the child to try to modify the likely outcome of the known handicapping condition or high risk status.

Any of the above terms may be used in some manner other than that outlined, either because of local custom or because state or federal financial support programs under a specific title. This latter factor is probably the most prevailing and persistent reason why these terms are not likely to become any less confusing in the near future. By general agreement, programming provided for any of the preceding categories of need may include direct services and/or training for parents. At certain levels parent education or training is the area of major emphasis; and when "education for high risk infants" is referred to, this properly includes a parent education component.

Historical development of early educational programs for disabled/handicapped children

Early childhood programs for the handicapped or those thought to be at risk have grown out of preschool programs established for nonhandicapped children. Although early work of European educators, such as Froebel and Pestalozzi in the 1800s, laid the foundation for later efforts, it was not until 1860 that Elizabeth Palmer Peabody established the first kindergarten program in the United States. Thirteen years later, kindergarten became a part of the public school system in St. Louis, Missouri, and early childhood education in the form of kindergarten was slowly but surely on its way to becoming an accepted part of the total educational spectrum.

This acceptance of kindergarten programs as part of the responsibility of the public schools was not without its disadvantages. As such, it was soon believed to be necessary to provide more emphasis on "academics" or "preparation for academics," so as to justify its existence as a part of an educational system dedicated to "reading, writing, and 'rithmetic." This emphasis is in considerable contrast to Froebel's original concern with the "whole child" and with social and emotional development. Over the years, nursery school and kindergarten programs have vacillated between emphasizing social/emotional components and academics or readiness for academics. In light of the many changes that have already occurred, it would be presumptuous to predict anything more than additional swings of the pendulum. Both of these areas of emphasis can be demonstrated to be of positive value, but two pertinent questions remain: (1) How much of each is needed? and (2) For which children?

The need for early childhood programs for the handicapped was first widely recognized in the United States for children with sensory impairments. By mid-twentieth century, there were a number of good programs for young children who were deaf or blind, provided in at least three types of settings: (1) in some of the more progressive public schools, especially in larger cities, (2) in state schools for the deaf and blind, and (3) in private schools. Because of the very obvious need for stimulating early childhood experiences, these deaf and blind children received the benefits of planned programs with results that were highly encouraging. The need for early training of parents to assist in these programs, especially as they interacted with their children at home, was soon established. With both the

Program areas of special concern

deaf and the blind, the fact that one sensory channel was inoperative led to the obvious conclusion that these children should receive additional stimulation and information through the other sensory channels. This, then, became one of the major points of focus of these programs. Blind children were encouraged to use the auditory and tactile/kinesthetic channels; deaf children were encouraged to use the visual and tactile/kinesthetic channels to expand their knowledge of their surroundings. In addition, each was encouraged and assisted in the use of any remaining ability in their area of disability. Through a review of individual case studies, it became abundantly clear that deaf or blind children who had lived in a highly protected, nonstimulating environment would almost always show dramatic increases (perhaps best described as "leaps") in overall functioning level after spending several months in a good early childhood program. This same sort of evidence suggested that the longer such special assistance to both child and parents was postponed, the less beneficial the intervention.

Although the value of such programming was established and accepted by mid-century and programs were in effect in some parts of the nation, other regions had few programs, and in many instances none was available outside of the state residential school. Unfortunately, this is still the case in some areas of the nation. Although PL 94-142 has done much to call the attention of both parents and educators to the need for such efforts, the law is written so that it permits states who do *not* provide preschool services to any other group of children to continue to overlook this important area of need.* In all fairness it must be noted that there are special incentives for programs for 3-, 4-, and 5-year-old children in PL 94-142, but it remains to be seen whether or not these will have the desired effect in all parts of the nation. Because of the constitutional principle that dictates that education remain the primary responsibility of the state, the federal government has felt compelled to proceed carefully in attempting to encourage the provision of good programs for the handicapped in the fifty states. This is perhaps a greater problem at the preschool level than at any other level of special education.

Structure and focus of early childhood programs for the disabled/handicapped

Educational programs for young children are held in a variety of physical settings. With the encouragement provided through PL 94-142, an increasing number of such programs will undoubtedly be housed in regular school buildings but may be provided in other settings under the auspices of agencies other than public schools. As noted in an earlier section, school-related programs have historically been provided in: (1) the regular public schools in specially built or adapted facilities, (2) in state-supported schools for the hearing or visually impaired, or (3) in private schools (including hospital-based programs).

Safford (1978) categorizes the settings for early childhood programs from both a physical location and a program focus point of view as follows:

---

*Many authors quote the part of PL 94-142 that indicates that not later than September 1, 1980, all handicapped children aged 3 through 21 must have available free, appropriate education. This statement is in the regulations for PL-142, but there is also a specific exception, which reads: "does not apply to a state with respect to handicapped children aged three, four, five, eighteen, nineteen, twenty, or twenty-one to the extent that the requirement would be inconsistent with state law or practice, or the order of any court, respecting public education for one or more of those age groups in the state." (*Federal Register*, Aug. 23, 1977, p. 42481, Sec. 121a.122 [c].)

1. Developmental day care programs (child care plus promotion of normal development)
2. Hospital-related programs (housed in and administered by a hospital)
3. Parent-child programs (focus on parent education and active role of parent)
4. Nursery school and head start programs (modeled after federally sponsored Head Start efforts)

Tjossen (1976) indicates that the need for early intervention may relate to identification as being at risk in one of three major categories: (1) established risk, (2) environmental risk, or (3) biologic risk.

Established risk refers to those cases in which there is a projection of delayed development, which may be related to a diagnosed medical condition. Established risk would include such conditions as Down's syndrome or other medical syndrome in which mental retardation is a major factor, and in known hearing or visual impairment. As will be seen in the examples of existing programs provided later in this chapter, it is in these established risk cases where we have seen some of the more notable examples of success.

Environmental risk is essentially the type of risk on which the original Head Start efforts were predicated. This includes those environmental conditions in which such early life opportunities as family care, health care, and physical and social stimulation are provided at only a minimal level. There are obviously many degrees or levels of environmental risk, and although this is intended to be separate from the established risk and biologic risk categories, in actuality, many young children who are considered at environmental risk are also at risk in one of the two other categories.

Biologic risk is indicated by prenatal, perinatal, neonatal, or early life events producing the likelihood of biologic disorders of the nervous system. This category is intended to be separate and identifiably different from environmental risk. However, as noted before, the two may well overlap. It is important that we note the existence of biologic risk as separate from environmental risk, since biologic risk is quite possible in cases where there is essentially no environmental risk.

A final way to characterize or categorize programs is in relation to either: (1) *known handicapping conditions* or (2) an *"at risk"* status. These might include programs for children known to be:

1. Visually impaired
2. Hearing impaired
3. Physically disabled
4. Mentally retarded or developmentally disabled
5. "At risk" (usually means likely to be mentally retarded or learning disabled)

In addition to the types of categorizations just reviewed, there is the matter of program philosophy or theoretical base. This is a very different consideration, and it is possible that any one of the types of programs just mentioned might fit into any of several variations in program philosophy. However, even though there are a number of variations, there are just two major theoretical bases for early childhood programs for the handicapped. These are (1) those programs involving a high percentage of planned, structured experiences and (2) those more like the early conceptualizations of Froebel, which were followed in establishing the first kindergartens. Safford (1978) considers these to be the two major program "streams" and characterizes the first (structured, oriented toward individual activity) as a Montessori type approach, and the second (more spontaneous, oriented toward group social interaction) as the traditional nursery school approach. In general, the traditional approach is more often used in general purpose nursery schools, whereas the more structured approach is more often used when specific goals are established for children, based on known handicapping conditions. It is also probably safe to say that as we enter the decade of the 1980s, the more structured approach (with many, many variations) will be used more frequently with very young handicapped children. However, as with other methodologic considerations, certain facets of both are often used.

As indicated in the foregoing discussion, there are many ways to characterize or categorize early childhood programs, and there is great variety in program approaches. All appear to have some value in some settings, and most could likely be called *intervention*-oriented programs in that their purpose is to intervene in the life of the child so as to effect positive change. The *type* of intervention will vary, based on differing needs and differences in philosophy of those who plan and provide the programs. The "why" of early intervention (that is, the critical need for intervention at an early age) is the major topic of consideration in the following section.

Critical need of handicapped children for early intervention

There is an obviousness about the need for early intervention in the case of young children who are known to have a handicapping condition, but there is additional research-based evidence of both the need for and the effectiveness of such efforts. One of the earliest reports that stimulated the interest of many who worked with young mentally retarded children was that of Skeels and Dye (1939). Their study was a by-product of an administrative decision, which today would be thoroughly condemned. Two 18-month-old children, classified as moderately to severely mentally retarded, were placed (because of lack of room in "proper" facilities) in an institution for the mentally retarded. These two illegitimate children were born of mothers classified as mentally retarded. The children's original IQs were estimated to be 35 and 46. After only 6 months in a ward for retarded women (18 to 50 years of age), their IQs were estimated to be 77 and 87. Several months later, each had an IQ in the mid-90s. This type of regular reevaluation of intelligence was not necessarily routine at that time, but because of their unusual placement, these children were more carefully observed, and the resultant IQ testing revealed these surprising results.

After learning of this situation, the investigators initiated a search for possible reasons for this amazing increase in IQ. It was discovered that both the ward attendants and the retarded women on the ward had responded to the presence of these infants by giving them an unusual amount of love and attention. Attendants had taken the children with them into the community on their days off, had purchased toys and books, and had provided other things that a normal child in a stimulating environment might have. Residents had spent a great deal of time playing with them, talking to them, taking them for walks, and in total, they had been flooded with stimulation.

Basing their request on this experience, Skeels and Dye were able to convince the state board of control that they should try an informal transfer of a number of 1- and 2-year-old mentally retarded children from the state orphanage to the state school for the retarded. A control population was retained in the orphanage. Children in the experimental group were placed with older girls in the state school for the retarded and, of course, were also the responsibility of specific employees of the state school.

Over a 2-year period, results were obtained supporting the earlier accidental findings with the two infants in the state institution. Children in the experimental group showed a mean IQ gain of 27.5 points; children in the control group; showed a mean IQ *loss* of 26.2 points. The obvious conclusion was that some preschool children who test as mentally retarded may in fact be potentially normal in intelligence and that a more stimulating environment may lead to the development of this potential intelligence. Later findings by Skeels substantiated these early results, and the value of early childhood education (enriched environmental opportunities) for the mentally retarded was established.

A number of research efforts over the next two decades tended to support Skeels and Dye's findings. In general, they indicated that, particularly in the absence of organic causes of mental retardation, early childhood efforts could substantially increase the level of intellectual functioning of young so-called retarded children, especially those from poor cultural or environmental settings. Then, Samuel Kirk, who was later to have considerable effect on some of our national political leaders, published a text on early education of the mentally retarded, which suggested not only that we might be able to increase IQ in some cases, but also that an inadequate cultural environment might be a cause for some mental retardation (Kirk, 1958).

The evidence presented by Kirk, coupled with similar evidence and opinions expressed by others, was given a further boost by the work of J. McVicker Hunt (1961) and the publication of his text, *Intelligence and Experience*. In composite, these various efforts were sufficiently compelling to lead to the federal funding of Project Head Start in 1965. Unfortunately, Project Head Start—for reasons that were more practical than based on theory—was initiated with 4-year-old children rather than with younger children.

Some of the original Head Start programs were successful, and most were undoubtedly of value in certain ways for many children, but the general impression, after the first few years of this type programming on a national basis, was that it was not a spectacular success. In retrospect, it appears that for many children, Head Start was initiated too late and that many individual Head Start programs had little direction.

Head Start programs have now improved; they have more specific program guidelines and they are certainly of value. Now, by mandate, Head Start programs must include handicapped children to the extent of at least 10 percent of their total enrollment. However, if we are to trust the implications of some of the research in early childhood education, Head Start may begin too late in the life of the child to have maximal value. Research on the plasticity of intelligence suggests that the earlier years are much more fruitful for any highly significant improvement in intellectual functioning. Efforts with the deaf in the area of language development lead to the same conclusion. For educators of the handicapped, the best demonstration of the need for and value of early education may be found in the results of various existing programs established specifically for the handicapped or children at risk. Several such programs will be outlined in the following section of this chapter.

Existing programs for children who are handicapped or at risk

In this section we shall review a number of existing programs; in the following section we shall attempt to gain a broader perspective provided through a comprehensive national study. Some of the programs mentioned are quite well known among those who work with young handicapped children; some are less visible nationally. Programs were selected to provide examples of efforts with somewhat different target populations and with different program approaches.

UNIVERSITY OF WASHINGTON MODEL PRESCHOOL CENTER FOR HANDICAPPED CHILDREN

Under the leadership of Alice Hayden, project director of the Down's syndrome programs at the University of Washington (Seattle), an exciting and apparently highly effective preschool program for Down's syndrome children has attained a considerable level of national visibility. This program, funded in part through the Handicapped Children's Early Education Assistance Act and Title I of the Elementary and Secondary Education Act, focuses on Down's syndrome children from birth through age 6. Down's syndrome children were chosen as a target group because: (1) the incidence of Down's syndrome is relatively high (thus a sufficient population could be obtained), (2) these children are almost always identified at birth (permitting the earliest possible intervention), and (3) there has been enough earlier work with Down's syndrome children to have a basis for predicting the "usual" or "expected" path of progress, thus providing a basis for comparing results of any special program efforts.

Certain basic objectives have been established for this program. These include:

1. Increasing the sensory, vocal, and motor development of children in the program to more nearly that of normal children
2. Increasing the subsequent rate of preacademic, academic, and social performance, so as to be able to include them in regular or special education programs of the public schools
3. Full involvement of parents in training of their children
4. Promotion of cooperation on the part of educators and nonhandicapped peers in the process of acceptance of these children in school and community
5. Maintenance of continuous measurement data on each childs progress, and use of these data as the basis for teaching activities
6. Provision of practicum training for special education students and teachers
7. Dissemination of information about the program through a wide variety of procedures

It is the hope of project directors that "procedures that provide accelerated development and remediation for the Down's child may well be effective in helping other children showing similar problems." (Hayden and Dmitriev, 1975, p. 195)

It may be noted that the first five objectives relate to accomplishing certain goals with the children included in the program; the last two relate to teacher training goals of the University of Washington and the goals of the federal government in providing much of the funding for this project. The goal concerning dissemination of information will be found in almost all federal projects (especially those considered "model" projects), and the training goal is common to programs carried out at universities. When these objectives are successfully achieved, the results of any project are carried far beyond the immediate effects to the boys and girls who are part of the project.

In establishing this program, the first step was identification of the desired "normal" sequential steps in physical, communication, cognitive, and social development. These steps were identified on the basis of verified research in early childhood development and were established as very small, sequential steps that must be accomplished. Target behaviors are established in each of the major areas of concern, and all teaching is directed toward attaining these target behaviors. As teachers interact with the children, target behavior is kept foremost in mind, and learning tasks are presented to maximize the likelihood of success. Appropriate and desired behavior is amply rewarded with smiles, a pat,

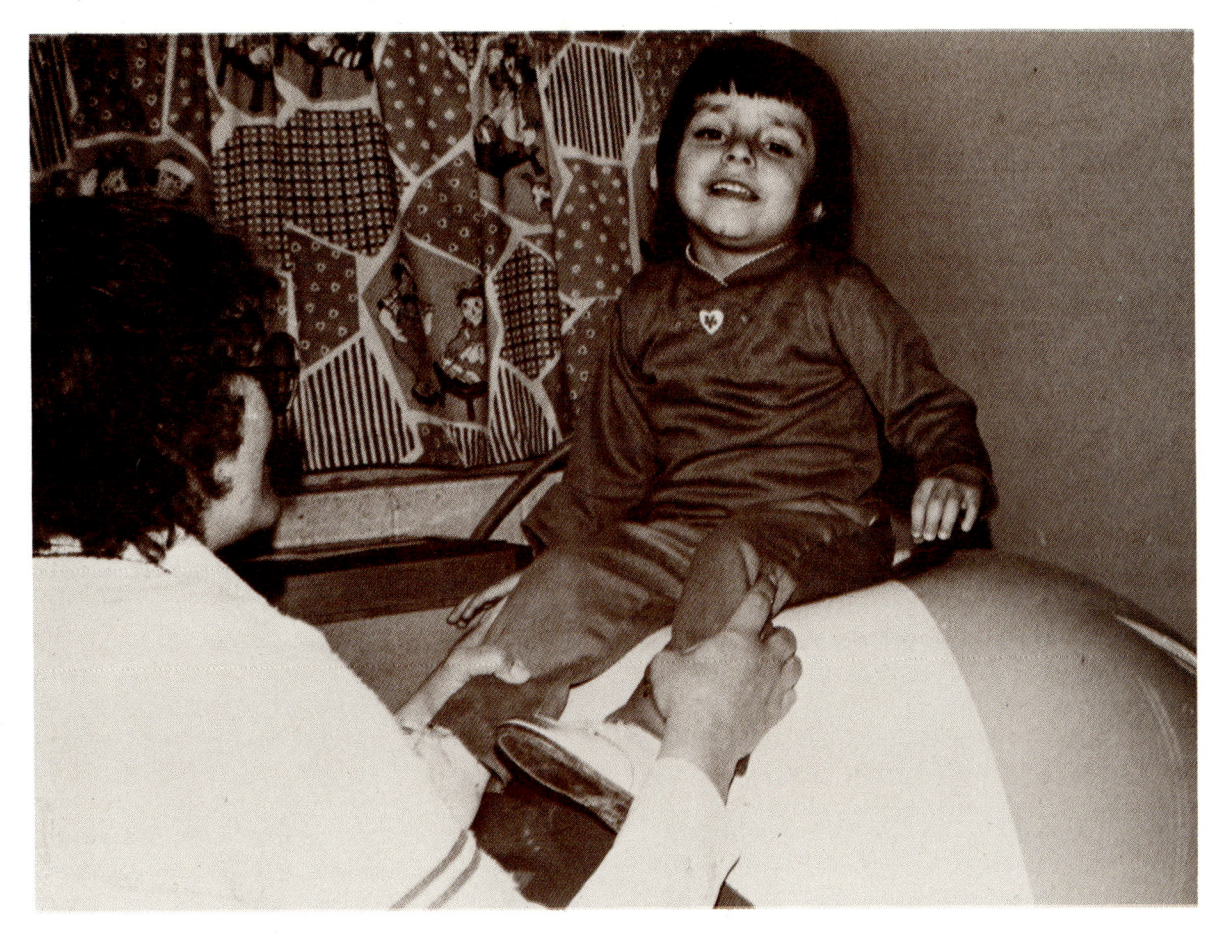

For this developmentally disabled child, further development of muscle tone and balance is a major goal.

or some form of readily evident social approval. Children who need additional motivation are given primary reinforcers as required—a piece of dry cereal, ice cream, etc. For the most part, use of primary reinforcers is saved for one-to-one situations and is most often used when pursuing language development goals or other preacademic tasks.

The program was organized into four classes: (1) infant learning program (5 weeks through 18 months), (2) early preschool (18 months through 3 years), (3) advanced preschool (3 through 5 years), and (4) kindergarten (4½ through 6 years). New children have been admitted, some of the older children have been moved into public schools, and present results of this well-organized, carefully monitored program are highly encouraging. How well these children progress on through the elementary grades and into the more advanced academic requirements of upper elementary years remains to be seen, but recorded data verify that, at least at the lower level of this program, Down's syndrome children are moving through the normal developmental steps at a rate considered highly unlikely, if not impossible, only a few years ago. It is now safe to say that "if the trend reflected in these data continues, we will feel justified in concluding that the programming . . . has succeeded in remediating the severe developmental lags usually exhibited by children in this population." (Hayden and Dmitriev, 1975, p. 212)

In summarizing this program we should note that it is highly systematic and highly behaviorally oriented. It includes extensive recording of individual behavior, and continuing efforts are based on the verified results of earlier efforts. The available staff is well trained and under excellent administrative and program direction and the presence of a number of university students provides even more enrichment in interactive opportunities for the children enrolled in the program. These are for the most part children who have been identified at a very early age and whose parents are interested and are participating in an ongoing training program. It is also fairly safe to assume (though not actually verifiable) that these parents carry out their recommended roles in the home, thus significantly extending the effectiveness of the school program. It may be difficult to actually duplicate these conditions in any large number of programs through the nation.

On the other hand, the information relating to the sequential development, the behavioral techniques, and the teaching methods designed to encourage and maximize success are commonly known and available to other program implementors. Thus the results attained in the Washington program should be attainable, at least to some extent, by all who will seriously strive to utilize this information and these techniques. What remains to be seen is the extent to which the children who received an earlier, more nearly normal start in life can maintain their momentum through the school program. It also remains to be determined just how greatly this type of program applies to children with other handicapping conditions.

MARIN COUNTY ATYPICAL INFANT DEVELOPMENT (AID) PROGRAM

The AID program of Marin County, California, like the University of Washington Down's syndrome program, is the result of a federal grant. The AID program is part of the "First-Chance" network, which is supported by the Bureau of Education for the Handicapped. The AID program is based on three fundamental assumptions (Nielsen and others, 1975):
1. The earliest possible identification and intervention is the best.
2. Parent training must be the central focus of any intervention program, since parents have the major effect on the development of infants.
3. The trans-disciplinary staff utilization model is the most effective with infant populations.

Because the AID program serves so many different needs, its program services are widely varied and are delivered in many different ways. Nevertheless, there are certain program components that are a part of nearly all types of service delivery variations, which will be described here.

Initial assessment is provided through evaluation by the pediatrician and the social worker, who determine general level of development and probable diagnosis and initiate the collection of information that may be pertinent to the development of a further plan of action. When developmental delay is suspected, the child is further evaluated by a teacher, psychologist, physical therapist, occupational therapist, and nurse. The purpose of this extended evaluation is better definition of deficit areas that may respond to special programming. This evaluation also provides information as to areas of normalcy or strength, which together with deficit information permits more meaningful initial planning.

Home visits are essential to the program and may occur even before initial evaluation, especially in cases of very young children or those whose parents indicate some interest but are apparently reluctant to bring the child to the center. In addition, if an infant or young child becomes a part of the AID program, home visits are carried out as long as the child is in the program. The nurse is often assigned as the primary home visitor, but other staff members may also be given this responsibility, depending on the unique needs of the child and the family. In all instances, the focus of home visits is assisting the parents to deal effectively with the child's special needs. Initially, home visits are made once per week, with frequency later reduced as the home situation permits. In most cases, those infants (and parents) visited at home are also part of either the parent-infant group or the prenursery group.

There are a number of important purposes of home visits. In addition to the management planning/assistance mentioned previously, it has been found that efforts to develop more positive, realistic attitudes toward the atypical infant may pay great future dividends. In conducting home visits, an effort is made to assess the parents' competence to handle the infant and thus provide a basis for future planning and counseling; but all such information is gathered with great care, with the focus remaining on the child. Home visitors are careful to relate to the child as they would to a nonhandicapped child, thus reinforcing the parent to act "normally" toward the child. This does not mean that special attention to procedures for dealing with a known handicap (such as deafness or blindness) are not discussed or demonstrated, but except for these very special needs, the normalcy of the child is stressed. Experience seems to indicate that such *demonstrated* attitudes are much more effective than verbalized attitudes.

Certain specific information about intervention strategies are provided once a good relationship is established with the parent(s). This may include such things as ways to encourage motor development as part of the daily routine or suggestions about language stimulation or feeding. The emphasis remains on things the parents can routinely do if they are aware of opportunities to do so.

The *parent-infant program* is another major thrust of the overall AID effort. In this component, parents spend 1 hour in a discussion group with a staff member while other staff members are working with the children in another room. This is primarily for infants relatively new to the program, and for the most part, this means infants less than 1 year of age. For parents, the purpose is to learn more about working with their child. Also, the opportunity to participate with other parents helps them all to understand that they are not alone in their concerns. Program officials note that these parent discussion groups "have been successful only when they were integrated into the program for the children and not conducted at a separate time." (Nielsen, p. 230) In addition to the benefits derived from the discussion with other parents and advice from professionals, the break from demands made by their children is an apparent motivation for these sessions.

The *prenursery group program* is attended by infants two to three mornings per week; entry age is usually 12 to 18 months. Although sometimes the process must be undertaken quite gradually, this program is for children alone, except for parent participation in feeding and certain other limited program aspects. It has been found that, in addition to certain respite-related benefits to parents, children in small groups learn from one another, with younger children modeling social skills of older children, despite the presence of the typically egocentric behavior expected at this age. And, even though the program focus remains parent involvement and management, this time period permits experienced staff to become involved in more intensive intervention as required.

Planned parent involvement in this program can be accomplished since parents deliver and pick up their children at the center. Parents can be involved in activities such as feeding the children lunch and can learn more about nutrition in the process. As required, parents may meet with staff members to discuss individual problems and concerns. They also have time to observe the program without actively participating, which may be a useful learning experience with guidance from the staff. In cases where an overly dependent relationship is developing, this time can serve to assist in reducing the problem.

The AID program is primarily for children under age 3, and the major single source of referral (approximately half) is from private physicians. Although absolute diagnosis at this early age is difficult, approximately one fourth of the children in the program have Down's syndrome, another fourth are diagnosed as developmental delay (unknown causes), and the remainder have various other conditions. Nearly half of the children in the earlier phases of this program were referred by the age of 12 months, with nearly 20 percent referred by 3 months of age. Estimates of intelligence (based on the Bayley Scales of Infant Mental Development) range from an IQ of less than 30 to normal, with the median IQ in the 50 to 65 range.

The essential content of the AID program is not too different from other infant and early childhood programs. For very young children parents are encouraged to make full use of the environment as a sensory-motor experience. It is assumed that these children may, because of restricted sensory or motor functioning, receive less than normal input from the environment, and thus this avenue for building a more normal learning base must be exploited to the fullest. In a similar manner, parents are shown how to provide maximal opportunities for the development of all of the various aspects of language development through enriched language experiences. In other words, all of the known basic requirements for later effective learning are analyzed, and parents are informed and shown how to increase their child's chances through very early promotion of these basic abilities. As was noted with regard to the University of Washington Down's syndrome program, the basic knowledge regarding what it needed to provide for maximal developmental opportunity is available. The problem is identifying the children who need additional help at a very early age and then assisting parents in providing the needed stimulation.

The AID program provides an excellent model for others to follow. The basic rationale is sound, the program is well organized and implemented, and present results indicate considerable success. Those who conceptualized and obtained the original funding for AID should be well pleased with the outcome of their efforts. However, the question of how to get these kinds of services to *all* infants and very young children who need them remains a major concern.

THE PORTAGE PROJECT

The cooperative service agency concept was initiated in Wisconsin in 1965 in an attempt to provide services to local school districts with relatively small school enrollments in sparsely populated areas of the state. Cooperative Educational Service Agency (CESA) 12 serves twenty-three such districts in south central Wisconsin and provides the cooperative structure within which school districts receive a variety of services on a more efficient, economical basis than would otherwise be possible. The Portage Project, provided through CESA 12, provides an example of early childhood programs in a geographic area much different from those considered in the previous two descriptions. Many times, educators in more sparsely populated areas are tempted to say, "We can't do that with our small population base," and at times this may be true. However, the Portage Project provides an example of how early childhood programs *can* be provided, even if the population base is small.

The Portage Project was originally funded in 1969 by the Bureau of Education for the Handicapped, U.S. Office of Education, to develop and demonstrate a model program for serving young handicapped children in a rural area. Today, it is funded by the public school districts that make up CESA 12 and the Wisconsin Department of Public Instruction. It was established through federal funding, but also in response to felt need, and now is needed to meet the requirements for early childhood education as mandated by Wisconsin Public Law 115.

The stated long-range objective of this program is: "Through early intervention, the project is designed to improve the child's school and home adjustment and achievement whether he is eventually enrolled in a regular class setting, a day care center, or a special education class." (Undated brochure, CESA 12, Portage, Wisc.)

Because of the large area involved (3,600 square miles) and the complications of both cost and responsibility in attempting to transport very young children over the great distances involved, it was decided in the very beginning that this would be a home-based program. In addition to cost and safety factors, staff members of the Portage Project believe that there are distinct educational advantages to their existing delivery system (Shearer and Shearer, 1976):

1. Because learning takes place in the home environment, there is no problem in transferring back to the home what has been learned in a clinic or school.
2. The home program base provides direct and constant access to behavior as it occurs naturally. Differences in cultures, lifestyles, and value systems can be incorporated into curriculum planning with relative ease.
3. It is more likely that learned behavior will generalize and will be maintained, because the behavior has been learned in the child's "normal" setting and has been reinforced by the natural reinforcing agent, the parent(s).
4. Teaching in the home provides maximal opportunity for full family participation in the teaching process.
5. The home setting provides access to a wider range of behaviors than might be observed in a more formal school setting.
6. It is possible (and is one goal of the program) that training parents to work with existing behaviors will prepare them to handle new behaviors and new situations as they may occur in the future.
7. Since the home teacher is working with only one child at a time, individualization is actually attained.

As with the previously considered early childhood programs, parent involvement is a key factor in the Portage Project. If the results of screening and evaluation efforts of the various local school districts' multidisciplinary teams indicate that a given child from birth to 6 years has exceptional educational needs, the child becomes eligible for services. The backbone of the professional effort is the home teacher, who conducts additional assessment to determine the child's specific needs. Parents are prime informants in this assessment, which forms the base for later contacts, including both program planning and implementation. Using a series of tests and developmental scales (these will vary depending on the age of the child and any obvious areas of disability), the child's present level of functioning is determined in (1) cognitive areas, (2) socialization, (3) motor development and/or skills, (4) self-help skills, and (5) communication skills. Based on this information and with the assistance of the Project Portage resource staff, initial activities are prescribed. This becomes the curriculum, and the parent is encouraged to provide suggestions that may be used to modify this program.

Based on this initial curriculum, the home teacher visits the home 1 day each week, bringing new ideas and materials to assist the parent in carrying out the prescribed activities. Normally, each weekly visit includes: (1) a review and discussion of the child's progress during the preceding week, (2) a description of the prescribed activities and goals for the

Happiness is a ball. The focus of many programs for children "at risk" is planned exposure to a wide variety of experiences.

coming week, (3) a demonstration of the methods or techniques required to carry out these new activities, or assistance with any activities that were a problem during the past week, (4) observation of parent-child interaction, including advice as needed, and (5) a summary of where the program presently stands, where it should be going, and the record-keeping required to provide meaningful monitoring.

The home teacher leaves necessary materials, written instructions as required, and progress charts for behavioral recording. These progress charts provide much of the basis of any program redirection that may be required during the year. In addition, the home teacher conducts formal reevaluation twice a year using appropriate tests and developmental scales.

The value of this program is enhanced by the parent's involvement, which should be of additional value after the child is no longer a part of the Portage Project. In addition, all of the records, including curriculum, progress reports, and evaluations, follow the child to whatever program he or she later enters. In fact, quite often the information precedes the child, and in either case it is not just "sent" but is rather taken by the home teacher, who interprets the information in a scheduled conference with the receiving teacher, the program administrator, or both.

Portage Project provides a valuable model for replication, especially in smaller school districts. It is a credit to CESA 12, and an example of what can result from a federal project and a state mandate for early childhood education for children with exceptional needs. In addition to its value to the handicapped children of rural Wisconsin, the Portage Project, through replication efforts supported by the Bureau of Education for the Handicapped, has been of benefit in similar settings throughout the nation.

UNIVERSITY OF ILLINOIS PROGRAM FOR GIFTED/TALENTED HANDICAPPED PRESCHOOL CHILDREN

The Institute of Child Behavior and Development at the University of Illinois (Champaign-Urbana) has developed a program called the *RAPYHT Program* (*R*etrieval and *A*cceleration of *P*romising *Y*oung *H*andicapped and *T*alented). RAPYHT is a "First Chance" project, funded by the Bureau of Education for the Handicapped and is part of another larger program involving fifteen rural Champaign County school districts. It is different from the other programs reviewed in that: (1) its point of focus is 3- to 5-year-olds, and (2) its major concern is handicapped children with obvious or hidden talents. In the RAPYHT program the term "talented" refers to six areas: (1) intellectual, (2) academic (math, reading, science), (3) creative, (4) artistic (art, music), (5) psychomotor, and (6) leadership.

Identification of gifted and talented children at the preschool level may be difficult even when it is not complicated by the fact that the search relates to handicapped children. However, since the RAPYHT program is part of a larger early education program for all handicapped children, the emphasis is on finding potential talent among the already identified or potentially handicapped.

When locating handicapped preschool children in the fifteen school districts, most of the accepted methods, such as media announcements, telephone census procedures, and nominations from local schools based on community information (often unusually effective in rural communities), are usually utilized. At the same time, information from parents and observation of children during screening are used to find clues to the existence of unusual talent among these children. Segments of the parent interview form used in the general search for handicapped or potentially handicapped children include questions about advanced vocabulary, special interests, social skills, and other information that might suggest potential talent. If this and other information gathered at the time of screening suggests potential talent, children are referred for more detailed study. When all information has been gathered, a staffing is held to attempt to reach consensus as to whether a given handicapped child should be considered potentially talented. If staff consensus about potential talent is reached, the child is placed, with the parent's consent, directly in one of the RAPYHT classrooms. Considerable follow-up observation is used as final verification, but if the initial impression was of potential talent, sufficient time is taken to give the child a chance for the talent to be evidenced.

RAPYHT is concerned with two specifically different approaches to educating potentially gifted/talented preschool children. The two approaches are similar in that each class meets for 2½ hours in the morning, each incorporates classroom assessment procedures as the basis for determining developmental levels, and each involves writing individualized educational programs (IEPs) and periodic charting of children's progress. Ancillary staff members serve as part of a planning and implementation team in each approach, and there is approximately the same total staff time expended in each approach.

However, because "it is generally agreed that there is no single best approach for educating any group of children, and this tenet holds for the gifted as well" (Karnes and Bertschi, 1978, p. 117), two approaches, based on two different theoretical rationales, are used. One, characterized as an open classroom approach, is informal and assumes that the children and teacher will together determine the direction, scope, and means whereby the educational process will proceed. This approach attempts to provide an environment through which the child is encouraged to explore, observe, and describe, and thus learn through experience. The teacher's major role is assisting the children to learn how to do these things.

In this setting children often decide both what they want to learn about and how they wish to proceed with the learning task. Teachers are of assistance and attempt to extend and expand this process when possible, but much of the program is child-paced, with program content child-selected to a considerable extent. The daily schedule is quite flexible, and many activities are taking place at any one time. Snacks are available throughout the day, and children may help themselves to various foods (illustrated on a menu card) when they are hungry. There is one specifically scheduled time period, a group meeting in which all children and teachers meet together, but other than this one time, it is an open, unstructured program.

A second, quite structured approach is also used. This approach is based on a specific interpretation of Guilford's structure of intellect (SOI) model, and thus on the assumption that children learn most effectively when each child's program is based on sequenced instructional objectives. These objectives are developed from information regarding that specific child's strengths, remedial needs, and the learning sequence concepts that are an outgrowth of the SOI. In this curriculum teachers use prepared materials chosen on the basis of the child's needs. Games, puppets, role playing, and the like are used, but it is a teacher-controlled, structured environment. The extent of planning, structure, and sequence might not be readily evident to an untrained observer, but it is there. A certain degree of freedom of action is part of the planned program, but for the most part it must occur within the context of planned activities. Each child has a separate envelope in which instructions and materials are kept; these tasks are called "workjobs" by the children.

A limited amount of self-selected activity is included in this program, but it is at times *scheduled* for self-selected activity. Certain less structured activity, such as music time, is alternated with the more structured time periods, and snacks are served at one given time, a time when social skills and expressive language development are encouraged.

The directors of this program indicate that "both approaches stimulate and nurture the talents of handicapped children as well as meet their special needs. Both are viable ways of providing programs." (Karnes and Bertschi, 1978 p. 119) They also indicate that "it may be more important to match the teachers with the approach than to attempt to match child and program."

The RAPYHT program is different from most other federally sponsored preschool programs in several respects. Its emphasis on discovery of the gifted and talented is one major aspect of difference, but perhaps of equal interest is the deliberate utilization of two quite different approaches, based on opposing theoretical bases. Implementors of this program are to be complimented on this well-planned, open-minded effort to further investigate differing approaches to education of young handicapped children.

A national perspective on early childhood programs for handicapped children and children at risk

Although early childhood programs are undergoing constant change, we may obtain a meaningful national perspective by reviewing the results of a recent national study of 103 such programs (Stramiello, 1978). These programs represent about 60 percent of the total number of early education programs funded by the Bureau of Education for the Handicapped. The purpose of this study was to bring into sharper focus the national "picture" regarding: (1) what was actually taking place (a facts-oriented view) and (2) what program directors of these programs believed to be their program's strengths and weaknesses (a subjective point of view). This study contains a great deal of information beyond what will be presented here, but the following should provide an enlightening look at these programs. Information has been selected to provide a type of status report in condensed form.

The Stramiello study contains adequate representation from all of the major geographic areas of the nation and from different sizes and types of communities. Directors' responses indicate that all programs were "developmentally based," and of the 103 programs, ninety-eight reported that they utilized *active* parent participation. In size, these programs ranged from one for only eight children to one that served 680 children. However, only thirteen of the 103 programs served over 100 children.

CHILDREN SERVED

In terms of major exceptionalities served, the most frequently reported were high incidence handicaps (mental retardation, learning disabilities, and emotional disturbance) and the multihandicapped. These represented 36 percent and 34 percent of the total programs, respectively, or over two thirds of the programs in total. Crippled and other health impaired, speech impaired, and the low incidence handicaps (hearing and visual impairment) were the point of focus of only 30 percent of the programs. Only eleven of the 103 programs included nonhandicapped children as part of their program.

Early in his report, Stramiello notes that there has been a dramatic increase in early education programs in the past several years,

Program areas of special concern

an observation borne out by his study. Of the 103 programs, all but thirteen had been serving children for 6 years or less. Although several of these programs were serving children for at least a year or two before they started receiving federal dollars, the advent of special federal funding was undoubtedly a major feature in this rapid program growth.

PROGRAM BUDGETS

Information regarding total budgets of these programs was also obtained in this study. Budgetary information is highly important in education for it reflects societal concern and commitment to the program under consideration. Budget information is indicated in Table 13-1.

In addition, the amount of "in-kind" contributions generated by the various projects was determined. The median figure was $20,000, but the range was from a low of $3,000 to a high of $600,000. This larger amount would seem to indicate that in some instances there are sources of assistance other than federal funds that may be available, if local units are sufficiently well organized, but the median figure of $20,000 indicates that these sources are limited or are not sufficiently well developed. Unfortunately, only 23 percent of the programs reported receiving direct local support (local government or school district), which would appear to indicate the need to develop local support potential for that time in the future when federal level funds are likely to be reduced or withdrawn.

UNIVERSITY AFFILIATION

Another question was that of affiliation with institutions of higher education. This would seem to be of particular interest in light of the history of the effectiveness of such programs, the potential for additional expert consultive help from university staff, and the direct program assistance often received from university students. Almost one third of the 103 programs indicated the existence of a formal affiliation, and another 47 percent indicated informal, unofficial ties. In total, 80 percent of the programs had viable affiliation with higher education.

AMOUNT (QUANTITY) OF PROGRAMMING

The amount or quantity of programming (months per year during which services are provided) is another question of interest. In his study, Stramiello found the following: (1) 22 percent served children on a 9-month basis, (2) 16.5 percent served on a 10-month basis, (3) 17.5 percent served on an 11-month basis, and (4) the remaining 44 percent served on a 12-month basis. Because early childhood programs are not usually all-day programs, another measure of quantity is the number of hours per month the child is actually served. To better understand these data, it is well to determine whether program services are provided in the home, the program center, or a combination of home and center. Table 13-2 provides this information.

TABLE 13-1
Total budgets for 103 early education programs funded by BEH*

Program budget	Number of programs	Percent
$200,001 and above	8	7.8
$150,001–$200,000	2	1.9
$100,001–$150,000	37	35.9
$ 50,001–$100,000	49	47.6
$ 50,000 and below	4	3.9
No response	3	2.9
TOTAL	103	100.0

*Data from Stramiello, A. *A descriptive study of selected features of handicapped children early education programs.* Greeley: University of Northern Colorado, 1978.

TABLE 13-2

Setting in which the early childhood program was provided (based on 103 programs)*

Setting	Number	Percentage
Center (only)	35	34.0
Home (only)	14	13.6
Combination (home and center)	54	52.4

*Data from Stramiello, A. *A descriptive study of selected features of handicapped children's early education programs.* Greeley: University of Northern Colorado, 1978.

The *maximum* amount of service per month was provided by two programs that followed the program center service delivery model. In these two programs, children were served 160 hours per month, an amount exceeding that provided to school-age children in normal public school programs. At the low end of the service continuum, some programs provided less than 10 hours of service per month. The data indicate an extremely large range of quantity (hours per month) of service. They also indicate that the center-based concept predominates on a ratio of approximately 6 to 1.

PARENT INVOLVEMENT

As we have seen, parent involvement is considered a key factor in almost all instances. In this study, program directors were asked: "To what extent are parents involved with the activities of your program?" Directors answered the question through the use of a five-point scale ranging from 1 (none) through 3 (somewhat) to (5) very much. One program director indicated "none," three directors indicated a "2," meaning somewhere between "none," and "somewhat." The other 99 directors indicated that parents were definitely involved, with over 50 percent indicating that parents were "very much" involved.

SOURCE OF REFERRAL

Another important question relates to source of referral. We must find the children who need assistance; and we must find them when there is opportunity for maximal results, given the program's emphasis and ability to provide service. In this study, six common referral sources were compared as to frequency of referral. Of these six sources, parents and social service agencies were the most effective by a large margin. The other four sources—hospitals, private physicians, public health nurses, and own staff—were much less effective.

PROGRAM EMPHASIS

One final aspect of this study, the question of program emphasis, also deserves consideration. Because emphasis will likely be different depending on the age of the children served, this question was approached from the point of view of major or "most important" program services for children ages birth to 3 years and for children ages 4 to 5 years. The following results should be considered significant in that they were very clear-cut choices. For children ages *birth through 3 years*, the five most important services or components were: (1) parent education, (2) infant stimulation, (3) diagnostic-prescriptive teaching, (4) home-based services, and (5) parent support. For children ages 4 and 5 years, the five most important services or components were: (1) language development, (2) diagnostic-prescriptive teaching, (3) parent education, (4) communication skills, and (5) developmental education.

• • •

The Stramiello study contains a great deal of additional information, but the preceding, along with the specific program descriptions in other sections of this chapter, should provide sufficient basic information to permit an understanding of thrust and scope of early childhood programs, plus an appreciation of the considerable variations that exist.

One other study deserves mention with respect to the value of preschool programs in the United States. A long-term follow-up of fourteen infant and preschool experimental programs was conducted by a consortium of investigators on behalf of the Administration on Children, Youth, and Families, Office of Human Development Services, U.S. Department of Health, Education and Welfare. (Lazar and others, 1977)

Among the conclusions of interest were that, within the limits of the results of this study, no "magic age" for intervention could be established. The report also suggested that "the tendency [of school districts] to adopt uniform policies and philosophies . . . mitigates against the capacity of many school districts to be responsive to individual and subcultural needs in the way a fifteen-child Head Start site can." (p. 110) This would be especially important where the target population included a number of culturally or ethnically different children. Perhaps the most significant conclusion of this research consortium report was that:

> Infant and preschool services improve the ability of low income children to meet the minimal requirements of the schools they enter. This effect can be manifested in either a reduced probability of being assigned to special education classes or a reduced probability of being held back in grade. Either reduction constitutes a substantial cost reduction for the school system. (Lazar and others, p. 107)

This would seem to be an appropriate final note for this chapter.

Summary

The national perspective based on the 1978 Stramiello study provided a summarization of what is happening throughout the United States with considerable accuracy. However, certain other comments are appropriate as we conclude this consideration of early childhood programs for the handicapped or children considered to be at risk. For example, we should again note that programs for handicapped, disabled, or at risk children, ages birth to 5, are among the fastest growing programs for the handicapped population today. Although there have been a limited number of early education programs for the visually or hearing impaired for many years, and more recent efforts such as Head Start have had the effect of serving many children who might have become mildly mentally retarded through environmentally related causes, the real push for these programs began in the early 1970s. Today, this emphasis includes all areas of handicap, plus the gifted and talented handicapped, and the end of this emphasis and interest is not yet in sight.

A great deal of the stimulation for these more recent programs has come from federal funding through programs administered primarily by the Bureau of Education for the Handicapped. Many states have joined this bandwagon through the provision of more adequate state-level funding, but other states have essentially no programs except those supported through federal funds. Although Public Law 94-142 encourages such early programs, it does not really require them, except as the state has other programs for preschool children. The question, then, is whether these less advanced states will continue such programs when federal funds are reduced or withdrawn. With sufficient parent pressure, they may; without such pressure and other well-planned advocacy efforts, programs for young handicapped children may not continue to develop and grow. With what is now known about the critical need for and benefits to be derived from such programs, a deceleration in the development of new programs would be a cause for alarm, and an actual reduction in the present level of programming would be a national disgrace.

This area of specialty and interest has great potential, both for those who may plan to spend their professional careers working with handicapped infants and young children, and for those who simply want a worthwhile cause to support and defend. It might be considered a type of educational "frontier," and it merits a great deal more deliberation and consideration.

focus

terminology

Early childhood education often means the range of educational programming from birth to age 5, but in some cases this might be considered to extend up through ages 7 or 8.

Preschool programs probably more often mean those that serve children of ages 3 to 5 or 3 to 6, but in some instances preschool programs funded by the federal government start with infants a few days or weeks old.

Nursery school means prekindergarten and programs are for children age 5 and younger.

Infant stimulation programs usually refer to programs for children from birth through age 2 or 3.

High-risk children usually means those children for whom certain factors, such as environmental deficits, delay in normal development, or the presence of a number of siblings who are handicapped, would seem to indicate considerably greater-than-usual likelihood of future handicapping conditions.

Intervention, as used in relation to programs for young children, means actual involvement in the life of the child to try to modify the likely outcome of the known handicapping condition or the high risk status.

By general agreement, programming provided for any of the preceding categories of need may include direct services and/or training for parents.

historical development of early educational programs

The need for early childhood programs for the handicapped was first widely recognized in the United States for children with sensory impairments.

structure and focus of early childhood programs

Established risk refers to those cases in which there is a projection of delayed development, which may be related to a diagnosed medical condition.

Environmental risk is essentially the type of risk on which the original Head Start efforts were predicated. This includes those environmental conditions in which such early life opportunities as family care, health care, and opportunities for physical and social stimulation are provided at only a minimal level.

a national perspective on early childhood programs

The Stramiello study contains adequate representation from all of the major geographic areas of the nation and from different sizes and types of communities. Directors' responses indicate that all programs were "developmentally based," and of the 103 programs, ninety-eight reported that they utilized active parent participation.

children served

In terms of major exceptionalities served, the most frequently reported were high incidence handicaps (mental retardation, learning disabilities, and emotional disturbance) and the multihandicapped.

university affiliation

In total, 80 percent of the programs had a viable affiliation with higher education.

parent involvement

Parent involvement is considered a key factor in almost all instances.

program emphasis

For children ages birth through 3 years, the five most important services or components in Stramiello's national study were: (1) parent education, (2) infant stimulation, (3) diagnostic-prescriptive teaching, (4) home-based services, and (5) parent support.

For children ages 4 and 5 years the five most important services or components were: (1) language development, diagnostic-prescriptive teaching, (3) parent education, (4) communication skills, and (5) developmental education.

References and suggested readings

Allen, F. Early Intervention. In *Hey, don't forget about me.* M. Thomas, (Ed.). Reston, Va.: Council for Exceptional Children, 1976.

Bangs, T. *Language and learning disorders of the preacademic child.* New York: Appleton-Century-Crofts, 1968.

Dmitriev, V. Motor and cognitive development in early education. In *Behavior of exceptional children: an introduction to special education.* N. Haring (Ed.). Columbus, Ohio: Charles E. Merrill Publishing Co., 1974.

Haring, N. Infant identification. *Hey, don't forget about me.* M. Thomas (Ed.). Reston, Va.: Council for Exceptional Children, 1976.

Hayden, A., and Dmitriev, V. The Multidisciplinary preschool program for Down's Syndrome children at the University of Washington model preschool center. In *Exceptional infant: assessment and intervention.* B. Friedlander, B. Sterritt, and G. Kirk (Eds.). Vol. 3. New York: Brunner/Mazel, 1975, pp. 193-221.

Hayden, A., and Haring, N. Early intervention for high risk infants and young children: programs for Down's Syndrome children. In *Intervention strategies for high risk infants and young children.* Tjossem, T. (Ed.). Baltimore: University Park Press, 1976.

Hunt, J. M. *Intelligence and experience.* New York: Ronald Press, 1961.

Jordan, J., and Dailey, R. (Eds.). *Not all little wagons are red: the exceptional child's early years.* Arlington, Va.: Council for Exceptional Children, 1973.

Karnes, M., and Bertschi, J. Identifying and educating gifted/talented nonhandicapped and handicapped preschoolers. *Teaching Exceptional Children,* Summer, 1978, *10*(4), 114-119.

Kirk, S. *Early education of the mentally retarded.* Urbana: University of Illinois Press, 1958.

Landreth, C. *Preschool learning and teaching.* New York: Harper & Row, Publishers, 1972.

Lazar, I., and others. *The persistence of preschool effects.* Department of Health, Education, and Welfare, Office of Human Development Services, Administration for Children, Youth, and Families, Washington, D.C., 1977.

Nielsen, G. An intervention program for atypical infants. In *Exceptional infant: assessment and intervention,* Vol. 3. B. Friedlander, G. Sterritt, and G. Kirk, (Eds.). New York: Brunner/Mazel, Inc., 1975, pp. 222-244.

Parker, R. (Ed.). *The preschool in action: exploring early childhood programs.* Boston: Allyn & Bacon, Inc., 1972.

The Portage Project. Undated brochure, CESA 12, Portage, Wisconsin.

Safford, P. *Teaching young children with special needs.* St. Louis: The C. V. Mosby Co., 1978.

Shearer, D., and Shearer, M. The Portage Project: a model for early childhood intervention. In *Intervention strategies for high risk infants and young children.* Tjossem, T. (Ed.). Baltimore: University Park Press, 1976.

Skeels, H., and Dye, H. A study of the effects of differential stimulation on mentally retarded children. *Proceedings of the American Association on Mental Deficiency,* 1939, 44 114-136.

Stramiello, A. *A descriptive study of selected features of handicapped children's early education programs.* Greeley, Colo.: University of Northern Colorado, 1978.

Thomas, M. (Ed.). *Hey, don't forget about me.* Reston, V.: council for Exceptional Children, 1976.

Tjossem, T. D. (Ed.) *Intervention strategies for high risk infants and young children.* Baltimore: University Park Press, 1976.

White, B. *The first three years of life.* Englewood Cliffs, N. J.: Prentice-Hall, Inc., 1975.

Peer tutoring is often quite effective with high school students. (From G. E. Marsh and B. J. Price. *Methods for Teaching the Mildly Handicapped Adolescent.* St. Louis: The C. V. Mosby Co., 1980.)

chapter 14

Education of handicapped adolescents: unique problems associated with secondary school programming

objectives

To understand the origins of secondary school programs for the handicapped.

To appreciate the conflicting expectations that exist as a result of differing societal perceptions of the role and function of secondary schools.

To consider how the nature of adolescence affects the focus of planning for secondary school students who are handicapped or disabled.

To describe a number of procedures or approaches to modifying educational programs or the educational environment in secondary schools to effectively educate handicapped adolescents.

To describe several major types of vocational training and consider guidelines for planning adapted vocational programs for the handicapped.

Introduction

There are many reasons for continuing concern about educational programs for handicapped or disabled adolescents. Among the major factors we find: (1) increasing awareness of the personal tragedy and national economic waste that is inevitable when we do not assist all persons to become productive, self-supporting citizens; (2) growing concern about the rights of each individual in our nation to have a chance for maximal development (this has been emphasized by the passage of Public Laws 93-112 and 94-142, and is now a matter of legal responsibility); (3) awareness that the secondary school is the last chance to assist many of these students before they attempt to enter the job market and assume the full range of adult responsibilities; and (4) growing evidence, provided by a limited number of effective secondary programs, that handicapped or disabled students *can* make significant progress in academic achievement, social adjustment, and vocational preparation. There are recognized reasons for the present state of affairs regarding secondary school programs for the handicapped or disabled, but these reasons can no longer be accepted as excuses. Among the more significant are the historic focus of special education on elementary schools and the development (or remediation) of basic skills, and an equally important emphasis, at the secondary school level, on "academic standards" and college preparation. A more recent vector of influence, the attack on what is perceived by some as a lowering of academic and behavioral standards, has also had some effect on the expansion of special education programs to the secondary level.

In addition to the composite effect of the above, when asked to initiate secondary programs, well intentioned but poorly informed special educators have often attempted to do so without understanding the structure of the secondary school, without carefully thinking through the differences in educational needs of the 15- to 18-year-old (as compared to younger children), and without understanding the nature of adolescence and its implications for the teaching/learning process. The disappointing results of some programs led some secondary educators to believe that special education had little to offer secondary age students. More recent efforts have led to greater success, but much remains to be accomplished.

In this chapter we will review the historical roots of secondary level programs for the handicapped, the manner in which the secondary school has evolved in the Western world, and the way the very nature of adolescence affects how we plan and implement programs. In addition, we will look at a number of approaches that have been successful at the secondary level and attempt to see why they have been successful. Finally, we will consider various types of vocational training programs and review guidelines for the initiation of such programs. In so doing, we will illustrate the potential of this level of educational programming, both from the point of view of benefits to the handicapped population and as an area of interest that holds much promise to special educators in training.

Historical roots of secondary level programs for the handicapped

As we search for roots that may be identified with programs and services planned specifically for the handicapped and administered in the secondary school, we discover the root structure is shallow and sparse. Special educational programming for the handicapped in the public schools was initiated almost exclusively for younger children, and the move into the secondary level has tended to be overlooked or resisted until the past decade or two. Specific observations will be made with respect to the various areas of handicap or disability which may, in total, summarize the historical origins of special programs for handicapped students at the secondary level. We will start by considering secondary programs for the hearing impaired.

Until well into the twentieth century, many deaf students did not progress into regular public high schools. There were secondary programs in state residential schools for the deaf, and hearing-impaired students who were brighter than average or who had unusually well-developed language skills were sometimes enrolled in public high schools. In general, however, the secondary level student was essentially ignored. More recently, the federal government has sponsored model programs for secondary-age deaf students and more school districts are providing resource assistance for hearing-impaired students at the secondary level. Public Law 94-142 can be interpreted in only one way with regard to this matter—the schools *must* make appropriate, special educational provisions for all handicapped adolescents.

Educational programs for the visually impaired at the secondary level are, in many ways, better than for any other handicapping condition. A significant percentage of blind persons who have no other handicapping condition graduate from high school and continue to complete at least one college degree program. Because many visually impaired children do well with academic tasks, and because the disability is obvious and more acceptable to the public than some other disabilities, secondary schools have tended to welcome visually impaired students to a greater extent than has been the case with other handicapping conditions. The nature of special programming for visually impaired children is such that it is carried over to the secondary level with a minimum of modifications. Certainly, some secondary school teachers do not want to bother with selecting materials in advance so that they can be brailled; also, a resource or consulting teacher for the visually impaired must work with six teachers rather than one or two, as is usually the case at the elementary level. However, the situation has often worked out quite well.

This segment of secondary education for the handicapped is more acceptable to the schools and more advanced in its state of evolution than many others for several reasons. There are organizations and associations to assist visually impaired students; visually impaired students do not present the kinds of behavior problems other handicapped students often do; and the number of visually impaired students is small.

There is, however, one area in which the schools have not provided sufficient assistance. This area of concern has considerable implication for vocational program planning. As discussed in Chapter 6, certain techniques of daily living (TDL) are often neglected by both parents and teachers of visually impaired children. Tuttle (1974) notes that, "to the nondisabled, these skills (TDL skills) seem superficial and elementary. To the visually impaired who are limited in the ability to learn by observation and visual imitation, such skills are stumbling blocks unless specifically taught and mastered." (p. 38) The lack of these daily living skills can be a serious detriment in obtaining and maintaining employment. This may also lead to serious difficulties in maintaining independence, even if efforts on the job are satisfactory. Therefore, although visually impaired students have fared better academically than students with other handicaps or disabilities, this one area of critical importance should be given specific attention through specially planned prevocational and vocational programs.

Like the deaf, the blind have had high school programs in state schools for many years, and these have tended to be utilized by students whose parents accepted or preferred placement away from home. In very recent years, as more visually impaired students have attended high school in the home school district, state school programs have come to include a growing proportion of multiply handicapped students, a trend that has led to rapid changes in programs in such schools. But overall, when compared to other handicapping conditions, secondary school programming for the visually impaired has been implemented for a longer period of time and is more nearly acceptable today in terms of program quality than programs for children with other handicaps.

Secondary level educational efforts for the learning disabled student are of very recent vintage because of the newness of the total field of learning disabilities. Like many of the other handicapping conditions or disabilities, the initial tendency is this area was to provide for younger children and ignore secondary-age students, apparently hoping they would "go away." This tendency was well illustrated in the results of a national study by Scranton and Downs (1975), in which thirty-seven states were included. At that time, 40 percent of the local school districts provided elementary level programs for the learning disabled; only 9 percent provided special secondary programs. This documented discrepancy repeats a pattern that has existed for many years in other areas of special education. The specific degree of difference in provision of service may have been reduced from this ratio of more than 4 to 1, but the difference still exists.

Mental retardation is an area where the effectiveness of secondary level work-study programs has been demonstrated on a nationwide scale. Starting in the 1950s, such programs became the standard practice for more progressive school districts across the nation if those districts had elementary level programs for the educable mentally retarded. Since the educable mentally retarded represented one of the largest self-contained special education programs and the earlier practice of leaving 16- and 17-year-old students in the elementary schools was becoming unacceptable, some type of program was essential. Work study programs grew in acceptance rapidly between 1950 and 1970 because of assistance in job placement and partial financial support by the Rehabilitation Services Agency. Although many excellent work-study programs continue today, in some areas, the segregated nature of such programs has caused difficulties. This conflict between philosophic concerns and apparently practical, effective program results remains to be resolved.

When we consider the history of secondary-age emotionally disturbed youth we find some apparently contradictory information. In their historical review, Rhodes and Head (1974) indicate that state institutions for the disturbed had begun to develop by the mid-nineteenth century and that various school districts began to establish special classes for disruptive children during the last quarter of that century. "Possibly the earliest effort in the public schools regarding deviant children was the creation in New Haven in 1871 of an 'Ungraded School' for mischievous and disruptive children." (p. 53) Within 5 years, similar programs were started in New York and Cleveland. Thus we find that special public school classes for disruptive children (certainly including adolescents) were started many years before public school programs for the mentally retarded. There is sufficient documentation to indicate that some sort of special programs for disruptive children were continued for several decades, but Shea (1978) states that "clinical and, especially, special educational services, are not available in quantity for high school students." (p. 11) It appears that, although public school programs for disruptive students were started nearly a quarter of a century before public school programs for the mentally retarded, by 1978 there were many programs for the mentally retarded but very few for socially maladjusted or emotionally disturbed students. This lack of programs extended from the preschool level through high school, but was most noticeable at the preschool, early elementary and at the high school levels. (Shea, 1978)

Certain major cities such as New York tried separate special schools for the emotionally disturbed or socially maladjusted, but these have been of questionable value. Started in 1946, these "600 schools," as they were known in New York City, have been repeatedly reviewed and reformed. They did provide a holding place for disruptive boys who caused real problems when enrolled in other schools, but it is questionable whether they should be considered as viable special education programs. They were, without question, schools which *housed* disruptive students, but they may have been little better than the special classes of the early twentieth century that were holding places for immigrant children and other disruptive students who did not fit into regular school programs.

Since about 1960, some improvement has occurred because of a combination of federal interest, increased concern with the rights of handicapped/disabled students, and the existence of more local social agencies to provide assistance in dealing with disruptive students. In some communities alternative schools have provided a vehicle for more appropriate management and educational provisions for some of these students. More deviance has been accepted in many schools as being within the range of "normal" behavior, which has made it possible to maintain some students with more mild problems in regular school programs. But the labels "emotionally disturbed" and "socially maladjusted" remain difficult for educators to accept as part of their normal responsibility and for parents to accept as an appropriate description of their child's behavior. In many sparsely populated areas where there are established programs for the learning disabled, mentally retarded, speech handicapped, and visually and hearing impaired, there are no special programs for the disruptive youngster or the student who is unusually withdrawn. This is true at both the elementary and secondary level, but as noted by Shea (1978), it applies more at the secondary level. Despite some early recognition of the special needs of these students, recent history is characterized by attempts to pretend the problem does not exist or to view it as a responsibility of an agency other than the schools.

In the other two widely recognized areas of disability, speech and physical disabilities, the historical status is little different from that outlined above. In speech pathology, programs have been primarily directed toward younger students, partly because a smaller percentage of secondary level students have speech problems, and partly because early public school speech programs were elementary level programs and there was insufficient motivation to change. One exception has been in the case of multihandicapped students with speech problems who are served in special classes or special school settings. In many instances these students receive an adequate level of assistance for speech and language problems. As for physical disabilities, although some schools made provisions for adapted physical surroundings (e.g., ramps, toilet areas, modified class settings) as long as 30 to 40 years ago, this area too has been neglected outside the adapted environment of the separate special school. It was not until the 1970s when federal monies for buildings were tied to the provision of such adapted surroundings that provisions began to be made on a nationwide basis.

In summary, then, the history of special educational provision beyond the elementary school has only one or two bright spots and generally speaking, has lagged far behind that provided for elementary-age children. Many handicapped or disabled students dropped out of school before the matter of special assistance at the secondary level became an issue, but with the coming of PL 94-142 and the Rehabilitation Act of 1973, a time for change was obviously at hand. Some change has already taken place, but in some areas it appears that school officials may try to use the concept of mainstreaming to avoid the need for adequate effective provisions for change. In commenting on efforts made in one state, Cole and Dunn (1977) warned that the least restrictive environment clause of PL 94-142 offers certain temptations to administrators who are pressured by budgetary problems, rejections of tax levies, and other similar concerns. They indicate that a number of superintendents admit to considering the possibility of retaining handicapped students in regular classes, with little or no special assistance, even after their unique needs are identified. This type of "mainstreaming" is not the intent of the law, and the situation must be closely monitored since the law strongly urges the least restrictive setting. Cole and Dunn argue that "this temptation could be avoided if schools could be guaranteed sufficient money to care for their handicapped students in resource-rich environments." (p. 6) This kind of hiding behind the wording of one section of the law in contradiction to its obvious intent is not likely to last for long if advocates for the handicapped decide to focus their full attention on the problem. The time for effective secondary programs is now, but to plan and implement them with maximal effectiveness, we must understand certain important characteristics of the secondary schools (compared to elementary schools) and of the students who attend these schools (compared to elementary age children).

The secondary school: conflicting concepts about its basic functions

Citizens in both the United States and Canada appear to have different expectations of secondary education that will be found in many European schools. Although there have been changes in the elitist concept in Europe in the past two or three decades, in the United States and Canada high school education for *all* students is the accepted goal for almost all parents, if not all students. This has not always been the case, for early high schools in the New World were also focused on preparation for college and were not intended for all students; but as early as 1918, the function of the high school in the United States was expanded to include preparation of students for successful employment in the community (Marsh, Gearheart, and Gearheart, 1978). This was an outgrowth of the report of the Commission on the Reorganization of Secondary Education, which developed the "seven cardinal principles of education"; health, command of fundamental process, worthy home membership, vocation, citizenship, worthy use of leisure time, and ethical character. This expanded version of the role of the secondary school was not immediately accepted in all quarters, but the essential message of this commission has been generally accepted over the past 50 years. However, certain concerns have surfaced over the years. Major among these have been: (1) lowering of academic standards (including grading controversies, concern about ability to read, write, and spell, and universal promotion practices), (2) lowering of standards of "discipline," (3) inadequate vocational or career preparation, and

(4) inadequate preparation for college. Quite often the schools in the same city during the same school year have been accused of being both too greatly college oriented at the expense of practical preparation for employment, and too greatly occupation/vocation oriented at the expense of good academic/college preparation. They have been asked to respond to the general call for greater accountability but have been given less voice in determining how they will reach the conflicting, multiple goals set for them by various segments of the general public, the school boards that govern them, and the legislative bodies that provide a large portion of their operating budgets.

> Criticism of the public schools seems to be related to their visibility and the need of patrons to exercise local control. Citizens . . . believe that they have little control over the national government. They react to and feel more a part of political issues at the state level, but cherish, and at times, fiercely protect their relationship with the neighborhood school and the local school system. It is an institution over which their control is immediately obvious—control exercised through interactions with teachers and administrators and support or opposition expressed at board meetings. (Marsh, Gearheart, and Gearheart, 1978, pp. 40-41)

Although the elementary schools receive a share of this criticism, the secondary schools seem to feel the major brunt of the continuing onslaught, and secondary educators become understandably sensitive.

Between 1970 and the present, two major concerns have been discipline problems and lowered scores on standardized achievement tests. Documentation of the scope and depth of these two concerns can be established by a review of daily newspapers, weekly news magazines, professional journals, and network specials on television. They are a fact of life to be reckoned with and have caused some secondary educators to become defensive if not almost paranoid. Concern with academic achievement scores has played the major role in establishment of competency examination requirements for high school graduation in an ever-growing number of states. Concern about test scores in the past led to questions about admitting or maintaining within the high school those students for whom we can predict much lower than average scores on academically oriented tests. Secondary administrators can truthfully state that at the very time when the public is calling for higher standards (equated with higher scores on competency examinations), federal regulations and advocates for the handicapped are asking them to accept more and more students whose test scores will almost invariably lead to lower average academic levels for the school as a whole.

In a similar manner, while school administrators are under pressure to require more acceptable, less violent behavior from secondary students, special educators are asking that disruptive students be admitted to and maintained within the public high school. Those responsible for responding to the charges of lax discipline and lowered standards on one hand are directed by law and the results of court action to accept students whose presence seems almost certain to tend to make these problems worse rather than better. In some cases, it is the very student who has been expelled or "counseled out" of school who now must be readmitted and provided special programming. The controversy does have two sides, and those responsible for planning and implementing more appropriate special education programs must understand the concerns of other educators if a broad range of high school programs for the handicapped is to become a reality. The role and function of the schools have been so greatly expanded that it sometimes appears almost impossible to meet all of the varied expectations; acceptance of more students who are handicapped or disabled only tends to make a bad situation worse in the minds of some educators.

On the plus side, ever-increasing numbers of high schools are having success with educational programs for the handicapped, and as more funds are provided for this specific purpose, additional programs are being implemented. In parallel efforts directed at a somewhat different population, "alternative schools" administered by the public schools are receiving growing acceptance throughout the nation. Their continued existence is another indication of a broadened concept of the function of the secondary schools, and their application, in some instances, to serve students who are officially part of the school's formal special education program justifies further consideration here.

The alternative school is just what the title indicates, an alternative to the regular, traditionally organized school program. Alternative schools have had varied acceptance in the nation, with more success in larger population areas, but there is growing acceptance in smaller communities. Such schools are truly nontraditional and do not fit any one alternative pattern, except that they are *not* like the "other" secondary school. In both theory and practice, it is agreed that the alternative school (which may be called by any of a variety of names) must be *obviously different* from "regular" schools.

Most alternative schools were organized to provide a place for high school students who had dropped out or were on the verge of dropping out of the traditional school program. Most alternative schools are not for students who are classified as a part of special education, although many high school students who have learning disabilities or are mildly emotionally disturbed or socially maladjusted are receiving their secondary educational program within the alternative schools. In some instances, a careful differentiation is made, with the alternative school very specifically *not* a special education program. Conversely, there are some alternative schools that enroll only those students who are officially a part of the special education program under state guidelines. This probably relates more to state reimbursement than any other single factor.

Alternative schools are typically smaller and less formal regarding such things as acceptable language in the classroom, but in other ways they are more structured (for example, in completing class assignments). Many tend to have a behavior modification orientation. In nearly all alternative schools the student is made to feel more on his own, that is, if the student wants to attend, he or she must conform to established rules. A very concerted attempt is made to make the rules simple, practical, understandable, and easy to monitor. Many teachers who do an excellent job in the traditional, comprehensive high school could not function well in the alternative school, but such schools have had notable success with some students. This has included both keeping students in school and in assisting them to continue learning. More individualized assignments with less group instruction is usually the pattern. If teachers have the required understanding and skills, and if sufficient flexibility is provided in materials and requirements for accomplishment of the steps leading to completion of courses (or units of study), the alternative school may serve some mildly or moderately learning disabled or emotionally disturbed students very effectively.

In summary, the secondary schools are presently going many different directions at the same time. Because of expanding demands they are attempting to prepare students for college, for employment, to be good parents, to be effective participants in the democratic process, and to be ready and able to use their leisure time wisely. While carrying out these and certain other basic functions, they are also attempting to keep all students in school through the twelfth grade and to reverse a downward trend in average academic achievement. In addition, they must attempt to respond to justifiable concern about a decline in acceptable behavior. This concern relates to much more than bad language or incidents in which youthful horseplay results in unintentional injuries. It includes an increasing number of serious assaults, rapes, knifings, and shootings and rising concern about the safety of both students and teachers in the halls and classrooms of modern secondary schools.

In the midst of these problems and increasing concern about inflation and the rising cost of education, secondary schools are being directed, through legislation and litigation, to adapt and modify existing programs to provide appropriate education for students with various types and degrees of handicaps or disabilities. The total of these influences is a considerable load to bear.

On the brighter side, there is some evidence of growing ability to adapt to the unique needs of the handicapped or disabled within the structure of the present educational program by modifying the program when needed. One variation, the alternative school, was established primarily for dropouts or potential dropouts, but in many instances serves the handicapped and disabled. This program, though not really a mainstream program, should be accepted as needed, for it is not a segregated program in the usual sense of the word. Rather, it is usually a self-selected alternative for most of the students enrolled.

Although many clouds remain on the secondary school horizon, there is some blue sky shining through, and the forecast seems to offer hope. The fact remains that the special educator who plans to work within the secondary school framework must understand some of the conflicts inherent in the total system to be able to effectively implement new programs for handicapped students.

Adolescence: implications for secondary school programming

Much of our knowledge in providing programs for handicapped students is based on successful experience with elementary-age children. When we attempt to plan for handicapped adolescents, we find that both the structure and goals of the school and the characteristics and drives of the students are different. Secondary schools are normally a part of the same local educational agency as that to which the elementary schools belong, but in many ways they are different. Their emphasis on subject content, the impersonality involved in a teacher seeing 150 to 200 different students per day, and other factors previously outlined in this chapter are significantly different from the elementary schools. Differences that are just as obvious and just as significant exist between a 15-year-old and a 10-year-old. Each is a *Homo sapiens* who has moved through only part of the physical, social, and emotional sequence that leads to maturity, but in many ways the period of adolescence is quite different from earlier childhood (Powell and Frerichs, 1971). Dictionary definitions characterize adolescence as the period between puberty and maturity, but this leaves a great deal unsaid. The length of the period of adolescence varies throughout the world, with the Western world having a longer period of adolescence because of the lengthy time required in preparation for employment. Although adolescents have certain characteristics similar to those of younger children, we must focus on their unique interests, needs, abilities, and problems if we are to plan effective, modified educational programs.

In addition to their general involvement with developing a workable self-concept and the stresses that sexual maturation may impose, there is, according to authorities such as Coleman (1971), an adolescent subculture, which has a value system quite different from that of adults. The adolescent usually is greatly influenced by the immediate peer group and by the larger peer subculture. This influence is often in direct conflict with the goals of parents and school authorities. In the case of secondary students who are achieving satisfactorily, the school may receive its share of attention, at least during class periods. Parents and teachers may be satisfied by acceptable grades, leaving the student to focus on what is immediately important in the remainder of his or her life. Life is segmented, and if academic requirements do not interfere too much with social requirements, this is an acceptable arrangement. Adolescents may feel that the most useful function of the school is to provide opportunities for varied social contact.

In the case of the secondary student who is not learning effectively within the normal school framework, another picture emerges. There is little satisfaction in the inability to complete school assignments, and if teachers use ridicule or sympathy to handle their part of the relationship, this is likely to lead to loss of prestige in the peer subculture. One reaction (which is accepted by some peers) is to become the class clown. Another is to become very belligerent. These do not promote learning and often lead to other difficulties with school authorities, but may be of value within the peer subculture. In many states, it is possible to drop out of school with few, if any, complications or repercussions. In fact, if a student begins to be a behavior problem, this may be encouraged by school authorities. In some instances, if the school cannot or will not adapt or modify the school program, the dropout may simply be reacting to the "facts of life." The school is in effect saying, "We provide a number of different programs; you must select among these and conform to our structure." The student is saying, "You don't really have anything to offer me—at least anything I find of value."

Adolescents, particularly those who are unsuccessful in school and can see little value in what is offered, are most interested in the approval of their peers and may not be particularly future oriented. They are not interested in having more failure experiences and they find little need to attend school to please adults. They have not developed the attitude (accepted by many persons with more maturity) which holds that we must take some routine, uninteresting, and perhaps even unfair events in life to be able to benefit from the more positive elements. They are interested in the here-and-now, and if school has little immediate value, the best plan is to drop out.

The manner in which adolescents relate to school cannot necessarily be generalized across the various handicapping conditions. Students who are learning disabled (if the disability is sufficient to prohibit successful participation in most of the existing program offerings of the secondary school) and disruptive students tend to be the biggest "problems" in many secondary schools. Both appear to be more normal in learning abilities (IQ, ability to learn through certain learning channels, perhaps successful achievement in some subject areas but utter failure in others), and thus may receive less special consideration from teachers and administrators who do not understand their disabilities. The mentally retarded are more likely to be accepted than the disruptive student and in many cases more accepted than the learning disabled. When they do cause discipline problems, they are not as "clever" in the way they do it. Their level of ability is recognized as lower, and planning is initiated on this basis. Hearing-impaired students are receiving increased acceptance as their impairments are becoming better understood by the public in general, including teachers. Visually impaired students tend to do well academically; however, educators have tended to overlook their needs beyond the academic arena. All handicapped adolescent students must be viewed first as persons, then as persons who are adolescents, then as adolescents who have a handicap or a disability. If we do this, we may be able to provide a program that is interesting, applicable, and thus of maximal value and benefit.

Various approaches to successful secondary school programming

There are many ways in which the topic of successful approaches may be considered. One is to view secondary programs in terms of the various handicaps or disabilities. Another is to consider types of programs such as remedial, compensatory, and the like. Still another is to relate to necessary modification of the physical environment. In the following presentation we will use a combination of these methods, for it seems more meaningful in considering all handicapping conditions. Some overlap is inevitable when such a multiple approach is used, but an attempt will be made to keep redundancy to a minimum and, when possible, to use it as a vehicle to promote better understanding of some of the program alternatives that may be utilized.

Modification of the physical environment may be the major need for students with certain disabilities. For some physically handicapped students, modifications that permit access to all floors of the building, to restroom areas, and to specialized learning areas such as chemistry laboratories (which may have to be lowered and adapted to wheelchair use) may take care of most special needs. Adaptations such as brailled information on doors to classrooms, offices, restroom areas, etc., may be required for blind students, and adapted learning materials may be needed by both the blind and the physically disabled. This type of effort is among the easiest to demonstrate a need for, and it takes less adaptation on the part of teaching staff; but building adaptations may be very costly and thus lead to budget problems. Nevertheless, this type of adaptation of physical environment, plus the provision of adapted learning material, is an obvious requirement of existing laws.

Remedial teaching approaches may be required by the secondary school student and is the approach probably most often conceptualized by non-special educators when they think of special education. Remedial teaching is the basic approach for many elementary school programs (depending on the handicap or disability) but seems to become less viable as students grow older, even for students to whom it was applicable at earlier ages. Remediation may focus on a skill area (mathematics or reading) or, it may be primarily concerned with some perceptual difficulty. Ordinarily, we do not think of "remedial social studies," "remedial auto mechanics," or "remedial consumer education"; at the secondary level we more often consider using some type of accommodation or a compensatory teaching approach.

Accommodation involves "any of a variety of methods of adapting the school organization, curriculum, or instructional methods to the learner." (Marsh, Gearheart, and Gearheart, 1978, p. 87) This concept is most successful when we think of adapting or providing accommodation *in relation to a specific student*, rather than providing an adapted program for a group of students. There may be need for a general framework for accommodation, but it is very important that we not initiate another curriculum, calling it "accommodation," only to find that it is insufficiently flexible to provide for individual differences.

The use of accommodation means that we are likely to be able to maintain the handicapped or disabled student in a normal setting for most of the day, but provide additional assistance as required by individual learning requirements. A number of accommodative techniques may be used, with some combination of techniques the most likely practice. In each case, the decision to use or not use any technique, approach, or procedure must be based on a careful analysis of the learning strengths and weaknesses of the individual as they interact with the educational goals for that segment of the curriculum.

One type of accommodation relates to planning student schedules and course loads. In such planning, careful attention should be given to a number of factors. In some cases, it may be a matter of making certain that the student does not take more than one "heavy" course per semester. Whether or not a course is particularly demanding may relate to the amount of reading or mathematical ability required, the degree of conceptualization involved, the number of formal written papers required, or other such factors or variables. *This must be considered with respect to each student.* In some instances, the total course load should be reduced, with specific assistance provided either through the resource teacher or a talented peer tutor.

In other situations, accommodation may mean advising the student to take alternative classes that are less demanding, or perhaps classes from a teacher who is known to be willing to provide alternative ways to completing course requirements. In a few instances the special (resource) teacher may offer a course section for a very small group of students who need much individual help. This latter procedure should be used only as a last resort, but where needed, such course supplantation may be the only way certain students can complete the high school program.

The use of modified teaching procedures and materials for hearing or visually impaired students is also considered as accommodative by some writers in the field, or this may be considered as a modification of the physical tools of teaching and related to environmental modifications. In a somewhat similar vein, substitute texts that present the same basic content and concepts in simplified form (usually lower reading level) may be considered a type of adaptation. It is important to note here that whereas learning disabled students may be able to relate to the same content and concepts as normal students if the reading level is lowered, mentally retarded students will usually require a lowering of conceptual level in addition to the lowered reading level.

In summary, we may say that there are many ways to implement accommodative procedures to assist the handicapped. Some secondary teachers may object to such attempts on the basis of academic principles, but many, if they understand the purposes and are assisted in initial implementation, will carry out such procedures willingly.

Special tutoring by the resource teacher is another method that may be quite effective in conjunction with some of the preceding program approaches or alternatives. This is different from course supplantation, in which the resource teacher actually teaches the troublesome course. In special tutoring, the teacher assists students in such special skills as note taking, outlining, preparing to give oral reports, and planning for homework. In a variation of this type of assistance, the resource teacher assists the students *in advance* with technical words that will be presented in the regular class in the near future, or with added oral discussion of abstract concepts introduced in reading assignments. Thus the student does not get so far behind or lose the continuity of the regular class. This type of assistance depends on close cooperation with the regular class teacher and may be one of several bases on which decisions as to class placements should be made.

One final type of tutoring that may be provided by the resource teacher relates to learning approaches and techniques. In addition to the fact that some students may have specific learning disabilities, may be behind in reading skills, and may not know how to effectively take notes, outline a lecture, or perform other learning-related skills, they may not know such things as different reading approaches required for different types of materials (i.e., skimming when first approaching new material or looking for references or resources; rapid reading when looking for major ideas; slower, more deliberate reading when problem solving, analyzing, and evaluating). Such learning comes without specific teaching to many students who are learning in a normal manner, and even if not fully mastered, it is not so critically important. To the handicapped or disabled individual, effective use of all available learning time is critical. Even if the overall reading rate is slower than average, the use of different speeds (within the existing range of ability) for different purposes is most important. This is only one of a number of study or learning skills that can be learned through individual or small group tutoring. This area obviously overlaps some of the accommodative procedures outlined earlier, but deserves separate attention in that it usually requires special tutoring by a teacher with special training. When successful, it results in a change in the learner (rather than in the surroundings or the learning structure) and may pay lifelong dividends to the student.

Career education or vocational preparation programs are successfully used with many handicapped or disabled students. Since in this chapter we are considering all areas of handicap or disability, we must note that some handicapped students, including many of the visually impaired and physically handicapped and some of the hearing-impaired, learning disabled, and emotionally disturbed, may go on to college. Most of the mentally retarded will not. On the other hand, as is the case with nonhandicapped students, many will enter the workforce immediately following completion of high school. For these students to successfully compete with nonhandicapped high school graduates, some special preparation for careers is essential. A wide range of specialized programs to assist these students to more successfully enter the adult work arena have been attempted. Some have been quite successful, some have been moderately successful, and some have failed miserably. This success or failure has been the result of many factors, and although such programs (except for work-study programs for the mentally retarded) are relatively new, some attempts to analyze them have been completed. The following discussion of vocational training programs for handicapped students provides guidelines for the development of a modified vocational program and a listing of errors or weaknesses common to such programs.

Vocational training programs for the handicapped

Vocationally oriented programs for the handicapped require specific planning and extensive program evaluation procedures. This is because of the known present disadvantages of these students (their handicaps or disabilities) and because there is even more likelihood than with nonhandicapped students that they have missed some of the incidental prevocational learning so essential to a good vocational program. This latter factor dictates that we plan prevocational components at the junior high level whenever possible.

Handicapped students should receive vocational education programming along with nonhandicapped students in existing vocational program components whenever feasible. This possibility will vary with the variety of existing vocational components in the regular school program, the type and degree of handicapping condition, and the level of acceptance developed on the part of vocational teachers in the regular program. This level of acceptance can be greatly increased by special educators who play their role properly and by "friendly" administrators, particularly building principals. Special educators can promote such acceptance as they relate to other staff members, carry their share of the extracurricular load without complaining about the difficulty of their special assignments, and, in general, show others that they are a part of the total secondary staff. They may increase the acceptance of handicapped/disabled students in a more concrete way as they follow some of the procedures outlined in the preceding sections.

Certain vocational skill components are of such nature that they must be taught by the special educator. One example is the orientation or mobility skills that a blind student must have to be able to get to this place of employment and move around successfully within the office building or factory. In the case of students at the lower end of the continuum of mental retardation or those who are multiply impaired, a great deal of one-to-one teaching may be required to attain certain learning objectives. It is impractical for the regular vocational teacher to attempt to provide such assistance within the framework of regularly assigned class loads.

Another program implemented primarily by special educators is the more traditional work-study program. For the most part, this may be most effectively accomplished by a trained special educator (work-study coordinator) working in conjunction with a rehabilitation counselor. However, the fact remains that many components of the vocational program can be planned in conjunction with existing vocational training programs, and students may participate in existing vocational programs as their needs and individual abilities permit. This joint planning should be initiated for each student as the IEP is developed each year and reviewed as a part of each formal IEP review. The concept of the least restrictive environment applies in vocational program planning as in all other parts of the school curriculum.

A technical manual has been developed for the Bureau of Education for the Handicapped,* which can provide assistance in the establishment of new programs and evaluation of existing programs. Part of the following discussion is based on this manual. In this discussion we will consider: (1) the major types of vocational training programs, (2) general guidelines that should be considered or utilized in planning an adapted vocational program for handicapped students, and (3) errors or weaknesses common to such programs.

MAJOR VOCATIONAL TRAINING PROGRAMS

The major types of vocational training programs are:
1. Low-cost skill training
   a. Work experience
   b. Work-study

---

*This manual, *Improving occupational programs for the handicapped*, is available from the U.S. Office of Education. It is further reviewed in Marsh, Gearheart, and Gearheart, 1978.

c. On-the-job training (OJT)
   d. Off-campus work stations
   e. Cooperative programs
2. High-cost skill training (usually very specific skills)

The descriptions that follow will be of assistance in differentiating between these various programs.

Work experience. This type of training is somewhat more advanced than prevocational programming. Its purpose is to guide the students toward general employment orientation. Simulated work experiences are presented to permit students to understand the tasks and responsibilities associated with various types of work.

Work-study. This includes both on-campus and off-campus work stations. In on-campus programs the student, over a 2- to 3-year period, may work with custodians, cooks, or in the library. In support of the work activities, classroom training is offered that deals with specific topics such as work conditions, completing application blanks, and keeping records. In off-campus work stations the student may work in a number of job situations under the supervision of actual employers. Part of the school day or week involves return to the classroom for training related to the student's experiences in the job stations. Although off-campus job stations may be specifically for training (in many instances employers are paid to participate), some employers may retain a student as an employee after graduation. The number and variety of such stations depend on the size of the community but should be as wide a representation of actual employment possibilities as can be arranged.

On-the-job training (OJT). This program is based on the concept that essential skills may be directly taught to trainees at the job site rather than having students exposed to a variety of job stations or general work experiences. This approach has been used with severely handicapped students because the training assistant can learn the job, bring work samples back to the school, and initiate basic training. There the assistant may then take the student to the job, work alongside the student, and eventually withdraw and provide less frequent supervision. If the student is able to meet the demands of the job and otherwise adjust, he or she may be formally employed.

Off-campus work station. This approach is also used with more severely handicapped students. An industry or business in the community provides work locations in the plant or office building where students are brought to work under the supervision of a coordinator employed by the school. Depending on the nature of the work required by the host employers, students may work there indefinitely and draw a wage. This is an intermediate arrangement between a sheltered workshop and actual competitive employment.

Cooperative programs. This type of program is suited for institutions that may need to secure services for their residential students because of prohibitive costs in establishing a program on the institutional grounds. In this instance, the institution enters into an agreement with a neighboring school or vocational-technical school so that students can be transported to the cooperating school for services. This would probably not be very useful for the majority of public school programs as presently constituted, but may become more valuable as schools enroll students with greater degrees of handicap or disability.

Higher-cost skill training. A high-cost program may be similar in most respects to other types of vocational training, but costs are increased by factors such as low pupil-teacher ratio (many professionals—teachers, counselors, aides, psychologists, work evaluators, etc.) or expensive equipment. Most public schools would not establish such a program except as they received outside funds for this specific purpose.

GENERAL GUIDELINES FOR ESTABLISHING AN ADAPTED VOCATIONAL PROGRAM FOR HANDICAPPED OR DISABLED STUDENTS

Although great care must be taken to recognize the heterogeneous nature of handicapped students and the resulting need for individual planning, certain general guidelines may be of value in establishing an adapted vocational program. The following guidelines indicate what should be considered in such program establishment and thus provide some idea of the actual program that might result. It should be noted that many of these guidelines are directed toward establishment of accurate information as to the target population; therefore, quite different programs will result if the nature of the population so dictates.

I. Establish an advisory committee.
  A. Organize a representative body with members having a variety of expertise, if possible. Be certain to include representatives of applicable advocacy groups.
  B. Select a chairperson and recorder.
  C. Charge the committee with the task of studying the problem.
  D. Organize meetings, study and research sessions, and subcommittees.
II. Define the target population.
  A. Establish which handicaps or disabilities are to be served.
  B. Estimate the number and location of students in the target groups.
  C. List potential students by age, sex, and grade.
  D. Estimate the incidence of any superimposed medical conditions.
  E. Estimate the number of target students who would be capable of meeting admission criteria for postsecondary programs.
  F. Identify the number and types of jobs that might be performed by students in the target group.
  G. Identify the jobs available in the community or in nearby communities.
III. Review all pertinent laws and regulations.
  A. Review state laws and guidelines pertaining to special education, vocational education, rehabilitation, and references to eligibility.
  B. Review laws pertaining to child labor, child abuse, peonage, minimum wage and working conditions, and general school laws.
  C. Summarize laws for target population as they relate to:
    1. Diagnosis.
    2. Evaluation.
    3. Treatment.
    4. Training.
    5. Education.
    6. Sheltered employment.
    7. Transportation.
    8. Restrictions on placement and training activities.
    9. Other.
IV. Determine demographic characteristics.
  A. Use a map of the community and indicate population density.
  B. Superimpose location of unit of interest (school, district).
  C. Locate junior and senior high schools on map.
  D. Locate and identify business and industrial job sites proposed for target population.
  E. Determine rate of unemployment by job category.

F. Contact employers (survey instrument) and determine employer needs (specialized training, etc.).
V. Review resources.
   A. Local sources.
      1. School budget.
      2. Possible private or nonprofit organizations.
   B. State sources.
      1. Rate of reimbursement for special education, vocational education, and support services.
      2. Search for others.
   C. Federal sources.
      1. Vocational education acts.
      2. Rehabilitation acts.
      3. The Elementary and Secondary Education Act.
      4. Developmental Disabilities Act.
   D. Grants
      1. Bureau of Education for the Handicapped.
      2. Bureau of Occupational and Adult Education.
      3. Social Services.
      4. Rehabilitation Services Administration.
      5. State grants.
      6. Private.
      7. Other.
VI. Space and equipment.
   A. Estimate equipment needs.
   B. Determine space needs and explore the possibility of finding low-cost or rent-free space in community.
VII. Community services.
   A. Determine scope and extent of community services.
   B. Determine possible input of labor and trade unions.
   C. Determine possible relationship with vocational-technical schools.
   D. Assess the nature and extent of existing vocational services in the schools and community colleges.
   E. Estimate possibility of cooperative programs.
   F. Other.
VIII. Determine tentative program type.
   A. Using the available data, propose program types that might be implemented (high-cost, low-cost, etc.).
   B. Project staff needs, budgets, space needs, and other significant costs.
   C. Estimate equipment needs and operating budget.
IX. Final report.
   A. Finalize report.
   B. Report to convening body.

The type and scope of program, how it is funded, and other related details of importance will be determined on the basis of the preceding data. Experience in establishing adapted or modified vocational training programs indicates that using a procedure such as the preceding is much to be preferred to simply deciding to start a program and doing so without a planned assessment of this type. After identifying the target population and making certain that the needs of students are well established, determining source of funding and making maximal use of all existing training facilities are of prime importance. Observation of program models in other areas of the state and in other states with similar characteristics will pay big dividends. There is no more need to reinvent the wheel in relation to vocational training programs for the handicapped than in any other area of education. The state department of education, the Bureau of Education for the Handicapped, or state or divisional offices of the Rehabilitation Services Agency may provide valuable help if asked to do so. Whenever possible, a prevocational program should be established to better prepare students for the vocational program, but if funds are available for immediate establishment of a vocational program, this should be done. The prevocational program can be established soon thereafter; often it requires less new funding than the vocational program.

One final point of importance. A plan for systematic reevaluation of any new program should be established even before the program is initiated. This should include specific input from those who work in the program, students, parents of students, and advocacy group representatives. If at all possible, it should also include evaluation by experienced persons from outside the area who can evaluate from a more unbiased point of view.

COMMON ERRORS AND WEAKNESSES OF VOCATIONAL TRAINING PROGRAMS FOR THE HANDICAPPED

Certain errors are common in establishing vocational training programs for handicapped students. These errors lead to predictable weaknesses relating to errors in judgment, lack of knowledge or information, lack of funds, or some combination of these and other factors. Some major weaknesses are:
1. Training based on achievement expectations that are too low
2. Lack of funds, good facilities, equipment, and materials
3. Too few effective instructors
4. Poor supervision and monitoring of student progress
5. Employment opportunities that are sexually stereotyped

In addition, it has been determined that vocational training programs tend to fail their clients (the student) in at least three important ways:
1. They fail to prepare the environment for the student and the student for the environment.
2. They fail to seek assistance from services or groups outside the program.
3. They fail to make programs relevant to the job market and environment where students must live.

With careful preplanning, with scheduled reassessment, and with knowledge of potential errors and weaknesses, program implementors should be able to serve students with much more effectiveness than in earlier times when there was little experience with this type activity and few precedents established. Unfortunately, some programs established very recently have been initiated with little real planning and have been of much less value than if the organizers had sought assistance. We may only hope that such haphazard practices will soon disappear.

Summary

Education of handicapped students at the secondary school level is recognized as a problem area by most special educators, and, although required by PL 94-142, it remains an area of minimal service provision in much of the nation. This situation has its origin in the fact that special education was historically focused on younger children and the basic skills, which are viewed as the province of the elementary school. Although some programs for handicapped adolescents were initiated before the start of the twentieth century, they did not grow at the same pace as services to younger children, and they represent a highly varied picture as far as the different handicaps and disabilities are concerned. Additional variation may be found when secondary programming is analyzed according to geographic areas of the nation.

With fiscal encouragement from the federal government, model and demonstration programs at the secondary level have been recently initiated in a number of states. The success of many of these programs, along with the mandate of PL 94-142, has led to increasing interest in secondary level programs, which must be matched by additional knowledge about program implementation and an increase in teacher-training programs for secondary level teachers of the handicapped and disabled. Programs for adolescent handicapped or disabled students must be initiated with full awareness of the idiosyncrasies of the secondary schools and the nature of adolescence. Certain approaches, such as various types of accommodation and special tutoring, seem to be more promising than the remedial approaches commonly used with younger children, although this must be further researched and verified. Although college preparatory programs are one viable option, a considerable number of secondary programs are vocationally oriented. These include a number of options: work experience, work-study, on-the-job training, off-campus work stations, and cooperative programs. Each may have application under certain circumstances, but no one alternative should be adopted as *the* vocational program for handicapped students.

Included in this chapter were guidelines for planning adapted vocational training programs, guidelines that begin with a careful determination of the nature of the target population and thus may lead to a variety of different programming options. Whatever the secondary program under consideration, accommodative, remedial, vocationally oriented, or some combination of these and other emphases, they are similar to programs for younger children in one very important respect: *Secondary school programs for handicapped or disabled students, like elementary school programs, can succeed only when they are individually planned and implemented.*

Program areas of special concern

focus

historical roots of secondary level programs for the handicapped

Special educational programming for the handicapped in the public schools was initiated almost exclusively for younger children, and the move into the secondary level has tended to be overlooked or resisted until the past decade or two.

Educational programs for the visually impaired at the secondary level are, in many ways, better than for any other handicapping condition. A significant percentage of blind persons who have no other handicapping condition graduate from high school and continue to complete at least one college degree program.

Mental retardation is an area where the effectiveness of secondary level work-study programs has been demonstrated on a nationwide scale.

It appears that, although public school programs for disruptive students were started nearly a quarter of a century before public school programs for the mentally retarded, by 1978 there were many programs for the mentally retarded but very few for socially maladjusted or emotionally disturbed students.

In speech pathology, programs have been primarily directed toward younger students, partly because a smaller percentage of secondary level students have speech problems, and partly because early public school speech programs were elementary level programs, and there was insufficient motivation to change.

The time for effective secondary programs is now, but to plan and implement them with maximal effectiveness, we must understand certain important characteristics of the secondary schools (compared to elementary schools) and of the students who attend these schools (compared to elementary age children).

the secondary school: conflicting concepts

Citizens in both the United States and Canada appear to have different expectations of secondary education than will be found in many European schools. Although there have been changes in the elitist concepts in Europe in the past two or three decades, in the United States and Canada a high school education for all students is the accepted goal for almost all parents, if not all students.

Between 1970 and the present, two major concerns have been discipline problems and lowered scores on standardized achievement tests.

While school administrators are under pressure to require more acceptable, less violent behavior from secondary students, special educators are asking that disruptive students be admitted to and maintained within the public high school. Those responsible for responding to the charges of lax discipline and lowered standards on one hand are directed by law and the results of court action to accept students whose presence seems almost certain to tend to make these problems worse, rather than better.

On the plus side, an ever-increasing number of high schools are having success with educational programs for the handicapped, and as more funds are provided for this specific purpose, additional programs are being implemented.

alternative school

In both theory and practice, it is agreed that the alternative school (which may be called by any of a variety of names) must be obviously different from "regular" schools.

Alternative schools are typically smaller and less formal regarding such things as acceptable language in the classroom, but in other ways they are more structured (for example, in completing class assignments). In nearly all alternative schools the student is made to feel more on his own, that is, if the student wants to attend, he or she must conform to established rules.

adolescence: implications for secondary school programming

Although adolescents have certain characteristics similar to those of younger children, we must focus on their unique interests, needs, abilities, and problems if we are to plan effective modified educational programs.

In addition to their general involvement with developing a workable self-concept and the stresses that sexual maturation may impose, there is an adolescent subculture that has a value system quite different from that of adults.

Adolescents, particularly those who are unsuccessful in school and can see little value in what is offered, are most interested in the approval of their peers and may not be particularly future oriented.

All handicapped adolescent students must be viewed first as persons, then as persons who are adolescents, then as adolescents who have a handicap or a disability.

various approaches to successful secondary school programming

Modification of the physical environment may be the major need for students with certain disabilities.

Accommodation involves "any of a variety of methods of adapting the school organization, curriculum, or instructional methods to the learner."

Special tutoring by the resource teacher is another method that may be quite effective in conjunction with some of the preceding program approaches or alternatives. In this procedure, the teacher assists students in such special skills as note taking, outlining, preparing to give oral reports, or planning for homework.

vocational training programs for the handicapped

Handicapped students should receive vocational educational programming along with nonhandicapped students in existing vocational program components whenever feasible. This possibility will vary with the variety of existing vocational components in the regular school program, the type and degree of handicapping condition, and the level of acceptance developed on the part of vocational teachers in the regular program.

The major types of vocational training programs are:
1. Low-cost skill training
    a. Work experience
    b. Work-study
    c. On-the-job training
    d. Off-campus work stations
    e. Cooperative programs
2. High-cost skill training

general guidelines for establishing an adapted vocational program

A plan for systematic reevaluation of any new program should be established even before the program is initiated. This should include specific input from those who work in the program, students, parents of students, and advocacy group representatives.

References and suggested readings

Ausubel, D. P., and Ausubel, P. Cognitive development in adolescence. In *Readings in adolescent psychology.* M. Powell and A. H. Frerichs (Eds.). Minneapolis: Burgess Publishing Co., 1971.

Cole, R., and Dunn, R. A new lease on life for education of the handicapped: Ohio copes with 94-142. *Phi Delta Kappan,* 1977, *59*(1), 3-6.

Colella, H. V. Career development center: a modified high school for the handicapped. *Teaching Exceptional Children,* 1973, *5,* 110-118.

Coleman, J. S. The adolescent subculture and academic achievement. In *Readings in adolescent psychology.* M. Powell and A. H. Frerichs (Eds.). Minneapolis: Burgess Publishing Co., 1971.

Elkind, D. *Children and adolescents.* 2nd ed. New York: Oxford University Press, 1975.

Erikson, E. *Identity: youth and crisis.* New York: W. W. Norton & Co., Inc., 1968.

Hogenson, D. L. Reading failure and juvenile delinquency. *Bulletin of the Orton Society,* 1974, *24,* 164-169.

Hoyt, K. B. An introduction to career education (DHEW Publication No. OE 75-00504). A policy paper of the U.S. Office of Education, 1976.

Inhelder, B., and Piaget, J. The growth of logical thinking from childhood to adolescence. New York: Basic Books, Inc., 1958.

Marsh, G., Gearheart, C., and Gearheart, B. *The learning disabled adolescent: program alternatives in the secondary school.* St. Louis: The C. V. Mosby Co., 1978.

Powell, M., and Frerichs, A. (Eds.). *Readings in adolescent psychology.* Minneapolis: Burgess Publishing Co., 1971.

Rhodes, W., and Head, S. (Eds.). *A study of child variance, Vol. 3: Service delivery systems.* Ann Arbor: University of Michigan Press, 1974.

Schloss, E. (Ed.). *The educators' enigma: the adolescent with learning disabilities.* San Rafael, Calif.: Academic Therapy Publications, 1971.

Schweich, P. D. The development of choices—an educational approach to employment. *Academic Therapy,* 1975, *10,* 277-283.

Scranton, T., and Downs, M. Elementary and secondary learning disabilities programs in the U.S.: a survey. *Journal of Learning Disabilities,* 1975, *8*(6), 394-399.

Shea, T. *Teaching children and youth with behavior disorders.* St. Louis: The C. V. Mosby Co., 1978.

Tuttle, D. In Napier, G., Kappan, D., and Tuttle, D. (Eds.). *Handbook for teachers of the visually handicapped.* Louisville, Ky.: American Printing House for the Blind, 1974.

U.S. Office of Education. *Improving occupational programs for the handicapped.* A technical manual prepared by the Management Analysis Center, Inc., of Washington, D.C. for the Bureau of Education for the Handicapped.

It is particularly important to have leisure time activities in which an individual can find pleasure and success.

chapter **15**

Programs and services for the adult handicapped

objectives

To describe and discuss variations in college programs for the handicapped.

To summarize information about residential programs for the handicapped adult.

To consider the value of the sheltered workshop and other vocationally related programs for a variety of handicapping conditions.

To review a number of community and/or personal adaptations that permit the handicapped adult to function more effectively in the community.

To summarize the legal rights of the adult handicapped citizen.

Program areas of special concern

Introduction

Although the major focus of this text has been the school-age exceptional individual, with emphasis on the handicapped, changes in societal attitude, accompanied by a number of legal provisions directed at providing better, more equitable opportunities for handicapped adults, dictates the consideration of programs and services for post–high school age handicapped. Gifted or creative students, often in need of modified educational programs to permit maximal development, are slowly being recognized by public school officials and some meaningful programming is now available. At the postsecondary level there is recognition of the unusually able individual in terms of academic or athletic scholarships, honors programs in institutions of higher learning, and other similar provisions, and for the most part, after high school graduation, these students are on their own. Therefore, we will not attempt to consider special programs for gifted or talented adults, but will focus on the manner in which adult handicapped persons are served through a variety of special programs and services and how recent legislative enactments should serve to better ensure their rights. This is a most important topic and merits our careful attention. As a rapidly expanding area of concern, it offers interesting employment potential for those who wish to enter this emerging field of interest.

For many years there have been programs for the adult mentally retarded in the form of institutions or residential facilities. These facilities, which at times were little more than holding centers, have been under a great deal of criticism for the past two or three decades, with the most serious attacks coming in the past 10 years. Serious problems remain with regard to general treatment of such residents. This includes concern about the lack of opportunity for maximizing existing abilities, use of residents as a source of cheap labor, and the overriding question of how original institutional placement is often made. Certain of these concerns have been addressed in Chapters 1 and 9 and topics discussed there will not be repeated here. But regardless of problems, concerns, and difficulties, residential facilities must be considered as a major part of the programming provided for the adult mentally retarded.

In a similar manner, residential programs for the adult mentally ill have been under considerable criticism, but they remain a major part of existing programs for this segment of the adult handicapped population. With both of these types of residential program we must be concerned with improving existing treatment and program facilities until such time as all large institutional facilities can be replaced by more acceptable substitutes.

One other program component that has been receiving increased attention and acceptance since about 1950 is the mental health center. These community-based centers provide outpatient treatment and preventive assistance for individuals with a variety of mental health problems. These will be considered briefly in this overview.

Programs for the adult handicapped take a variety of other forms, including some that are primarily continued basic education and are designed to permit a continuation of learning beyond the high school level. This would include efforts to assure access to physical facilities for the physically handicapped, and programs that provide additional taped or brailled materials for the visually impaired and materials or special assistance for the hearing impaired. These programs are designed to assist the handicapped to pursue a program of higher education or continue a self-improvement process in their own homes after work. Other efforts include specially designed post–high school vocational preparation programs that take into account the handicapping condition and provide appropriate training. Sheltered workshops or other sheltered employment are now provided for the mentally retarded and multihandicapped with some expansion to other areas of disability. Such programs may be established at various levels, reflecting the level of ability and need of the clients served. With continued emphasis on deinstitutionalization, a wide variety of efforts of this nature is required.

An increasingly important facet of any consideration of programs or services for the adult handicapped is the matter of legal rights. Although this concern overlaps all of those previously mentioned, it deserves consideration in its own right. Its implications are broad; it will serve to ensure the establishment of those types of programs and services already mentioned and, in addition, will help assure an equal (fair) opportunity for handicapped persons in such areas as employment, transportation, and housing. Without affirmative action laws in this area, programs that prepare the handicapped for employment would be to no avail in many instances. As a matter of fact, as better training programs to prepare the handicapped for gainful employment were in the planning stage, the question of who would employ them—even if they were competent—was often raised, though less often put into writing. Fortunately, advocates for the handicapped *did* raise the question and safeguards and assurances are now provided, at least in some states. In addition, federal assurances are provided, and may be enforced, *if* all concerned are aware and are willing to raise the issue.

Various adult programs and services will be considered in this chapter, with respect to the traditionally recognized handicaps and disabilities, but a more general, cross-categorical grouping will be used as a general framework for discussion. This framework includes the following major subareas: (1) *college programs,* including any program housed within existing higher education programs, but emphasizing those programs most like college programs for nonhandicapped individuals, (2) *residential programs,* including any program in which special living arrangements are provided, (3) *vocational programs,* including any program in which vocational training, retraining, or work-as-therapy is provided, (4) *community or personal adaptation programs,* including those in which the environment in general is modified or where special personalized adaptations are provided on an individual basis, and (5) *temporary or intermittent support services,* including those (such as may be provided in a mental health center) designed to permit the individual to cope with the environment with little or no additional support. Assistance within these categories is needed by individuals who have very different primary handicaps, although certain general categories are more applicable to one handicapping condition than others.

Finally, following the consideration of programs and services, we will review certain aspects of the general legal framework within which these services are provided and the rights of the adult handicapped presently provided by law.

College programs for handicapped and disabled adults

College programs for the handicapped or disabled fall into a number of broad general classifications. One such classification involves the adaptation of materials, class presentation, test administration, and the physical environment, so that handicapped or disabled students may attend and benefit from the regular college program. For students in wheelchairs, this means ramps, elevators, modifications to doorways, toilet areas, and laboratory facilities, and other similar adaptations. The Rehabilitation Act of 1973 requires this type of provision, and this need is being met at at relatively rapid pace.

College programs have been well attended by blind students for many years, and the type of adaptations provided in the elementary and secondary schools are generally applicable at the college level. Certain states provide special state funds for "readers," that is, other students who will read to the blind student when this is required; for the most part, college programs for the blind are much more satisfactory than those for students with other types of disability.

Adaptations for students with learning disabilities are not as widely provided, and there are more questions as to what can and should be done to provide for such students effectively. Because the learning-disabled adult may exhibit a wide variety of special needs, most of the existing programs actually make provision for only part of the total learning-disabled population. Several program ideas (which may be effective in post secondary programs) are presented by Marsh, Gearheart, and Gearheart (1978), including:

1. Use of tape recorders for recording notes and responding to class assignments
2. Use of tape recorders for responding to test questions
3. Peer tutoring
4. Special counseling for both program planning and vocational goals
5. Special instruction in how to study

These and other adaptive and compensatory techniques have been used to good advantage, but there remains a severe shortage of organized programs specifically designed to serve the college-age learning disabled.

In contrast to college programs provided

The development of new college programs for the hearing impaired*

In 1975, there were 63 known programs [which served deaf college students and provided specialized educational assistance] in the United States and 5 programs in Canada. Twenty-three states, the District of Columbia, and two provinces had one or more programs; California had the largest number of programs (9).

A total of nearly 3000 hearing impaired students were in full-time attendance in college programs in 1975; approximately half were at Gallaudet or the National Technical Institute for the Deaf (NTID).

In 1975, two-thirds of the programs had been in operation less than five years.

75% of the programs had some type of preparatory program for entering students. Such programs ranged from a few days to as much as a year.

Curriculum emphasis included:
26% relating to Business and Office
20% in Fine Arts and Humanities
11% in Public Service
11% in Communication and Media
11% in Manufacturing
 5% in Health Careers
16% in a variety of other career areas.

*From Rawlings, B. *Update on Postsecondary Programs for Hearing Impaired Students*, Office of Demographic Studies, Gallaudet College, Washington, D.C. (mimeographed report), 1976.

through adaptive and compensatory techniques applied in regular college classes, special college programs for the hearing impaired have historically been provided in a separate setting, at Gallaudet College in Washington, D.C. This situation is slowly changing so that today there is an increasing number of post-secondary institutions that provide some type of college program for the hearing impaired. According to Rawlings (1976):

> For almost a century, hearing impaired individuals who sought postsecondary education with the provision of special educational services had only one choice of an institution, and that was Gallaudet College. Their choice was also limited to the liberal arts curriculum which Gallaudet offered. Then, in the early 1960's, a number of postsecondary institutions began providing special educational services for deaf youth, and with this there existed a broadened facet to the education of our hearing impaired young people.

Information on the manner in which college programs for the hearing impaired have broadened since the early 1960s is provided in the box on p. 438. This type of provision of special services for the hearing impaired may well indicate a trend and may soon be followed with respect to other handicapping conditions.

These special programs for hearing-impaired college students tend to be much more "special" than programs offered for the visually impaired, the learning disabled, or the physically handicapped. This is essential, because of the unusual educational needs of hearing impaired students relating to inadequate language development and the additional need of many students for some type of manual communication. A review of the annual statistical summaries of educational programs and services provided in *American Annals of the Deaf** indicates that the trends outlined in the Gallaudet report are continuing with small yearly fluctuations in the number of college programs offered and some slight increase in the breadth of course offerings for the deaf.

A third type of program for the handicapped is not a college program in the usual sense of the word, but it is a special program provided in a college setting. The number of somewhat similar programs in which a college provides special, non–college level classes appears to be growing throughout the United States. This occurs more often in community colleges and the multipurpose 2-year institutions, which provide many other nontraditional adult classes and programs. The educational responsibilities assigned to such institutions by state legislative bodies are consistent with such offerings, and some of these colleges appear to be doing an excellent job of providing relevant post secondary education for handicapped adults.

Broward Community College in Fort Lauderdale, Florida, is one school that apparently is having great success in continuing education programs for the handicapped. The Broward program is the outgrowth of classes initiated in 1974, which received enthusiastic support once the goals were understood and administrative support established. Educa-

---

**American Annals of the Deaf* is a national professional journal for teachers, specialists, and administrators working in education of the deaf. One issue each year is dedicated to the provision of a directory of programs and services for the deaf, including a complete listing of educational programs, rehabilitation programs, teacher training programs, specialized community agencies, and other directory-type information. This information relates to programs and services in both the United States and Canada.

tional Programs for Exceptional Adults (EPEA) at Broward Community College is a multifaceted program providing opportunities for educable and trainable mentally retarded and orthopedically handicapped students to attend a variety of classes, many of which directly parallel those classes attended by the regular student body (Wood, Meyer, and Grady, 1977). EPEA is a noncredit, continuing education program with enrollees using all college facilities and services and participating in the normal range of student events (concerts, dramatic productions, etc.). Admission and registration parallel standard Broward procedures, and in every way possible this special program is similar to the regular program. The EPEA curriculum is flexible, and includes courses such as basic business, food and nutrition, communicative arts, cosmetology, creative arts, health education, consumer education, human growth and development, folk and square dancing, and others.

Financial aid is provided through the Office of Vocational Rehabilitation and various community agencies assist in various aspects of the program. Parents of these exceptional adults are involved to a degree that would be unusual for regular college students, but their involvement and participation have led to a number of program improvements. This is not a degree-granting program, or even a certificate-granting program in the usual sense of the word, but the administration has developed a special certificate for those who complete specified aspects of the EPEA program, and commencement ceremonies are held at appropriate times.

As indicated earlier, the EPEA type program is not a college program in the same sense as programs mentioned earlier in this section, but it provides an organized set of learning opportunities within the college setting, and appears to have led to many meaningful experiences for the handicapped students in the program. EPEA participation appears to have led to greater independence on the part of students, improved job skills (which may lead to more normal employment opportunities later in life), and improved self-image. Since these are accepted goals for other college students, it would seem that EPEA and similar programs are serving an important role in providing meaningful programs for the adult handicapped.

The various types of college programs outlined in this section represent only a small segment of the total spectrum of programs and services for handicapped adults. In the following sections, we will consider other types of programs, which, for the most part, are not educational in the traditional sense of the word. Some are overlapping, and some, such as adaptive programs, may be an integral part of programs reviewed in this section, but each of these other areas has importance and impact beyond the more normal college program. Residential programs will be considered first. As will be noted from the discussion which follows, "residential" may mean many different things when we consider the various handicapping conditions and disabilities.

Residential programs for the handicapped

Early residential programs for the adult handicapped meant 24-hour programs in which the handicapped were segregated and "protected." One motivation for such institutionalization was to remove such persons from the sight—and minds—of others in the community. In addition, there was the hope that some might be able to return to the normal community setting. A more specific history of various types of residential programs has been presented in earlier chapters concerning children and youth who are hearing impaired, visually impaired, mentally retarded, or emotionally disturbed. Usually, the hearing impaired and visually impaired (with no additional handicaps) do not remain in the residential setting after completion of formal schooling, thus we will not further discuss these disabilities in this section. In contrast, the mentally retarded, the mentally ill (the term more often used with emotionally disturbed adults), and multihandicapped adults who have significant components of mental retardation or mental illness are often found in an institutional setting. The mentally retarded, the mentally ill, and the multihandicapped will be our concern as we further pursue the topic of residential programs.

PROGRAMS FOR THE MENTALLY RETARDED

There is considerable evidence that the large residential facility is in disrepute in many quarters and that other residential alternatives must be further explored and systematically developed (Blatt, 1970; Wolfensberger, 1972). Both the President's Committee on Mental Retardation (PCMR) and the National Association for Retarded Citizens (NARC) have established goals calling for a substantial reduction in the number of persons who are residents of such institutions. In addition, litigation over the past 10 years has emphasized both actual and potential problems with such large facilities. The results of such litigation have ranged from decisions or agreements that have significantly reduced the population of certain institutions (and assured much better care and treatment of those who remain) to those that direct the actual closing of others. However, the rate of decrease in total residential populations in public facilities for the mentally retarded has been relatively slow, with wide variations among the states. As reported by Stramiello (1979) the overall rate of decrease between 1970 and 1975 was 10 percent nationally, with the state level changes in population widely varied. For example, Michigan, Montana, and Nebraska all reported decreases of 40 percent or more. However, in the same 5-year period, Mississippi reported a 74 percent *increase*, and Georgia reported an amazing 91 percent increase. This contrast is an excellent example of the manner in which national trends can be misleading when generalized to a more limited geographic area.

Although different in some ways from the trends that have shaped educational programs for handicapped minors, there are important similarities in recent trends affecting adult residential programs. As with younger handicapped persons, the major trend relates to a return to the mainstream of society. This concept, implemented as part of the principle of normalization (see pp. 26-27 and 274) has led to the initiation of a variety of residential options other than the large (often 3,000 to 4,000) residential facility. In discussing such options, Stramiello (1979) mentions apartment settings, group homes, adoptive homes, and foster homes. He also mentions that in many cases, return to the individual's real home may be possible if sufficient community support services are available. Return to the real home would not usually be called a "residential program," but certainly it is one alternative to the various types of residential program options. Regardless of what the alternative programs may be called, it is clear that the present trend is toward smaller, more diversified residential programs in a wide variety of community-based settings.

PROGRAMS FOR THE MENTALLY ILL

Another area of disability in which we have seen much utilization of residential facilities for adults is mental illness or psychiatric disorders. The return-to-the-community trend is also very evident here, but unlike mental retardation, there appears to be a significant incidence of former patients returning to the institution. This is undoubtedly the result of the existence of known, temporary remission in the case of mental illness, a circumstance that does not apply in mental retardation. In a discussion of community acceptance of returned mental patients, Graham (1977) notes that the State of Illinois had 49,000 patients in 1959, but fewer than 13,000 in 1977; New York's inpatient population was only 26,700 in 1977, compared to 85,000 in 1964; California's mental hospital population was reduced from 36,000 in 1967 to 16,000 in 1977. These highly significant changes came about as a result of changing attitudes and changing treatment procedures, and at least in part in response to the strong recommendations of the 1961 Report to the President of the Joint Commission on Mental Illness and Health. This report called for "a reduction in size, and, where appropriate, the closing of large State hospitals." (Report to the President from the President's Commission on Mental Health, vol. I, 1978, p. 3) In addition, the 1961 report called for the development of a wide variety of mental health facilities and an upgrading of the quality of care in those smaller state hospitals that were maintained. Further verification of this trend is provided in *The Disorganized Personality* (Kisker, 1977). In prefacing this third edition of a text first published in 1964, Kisker states that information on comparative admission rates to public mental health hospitals is no longer presented. "The reason is that the increasing availability and use of mental health services in the local community make admissions to public mental hospitals an uncertain index of the true prevalence of mental disturbance." (p. xiii)

Results of the continuing emphasis on a reduction in the number of hospitalized mentally ill adults are apparently mixed. In some areas of the nation, a wide range of community support facilities have permitted patients who are released from mental hospitals to achieve effective reintegration into the community. Where such services exist, there seems little question as to the merit of this deinstitutional trend. In other areas of the nation, patients are released with little or no potential for continued support. According to Graham (1977), many of these persons eventually return to the mental hospital, with some resorting to considerable lengths (drinking hair tonic, slashing their wrists, etc.) to gain readmittance to a full-time residential facility. As might be expected, with more efforts directed toward deinstitutionalization, there is an increasing rate of readmission.

We may summarize this consideration of the need for and utilization of residential programs for the handicapped adult by indicating that since about 1960, there has been a broadening of the concept of residential facilities to include a number of community based alternatives, such as apartment settings, small and large group homes, adoptive settings, and foster settings. There has been a related effort to ensure that existing state schools become much smaller. It is predictable that if present trends continue, "large," which once meant several thousand residents, may come to mean 200 to 300 residents or perhaps even fewer.

The reduction in large residential facilities and the increased use of alternate residential models has led to the need for other community services and for increased community awareness, understanding, and acceptance of this population as part of the community. A variety of organizations have supported this general change of direction, and the federal government, through public information efforts and funds for certain specific demonstration programs and support services, has played a leadership role. Nevertheless, general public acceptance remains mixed. According to Graham, some of the mentally ill who have been returned to the community with less than adequate support services "are recruited into migrant labor camps or prostitution. Many are victims of crime, poverty, hostility, or indifference." In some instances, the problem of appropriate community services relates to the fact that the same dollars that made services possible in the institution cannot follow the individual into the community setting. We can only conclude that services to the handicapped adult, provided through some type of residential service model, are in a state of flux. Much additional attention is required if the goals of present deinstitutional thrusts are to be realized. Most of the needs of the handicapped individuals involved can be met through the development of greater community support and understanding and more effective development and utilization of vocational preparation programs, community and personal adaptation programs, and support services, as will be outlined in the three following sections.

Vocational programs for the adult handicapped

The term "vocational program" can mean many different things when applied to education in general, and similar variety exists when applied to special education. For the adult handicapped, vocational programs will vary, depending on the major goals of the program, the type of handicap or disability, the age and level of intelligence of the individuals involved, previous educational and/or vocational training experiences, and the orientation of the agency planning such programs. Because a great deal of information about the Rehabilitation Services Agency and the process of rehabilitation will be provided in Chapter 16, only a minimum of information about the workings of this specific agency will be given here. Rather, we will consider the basic types of vocationally related programs that may be provided the adult handicapped or disabled, the settings in which they may be provided, and the general characteristics and goals of such programs.

It might first be noted that a number of highly effective vocational preparation programs for the adult handicapped or disabled are implemented by various colleges, junior colleges, technical schools, or specialized programs such as the National Technical Institute for the Deaf (NTID). Certain of these programs were reviewed earlier. Our emphasis in this section will be noncollege programs; in general, the population served by such programs has tended to be those with more severe handicapping conditions. There are exceptions to this generalization, but if the functions of the community colleges of this nation continue to broaden and expand, specialized vocational training programs for the more capable handicapped adults may eventually be included within the framework of the community college structure to an increasing degree.

THE SHELTERED WORKSHOP

Perhaps the most widely recognized type of vocationally related program is the sheltered workshop. The sheltered workshop was initiated in the United States in 1837 with the establishment of a workshop for the blind near Boston. This workshop was established to train the blind for productive, self-supporting employment, but from the very beginning there were problems in encouraging the worker-clients to leave the sheltered setting. This problem, plus the fact that such workshops have seldom been self-supporting, has been a continuing source of concern through the years. More recently, however, it has been accepted that the sheltered workshop may serve several different functions and that they will not be self-supporting. Recognition of the varied functions of the sheltered workshop has been promoted by the fact that the federal government will allow placements (by rehabilitation counselors) in workshops for a variety of purposes, and if the facility is accredited, it may obtain significant federal support for these various services.

It is generally recognized that although there are a number of potential functions of the sheltered workshop, these are usually related to two basic functions: (1) training for employment in competitive (outside) jobs, and (2) terminal (permanent) employment for adults who cannot successfully function in outside, competitive employment situations (Bolanovich, Drought, and Stewart, 1972). Some authorities characterize the principal function of the sheltered workshop as the development of "work adjustment," and, according to Bitter (1979), "A principal vehicle for developing work adjustment in the disabled is the use of production work." (p. 222)

Work adjustment is training to work; it is orientation to the demands of employment and has little to do with academic skills or the usual orientation of an educational program. Work adjustment precedes on-the-job training and also is an integral part of it. For some clients it may relate to the requirements of punctuality, cooperation, and perseverance at an assigned task. For others it may be the normal requirements of courtesy or cleanliness. Very simply, lack of work adjustment may be the basic reason that a person is fired, even if he or she has the academic and physical skills to do the job. Vocational preparation programs provided through the sheltered workshop *must* emphasize work adjustment skills for all clients, whether they are destined for outside competitive employment or continued employment within the sheltered workshop.

Bluhm (1977) has pointed out that although vocational success of the retarded has been extensively studied, the findings are often contradictory. At least to some extent, the same thing applies in other areas of disability. However, there is one finding that is relatively well agreed upon. For many disabled workers, it is *not* lack of mental ability, physical skills, or level of academic achievement (basic reading or mathematical ability) that prevents success on the job. Rather, the problem is work adjustment. Thus this will apparently remain a major area of emphasis in vocational training in the sheltered workshop and, for that matter, in other training settings.

In addition to work adjustment skills, a number of both general and specific work skills are taught in the workshops. Through continuing study of the skills required for the various jobs usually available to the handicapped or disabled, those who conduct the sheltered workshop type programs have catalogued the necessary physical/motor skills. Likewise, the required basic reading and mathematical skills are known. Professionals who specialize in the various areas of handicap or disability know which skills are more likely to be underdeveloped among clients who have the various disabilities, and this knowledge is brought into play when completing the individual planning essential for each client. Evaluation on the job, whether in the workshop or outside employment, leads to additional information that is incorporated in the training plan. This information, as regularly revised and updated, becomes the individual training plan.

One relatively new force in the sheltered workshop movement deserves mention here; its long-term effectiveness remains to be determined, but its potential for impact appears to be great. In 1938, through the Wagner-O'Day Act, the federal government established a special status for workshops for the blind. This law mandated that certain products be purchased (for federal use) from such workshops, thus providing a special type of government subsidy. The National Industries for the Blind was created to coordinate purchases of products made by the blind. In 1971, the Javits-Wagner-O'Day Act expanded this concept to include other disabling conditions. As a result, in 1974, six national volunteer agencies—Association of Rehabilitation Facilities, Goodwill Industries of America, National Association of Jewish Vocational Services, National Association for Retarded Citizens, National Easter Seal Society for Crippled Children and Adults, and United Cerebral Palsy Association—established a nonprofit corporation called National Industries for the Severely Handicapped (NISH). NISH is now involved in the identification of ways in which the federal government's expressed interest in the sheltered workshops can be facilitated. As may be inferred from the list of volunteer agencies involved in NISH, the sheltered workshop is a concern of advocates for most of the recognized handicapping conditions, but especially the mentally retarded, the very seriously physically handicapped, and the multihandicapped. Certain versions of the sheltered workshop are also of increasing importance to another group of adults, the mentally ill, as will be seen in the following discussion.

With the increasing rate of return from the mental institutions and with much lower rates of admittance, it has become increasingly important that a wide variety of community services be provided individuals who need temporary or intermittent support. More will be said about this support concept in a later section, but it is pertinent to note here that some type of sheltered employment may actually be an important step in the treatment of the mentally ill. The work-as-therapy concept is apparently growing, and it is a concept with a commonsense support base. Given the fact that mentally ill persons cannot handle what would usually be called normal interactions with "normal" people (demonstration of this lack of ability is what leads to their being called mentally ill), it is certainly reasonable to believe that they must *learn* to handle such interactions. What more logical place than in a sheltered employment setting? From the point of view of treatment theory, this might be called a type of resocialization (social learning in a real-life situation) or behavioral rehearsal, both accepted as potentially valuable types of behavioral therapy for the mentally ill (Kisker, 1977). For the mentally ill on the road to reintegration in the mainstream of society, the opportunity to practice work skills in an environment where an error in judgment or erratic behavior becomes a learning situation rather than a trigger for more rejection may be of critical importance. Work-as-therapy, whether within the framework of an established sheltered workshop or provided in some other manner, is certainly a type of vocational training (or retraining) and undoubtedly deserves more research and attention than it has presently received.

Community and/or personal adaptation programs

There are a number of ways in which the adult may more successfully participate in the community through the use of various adaptive techniques or hardware, or through adaptations in the environmental surroundings. Many of these adaptations have been mentioned in preceding chapters with respect to educational programs for handicapped/disabled students, but they will be outlined again as they relate to adults. In general, the various personal adaptations are those that must be obtained by the individual. Some of the adaptive devices are very expensive, and low-income adults may need assistance from social service agencies or advocacy organiza-

Program areas of special concern

tions. Some environmental adaptations are also expensive, especially if they involve renovation of existing buildings but many are not particularly costly if incorporated into the design of new buildings, streets, and sidewalks. It is primarily a matter of awareness and the not-too-costly (but often difficult to achieve) changes in city ordinances, building regulations, and so on. These latter changes require strong support from the public, a responsibility that the readers of this text must assume as informed citizens.

Personal adaptations range from such things as simple hearing aids (perhaps not available to some adults because of the cost) to devices that permit the deaf to know when a doorbell rings through the use of visual signals. Other examples include the familiar seeing-eye dog and the less familiar use of the dog to assist the deaf to live in more comfort and safety. Assistance such as a battery-operated wheelchair, the right prostheses and training to use them, a wide variety of mechanical devices for use by the severely physically impaired, modified automobiles for use by the physically handicapped, equipment that converts print to sound, and specialized lenses that permit the legally blind to see (under certain circumstances) may make a tremendous difference in the life of the handicapped or disabled. Unlike the handicapped child who has school personnel who are directed by law to consider the handicap, adults who are not aggressive in seeking help may be overlooked and have a much less than satisfactory existence, when simple assistance could make a great difference.

The list of possible adaptations, though not endless, is too extensive to consider here. However, we will consider two specific areas in which adaptations can be made, which represent examples of the complexity of such adaptations and the degree to which the needs of the handicapped have been addressed in certain parts of the nation. The large majority of all such adaptations and the efforts underway to make them available to a larger proportion of the handicapped population are the result of joint efforts of advocacy groups and federal agencies.

ENVIRONMENTAL ADAPTATIONS

One important area in which specific adaptive planning is highly essential is the environment in which handicapped persons (either children or adults) live, attend school or other training program, work, shop, pay bills, conduct business or attend worship services. Unless certain adaptations and modifications are made, many handicapped persons do not have equal access to housing, city, county, or federal service agencies, hospitals, places of entertainment, restaurants, and many other aspects of the normal environment. They may be denied equal opportunity for employment because the office building or factory is not accessible.

Federal law prohibits discrimination against any handicapped person who is otherwise qualified and specifically relates to the question of access, but this applies only to those programs or activities receiving federal funds. Fortunately for the handicapped, most local and state agencies receive some federal funds and therefore are covered by this law (Public Law 93-112, Section 504), but in many cases, unless a complaint is filed, such discrimination continues to exist. It is also fortunate that many states have parallel laws that may be even more specific, but problems remain, especially in older buildings and in rural areas of the nation. The following partial list will indicate some of the types of environmental modifications or additions that are needed just with respect to buildings:

Ramps
Elevators
Modified drinking fountains

446

Modified restroom areas
Brailled signs (directories, door signs, etc.)
Handrails
Modified cafeteria facilities

In addition, certain specialized modifications, tailored to the unique needs of a particular individual, may be required, which could include modifications in work areas (desks, tables, telephone, typewriters) or other special provisions. In areas outside of public buildings, offices, or other places of employment, special parking provisions may also be required.

In an effort to more effectively illustrate many of these environmental adaptations, a training project called the Center for Architectural Planning and Design for Handicapped People has been established at the Massachusetts College of Art in Boston. This project was designed to train or retrain personnel who serve those with special needs with respect to the many ways in which the environment can be designed to facilitate rather than impede program participation and learning. The emphasis is on designing for people with handicaps, a concept that is the topic of a special annual regional institute. This training is provided through special meetings conducted by the staff; slide presentations and other media that illustrate adapted areas in offices, schools, homes, and hospitals; and other activities. In addition to its valuable training function directed toward teachers, nurses, occupational therapists, physical therapists, parents, and other consumers, the Center will provide a permanent setting in which adapted environments can be shown to visitors. This permits a much better idea of what to do and how to do it than written descriptions; there is also the advantage of having this variety of resources under one roof. An adaptive environments library is also available at the Center, and design specialists are members of the Center staff. This is a relatively new program (initiated in 1978 and undergoing further development since that time) and promises much in this area of need.

ADAPTED TRANSPORTATION FACILITIES

Another related but distinctly separate area of concern will be considered as our second example of the variety of adaptive needs of the handicapped. This is the area of transportation-related needs. The basic need for transportation can be easily conceptualized, but the kinds of adaptations required and the cost of these adaptations are not always so easily "sold" to those who can provide assistance. Even though we have the appropriately adapted barrier-free environment (for example) at the place of employment, how effectively can the handicapped get there? This question must be faced squarely, or the considerable effort and cost involved in preparing the handicapped for the world of work and adapting work settings to their needs are wasted for many handicapped persons; thus this is a most important consideration. This question can be considered within two major categories, public transportation and personal transportation. Each has its place, and we shall review these two areas separately.

Public transportation facilities involve community-supported adaptation; that is, supported by public funds, used by handicapped persons with a number of differing needs and adaptive requirements, and involving national level planning. The so-called "transbus" specifications would make all urban transit buses much more accessible for use by the elderly and the handicapped. According to a Transportation Department report in Congressional committee hearings (Sept. 1978), $27 million had already been spent by the fall of 1978 on the development of a practical "transbus," and serious problems remained. The seriousness of these problems can be inferred from the fact that in late 1978, two of the three firms that had earlier informed the Transportation Department that they were interested in bidding on the transbus construction contracts had essentially withdrawn from competition. Also, at about that time, three major cities that had formed a consortium to buy 500 of the planned transbuses dropped their purchase plans. Among the major problems cited by the manufacturers were requirements for a front door ramp, a back door hydraulic lift, and a lower floor height than existing buses. A coalition of thirteen organizations representing the elderly and the handicapped has pushed for the development of buses that could serve their needs, and certain compromises between what coalition members were demanding and what the manufacturers believed could be done appear to have gotten this project back on track; but at best, it will be completed several years later than earlier projected.

Efforts such as the transbus project have tremendous implications for the adult handicapped, especially the physically handicapped. In some special transportation efforts, communities operate one or two special buses throughout the city on a schedule that permits transportation to, for example, a downtown area, once or twice each day. This may be useful for some retired persons or those with no time schedule requirements, but for the handicapped who cannot ride the regular bus, have limited funds, but need to get to work to earn a living, this is almost useless. They do not have a fair chance to utilize their work skills, or if they do, it is at a considerable cost for special transportation.

The federal government, through the Department of Transportation, is able to establish guidelines for bus purchases for those cities that use federal funds in purchasing buses. This includes most of the major cities and many smaller ones. The whole question is a multimillion dollar one. It will slightly increase the cost of transportation for all citizens but will enable the handicapped and the elderly to participate in society in a way never before possible. Many problems remain before this matter is settled satisfactorily to all concerned, but this provides an excellent example of community adaptation in the area of transportation, which can make a great deal of difference to the handicapped and bring them one step closer to full participation in all aspects of the world in which they live.

Personal transportation may also be adapted for use by the handicapped. This issue has to do with both the provision and licensing of private automobiles for the disabled. As with the public transportation/transbus issue, federal agencies are the funding source for most such efforts, with major leadership provided through two agencies, the Veterans Administration and the Rehabilitation Services Administration. One example of their joint support is a 200 page publication, *Personalized Licensed Vehicles for the Disabled*, an illustrated report on the latest in adaptive systems available through various manufacturers. This publication was the outgrowth of a national worshop held at the Rehabilitation Engineering Center (REC) at Moss Rehabilitation Hospital in Philadelphia, and is available from that source (Programs for the Handicapped, 1977).

This workshop, sponsored by the VA and RSA, brought together representatives of the community of disabled persons, rehabilitation researchers, government officials, representatives of the automobile industry, and representatives of various companies that manufacture adaptive systems. Conference topics were structured to provide information regarding both what is presently available and what is needed by disabled persons. Topics such as human factors of driver capability, driver training, and biomechanical requirements relating to strength, range of motion, and control sensitivity were considered in depth. Other topics, such as legal matters involved in licensing, liability, and insurance, were also considered. These latter concerns must be addressed in many cases on a state-by-state basis, since they are controlled primarily by state law or regulation. Without careful consideration of these legal matters, in some states certain handicapped or disabled persons will not be able to drive, regardless of the effectiveness of adaptive developments.

• • •

It should now be evident that even this one topic, transportation, is a very complex one and requires much additional attention. At the federal level, continued pressure must be applied to win the battle to assure equal access to public transportation. Additional efforts at the local and state levels are also required and have been underway for several years. These include the more evident "sit-ins" and street blockades (usually by persons in wheelchairs) that have taken place in many major cities, and the behind-the-scenes political maneuvering that is an integral part of the American system of government. Concerning personal vehicles, it appears that the Veterans Administration and the Rehabilitation Services Administration, along with manufacturers, are making real strides with mechanical adaptations. However, additional efforts are required, primarily at the state level, to establish realistic laws, regulations, and practices with regard to such matters as licensing, liability, and insurance. This may be a lengthy process and may best be attained with the strong support of key state legislators. In summary, the conflict on this particular front is well underway. Significant major battles have been won, but many remain to be fought. And there are many other areas of concern related to the overall question of modifying or adapting the environment so that the handicapped may participate fully in all aspects of society.

Temporary or intermittent support services

There are certain types of service that may be viewed as temporary or intermittent. These services must be available at all times, and thus are not "temporary" in this respect, but rather the individual who needs them may need them only on a temporary or intermittent basis. Most of these services have been established rather recently. They are part of a variety of attempts to permit the handicapped or disabled to be maintained within the community rather than in a residential setting.

One of the more common of such services is provided through the mental health centers. Although the scope and quality of service vary widely, this is one type of service found in almost all geographic areas. Staff composition of the centers may also vary, but according to Kisker (1977), "the traditional mental health team is made up of the clinical psychologist, psychiatrist, psychiatric social worker, psychiatric nurse, and psychiatric aide." (p. 14) The role of mental health centers is usually to reduce personality and/or behavior disorders or problems, and thus reduce the need for institutional treatment. They may serve this role in a wide variety of ways. For some it is a matter of providing support during a particularly stressful period of life, and thus preventing the need for residential treatment. For others, who have been in a residential setting or psychiatric ward of a local hospital, their service may eliminate the need to return to these settings.

The concept of the mental health center appears to be steadily gaining in acceptance, and the functions of such centers are expanding. Some of this expanded role is filled by an increase in the numbers of staff members with professional job descriptions, as indicated before. However, there is increasing use of paraprofessionals who fill a variety of mental health roles. These paraprofessionals include persons ranging from teenage to retirement ages, who serve as teacher aides, home visitors, special skill instructors, recreation assistants, foster parents, nursing aides, physical or occupational aides, and general group activity assistants. This rapidly expanding vocational area presently appears to be moving in many different directions at once, with no readily evident trends indicating where or when the limits of paraprofessional assistance will be reached. In contrast to most of the professional staff members of the mental health team who come from disciplines that subscribe to increasingly stringent licensing practices, the paraprofessionals are "just people," who exhibit interest, warmth, and patience, or—put simply—who care. The mental health center is a most interesting phenomenon of the last half of the present century and appears to have won rapid acceptance in its role of prevention and intermittent support.

Another type of intermittent support is represented by the type of assistance provided the deinstitutionalized mentally retarded, designed to assist them in handling a number of daily affairs we commonly assume that persons with normal intelligence can handle alone. This includes (but is not limited to) assistance in planning purchases and in planning meals and advice as to family or marital planning. Some of these types of counseling services may be provided in a mental health center, but special funding may be available to establish agencies to assist only the mildly or moderately mentally retarded. Also, they may be working primarily with the mentally retarded who were formerly institutionalized. As the public schools assume more of their rightful role in these areas, the need for such assistance will be reduced, but it is likely that there will always be a need for someone for the mentally retarded to turn to (someone they can trust, who will not take advantage of them) to discuss matters such as installment purchases, life insurance, minor personal interaction problems, and other similar matters. A number of states have established such offices or centers, and those who serve in this capacity are a combination advocate, consumer adviser, and substitute big brother or sister to those needing help. Without such help, many of these retarded individuals would soon be in serious legal, financial, or other difficulties. Unlike the better established mental health center concept, this type of counseling and advocacy role—as an established governmental function—has not reached all areas of the nation. It must be expanded if we are to achieve the deinstitutionalization goals that have been accepted in much of the nation. Present indications are that they are highly viable, both from a self-realization (on the part of the client) and a financial (on the part of society) point of view.

Legal rights of the adult handicapped or disabled

The rights of the adult handicapped, like the rights of handicapped students, are established through state or federal constitutional interpretations, through specific laws, and through litigation. However, unlike the handicapped student, the adult handicapped have no one agency primarily responsible for ensuring these rights or providing the indicated opportunities or services. Fortunately, certain societal events indicate increased general interest and concern for the rights of the adult handicapped. This interest and concern apparently parallels the intensified interest and concern expressed on behalf of handicapped students, and although it developed somewhat later, it may well have equally significant effects.

One indication of this concern was the relatively recent (1973) expansion of the official focus of the National Association for Retarded Children, reflected in the renaming of that group as the National Association for Retarded Citizens. During the past 15 to 20 years, the interest of key leadership persons in the federal government was indicated by the calling of national conferences and the initiation of federally sponsored projects on behalf of adults who are mentally retarded or mentally ill. The hearing impaired and the visually impaired had been the recipients of a variety of federally supported efforts for many years, and most of these efforts were expanded during this time.

Increased interest in the handicapped or disabled adult was evident, but how was this interest to be maintained and expanded? The answer, which was obvious to those who were fully aware of the way in which such "voluntary" governmental or societal interests tend to wax and wane, was mandatory legislation.

The legal rights of the handicapped or disabled adult, as established by the enactment of state or federal law, will be the topic of concern of this final section of this chapter. Basic federal provisions will be reviewed first, followed by examples of rights established through state legislation. Our purpose will be to understand the considerable range and complexity of such legislation rather than to comprehensively overview or sample all of the legislative facets or components involved. It is hoped that certain of the state legislative enactments that are now common to only a few of the fifty states will have spread to many more states before this text is first revised. Therefore, rather than indicate the state in which each of these laws was passed, we will simply consider the subject of these laws. We will then hope that these and other legal rights will spread rapidly, thus more nearly assuring that the handicapped may eventually become first-class citizens in all respects.

Among the major federal enactments that in some way affect more handicapped adults than any other are those that together provide the framework for rehabilitation services. Certain of these laws, particularly the Rehabilitation Act of 1973, have been mentioned in various places throughout this text. The sequence of enactments that preceded the Rehabilitation Act of 1973, and the amendments that have passed since that time will be reviewed in some detail in the following chapter; therefore, they will not be detailed here. However, when speaking of the legal basis for services for handicapped adults, we should mention these federal vocational rehabilitation first, because they are basic to so many of the adult services now provided.

In addition to the federal laws quite specifically related to rehabilitation, those laws relating to vocational education have provided for a number of additional services. One early example was the Smith-Hughes Act of 1917. This law was essentially a vocational education law, and along with other vocational provisions, it created a Federal Board for Vocational Education, which was responsible for vocational rehabilitation of veterans. Further information about this act and others relating to veterans benefits and vocational education will be presented in Chapter 16.

RIGHTS GUARANTEED BY FEDERAL LAWS

As a result of federal law, disabled persons have specific rights in the areas of employment, health care, social services, rehabilitation services, and all other public or private services that are wholly or in part supported by U.S. tax dollars. These rights are outlined in a federal brochure entitled *Your Rights as a Disabled Person* (see pp. 452-454).

It is important to repeat that these rights, although established by law, may not be actually accorded to the handicapped in many

Program areas of special concern

Your rights as a disabled person

Are you disabled? Or the parent or guardian of a disabled child? If so, federal law is on your side.

As a physically or mentally disabled person, you have the same right as anyone else to:
- Education
- Employment
- Health care
- Senior citizen activities
- Welfare

and any other public or private service that *U.S. tax dollars help to support*.

If you are otherwise qualified—for a job, college, welfare, or other activity or service—your disability doesn't count. That's the law. It's Title V, section 504, of the Rehabilitation Act of 1973 (Public Law 93-112).

Remember: Your rights are protected by section 504 if your employer, school, college, hospital, or other service provider receives federal assistance. That means federal money, services, or property.

If you're not sure your employer must comply with section 504, ask your supervisor if the activity receives federal assistance. If the answer is "yes," your rights are guaranteed.

If you're not sure your college, hospital, social service agency, or other place that provides services to you must comply with section 504, ask your service representative if the activity receives federal assistance. Again, if the answer is "yes," your rights are guaranteed.

If you are the parent or guardian of a physically or mentally disabled child, you have the right to *demand* that your federally assisted local public school system provide a free education appropriate to your child's needs.

That's the law. In fact, it's two laws: section 504 of the Rehabilitation Act, and the Education for All Handicapped Children Act (Public Law 94-142).

Again, federal assistance is the key. If the public school district in which you live benefits from the use of federal funds, services, or property—and nearly all public school districts do—your disabled child's right to a free appropriate education is assured.

This pamphlet is about your rights under both laws:
- Your section 504 right to work, study, or be served by an institution that receives federal assistance under Department of Health, Education, and Welfare (HEW) programs.
- Your section 504 right to have your disabled child educated at public expense.
- Your right under the Education for All Handicapped Children Act to participate with the public school in planning and evaluating an appropriate learning program for your disabled child.

*Department of Health, Education, and Welfare, Washington, D.C., 1978.

Your right to employment

As a disabled job applicant or employee, you have the same rights and benefits as nonhandicapped applicants and employees.

Your ability, training, and experience must be considered. Your disability must *not* be considered—unless it keeps you from doing the job adequately.

An employer receiving federal assistance may not discriminate against you in:
- Recruitment, advertising, or processing of applications for employment.
- Hiring, promotion or demotion, transfer, layoff, or rehiring.
- Job assignments or career ladders.
- Leaves of absence, sick leave, training programs, and other fringe benefits.

Once hired, your employer is required to take reasonable steps to accommodate your disability unless they would cause the employer undue hardship. That may mean supplying, for example:
- A reader if you are blind and the job includes paperwork.
- An interpreter if you are deaf and the job requires telephone contacts.
- Adequate workspace and access to it if you use a wheelchair.
- Minor adjustment in working hours if you are required to visit a methadone clinic daily.

Your right to health care

Hospitals are the largest group of health care providers affected by the section 504 regulation.

As a disabled person, you are entitled to all medical services and medically related instruction available to the public. Hospitals receiving federal assistance (including Medicare payments) must take steps to accommodate your disability.

Among other things, hospitals must:
- Provide an emergency room interpreter or make other effective provisions for deaf patients.
- Treat the physical injury of a person under the influence of alcohol or drugs.
- Admit disabled persons to natural childbirth, anti-smoking, and other public-service programs of instruction.

If you are a Medicaid patient, your private physician must:
- Have an office physically accessible to you,
- Treat you in a hospital or your home, or, if this is not possible,
- Refer you to another physician whose office is accessible, after conferring with you.

Your right to social and rehabilitation services

As a disabled person, you have the right to participate in vocational rehabilitation, senior citizen activities, day care (for your disabled child), or any other social service program receiving federal assistance on an equal basis with nonhandicapped persons.

For example, you *may not*:
- Be denied admission because you use a wheelchair and need access to classrooms, recreation areas, or buses.
- Be excluded from vocational training because you are blind, mentally retarded, or paralyzed and may need more training for paid employment than students with other disabilities.

Continued.

Program areas of special concern

Your right to an education

As a disabled young person or adult, you have the same right as anyone else to go to college or enroll in a job training or adult post-high school basic education program.

The college, job-training, or adult basic education program you select must consider your application on the basis of your academic and other school records. Your disability is not a factor.

A college or training program *may not*, for example:
- Ask you to take a pre-admission test that inadequately measures your academic level because no special provisions were made for the fact that you are blind, deaf, or otherwise disabled.
- Inquire about any disability before admitting you, unless it is trying to overcome the effects of prior limitations on enrollment of handicapped students, and you are willing to volunteer the information.
- Limit the number of handicapped students admitted.

Colleges are *not* required to lower academic standards or alter degree requirements for you. But, depending on your disability, they *may* have to:
- Extend the time allowed for you to earn a degree or substitute one elective course for another.
- Modify teaching methods and examinations so you can fully participate in a degree program.
- Provide braille books or other aids for you if they are not available from other sources.

---

instances. Unfortunately, this is the case with all rights and legal assurances and is the reason why active advocacy efforts are so very important. The same principle applies in the case of rights established at the state level and thus must be considered with respect to the various state-mandated rights outlined in the following section.

RIGHTS GUARANTEED BY STATE LAWS

In examining state laws that establish the rights of the handicapped or disabled, it will be noted that in many cases the state law is very similar to the federal law. Why then do we need the state law? It is because in many cases the federal law is applicable only as federal funds are used in whatever activity is under consideration. In a few instances, confusion might result from such dual legislation, but for the most part, the existence of two laws (for example, relating to the right of access) has a strengthening effect. In many instances the state law is even more specific and pertinent (in that state) than the federal law. We should also note that certain types of laws are the province of *only* the state or *only* the federal government. The licensing of drivers, for example, is purely in the jurisdiction of the state; rail transportation is a matter left to the federal Congress. In the following, a number of state laws guaranteeing specific rights to the handicapped will be discussed. This information will be provided in outline form to illustrate the essential thrust of the law and the guarantees provided, without becoming involved in a plethora of legal language.

The right of access

If otherwise qualified, no handicapped person shall, because of his or her handicap, be de-

nied the full use of streets, sidewalks, public buildings, public facilities, and public places.
Includes all public accommodations (airplanes, railroads, buses, boats, etc.) that are generally open to the public.
Cannot be denied equal enjoyment of goods, services, and facilities offered in places of public accommodation.

Architectural barriers *(related to the "right to access" but somewhat different; has to do with architecturally determined accessibility)*

Must provide facilities for the handicapped (i.e., ramps, handrails, elevators, wide doors, specially treated floor surfaces, and other design features and conveniences that facilitate the health, safety, or comfort of the handicapped person)
Applies to buildings and to transportation facilities.
All new buildings (not just public facilities), except single family dwellings must be built to be accessible to the physically handicapped.*
In general, applies only to new or remodeled buildings.

Voting rights

Qualified voters who are physically unable to appear at designated places of registration may request "special registration."
Persons unable to see, read, or write may be assisted in completing registration.
Blind or otherwise disabled voters who are unable to mark their ballot or operate the voting machine may have assistance in actual voting.
Voters needing assistance have specific guarantees against disclosure by those who assisted them as to how they voted; prompting or suggestion by those assisting is also prohibited.
Special provisions for absentee voting apply to the handicapped.

Special rights of the blind

Any place open to the public must admit the dog guide. (However, the dog's owner is liable for property damaged by the dog.)

---

*This is a controversial proposal under consideration in certain states.

A number of special provisions relating to the absolute right-of-way of the blind (over vehicular traffic) are spelled out in some detail.*

Special rights of the deaf

When a deaf person is a party to or witness at a court proceeding, he or she shall have the right to a court appointed interpreter. This interpreter is paid by the court.
Similar rights apply at insanity or mental health commitment proceedings, or at a police station in case of arrest.

Special rights of the mentally ill†

Right to communicate by sealed mail with individuals and official agencies.
Right to actual planned treatment.
Right to be free of mechanical restraints, except as specifically prescribed by a physician.
The hospital administrator is responsible to see that all patients admitted for mental illness receive a written statement of their rights and release procedures. This statement must also explain the procedures by which persons may be declared legally incompetent; all of the preceding information must be written in simple, nontechnical language.

Other rights in some state statutes include those relating to: (1) the right to employment without discrimination, (2) the right to special parking spaces, and (3) the right to a driver's license (a license is not categorically prohibited on the basis of handicap as once was the case, but applicant must meet certain requirements).

LITIGATION AND LEGAL RIGHTS

Litigation to establish and further define the rights of individuals or groups of individuals is also highly important and was dicussed in the first section of this text. Much

---

*Rights of the blind are often included in what is called "white cane law" and tend to be very similar from state to state.
†In general, these also apply to the institutionalized mentally retarded.

of the more important litigation presently underway relates to rights guaranteed by the Rehabilitation Act of 1973 or rights of individuals who are institutionalized. Additional categories or types of litigation that are more generally applicable to adults were reviewed on pp. 17-18. One other area of concern that has received very recent attention is the right of mental patients to refuse treatment. Plotkin (1978) notes that the mentally ill are regularly confined for "treatment" for an indeterminate period of time, without the benefit of a trial. "While so incarcerated they are subjected to a veritable orgy of 'therapeutic techniques' with uncertain consequences." (p. 8) According to Plotkin, psychiatrists have tended to oppose legal regulation of treatment, wanting to rely on the principle of the "best judgment" of the physician. This has led to decisions which, although based on the best interests of the patient's *health*, have often overlooked the individual's rights as they relate to *liberty* and *freedom*. With increased availability of new drugs and psychosurgical procedures, these questions must soon be faced. The potential conflict of interest between health, liberty, and freedom will undoubtedly be the scene of a variety of litigation of interest.

In concluding this discussion of the legal rights of the handicapped or disabled, we will consider the words of Harold Russell, taken from the foreward of *A Handbook on the Legal Rights of Handicapped People* (1976):

> We're proud to point in America to "a government of laws and not of men . . ." But the laws—however fair, well-written and inclusive—are only as effective as they are known to the people for whom they are intended.
>
> A good deal of legislation has been enacted by the Federal and state governments to insure legal rights and provide beneficial services to handicapped individuals. To partake of these programs and services requires a working knowledge of their availability and eligibility requirements.
>
> It is important that handicapped persons become aware of laws enacted at all levels to assist them in overcoming the problems they face daily in such areas as employment, education, housing, transportation, and so forth . . . Equipped with knowledge of their legal rights, handicapped persons will be in a better position to obtain full citizenship and full employment.

We might add that in addition to the need for the handicapped to possess full knowledge of their legal rights, it is most important for all professionals who work with the handicapped to be equally aware of these rights.

Summary

After centuries of no treatment, mistreatment, or inadequate treatment, society has recently begun to modify its general attitude regarding the potential and the rights of handicapped adults. We have learned that many handicapped persons have full potential for independence and self-support, given the right training and special assistance. We have concluded that although some handicapped persons may require residential-type services, the "warehousing" of a few decades ago is totally unacceptable. A number of programs and services for handicapped adults have proved to be effective; certain of these programs have been outlined in this chapter.

College programs for the handicapped take many forms, including (1) regular academic programs provided in regular colleges and universities, with adaptations as needed by the handicapped student; (2) academic programs delivered in a special setting (such as at Gallaudet College) with more extensive modification or adaptations; (3) short-term vocational or technical programs, often provided in community college or vocational-technical schools; and (4) nondegree programs organized to provide a more normal setting for instruction, but not comparable in content to postsecondary programs for the nonhandicapped. These latter programs are more often for the moderately or severely mentally handicapped or multihandicapped and might be described by some as non–college level programs provided in a college setting.

Residential programs for the handicapped have been the object of a great deal of negative comment, and the general trend is toward deinstitutionalization. Reductions in institutional populations in the past 20 years have been greater for the mentally ill than the mentally retarded, but in both areas institutions may continue to exist for some time. There is general agreement that most existing institutions should be reduced in size and programs within the institution improved. Some persons would suggest closing all existing large institutional facilities, but this is not necessarily a consensus of all professionals or all members of advocacy groups who are concerned with the needs of the handicapped.

One of the more common vocational programs for the handicapped or disabled is the sheltered workshop, a concept that has been described in earlier chapters. It appears that the sheltered workshop or some type of sheltered employment setting is gaining in acceptability, with recognized value as preparation for later employment in a nonsheltered setting, as a technique to improve mental health and emotional adjustment, or as a place of permanent employment.

Personal adaptations may be of great value in assisting some handicapped adults toward more normal participation in society. These may relate to sensory impairment or to physical disabilities. Several of these adaptations were discussed in this chapter as examples of the various types of adaptive possibilities. In addition, certain environmental adaptations, such as modified buses or automobiles and modifications in buildings were mentioned as representative of a wide range of such adaptations.

Temporary or intermittent support services are becoming of increasing importance, particularly in relation to the deinstitutionalization movement. Such support services include mental health centers and various other agencies organized to assist the handicapped adult to cope with the environment. This might include consumer counseling, assistance in obtaining a new job, help with problems on the job, or whatever is required for the handicapped individual to more successfully manage his or her surroundings.

Legal rights of handicapped persons are beginning to be well established but are not always recognized and understood. These rights, established by federal and state laws, are highly important, but it is equally important that the handicapped and those who work with them be fully aware of these rights.

Program areas of special concern

focus

college programs for handicapped and disabled adults

College programs for the handicapped or disabled fall into a number of broad general classifications. One such classification involves the adaptation of materials, class presentation, test administration, and the physical environment, so that handicapped or disabled students may attend and benefit from the regular college program.

Programs for hearing-impaired college students tend to be much more "special" than programs offered for the visually impaired, the learning disabled, or the physically handicapped. This is essential because of the unusual educational needs of hearing-impaired students, relating to inadequate language development, and the additional need of many such students for some type of manual communication.

programs for the mentally retarded

There is considerable evidence that the large residential facility is in disrepute in many quarters and that other residential alternatives must be further explored and systematically developed.

Regardless of what the alternative programs may be called, it is clear that the present trend is toward smaller, more diversified residential programs in a wide variety of community-based settings.

programs for the mentally ill

Another area of disability in which we have seen much utilization of residential facilities for adults is mental illness or psychiatric disorders. The return-to-the community trend is also very evident here, but unlike mental retardation, there appears to be a significant incidence of former patients returning to the institution.

We may summarize this consideration of the need for and utilization of residential programs for the handicapped adult by indicating that since about 1960 there has been a broadening of the concept of residential facilities to include a number of community-based alternatives, such as apartment settings, small and large group homes, adoptive settings, and foster settings.

The reduction in large residential facilities and the increased use of alternate residential models has led to the need for other community services, and for increased community awareness, understanding, and acceptance of this population as part of the community. Some of the mentally ill who have been returned to the community with less than adequate support services "are recruited into migrant labor camps or prostitution. Many are victims of crime, poverty, hostility, or indifference."

the sheltered workshop

It is generally recognized that although there are a number of potential functions of the sheltered workshop, these are usually related to two basic functions: (1) training for employment in competitive (outside) jobs and (2) terminal (permanent) employment for adults who cannot successfully function in outside, competitive employment situations.

The work-as-therapy concept is apparently growing, and it is a concept with a commonsense support base. Given the fact that mentally ill persons cannot handle what would usually be called normal interactions with "normal" people, it is certainly reasonable to believe that they must *learn* to handle such interactions.

community and/or personal adaptation programs

Unlike the handicapped child, who has school personnel who are directed by law to consider the handicap, adults who are not aggressive in seeking help may be overlooked and have much less than satisfactory existence, when simple assistance could make a great difference.

environmental adaptations

Unless certain adaptations and modifications are made, many handicapped persons do not have equal access to housing, city, county, or federal service agencies, hospitals, places of entertainment, restaurants, and many other aspects of the normal environment. They may be denied equal opportunity for employment because the office building or factory is not accessible.

Federal law prohibits discrimination against any handicapped person who is otherwise qualified and specifically relates to the question of access, but this applies only to those programs or activities receiving federal funds.

temporary or intermittent support services

There are certain types of service that may be viewed as temporary or intermittent. These services must be available at all times and thus are not "temporary" in this respect but rather the individual who needs them may need them on only a temporary or intermittent basis. One of the more common of such services is that provided through the mental health centers of the nation.

The concept of the mental health center appears to be steadily gaining in acceptance and the functions of such centers are expanding.

rights guaranteed by federal law

As a result of federal law, disabled persons have specific rights in the areas of employment, health care, social services, rehabilitation services, and all other public or private services that are wholly or in part supported by U.S. tax dollars.

These rights, although established by law, may not be actually accorded to the handicapped in many instances. Unfortunately, this is the case with all rights and legal assurances and is the reason why active advocacy efforts are so very important.

rights guaranteed by state laws

In examining state laws which establish the rights of the handicapped or disabled, it will be noted that in many cases the state law is very similar to the federal law. Why then do we need the state law? It is because in many cases the federal law is applicable only as federal funds are used in whatever activity is under consideration.

litigation and legal rights

"It is important that handicapped persons become aware of laws enacted at all levels to assist them in overcoming the problems they face daily in such areas as employment, education, housing, transportation, and so forth . . . Equipped with knowledge of their legal rights, handicapped persons will be in a better position to obtain full citizenship and full employment."

In addition to the need for the handicapped to possess full knowledge of their legal rights, it is important for all professionals who work with the handicapped to be equally aware of these rights.

References and suggested readings

Architectural and Transportation Barriers Compliance Board. *Resource guide to literature on barrier-free environments.* Washington, D.C., 1978.

Bitter, J. *Introduction to rehabilitation.* St. Louis: The C. V. Mosby Co., 1979.

Blatt, B. *Exodus from pandemonium—human abuse and a reformation of public policy.* Boston: Allyn & Bacon, 1970.

Bluhm, H. The right to work: employers, employability, and retardation. In *Mental retardation: social and education perspectives.* C. Drew, M. Hardman, and H. Bluhm (Eds.). St. Louis: The C. V. Mosby Co., 1977.

Bolanovich, D., Drought, N., and Stewart, D. *Full employment for the mentally retarded.* St. Louis: The Jewish Employment and Vocational Service, 1972.

Clements, H. NISH finds its niche. *Journal of Rehabilitation,* 1977, *43*(2), 16-20.

Cull, J. and Hardy, R. (Eds.). *Vocational rehabilitation: profession and process.* Springfield, Ill.: Charles C Thomas, Publisher, 1972.

Graham, V. Community rejects returned mental patients. Associated Press, Dec., 1977.

Kisker, G. *The disorganized personality.* 3rd ed. New York: McGraw-Hill Book Co., 1977.

Marsh, G., Gearheart, C., and Gearheart, B. *The learning disabled adolescent.* St. Louis: The C. V. Mosby Co., 1978.

Nelson, N. *Workshops for the handicapped in the United States.* Springfield, Ill.: Charles C Thomas, Publisher, 1971.

Plotkin, R. Mental patients' right to refuse treatment. *The Mental Health Law Project,* Summer 1978, *4*(1), 8-9.

President's Commission on Mental Health. Report to the President Vol. I. Washington, D.C.: U.S. Government Printing Office, 1978.

President's Committee on Employment of the Handicapped. *A handbook on the legal rights of handicapped people.* Washington, D. C.: U.S. Government Printing Office, 1976.

Programs for the handicapped, Office for Handicapped Individuals. 1977-2. Washington, D.C.: Department of Health, Education and Welfare, 1977.

Programs for the Handicapped, Office for Handicapped Individuals, 1978-3 and 1978-4. Washington, D.C.: Department of Health, Education and Welfare, 1978.

Rawlings, B. *Update on postsecondary programs for hearing impaired students.* Washington, D.C.: Office of Demographic Studies, Gallaudet College, 1976. (Mimeographed report.)

Schulman, E. *Focus on the retarded adult.* St. Louis: The C. V. Mosby Co., 1979.

Stramiello, A. In *The trainable mentally retarded.* 2nd ed. B. Gearheart and F. Litton. St. Louis: The C. V. Mosby Co., 1979.

Wolfensberger, W. *The principle of normalization in human services.* Toronto: National Institute on Mental Retardation, 1972.

Wolfensberger, W. The origin and nature of our institutional models. In *Changing patterns in residential services for the mentally retarded.* R. Kugel and W. Wolfensberger (Eds.). Washington, D.C.: President's Committee on Mental Retardation, 1969.

Wood, L., Meyer, B., and Grady, S. Exceptional adults learn in Broward Community Colleges' Continuing Education Program. *Teaching Exceptional Children,* Sept. 1977, *10*(1), 7-9.

Your rights as a disabled person, Washington, D.C.: U.S. Government Printing Office, 1978.

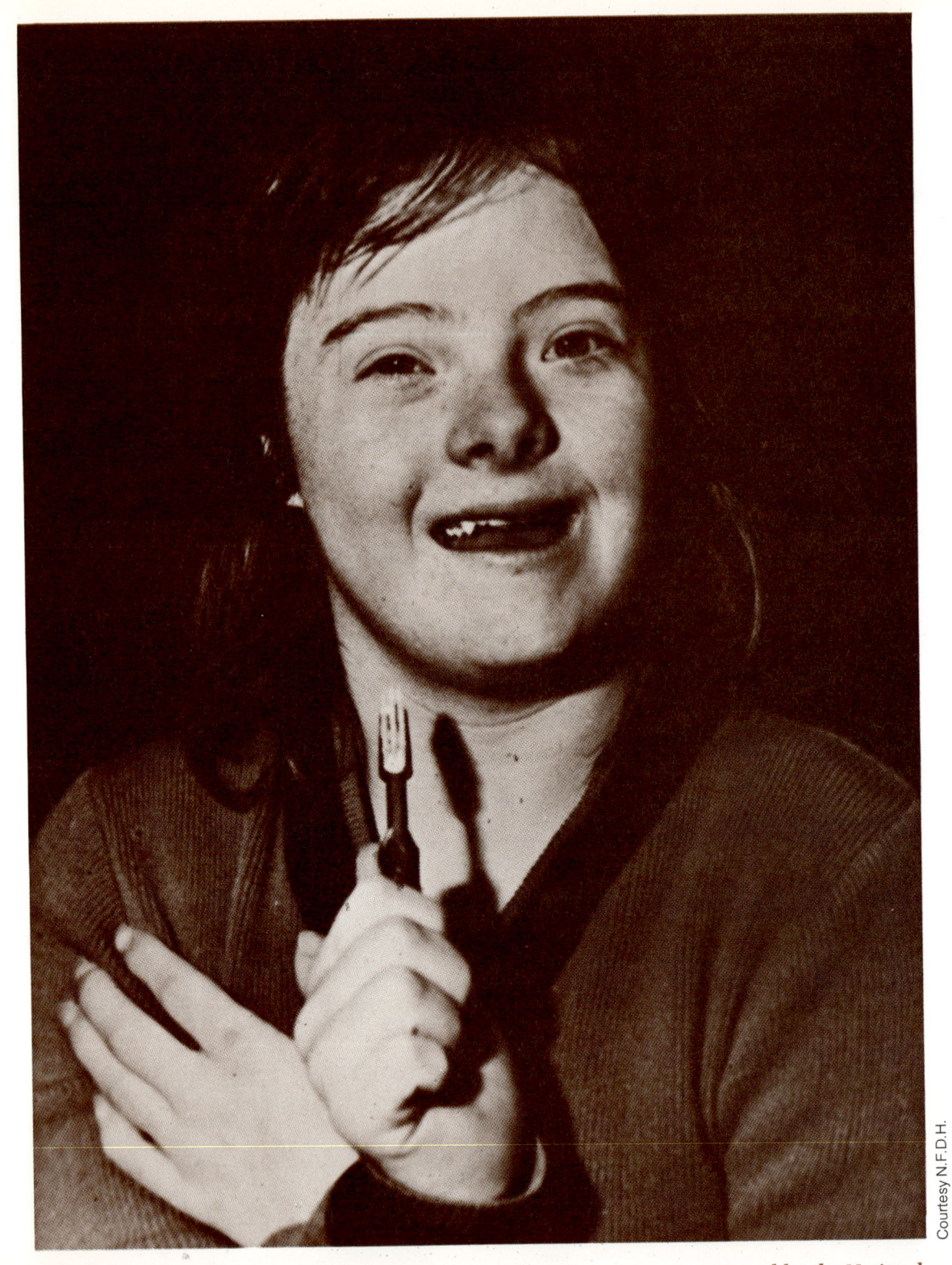

This young lady is learning about proper dental care through a program sponsored by the National Foundation of Dentistry for the Handicapped.

Courtesy N.F.D.H.

chapter 16

Rehabilitation and other programs and resources for the handicapped

objectives

To develop an understanding of the broad scope of rehabilitative services and their historical origins.

To appreciate the basic philosophy of rehabilitative programs.

To provide examples of various specialized community programs for the handicapped.

To consider the need for better, more comprehensive parent counseling programs.

To discuss the unique skills required for effective parent counseling.

Introduction

This final chapter is designed to present an overview of certain programs and resources that are highly important to successful total life planning for the handicapped. Rehabilitation services are foremost among these programs, and although mentioned in various places in preceding chapters, we will provide a more complete, integrated view of these services, including the legislative history leading to their present state of development. In addition, other community, state, and federal program efforts will be outlined to illustrate an even larger number of such programs that actually provide this wide variety of assistance. Many of these programs are private, nonprofit organizations, which have been established to serve some unique, special purpose. Most of them have been the recipients of some state or federal assistance through grants of some type, but they remain private agencies, dedicated to specific purposes or goals. Many of these same agencies are interrelated with the Rehabilitation Services Agency; that is, they provide services through some type of contractual agreement with RSA. In composite, these resources are of considerable importance to the provision of meaningful services to the handicapped, and special educators should be familiar with their scope and function.

Historical development of publicly supported rehabilitation programs in the United States

In other chapters we have outlined the historical events leading to programming for students with various handicaps and disabilities. We have also reviewed the legislative and fiscal bases for programs for the handicapped of disabled, again focusing on programs that are primarily educational, and that, for the most part, are provided through the public schools. As we approach the topic of rehabilitation programs, we must consider the history from a somewhat different point of view.*

Admittedly, the sheltered workshops provided for the blind and mentally retarded were forerunners of present rehabilitation programs and services, but the rehabilitation programs of today are primarily dependent on federal legislation for their existence. In contrast to public school programs for the blind, deaf, and mentally retarded, which were started long before the type of encouragement now provided by federal legislation, the history of vocational rehabilitation, and our presently expanded concept of rehabilitation services, can only be told with accuracy by reviewing the federal legislation which gave it birth. Thus the historical review that follows is a review of the major legislative enactments leading to our present joint federal-state rehabilitation programs.

According to Bitter (1979), rehabilitation legislation was initiated with the passage of the National Defense Act of 1916. This act provided for vocational training for returning soldiers and was "the beginning of a congressional attitude toward rehabilitation which would result in the large national program of today." (p. 15) Then, in 1920, the Smith-Fess Act (Public Law 66-236), commonly called the Vocational Rehabilitation Act of 1920, became the first federal law specifically and exclusively related to rehabilitation services and not limited to soldiers or former soldiers. This act was to provide vocational guidance, training, occupational adjustment, prostheses, and placement services to the physically disabled. The Smith-Fess Act did not specify a minimum age, but because it related to vocations, it was interpreted to mean that it applied only to those persons within each state who were over legal employment age.

---

*The sources for most of this historical information are Bitter (1979) and Lassiter (1972).

The Smith-Fess Act established a precedent that is followed to this day; that is, a partnership on the part of the state and federal government in the administration and funding of rehabilitation services. The need was sufficiently obvious (even in those days of greater reluctance on the part of states to accept federal aid and controls) that within 18 months of the passage of the Smith-Fess Act thirty-four states had passed enabling legislation permitting them to establish a state agency that could accept federal funds on a 50-50 matching basis.

Between 1920, when the Smith-Fess Act was passed, and 1935, the federally sponsored rehabilitation program was in some respects an "on-and-off" program since it was continued only as Congress saw fit to extend it for short time periods. In fact, it lapsed for a period of time, but most of the states kept their programs going on a limited basis with state funds (Lassiter, 1972). But with the passage of the Social Security Act of 1935, a permanent base for federally sponsored vocational rehabilitation programs was established. This act included provisions that continued and strengthened earlier provisions for the pshysically disabled and included assistance for the blind. This provided the first continuous authorization for a program that was to grow into the provision of a wide variety of services for persons with various handicapping conditions.

The Vocational Rehabilitation Act Amendments of 1943 (Public Law 78-113) led to a number of important changes in the coverage and funding of vocational rehabilitation in the United States. This included an expansion of services to include such items as corrective surgery, prosthesis training, medical examinations, therapeutic treatment, occupational tools, equipment, licenses, and transportations costs. Rehabilitative services were extended to the mentally ill and the mentally handicapped, and the federal government began to pay considerably more than half of all rehabilitative costs.

The Vocational Rehabilitation Act Amendments of 1965 (Public Law 89-333) further increased the federal share of rehabilitation to 75 percent, provided construction assistance for building rehabilitation centers and workshops and encouraged more client evaluation. It created a broader service base, including socially handicapping conditions, and eliminated economic need of the client as an absolute prerequisite for eligibility for services. An amendment in 1967 provided services for migratory workers and eliminated residency requirements for any person otherwise eligible who needed services. An additional amendment in 1968 changed the federal share of funding from 75 to 80 percent and provided a number of additional expansions of coverage and authorizations for capital expenditures.

Public Law 93-112, the Rehabilitation Act of 1973, has been mentioned a number of times in this text, and several of its provisions are outlined on pp. 452-454. They should be reviewed to provide a better perspective of the evolution of rehabilitation as it exists today. Not mentioned earlier is the fact that this was the time when the Rehabilitation Services Administration was established by statute, and the term "vocational" was officially dropped from the title of the Act. This reflected much more than a simple change of terminology. It indicated a recognition of the fact that for some individuals, a true vocational goal is not actually feasible. This act emphasized the priority that should be given the more severely handicapped (which in itself dictated a retreat from the concept of "vocational" rehabilitation for all) and provided for special studies to better determine how to serve those for whom vocational goals were not feasible.

In 1974, the Rehabilitation Services Agency was moved from the Social and Rehabilitations Service to the office of Secretary of Health, Education and Welfare, and the RSA commissioner was appointed directly by the President, with the consent of the U.S. Senate. In addition, the 1974 amendments (PL 93-516) provided for a White House conference on handicapped individuals within 2 years to develop a more complete comprehensive plan to meet the needs of all handicapped persons. In 1978, the Ninety-Fifth Congress passed PL 95-602, which further improved the funding base for rehabilitation services and authorized a comprehensive program of independent living services for severely handicapped persons.

In summary, we see that the early legislative concept of vocational rehabilitation for the physically impaired has been expanded over the years to include a very broad range of rehabilitative services for persons who are handicapped or disabled. The publicly supported funding base has been shifted more and more heavily to the federal government, and the authorizations have been increased dramatically. Over the years the offices that administered federal programs have been: (1) a separate federal board, (2) the Department of Interior, (3) the Federal Security Agency, and finally (4) the Department of Health, Education and Welfare.

Private rehabilitation programs and resources

Private rehabilitation programs were started almost 100 years before public-supported programs were initiated; the first programs in the United States were for the blind (see pp. 443-445). These early programs were primarily sheltered workshops, and all had similar difficulties; they could not develop into self-supporting units, and even those workers-in-training who did develop marketable skills often wanted to stay in the sheltered community setting. Near the close of the nineteenth century, various religious organizations began a variety of multipurpose programs that served a rehabilitative function. These included organizations such as the Salvation Army and the Goodwill Industries, which were not specifically directed toward the handicapped, in the sense the term has been used in this text, but rather toward anyone who was "down-and-out." Their programs were (and are) directed toward a combination of spiritual and rehabilitative goals. These two organizations, later joined by the Society of St. Vincent de Paul, have been involved for many years in the collection and renovation of clothing, furniture, and other resalable materials. This type agency is at times used by the public rehabilitation agencies for training purposes, with Goodwill Industries used more often than the others.

Other groups, such as the United Cerebral Palsy Association, Inc., the National Association for Retarded Citizens, and the National Society for Crippled Children and Adults, have also been active in initiating and maintaining a variety of rehabilitative facilities. These groups often operate with the assistance of federal grants or with direct training funds from the Rehabilitation Services Administration or state education or institutional agencies. The Jewish Vocational Service Agencies have served a rehabilitative function in a similar manner with a strong emphasis on vocational adjustment.

In addition, there are many rehabilitation facilities that are part of a larger hospital setting. These facilities range from those with over 100 paid employees, hundreds of volunteers, and multimillion dollar budgets to smaller units with three or four staff members. Some of these facilities are quite specialized and others are very broad and comprehensive in their scope of service. Most of these facilities embrace the same general philosophy of rehabilitation, which will be reviewed in the following section.

Scope and philosophy of rehabilitation programs

Although the effectiveness of rehabilitation services is greatly enhanced by the presence of a number of valuable private rehabilitation facilities, the scope of rehabilitation services can best be described by outlining the structure of the present federal-state rehabilitation program. As noted in the preceding historical review, many of the private rehabilitation facilities are heavily supported by this federal-state public system.

The Rehabilitation Services Administration, headquartered in Washington, D.C., with ten regional offices located throughout the United States, provides major leadership for state rehabilitation agencies. There are state agencies in the fifty states, plus the District of Columbia, Guam, Puerto Rico, American Samoa Trust Territory, and the Virgin Islands. In addition, there are twenty-eight separate state rehabilitation agencies for the blind.* In those states where there is no separate state agency for the blind, that function is assumed by the general rehabilitation agency (Bitter, 1979).

The federal program is directed by a commissioner, and each of the ten HEW regions in the nation has a director, who is given considerable authority within the region. Bitter (1979) describes the services provided to disabled persons as follows:

> Under the federal-state program of rehabilitation, a wide range of services is provided to individual disabled persons. Eligibility is based on the presence in the individual of a physical or mental disability which constitutes a substantial handicap to employment but for which there is a reasonable expectation that vocational rehabilitation services will enable the individual to engage in a gainful occupation. As determined by a particular client's needs—the services may include (1) comprehensive evaluation, including medical studies and diagnosis and psychological, social, educational, and vocational studies, (2) medical, surgical, and hospital care and related therapy to remove or reduce a disability, (3) prosthetic and orthotic devices, (4) counseling and guidance, (5) training, (6) services in rehabilitation facilities, (7) maintenance and transportation during rehabilitation, (8) tools, equipment, and occupational licenses, (9) initial stock and supplies in managing a small business, (10) readers for blind persons and interpreters for the deaf, (11) recruitment and training to provide new careers for handicapped people in the field of rehabilitation and other areas, (12) services which contribute to a group of handicapped people though perhaps unrelated directly to the rehabilitation of any one person, (13) services to the families of handicapped persons that will contribute substantially to the rehabilitation of the handicapped client, (14) job replacement assistance including follow-up to aid handicapped individuals in maintaining their employment, and (15) any other goods or services which may be necessary to render a handicapped person employable.
>
> Generally services must be made available by state agencies on a state-wide basis. A state agency may obtain a waiver from this requirement, however, to take advantage of an opportunity to increase a service in a geographic area where local funds are available to supplement the state appropriation. Besides this waiver provision, a state rehabilitation agency can, in order to expand its services, enter into financial arrangements with other public agencies whose services relate to the needs of handicapped persons. Such arrangements are known as third-party agreements. Third-party agreements enable rehabilitation services to be offered simultaneously with the services of another agency or to expand services beyond those which are normally the responsibility of another agency. (p. 7)

The philosophy of rehabilitation is implied in the definition of the term; in almost every

---

*Whether a state has one state rehabilitation agency, serving all handicapped persons who are eligible for such services, or two agencies, one for the blind and one for all other handicapping conditions, is a matter of state choice.

instance the word "restoration" is featured. The concern of rehabilitation services is the correction or minimizing of the disability under consideration, and the method of restoration may be any authorized or permitted under the legislation enacted by the U.S. Congress, the rules and regulations approved to carry out this legislation, or the guidelines of any regional or state office. Most actual rehabilitation services are provided through private sources, with services purchased by the state agency counselor. Such resources include hospitals, clinics, rehabilitation centers, or educational/training facilities. In some cases, services may be purchased from an individual such as a physician, a physical therapist, a reader for the blind, an interpreter for the deaf, or other specialist. Such services must be consistent with the Individualized Written Rehabilitation Program (IWRP), which is required by federal regulations. This IWRP is similar to the IEP required for handicapped children, mentioned in many places throughout this text. The IWRP is developed during the first stage of program services, the evaluative stage, and is critically important to all that follows.

The rehabilitation process, as envisioned by all knowledgeable authorities in rehabilitation, is a team process, with the rehabilitation counselor serving as initiator, coordinator, and facilitator of program services. It is most important that the possible need for various professionals (dentists, physicians, psychologists, physical or occupational therapists, speech pathologists, audiologists, orthotics-prosthetics specialists, mobility instructors, social workers, recreation specialists, nurses, or others) be carefully considered. The various restorative areas (physical, social, psychologic, educational, and vocational) must be systematically evaluated, so that piecemeal efforts do not result in failure or only partial success. According to Bitter (1979),

"vocational rehabilitation offers economic benefits which are worth at least eight times the cost, and perhaps as much as thirty-three times the cost." (p. 11) However, the *reason* for the recent increase in provision of rehabilitative services has not been economic. It is rather an increasing conviction on the part of congress and the citizens of the nation that equality of opportunity for participation in the benefits and responsibilities of this nation is the inherent right of all citizens.

Other community programs and services

The variety of community programs and services for the handicapped is not endless in the literal sense of the word, but with the added attention received by handicapped children, youth, and adults in the past 15 to 20 years, it is certainly very great and is expanding daily. Such programs and services as genetic counseling, free or low-cost transportation services, special dentistry programs, the efforts of community advocacy and volunteer organizations, and many others represent giant strides in community-level services for handicapped or disabled persons. In this section we will consider several specific programs in some detail and then note the sources of other community programs and services. In total, these services are of tremendous value to the handicapped and disabled; they are services of which special educators must be aware if they are to serve their students or clients effectively, and they provide additional opportunities for future employment that should not be overlooked.

Genetic counseling is rapidly growing in acceptance, and with the stated interest of such groups as the President's Committee on Mental Retardation and the National Association for Retarded Citizens, it seems certain to be the subject of continued emphasis for the foreseeable future. Genetic counseling offers one of the better available opportunities for prevention and thus has almost automatic approval from a majority of federal agencies and parent or advocacy groups.

According to Carter (1975), genetic counseling has three main objectives:

1. To answer parents' questions on risks of recurrence in another child when one member of the family has some malformation or disease that might be genetically determined. A basic premise of genetic counseling is that parents are entitled to be informed about the risks for the birth of another defective child. Risks of recurrence and incidence are not to be confused. "Risk of recurrence" refers to the chances of the defect appearing in a particular family after one defective child is born. The "risk of incidence" refers to the chances of occurrence in the total population.

2. To call attention to a special risk that may result in a child born with a genetically determined disease so that early diagnosis and treatment are possible. A genetic counselor must be ready to alert other medical professionals to special risk cases with genetically determined disorders. Certain conditions are amenable to early treatment and need particular attention.

3. To prevent an increase in the frequency of children born genetically predisposed to serious handicap. The ultimate objective here is a reduction in the number of genetically defective individuals. This goal is usually accomplished in one of two ways: by screening for carriers of defective genes or by terminating a pregnancy.

Therapeutic abortion is highly controversial because of moral, social, legal, and religious involvements, but medical techniques such as amniocentesis for detection of chromosome abnormalities and inborn errors of metabolism have made this an alternative to be considered.

In most cases, the genetic counselor is a physician whose specialty is medical genetics. The counselor is concerned with diagnosing genetic disorders and giving genetic advice. Physicians who specialize in various medical disciplines relating to the genetic disorder may be involved in genetic counseling. For example, genetic counseling about some birth defects might be performed by an obstetrician or a pediatrician, and counseling about chromosomal disorders might be performed by a physician whose area of emphasis or interest is cytology (that branch of biology concerned with formation, structure, and functions of cells) or cytogenetics (that branch of biology concerned with the study of heredity from the points of view of cytology and genetics).

The number of genetic counseling centers has increased rapidly in recent years. Most counseling services are housed in a medical complex or center, so that a "genetic team" is available to ensure complete, quality counseling. These centers are selective in the number of patients they assist because of limited funds, time, and manpower. As additional centers are opened, this situation should ease. Centers usually require a recommendation from a practicing physician who is familiar with the patient's disorder and background. The cost of genetic counseling varies according to the specific services. Some centers use a flat fee for tests required, whereas others base the fee for service on a sliding scale based on ability to pay.

Special transportation services for the handicapped or disabled are another type of community provision that is gaining acceptance. In addition to adaptations provided in regular transportation system units, many communities have some sort of "handibus" available for the handicapped or elderly. This type service is sometimes on a scheduled basis or may be "on-call." It may be provided through some sort of federal grant or can be part of a city or county service supported by tax dollars. Such services are often administered by a local department or division of the city government, with an increasing number of such departments called the "department of human resources" or some similar name.

In addition this type of regularly organized special transportation system, there are other programs provided by volunteer agencies. With increasing recognition of the fact that transportation can play such a vital role in providing for full participation of the handicapped in community activities, this type of service will undoubtedly grow in importance.

A special dentistry program for the handicapped is an outgrowth of the work of the Academy of Dentistry for the Handicapped. This is an excellent example of a highly specialized program, initiated and conducted primarily by a concerned professional group. This program illustrates the manner in which interest and dedication on the part of a few individuals can grow into a program that affected some 12,000 handicapped persons (approximately 50 percent adults, 50 percent children) in 1978 (Leviton, 1978).

The National Foundation of Dentistry for the Handicapped (NFDH) was established in 1974 to decrease the need for dental care among handicapped people by controlling the incidence of oral disease and by sensitizing dental caregivers to the needs of disabled individuals. NFDH was incorporated by the Academy of Dentistry for the Handicapped, a professional organization that has been concerned about dental care for the handicapped population since 1952.

The philosophy on which all NFDH programs are based is that a dental delivery system must maintain a comprehensive coordinating effort at the community level to be responsive to the needs of handicapped people. If a health-oriented philosophy is to replace the oftimes crisis-motivated method of care to the disabled population, dentistry must reach out in an organized manner into the community-based programs—the schools, workshops, and homes where many handicapped people learn, work, and live.

Most NFDH efforts focus on further developing its "campaign of concern." Funded by a $17,500 grant from the Colorado Developmental Disabilities Council, a model preventive outreach system, predicated on the NFDH program philosophy, was initiated in Denver in March, 1975. As a result, significant improvements were effected in the oral hygiene of over 1,500 noninstitutionalized developmentally disabled people (i.e., those with mental retardation, cerebral palsy, epilepsy, or autism). Moreover, NFDH was able to improve the accessibility of dental treatment to more than 500 of these people by referring them to dentists in the community for needed care. Upon completion of this model project, the Colorado legislature appropriated general revenue funds to provide long-term and statewide expansion of the program.

In 1975, the Foundation received a 3-year grant from the Developmental Disabilities Office of the U.S. Department of Health, Education and Welfare to replicate this program in at least nine cities across the country. This project is now well underway.

In each participating community, a dental hygienist has been retained to develop a structured daily oral hygiene program in facilities serving disabled persons. Individuals needing definitive treatment are referred to private practitioners or clinics identified through a survey as accepting handicapped patients. By integrating preventive measures, periodic screening evaluations to identify disease in the incipient stages of development, and therapeutic intervention when necessary, the incidence and severity of dental disease are being reduced.

In developing systemization of care and preventive initiatives, government officials, philanthropic foundations, and service organizations have geen approached for support. During meetings with such groups, the Foundation has found the general public unaware of the oral health problems experienced by many handicapped individuals. The issue has not been visible and, consequently, few people have given it adequate consideration. The Foundation has prepared, and has available for free distribution, a number of informative brochures, booklets, and leaflets, including two pamphlets in braille for blind persons. Additional videotape and slide/tape presentations are available on a loan basis. The national office staff works with interested dental practitioners and advocacy groups for handicapped people in helping to develop preventive dentistry programs that will meet the unique needs of the community or geographic area in question.

The efforts of the National Foundation of Dentistry for the Handicapped provide an excellent model that hopefully may be followed by other professional groups who deal with other health needs of the handicapped. The key to their success is providing services to the people who need them in the setting in which handicapped persons are found.

Community advocacy and volunteer organizations are a highly important source of community assistance. Their support is often a major factor in the success of other efforts, including the transportation and special dentistry programs just discussed. Their efforts may take any of a wide variety of paths, depending on local needs and the energy and dedication of the local membership. Such groups include parent groups (such as the Association for Retarded Citizens), service clubs (such as the Lions, Kiwanis, Rotary), educationally oriented groups (such as the Epilepsy Foundation), fraternal groups (such as the Elks, Moose, and Masons), emergency intervention organizations (such as the American Red Cross), church/synagogue-related organizations, and others. In any given community, because of the interest of one or two community leaders (often someone who has a relative who is handicapped or disabled), specific types of worthwhile assistance will be provided that are not typical of other communities or areas of the nation. Senior citizens groups have served as "special grandparents" to handicapped children, and church or synagogue groups may take on projects such as providing respite babysitting services for parents who have handicapped children.

In communities where there is a college or university, a number of worthwhile services may be provided by college students, especially if the school has a special education department. Some YMCAs and YWCAs have established special programs for the handicapped, and youth groups such as Boy Scouts, Girl Scouts, Campfire Girls, Boys Clubs, and others may have special programs. (In many cases these groups do not presently have such programs, but with encouragement and assistance from parent and advocacy groups, they often can be started.)

This listing of sources of community assistance could be further expanded but those indicated above may be found in various parts of the nation and should suffice to illustrate this type of assistance. In states where broad range special education programs are a well-established part of the public schools, the local director of special education may be the best single source of information regarding available services, but this is not always the case. In any event, this type of community service must be understood, encouraged, and coordinated to prevent needless overlap of service if its potential is to be fully realized.

Counseling parents of the handicapped may well be one of the most needed community services for the handicapped. As noted in Chapter 13, experts in early childhood education believe that preparation of parents to successfully manage and provide maximal experiences for their own children may be the most effective way to provide meaningful early education. Since most parents who have handicapped children were not prepared for the birth of a handicapped child, there is a great need for very special counseling.

The purpose of this closing section of the final chapter of this text is to emphasize the need for better training for professionals who provide services to parents of the handicapped and to support the need for more counseling services within the community. The counseling process is not simple and should be carried out only by those with specific training. Some parent groups provide counseling services for those who will actively seek them, and some physicians, social workers, or others employed by hospitals or community agencies may provide adequate counseling services, but this is an area of great, essentially unmet need. It is a need that cuts across the various areas of handicap and requires differing skills at different age levels.

Special education teachers need to learn how to relate to parents with regard to the areas of handicap that they serve, and with respect to the general age range with which they work. For example, counseling with regard to vocational planning for the mentally retarded may require different knowledge and skills than counseling with regard to behavioral management of a young mentally retarded child. Similar differences exist with respect to other areas of handicap. Differences in counseling approaches are also dictated with respect to the age at which the handicap is recognized by the parent. With mild handicapping conditions, parents may not be aware of the problem until the child is 7 or 8 years of age. This creates a very different problem from that relating to a severely handicapped child whose parents have been aware of the handicap since birth. Teachers in training must become acutely aware of parent counseling needs and study all available information that will better prepare them to deal with this skill, which may, in many instances, have significant effects on the educational progress of handicapped children. When parents have realistic expectations, understand the child's unique needs, and are accepting of the child despite the handicap, learning will proceed more effectively.

An additional need that is more likely to be a factor in the case of severely handicapped children is parent counseling during early childhood. The teacher of school-age children will not likely have much direct contact with this function but can and should play a role in initiating such counseling services within the community. This is badly needed for the sake of both child and parents. If such counseling is provided, it will tend to make the teacher's job easier when the child is enrolled in school.

An understanding of the forces in effect when the parents of a very young child learn that their child is handicapped is essential if this counseling function is to succeed. Such an understanding also provides insight for the teacher who may counsel with parents at some later date. The description of these forces by Chinn, Winn, and Walters (1978) is undoubtedly among the more accurate and effective descriptions available in the literature:

> The family is like a miniature society. It develops its own set of norms, values, and expectations for its members. It develops rules and procedures to regulate the behavior of its members in terms of those standards and to maintain the system itself. The basis for family style seems to be the family backgrounds and self-concepts of the founders of the family system and the accommodative relationship they develop. As they establish the marital relationship, make decisions about who is to do what, how and when, and work out together the patterns of interaction and communication, a basic orien-

tation evolves. An "open" orientation is one in which growth of individual members, as well as growth of the system, is a major family goal. Differences and differentness among family members are accepted as normal and are used to enhance the system. Families with a "closed" orientation or style scene, in contrast, tend to be primarily devoted to maintaining the system's status quo. One result is that differences and differentness among family members are suppressed—they pose a threat to the status quo.

Entry of a new member—the birth of a child—into the family is an event that has considerable social, economic, and emotional impact on the existing system. How the family system adapts to the event and the new member permanently affects its subsequent operation as a unit—its family style. Even if the infant is a normal, healthy child, the adjustments required are significant . . . the birth of a child with a handicap can have a devastating impact.

The list of complications, inconveniences, expenses, and changes in life-styles brought on by a new child is endless. Many, if not all, of these negative aspects of parenthood are often overshadowed by the sheer joy and pleasure that the child brings to the new parents. The displeasures of diaper changing and the sleepless nights owing to the infant's crying may tend to fade away with the first smile, the first step, and the first spoken word. With these first accomplishments, parents may begin to envision a fruition of their dreams and hopes of parenthood—healthy, bright, capable, beautiful children doing all the things that their parents did or wished they could have done.

The child who is blind may not be able to see well enough to smile in response to parents when most seeing children do. The child who is deaf may not be able to mimic the voices or sounds a normal child would have heard. The physically impaired child may never make that first step. The profoundly retarded child may never be able to say the first word. The parents of handicapped children may find few of the typical joys that compensate for the frustrations and inconveniences imposed by their child. Dreams and hopes regarding the child's future are often shattered. The child who was to represent the extension of his parents' egos serves instead as a deflation of their egos. He or she may serve as a threat to the parents' self-esteem and feelings of self-worth and dignity. Many individuals view the procreation of normal, healthy children as one of the main purposes of existence. In producing a handicapped child, they may view themselves as failures in what they consider one of their most fundamental purposes in life. (pp. 3, 17)

The feelings of parents as they first begin to fully realize the potential effect the handicapped child will have on the family have been variously described to include anger, depression, despair, disappointment, embarrassment, frustration, fear, rejection, self-blame, and shock (Gearheart and Litton, 1979). But beyond this mix of feelings, a certain sequential series of stages of adjustments to the presence of the handicapped child may be predicted. These stages are: (1) awareness, (2) denial, (3) recognition, (4) search for a cause, (5) search for a cure, and finally (6) actual acceptance. Differences in the amount of time required to move through these stages are to be expected, but for most parents some version of each of the first five stages must be experienced before the final stage, actual acceptance, can be reached. One of the major goals of counseling is to provide the parent(s) assistance in the personal adjustments involved in moving through these stages of adjustment. As noted earlier, it is not our intent, in this very brief discussion, to attempt to tell the reader *how* to counsel parents. It is our intent to build some understanding of the considerable importance of the counseling function and, to encourage those who enter the field of teaching the handicapped to learn more about this specialized need.

We will close this section with advice from a parent of a handicapped child. In an article entitled "Some pointers for professionals," Patterson (1956) makes a number of valuable suggestions:

1. Tell parents about the nature of the problem at the earliest possible time. Try to talk to both parents.
2. Help parents see that this is *their* problem, but be informed and supportive regarding available resources.
3. Remember the importance of attitudes. Remember that parents of the handicapped are just people; never put them on the defensive.
4. Be careful about the language used in parent conferences; be especially careful about the use of "professional jargon."

The value and logic of this simply stated advice from the parent of a handicapped child should be obvious. The critical importance of having professionals prepared to respond to this need should be self-evident.

Summary

One resource for the handicapped or disabled that is too little understood by many special educators is rehabilitation. Although there are a number of excellent private rehabilitation facilities in various parts of the nation, it is the publicly supported federal-state rehabilitation program that directly affects a large number of handicapped persons, especially adolescents and adults. In this chapter we have reviewed the manner in which federally sponsored rehabilitation programs got their start during World War I and how they have grown since that time. Today they reach into almost all communities and provide essential services to the adult handicapped, plus vocational preparation assistance for certain high school students. This program is administered through state level programs (even though the federal government pays most of the costs) and may provide such services as evaluation, medical, surgical and hospital care, prosthetic devices, training, transportation, tools and equipment, readers for the blind, interpreters for the deaf, family services, and job placement assistance.

The basic concept of rehabilitation services is restoration, with correction or minimization of the disability the major goal. All early rehabilitative efforts were directed toward *vocational* rehabilitation, and this remains the major thrust of the Rehabilitation Services Administration. However, recent legislatively mandated emphasis on the more severely disabled has led to some redefinition of rehabilitation goals to include goals that would not have been accepted as appropriate 15 or 20 years ago. It is essential that special educators understand the services that may be provided through the rehabilitation counselor; otherwise, their own teaching, planning, and counseling may not be fully effective.

Other programs considered in this chapter included the growing area of genetic counseling, which should be of value with respect to prevention of handicapping conditions. Better understanding of potential risks and early knowledge and understanding of the handicapping condition are other benefits of such counseling. Although most would agree that genetic counseling can be of great benefit, the issue of therapeutic abortion (in cases where it is confirmed that the fetus is defective) continues to cause heated debate.

Special transportation services, a special dentistry program, and the potential assistance provided by community advocacy and/or volunteer organizations were also discussed. Each of these areas of community service is well developed in certain areas of the nation but poorly developed or even nonexistent in others. This variability of service is a proper target for concerted effort on the part of all who are concerned with the needs and rights of the handicapped and disabled population of the nation.

Better counseling for parents of the handicapped is needed to help them come to terms with the very real problems of having a handicapped child. The birth of a handicapped child may be a very traumatic event, and the parents should have assistance as they move through the various stages of adjustment toward realistic acceptance of the handicapping condition.

focus

scope and philosophy of rehabilitation programs

The Rehabilitation Services Administration, headquartered in Washington, D.C., with ten regional offices located throughout the United States, provides major leadership for the state rehabilitation agencies. There are state agencies in the fifty states, plus the District of Columbia, Guam, Puerto Rico, American Samoa Trust Territory, and the Virgin Islands. In addition there are 28 separate state rehabilitation agencies for the blind.

The concern of rehabilitation services is the correction or minimizing of the disability under consideration, and the method of restoration may be any authorized or permitted under the legislation enacted by the U.S. Congress, the rules and regulations approved to carry out this legislation, or the guidelines of any regional or state office.

The rehabilitation process is a team process, with the rehabilitation counselor serving as initiator, coordinator, and facilitator of program services. The various restorative areas (physical, social, psychologic, educational, and vocational) must be systematically evaluated, so that piecemeal efforts do not result in failure or only partial success.

other community programs and services

Genetic counseling has three main objectives: (1) to answer parents' questions on risks of recurrence in another child when a member of the family has some malformation or disease that might be genetically determined, (2) to call attention to a special risk that may result in a child born with a genetically determined disease so that early diagnosis and treatment are possible, and (3) to prevent an increase in the frequency of children born genetically predisposed to serious handicap.

Special transportation services for the handicapped or disabled are another type of community provision that is gaining acceptance.

Community advocacy and volunteer organizations are a highly important source of community assistance.

Community service must be understood, encouraged, and coordinated to prevent needless overlap of service if its potential is to be fully realized.

counseling parents of the handicapped

The feelings of parents as they first begin to fully realize the potential effect the handicapped child will have on the family have been variously described to include anger, depression, despair, disappointment, embarrassment, frustration, fear, rejection, self-blame, and shock. But beyond this mix of feelings, a certain sequential series of stages of adjustment to the presence of the handicapped child may be predicted: (1) awareness, (2) denial, (3) recognition, (4) search for a cause, (5) search for a cure, and finally (6) actual acceptance. One of the major goals of counseling is to provide the parent(s) assistance in the personal adjustments involved.

References and suggested readings

Bitter, J. *Introduction to rehabilitation.* St. Louis: The C. V. Mosby Co., 1979.

Carter, C. *Handbook of mental retardation syndromes.* 3rd ed. Springfield, Ill.: Charles C Thomas, Publisher, 1975.

Chinn, P., Winn, J., and Walters, R. *Two-way talking with parents of special children.* St. Louis: The C. V. Mosby Co., 1978.

Cull, J., and Hardy, R. (Eds.). *Vocational rehabilitation: professional and process.* Springfield, Ill.: Charles C Thomas, Publisher, 1972.

Gearheart, B., and Litton, F. *The trainable retarded: a foundations approach.* 2nd ed. St. Louis: The C. V. Mosby Co., 1979.

Lassiter, R. History of the rehabilitation movement in America. In *Vocational rehabilitation: profession and process.* J. Cull and R. Hardy (Eds.). Springfield, Ill.: Charles C Thomas, Publisher, 1972.

Leviton, F. Personal communication, Nov. 30, 1978.

Milligan, G. Counseling parents of the mentally retarded. In *Mental retardation: readings and resources.* 2nd ed. J. Rothstein (Ed.). New York: Holt, Rinehart & Winston, 1971.

National Foundation of Dentistry. *Public Information Brochures,* undated.

Noland, R. *Counseling parents of the mentally retarded: a sourcebook.* Springfield, Ill.: Charles C Thomas, Publisher, 1970.

Patterson, L. Some pointers for professionals. *Children,* 1956, *1*, 13-17.

Rehabilitation Act of 1973. Public Law 93-112, 93rd Congress, Washington, D.C., 1973.

Glossary

acceleration A term used in relation to the gifted, talented, or creative indicating more rapid movement through school programs than normal; involves such procedures as early entrance, skipping a grade, and advanced courses.

accommodation A term referring to a variety of adaptations of school organization, curriculum, and/or instructional methods to meet the needs of a student.

acquired aphasia Inability to speak or understand language after such skills have been acquired.

adaptive behavior A wide range of skills and competencies utilized by individuals to meet the needs of their environment. Included are aspects of motivation, social behavior, physical abilities, intellectual functioning, and others. Standards for adaptive behavior are generally age related.

adventitiously deaf Deafness acquired at some time after birth (also called postlingual deafness).

alternative school An academically, remedially, or skill-oriented program for adolescents that is markedly different from traditionally organized secondary schools.

American Sign Language (ASL) A method of communication used with and by deaf persons. It is concept-based and does not necessarily conform to individual English words.

amniocentesis A procedure utilizing analysis of the amniotic fluid of the uterus, which can aid in identification of Down's syndrome and other congenital defects.

anomie Condition of rootlessness or a state of lack of social norms and/or values.

anoxia A lack of oxygen in the blood resulting from a variety of causes, which, depending upon the degree, results in damage to brain tissue or other parts of the organism.

aphasia Impairment or loss of the ability to comprehend language caused by brain injury or disease. Can be manifested by the inability to speak, understand, or write.

arthritis A disease affecting the joints and muscles, resulting in pain and inflammation.

articulation Refers to movements of the vocal tract including the stream of breath producing voiced and unvoiced sounds, enunciation of words, vocal sounds, and movements of the jaws, lips, and tongue.

articulation disorders Any impairment of the vocal tract that affects the production of speech, the enunciation of words, or vocal sounds.

assessment A process employing mental, social, psychologic, or educational tests and observations to determine an individual's strengths and weaknesses.

asthma A respiratory condition manifested in episodes of breathing difficulties.

astigmatism An eye condition in which a refractive error results in blurred vision.

ataxia Refers to one type of cerebral palsy; unsteady balance and gait, lack of coordination of muscles, eyes, etc.

athetosis A type of cerebral palsy characterized by twisting or writhing movements and facial grimaces.

audiogram A graphic representation of decibel loss, by frequencies, for each ear.

Glossary

audiology The science of diagnosing hearing impairments and assisting in remedial planning.

audiometry The use of tests to measure or assess hearing.

auditory acuity How well one hears.

auditory expressive language Broad term referring to the ability of an individual to use words and language.

auditory global method Method of providing information to the hearing impaired that is primarily auditory.

auditory memory Ability to retain and recall what has been heard.

auditory perception Ability to interpret or organize what is heard.

auditory-receptive language General term referring to the ability to understand what is heard.

auditory training Systematic method to train the hearing impaired to utilize all of their residual hearing for the purpose of developing language.

aura A sensation, including sounds, images of light, odors, etc., that precedes the onset of an epileptic seizure.

aural Refers to the sense of hearing or to the ear.

auricle The external portion of the ear, which collects sounds and funnels them to the inner ear; composed of cartilage.

autism A childhood psychosis rendering the child noncommunicative, withdrawn, self-stimulating, and often with cognitive and perceptual deficits.

behaviorism School of psychology that explains causes of emotional disturbance in terms of learned behavior; in treatment, applies principles of respondent and operant conditioning.

binocular vision Ability to fuse the images coming through the eyes into a single image.

biochemical imbalances Term used in relation to emotional disturbance to indicate disorders involving metabolic processes.

biophysical theory Theory that attempts to explain causation of emotional disorders based on biologic factors.

blind A general term that can refer to no vision or to limited vision.

bone conduction The transfer of sound waves to the inner ear through the vibration of the bones of the skull.

braille A system of raised dots which are translated into letters, used by the blind to read and write. The raised dots are in a two dot by three dot cell.

braillewriter A machine, similar to a typewriter, used to produce braille.

brain damage Any injury to the tissues of the brain that can be located or identified.

brain dysfunction Term used to describe a suspected malfunctioning of the brain.

brain injured Refers to one who before, during, or after birth has received an injury to the brain. The injury can be the result of trauma or infections. Usually affects learning.

career education A general term referring to the procedure of teaching about various jobs early in school, which may be followed by more specific training in relation to a particular job.

cathartic method Method in which repressed traumatic experiences are discharged by "talking it out."

cerebral palsy A complex condition in which various motor disturbances such as spasms, weakness, and incoordination are present; usually said to be caused by brain damage.

cerumen Ear wax; useful in preventing foreign matter from entering the ear.

child abuse Physical or mental injury to a child under 18 years of age through negligence or maltreatment.

choroid The vascular membrane between the sclera and the retina of the eye.

cleft palate A rift or split in either the soft or hard palate. Generally present at birth but can be caused by injury.

cluttering Garbled speech, including difficulty in fluency, poor rate or rhythm, and sound transpositions.

cochlea Major organ in the inner ear, shaped somewhat like a snail.

commitment The act of placing an individual in the charge of others as in the commitment of a person to an institution for the mentally retarded or mentally ill.

communicative disorders Any significant impairment or disability in the ability to communicate.

conductive loss Hearing impairment caused by reduced or impaired conduction of sound in the outer or middle ear.

congenital aphasia Inability to produce or to comprehend language; present at birth.

congenitally deaf Deafness present at birth (also called prelingual deafness).

continuum of educational services The full range of services available for handicapped students. The range extendes from full-time residential placement, which is the most restrictive, to full-time placement in regular classrooms, which is least restrictive.

cooperative plan The term used to describe the services provided for handicapped students in which the student receives a portion of the daily instruction in the regular classroom and the remainder in a special classroom.

cooperative program An organizational plan that provides educational opportunities and technical training for severely handicapped students. This type of arrangement may be made between an institution and a vocational-technical school.

cornea The transparent outer covering of the eyeball, in front of the iris and pupil.

Council for Exceptional Children A national professional organization for all who work for and with gifted and handicapped persons. Included within the broad organization are divisions for each area of exceptionality.

countertheories Those theories relating to emotional disturbance that are not associated with or are in contradiction to the more recognized theories of causation or treatment of mental illness.

creative Ability to develop unique ideas and/or solutions to problems; high degree of flexibility in responses.

cretinism Condition resulting from a thyroid gland disorder. Characterized by hoarse voice, short thick hands, delayed bone development, muscular enlargement, and mental retardation.

cultural transmission theory The belief that deviant behavior is taught to succeeding generations much the same as the other traditions might be taught.

deaf The condition in which the sense of hearing either does not function or functions so minimally that the individual does not hear.

decibel Unit of intensity or loudness of sound.

delayed language Failure to develop language at the normal time expected. Refers to the ability to understand as well as speak a language.

dependent retarded *see* **severely retarded.**

developmental aphasia Impairment or loss of the ability to comprehend written or verbal language.

developmental disabilities Identifiable delay in normal development.

developmental period In reference to mental retardation, the ages between birth and 18 years.

diabetes A metabolic disorder in which the pancreas fails to produce a sufficient amount of insulin resulting in an abnormal amount of sugar in the blood and urine.

differentiated services Related to the gifted, creative, and/or talented, services provided to enhance the specific area of excellence.

diplegia Dysfuction or paralysis of all four bodily extremities.

directionality The ability to recognize directions involved in the environment, such as up from down, front from back, under from on, etc.

distortions Faulty articulation resulting in altered speech sounds, such as "shlide" for slide.

dog guides A dog specially trained to detect obstacles that may hamper the mobility of a visually impaired person.

Down's syndrome A specific type of mental retardation resulting from a chromosomal irregularity. Usually apparent in various physical aspects such as slanted eyes, thick tongue, etc.

Duchenne Type of muscular dystrophy in which there is progressive muscle fiber deterioration; this hereditary disease usually attacks children between the ages of 1 and 6 years and is generally considered fatal.

dysacusis A difficulty in understanding speech caused by an inner ear condition.

dysgraphic One who demonstrates extremely poor handwriting.

dyslexia An inability to read despite normal intelligence, appropriate experiences, and conventional teaching methods.

eardrum The thin membrane that separates the middle ear from the external ear, which vibrates when struck by sound waves.

early childhood education Educational efforts for young children, generally from birth through 8 years of age.

ecologic theory A compilation of various views of causation and treatment procedures for emotional problems, which have their basis in the

Glossary

ecologic theory of interrelatedness between an organism and the environment.

educable mentally retarded Term used in educational circles referring to individuals who generally can learn academic skills and can become self-sufficient; usually have a measured IQ between 50 and 70. To be diagnosed as educable mentally retarded, an individual must also demonstrate adaptive behavior that is consistent with the measured IQ.

electronic devices Various devices used by visually impaired persons to detect obstacles in their environment.

emotionally disturbed A broad term used to describe individuals whose major difficulty is managing their emotions and maintaining them within the range of acceptability.

environmental control An effort to use and control the space and circumstances for an individual in order to maximize learning or to control behavior. Can refer to learning disabilities or emotional disturbance.

epilepsy A recurrent central nervous system disorder characterized by convulsions and seizures.

erythroblastosis fetalis Condition resulting from Rh factor incompatibility. Includes the destruction of the red blood cells of the fetus and the secretion of bilirubin (reddish yellow pigment in the bile) which, if not treated, results in damage to the basal ganglia of the brain.

etiology The study of the causes of disorders and diseases.

external auditory meatus The external passage of the ear.

figure-ground perception The ability to attend to one aspect of the visual field while relegating all other aspects to background position or status.

flexibility disorders Impairments of disabilities caused by rigidity and/or stiffness in articulation, pitch, or quality of voice.

functional disorders Diminished speech ability with no known organic cause.

galactosemia A hereditary disease characterized by the inability of the body to convert the galactose portion of the lactose molecule in milk to glucose for utilization. If not treated, it can result in mental retardation, cataracts, or other disorders.

genetic blueprinting The hereditary characteristics transmitted by parents to their offspring by means of the genes or the chromosomes.

genetic counseling Information provided to parents or prospective parents regarding the probability of an offspring inheriting a handicapping condition. The information is based on various factors such as chromosome aberrations, probability statistics, etc.

gifted Refers to persons possessing high level cognitive abilities. Intellectual superiority must be sufficient to set the individual apart from normal or average.

glaucoma A condition of unknown cause resulting in excessive internal pressure in the eyeball. If left untreated, it usually results in reduced vision or blindness.

grand mal seizure A severe form of epileptic seizure in which the person loses consciousness for a period of time.

hard of hearing A term used to describe individuals who have reduced auditory acuity. There are many degrees of this condition.

health impairments Conditions existing in children that may require special procedures, equipment, or adaptations. Among such conditions are cystic fibrosis, muscular dystrophy, diabetes, and arthritis.

hearing aid Device used to amplify, collect, or conduct sound waves. Used by persons to enable them to utilize whatever vestiges of hearing remain.

hearing handicapped The condition of reduced hearing acuity of sufficient magnitude to interfere with the normal activities of the individual.

hearing impairment General term that includes all degrees of hearing loss.

hemiplegia Paralysis of one side of the body

hemolytic disease *see* **Rh incompatibility.**

high-risk children General term used to describe children who, because of various environmental deficiencies, delayed normal development, or other factors, may experience a more-than-normal likelihood of future handicaps.

homebound service Refers to educational instruction provided in the home.

hospital service Educational instruction provided in a hospital.

hydrocephalus A condition of excess cerebrospinal fluid accumulation in the cranial cavity usually resulting in an enlarged head. Can result in brain pressure and/or mental retardation.

hyperactive A condition characterized by excess motor activity, inattention, or impulsivity.

hyperopia Farsightedness; poor close vision caused by shortened eyeball. Can usually be corrected by a convex lens.

hypoactivity A condition characterized by lethargy and lack of activity. Opposite of hyperactivity.

hypoglycemia A condition in which there is an abnormally low glucose content in the blood.

impairment A general term that describes a less-than-normal functioning; implies injury or deficiency.

incoordination Lack of coordination.

incus The anvil-shaped bone in the middle ear.

individualized education program A written plan of instruction that includes a statement of the child's present level of functioning, specific areas needing special services, annual goals, short-term objectives, and method of evaluation. Required for every child receiving special educational services under the conditions of PL 94-142.

infant stimulation programs Programs designed for severely handicapped children from birth to 3 years of age.

inner ear Interior portion of the ear including the cochlea and the vestibular mechanism.

insulin The hormone that regulates sugar metabolism in the body; produced by the pancreas. Can be produced synthetically and used in the treatment of diabetes.

intervention Refers to actual involvement in the life of a child to modify the likely outcomes; usually begun because of a suspected or actual handicap.

intoxications In referring to mental retardation, includes poisoning by toxins such as arsenic, mercury, alcohol, and narcotics, which may result in deficient intellectual development.

iris The colored portion of the eye, functioning somewhat like a camera shutter; opening or closing depends on the amount of light striking it.

itinerant services Those services provided by specialists who travel among schools, homes, hospitals. The services may include academic instruction, counseling, or therapy.

itinerant specialists Those who travel from school to the home or hospital to provide special services for the handicapped.

jacksonian seizures Epileptic seizures that affect limited regions of the body.

juvenile delinquency Law-breaking behavior, as defined by statute, on the part of minors.

juvenile rheumatoid arthritis A chronic form of arthritis; in severe forms can even cause paralysis. Children are the usual victims.

kernicterus Severe form of erythroblastosis fetalis that is usually fatal during the neonatal period.

kinesthetic talent Above normal ability in areas such as athletics or dance.

labeling The assignment of a general name or term to a handicapping condition (such as mentally ill or emotionally disturbed).

labeling theory A statement of principles, stemming from sociology, which pertain to the selection of individuals within a society for a deviant role. Related to emotional disturbance.

language The ability to communicate thoughts and feelings through sounds (primarily words), gestures, and written symbols.

larynx The area of the throat containing the vocal cords.

laterality Ability to correctly interpret the position and sidedness of the body. Often refers to right- and left-sidedness.

learning disabilities *see* **learning disabled.**

learning disabled A general term used to describe individuals who demonstrate a discrepancy between the expected level of achievement and their actual achievement. Usually implied is lower-than-average ability to understand or use spoken and written language.

least restrictive environment a concept dictating that a handicapped student should be educated within the environment that is most like that in which he or she would be educated if *not* handicapped. In laws and legal opinions, this refers to the least restrictive environment in which an *appropriate* or *effective* educational program can be provided. For example, a child in a wheelchair, with no intellectual disabilities, should be educated with peers in a regular classroom with physical accommodations made for the wheelchair.

legally blind 20/200 vision in the better eye after correction, or 20 degrees or less in the visual field.

legislation Act of passing laws or the laws themselves.

lens The portion of the eye that changes and, if need be, refines the focus of the light rays.

Linguistics of Visual English (LOVE or LVE) A system of manual signs that follows English word order and was developed for use with preschool and primary-age children with hearing impairments.

litigation The act or process of resolving a dispute in a court of law; also may refer to the actual lawsuit.

long cane A stick usually about 4 or 5 feet long, made of aluminum or fiberglass, used by visually impaired persons to locate obstacles or changes in the terrain as they move about the environment.

low vision The term applied to persons who are visually impaired but have some residual vision.

mainstreaming The practice of providing handicapped persons an education with their nonhandicapped peers to the greatest extent possible.

malleus Hammer-shaped bone in the middle ear.

manual When used in reference to the system of communication of the deaf includes fingerspelling and sign language.

manual communications systems Fingerspelling and sign language used by the deaf to communicate; used in place of speech.

mastoid bone That portion of the skull extending down behind the ear.

maternal rubella A viral disease (german measles), which, when present in the female during early stages of pregnancy, results in a high probability of severe handicaps in the child.

megavitamin Refers to various types of treatment consisting of large doses of vitamins.

meningitis A bacterial or viral inflammation of the membranes that encase the brain and spinal cord.

mentally retarded A term describing persons who have subnormal intellectual functioning and are deficient in adaptive behavior, both of which are manifested during the developmental period.

metabolism A general term referring to all the chemical processes and changes involving cells and tissue that maintain life.

microcephalus An inherited condition resulting in small head and brain size and severe mental retardation.

middle ear The portion of the ear housing the eardrum and the malleus, incus, and stapes (hammer, anvil, and stirrups).

minimal brain dysfunction A general term referring to a diagnosed or suspected malfunction in the central nervous system. Usually related to children who may also be called learning disabled.

mixed loss Hearing impairment caused by both sensorineural and conductive loss.

mobility training Refers to training provided for visually impaired persons, which enables them to detect various potential obstacles (such as objects or inclines) in their environment and to successfully move themselves from place to place.

modeling Providing a demonstration of a particular behavior.

monoplegia Dysfunction or paralysis of one limb.

multihandicapped A term to describe persons with more than one handicap; for example, blind and mentally retarded.

multisensory A term referring to training or teaching procedures that simultaneously utilize more than one sensory modality. Often means the use of three or more modalities.

muscular dystrophy Disease of the muscles characterized by weakness and deterioration of the skeletal muscles resulting in increasing disability and deformity.

myopia Poor distance vision resulting from a too long eyeball; usually corrected by concave lens.

neurologically impaired A general term referring to a number of conditions that result from an injury to or a dysfunction of the central nervous system.

nursery school Generally refers to programs especially for prekindergarten age children.

nystagmus Continuous, involuntary movements of the eyeball, often resulting in impaired vision.

off-campus work station An educational practice whereby employers provide jobs for students with the understanding that an employee of the school will directly supervise and teach additional skills as needed.

omissions Related to speech, an impairment characterized by omitted sounds (such as "ed" for "bed").

on-the-job training The educational practice

whereby skills relating to a particular employment are taught primarily at the job site.

ophthalmia neonatorum An inflammation of the forepart of the eyeball occurring during the first weeks of a baby's life.

ophthalmologist A physician who has additional training in treatment of diseases of the eyes. Can prescribe medication or perform surgery in addition to measuring refraction and prescribing lenses.

Optacon An electronic device for converting print into vibratory images, which visually impaired persons can "read."

optic nerve The nerve located in the brain that carries impulses of sight.

optometrist A nonmedical person trained in the functioning of the eyes. Can measure refraction and prescribe lenses.

oral When used in reference to the deaf, a system of communication that excludes fingerspelling or sign language. It includes speech reading, writing, and spoken language.

organ of Corti Portion of ear in which the sensory cells are located.

orientation In relation to the blind, it refers to the ability to establish one's position in space relative to other objects in the environment without the use of visual cues.

orofacial Pertaining to the face and mouth.

orthopedically handicapped (or impaired) Refers to those with disabilities or reduced functioning of joints or muscles. Can also refer to those with bone problems.

ossicles Small bones within the middle ear that transmit sound. The bones consist of the malleus, incus, and stapes.

otitis media Inflammation of the middle ear, which, without treatment, can cause a conductive hearing loss.

otology Term referring to the medical aspects of the ear.

otosclerosis Disease characterized by new bony growth in the areas surrounding the inner ear.

outer ear The visible portion of the ear external to the head.

overattention The act of focusing attention on one particular object or task and the seeming inability to break the focused attention.

paraplegia Dysfunction or paralysis of both legs.

parent groups Oganizations of parents of exceptional children, usually organized to achieve educational, recreational, or other benefits for their children.

perceptual disorders Inability to interpret or organize information received through any one or combination of the senses.

perceptual-motor approaches Those approaches to learning disabilities which focus on the interaction of perception and motor activities. Most common of the perceptual areas utilized are visual, auditory, kinesthetic, and tactual.

perseveration The inability to stop repeating a word or action, although it is no longer goal-directed and has lost its usefulness or initial meaning.

petit mal seizure An epileptic seizure characterized by dizziness or blackout, usually of short duration and occurring with varying frequency. Such seizures may go unrecognized by teachers or peers for long periods of time.

phenylketonuria (PKU) A condition in which certain protein-digesting enzymes are absent, resulting in increased toxins in the blood and urine of the infant. If not treated, results in mental retardation.

phonation The production of sounds by the larynx.

physically handicapped Refers to individuals with defects of the limbs or other health problems. As generally used in special education, does not include conditions such as mental retardation, emotional disturbance, blindness, deafness, or learning disabilities.

pinna External portion of the ear.

pitch disorders Impairments in ability to regulate high or low voice qualities.

poliomyelitis An inflammation of the nerve cells of the spinal cord or brainstem, in severe cases results in paralysis.

postlingual deafness Deafness occurring after speech and language have been developed (also called adventitious deafness).

preliminary injunction An initial legal order from a court prohibiting a certain action or commanding that an action be performed.

preliminary review Refers to the introductory or first examination of the information collected regarding a child experiencing some difficulty in school.

prelingual deafness Deafness present at birth or occuring prior to the development of speech and language. (If occurring before birth, also called congenital deafness.)

presbycusis A lessening of the sense of hearing as a result of aging.

preschool programs Programs for children either from ages 3 to 6 or birth to 6.

psychoanalysis Method of treatment of mental illness developed by Sigmund Freud.

psychoanalytic theories Broad term generally used to denote causation or treatment of mental illness primarily based on freudian principles.

psychochemicals Drugs that produce temporary changes in brain functioning and thus influence behavior.

psychomotor seizure A type of epilepsy, including erratic and inappropriate actions, such as chewing, arm-rubbing, etc., resulting from a particular type of epilepsy. Although usually there is not complete loss of consciousness, the person cannot remember what happened.

psychoneurologic learning disabilities Refers to learning problems that are related to central nervous system dysfunctions.

psychosocial talent Refers to above-normal ability to lead others in intellectual, social, political, religious, and similar pursuits.

pupil The opening in the middle of the iris.

quadriplegia Dysfunction or paralysis of both arms and both legs.

quality disorders As related to speech, impairments of the voice characterized by hoarseness, nasal tones, etc.

referral The process of informing the appropriate specialist(s) about an individual for the purpose of collecting further information and considering the possible need for special educational services.

refractive errors Dysfunction or abnormality in the functioning of the eye resulting in distorted images on the retina.

rehabilitation A general term referring to the assistance provided for handicapped persons. It may refer to providing hearing aids, and prosthetic devices, counseling, job placement, psychologic, social, and/or educational evaluations, and other related services.

reinforcer Reward that increases the likelihood of a behavior being repeated. May be food, free time, or other activity.

residential school A facility in which an exceptional individual resides for 24 hours each day. The mentally retarded and mentally ill are most often in need of this type of service.

resource room A service delivery model characterized by the provision of assistance to a child by a specialist for some portion of the school day. The room in which this assistance takes place is usually referred to as the resource room.

retina The back portion of the eye containing the sensitive nerve fibers connected to the optic nerve.

retinal defects Malformations or malfunctioning of the retina.

retinitis pigmentosa A hereditary disease of the retina that usually results in total blindness.

retrolental fibroplasia Disease in which there is growth of scar tissue over the retina of the eye, resulting from excessive oxygen administered shortly after birth.

Rh incompatibility A reaction to opposite Rh factors (in the mother and the fetus) that results in the destruction of red blood cells in the fetus and the release of large amounts of reddish yellow pigment in the blood (bilirubin). If not treated this condition often results in severe handicaps for the child caused by brain damage.

rheumatic fever A disease characterized by painful swelling of joints, skin rash, and fever; usually follows strep throat or scarlet fever and often results in heart damage.

rigidity In cerebral palsy refers to diminished movement of limbs.

Rochester method Method of teaching the deaf to utilize speechreading and fingerspelling to receive information.

rubella German measles. If contracted by a pregnant woman, especially during the first trimester, serious birth defects can result, including deafness, visual impairments, heart defects, and mental retardation.

screening Broad-scale testing procedures used to identify children who may need more intensive assessment. Vision and hearing screening procedures are among the more common utilized in most schools.

Seeing Essential English (SEE$_1$) A system of manual signs used in communication by hearing-impaired persons in which the signs parallel (syntactically) the English language.

semicircular canals Portion of the inner ear that provides a sense of balance.

sensorineural loss Hearing impairment caused by some malfunctioning of the inner ear.

sensory Term relating to the information received through sight, hearing, touch, taste, or smell.

severely retarded Individuals who will need lifetime supervision in social and academic functioning and daily living skills. They usually have a measured intelligence of below 25.

shaping A procedure of reinforcing responses resembling the desired one, providing reinforcement for increasingly closer approximations, until the final desired response is attained.

sheltered workshop An employment facility with specific types of work for individuals unable to function in competitive employment. The environment is controlled and the jobs carefully supervised by those who fully understand the limitations of the employees.

sighted guide A sighted person serving as a guide to a visually impaired person who "reads" the messages of the sighted person's body when moving from place to place.

Signed English Manual signs for 800 words that were not included in other signing methods but were felt to be important for young deaf children. This system follows English word order.

Signing Exact English (SEE$_2$) A system of manual signs used in communication by the hearing impaired, which is presented in printed form by a series of drawings. This system is similar to American Sign Language.

Snellen chart An instrument used to measure visual acuity. Black symbols on a white background are large at the top and smaller at the lower portions of the chart.

social disorganization theory Theories suggesting that disrupted social patterns may result in mental illness for some people.

socially maladjusted Individuals who display a lack of social responsibility and inability to conform even minimally to social norms.

sociologic theories Broad term used to describe causation and treatment of emotional disturbance based on social factors that affect the behavior of individuals and groups.

spasticity Muscular incoordination resulting from sudden, involuntary contractions of the muscles. Can refer to a type of cerebral palsy.

special class Class organized, usually by a particular diagnostic label (such as emotionally disturbed or learning disabled), which has a full-time teacher and in which the students receive most of their instruction. Students are integrated into the regular class for only short periods of time or not at all.

special day school Provides day long educational experiences for children. Often private; may be limited to one handicap, or may accept children with various handicaps.

speech The mechanical (vocal) operations that produce audible, identifiable sounds and words.

speech clinician *see* **speech pathologist.**

speech correctionist One who is trained in providing instruction to individuals with deficiencies or difficulty in producing spoken language. May also be called speech therapist or be used interchangeably with speech clinician or speech pathologist. Terminology may depend on regulations or statutes in effect in any given state.

speech flow The voice movement from sound to sound, syllable to syllable, and word to word. Also includes sequence, duration, rhythm, rate, and fluency.

speech handicapped Those whose speech interferes with communication, calls attention to themselves, or causes the person maladjustment or anxiety. The problems in speech may be caused by organic defects, malfunctioning muscles, faulty articulation, or other factors.

speech pathologist A professional trained in the study of human communication, its normal development, and its disorders.

speech pathology A discipline relating to the diagnosis and treatment of speech impairments or delayed development of speech.

speech therapist One who is trained in providing language-based services, such as speech correction, articulation improvement, and voice quality. This title is still in limited use, but is in disfavor with professional speech pathologists.

speechreading Method used by the deaf to decode lip movements and facial expressions in order to understand spoken language.

spina bifida A congenital defect characterized by a

Glossary

lack of closure at the base of the vertebral column. In severe cases results in paralysis of the legs and lack of bowel and/or bladder control.

staffing A term commonly used to describe an officially scheduled meeting of various concerned persons regarding the placement or education of a particular child.

stapes Stirrup-shaped bone in the middle ear.

strabismus A condition characterized by the failure of both eyes to focus on an object simultaneously. Usually caused by weak eye muscles.

Strauss syndrome A condition characterized by hyperactivity, incoordination, and inattention. Named for A. A. Strauss who pioneered in research on the brain injured.

stuttering A speech impairment characterized by hesitations, repetitions, or spasms of breathing; can be accompanied by facial distortions indicative of the struggle to speak.

subaverage intelligence In referring to mental retardation, 2 or more standard deviations below the mean on individual intelligence tests.

substitutions A speech impairment characterized by inaccurate sounds being substituted for the accurate ones, as in "wabbit" for "rabbit.

sweep test A screening test that utilizes an audiometer to detect hearing loss.

systematic sign language A system of manual signs used in England.

talented A term used to describe individuals who have highly developed skills, abilities, or aptitudes without necessarily possessing a high degree of intelligence.

techniques of daily living (TDL) Refers to skills such as living independently, performing on the job, management of personal affairs, (grooming, personal hygiene), and traveling independently, which must be specifically taught to the visually impaired.

terminal employment A term used in relation to sheltered workshops to indicate permanent employment in this type of setting for certain individuals.

tinnitus The clinical term used for what is commonly called "ringing in the ears."

total communication A philosophy espoused by various professionals involved in teaching the hearing impaired, which includes use of aural, manual, and oral methods to ensure effective communication.

trainable mentally retarded Term used in education related classifications; refers to individuals who will have limited success in basic academic skills and will usually require controlled work and living situations. Measured IQ is approximately 25 to 50. To be diagnosed as trainable mentally retarded, an individual must also demonstrate adaptive behavior that is consistent with the measured IQ.

trauma Refers to a wound or injury that is violently produced. Also refers to the condition, physical or mental, that results from shock.

tremor Involuntary vibration in large muscles such as arms, legs, etc.; relates to cerebral palsy.

triplegia Dysfunction or paralysis of three limbs.

tympanic membrane Thin membrane between the outer and middle ear; often referred to as the eardrum.

vestibule Upper portion of the inner ear, which contains the semicircular canals; responsible for the sense of balance.

visual acuity How well one sees. Can refer to close

or far vision as well as clarity in distinguishing various characteristics.

visual efficiency The ability with which one can utilize eyesight.

visual impairment A term used to describe any deviation in or malfunctioning of the eye.

visual memory Ability to retain and recall what is seen.

visual perception Ability to interpret and organize information provided by sight.

visualization Ability to recall and "picture" in the mind what has been seen or heard.

visually handicapped A general term used to describe individuals whose vision is sufficiently impaired that they require special provisions for their education. Can also include legally blind.

visuomotor model Term used to describe the manner in which higher level intellectual abilities develop from lower level motor systems. Conceptualized by Gerald Getman.

vocational training Specific planned teaching of skills prerequisite to employment. A portion of the training may be incorporated in the initial stages of employment.

voice disorders Impairments in spoken language, such as unusual pitch, quality, etc.

voiceless sounds Those sounds, such as /h/ and /s/, that are produced when the larynx is open and air turbulence is generated in the vocal tract.

work experience An educational procedure whereby simulated work experiences are presented to teach students skills or responsibilities related to a variety of types of work.

Name index

A
Abeson, A., 39, 43
Alley, G., 67
Anastasi, A., 9
Apgar, V., 265

B
Bailey, E., 180, 181
Baker, E., 289
Balow, B., 306
Barbier, C., 156
Barr, M., 248
Barraga, N., 148, 149, 150, 151, 160, 161
Beck, J., 265
Bell, A. G., 9, 114
Bell, A. M., 216
Bergman, G., 94
Berman, J., 261
Berry, H., 261
Bertschi, J., 402, 403
Best, G., 318
Beuree, G., 91
Biklen, D., 133
Birch, J., 362
Bitter, J., 444, 464, 467, 468
Blatt, B., 441
Bliss, C. K., 102
Bluhm, H., 444
Blum, A., 302
Bonet, J., 112
Bourne, R., 309
Bower, E., 291, 293
Braddock, D., 37
Bradfield, R. H., 66
Braidwood, T., 112, 113
Braille, L., 155, 156
Bryan, J., 309
Bryan, T., 309

Buckley, R., 202
Bullock, L., 306
Bush, J., 261

C
Cain, L., 21
Carter, C., 469
Chalfant, J., 220, 221
Charleston, L., 326
Chen, M., 261
Chinn, P., 472, 473
Clarizio, H., 294
Clerc, L., 113
Cole, R., 416
Coleman, J. C., 5, 285, 287, 295, 296
Coleman, J. S., 420
Collins, E., 371
Conant, J., 351
Cornish, R., 362
Cott, A., 201
Coulter, W., 254
Cratty, B., 195
Craviato, J., 296
Crook, W., 202
Cruickshank, W., 187, 188, 196

D
Dale, P., 219
Dalgarno, G., 112
Davies, S., 249
Davis, H., 111, 112, 122, 126, 131
Deland, S., 112
Dember, W., 176, 177
Denhoff, E., 326
DesJarlais, D., 300, 302, 303
Deutch, A., 287
Dix, P., 7, 8, 287
Dmitriev, V., 394, 396

489

Name index

Doll, E., 249
Doris, J., 252, 258
Down, J., 263
Downs, M., 414
Dunham, H., 304
Dunn, L., 70
Dunn, R., 416
Durkheim, E., 302
Dye, H., 392, 393
Dykes, M., 306

E

Eckstein, H., 262
L'Epee, Abbe de, 112, 113, 145

F

Faris, R., 302, 304
Farrel, G., 146
Fernald, G., 184, 186
Fine, R., 296
Ford, R., 261
Foster, C., 67
Foster, G., 306
Fox, V., 308
Freud, S., 296, 298
Froebel, F., 389, 391
Frostig, M., 195

G

Gall, F., 176, 177
Gallagher, J., 370, 379, 380
Gallaudet, E. M., 114
Gallaudet, T. H., 113, 114, 115
Garretson, M., 125
Gearheart, B., 7, 16, 59, 177, 184, 199, 271, 473
Gelles, R., 309
Getman, G., 190, 191
Getzels, J., 354, 358, 360
Gillingham, A., 186, 187
Gottlieb, J., 70
Gove, W., 302, 303
Gowan, J., 363, 365
Grady, S., 440
Graham, V. 442, 443
Grossman, H., 253, 254, 271
Guilford, J. P., 358
Guthrie, O., 285

H

Hallahan, D., 187, 196
Halperin, M., 309
Hansen, H., 261
Hardy, M., 87
Haüy, V., 145
Hawley, C., 202

Hayden, A., 394, 396
Head, H., 176
Head, S., 414
Healy, W., 289
Heinicke, S., 112, 113
Helfer, R., 309
Henry, G., 5, 8
Hewett, F., 5
Hinshelwood, J., 177
Hippocrates, 285
Hobbs, N., 69
Hoffer, A., 201
Hoffman, E., 287, 288
Hoffman, H., 261
Holder, W., 112
Holmes, L., 263
Howe, S. G., 7, 114, 146, 156, 287
Hunt, J. M., 393

I

Itard, J., 7, 250

J

Jackson, P., 354, 358, 360
Jacobs, J., 361, 362
Jensema, C., 334
Johnson, D., 196

K

Kanner, L., 248, 249
Karchmer, M., 135
Karnes, F., 370
Karnes, M., 402, 403
Kauffman, J., 287, 288, 289, 293, 295, 298
Kelly, L., 255
Kelly, T., 306
Kendall, D., 88, 105
Kennedy, J. F., 13, 70, 252
Keogh, B., 188
Kephart, N., 190, 194, 195
Kerr, J., 177
King, M., 85
Kirk, S., 178, 198, 199, 318, 322, 332, 393
Kisker, G., 442, 445, 449
Kott, M., 249, 251
Kraepelin, E., 295

L

Lambert, N., 291
Lassiter, R., 464
Lazar, I., 406
Lehtinen, L., 187
Lewis, N., 285
Lindman, F., 248
Lin-Fu, J., 260

Little, D., 85, 105
Litton, F., 7, 16, 270, 271, 473
Long, B., 220, 221, 222
Lorenz, K., 304
Lovitt, T., 201
Lowenfeld, B., 144, 145, 146, 155, 156
Lundeen, D., 215, 216, 227

M

Maclellan, E., 91, 92
Magnuson, R., 92
Mann, H., 114
Marland, S., 357, 366, 369
Marsh, G., 204, 417, 421, 438
Matza, D., 302
McCoy, G., 294
McGuigan, J., 89
McIntyre, K., 248
McKay, H., 302
McMillan, D. L., 70
McNaughton, D., 102
Mercer, C. D., 70
Meyer, B., 440
Montessori, M., 391
Moores, D., 64, 110, 111, 112, 114, 120, 124, 132, 133
Morgan, W., 177
Morin, J., 92, 93
Morrow, H., 254
Moser, H., 258
Mowrer, D., 226
Myklebust, H., 196, 198

N

Napier, G., 146, 156
Nelson, A., 189
Newberger, E., 309
Newland, T. E., 356, 357
Newns, G., 262
Nielsen, G., 376

O

O'Donnell, P. A., 66
Oliver, J., 263
O'Rourke, T., 127
Orton, S., 186
Osborne, R., 161

P

Paden, E., 215, 216, 217
Patrick, D., 261
Patterson, L., 473
Pauling, L., 201
Pavlov, I., 297, 298
Payne, J., 70
Peabody, E., 389

Peet, H., 111
Pegnato, C., 362
Perkins, W., 214, 217, 223, 225, 227-229, 235, 237, 239
Pestalozzi, J., 389
Pinel, P., 287
Plato, 285
Plotkin, R., 456
Pollin, W., 295
Ponce de Leon, 111

Q

Quay, H., 294

R

Raiti, S., 262
Randel, H., 326
Rawlings, B., 438, 439
Rein, R., 296, 305
Rhodes, W., 294, 414
Rice, J., 350, 355, 361
Rich, L., 306
Rimland, B., 295
Roberts, C., 87
Rosenthal, D., 295
Rubin, R., 306
Rush, B., 287
Russell, H., 456

S

Safford, P., 388, 390
Sarason, S., 252, 258
Sardharwalla, I., 262
Scheerenberger, R., 258
Scheff, T., 303
Scherr, M., 326
Scranton, T., 414
Seguin, E., 7, 250, 251, 287
Seligman, T., 326
Selling, L., 284, 287
Shaw, C., 302
Shea, T., 291, 294, 297, 300, 414, 415
Shearer, D., 399
Shearer, M., 399
Sheffelin, M., 220, 221
Silverman, S., 111, 112, 122, 126, 131
Simpson, D., 189
Sisk, D., 374
Skeels, H., 392, 393
Skinner, B., 299
Smiley, W., 308
Smith, D., 263
Smith, E., 219
Solenberger, E., 318
Stern, C., 258

Name index

Stevens, J., 326
Stramiello, A., 403, 404, 405, 441
Strauss, A., 187, 188
Stullken, E., 289
Stutt, H., 105
Sutherland, E., 302
Swallow, C., 293
Syphers, D., 356

T

Terman, L., 9, 350, 361
Tillman, M., 161
Tisdall, W., 161
Tjossen, T., 391
Torrance, E. P., 358, 360, 367, 368
Townsend, J., 85
Treherne, D., 87, 105
Trybus, R., 135, 136
Tuttle, D., 163

V

Vassar, W., 373
Vergason, G., 255

W

Wallis, J., 112
Walters, R., 472, 473
Watson, J., 298
Weishahn, M., 59, 159
Whitney, A., 249
Wiederholt, L., 176
Wilkin, W., 39
Wilkins, D., 262
Wilson, D., 261, 263
Winn, J., 472, 473
Witkin, H., 161
Wolf, P., 258
Wolfensberger, W., 102, 441
Wolman, B., 293
Wood, L., 440
Woody, R., 291
Wunderlich, R., 202

Y

Yamamoto, K., 358
Ysseldyke, J., 68, 306

Z

Zettel, J., 39, 43
Zilboorg, G., 5, 8

Subject index

A

Access, right to, 454
Accommodation, in secondary school, 421-422
Adaptations for the handicapped or disabled, 445-449
   environmental, 446-447
   transportation, 447-449
Adapted materials and equipment for visually impaired, 163
Addition, errors of, 226
Adolescence, implications for secondary school programs, 419-421
Adults, programs for handicapped or disabled, 436-457
   college programs, 437-440
   community programs, 445-449
   residential programs, 440-443
   vocational programs, 443-445
Alberta, special education in, 98-100
Allergies related to asthma, 325-326
Alternative school programs, 418, 419
American Association on Mental Deficiency (AAMD), 25, 251, 254, 255
American School for the Deaf, 113
American Sign Language (ASL), 127
American Speech and Hearing Association (ASHA), 25, 216, 217, 223, 224, 232-233, 238
Amniocentesis, 264
Amputations, 323-324
Anoxia, 260
Aphasia, 231-232
Architectural barriers, litigation related to, 17
Aristotle, 111
Arthritis, 324-325
Articulation disorders, 225-277
Assessment, 56-58
   bias in, 68
   flow chart for, 57-58
   nondiscriminatory, 67-68
Association for Children for Learning Disabilities (ACLD), 22, 179, 180

Asthma, 325-326
Astigmatism, 151
Asylums, 7
Ataxia, 327
Athetosis, 327
Atlantic Provinces Special Education Authority, 88, 90, 91, 92
Atypical Infant Development (AID) program, 396-398
Audiograms, 119
Audiologist, role of, 122
Auditory canal (meatus), 115
Auditory system, 115-117
Auditory training, 130-131
Auricle, 115
Auxiliary Classes Act, 89

B

Bayley Scales of Infant Mental Development, 398
BEH; *see* Bureau of Education for the Handicapped (BEH)
Behavior modification, 200-201
Behavioral theories, 298-300
Bias in assessment, 68
Bicetre of Paris, 249
Binet-Simon Scales, 9
Biochemical imbalances, 296
Biologic risk, 391
Biophysical approaches to emotional disturbance, 294-296
Blind, special rights of, 455; *see also* Visual impairment (or visually impaired)
Blissymbolics Communication Foundation (Bliss Symbols), 102
Bonnaterre, Abbe, 249, 250
Braille, 156
Brain
   plasticity of, 221
   role in language function, 220-221, 222
Brain damage, 295
British Columbia, special education in, 100-101

Subject index

British North America Act, 82, 83
Broward Community College Program for Exceptional Adults, 439-440
Bureau of Education for the Handicapped (BEH), 284, 371, 399, 401

C

Canada, 82-105
    CEC in, 86-87
    education in, 83-87
    government structure of, 82-83
    population of, 87
    size of provinces of, 87
    special education in, 88-105
Career education, 423
Center for Architectural Planning and Design for the Handicapped, 447
Cerebral palsy, 326-329
Cerumen, role of, 115
Choroid defects, 151-152
Classification, litigation related to, 17
Cleft palate, 235-236
Cluttering, 229-230
Cochlea, 116-117
College programs for handicapped or disabled adults, 437-440
Commitment, litigation related to, 17
Competency examinations for graduation, 417
Conceptualization, 198
Conductive hearing loss, 118
Connecticut, program for gifted in, 374-379
Conseil du Quebec de l'Enfance Exceptionnelle (CQEE), 87
Continuum of services (full continuum); *see also* specific exceptionality
    chart of, 60-61
    general concept of, 59-63
Convulsive disorders, 329-330
Cooperative Plan, 62
Cooperative programs (vocational orientation), 425
Cornea, 147-148
Council for Exceptional Children (CEC), 22, 24, 25
Counseling parents of handicapped, 471-474
Cove Schools, 187
Creative students, 348-384
Crippled and other health impaired, prevalence of, 54; *see also* Physical disabilities
Cultural transmission theory, 302
Custody, litigation related to, 17

D

Deaf, special rights of, 455; *see also* Hearing impairment (or handicap)
Delayed language, 230-231
Dental care for handicapped, 470-471
Developmental delay, 388-389

Diabetes, 330-332
Diana v. State Board of Education, 20
Diplacusis, 119
Diplegia, 327
Distortion, errors of, 226
Dog guide, 160
Down's syndrome, 263-264

E

Early childhood education
    for handicapped, 388-409
    Stramiello study of federally funded programs for, 403-406
Early intervention, 392-393
Ecologic theory, 304-305
Educable mentally retarded, 266-269
Education
    adults' right to, 454
    litigation related to, 17, 18-21
Emotionally disturbed
    characteristics of, 292-293
    definitions of, 291-292
    historical origins of education for, 284-291
    prevalence of, 54, 293-294
Employment
    litigation related to, 17
    protection in, 44
    right to, 453
Environmental control, 189-190
Environmental risk, 391
Epilepsy, 329-330
    suggestions for management of grand mal seizures, 330
Established risk, 391
Expressive language, 198

F

Federal aid to education, 37-38
Financial structure of public schools, 37-39
First-Chance Network, 396, 401
Flexibility, disorders of, 228
Fluency disorders, 228-230

G

Galactosemia, 261-262
Gallaudet College, 114, 439
General motor development, 192
Genetic blueprinting, 295
Genetic counseling, 468-469
Gheel, 249
Gifted (including creative and talented), 348-384
    characteristics of, 366-369
    definitions of, 353-358
    federal assistance for, 44-45, 371
    history of, 4, 349-353
    identification of, 360-366, 377-378

Gifted (including creative and talented)—cont'd
  prevalance of, 54, 369
  state leadership for, 371-374
  teachers of, 369-370
Glaucoma, 153
Glidewell, J., 293
Grand mal seizures, 329
  suggestions for management of, 330
Guardianship, litigation related to, 17

H

Head Start programs, 393
Health care, right to, 453
Hearing, process of, 117
Hearing aids, 130
Hearing impairment (or handicap), 109-141
  causes of, 120-121
  characteristics of children with, 123-124
  college programs for, 438-439
  degrees of, 117-120
  historical origin of programs for, 111-115
  prevalence of, 54, 122-123
  surgical treatment for, 121
  types of, 117-120
Hemiplegia, 326
Hemispheric specialization of brain, 220-221
  tabular representation of, 223
Hemolytic disease, 259
High-cost skill training, 425-426
High-risk children, 388-391
High school programs; *see* Secondary school programs for handicapped
Home visits in early childhood programs, 397
Homebound service, 63
Hospital service, 63
Hydrocephalus, 262
Hyperactivity, approaches to and theories of, 187-190
Hyperopia, 151
Hypoglycemia, 201-202

I

Illinois Test of Psycholinguistic Abilities (ITPA), 199-200
Imagery, 197
Independent travel, 159
Individualized Educational Programs (IEP), general description of, 41-42
Innate responses, 190-191
Inner ear, 116-117
Inner language, 197
Intensity, disorders of, 227-228
Iris, 147, 148
Itinerant services, 60-61

J

Jacksonian seizures, 330

Juvenile delinquency, 308-309
Juvenile rheumatoid arthritis, 324-325

K

Kendall report, 88-89

L

Labeling
  negative aspects, 69
  positive aspects, 69
  problems associated with, 69-72
Labeling theory, 302-303
Labrador, special education in, 90-91
Language development, 218-221
Language disorders, 221-225, 230-232
Larry P. v. Riles, 19-21
Lead poisoning, 260
Learning disabilities, 175-205
  definition of, 179, 180, 181
  educational provisions for, 202-204
  historical origins of, 176-179
  hyperactivity in, 187-190
  identification of, 181-183
  as language disorder, 232
  perceptual-motor approaches, 190-196
  prevalence of, 54, 180-181
Legal basis for education, 35-36
Legal rights of adult handicapped or disabled, 451-456
  access, 454-455
  of blind, 455
  of deaf, 454
  to education, 454
  in employment, 453
  to health care, 453
  of mentally ill, 454
  to rehabilitation services, 453-454
  in voting, 455
Legally blind, 150
Legislation; *see also* Litigation
  on behalf of gifted, 25-26
  relating to the handicapped, 13-16
    Public Law 85-926, 13
    Public Law 88-164, 14, 290
    Public Law 89-10, 14
    Public Law 89-750, 15
    Public Law 91-230, 15, 352
    Public Law 93-112, 16, 412, 446, 465
    Public Law 93-380, 16, 353
    Public Law 94-142; *see* Public Law 94-142
Lens abnormalities, 151
Linguistics of visual English, 127-128
Litigation; *see also* Legislation
  description of, 16-21
    architectural barriers, 17
    classification, 17

Subject index

Litigation; *see also* Legislation—cont'd
  description of—cont'd
    commitment, 17
    custody, 17
    education, 17, 18-21
    employment, 17
    guardianship, 17
    protection from harm, 18
    sterilization, 18
    treatment, 18
    voting, 18
    zoning, 18
  effect of, on legislation, 35
  forces preceding, 12-13
  specific cases
    Diana v. State Board of Education, 20
    to establish legal rights of adults, 455-456
    Larry P. v. Riles, 19-21
    Mills v. District of Columbia, 19
    P.A.R.C. v. Commonwealth of Pennsylvania, 18-19
Long cane technique, 159
Low vision, 149

M

Mainstreaming, 64-65
Manitoba, special education in, 96-97
Manual alphabet, 128
Manual approach to teaching deaf, 112-115
Manual communication systems, 126-128
Marin County AID program, 396-398
Medical specialists, role of, in management of physical disabilities, 335-336
Mental health centers, 449-450
Mental retardation
  definition and terminology in, 253-257
  educational classification system of, 256
  educational placement in, 271-273
  historical origin of programs for, 4, 248-253
  identification of, 264-266
  levels of, 253-254
  prevalence of, 54, 257-258
Mentally ill, special rights of, 455
Microcephalus, 262-263
Middle ear, 115
Mills v. District of Columbia, 19
Minority students, assessment of, 67-68
Mobility, 157
Modeling, 299
Monoplegia, 327
Multihandicapped, prevalence of, 54
Multiple disabilities, 334-335
Multisensory approaches, 183-187
Muscular dystrophy, 332

Myopia, 150-151

N

National Association for Gifted Children, 351
National Association for Retarded Citizens (NARC), 21-22, 248, 252, 274
National Defense Education Act (NDEA), 351
National Easter Seal Society, 319
National Foundation of Dentistry for the Handicapped, 470-471
National Industries for the Severely Handicapped (NISH), 445
National Institute on Mental Retardation, 102
National Society for Crippled Children, 21
National/State Leadership Training Institute for the Gifted and Talented, 370
New Brunswick, special education in, 88-90
Newfoundland, special education in, 90-91
Nondiscriminatory assessment, 67-68
Nova Scotia, special education in, 91
Nystagmus, 152

O

Ocular motor development, 192
Off-campus work stations, 425
Office of Gifted and Talented, 371-374
Official Languages Act of 1969, 86
Omission, errors of, 225-226
Ontario, special education in, 95-96
On-the-job training, 425
Operant conditioning, 299
Ophthalmia neonatorum, 153
Optacon, 157
Oral approach to teaching deaf, 112-113, 114, 115, 124-125
Orientation training, 157
Orton-Gillingham approach, 186-187
Otitis media, 120
Otosclerosis, 120
Outer ear, 115

P

Paraplegia, 327
Parent groups, influence of, 21-24
Parent involvement in early childhood programs, 405
Parent permission, 57-58
Pennsylvania Association for Retarded Children v. Commonwealth of Pennsylvania, 18-19
Perception, 193-197
Perceptual-motor approaches, 190-196
Perceptual-motor match, 194
Perkins School for the Blind, 7
Petit mal seizures, 329-330
Phenylketonuria, 261
Philosophy of education
  for exceptional children and youth, 52-53

Philosophy of education—cont'd
  related principles in, 53
Physical disabilities
  definition of, 323
  educational settings for, 336-339
  guidelines for educational programming for, 321-322
  history of programs for, 318-321
  medical involvement in, 335-336
  prevalence of, 54
Pinna, 115
Pitch, disorders of, 227
PKU, 261
Placement in special programs
  decision about, 59
  variables affecting, 63
Poisons, 259-260
Poliomyelitis, 332-333
Portage Project, 398-401
Postlingual deafness, 118
Preliminary review, 56-57
Prelingual deafness, 118
Presbycusis, 120-121
Preschool programs, 388
Presidents' Committee on Mental Retardation (PCMR), 264-274
Prevalence of exceptional children
  percentage limitations under PL 94-142, 54
  table of, 54
Prince Edward Island, special education in, 91-92
Professional groups working with handicapped, 24-25
Prosthetic devices for speech problems, 236
Protection from harm, litigation related to, 18
Psychiatric support, temporary, 449-450
Psychoanalytic theories, 296-298
Psychochemicals, 202
Psychomotor seizures, 330
Public Law 94-142
  children served by, 40
  financial provisions for, 42-43
  individualized educational program and, 41-42
  other provisions of, 388, 390, 412, 413
  purpose of, 40
  related services with, 40-41
  summary of, 39-43
Public transportation for handicapped, 447-448

Q
Quadriplegia, 327
Quality, disorders of, 228
Quebec, special education in, 92-94

R
RAPYHT (Retrieval and Acceleration of Promising Young Handicapped and Talented) project, 401-403
Receptive language, 197-198

Referrals, 55-56
  source of, for early childhood programs, 405
Refractive errors, 150-151
Rehabilitation services
  history of, 464-466
  philosophy of, 467-468
  right to, 453-454
Reimbursement in special education, 38-39
Remedial teaching in secondary school, 421
Residential programs
  for handicapped adults, 440-443
  for mentally ill, 441-443
  for mentally retarded, 441
Residential schools for handicapped, 10-11, 63
Resource room services, 61-62
Retina, 147-148
Retinal defects, 151-152
Retinitis pigmentosa, 152
Rh incompatibility, 259
Rheumatic fever, 333
Rights of adult handicapped; *see* Legal rights of adult handicapped or disabled
Rigidity, 327
Risk
  biologic, 391
  environmental, 391
  established, 391
Rome, treatment of retarded in, 248-249
Rubella
  as cause of blindness, 153
  effects in mental retardation, 258-259
  study of children after, 334

S
St. John's Learning Disabilities Centre, 90
Saskatchewan, special education in, 97-98
School boards, legal responsibility of, 35-36
Screening for possible need for educational assistance, 55
Secondary school programs for handicapped
  history of, 413-416
  various approaches to, 421-423
  vocational training programs for, 423-428
Section 504: Vocational Rehabilitation Act of 1973; *see* Vocational Rehabilitation Act of 1973
Seeing Essential English (SEE$_1$), 127
Sensorineural hearing loss, 118
Sensory impairments, 107-108, 109-172
Shaping, 299
Sighted guide technique, 159
Signed English, 129
Signing Exact English (SEE$_2$), 127
"600 schools," 290
Skeels and Dye study, 392-393
Snellen chart, 154-155
Sociologic theories, 300-304

Subject index

Spasticity, 327
Special classes
  history of development of, 8-10
  as part of continuum of services, 60-61, 62
  trends in, 11
Special education
  history of, 4-13
  scope of, 4
Special motor development, 192
Special schools for children with physical disabilities, 320-321
Speech, development of, 217-218
Speech disorders, 221-223, 225-230
  classifications of, 221-223
Speech flow, 218
  disorders of, 228-230
Speech/language disorders
  assessment of, 236-237
  causes of, 233-235
  history of, 215-217
  identification of, 233
  medical/surgical treatment of, 235-236
  prevalence of, 54, 232-233
  remediation of, 237-238
Speech reading, 131-132
Speech remediation models, 237-238
  "bad habit with benefits" model, 238
  "bad habit" model, 237
  "symptomatic disorder" model, 238
  "vicious cycle" model, 237-238
Spina bifida, 333-334
Staffing procedures, 57, 58-59
Stanford-Binet Intelligence Scale, 9
Sterilization, litigation related to, 18
Strabismus, 152
Stuttering, 228-229
Substitution, errors of, 226
Superstition, role of, in treatment of handicapped, 5
Symptoms of visual difficulties, chart of, 154

T

Talent, classifications of, 355-356
Talented students, 348-384
Taxes as sources of support of education, 38
Tinnitus, 119-121
Torrance tests of creative thinking, 360
Total communication method of teaching deaf, 125-126
Trainable mentally retarded, 269-270
Transportation for handicapped, 447-449, 469-470
  private, 448
  public, 447-448
Trauma, 261
Treatment, litigation related to, 18
Tremor, 327

Triplegia, 326
Tutoring in secondary school, 422-423
Tympanic membrane (eardrum), 115

U

United Cerebral Palsy Association (UCP), 22, 319

V

VAKT approaches, 184-187
Victor (wild boy of Aveyron), 7, 249-250, 287
Vision, process of, 148
Visual acuity, 149-150
Visual efficiency, 150
Visual impairment (or visually impaired)
  causes of, 150-152
  definition of, 149
  identification of, 155
  medical and surgical treatment of, 153-154
  prevalence of, 54, 152-153
  techniques for daily living for, 163-164
Visual perception, 150
Visual system, anatomy and physiology of, 147-148
Visualization, 192-193, 197
Visually handicapped; *see* Visual impairment (or visually impaired)
Visually limited, 149
Visuomotor model, 191
Vocational programs for handicapped, 423-428, 443-445
  cooperative programs in, 425
  general program guidelines on, 426-428
  high-cost skill training in, 425-426
  in off-campus work station, 425
  in on-the-job training, 425
  in sheltered workshops, 443-445
  in work-experience programs, 425
  in work-study programs, 425
Vocational Rehabilitation Act of 1973, Section 504
  general discussion of, 43-44
  employment protection under, 44
Voice disorders, 227-228
Voiced sounds, 217-218
Voiceless sounds, 218
Voting, litigation related to, 18
Voting rights, 454

W

Wagner-O'Day Act, 444-445
Washington, University of, Down's syndrome program, 394-396
Wild boy of Aveyron, 7, 249-250, 287
Work-experience programs, 425
Work-study programs, 425

Z

Zoning, litigation related to, 18